$47

Writing and Reporting News
A Coaching Method

From the Wadsworth Series in Mass Communication and Journalism

General Mass Communication

Communications Law: Liberties, Restraints, and the Modern Media, 2d ed., by John D. Zelezny
Communications Media in the Information Society, updated edition, by Joseph Straubhaar & Robert LaRose
Ethics in Media Communications: Cases and Controversies, 2d ed., by Louis Day
International Communications: History, Conflict, and Control of the Global Metropolis,
    by Robert S. Fortner
The Interplay of Influence, 4th ed., by Kathleen Hall Jamieson & Karlyn Kohrs Campbell
Media/Impact: An Introduction to Mass Media, 3rd ed., by Shirley Biagi
Media/Reader: Perspectives on Media Industries, Effects, and Issues, 3rd ed., by Shirley Biagi
Mediamerica, Mediaworld: Form, Content, and Consequence of Mass Communication, updated
    5th ed., by Edward Jay Whetmore
Women and Media: Content, Careers, and Criticism, by Cynthia Lont

Journalism

Crafting News for Electronic Media: Writing, Reporting, and Production, by Carl Hausman
Creative Editing for Print Media, 2d ed., by Dorothy Bowles and Diane L. Borden
Free-lancer and Staff Writer, 5th ed., by William Rivers
Interviews that Work: A Practical Guide for Journalists, 2nd ed., by Shirley Biagi
News Writing, by Peter Berkow
The Search: Information Gathering for the Mass Media, by Lauren Kessler & Duncan McDonald
When Words Collide, 4th ed., by Lauren Kessler & Duncan McDonald
Writing and Reporting News: A Coaching Method, 2nd ed., by Carole Rich

Photography & Design

Design Principles for Desktop Publishers, 2nd ed., by Tom Lichty
Desktop Computing Workbook, by Paul Martin Lester
Introduction to Photography, 4th ed., by Marvin J. Rosen & David L. DeVries
Visual Communication: Images with Messages, by Paul Martin Lester

Public Relations & Advertising

Advertising and Marketing to the New Majority: A Case Study Approach, by Gail Baker Woods
Creative Strategy in Advertising, 5th ed., by A. Jerome Jewler
Electronic Public Relations, by Eugene Marlow
International Advertising: Communicating Across Cultures, by Barbara Mueller
Public Relations Cases, 3rd ed., by Jerry A. Hendrix
Public Relations Writing: Form and Style, 4th ed., by Doug Newsom & Bob Carrell
This is PR: The Realities of Public Relations, 6th ed., by Doug Newsom, Judy VanSlyke Turk & Dean Kruckeberg

Research & Theory

Communication Research: Strategies and Sources, 4th ed., by Rebecca B. Rubin, Alan M. Rubin & Linda J. Piele
Mass Communication Theory: Foundations, Ferment and Future, by Stanley Baran & Dennis Davis
Mass Media Research: An Introduction, 5th ed., by Roger D. Wimmer & Joseph R. Dominick
The Practice of Social Research, 7th ed., by Earl Babbie
Surveying Public Opinion, by Sondra Miller Rubenstein

Writing

and

Reporting

News

A COACHING METHOD

Second Edition

Carole Rich

University of Kansas

Wadsworth Publishing Company
I(T)P™ **®** **An International Thomson Publishing Company**
Belmont • Albany • Bonn • Boston • Cincinnati • Detroit •
London • Madrid • Melbourne • Mexico City • New York •
Paris • San Francisco • Singapore • Tokyo • Toronto •
Washington

Communication and Media Studies Editor: Todd R. Armstrong
Project Development Editor: Lewis DeSimone
Editorial Assistant: Michael Gillespie
Production Services Coordinator: Debby Kramer
Production: Mary Douglas/Rogue Valley Publications
Designer: Cloyce Wall
Print Buyer: Barbara Britton
Permissions Editor: Robert Kauser
Copy Editor: Rebecca Smith
Illustrator: Teresa Leigh Roberts
Cover Designer: Three Communication Design/Norman Rice
Compositor: G & S Typesetters, Inc.
Printer: Quebecor Printing Book Group/Fairfield
Cover Printer: Phoenix Color Corporation

Printed in the United States of America
 3 4 5 6 7 8 9 10

For more information, contact Wadsworth Publishing Company:

Wadsworth Publishing Company
10 Davis Drive
Belmont, California 94002, USA

International Thomson Publishing Europe
Berkshire House 168-173
High Holborn
London, WC1V 7AA, England

Thomas Nelson Australia
102 Dodds Street
South Melbourne 3205
Victoria, Australia

Nelson Canada
1120 Birchmount Road
Scarborough, Ontario
Canada M1K 5G4

International Thomson Editores
Campos Eliseos 385, Piso 7
Col. Polanco
11560 México D.F. México

International Thomson Publishing GmbH
Königswinterer Strasse 418
53227 Bonn, Germany

International Thomson Publishing Asia
221 Henderson Road
#05-10 Henderson Building
Singapore 0315

International Thomson Publishing Japan
Hirakawacho Kyowa Building, 3F
2-2-1 Hirakawacho
Chiyoda-ku, Tokyo 102, Japan

Library of Congress Cataloging-in-Publication Data
Rich, Carole.
        Writing and reporting news : a coaching method /
Carole Rich. — 2nd ed.
                    p.   cm.
        Includes index.
        ISBN 0-534-50879-0
        1. Journalism—Authorship.   2. Reporters and
        reporting.   I. Title.
PN4781.R42   1997
808′.06602—dc20   96-11681

Brief Contents

Detailed Contents

Preface

Writing news can be fun. Writing news is also a crucial skill. Technology has reduced the world to a global village where people can communicate with as much speed and ease as though they lived next door to each other. But the amount of information available is of galactic proportions. No matter what medium is used to convey the information—computers, television or paper—journalists who know how to gather and write information clearly will be needed more than ever as the world of communication continues to expand. This book is devoted to teaching you how to acquire those skills.

Writing and Reporting News: A Coaching Method, Second Edition, uses the principles of the writing coach movement in newspapers to bring coaching into the classroom. Teachers and good editors have always helped writers improve their stories by offering suggestions during the reporting and writing process. But in many newsrooms editors became too busy to confer with writers before the stories were submitted for editing. The writers often received little or no feedback about how they could improve their work.

Concerns about the quality of writing in newspapers have prompted many editors to hire writing coaches to help journalists improve their skills. The coaching movement was initiated at the Poynter Institute for Media Studies in St. Petersburg, Florida, which offers training programs for journalists. Two of the institute's directors, Roy Peter Clark and Don Fry (who is now an independent writing consultant) trained journalists from all over the world in coaching methods.

But what is coaching? Coaching is a way of helping writers help themselves. A coach doesn't stress how you failed to write a good story. A coach stresses how you can succeed. A coach helps you discover your writing problems and suggests how you can find solutions. An editor may concentrate on the end results of your writing; a coach concentrates on the process of your writing. A coach asks you what techniques worked well for you in your story and where you struggled. Then a coach helps you find ways to report and write more effectively by encouraging you to try new approaches and take risks. Like a basketball coach who trains players how to improve their techniques on the court, a writing coach trains writers how to perfect their techniques in the craft.

This book aims to serve as a writing coach by anticipating problems writers have and offering solutions. It describes techniques writing coaches use at newspapers. Many other techniques in this book are an outgrowth of my experiences teaching journalism students at the University of Kansas and of my work as a visiting writing coach at several newspapers.

Each chapter begins with coaching tips so you can learn how to be your own writing coach and gain confidence as a writer. No book can substitute for your instructor. This book attempts to supplement what you learn in the classroom by providing you with hundreds of examples and tips from award-winning writers.

I have chosen the examples carefully to provide stories that not only illustrate the techniques in the chapter but are also fun to read. I have also included examples that reflect our multicultural society in subject matter as well as in the choice of writers. Newspapers and magazines contain some remarkably good writing. I hope you will agree when you read some of the excerpts and full text articles from them. Newspapers also publish some dreadful writing. I hope you will learn what to avoid from the bad examples.

This second edition of *Writing and Reporting News: A Coaching Method* contains many new features, such as:

• a new chapter on beat reporting

• a new chapter on computer-assisted journalism featuring detailed instructions for finding information on the Internet (as well as references throughout the book to on-line journalism sources and skills)

• a revised chapter on the changing concepts of news

• a revised disaster chapter featuring the Oklahoma University student newspaper's coverage of the Oklahoma City bombing

• a revised chapter on storytelling techniques, incorporating features and specialty stories

• a revised chapter covering government and statistical stories

• an expanded chapter on accuracy and libel

• an appendix of on-line sites useful to journalists

• many new exercises

The book also emphasizes current trends in news writing, such as the emphasis on graphics. You will learn how visual and verbal elements work together and how to use graphics as a writing tool.

How the Book Is Organized

The first three parts of this book are devoted to teaching you the techniques of reporting and writing—from generating story ideas to developing a writing process. Writers have many different ways of working. No one way works for everyone. This book offers you many tips so that you can choose the ones that work best for you. It encourages you to take risks and to find your own style. It urges you to consider revision as a crucial part of the writing process. If you learn the techniques of good writing, you can apply them to a variety of stories.

The fourth part of the book provides you with opportunities to apply those skills to many types of stories. It offers tips for solving problems you might encounter covering crime and court stories, government, disasters and a variety of other stories. This part of the book also offers a chapter on how to apply for a job.

Although the book is arranged sequentially to take you through the steps from conceiving the idea to constructing the story, you do not need to study the book in the order it is written. Each chapter is self-contained so that your instructor can design the course to fit the needs of the class and so that you can use chapters of most interest to you.

The greatest frustration I experience as a teacher is that there is too much information to teach in a basic reporting course. With the increasing use of technology and such resource tools as the Internet, the journalistic skills you need to master multiply as well. There is no way you can learn all the skills you need in one semester. But I hope that you find this book helpful in teaching you the techniques you need now and that you will use this book as a reference for information you may need in the future.

Basic and Advanced Techniques

This book is geared to beginning and advanced journalism students. If you are a beginning journalism student, you will find detailed explanations about how you can develop reporting and writing skills. If you are an advanced journalism student, you can study more complex writing techniques, such as those in the chapter on storytelling or the use of data bases in the chapter on computer-assisted reporting. You will also find many models of sophisticated writing styles by journalists who have won numerous awards.

Although the primary focus of this book is newspaper writing, the techniques of reporting and writing presented here will serve you well if you are planning a career in magazines, public relations or broadcasting.

I hope the coaching tips and writing examples in this book entice you to try many techniques so your writing becomes a very rewarding experience for you and your readers. I welcome your suggestions for improvement.

Acknowledgments

First, I thank my students for encouraging me to write this book. Second, I also thank many others: my editor, Todd R. Armstrong and other editors at Wadsworth Publishing Company; production editor Mary

Douglas; Don Fry, a writing consultant who taught me the coaching method; Dick Thien, University of Nebraska journalism professor, for urging me to write about writing and for giving me my first job as a writing coach when he was a newspaper editor; my colleagues, Max Utsler, Adrienne Rivers, Tom Volek, Ted Frederickson, John Broholm and Bill Dickinson; my former journalism students, Katy Monk, Lara Gold, Patricia Rojas, David Silverman, Lee Hill and so many others who have given me the joy of teaching them and learning from them. I also thank the many journalists who shared their time and their expertise to provide tips for this book. Some of these journalists have changed jobs between the time they were interviewed and the publication of this book.

I also thank the reviewers of this book whose comments and suggestions were invaluable: Charles Adair, State University of New York at Buffalo; Roy Atwood, University of Idaho; Maurine Beasley, University of Maryland, College Park; Retta Blaney, New York University; Ray Chavez, University of Colorado; Lynne Flocke, Syracuse University; Sandra Haarsager, University of Idaho; Bruce Johansen, University of Nebraska–Omaha; Lee Jolliffe, University of Missouri; Robert C. Kochersberger Jr., North Carolina State University; Linda L. Levin, University of Rhode Island; Gary McLouth, College of St. Rose; Beverly Merrick, New Mexico State University; David C. Nelson, Southwest Texas State University; W. Robert Nowell III, Chico State University; Marshel Rossow, Mankato State University; Linda N. Scanlon, Norfolk State University; Norman Sims, University of Massachusetts; Martin D. Sommerness, Northern Arizona University; and Carl Stepp, University of Maryland, College Park.

About the Author

Carole Rich is an associate professor of journalism at the University of Kansas. She began her career in 1970 as a reporter specializing in education and government at the *Philadelphia Bulletin.* She later worked for the *Fort Lauderdale* (Fla.) *News/Sun-Sentinel* as a reporter, food editor and city editor. She also worked at the *Hartford* (Conn.) *Courant* as deputy metropolitan editor for two years before she began her teaching career in 1985. Rich has been a visiting writing coach at more than a dozen newspapers and has conducted writing seminars throughout the country.

Writing and Reporting News
A Coaching Method

Introduction: Tips From Award-winning Journalists

Make the reader see. Make the reader care. Follow those two principles, and you will have the makings of an award-winning journalist.

Eugene Roberts, a former editor at *The Philadelphia Inquirer* and *The New York Times,* tells this story about how his editor influenced him to make the reader see. Roberts was a reporter at the *Goldsboro News-Argus* in North Carolina. His editor, Henry Belk, was blind. Many days Belk would call in Roberts to read his stories to him, and Belk would yell: "Make me see. You aren't making me see."

Advice from Roberts: "The best reporters, whatever their backgrounds or their personalities, share that consummate drive to get to the center of a story and then put the reader on the scene."

Roberts should know. During the 18 years he was executive editor of *The Philadelphia Inquirer,* the newspaper won 17 Pulitzer Prizes.

How do you become one of the best reporters? Observe. Gather details. Ask questions. Be curious. Then write word pictures that make the reader see and experience the action, and plan photos or graphics to accompany your stories.

In the future, as broadcast and print media converge, you may be mixing video images and sound bites with written words. But Roberts' advice will still apply. Make the reader care. Make sure the story has a "so what" element. Write a compelling story that touches the reader's emotions. Use facts, quotes, and visual and verbal images that make the reader angry, sad, happy, relieved or more informed about an issue.

Ken Fuson, who has won several awards for outstanding writing at *The Des Moines* (Iowa) *Register,* has this advice: "Don't turn in a story you wouldn't read. If you tell a good story, people will want to read it. If you don't think many people will want to read it, make it short." Fuson is convinced that even stories about government meetings can be made readable with storytelling techniques. "Look for ways to show conflict; try to describe the mood," he says.

He worries that newspaper editors are too concerned about making stories shorter to appeal to impatient readers and to conserve space in the paper. "Some stories are better if they're long," Fuson says. "You could probably make *Moby Dick* a lot shorter, too. But I still think people will read a good tale."

For Fuson, the ending is even more important than the beginning of a story. "When I was a kid, the stories that would make me go back and read again were the ones that had the best endings," he says. "I know most newspaper readers don't read all the way to the endings. But I tell myself if I do it well enough, they'll read mine."

Julie Sullivan is more certain readers will get to the end of her stories. Her prize-winning stories run only 8 inches. Sullivan is a reporter for *The Spokesman-Review* (Wash.). She packs a wealth of descriptive detail into short sentences without resorting to adjectives. Like Fuson, she strives for strong endings, especially in short stories.

"You are trying to make a point with every paragraph," Sullivan says. I think the last one is the one people remember." Her last paragraph in one story is a simple statement that makes a powerful point about the daily dangers an 82-year-old man faces in a deteriorating, low-income apartment complex in Spokane. His watch had been stolen by a drug addict.

"I'll get it back, you watch and see," he fumed later.

He did. The $50 Seiko was returned without explanation Thursday morning.

That night, they stole his food stamps.

Sullivan also thinks there is a place for longer stories, but she says the trend now is for brevity. Her advice: "Trust your instincts. Ask yourself what is important and what struck you during the interview. Then write what you remember. Then rewrite. Go back over the story and take out every word that is extraneous."

And some advice from that master storyteller, Edna Buchanan, Pulitzer Prize–winning former police reporter for *The Miami Herald.* Here is what she says in her book *The Corpse Had a Familiar Face:*

What a reporter needs is detail, detail, detail.

If a man is shot for playing the same song on the jukebox too many times, I've got to name that tune. Questions unimportant to police add the color and detail that makes a story human. What movie did they see? What color was their car? What did they have in their pockets? What were they doing the precise moment the bomb exploded or the tornado touched down?

Miami Homicide Lieutenant Mike Gonzalez, who has spent some thirty years solving murders, tells me that he now asks those questions and suggests to rookies that they do the same. The answers may not be relevant to an investigation, but he tells them, "Edna Buchanan will ask you, and you'll feel stupid if you don't know."

A question I always ask is: What was everybody wearing? It has little to do with style. It has everything to do with the time I failed to ask. A man was shot and dumped into the street by a killer in a pickup truck. The case seemed somewhat routine—if one can ever call murder routine. But later, I learned that at the time the victim was shot, he was wearing a black taffeta cocktail dress and red high heels. I tracked down the detectives and asked, "Why didn't you tell me?"

"You didn't ask," they chorused. Now I always ask.

Writers like Edna Buchanan take risks. They try new approaches to make the reader want to read their stories.

This book is about risk-taking writing, the kind of writing that tells stories people want to read. It is about writing to make readers see and care. It is about the kind of reporting and writing that makes reluctant readers read.

Here are some general tips for good writing:

- Show people in action whenever possible. Show and tell.
- Use simple sentences. Favor a subject-verb-object construction. If you write long sentences, follow them with short ones.
- Use strong action verbs.
- Translate jargon into simple English that the reader will understand.
- Use specific details instead of adjectives. Don't write about a large dog; write about a 250-pound St. Bernard named Churchill.
- Take risks. Try new styles. The writer who takes no risks is taking the biggest risk of all—the risk of being mediocre.

ONE

Understanding
News

COACHING

TIPS

To find your focus, ask yourself: What is the story about? Answer in one sentence.

To find your lead, ask yourself: What was most interesting?

Plan photos, maps, graphics or boxes of information to accompany your story.

Write the story as though you were telling it to a friend.

Write From the Start: A Coaching Method

1

Lee Hill burst into her classroom to tell her professor about the dream she'd had the previous night.

"I dreamed I was on a basketball court, and you were coaching on the sideline," she said. "You were yelling, 'Focus, focus, focus.' I kept running around the court, and then I focused on the basket."

"Did you make the basket?" the professor asked.

"I can't remember," she said, laughing. "All I remember was you yelling, 'Focus.'"

Hill, a graduate student at the University of Kansas, was taking a writing course taught by a coaching method. She had been learning how to construct her news stories around a main theme called the focus. Like a basketball coach who guides you from the sidelines, a writing coach doesn't fix the story for you; a coach helps you discover ways to fix it yourself. A coach asks questions and makes suggestions that help you understand how you can improve your writing. Hill likened the coaching process to cheerleading. It gives the reporter confidence to write, she said.

An outstanding reporter, Hill would gather reams of information. But like many professional writers, when she began to write her story, she would struggle to decide how to begin, what to include and in what order. The professor would coach her by asking her to describe the main point of her story—in one sentence. Once Hill established this focus, she could select the most important information related to that focus and discard unrelated material. Then the professor would ask a few more questions, such as what struck Hill as most interesting or important, to help her determine

Coaching skills are essentially reporting skills: asking good questions and listening to the answers.

Roy Peter Clark and Don Fry,

Coaching Writers: Editors and

Reporters Working Together

the lead and the order for her story. Those are the same techniques that writing coaches use at newspapers.

Now imagine that you have your own writing coach to help you with all your news stories. Your coach would ask you some leading questions to help you discover the best way to write your story. If you learn to ask yourself those questions before you write, you can be your own writing coach. That is one of the goals of this book. Even if you have never written a news story, you can begin reporting and writing by following some simple coaching tips that are presented in this chapter.

The Reporting and Writing Process

The coaching method in this book has four phases:

1   Conceive: At this stage you develop the idea for the story. If you are covering an event, such as a meeting or an accident, you need to start with the idea—the main point of what occurred. If you are writing a news story about a problem in your community, you still start with a central idea, which is the focus of your story. Once you begin reporting, you may discover some information that is more important than your original focus. Thus you should be flexible and decide the focus for writing after you collect the material.

2   Collect: This is the reporting stage. You interview sources and gather as much information as you can about your topic. Don't rely on one source; seek several points of view. Ask more questions and take more notes than you plan to use. You should also jot down your observations and gather as many details as possible.

3   Construct: This is the writing stage. You begin with a plan for your story developed around the focus. Then go through your notes and mark only the information related to that focus. Like a carpenter building a house, you need a blueprint. A good writer does not write a story without a plan. Jot down a few key words to indicate how you will organize your story. Then write a first draft of your story. You may revise your original draft in the next step.

4   Correct: This is the revision stage. After you have written your story, read it and make any changes you think are necessary. You may decide to add or delete information or to completely reorganize the story during this stage. You should also check the spelling of all names and the accuracy of facts, and you should correct grammar, style and typing errors.

These four steps compose the basic process for all news stories. In the coming chapters you will learn many techniques for reporting and writing news. But how do you get started now?

How to Be Your Own Writing Coach

Many news-writing courses start by teaching leads (the beginning of the story) and the organization of news stories. But there are several ways to write a lead or to organize a story. Too many writers spend their time agonizing over the perfect lead without thinking about the whole structure of the story.

A news story is based on one main idea with supporting points. That's why it is important to establish that central focus. Once you get your focus, you should select only the information that supports the basic idea. It is the key to organizing your story. There are some exceptions, such as stories about meetings that involve several unrelated actions, but even those news stories should be organized around a primary focus.

Determining Your Focus

The coaching method for determining your focus involves two simple steps: deciding what the story is about and thinking about how you would tell the story to a friend. These steps will also help you find a lead and a structure for the story.

What's the story about?   This is the first question to ask yourself. You should be able to write the answer in one sentence, preferably in fewer than 35 words. That is your focus statement. Put this sentence at the top of your story to remind you of the focus. This statement could be your lead if you decide you want the first sentence to get directly to the point of your story. If you prefer a more creative lead, this statement will become your focus paragraph—also called a "nut graph." Because readers are impatient to find out why they are reading a story, it is preferable to place this focus graph within the first five paragraphs of your story.

How would you tell the story to a friend?   The "tell-a-friend" technique is a natural, conversational storytelling method. It also works for broadcast journalists, who must tell their stories anyway. In fact, the conversational method is a cornerstone of broadcast writing.

Imagine that your friend asks what the story is about and what happened. Chances are you might talk about the most interesting information first. Thinking in these terms will give you a clue for your lead and your organization.

If you mention something that isn't clear, a friend will probably ask you to explain. That's another clue for organizing your story. When you write one paragraph that raises a question in a reader's mind or has supporting material to explain it, follow it immediately with information that answers the question or substantiates the point, either with quotes or facts.

You also can use the tell-a-friend technique in the reporting stage. If you were trying to relate a story to a friend, what information would you need to know? What would you want to know? Let your natural curiosity be your guide when you are gathering information.

Almost all stories answer some basic questions: who, what, when, where, why and how. Add the question "so what" to make sure you have a story that will make a reader care.

Before you begin writing your story, don't forget to make a rough plan. Jot down some key words to remind you of the order you want to use. If you need more questions to determine how to start your story (the lead), try asking yourself these:

What struck you as most interesting about the story?

What do you think is the most important idea?

What do you think the reader wants to know?

What do you think might hook the reader?

Now write a first draft of your story. You'll revise it later, so don't struggle until you get the perfect words for the lead or for each paragraph. Write the story as quickly as you can. Then go over the story and change anything you don't like. In this revision stage, make sure you check the accuracy of all the names, facts and spelling.

Putting It All Together

Here is how Leslie Barewin used the coaching method to write her first news story when she was in journalism school at the University of Kansas. Barewin got the idea for the story when she went to the university health center because she had been feeling ill. The nurse stuck a thermometer in her ear. Barewin was surprised. She had never seen a thermometer like that. She decided that other students might be unaware of that type of thermometer and so it would make a good news story.

She started by asking herself what the story's about and wrote this focus statement at the top of her story:

Temperature probes are being used to
take patients' temperature through the ear
at Watkins Memorial Health Center.

Then she used the tell-a-friend technique to write her story. Although you might tell your friend this story in a different order, the style is basically a conversational storytelling method.

Barewin's original lead on her first draft was as follows:

You might not have to waste three minutes of your time at Watkins Memorial Health Center.

After she wrote her story, during the correcting/revising process, her professor asked her this coaching question to brighten the lead: What struck you as most interesting about this story? Barewin said it was the fact that the probes were used in the ear, the concept she had written in her focus statement.

That was what gave her the idea for her revised lead on the story. The focus statement on top of the page was not printed with the story. It was there only to help Barewin determine the main point and other information to include in her story.

Here is the revised version:

Focus statement: What's the story about?

Lead: What struck you as most interesting about these thermometers?

Focus/nut graph: What's the story about? Note the similarity to the focus statement.

Supporting material: How does it work? This paragraph raises a question answered in the next paragraph.

Description of ear probe

Temperature probes are being used to take patients' temperature through the ear at Watkins Memorial Health Center.

Don't be surprised if a nurse at Watkins Memorial Health Center tells you to stick it in your ear.

It's the current method of taking your temperature at the center.

Watkins is using the latest in thermometer technology. For more than a year, temperature probes have been used to take a patient's temperature through the ear instead of through the mouth or rectum.

"This thermometer tests the temperature of the skin in the ear canal, not the eardrum itself," said Jody Woods, director of nursing.

"The temperature of the ear is close to brain tissue," Woods said. There is a concern in the medical profession that excessively high temperatures may cause brain damage.

"A fever is the body's way of trying to release heat," Woods said.

The electronic ear probe resembles an electric shaver. The smooth white base curves slightly upward and rests comfortably in the hand.

Several buttons and a small digital screen that displays the temperature are on the front of the probe.

On the opposite side is the scanner. Covered by a plastic disposable cap, the scanner measures the body's temperature within 15 seconds.

The used cap is popped off, a new cap is installed, and the probe is ready for the next patient.

Woods said that rectal thermometers were the most accurate but that most students preferred other methods.

Because the ear probes are relatively new to nurses, there is a tendency to question them a bit more, Woods said.

Each new probe costs about $450 and is issued by the state, Woods said.

Lori Zito, a sophomore from Omaha, Neb., had her temperature taken with the ear probe recently.

"It's quicker," she said. "It only takes a few seconds. You don't have to sit there for two minutes with something in your mouth while trying not to cough."

Leslie Barewin, *The University Daily Kansan*

More elaboration about how the thermometer works

How does it compare to other thermometers?

Supporting material: cost

Reaction from a student

Adding Visual Elements

Barewin's story was accompanied by a photograph. Visual elements such as photographs, charts and other graphic illustrations are crucial to news presentation. Research shows that 98 percent of readers are drawn first to a photograph on a newspaper page. Visual elements, then, are an essential factor to consider when you are planning a story.

Photographs and other graphic illustrations not only help make your story look good, they can also make it easier to read. Many of the visual elements—such as headlines, boxes of information and summary sentences—are written by copy editors, and decisions about display are made by these editors or by page designers. However, reporters are expected to plan photos for their stories and to provide information for some of the graphics.

When a chart, a graphic or an information box will accompany your story, you need to consider whether the story needlessly duplicates information that could be presented visually. So in the writing process, don't just think about information to put into your story; think about information to pull out for visual devices.

The following sections describe the most common visual devices used with news stories.

Point of entry   The term "point of entry" indicates where the reader "enters" a story or where the reader can be lured to look. Points of entry include headlines, photographs, illustrations, facts boxes, captions and subheads (small titles or captions within a story).

Summary blurb   A paragraph or sentence summarizing the story is called a "summary blurb." It is placed below the headline. When you ask yourself what the story is about, you are really writing a summary blurb. Even though copy editors write the summary blurb, you should use the concept to write your focus statement.

Here is an example of a summary blurb on a story about a term paper scandal at the University of South Florida:

Papers a lesson in criminology	*Headline*
A USF professor follows a paper trail to a former student, wanted on charges he sold term papers to criminology majors.	*Summary blurb*

If the story is topped by a summary blurb, the lead should not repeat the exact wording of the summary. As a result, the writer can be more creative in the lead. Here is the lead on the term paper story:

A. Engler Anderson's term papers weren't just bad. They were a crime, said one professor.

Anderson, 31, is wanted on charges that he sold term papers to two University of Florida students.

Their major?

Criminology.

The charge—selling a term paper or dissertation to another per-son—is only a second-degree misdemeanor, but if he is caught, Anderson will be held without bail because he failed to appear for a court hearing this week.

St. Petersburg (Fla.) *Times*

The story then explains how William Blount, chairman of the USF Criminology Department, received two papers that he thought were "awful" and then discovered they were written by Anderson, a former student.

Facts box   Information from a story is sometimes set off in a "facts box" for reading at a glance. A facts box is also called a "highlights box," meaning that it highlights the key points in the story. For example, when basketball star Earvin "Magic" Johnson announced that he had the AIDS virus, many newspapers ran boxes containing highlights of his career. Others ran facts boxes containing information about AIDS, or acquired immune deficiency syndrome.

A facts or highlights box can include key dates in a chronology, the main points of a new proposal or any other crucial information. It is especially useful for breaking statistics out of a story. Although some information from a facts box may be crucial to the story itself, the writer should guard against too much repetition.

This example illustrates why the writer, as well as the copy editor, should consider the facts box as part of the story content, not just a graphic illustration:

Nevada regents OK raises

Professors, administrators: Contracts force pay hikes despite budget crisis.

While 23,000 other state workers sit and wait for their pay hike, professors and administrators in the University of Nevada System will get a 4 percent raise.

Headline

Summary blurb

Lead

> The Board of Regents' 6-2 vote Thursday for a pay increase beginning Oct. 15 came a week after a state board chaired by Gov. Bob Miller delayed all state pay raises until January to avert a budget crisis.
>
> But regents, faced with signed contracts, are obligated to pay the raises, said Chairwoman Carolyn Sparks of Las Vegas.
>
> "If we don't, we're up against thousands of lawsuits," she said.
>
> *Reno* (Nev.) *Gazette-Journal*

Here are the two facts boxes that accompanied the story, the first on the front page and the second on the "jump page" (the page on which the story continued):

University pay raises

Who gets them

About 2,000 professional employees on contract with the Nevada System, including

- 972 UNR professors and administrators
- 219 at Truckee Meadows Community College
- 88 at Western Nevada Community College

Who doesn't

- All university system classified employees, including secretaries, clerical and support personnel employed by the state

---

UNR salary ranges

- **President:** $141,400 now; $147,056 with 4 percent raise
- **Dean:** $53,772 (minimum) now; $55,772 with 4 percent raise
- **9-month professor with Ph.D.:** $51,589 (minimum) now; $53,652 with a 4 percent raise

---

The statistics in these facts boxes were not repeated in the story.

Empowerment box An "empowerment box" contains information that lets readers know where they can call for help or whom they can contact for more information related to the story.

This is an example from another story in the *Reno Gazette-Journal* about an increase in nursing home complaints. The empowerment box contained this information:

Help for seniors
How to complain

To report a complaint about a nursing or group-care home, call these representatives of the Nevada Aging Services Division:

- **Northern Nevada:** Earl Yamashita at 688-2964
- **Southern Nevada:** Gilda Johnstone or Lisa Selthofner at 1-486-4545

Pull quote   A good quote might be broken out of the story, placed in larger type and used as a point of entry to entice the reader. Although a copy editor will decide which quotes to pull for graphic display, when you write your story, consider which quotes could be used to entice readers. Then use your best quotes high in your story.

When Magic Johnson announced that he was retiring from basketball because he had contracted the AIDS virus, *The Washington Post* used this "pull quote" for emphasis:

"This is not like my life is over because it's not."
—Magic Johnson

Infographic   A chart, map, graph or other illustration meant to provide information, not just to make the story look good, is an "infographic." *USA Today* provides daily infographics in the bottom left-hand corner of its sections to explain some interesting statistical information about American life (see Exhibit 1-1). Other examples of infographics are diagrams of plane crashes or major accidents and illustrations explaining how something works.

The most common type of infographic, called a "location map," pinpoints the location of an accident, a crime or any other major news event. It is the reporter's responsibility to supply the information for those maps. So when you report a story that may need a map, make sure you gather information about the exact location of the event by noting the streets, the number of feet or yards from a spot where an explosion or major crime occurred, or any other crucial information that would help readers visualize the location.

Exhibit 1-1

Infographic from
USA Today
©1992 *USA Today.*
Reprinted with permission

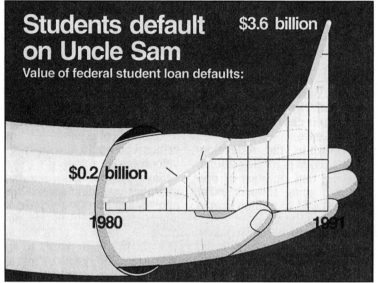

USA SNAPSHOTS®

A look at statistics that shape the nation

Students default on Uncle Sam

Value of federal student loan defaults:

$3.6 billion

$0.2 billion

1980   1991

Source: Department of Education   By Elys A. McLean, USA TODAY

Exercises

1 **Visual and verbal exercise:** Write a story based on the following information. Before you write the story, place your focus statement at the top. For this story, your focus sentence should be the results of the study. If you want a lead that gets directly to the point, your focus sentence could also be your lead. Once you've written a focus sentence, add a suggestion for visual presentation—a photograph, chart, facts box or other graphic illustration. Decide what facts, if any, should be duplicated in the story and the graphic. Then use the tell-a-friend technique to relate what you thought was the most interesting information. The following material is based on a story from *The* (San Bernardino, Calif.) *Sun.*

Who/what: A study comparing the death and accident rates of left- and right-handed people

When: Study was conducted last year and was reported in today's edition of the *New England Journal of Medicine.*

Where: Study was conducted by Diane Halpern, a psychology professor at California State University at San Bernardino, and Stanley Coren, a researcher at the University of British Columbia.

Why: To determine why fewer left-handed people are among the elderly population

How: Researchers studied death certificates of 987 people in two Southern California counties. Relatives were queried by mail about the subjects' dominant hands.

Backup information: The following points are not necessarily in the order they should be used in your story.

The researchers found that the average age at death for right-handed people was 75, for left-handed people 66; left-handed people represent 10 percent of the U.S. population; right-handed females tend to live six years longer than left-handed females, and right-handed males live 11 years longer than left-handed males; left-handed people were four times more likely to die from injuries while driving than right-handers and six times more likely to die from accidents of all kinds.

Halpern said, "The results are striking in their magnitude."

Halpern is right-handed.

She said her study should be interpreted cautiously. "It should not, of course, be used to predict the life span of any one individual. It does not take into account the fitness of any individual."

Left-handed women die around age 72; right-handed women die around age 78. Left-handed men die about age 62; right-handed men die about age 73.

"Some of my best friends are left-handed," Halpern said.

"It's important that mothers of left-handed children not be alarmed and not try to change which hand a child uses," she said. "There are many, many old left-handed people."

"We knew for years that there weren't as many old left-handers," Halpern said. "Researchers thought that was because in the early years of the century, most people born left-handed were forced to change to their right hands. So we thought we were looking at old people who used to be left-handed, but we weren't. The truth was, there simply weren't many left-handers left alive, compared to right-handers."

"Almost all engineering is geared to the right hand and right foot," Halpern said. "There are many more car and other accidents among left-handers because of their environment."

2   Reaction story: Interview at least three students on campus who are left-handed. Ask them what problems they encounter because they are left-handed. Using the study in Exercise 1 as a focus for your story, write a reaction story with the students' comments. Make sure you get the full names of the students, their majors and year of study (freshman, sophomore, and so on) so you can identify them properly in the story.

COACHING

Ask people in your community what they want to read in the newspaper.

Seek to include multicultural sources in your stories.

Ask yourself how your story affects your readers.

Consider whether your story needs a photograph or graphic.

Changing Concepts of News

2

I n Vancouver, Wash., reporters work on the "Glue Beat." In Wichita, Kan., they work on the "Public Life" team. At both newspapers, reporters with these assignments cover government—but not the way they have in the past.

The nature of news is changing. Traditional coverage of police departments, city councils and school districts hasn't disappeared, but a new concept of news is emerging. Increasingly, the emphasis in the print and broadcast media is on making news relevant to readers and viewers.

Thus the Glue Beat at *The Columbian* in Vancouver is defined as news about government and other agencies that hold or "glue" a community together. Reporters on this beat have shifted from covering meetings to writing stories that untangle red tape and show how people are affected by government.

The Wichita Eagle interprets its Public Life team in a similar way, emphasizing stories that show how to bring government and people together to solve problems. For example, the front page of one Sunday newspaper featured "A formula for safety," a story explaining how crime was decreasing in neighborhoods where citizens were helping police by identifying crack houses and conducting "block watches" to reduce crime. Indicative of the reader-involvement approach was a box accompanying the story: "How you can get involved."

Successful newspapers frequently will review their definitions of news, adjusting the mix of content to meet the requirements of the audience they wish to reach. This does not mean that bad news will be avoided or sugar-coated. This does mean that readers will receive a newspaper containing both what they need to know and what they want to know.

Burl Osborne, editor,

The Dallas Morning News

The Changing Newsroom Structure

The Eagle is one of many newspapers that not only changed the content of its news but also the structure of its newsroom in the mid-1990s. Instead of traditional departments—such as City Desk, Features and Business—teams of reporters and editors are assigned to cover such topics as relationships, leisure, religion and health. The last two topics are now part of the newspaper's Body and Soul team.

"The Body and Soul team will focus on the most important relationship each of us has in our lives—the relationship with ourselves," says a newsroom memo. "The team will look at our faith . . . the ways we try to grow spiritually. It will bring us stories on health and fitness, the ways we try to improve our physical condition. This team will endeavor to connect with our readers' personal concerns."

The (Portland) *Oregonian* also reorganized its newsroom with teams and topics; for example, the Shopping and Apparel team covers fashion and shopping patterns. Some other teams include the Tax team, which covers the impact of state and local taxes on readers, and the Kids' and Family Rights team. From planning the story idea to designing how it will appear in the newspaper, teams at *The Oregonian* are supposed to answer this question for readers: "Why should I care?"

These were just a few of the changes that took place at scores of newspapers in the United States during the 1990s as they tried to cope with declining circulation and competition for readers' time. Many broadcast news programs also expanded local news coverage to capture viewers and advertisers as competition increased from cable television and other local stations. In fact, the buzzwords in newsrooms at the end of the 20th century were *restructure, revamp, rebuild, reorganize, redefine,* and *reinvent.* After decades of complacency, newspapers, in particular, were seeking to change their definitions of news.

Previously, most newspaper editors and reporters chose to cover news that they thought readers needed to know. Although that is still true to a great extent, the emphasis at many newspapers shifted in the '90s to what readers wanted to know.

Concepts of news changed because people's needs changed. More women had entered the work force, and they had less time to devote to newspapers. But they had more buying power, so many newspapers started addressing women's concerns. Television became more of a competitive force, especially during major news events, when viewers were able to watch events as they occurred on the cable news network, CNN. In addition, newspapers faced competition for readers' time from videotapes, magazines, computer services and other leisure activities. As newspapers lost readers, advertisers switched to radio, cable television and direct mail to reach more people. Newspapers had to figure out a new role for themselves.

Public Journalism

One new role adopted by some newspapers, such as *The Charlotte* (N.C.) *Observer,* was called "public journalism" or "community-assisted journalism," shaping news coverage based on readers' concerns instead of reacting to news events. For example, in one presidential election, *The Observer* conducted polls jointly with a local television station and asked voters what issues they wanted politicians to discuss. Reporters then interviewed candidates about those issues instead of letting candidates discuss their own agendas. The first story of the election coverage began this way:

Listen, candidates, your neighbors are worried.

Worried about losing their jobs, their health insurance and even the moral values that glue their communities together. . . .

As a new election year unfolds, a Charlotte Observer/WSOC-TV poll of 1,003 Carolinians found people are deeply troubled about the future. And nine out of 10 in the 140-county Charlotte region doubt their elected leaders are in touch with the powerful forces tearing at their lives.

They want their worries heard. They want them to become the priorities of politicians.

Not everyone in the media approves of this approach to news. Newspaper editors involved in public journalism call it community leadership because they are setting the agenda for solving local problems. Critics call it advocacy journalism or biased journalism, which contradicts the traditional newspaper role of remaining objective and uninvolved in the news.

News 2000

On a similar but broader scale, the Gannett Co., which owns *USA Today* and more than 140 other daily newspapers, has redefined news to reflect the concerns of readers. The company calls its approach News 2000, a concept of planning news based on a pyramid of concerns (see Exhibit 2-1). The most important block, community interest, forms the base. Editors at each Gannett newspaper conducted surveys to determine the major interests of readers in their communities and then developed plans to cover those subjects more extensively. Some of the other building blocks require the newspapers to interact with readers, present news with graphics, use multicultural sources and write stories that evoke emotions. News 2000 is another way of trying to give readers what they want instead of what editors think they need.

ANTICIPATES
CHANGE

EMPHASIZES
IMMEDIACY

FOSTERS
INTERACTION
WITH
READERS

PROVIDES
INFORMATION
PEOPLE
NEED

EVOKES
EMOTIONS

MAINTAINS
CONSISTENCY

UPHOLDS
FIRST
AMENDMENT
RESPONSIBILITIES

REQUIRES
DIVERSITY

UTILIZES
COMPELLING
PRESENTATION

CENTERS ON
COMMUNITY INTEREST

Exhibit 2-1

The News 2000 concept

Courtesy of The Gannett Co., Inc.

Judy Pace, editor of the Gannett-owned *Jackson* (Tenn.) *Sun,* explained the changes this way: "The days of spinach journalism—read this, it's good for you—are gone."

The Need For Change

If there were a wizard of change, it would be Jean Gaddy Wilson. She is executive director of New Directions for News, a University of Missouri–based organization that conducts roundtable discussions with editors throughout the country to find solutions to problems facing the newspaper industry. Wilson says newspapers must change the way they present news.

"Readers are saying, 'Don't give me all this stuff that you have been throwing at me like a ball machine; give me stuff I can understand about a complex world,'" Wilson says. "I think the content will change. I don't think it's a matter of shortening up the same old stuff. Local news will remain important, but it is not going to be the same ho-hum news. We can still report about city hall. We just haven't written about it compellingly to show how it affects people's lives. Journalists need to use investigative powers—not just to go get the damn rascals—but to investigate what a community is looking for, what people do and how to serve their needs."

That is precisely what many journalists in print and broadcast news are doing. Through access telephone numbers, electronic mail, polls, town meetings, fax numbers and focus groups (interviews with small groups of readers), newspaper and television news editors are seeking to interact with readers and viewers. Electronic newspapers use "chat" features or bulletin boards to interact with readers.

The Impact of Technology

Technology is one of the biggest causes of change in the media. Despite concerns that newspapers will become dinosaurs in a Jurassic Park of journalism, such obsolescence is not imminent. The form of newspapers may change, but journalists will be needed more than ever to sort out and clarify news in an age of information overload.

To ensure their survival, many newspapers, magazines and broadcast programs—MTV and ABC News, for example— have produced electronic versions that people can access with their computers via commercial services, such as America Online, and via the Internet, a massive computer network of information. Advertisers have also begun using computer services as direct-order shopping centers, much like the shop-at-home channels on television.

But do you have to sit in front of a computer to read your newspaper or magazine?

No, says Roger Fidler, a media visionary who has developed a portable, flat-panel computer about the size of a magazine by which readers may receive their newspaper. It weighs less than two pounds and resembles a self-contained screen of a notebook computer. The paperless newspaper provides touch-sensitive boxes so readers can select the news they want, order goods from advertisers and perform other interactive functions with the newspaper by using a special electronic pen or their fingers.

"The last vestige of the Industrial Age is the printing press, and that is about to change," Fidler says. "I am convinced that sometime within the first decade or two of the new millennium, pigmented ink and pulp paper will finally begin to give way to digital ink and silicon paper in the form of portable information appliances."

Fidler predicts that for a while newspapers will continue to simultaneously publish printed and electronic versions, much as the *San Jose* (Calif.) *Mercury News, Chicago Tribune* and other papers do. Even if the paper versions eventually disappear, Fidler is optimistic about the future of newspapers and opportunities for journalists. "I think newspapers in the next century will be the dominant medium," he says.

But the newspapers that he envisions will mix text with animation, full-motion video clips, sound bites and even a speaker option.

"Suppose you want all these stories read to you as you jump into your car," he says. "You could use the speaker option. If you are bored with a story, just say 'Next.'"

Many features on the Internet already combine sound and motion. As technology continues to improve, more publications will offer text, sound and video. Scores of newspapers, such as *The Orange County* (Calif.) *Register,* already provide cable news and audiotext, which provides recorded stories and information for readers who call the paper. As a result, most media futurists insist that journalists need to be trained in both broadcast and print media.

Computers have also made it possible for journalists to interpret huge data bases of statistics and other government documents. Computer-assisted reporting, reserved in the past for major investigative projects, is now being used more for a variety of stories. For example, the *Dayton* (Ohio) *Daily News* was the first newspaper in the country to be directly wired to the county's computers, giving the paper instant access to police reports, court files, property records and other county data. In one project, the newspaper analyzed a data base of 58 million court records to find the state's worst drunken drivers. Other newspapers, like the (Raleigh, N.C.) *News & Observer,* routinely use data bases for features and daily stories as well as projects.

Access to computerized records can be costly, however, because government agencies can charge high fees for providing the data. But these data bases may totally replace paper police reports and other records in the future, making computer-assisted reporting an important tool in journalism training.

Despite all the technology, Fidler says content is still the most important factor. "Forget technology; technology will adapt to you. We need to step back and ask what would you as a reader really want."

All these efforts to give readers what they want worry some editors. Geneva Overholser, ombudsman for *The Washington Post,* said that newspapers are so afraid of offending anyone that they seem to have a new slogan: "All the news that doesn't displease anyone."

"We have this notion that we must make sure that no one suffers," Overholser says. "That is not the newspaper editor's role. It is to make sure the truth is told, that word goes out, that the whole picture is presented. Let us have confidence in what we know how to do—tell a story that brings tears or laughter. To explain a dilemma. To bring the unknown to light. Let us not care what one individual thinks of us on one given day. For truth-telling will have its victims."

Regardless of how and where the information is presented, writing still must be compelling, and some of the basic definitions of news will remain valid.

Hard News and Features

News falls into two basic categories: hard news and soft news. "Hard news" includes stories of a timely nature about events or conflicts that have just happened or are about to happen, such as crimes, fires, meetings, protest rallies, speeches and testimony in court cases. The hard approach is basically an account of what happened, why it happened and how readers will be affected. These stories have immediacy.

"Soft news" is defined as news that entertains or informs, with an emphasis on human interest and novelty and less immediacy than hard news. For example, a profile about a man who designs model airplanes or a story about the effectiveness of diets would be considered soft news.

Soft news can also be stories that focus on people, places or issues that affect readers' lives. These types of stories are called "feature stories." A story about the growing number of babies suffering from AIDS could be considered a soft-news story. It isn't less important than hard news, but it isn't news that happened overnight. However, a feature story can be based on a news event. Instead of being just a factual account of the event, it features or focuses on a particular angle, such as human interest reactions.

If the action or event occurred the same day as or the day before publication of the newspaper, the event is called "breaking news." Here is an example of the lead of a breaking-news story from a Saturday edition:

> Tornadoes rapped Topeka and southeast Shawnee County Friday afternoon, damaging seven homes and sending residents scurrying for cover.
>
> No one was injured by the short, severe storm that struck unexpectedly.
>
> Steve Fry, *Topeka* (Kan.) *Capital-Journal*

The preceding example of a hard-news story tells readers what happened. The newspaper also printed this feature story focusing on people affected by the storm:

> Becky Clark of Topeka was told the tornado sirens that sounded Friday afternoon were a false alarm.
>
> Then she got home from work and saw her back yard at 2411 S.E. Gemini Ave. in the Aquarian Acres neighborhood.
>
> "I couldn't believe it," she said.
>
> A tornado had lifted up the family pontoon boat, which was parked in the back yard, and tossed it into the family swimming pool, crushing part of the boat.
>
> "It just wanted to get in the water," said Joe Clark, Becky's husband.
>
> "I guess it was tired of being in dry dock. . . ."
>
> Joe Taschler, *Topeka Capital-Journal*

The hard-news story about the storm was the main story, called a "mainbar." Because the accompanying feature story was a different angle on the same topic, it was a "sidebar" packaged with the main story.

But many other features in a newspaper do not have a breaking-news peg. They simply focus on interesting people or topics. For example, the *Boca Raton* (Fla.) *News* printed a feature story on the growing popularity of waterbeds, a topic of interest to its readers.

Qualities of News Stories

Definitions of news are changing. But these are some of these traditional qualities of both hard- and soft-news stories:

Timeliness: An event that happened the day of or day before publication or an event that is due to happen in the immediate future is considered timely. Some events that happened in the past also may be considered timely if they are printed on an anniversary of the event, such as one, five or 10 years after the incident. Timeliness answers this reader's question: Why are you telling me this now? This story was timely because it was published the day after the accident:

> A bus loaded with elementary school children crashed head-on into a compact car in southwestern Jefferson County yesterday, injuring 24 students and the two drivers.
>
> The (Louisville, Ky.) *Courier-Journal*

Proximity: An event may be of interest to local readers because it happened in or close to the community. This story would be of particular interest to residents in the Oregon community where this man lived:

> A 71-year-old former psychologist received an eight-year prison sentence Monday for running the most sophisticated indoor marijuana-growing operation ever discovered in Clackamas County.
>
> Authorities said Arvord E. Belden of Estacada may be the oldest man ever sentenced to federal prison for a drug crime in Oregon.
>
> Dave Hogan, *The Oregonian*

Unusual nature: Out-of-the-ordinary events, a bizarre or rare occurrence, or people engaged in unusual activites are considered newsworthy, as in this story:

Man ticketed for walking his lizard

FORT LAUDERDALE, Fla.— Walking your dog along the beach here is illegal—and so is lounging with your lizard, Chris DeMango found out. Mortimer, DeMango's 20-pound purple-tongued monitor lizard, complete with matching pink doll sweater and leash, was out for exercise Monday. DeMango said a walk makes Mortimer more docile, but police said it makes him an illegal lizard—animals are banned on the beach. DeMango was ticketed, and his lizard law violation could cost him 60 days in jail and a $500 fine, said police spokesman Ott Cefkin. DeMango was not amused. "I would think that would be the most absurd thing, if I were to go to jail for this," he grumbled.

St. Petersburg (Fla.) *Times*

Celebrities: People who are well-known for their accomplishments— primarily entertainers, athletes or people who have gained fame for achievements, good or bad—attract a lot of attention. This story ran on the front page because of the celebrity status of the entertainer:

Michael Jackson, whose inventive dancing and pop vocals have earned him worldwide fame and millions of dollars, did a new move Friday: He apologized.

Rocked by a barrage of viewer complaints about a sexual and violent segment of his "Black or White" music video, Jackson and Fox Broadcasting Co. said they were sorry and agreed to cut the offending segment from the video.

The video, which premiered Thursday night on Fox, will be rebroadcast Sunday night—minus a final sequence in which Jackson materializes into a panther and launches into a primal dance during which he grabs at his genitals, unzips his pants and smashes the windows of a car with a crowbar.

Ray Richmond and Anne Valdespino, *The Orange County Register*

Human interest: People like stories about people who have special problems, achievements or experiences. These stories can be profiles or unusual stories about people that make readers care about their plight. This example about a couple who spent $6,000 looking for their lost cat combines human interest and an unusual story:

Five-year-old Marble used to hide in the box springs of a spare bed in Bill and Carol Deckers' Denver home.

Now the Deckers' cat is hiding somewhere in the woods near Carthage, Mo.

Since Marble escaped from the couple's recreational vehicle Aug. 18, the Deckers have spent more than $6,000 trying to get her back.

"We taught her to live with us and we owe it to her," said Carol Decker, 41, a part-time accountant who gave up her job to look for Marble. . . .

Since losing Marble, the Deckers have put up posters and placed newspaper ads in Colorado, Missouri and Oklahoma, and contacted a psychic to locate her, to no avail.

The Deckers have returned to the site, often sleeping outdoors in the hope that their presence would draw Marble to them.

Tillie Fong, *Rocky Mountain* (Denver) *News*

Conflict: Stories involving conflicts people have with government or other people are often newsworthy, especially when the conflict reflects local problems. This example affected people in Chicago:

> Hundreds of protesters descended on the Chicago School Board's headquarters Tuesday to oppose school closings that they contend will drive hundreds of students away from school and endanger the lives of others.
>
> David C. Rudd and John Kass, *Chicago Tribune*

Impact: Reaction stories to news events or news angles that affect readers have impact. During the confirmation hearings for Supreme Court Justice Clarence Thomas, who was accused of sexual harassment by University of Oklahoma law professor Anita Hill, reaction stories abounded. Here is one example:

> Anita Hill is not alone. Working women around the country have joined her, crossing beyond confusion and fear about sexual harassment to share their experiences.
>   "We've had a real outpouring of calls," said Barbara Otto of 9 to 5, the National Association of Working Women. "It's like they're coming out of the closet to tell their dirty secret. They're saying, 'Enough!'"
>
> The Associated Press

Some additional qualities of news to consider:

Helpfulness: Consumer, health and other how-to stories that help readers cope with their lives.

> If your head spins at the torrent of medical studies that fills newspapers, magazines and TV, join the club. It seems that each day brings another round of studies contradicting last month's hot results.
>   One day vitamin E is found to prevent cancer. Next, it is suspected of causing it.
>   Margarine is good. No, it's bad.
>   One can almost hear a collective scream of frustration across the land.
>   Studies are the cornerstone of medical progress, showing doctors and patients the way to longer, healthier lives. But they can also lead us astray.
>   To try to help you through the hype and hustle, here's a basic outline of what studies are, how they differ, what they can tell us and where they can go wrong. Call it A User's Guide to Medical Studies. Or, How to Follow Health News Without Having a Stroke.
>
> Phillip E. Canuto, Knight-Ridder/ Tribune News Service

Entertainment: Stories that amuse readers, make them feel good or help them enjoy their leisure time have entertainment value. In a broad sense, many of the news features in sports and lifestyle sections can be classified as entertainment. Entertainment stories often involve celebrities or have human-interest qualities. This story combines news qualities of human interest and unusual nature to entertain or amuse readers.

ODESSA, Texas—When Elbert Lewis got his draft notice, he told his wife goodbye. Then he thought of his children. And his seven grandchildren. And his great-grandchild.

The Selective Service was cracking down on potential draft dodgers, and government records showed Lewis failed to register as required by law when he turned 18 in November.

The problem: Lewis turned 18 in November 1932.

The records showed his birth-date was Nov. 11, 1976, instead of in 1914, which makes him 80.

What's more, Lewis did register for the draft—in 1941. He served on a Navy anti-aircraft cruiser during World War II and received a Purple Heart.

When Lewis got the draft compliance notice Saturday, he broke the news to his wife, Janie.

"He came into the den and said, 'Well, I have to tell you goodbye,'" she said. "Then we called our kids. We just cut up and acted silly about it, really."

"We really got a laugh out of it, and so did all four of my kids," Lewis said.

He dashed off a copy of his birth certificate and honorable discharge to the Selective Service. The agency removed his name from its list, spokesman Lou Brodsky said.

The idea of being 18 again was appealing, to a degree.

"I wouldn't mind it, take away the war," Lewis said.

The Associated Press

Inspiration: Stories about people who overcome difficulties also have human interest as a news quality.

Until a few months ago, the only image most people had of Rachel Barton was of a 20-year-old violin prodigy performing raptly on the formidable stage at Orchestra Hall.

Then she was nearly killed in a freak train accident that severed one of her legs.

Now, another image has emerged. It is of Barton wearing a radiant red dress that covered her remaining leg, beaming a confident smile and playfully bragging about the flowers she received while in the hospital.

Were they from Itzhak Perlman?

No, she giggled, they were from Slash, the lead guitar player for Guns N' Roses, "my favorite heavy metal group."

Two months after she was nearly killed, Barton spoke publicly for the first time Tuesday about the accident, her faith and the long rehabilitation ahead.

Michael A. Lev, *Chicago Tribune*

Special interest: Some stories appeal to people's interests in such subjects as science, business or religion or to such special groups as women, minorities, disabled people, veterans, college students or other groups with particular interests. The *Chicago Tribune* specifically targets women in a section called Womanews with stories like this:

A card table and two chairs hang suspended from a ceiling above menacing yellow and orange flames. That was how Hollis Sigler felt when she waited for test results that would reveal whether her breast cancer had spread to her bones, which it in fact had.

So that was what Sigler depicted in oil pastel on paper in a work that forms part of a series titled "The Breast Cancer Journal."

Sigler is one of a growing number of artists whose experiences with breast cancer are finding expression in their art.

Barbara Brotman, *Chicago Tribune*

Issues or problems in the community: These stories usually include qualities such as conflict and proximity. The *St. Cloud* (Minn.) *Times* combined the trends of reader involvement with issues important to minorities in a series called "Open or Intolerant?" The newspaper sought opinions from teen-agers of different races as well as from police, city leaders and residents about police treatment of young people of color.

Since moving to St. Cloud three years ago, Jacob "Cisco" Owens says he has been hassled, detained, pulled over and provoked by St. Cloud police officers more times than he can remember.

Owens, a 16-year-old Apollo High School junior, admits he's been in trouble a few times for minor things. But for every time he's done something, anything, wrong, he swears he can identify seven more times he's been confronted by police when he's done nothing at all.

"And almost all the time they ask me if I'm in a gang. It makes me angry that they just assume. It's just a given that I'm treated like that," he says. "Just because I'm young and black, I'm treated like a thug."

Dozens of young people of different races in St. Cloud say it's no secret: Police here are known for targeting minority youth for bogus traffic stops, tough talk, and sometimes, rough treatment when responding to calls.

Lee Rood, *St. Cloud Times*

Trends: Stories may indicate patterns or shifts in issues that influence readers' lives, such as increases in crime, social issues and other forces in society.

Many Milwaukee area public libraries no longer have strict "SH!" policies.

Libraries are shedding their image as quiet, somber places for bookworms and students only. Instead, today's libraries offer a wide variety of materials and programs in an effort to appeal to more people.

Lawrence Sussman, *The Milwaukee Journal Sentinel*

The Importance of Graphics

The presentation of a story with photographs or graphics is crucial. Studies by the Poynter Institute for Media Studies in St. Petersburg, Fla., show an increased emphasis on graphic devices and color.

In one study, called "Eyes on the News," researchers measured the movements of people's eyes as they read the newspaper. The results of this study, also known as the Eye Trac study, show that readers are drawn to color photographs first, then headlines, cutlines (captions), briefs (stories abbreviated to one to three paragraphs) and a number of other graphic devices called points of entry—points where the reader enters a story. Some of those eye-catching points include subheadlines and quotations displayed in larger type within the story.

The study also concludes that most people only scan the newspaper, looking at headlines and graphics, and that they read very few stories all the way through. The average reader skims about 25 percent of the stories in the newspaper but thoroughly reads only half of those (about 12 percent), the study concludes.

To grab readers' attention, news stories now are a mix of visual and verbal information. Graphics have become so important in news presentation that some newspapers, including *The Orange County Register* and *The Dallas Morning News,* have graphics reporters. When a major story such as an airplane crash occurs, these graphics reporters go to the scene with other reporters to gather information for the graphic. While the regular reporters gather facts, quotes and other materials, the graphics reporters seek such details as how many feet the plane skidded, for scale drawings.

Because most newspapers do not have special reporters to gather information for graphics, those responsibilities often belong to regular reporters. In addition, all reporters need to consider the graphic devices that may accompany the story, so information is not duplicated.

That is the emphasis at the *Reno* (Nev.) *Gazette-Journal,* a Gannett newspaper that makes extensive use of graphics. Reporters are expected to visualize their stories as a total package involving photos and graphics. The emphasis is on using verbal and visual tools that will make information clear to readers.

For example, a story about water rates explained the effect on readers in the lead and in this summary box above the story:

Water shock

What it means to you

- By 1994 a $15.41 monthly increase for the average residential customer
- By 1996 another $12.40 monthly hike

The story then began with this impact lead, which explains how the increased water rates will affect readers:

> You may be paying almost 150 percent more for water in 1996 to cover costs caused by new federal drinking water standards and area growth.
>
> That's a $71.50 monthly bill for average residential customers and "the reality of what's facing the area," Phil Seges, Westpac Utilities president, said Friday.

Mike Norris, *Reno Gazette-Journal*

The graphs in Exhibit 2-2 were another piece of the total package.

Mario R. Garcia, an associate director in charge of graphics and design programs at the Poynter Institute for Media Studies, says the majority of readers today do not remember life without television, so visual elements are crucial in a newspaper. "The marriage of visual and words has to begin early—from the first time you learn reporting," he says.

Garcia, considered the leading authority on graphics, has redesigned more than 100 newspapers throughout the world. He says that redesigning a newspaper for appearance without considering the writing content is like cosmetic surgery. "It's like giving someone a new nose but you have the same old boring personality," he says.

There must be a renewed emphasis on good writing, Garcia says. "We have not lost the readers; what we have lost is good stories." His solution for the future is more of what he calls "invisible stories," the kinds

Exhibit 2-2

Infographic for story on water rates

Courtesy of the *Reno Gazette-Journal*

of news stories a newspaper develops through investigative or enterprising reporting. "Visible news comes to you—police reports, meetings, etc. It's there, but television also hears the sirens and gets it sooner." He says newspapers must develop angles to stories and find unusual stories television doesn't have.

All these kinds of stories have their place in the newspapers of today and of the future. And editors will continue to grapple with an old dilemma: Should they give people what they want or what they need? As Burl Osborne, editor of *The Dallas Morning News* says, a good newspaper contains both kinds of stories. Many will be short; others will be in-depth. Journalists will still need to learn how to present information to keep readers informed and interested.

Exercises

1   Try this experiment to test your reading habits. Bring to class a copy of a newspaper you haven't read. Read the newspaper as you would for pleasure. Place a check on the first item you look at—a picture, graphic, headline or story. Mark the stories you read, and place an X at the point in the story where you decide to stop reading.

Where did your eye go first? Why are visual elements so important? Now analyze which stories you read and how much of them you read. Where did you stop on most stories? Why?

Because you are a journalism student, you may read more than the average reader. Guess how many seconds the average reader spends on a story before deciding to continue or switch to another story. (The answer is at the end of Exercise 5.)

2   Keep a journal of your reading habits for three days. Write a paragraph each day about the kinds of stories you read and didn't read, how many you read all the way through, and how many you read just through the headline or the first few paragraphs. Clip some of the stories you liked and didn't like, and analyze your preferences. Record the amount of time you spent reading the newspaper for pleasure, not for an assignment. Then interview three other people—students, neighbors or strangers—and ask them what kinds of stories they do and don't read. Write a summary of your findings.

3   **On-line news ideas:** Either in small groups or as a class, brainstorm topics and ideas that you would want to read in an electronic newspaper or magazine. Discuss the advantages and disadvantages of reading your newspaper or magazine on a computer screen.

4   Analyze the role of graphics—maps, facts boxes, illustrations, photos—in your local or campus newspaper. Find stories that could benefit from more graphics.

5   **Role of technology:** Working individually or in groups (if your instructor prefers), interview one or more sources in your field of journalism about the role technology will play in the presentation of information in that area of the media.

Check your sources with your instructor before you conduct interviews to make sure several students are not interviewing the same person. Ask your sources about on-line technology, e-mail, faxes and any other changes in their field. Also ask your sources what skills they think journalists in their field will need in the future. Write a story based on your findings.

(The answer to the question in Exercise 1 is three seconds. Now you can see why you must write compelling news stories that make the reader want to continue reading.)

COACHING

State the main idea of your story in one sentence.

Visualize your story with text and graphics or photographs.

Make sure your quotes don't repeat your transitions.

Test the quality of your quotes: Are they good enough to be used as pull quotes?

The Basic News Story

3

The basic news story is told upside down. It usually is called a hard-news story. That doesn't mean it should be hard to read. Quite the contrary. It really should be called an easy news story, because the facts are presented in a direct form that makes it easy for the reader to get the most important information quickly. A hard-news story often presents the end result of a news event first, so the key facts are in the first few paragraphs. If a news story were a mystery story, you would solve the mystery in the beginning and then devote the rest of the story to telling the reader how and why it happened. Dan Henderson, the late assistant managing editor of *The Commercial Appeal* in Memphis, Tenn., described it this way: "A basic news story is similar to a formula for writing a novel about the Old West: Shoot the sheriff in the first paragraph."

For example, if the state officials who regulate higher education—often called the Board of Regents—had met yesterday to discuss an increase in tuition at universities in your state, you wouldn't write that the Board of Regents met to consider a tuition increase. You would give the end results. What did the regents decide? This is a direct approach: "The Board of Regents voted yesterday to raise undergraduate tuition next fall at state universities by $100 to $4,700." Or you might say, "Tuition will increase next fall by $100 for undergraduate students at the state's universities." Then you could explain that the decision was made yesterday by the Board of Regents and give details about the tuition increase and its impact. Here is how one newspaper actually reported such a story:

Too many stories fail to answer the reader's most challenging question: So what?

Roy Peter Clark, writing coach and author

> The cost of sending an undergraduate to Stanford University will climb in the fall to $21,262 for tuition, room and board, officials announced yesterday.
>
> Tuition will go from $14,280 to $15,102, an increase of 5.75 percent, and room and board will increase 3.9 percent to $6,160.

San Francisco Chronicle

Not all basic news stories have to start with such a direct approach. There are many other ways of writing news stories and still delivering the information to readers in a quick, easy form. But all news stories answer some basic questions: who, what, when, where, why and how? As newspaper readership declines, editors increasingly want the answer to another question: so what? What is the significance to readers? What information does the story contain that will make readers care?

Conflict and Resolution

Most hard-news stories are about a conflict or a problem and the attempts to resolve it. Consider all the stories about crime, courts and government. The majority involve problems created or being resolved by the people who are involved.

The qualities discussed in Chapter 2—such as timeliness, unusual nature, celebrity and human interest—also help provide answers to the "so what" question. Here's one example of a conflict that is also unusual:

> The family expected to mourn Anthony Romeo, who died of heart disease in September at his Seffner home. Instead, they found a stranger in his coffin.
>
> The Hillsborough Medical Examiner's Office had shipped the wrong body to the funeral home.
>
> The mix-up so upset Romeo's son Joseph that he filed suit Monday against Hillsborough County, the Brandon funeral home and the private courier that delivered the body.

Conflict

Resolution

Rachel L. Swarns, *St. Petersburg* (Fla.) *Times*

Elements of the Basic News Story

Although a news story can contain a wealth of information, it should have one main idea. You should be able to identify the main idea in a sentence. All the other information should then support that central concept.

Like all stories, the basic news story has a headline and three general parts: a beginning called the "lead," a middle called the "body" and an ending. Other elements are backup for the lead, nut graph, impact, attribution, background and elaboration.

Headline

The headline is the line on top of the story that tells the reader what the story is about. It usually is written by a copy editor or editor, except at very small newspapers where the editor also may be the reporter/writer. For a basic news story, the copy editor bases the headline on the main points of the story, which the reporter is expected to write in the first few paragraphs.

With the increased emphasis on graphics, more newspapers today are using secondary headlines, called "deck heads" or "summary lines," under the main headline. The two headlines together give the reader a quick overview of the story's content. Here is an example from a newspaper that uses summary lines on most of its major stories:

Salmon spawn a new crisis	*Headline*
Dwindling numbers and fading strength threaten to add the fish to the list of endangered species. But some question if the Northwest will pay the price to save the animals.	*Summary line*

Los Angeles Times

Even though you won't write the headlines for your own stories, you can use the concept as a writing tool. If you are having trouble identifying the main point of a story, think of a headline for it.

Lead

The beginning of the story, the hook that tells the reader what the story is about, is the "lead." A good lead entices the reader to continue reading. In a hard-news story, the lead usually is written in one sentence—the first sentence of the story—and gives the most important information about the event. But even a basic story can have a creative lead, called a "soft lead."

The most common type of lead on a hard-news story is called a "summary lead" because it summarizes the main points about what happened. It answers the questions of who, what, when, where, why and how. The rest of the story elaborates on what, why and how.

Hard-news leads do not have to answer all those questions in the first sentence if doing so would make the lead too long and difficult to read. Shorter leads of fewer than 35 words are preferable, but that number is only a guideline. The writer has to decide which elements are most important to stress in the first sentence. This summary lead stresses who, what, where and when; the rest of the story gives more details, such as the names of the professor and the suspect.

> A Northwestern University professor of hearing sciences was shot and seriously wounded in a university parking lot Thursday.

Backup for the Lead

The lead should be backed up, or supported, with explanation that substantiates information in the lead. The "backup" should contain statements or quotes to explain your key point. Here is an example:

> GAINESVILLE, Fla.—A University of Florida law student suffering from amnesia after mysteriously disappearing in July has recalled her abduction under hypnosis, authorities said.
>
> Elizabeth "Libby" Morris, 32, slowly has regained memory of her life before her disappearance from the Oaks Mall parking lot but has never consciously remembered what occurred during the five days she was missing, said Lt. Spencer Mann, a spokesman with the Alachua County Sheriff's Office.

Summary lead

Backup

The Associated Press

Nut Graph

The nut graph is a sentence or paragraph that states the focus—the main point—of the story. It should tell in a nutshell what the story is about and why it is newsworthy. Although a news story may contain many comments and points, it should be developed around one major theme or concept, and all other information should relate to that focus.

In a hard-news story with a direct summary lead, the lead contains the focus, so you don't need a separate nut graph. When the lead takes a softer, more creative approach and does not immediately explain the main point of the story, the nut graph is a separate paragraph. The nut graph is even more crucial when a story starts with a softer feature lead, because the reader has to wait for a few paragraphs to find out the reason for the story.

The nut graph should be placed high in the story, generally by the third to fifth paragraph. But if the lead is very compelling, the nut graph could come later. Rigid rules can ruin good writing.

Here's an example:

RAVENNA, Ohio—There's no room at the Portage County Jail for Matthew P. Dukes—and he's trying hard to get in.	*Lead*
The Newton Falls resident has tried six times in 15 months to serve a 30-day sentence for driving while intoxicated. But each time, deputies have turned him away.	*Backup*
The jail is full, they say. Come again.	
But Dukes has gone to court, filing a federal suit against the county sheriff and alleging that he is suffering cruel and unusual punishment by being prevented from going to jail.	*Nut graph*
Several area lawyers say it may be one of the first cases of its kind—a test of civil liberties that may pave the way for others who are idling away the hours while they wait to serve sentences in filled-to-capacity facilities for crimes such as shoplifting, theft or drunken driving.	
For Dukes, 26, the unserved sentence is a constant source of frustration and embarrassment, a situation that he said has helped to turn him away from a hard-drinking lifestyle.	
He said that he had not had a drink in a year and that he wanted to put the sentence behind him.	

Carol Biliczky, Knight-Ridder/Tribune News Service

Lead quote

The first quote that backs up the lead is called the "lead quote" or the "augmenting quote." It is usually the strongest quote you have, and it supports the concept in the lead without repeating the same information or wording. A lead quote isn't required in all stories, but a strong quote placed within a paragraph or two after the lead helps make the story interesting.

PENSACOLA, Fla. (AP)—Soon-to-be graduate student Michael Kearney hasn't chosen a major yet—but give him time, he's only 11.

Michael will begin tackling graduate studies at the University of West Florida in Pensacola this summer.

"We don't push him," said his mother, Cassidy Kearney. "He pushes us. We just try and keep up with him."

The Associated Press

Impact

Whenever possible, the writer should explain how the news affects readers. The "impact" sentence or paragraph should answer the question: "What is the significance of this story? What in the story makes the reader care?" Sometimes the impact is explained in the lead or in the nut graph; sometimes it is lower in the story, in an explanatory paragraph.

In the story about the man who can't get into jail, the impact is the significance of his lawsuit. The significance is explained in the paragraph following the nut graph.

Not all stories can show direct impact on readers, but they should all have a clear paragraph explaining the reason for the story. In some stories, such as police stories, the impact is that the news happened in the community and should be of interest to local residents.

When Oregon's mandatory automobile seat belt law goes into effect Dec. 7, police won't have any trouble enforcing it—all they have to see is a shoulder harness or a lap belt dangling unused. — *Lead*

"Police officers routinely tell us that safety belt laws are easy to enforce," said Geri Parker, safety belt program coordinator for the Oregon Traffic Safety Commission. — *Backup*

Oregon voters approved a ballot measure Nov. 6 to extend mandatory seat belt use to people age 16 and older. Seat belts or safety seats already are required for everyone under 16.

Beginning Dec. 7, everyone in the front and back seats of a car will need to buckle up—if belts are available—or face a fine of up to $50. — *Impact*

Phil Manzano, *The* (Portland) *Oregonian*

In the following example, some of the impact is in the lead, and more is in the second paragraph:

The federal education budget includes more money for cash grants to college students, and new guidelines will push most of it to students from low-income families.	*Lead*
Losers in the already-difficult scramble for the Pell education grants could be students from middle-income families.	*Impact*

USA Today

Attribution

Where did you get the information? Who told you these facts? How can the reader be sure what you say is true? The "attribution" provides those answers. You need to attribute all quotes—exact wording of statements that people made—and much information that you did not witness. If the information is common knowledge or indisputable, you do not have to attribute it. (A more complete discussion of how to use quotes and attribution comes later in this chapter.)

The attribution should be in the lead for controversial or accusatory information, but in many other cases it can be delayed so it doesn't clutter the lead. Police stories often have attribution in the lead, especially if you get the information by telephone or if the information is accusatory:

ST. PETERSBURG, Fla.—A 15-year-old boy was stabbed twice in the chest Thursday afternoon when he apparently tried to break up a fight in a crowded parking lot at Northeast High School, authorities said.	*Lead with attribution*
Police and school officials said the stabbing, believed to have occurred after one student took another's hat, was the first they could recall at Pinellas County schools.	*Backup*

St. Petersburg Times

In the next example, general attribution is in the lead, but the specific attribution is in the second paragraph. The names of the groups that did the study are too cumbersome to use in the lead.

U.S. college students, criticized as over-materialistic in the 1980s, are showing increased interest in social causes such as the environment and less interest in making money, a new study says.

Lead with general attribution

The 25th annual survey of college freshmen, conducted by the American Council on Education and the University of California, Los Angeles, shows steadily changing attitudes.

Backup with specific attribution

USA Today

Background

Is there any history or background the reader needs in order to understand how a problem or action occurred? Most stories need some background to explain the action, as in this example:

Lock your doors.

Lead

That's the advice of University of Iowa security chief Dan Hogan in light of recent reports of a prowler slipping into unlocked dormitory rooms at night.

Nut graph

"I can't stress that enough," he said. "It's a very serious situation."

Backup with lead quote

Since Aug. 24, there have been six reports of a man entering women's rooms between 3 a.m. and 5:30 a.m. Five incidents were in Burge Hall and one was in Currier Hall.

Background

Two times the man touched the sleeping women, Hogan said. But there was no force or violence. In each instance the man ran when the woman discovered him.

More recently, a woman in Burge Hall heard someone at her door. She opened it and saw a man running down the hall, Hogan said.

Valoree Armstrong, *Iowa City Press-Citizen*

Elaboration

Supporting points related to the main issue constitute "elaboration." These can be statements, quotes or more detail to explain what happened, how and why the problem or action occurred, and reactions to the event. In this part of the story, seek other points of view to make sure you have balance and fairness. A story based on one source can be too biased.

The preceding story about the University of Iowa continued with more explanation:

| George Droll, director of residence services, said main doors to the halls were locked from midnight to 6 a.m. But each resident has a key. Some floors have 24-hour visitation. | ***Elaboration*** |
| Often students feel more secure than they should because the buildings are large and are home to many of their friends, he said. | |

Ending

The most common type of ending includes one of these elements: future action, a statement or quote that summarizes but does not repeat the previous information, or more elaboration. If the future action is a key factor in the issue, it should be placed higher in the story. Avoid summary endings that repeat what you have already said. In a basic news story, end when you have no more new information to reveal.

The ending on the Iowa story follows the residence director's comments about why students feel secure in large buildings where they have friends:

| "That's a strength, but it can also be a weakness in terms of people securing their rooms," Droll said. | ***Summary quote ending*** |

Here is the ending from the story about the prospective inmate who wants to go to jail to serve his sentence for drunken driving:

| Although a new, 184-bed facility costing about $15 million is planned, that does nothing to stem the tide of today's inmates, who Howe said are coming in record numbers. | ***Future action pending*** |

Graphics

Remember to consider a photograph, chart or other graphic device as a crucial part of your story. A copy editor may write the highlights box, an artist will design the graphic, and a photographer will shoot the picture. But the way the story is presented visually will affect the length of your text, and it will help you determine what information you can include or leave out.

Examples of Basic News Stories

The following examples will show you how elements of the basic news story fit together. The first example is a standard news story with a summary lead. The content involves conflict and a group's attempts to resolve it. The story is organized in inverted pyramid form, giving the most important information first and the rest in descending order of importance. (This form will be discussed in Chapter 12.) This story contains most of the basic news elements described in this chapter:

Thousands gather on Capitol steps for animal rights

By Joan Mower
The Associated Press

Summary lead: who, what, when, where, why

WASHINGTON—Thousands of animal rights activists rallied in the nation's capital yesterday, seeking to promote the humane treatment of animals in the wild, on farms and in research laboratories.

Backup for lead, with differing opinions about crowd size

U.S. Capitol Police said an estimated 24,000 people attended a rally on the steps of the Capitol after a one-mile march down Pennsylvania Avenue under sunny skies. Organizers said more than 50,000 people from around the country showed up.

Elaboration

Marchers chanted, "Animal rights—now." Many carried banners and placards with pictures and slogans saying things such as "Fur Is Dead" and "Animals Have Rights, Too." Some brought their dogs.

Organizers said "March for Animals"—the first event of its kind—

Background

was a milestone in a movement they said was once viewed as outside the mainstream.

Among the groups participating were the American Society for the Prevention of Cruelty to Animals, People for Ethical Treatment of Animals, the U.S. Humane Society and the Doris Day Animal League.

Peter Linck, coordinator of the march, said the ultimate goal of the animal rights activists was to stop the use of animals in scientific research. However, he conceded it was unlikely the public would adopt that stance.

Impact

"In the meantime," he said, "we want to improve the condition of animals and promote alternatives to reform society."

Elaboration

The event attracted a wide variety of animal supporters, Linck said. They ranged from those who want protection of species, such as elephants, to those seeking to end medical testing on animals. Many were seeking changes in the way animals are raised for slaughter, as well as a ban on fur clothes.

Reaction: balance from different points of view

Health officials are particularly sensitive about efforts to end animal testing, a move they say could be disastrous for science.

Health and Human Services Secretary Louis W. Sullivan has criticized the animal-rights advocates who use violence and intimidation to block testing of animals.

"They are on the wrong side of morality," he said last week.

Sullivan said some of the greatest advances in medicine, such as the cure for polio, never would have been achieved had animals not been used in tests.

Ending: future action

Participants in yesterday's march planned to lobby Congress today in support of bills that deal with animal issues.

The second example is a basic news story with a softer lead that stresses the impact of the story. The nut graph gives the crucial information. It states the problem, the "so what" of this story. Attribution is limited in the beginning because the backup for the lead is factual: a law that has been enacted. Note, however, that quotes and opinions are attributed.

Throw the book at them

Law could lead to arrests for over-due library books

Deck headline

Soft lead

BOSTON—Drop the novel. Step away from the car. You're under arrest for having an overdue library book.

Nut graph: what, why, when, so what, impact and background

Starting Thursday, overdue books could land you in police custody. A law signed by Gov. Michael S. Dukakis in June would allow the arrest of library scofflaws if they had received notice that their books were 30 days overdue.

The law also raises the maximum fine for an overdue book from $50 to $500.

Elaboration

Although the law makes no provision for an overdue book, it allows for up to five years in prison and a fine of $25,000 for the theft of library property worth more than $250.

Reaction

Gregor Trinkaus-Randall, a collection management consultant for the Massachusetts Board of Library Commissioners, said librarians needed tough enforcement tools.

"Any library book that is not returned therefore has to be replaced by the library, and that is money out of the town's pocket that could be spent on other materials," he said.

Attribution for quote

David Linsky, a defense lawyer in Cambridge, criticized the measure.

More reaction

"I think the police are having enough trouble chasing down murderers and rapists without having to keep up with people who have overdue library books," he said.

Linsky said that the law allowed the arrest of library scofflaws without a warrant, something that could not be done with an offense such as assault and battery. He said the measure was unenforceable.

"If the police are told by an employee of the library that you have an overdue library book, then the police can arrest you in any public place and put the handcuffs on you," he said. "That's the real horror show of this thing."

Ending: reaction quote

The Associated Press

Quotes and Attribution

Coaching Tips

Ask yourself: Is the quote memorable without referring to your notes? If so, it's probably a good quote.

Do your quotes repeat your transitions? Could the quote or the transition be eliminated?

A guide to attribution: If you don't attribute the statement to a source, are you sure it is a fact that can be substantiated by records or officials or that it is common knowledge?

Can you state the information better in your own words? If so, paraphrase.

Does the quote advance the story by adding emotion, interest or new information?

Are you including the quote for your source or for your readers? That is the most important question of all. The readers' interests always take priority.

Janet Malcolm called herself "a compulsively careful" writer. Jeffrey Masson called her a liar. And for 10 years the two of them slugged it out in court.

Masson, a psychoanalyst who gained fame for his critical views of Sigmund Freud, said Malcolm fabricated quotes that she attributed to him in a profile she wrote about him in *The New Yorker* magazine. He sued her for libel. Malcolm, who reconstructed one quote from memory and condensed others, insisted that she followed a common journalistic practice and only clarified his statements. At issue in the landmark case was whether journalists could slightly change the wording in quotes without legal repercussions.

Although it is common practice to clean up quotes for grammar, major changes in wording are not acceptable. The case went to the U.S. Supreme Court, which ruled in 1991 that altering a quote for grammar and syntax is not grounds for libel unless the changes alter the meaning and make the statement false.

Libel is defined as a false and defamatory written attack on a person's character. According to First Amendment precedents in libel cases, a public figure must show that the publication that injured his or her reputation was not only incorrect but also published with "actual malice," which is legally defined as publishing with knowledge of falsity or with reckless disregard for the truth.

By its ruling, the Supreme Court upheld previous legal standards for libel and refused to create a new libel category for quotations. But the court also refused to rule on specific quotes in contention and sent the case back to a lower court for a decision on whether those quotes were libelous. In 1994 a federal court in California ruled that even though some of the disputed quotes were false, they were not libelous because Malcolm did not knowingly write them with "reckless disregard" for the truth.

The upshot is that minor grammatical changes in quotes are OK if the quotes accurately reflect what the source said. The quotation marks are a signal to the reader that those are the source's words, not an interpreted version. If a quote has to be substantially changed to correct its grammar, paraphrase it and attribute it to the source without quotation marks.

When to Use Direct Quotes

Good quotes can back up your lead and substantiate information in your story. In addition, good quotes let the reader hear the speaker. They add drama and interest to your story. But boring quotes can bog down stories. If they repeat what you have already said, it's better to paraphrase or to eliminate the quotes altogether.

What is a good quote? One that is vivid and clear and that reveals strong feelings or reactions of the speaker. For example, Supreme Court Justice Clarence Thomas said at his confirmation hearing, "I'd rather die than withdraw." That's a statement worth remembering.

In deciding whether to use a quote, the key is whether it is emotional or adds new information. Too many writers use quotes just to prove that they spoke to a source.

Susan Ager, a columnist and writing coach for the *Detroit Free Press,* said reporters should consider quotes as the spice of the story, not the meat and potatoes. "Readers come to the newspaper the way they come to a party," she said. "They want to talk to interesting people. Long quotes usually are not very interesting."

Here are some guidelines for deciding when to use quotes:

• When the quote is interesting and informative (example from a story about a woman who drank too much water before a urine test)

> "As more people are subjected to urine drug testing, more people are going to accidentally drink too much water for their own good and become ill," said David Kloniff, a specialist in chemical and hormonal imbalance.
>
> Knight-Ridder/Tribune News Service

• To back up the lead, the nut graph or a supporting point in your story

> ATLANTA—The signs of dangerous cults are everywhere, including colleges, a cult expert told campus police officials.
>
> "You may not think it's a problem on your campus, but you have it," Marcia Rudin, director of the International Cult Education Program, said Friday at a meeting of the International Association of Law Enforcement Administrators.
>
> "We're concerned," Rudin said. "It's been 10½ years since Jonestown. People ask us, 'Haven't they gone away?' Unfortunately not."
>
> The Associated Press

• To reveal the source's opinions or feelings (quote by the president of a nudist club protesting laws that prohibit nude bathing in the St. Petersburg area)

> "I think the rules are silly. In most of Europe on the beaches you can go either nude or topless or clothed; it's entirely up to you."
>
> *St. Petersburg Times*

• If the quote is very descriptive or dramatic (example from a story about the aftermath of an earthquake)

> "This is what the end of the world must look like," said a factory worker.
>
> David Remnick, *The Washington Post*

• To express strong reactions from a source (quote from the mother of a 2-year-old shot by a 3-year-old playmate who found a gun under a pillow in the house)

> "My God, it was an accident. . . . I never in my life dreamed this could happen. I just wish it was me instead of my baby. I can't stand to think of him in pain."
>
> *The Seattle Times*

• To convey dramatic action

> A 24-year-old Wichita woman chased a burglar through her house Thursday morning before he managed to flee the house with less than $100 in cash.
> "I woke up to see someone peering through my bedroom door," said the woman, who did not want to be identified. "I rushed the door and smashed his arm between the door and the door frame."
>
> *The Wichita* (Kan.) *Eagle*

• When you use first-person singular or plural pronouns (*I, we, us*) in a source's comments

> "I wish the professor had told us we were going to lose points for punctuation errors," she said.

If you paraphrase, use *she, he* or *they:* "She said she wished the professor had told them they were going to lose points for punctuation errors."

Good quotes enhance a story, but worthless ones just take up space. Here are some types of quotes to avoid:

• Avoid direct quotes when the source is boring or the information is factual and indisputable. For example, a city official who says, "We are going to have our regular monthly meeting Tuesday night" is not worth quoting directly.

• Avoid any direct quote that isn't clearly worded. If a government official says something in bureaucratic language that you don't fully understand, ask for clarification and paraphrase. Here's an example of a bad quote:

> The House on Wednesday over-whelmingly approved mandatory drug and alcohol testing for as many as 6.3 million transportation workers.
>
> "People have a right to know that those to whom they're consigned in the area of mass transportation are free of substance abuse and sober," said Rep. William Hughes, D-N.J.
>
> The Associated Press

• Avoid quotes that don't relate directly to the focus and supporting points in your story. Some of the best quotes a source says may have nothing to do with your focus. It's better to lose them than to use them poorly.

• Avoid accusatory quotes from politicians or witnesses of a crime. If you intend to include any accusations, get a response from the person accused. A direct quote does not save you from libel. If police or other criminal justice officials make accusations in an official capacity, you may use direct or indirect quotes, providing you attribute them carefully.

How to Write Quotes

On the surface, writing quotes may seem easy: You just write down what somebody else has said. But in reality, you must observe the following guidelines if you want to use quotes correctly and effectively:

• Always put commas and periods inside the quotation marks:

> "There are no exceptions to that rule," the professor said.

• A question mark and other punctuation marks go within the quotation marks if the punctuation refers to the quoted material; otherwise, they go outside the quote marks:

> He asked, "When does the semester end?"

> Who said, "I hope it ends soon"?

• Each new speaker must be quoted in a separate paragraph:

> "Never place quotes from two speakers in the same paragraph," Professor Les Polk said.
>
> "Even if it's short?" Janet Rojas asked.
>
> "Yes," Polk answered.

• Don't attribute a single quote more than once. If you have two quoted sentences from the same speaker in the same paragraph, you need only one attribution:

> "You must study your Associated Press Stylebook," the professor said. "You will have a test Tuesday on material in the first 30 pages."

• Place the attribution after the first sentence in a quote:

> "When the quote is two or more sentences in the same paragraph, attribute it after the first sentence," Carol English said. "Don't make the reader wait until the end of the paragraph to discover who is speaking."

• Attribution in the middle of a quote is acceptable but not preferable if it interrupts the thought:

> "It isn't the best way," he said, "to use a direct quote. But it is all right if the quote is very long. However, it's better to put it at the end of a complete sentence."

• When you are continuing a quote from one speaker into another paragraph, don't use closing quotation marks after the first paragraph. Put quotation marks at the beginning of the next quote, and attribute the quote again in the second paragraph, as in this excerpt from a story about the Supreme Court ruling on quotes:

> Justice Kennedy said, "We reject the idea that any alteration beyond correction of grammar or syntax by itself proves falsity in the sense relevant to determining actual malice under the First Amendment.
>
> "A deliberate alteration of the words uttered by the plaintiff does not equate with knowledge of falsity," he added, "unless the alteration results in a material change in the meaning conveyed by the statement."
>
> *The New York Times*

• Don't string together quotes from different people. Place the attribution at the end of the quote in most cases. But when you quote a new speaker immediately after the previous one, introduce the new speaker in a new paragraph with a transition. In this example from a story about a bus accident in which 39 students were injured, the first paragraph of quotes is correct. But look how confusing it can be to change speakers without any introduction:

"I heard a big bang and then I hit the seat in front of me," said Felicia Slaughter, 17, an 11th-grader at Henry County Senior High School. "I saw a big flash of light as soon as I hit."

"Everybody hit something—either a window or the seat in front of them," said Peggy Brooks, 16, an 11th-grader, whose left arm was in a sling. "Everybody remained pretty calm, but we started complaining about where we were hurting."

Atlanta Constitution

It's easier for the reader if you introduce the new speaker in one of two ways:

Peggy Brooks, another 11th-grader, said, "Everybody remained pretty calm. . . ."

Peggy Brooks, an 11th-grader, also was injured in the crash. "Everybody remained pretty calm," she said.

• Quotes within quotes take a single quotation mark, followed by a double quotation mark:

The woman testified, "He ordered me to lie on the floor, and then he said, 'I'm going to kill you if you go to the police.'"

• Don't tack on long explanations for the quote. If the quote isn't clear by itself, paraphrase. For example, avoid the following:

When asked how he learned about the fire at his apartment complex, he said, "I heard the news on the television."

"I heard the news on the television," he said when asked how he learned about the fire at his apartment complex.

Instead, introduce the quote with a transition:

He was at a friend's house when the fire broke out at his apartment. "I heard the news on television," he said.

• Don't overuse transitions to set up quotes. If the quote follows your previous thought naturally, you don't need to introduce it with a transition:

> One in five people over 60 has had an adverse reaction to a prescription drug, causing serious problems for 43 percent of them, a new survey says.
>
> "This is clearly a big public health problem and could get worse as the population ages," says gerontologist Beverly Lowe, University of Southern California in Los Angeles.

• Limit the use of partial quotes. They are acceptable when the whole quote would be cumbersome, but too many partial quotes make a story choppy. And the reader wonders what was left out. If you follow a partial quote with a full one, you must close the partial quote:

> McDonald says he sees the government as "weak and inept" and fraught with "major-league problems."
>
> "There's a crisis in our leadership," McDonald said.

• Limit the use of ellipses, sets of dots that indicate part of the quote is missing. Use three dots for the middle of a sentence, four (one of which is the period) for an ellipsis at the end of the sentence. Use the ellipsis when you are condensing whole quotes or long passages from which you delete several sentences. It's useful for stories about speeches or excerpts from court rulings. Be careful not to leave out material that would change the speaker's meaning.

> Four days before he was killed, the Rev. Martin Luther King Jr. stood before 4,000 people in the still unfinished Washington Cathedral and declared: "We must find an alternative to war and bloodshed. Anyone who feels . . . that war can solve the social problems facing mankind is sleeping through a revolution."
>
> *The Washington Post*

> "We must find an alternative to war and bloodshed. . . ."

Do not use an ellipsis at the end of a quotation that closes with attribution. This is improper:

> "We must find an end to war and
> bloodshed . . . ," King said.

Use this instead:

> "We must find an end to war and
> bloodshed," King said.

• Avoid stutter quotes, quotes that repeat the transition almost verbatim:

> Officials said some of the students
> selling drugs were the cause of vio-
> lence at the school.
>   "Some of the students involved
> in selling drugs have been respon-
> sible for the violent incidences on
> campus," said School Superinten-
> dent Howard Humes.

• Avoid quotation marks around words that you want to emphasize. Unless someone said it, don't enclose it in quotes.

> The school has had a "whopping" in-
> crease in enrollment.

When to Use Attribution

All quotes must be attributed to a speaker. In addition, you need to attribute information you paraphrase.

Plagiarism   Copying the words of other writers is plagiarism, a cardinal sin in journalism. In one recent case of plagiarism, a reporter copied
a source's quote from another newspaper but failed to attribute it to that
paper. Because electronic data bases now allow ready access to many
newspapers, plagiarism is easier than ever. Even if you paraphrase information you receive from other publications, you are plagiarizing if you
don't attribute it.

Plagiarism is grounds for dismissal at most newspapers. So if you
take information from a written publication, make sure you attribute it to
that source.

When all the information you gather is from your own sources, you
still need to tell the reader where you got your material. However, you
don't need to attribute everything. Here are some guidelines:

• You don't need to attribute facts that are on record or are general
knowledge:

> The trial will resume tomorrow.

> A suspect has been arrested in
> connection with the slaying of a
> 16-year-old girl in Hometown last
> week.

• You don't need to attribute information that you observed directly:

> The protesters, carrying signs and chanting songs, gathered in the park.

• You don't need to attribute background information established in previous stories about the same subject:

> The defendant is accused of killing the three Overland Park women whose bodies have never been found.

• You do need to attribute information you receive from sources if it is accusatory, opinionated, and not substantiated and if you did not witness it—especially in crime and accident stories. However, you don't always have to attribute everything in the lead. The following statement is factual, so no attribution is needed:

> A 2-year-old girl escaped injury when a mattress she was sitting on caught fire and engulfed the studio apartment at Wheatshocker Apartments in flames.

• Attribution is needed here, however, because the cause of fire is accusatory and the amount of damage is speculative:

> A 2-year-old girl playing with a lighter started the fire at the Wheatshocker Apartments near Wichita State University that caused about $400,000 in damages, fire authorities said Thursday.
> "She was just kind of flicking it, and she caught the bedding on fire," said fire Capt. Ed. Bricknell.

The Wichita Eagle

Wording of attributions   For most hard-news stories, the word *said* is preferable. Although there are many synonyms for *said,* they make the reader pause. *Said* does not. Don't worry about overusing the word.

• Strictly speaking, *said,* the past tense, should be used if someone said something once. If someone always says the same thing, use *says,* the present tense. However, that rule is very restrictive. You could also just use *said* for most hard-news stories and use *says* for feature stories (if *says* seems appropriate to the context). In either case, keep the tense you choose throughout the story; if you start with *says,* continue using it for the rest of the story.

• Avoid substitutions for *said,* such as *giggled, laughed* or *choked.* It's almost impossible to giggle, laugh or choke at the same time you are speaking. If you want to convey the emotion, write it this way:

> "I'm going to try out for the circus," she said, laughing.

• Use *according to* when you are referring to inanimate objects: "*according to* a study." It is acceptable to say "*according to* police" but not preferable. People talk. Use *said* or *says* when you attribute to people; *according to* is vague.

• Normal speaking order is preferable. That is, you should place *said* after the name or pronoun. If the person has a long title, *said* can be placed before the name and title. The example on the left is awkward, the one on the right preferable:

Awkward	**Preferable**
"Normal speaking order is preferred," said the professor.	"Normal speaking order is preferred," the professor said.

Overview attribution   A technique that allows you to attribute information to one speaker for a few paragraphs, without attributing each statement or each paragraph, is useful when you are giving a chronology of events, as in a police story. But if you change speakers, you need to use attribution for the new speaker. Overview attribution is a brief statement followed by a colon. Here are some ways of starting an overview attribution:

> Police described the incident this way:

> Witnesses said this is what happened:

> Police gave this account:

Second references   The second time you refer to a source in your story, use the last name only. If you have several sources—or two sources with the same last name, such as a husband and wife—use the full name again or an identifying phrase.

> James Jones, the director of public safety, was injured in a three-car crash yesterday. Jones was taken to Memorial Hospital, where he was treated for bruises and released.

If you have mentioned several other people and want to get back to Jones later in the story, remind the reader who Jones is by using his title:

> Public Safety Director Jones said he
> would return to work Monday.

Titles   When a person's title is used before the name, capitalize it, as in the preceding example. When it is used after the name, use lowercase letters:

> Police Chief Ron Olin said the crime
> rate has gone down.

> Olin, police chief of Lawrence, said
> the crime rate has gone down.

Courtesy titles   Most newspapers no longer use courtesy titles—Mr., Miss, Mrs. or Ms.—before the names. There are exceptions. *The New York Times* and *The Wall Street Journal* still use courtesy titles. Other newspapers use them in obituaries. For general purposes in this book, courtesy titles will be eliminated unless they are contained in examples from newspapers that still use them.

Exercises

1   Basic news story 1: Here are some reminders about writing a basic news story:

Lead: Ask yourself what the story is about. Try stating that idea in one clear sentence of fewer than 30 words.

Statement of the problem or conflict: What caused the action in the lead?

Backup for lead: Provide details about how and why.

Impact: Was there any impact on the reader? What is the significance of the story?

Background: What background was relevant to current action?

Attribution: Make sure you tell the reader where or from whom you got the information.

Ending: Put whatever information you think is appropriate at the end—the least important point, the final action or the next step.

Now try writing a basic news story based on the following information, which is from a story in *The Des Moines* (Iowa) *Register:*

Who: Iowa State University officials and leaders of the Heterosexual Society

What: Officials won't permit the Heterosexual Society to be a registered campus group; officers of the group object.

When: Use yesterday for the purposes of your story, but name which day of the week came yesterday.

Where: At the university

Why: University officials say the group discriminates against homosexuals, who can't be full members.

How: Lisa Norbury Kilian, assistant dean of students, said the university turned the group down because it refuses to admit homosexuals as full members. No registered campus group can discriminate on the basis of age, color, handicap, nationality, race, religion, marital status or sexual orientation, she said.

Significance: Group officers say the decision violates their rights of free speech and freedom of association.

Attribution: Most of the comments come from Dee Backes, a member of the group, and from Kilian.

Backup information: Put this information in the order that you think makes sense and would be most readable.

Backes, a senior from Decorah and a member of the Heterosexual Society, said she suspects the group already has a gay member, but she thinks he is a plant from one of the two gay campus groups. She said homosexuals can join the group's two lower levels of membership, but to be promoted to the top two levels, members must sign forms promising that they are straight.

Backes said the Heterosexual Society would bring in speakers, sponsor a heterosexual pride week and have other activities "to fight the misinformation on homosexuals and AIDS." She insisted that the university decision violates her rights of free speech and freedom of association. "We want to be a registered group because we have the right to be a registered group."

Kilian said that giving special membership privileges and rank to only particular members of a group because of sexual orientation is against ISU policy. Except for fraternities and sororities, which are allowed to discriminate by gender, no other group can exclude a particular group from its ranks.

2 **Basic news story 2:** Write a brief news story based on this information. Write a focus sentence at the top of the story. Consider whether you would use a chart or other graphic for some of the statistics. If you plan to use a graphic, write a paragraph under your focus sentence explaining what information your graphic will contain.

This information comes from a survey that was published in a book, *The Day America Told the Truth.* The book was just released and is arriving in area bookstores this week. The survey says 90 percent of people in the United States lie routinely; 36 percent confess that they tell important lies.

Co-author James Patterson said in an interview with you: "Americans are willing to lie at the drop of a hat. Lying is part of their lives. People say what others want to hear."

He classifies lies as "dark lies," the ones that hurt other people, and "trivial lies," those that include insincere compliments on dinner or clothes.

Patterson found that 86 percent lie regularly to parents, 75 percent lie to friends, 73 percent lie to siblings, and 69 percent lie to spouses.

He also found that 81 percent lie about their feelings, 43 percent lie about their income, and 40 percent lie about sex.

The survey also asked people what they tell the truth about. These are the findings: 51 percent say there is no reason to marry, 29 percent say they aren't sure they still love their spouse, and 31 percent admit they are having or have had an extramarital affair.

3 Quotes and attribution exercise: Check the appropriate column if you think attribution is or is not needed:

Needed	Not needed	
_____	_____	**a** Two leading figures in the growing national debate about political correctness on American college campuses will be at the University of South Florida in Tampa tonight.
_____	_____	**b** Dieting doesn't work for the vast majority of people.
_____	_____	**c** A 40-year-old woman went berserk in her ex-boyfriend's apartment early Monday, shooting him to death with seven shots from two guns.
_____	_____	**d** Members of a local gay rights group protested Thursday in support of a gay University of Tampa student's efforts to take an Army ROTC class.
_____	_____	**e** City council members voted unanimously Thursday to increase city fines for prostitution.
_____	_____	**f** A York College sophomore died early yesterday after drinking at a dormitory party.
_____	_____	**g** Alumni members of Skull and Bones, an all-male secret society at Yale University, have voted to admit women.

The next three statements are from the same story. You may want to read all three before making your decision.

_____	_____	**h** A Temple University student was gang raped during an off-campus party early Thursday at a fraternity house.
_____	_____	**i** Philadelphia police have arrested a fraternity member and a former student on charges that they raped the woman, 19, on a pool table in a first-floor common area.

_____   _____   **j** The university and the fraternity's national organization immediately suspended the local chapter.

4   Enterprise: Attend an event on your campus, and write a basic news story about it. (Look in your campus newspaper for a list of activities that will take place during the week, or check bulletin boards for notices of activities.) Talk to friends about other story possibilities. Here are some other possible topics for a news story at the start of the semester: a new course, problems students are having enrolling in certain courses, a new club or organization on campus, a student support group.

COACHING

Does your idea have a strong news element, so you can answer the question "What's new?"

Does your story pass the "so what" test?

Can you state the story idea in one sentence with a single focus?

Have you considered a photo-graph, map, chart or other graphic illustration that would enhance your story?

Story Ideas

4

W hen Vikki Porter clips coupons from her newspaper, she isn't trying to save money at the supermarket. She's getting story ideas from readers.

Porter, executive editor at *The Olympian* in Olympia, Wash., prints coupons almost every day for readers to return with their ideas. For example, one coupon asked readers for their views about whether laws on endangered species help or hurt the Northwest. Reporters then used readers' responses for story ideas and sources in a special section on endangered species. Readers' comments also were woven into stories and were featured in one part of the section called Voices.

In addition to using coupons to generate ideas, Porter routinely sends reporters into the community to ask people about their interests and concerns. Porter calls these excursions field trips. "We ask them what we should be writing about and what issues we should be addressing," Porter says. "Reporters come back and pull out story ideas."

On one field trip, for example, a team of three reporters and an editor talked to 100 people in a growing suburb of Olympia about the changing nature of their community. In another project about the economy of the area, Porter conducted newspaper forums with residents to get their ideas.

Porter also has created several reader advisory panels, groups of readers who consult with reporters and editors about issues in the community. "A story on the growing number of guns in the schools was sparked by an education roundtable. Parents, teachers and students are helping us decide the best questions to ask to find

If you can't write your idea on the back of my calling card, you don't have a clear idea.

David Belasco, theater producer

Vikki Porter, executive editor, The Olympian

out how the education system really works. Our diversity panel members have suggested a wealth of ways to track success or failure of state or local affirmative action plans." Those are just some of the modern ways journalists are getting story ideas.

Stories based mainly on events are giving way to stories based on issues and trends that affect readers' lives. For example, at the Minneapolis *Star Tribune,* editors and reporters are urged to have "daily life" discussions. The premise is that the concerns staff members have in their daily lives could be concerns that readers have and might make good ideas for news stories.

But communities are very diverse, and a reporting staff may not be representative of the newspaper or television audience. Therefore, when you seek ideas, you should contact different groups of people. When you are in a supermarket, a shopping mall, a self-service laundry or any other gathering place on campus or in your community, ask people what they are concerned about and what type of news stories they want. That is a starting point for getting story ideas.

Let your curiosity be your guide to good story ideas. When you see or hear something that strikes you as interesting or unusual, perhaps it will have the same effect on your readers or viewers.

Because the nature of news is changing by placing more emphasis on how people live, work and play, the range of story ideas is increasing. One of your first considerations should be the "so what" factor—whether the story idea you have will affect your audience. For example, the coupon, "Mood of South Sound," shows how Porter asked readers to suggest stories about religion and spirituality that would affect their lives.

Endangered Species coupon from *The Olympian*

Endangered species thoughts

How has the Endangered Species Act helped or hurt the Northwest? How effective has it been in protecting plants, fish, and wildlife?

_____

_____

_____

_____

_____

_____

Name: _____ **City:** _____ **Phone:** _____

Send your response by April 7 to: **Endangered Species, c/o The Olympian, P.O. Box 407, Olympia, Wash. 98507**; or fax them to **357-0202**. Your answers may be published in a future edition of The Olympian.

Mood of South Sound
coupon from *The Olympian*

Mood of South Sound

☐ THE TOPIC: RELIGION AND SPIRITUALITY

More people turn out for worship in one month than those who attend all sporting events in an entire year. Religious contributions nationally outpace revenue from major league baseball, football and basketball 14-1. Money contributed to religion totaled $56.7 billion in 1992, compared to just $4 billion spent on the three biggest sports.

The Olympian is committed to covering all aspects of issues relating to religion and spirituality in the South Sound region. We ask readers to complete the following questionnaire. Your responses will help us formulate strategies for covering this important topic in the future.

☐ **What types of religious/spiritual activities do you participate in and how frequently?**

_____

_____

_____

☐ **How does this experience affect your daily life?**

_____

_____

_____

☐ **How would you describe yourself in terms of your religious affiliation? (Baptist, Lutheran, Assembly of God, Catholic, Jewish, Buddhist, Muslim, Mormon, Ramtha teachings, agnostic, nonbeliever, etc.). What draws you to this particular belief?**

_____

_____

_____

☐ **If you are not involved in any organized religion, why?**

_____

_____

_____

☐ **What kinds of stories on religion and spirituality would you like to see printed in The Olympian?**

_____

_____

_____

☐ **Do you read Pastor's Perspective and Church Notes Saturdays in The Olympian? What's your impression of those regular features, and what changes would you suggest?**

_____

_____

_____

☐ **Would you be willing to serve on a focus group discussing religion and spirituality in South Sound?**

_____

_____

_____

☐ **What specific story ideas would you suggest today?**

_____

_____

_____

☐ ☐ ☐

Name: _____ **Age:** _____

City: _____ **Telephone:** _____

Send your comments to Religion, c/o The Olympian, P.O. Box 407, Olympia, Wash. 98507, or send us a fax to 357-0202.

Ways to Find Story Ideas

Some of the traditional ways of finding news are still important. The basic concepts for news—local interest, human interest, timeliness, unusual events, conflict, celebrity, impact of news events—can generate story ideas. A major national or local news event might be worth a local reaction story. If you are on a college campus, you are surrounded by experts in many fields. Professors can be good sources for national stories that need a local angle or interpretation.

The primary way to get story ideas, especially if you are assigned to a beat, is to contact your sources regularly and ask them what is going on in their workplace. Another way of getting story ideas is to examine records related to your beat, such as government documents.

Many good stories result from observation. Do you notice anything unusual or different on campus or in your community? Photojournalists usually excel at observing people and places for good pictures. An idea for a good photograph might also be an idea for a good story.

The visual concepts are as much a part of the story idea as the verbal concept. Does the story need a photograph, graphic illustration (such as a chart or map) or highlights box? Think about those elements when you devise your story idea.

Here are some other suggestions for ways to find stories:

Brainstorm: Discuss ideas for stories with other students and with people in your community. What topics on campus or in your community are of interest to people? Does anyone have an unusual course, a professor worth a profile or interest in an organization that is newsworthy? Think of consumer stories—how to get the best buys on books or how to get scholarships and loans.

Check data bases: Check clip files or computer data bases of other stories. When you begin a beat or a major story, check for sources and angles in previous articles about the subject in your own publication and in other newspapers and magazines. Be careful not to copy information or quotes—that's plagiarism—but use these stories for ideas.

Map the topic: "Mapping" is a form of brainstorming suggested by researchers who have studied the functions of the left side of the brain (the logical reasoning part) and the right side (the creative part). It is a creative process of word association that helps you explore different facets of a topic of interest to your readers. Draw a circle or a trunk of a tree for the main topic, and list the related ideas as spokes or branches; or just write a list.

For example, you might want to explore whether tuition is increasing. Tuition is the topic in the center of the circle or on the trunk of the tree. The related topics might be effects on out-of-state students, where the money goes, a comparison to other colleges and so on. Once you

Exhibit 4-1

*Story ideas generated
by mapping*

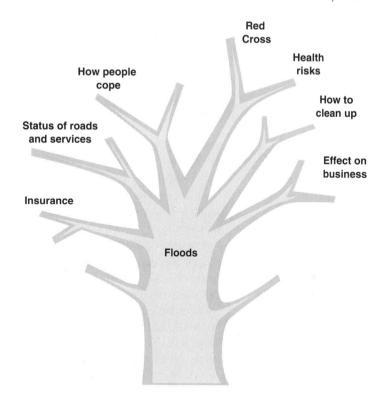

Red
Cross

Health
risks

How people
cope

How to
clean up

Status of roads
and services

Effect on
business

Insurance

Floods

have generated all the ideas you can that are related to the main focus, you can eliminate the ideas that don't seem worthy of a separate news story.

Another topic for possible mapping is a holiday. How many ideas can you devise for stories related to Thanksgiving, spring break or Valentine's Day?

Try this technique with the weather. If your area has had floods or an extended drought, think of all the people, businesses and other groups affected by the weather. Exhibit 4-1 shows how the topic of floods could be mapped.

Assume other points of view: This technique is similar to mapping. Take an issue and role-play to discover how other people might think about it. Does that process give you an idea for a feature or a profile about someone who is affected by the issue? If the state cuts its funding to your university, how are students, programs, departments and related campus activities affected?

Another potential source of ideas is special interest groups. What groups of people don't get much coverage in your newspaper? Do minorities on your campus have concerns that could generate news stories? What problems do the elderly residents in your city have? Do women's groups in your school or town have special problems and interests that would make good ideas for news? What are the needs of people with disabilities? Do veterans in your community have special needs that are newsworthy? Do you have an active gay rights group on campus? Contacts with members of these groups can generate scores of story ideas.

Observe: Look at bulletin boards on campus or in local government offices. Look around your city. Are there new stores or buildings that are worth telling the reader about? Are there old buildings, landmarks or stores that are closing, such as a famous hangout? Does anything make you curious? Do you notice something new? Is there a program or event that might be newsworthy?

Talk to people: Ask your friends what interests them. Eavesdrop at lunch to find out what people are talking about. When you are out in the community, ask people what they read in newspapers and what they would like to read.

Check directories: Universities and many government agencies have directories listing departments and personnel. Do any people, places or programs seem newsworthy? Does your school directory list organizations or departments that sound unusual or worthy of a feature?

You could also check the yellow pages of your telephone book for ideas about interesting services and places. For example, how many escort services are advertised in your city? In Fort Lauderdale, Fla., the yellow pages list more than 20 escort services. Dan Lovely, a former reporter at the *Sun-Sentinel* in Fort Lauderdale, began by checking out the escort services and ended up writing an investigative story about some of the escort services that were a front for a prostitution ring.

Read local newspapers: Does a news story suggest angles that could be developed into a separate story? Does it name people who could be profiled? Sometimes the best feature stories are offshoots of a breaking news story.

Is there a larger story to be developed from a news event? If a nursing home in your community is cited for improper procedures, is there a larger story about problems and licensing in nursing homes?

When a big story breaks in your community, are there experts or other people affected by the problem who would be worth a separate story? For example, if the teachers in your town are on strike, consider all the different people who are affected. Is there an expert on campus or in your city who is worth a feature because of his or her views on the issue?

Almost all major stories affecting your community—such as disasters, strikes, crimes and court rulings—need follow-up stories to explain the next step or action resulting from the issue.

Read classified advertisements: Look for unusual items. An advertisement in a campus newspaper about services to provide term papers could make a good investigative story. Other ads about adoption, unusual research offers or new services could generate news stories. Also look in the lost and found column. Is there a human interest story behind a lost pet or other item?

Patricia Rojas, a former reporter for *The Des Moines* (Iowa) *Register,* was scanning the classified section of her newspaper when this ad caught her attention:

> LOST WARRIOR, blue tick Coon-hound, male, stupid but friendly.

"When I saw 'stupid but friendly,' I had a feeling there was a good story behind this ad," Rojas said. There was. The dog had wandered two blocks from home and couldn't find his way back. It turned out that the dog had led a difficult life. One time he was stolen from his owner, Lisa Volrath of Des Moines, and he nearly starved after his captor abandoned him. This time he was luckier. Someone found him and took him to an animal shelter. Rojas ended her story with this quote from Volrath after she had recovered her dog:

> "I could tell from his stupid expression that he was my dog," Volrath said.

It was just a little story, but people enjoy reading about dogs. And Rojas said her editors enjoyed her initiative in finding the story.

An advertisement for a lost pet cobra turned into a fun story for another reporter. This story could be broadened into a feature about unusual pets.

Localize national news: Is there a national story that you can apply to your area? What are the local angles? What are the reactions of people in your community?

Seek profiles: Is there a person who is in the news or someone who should be in the news because of his or her accomplishments? Is someone mentioned in a story as an expert worthy of a separate profile?

Can you find stories about people who have accomplished something special, triumphed over adversity, or experienced pain or joy in relation to a news event or stories about people who represent a particular aspect of a news event? Such stories often make good human interest features.

Track programs and events: Is there a campus or government program that would be of interest to your readers? Is it a new program? Is an old program approaching an anniversary? Has it been effective or ineffective? Is there a program that a private citizen or group is trying to establish? Is the program related to the season or an event in the news? For example, is there a program affected by budget cuts at your university?

Holidays, news events and anniversaries of major news events also make good features. Plan ahead and think of stories related to these topics.

Check your newspaper's files or microfilm of major stories from previous years. Do they merit follow-up stories? Good newspaper editors and reporters keep tickler files, which are organized by weeks or months to remind them about stories that should be followed. When you are reporting, especially on a beat, you should start your own tickler file so you can remind yourself about stories you should follow. You could start a computerized tickler file listing the months and story ideas that need updates during those months.

Rewrite press releases: Government agencies, organizations in your community and campus organizations issue press releases about news events. These press releases often contain ideas for features. If you are assigned to cover a specific beat, ask the key sources to send you any press releases they issue. (More about using press releases follows in this chapter.)

Follow issues and trends: Are there problems on campus or in your community that reflect national problems? Do any local news events reflect a larger problem? For example, if four women have been attacked on campus in separate incidents, is there a larger story about rape on campus or lack of security?

When you write issue stories, make sure you have a narrow focus. A topic such as AIDS or homeless people is too broad. Focus the story on one aspect of the problem. You might do a story about the growing number of AIDS cases on your campus or a story about how your city is or isn't handling the problem of caring for AIDS patients. Or you might do a story about an aspect of the homeless problem in your city, such as an increase in the number of homeless women with children.

Be curious and concerned: These qualities, above all, will lead you to good stories.

Press Releases

Coaching Tips

Remember that a press release is written by an advocate for the organization. It is not a balanced news story.

Check the information with sources listed in the press release.

Seek other sources to confirm, deny or give other points of view.

A press release is an announcement or a story written by a public relations officer or employee of some organization. The organization that sends it hopes a newspaper, magazine, radio or television station will use it—either as an idea for a story or just as it is written. Videotaped press releases are also becoming popular as a way for corporations to promote their views, and some television stations have been using these prepackaged news stories.

Even though you may copy information in the release without fear of plagiarizing, you should always check the information. Good reporters use a press release only as a starting point for a story. Then they seek additional information.

Remember that a press release is not a balanced news story. It is a story to promote the organization or person in the release. Any critical or controversial information is likely to be missing.

It is not illegal to use press releases as written, but it is unethical to use them without stating that the information was from a release. Readers and viewers should not get the impression that the news was gathered by unbiased reporters. By not informing the audience that the news was produced by a promotional source, the station or newspaper jeopardizes its credibility.

In many cases, the press release contains quotes from an official or source within the organization. If you can't reach the source to get comments yourself, you may use the quotes. But you should attribute them to the press release. For example, write "the chancellor said in a press statement" or "according to a press release."

Here is an example of a press release issued by the University of Kansas public relations office and a local newspaper story that was based on it. Compare the story to the press release. What information came directly from the release, and what came from interviews? Note that the newspaper story contains more sources than the press release, including an interview with a campus police official.

Press release

A survey to measure the extent and impact of sexual violence on the University of Kansas Lawrence campus will be mailed to a random sample of students during the week of April 8.

The survey is intended to gather data about attitudes and assumptions about sexual violence at KU as well as numbers of incidents known by the responding students.

The Office of Student Affairs Research Committee is conducting the survey, developed specifically for KU, according to David Ambler, vice chancellor for student affairs. Stanford University conducted one of the first surveys on sexual violence on campuses.

KU's survey seeks to answer some of the most-asked questions about sexual violence, rape, and sexism.

KU officials expect that the facts and data from the survey will become the basis for future educational activities and programs designed to change attitudes that allow sexual violence to persist on campus and in society.

Students receiving the survey in the mail are asked to complete it anonymously and return the answer sheet in the envelope provided.

No individual, group or population has been chosen for the survey. It is a representative sample of the student body, making participation by every individual important.

Results will be released publicly during the fall 1991 semester after all data have been analyzed.

Contact:

Caryl K. Smith, associate vice chancellor for student affairs (913) 864-4060

or Jeff Weinberg, assistant vice chancellor for student affairs (913) 864-4381

Newspaper story

Comprehensive surveys about sexual violence were sent to 1,500 Kansas University students on Monday, and an official with the student affairs office today said he hoped students would take the surveys seriously.

The Office of Student Affairs Research Committee is conducting the survey. Jeff Weinberg, assistant vice chancellor for student affairs, said the survey was sent to a random sampling of students.

No individual, group or population was targeted in the survey, which is intended to gather data about attitudes and assumptions about sexual violence at KU as well as incidents known by the responding students.

Students were asked to complete the survey anonymously, and Weinberg said the mailing list already has been destroyed.

He said the Office of Institutional Research and Planning assisted student affairs with the survey, which he hopes will help KU officials determine how to confront sexual violence on campus.

"Certainly, we have been concerned about the problems of sexual violence," Weinberg said. "There's been an awful lot of time and money spent on lighting, transportation and escort services on campuses. But there's never enough money. Throwing money at the problem doesn't get to the root of the problem, which is attitude."

Students targeted in the survey will be asked about their attitudes on sexual violence, rape and sexism. Weinberg said the survey also will allow students to make any comments they wish to about sexual violence.

Weinberg said the survey is patterned after a 1988 survey at Stanford University, the final report of which he said was released about eight weeks ago. However, he said KU's survey was developed specifically for the Lawrence campus.

The student affairs research committee was restructured in the summer and began reviewing literature on sexual violence in September, Weinberg said. He added that the office hopes to be able to release survey results during the fall semester.

"The most important thing is to use the facts to identify on our campus those changes that we have to make in our educational programs here," Weinberg said. "We are hoping students will take the survey as seriously as it certainly is."

Students have been asked to return the surveys by April 22.

Lt. John Mullens of the KU police department said that because the surveys are confidential, police would not be able to respond to any incidents reported in the surveys.

"The individuals would have to come to us with incidents," he said.

No rapes were reported on the KU campus during 1990. Two rapes have been reported to KU police this semester. One occurred in March, and the other occurred in mid-January and was reported later that month.

Deb Gruver, *Lawrence* (Kan.) *Journal-World*

Idea Budgets

Some story ideas are assigned by editors, but most editors expect reporters to provide their own story ideas, especially if the reporter covers a beat. The daily "story budget" contains a brief description of each story planned for the next day's newspaper. Each budget item, or "budget line," begins with a "slug" (a one-word title) and is followed by a few sentences describing the story. Many newspapers also use a planning story budget, describing story ideas for the week and long-range stories.

Of course, reporters can't plan for unexpected, breaking news. Newspapers expect to respond to those stories.

The budget line also is a tool to help you focus your ideas. As you write your budget lines, you should be keeping the focus—the "so what" factor—in mind. Your budget line is your way of selling the story idea to your editor, so you need to make it sound like an essential news story or a compelling idea.

To write a budget line, give your story a slug, and describe the idea in a paragraph or two. Include potential sources and possibilities for photos or graphics. Here's an example of a budget line by Buddy Nevins, a reporter who covered the transportation beat for the *Sun-Sentinel* in Fort Lauderdale, Fla.:

Pedestrians: Broward has one of the highest rates of pedestrian deaths in the nation. One problem is that the roads haven't been designed for pedestrians, and many don't have sidewalks or crosswalks because of a lack of money. What is being done to solve the problem?

Graphics: Charts, maps of worst roads

Here is an example of a budget line written by a student for the story in Chapter 1 about a new type of thermometer:

Thermometers: Watkins Memorial Health Center is using a new type of thermometer, called a probe, to take patients' temperature through the ear instead of the mouth.

Sources: Watkins nursing director Jody Woods and students who have had their temperature taken by the probe

Graphics: Photo of a student having his or her temperature taken with the probe

Anatomy of a College Project

The topic was broad: college drinking. That was the starting point for a project a journalism class was doing for the local newspaper in a small city centered around the university. Drinking was part of the college culture. It was also big business. State liquor tax records showed $26 million in sales of beer, wine and liquor a year in this city, which had more than 40 bars catering primarily to students. Each of the 18 students in the class would do at least one main story and a sidebar. But what would those stories be?

Imagine that you are designing a similar project for your campus or community newspaper. Where do you start? What kinds of stories do you do?

Focus

The first step in starting any project is always the same: Identify the focus and define what you are trying to accomplish. Although the focus may change as you begin your reporting, when you are brainstorming ideas, you need to have a starting point.

Using some of the concepts discussed in this chapter, the students working on this project purposely started with a broad topic so they could brainstorm a lot of related ideas. They decided that the project should not focus on the dangers of drinking, nor should it have a preachy tone. Too many stories like that had already been done. Instead, they wanted the project to be a portrait of the drinking life in this university city—how and why college students drink. They wanted to capture scenes and feelings from the student point of view, which had not been revealed before in many news stories. And they wanted the local angle.

Although the idea was still broad, the project was taking shape. All the stories had to relate to the focus of college students' drinking customs—a behind-the-scenes look at the real world of college drinking.

Audience

Another important initial step in planning any story is to consider your audience. Who will the readers be, and why should they care about the story?

Because the audience for the student project would be readers of the community newspaper, not the campus newspaper, the concept was to reveal the students' drinking customs that people in the community might not know about or understand. The "so what" factor would be addressed by stressing that the community was affected, economically and culturally, by students' alcohol consumption. Although the same concept could work for stories on this topic in a campus newspaper, some of the stories could take a different approach if the audience were primarily students.

Field Trips

As a preliminary way to get some ideas about students' experiences and feelings about drinking, the journalism students talked to friends and other students. Some student sources thought the project was a stupid idea, and they were annoyed that the journalism students would even think of revealing some things, such as how to get and use false identification. Other sources thought it would be interesting to read stories about a subject that was part of their lives, and they shared many anecdotes and ideas. Journalism students came back with scores of ideas and were ready for brainstorming in class.

Mapping

The trunk of the map, or focus, was the drinking culture in the local community. Then students began listing story ideas. One was that each student would do a vignette, a brief profile, of a college student drinking at a local bar. The point would be to show a cross section of the types of students who drink and some of their experiences. Some of these brief profiles later turned into major stories, such as a story about a student who was wrestling with alcoholism.

Some other ideas for major stories included 21st-birthday drinking customs, foreign students' views of U.S. students' drinking habits, students' memories of the first time they got drunk, local and national studies of college drinking, ways that underage students sneak into bars, illegal drinking in dormitories, fraternity keg parties, nondrinking students and ways to cope with hangovers.

Initially, students chose 50 ideas. Then each student chose two ideas to pursue personally. Many of the students' initial ideas did not work because sources were uncooperative or the stories just didn't turn out to be as interesting as they sounded in the idea stage. And many other story ideas developed once the reporting process began.

Visuals

From the start, students began thinking about facts boxes, photographs, sidebars and graphics that would accompany the stories to make the package interesting and presentable. The visuals were an important part of the planning process, because they would affect the reporting and writing.

The class decided to avoid anonymous sources so credibility of the stories would not be jeopardized. As a result, the students interviewed had to be willing to have their names and pictures in the newspaper.

Visual sidebars that the students planned included a lexicon of drinking terms students use, results of a survey of students' favorite beers and the amount they drink and spend in a week, a list of places to go for help with a drinking problem and penalties for using fake identification.

Reader Interaction

To get readers involved, the students also planned to include a question about drinking for readers to respond to. The access telephone number would be printed daily in the newspaper.

Clips and Data Bases

Students checked the university archives and data bases in the library for other stories about campus drinking before they began working on their stories. Because the students were merely trying to avoid duplication of stories that already had been published, this process had limited value. The most useful information they found was from a story on national and local studies; previous clips generated sources they could use in their own stories.

The Internet

Students checked news groups on the Internet and searched the World Wide Web for studies or information about college drinking. (More about how to do an on-line search will be included in Chapter 26.) They found a news group devoted to beer and wine making but little other information of value. If the series had had a broader national scope, the Internet might have been more useful.

Computer-assisted Reporting

Each journalism student interviewed 15 students about how much they drank and spent on alcoholic beverages each week and what their favorite brews were. Pooling their results, the journalism students ended up with a data base of results from 270 students. The statistical information also generated a short story on the class survey.

Ethics

In planning the project, the students set ground rules: no anonymous sources, no undercover journalism, no illegal means of getting stories. One student raised concerns about balance; she thought the package was glorifying drinking. So the class added a few stories about nondrinkers and the dangers of alcohol abuse. Students also discussed whether to use their friends as sources, and they decided this practice would jeopardize their friendships and the credibility of the reporting.

Other ethical issues arose as the reporting process got under way. Sources refused to go on record for a good story about drinking in the dorms, so the students decided to grant anonymity in this case. Nevertheless, ethical considerations, particularly ground rules about anonymous sources, should be discussed at the start of a project.

Results

The students wrote 38 stories, and 17 were published. The stories, photographs and graphics ran on four full pages in the local newspaper and were grouped by topics: who's drinking, how they drink and what the consequences of drinking are. From idea to completion, the students learned at least one lesson about project planning: Be flexible.

Exercises

1 Field trips: Talk to people on your campus and in your community about what they read or don't read in the campus or local newspaper and what kinds of stories they would like to see in their newspaper.

2 Analyze your local or campus newspaper. Try to determine its primary audience from the kinds of stories it runs. Discuss whether the newspaper includes stories targeted for certain audiences, such as college students, minorities, women and other special groups. Perhaps one student or a group could interview the editor about his or her vision of the community.

3 Daily life brainstorming: Working in groups of three to five students, have a "daily life" discussion, such as those by teams at the Minneapolis *Star Tribune,* and see how many story ideas you can generate. You could also try this exercise with a group of friends.

4 Look in your local newspaper for ideas for profiles. People used as sources might be interesting subjects for a separate story.

5 Read the classified advertising section of your newspaper and look for items that could generate stories of human interest, new businesses, trends or unusual news.

6 Write a story budget with three ideas for stories you would like to cover. Identify some sources you would interview, and consider photo or graphic possibilities. Use the story budget format in this chapter, or modify it as you or your instructor wishes.

7 Take a walking tour of your campus or your community (individually, in small groups or as a class). Write as many story ideas as you can based on your observations.

8 Localize a news story based on a national issue. For example, localize a story about problems and legal issues of gays in the military. How would you localize your story, and whom would you contact?

9 Enterprise: Write a news story from one of your story ideas. If you are still having trouble, consider a story about an upcoming holiday. You might get some other ideas if you check the office of institutional research at your college or university for any studies the office has done, check some club sports that don't regularly get covered in your campus newspaper, or check clubs and support groups on your campus or in your community. Who are some of the people behind the scenes who perform valuable services in your community? You could do profiles such as a day in the life of a postal carrier, the city clerk, a sanitation worker or other people in service jobs.

10 Plan a project. Using the idea of drinking on campus or any other idea of interest to you, brainstorm a project in class. Use some of these planning topics: focus, audience, field trips, mapping, visuals, clips and ethics.

TWO

Collecting Information

Curiosity and Observation

Sources of Information

Listening and Note-Taking Skills

Interviewing Techniques

COACHING

TIPS

Imagine yourself as an eyewitness at the scene of the story you are covering. How would you describe the situation if you were being interviewed?

Using all your senses, record the sights, sounds, smells and other details you can observe when you are reporting. Use concrete nouns; avoid adjectives.

When you are gathering information, ask yourself what vivid action verbs could describe your observations.

Curiosity and
Observation

The blood spots made the difference.

A woman shot her boyfriend. He fled to a nearby store to seek help, and he died two hours later in a hospital.

It was just a basic news story for Martha Miller, then a police reporter. But when she went to the scene, she saw the blood spots. First Miller measured the spots with a dime. But they were larger than that. So she tried a nickel. That fit. Then she counted the spots. She wrote a hard-news lead stating that the woman had shot and killed her boyfriend, and in the middle of the story she wrote this:

> Brown, who was shot several times, staggered out of the apartment and down two houses to the Waystation convenience store on Virginia Street—his path, easily traceable by 41 nickel-size blood splotches that dotted the sidewalk.

Martha Miller, *Reno (Nev.) Gazette-Journal*

Why bother measuring and counting the blood spots? "I was curious," says Miller, now a magazine writer and editor. "I saw them and I wanted to follow where they led. I wanted to show how he fled and that he was dripping blood. I wanted the reader to picture that."

The technique is one you learned in kindergarten: Show and tell.

You tell your readers a story by not telling them. You show it. You write it so they feel it. Use all of your senses to put the reader there. Get in the smells and the sounds.

Martha Miller, reporter

Martha Miller, reporter

Curiosity

A good reporter also possesses a trait you had in kindergarten—curiosity. You probably badgered your parents with questions: What's that? Why? Those are still good questions for gathering news. Just add a few more: who, when, where, how and so what?

Most writing teachers tell you, "Show, don't tell." But you need to do both. To show, you need to observe. To show and tell, you need to be curious. You need to ask questions the reader will want answered in the story.

How do you know what questions to ask, what to observe and report? Start with the basics:

Who: Get the full names of people involved, complete with middle initials, and always check the spelling.

What: Get an account of what happened. In some stories, especially police stories, you may want to recount the sequence of events. You don't have to write the story chronologically, but you need to understand the sequence.

When: Note the day and time of the event.

Where: Get the location. Describe the scene.

Why: Understand what caused the event. What was the conflict and the resolution, if any?

How: Seek more information about what happened. How did it occur? In what order did events unfold?

So what: What impact did this event have on the participants? What impact could it have on readers?

Now for the harder questions: What does the reader need to know to understand and care about your story? You can't explain the event unless you understand it yourself, and you can't understand it unless you dig for answers. The key is to unleash your curiosity. Here are some techniques for developing your curiosity:

Role-playing: Put yourself in the role of the reader. What makes the story important and interesting? If you were affected by this story, what would you want and need to know?

Imagine that you are a reporter for your campus newspaper. The phone rings. The caller tells you there is a fire and then hangs up. You call the fire department. A dispatcher gives you the address of the fire. It's your address. What are the first questions that come to your mind? If you have a roommate, chances are you would want to know if he or she was injured. Was anyone else in the building killed or injured? Is your cat OK? Was your apartment or room destroyed? What was the extent of the damage? What caused the fire? When did it start? How long did the building burn? Where will residents of the building live if their apartments were destroyed or heavily damaged? Then you might be concerned about other questions. How long did it take to put the fire out? Were there eyewitnesses? Who called the fire department? How quickly did the department respond? Is this the first time this building has been struck by a fire? Did the building have sprinklers? If so, did they work?

The list could go on. That's the basic concept of role playing, and it can generate scores of questions for you in many stories.

Using time lines: Another method of using curiosity to generate questions is pinning down the sequence of events. Start with the present, then go to the past and then to the future. What is happening now? How did this action develop? In what order did the event evolve? What is the next step?

Questions involving time sequence will give you answers for background and chronology in your stories.

Being a detective: Imagine that you are a detective at the scene of a crime, a protest rally, or any other event that involves a mystery or conflict. What questions would you ask to solve the crime or the problem? These questions will center on what happened, the motives, consequences and clues to uncovering the truth.

Brainstorming and mapping: These are the same techniques discussed in Chapter 4, but you can use them to generate reporting questions as well. Make a list of all the questions that come to your mind about your story idea. Using all of the techniques above, just start thinking of key points you want to cover in the story.

Observation

Nothing prepared David Remnick for what he saw when he went to the little town of Spitak in Armenia five days after a massive earthquake in 1988. In fact, that's exactly what he wrote in this story, which is based largely on his observations:

In Spitak, the living are searching for the dead.

One young man in his 20s walked up and down the rows of coffins today, opening their lids, looking for his brother. Finally, he found what he did not want to see, and at the sight of his brother, he climbed into the coffin with him, ready to join the dead.

Nothing prepares you for Spitak. Nothing prepares you for a small town stadium filled with coffins and bodies left out in the cold. A town of 20,000, surrounded by the Armenian Caucasus Mountains, Spitak was a beautiful place to live a week ago, people here say. But then the earth moved beneath it, and in minutes Spitak was destroyed. At least half its people are dead. Eight kindergartens, eight schools, factories for soap, sugar, and ele-vators—all of them are rubble.

On every street, the curbs are lined with coffins and the detritus of ordinary life: a stack of Armenian novels, a pile of cabbages, a boot, a half-eaten loaf of bread, a torn reproduction of a portrait. And everywhere the smell is of smoke and snow and the dead, rotting in their makeshift coffins of rough pine.

David Remnick, *The Washington Post*

Nothing prepares the reader to see, think and care about a story as well as such details. They help a writer show and tell.

Good writers must be good reporters first. And good reporters show and tell by observing and gathering details with all their senses: sight, sound, smell, and less often, taste and touch.

That's what Ron Davis did to reveal conditions in the Laclede County Jail:

"Hey! Turn up the damn heat!"

The voice ricochets down the concrete and steel halls of the Laclede County Jail and is immediately followed by a series of violent booms, as an inmate pounds on the walls. Something is wrong with the heating system at the Laclede County Jail. But what's new? The inmates say this happens every night.

It's 38 degrees outside on this March night, and the men in the upstairs security cellblock are too cold. They always are; no matter how high the guard at the main level dispatch desk cranks the thermostat, the heat never makes it to the security wing. . . .

In the basement is the drunk tank, a cavernous bunker that reeks of urine and vomit. A hole in the floor serves as toilet and trash can.

The tank is empty tonight, but its stench overpowers the smell of food from the adjoining pantry. . . .

Ron Davis, *The* (Springfield, Mo.) *News-Leader*

Observation does not have to be limited to tragedies and the grim side of life. You can use your observation powers in any story—from a fire scene to a county fair.

Mary Ann Lickteig turned an ordinary story about the Iowa state fair into a fun one by observing these details:

Off in an exhibit room, Nancy Pelley, a home economist from Tone Brothers spice company, looked over five cakes. One of them looked back. It had teeth and a tongue hanging out between the layers. "Isn't that something," Pelley mused. "What category is that?"

It was the Ugliest Cake category. A green one with gummy worms on top won first place. Eight-year-old Jonathan Eddy of Des Moines named his entry "Green Mean Wormy Machine."

To satisfy the requirement to include his recipe, Jonathan penciled on an attached card: "I made a cake. I frosted my cake. I made it ugly."

Mary Ann Lickteig, *The Des Moines* (Iowa) *Register*

The Show-in-action Technique

If you want the reader to visualize your source or the scene, one of the best techniques is to show the person in action. This technique is more commonly used in feature stories with descriptive writing. But it also can be used in hard-news stories or for a soft lead on a news story. Regardless of the type of story, you need good observation skills. Here is an example of the show-in-action technique:

The softball lands with a disappointing thud on the gym floor.

"Come on, Dan. You can do better."

This is an important practice for Dan Piper. In one week the eighth-grader will represent his Ankeny school at a track meet. If he is to win a blue ribbon, he must improve.

Jim Mollison knows this. He is coaching Piper in the long jump and the softball throw. He urges Piper to throw the ball from one end of the gym into a net halfway across it.

"Try it again," he said.

By now a crowd has gathered, about two dozen junior high school students on their way to gym class.

They are healthy, robust students, for whom throwing a softball is about as hard as chewing gum, but they care about this throw because they know how much effort it requires.

Dan Piper, 16, is not like other students. He is mentally retarded, born with Down's syndrome.

Jim Mollison, 13, is not like other coaches. He's an eighth-grader, a bright student, a talented athlete and Dan Piper's best friend. He is helping Piper prepare for the Special Olympics.

The students root along the sidelines.

"Go, Dan!"

"You can do it, buddy!"

"All the way, Danny boy!"

Piper grimaces, reaches back and fires. Like most youngsters born with Down's syndrome, a genetic defect caused by an additional chromosome, his features are slightly out of proportion—the eyes set a little too close together, the ears a little too small, the tongue a little too large. He does not simply set forward and fling a softball. He heaves his entire body into the motion.

Higher and higher the ball soars, not just into the net but over it, landing a mere two linoleum tiles short of the far wall. Piper raises his arms in triumph, then slaps hands with Jim Mollison.

Ken Fuson, The Des Moines Register

Hard News Versus Soft News

You need good observation for both hard-news and feature stories. Although descriptive detail based on observation is more common in feature stories, such as the stories about the county fair and the Special Olympics, you can use the same observation techniques in gathering information for hard-news stories. Stories about weather disasters, fires and other events where the scene is crucial especially lend themselves to descriptive detail based on observation. At a protest, use observation to report what signs the protesters carried and what they were chanting. At a trial, use observation to help the reader see how the defendant and other people in the courtroom reacted.

Here is an example of descriptive detail based on observation by reporters in a hard-news story about a train wreck. SEPTA stands for Southeastern Pennsylvania Transportation Authority, well-known to Philadelphians, so this acronym is not defined in this story.

A SEPTA train crowded with morning rush-hour passengers derailed beneath Market Street yesterday, killing three people and injuring more than 100 others in the underground wreckage.

In what sounded like scenes from a mine disaster, witnesses described flashlights playing in the darkness over knots of terrified victims, a rail car disemboweled by tunnel girders and passengers' cries for help in the damp cold just on the west side of the Schuylkill River.

Amid the subterranean chaos of the deadliest SEPTA disaster ever, doctors wearing green scrubs and firefighters in yellow helmets used knives and power tools to cut flesh and metal in order to free trapped victims, while a policeman asked surviving passengers to pray. . . .

Physicians and paramedics wriggled through the jagged wreckage to inject victims they could barely reach with pain-killing morphine and saline solutions.

Michael E. Ruane, The Philadelphia Inquirer

Fact Versus Opinion

Observing action and the details that you will include in your story is not the same as voicing your opinion. You need to use your senses to gather the information, but you should not express your opinions about what you saw. In news stories, all opinions, judgments and accusations must be attributed to a source. Reporters should keep their views out of the story. The only places for reporters' opinions or interpretations are in columns, stories labeled "analysis" or first-person stories, which are usually labeled or preceded by an editor's note.

A few newspapers have been allowing reporters to insert first-person references (*I* or *me*) in feature stories, but that is a technique usually reserved for magazines. Most newspaper editors insist that the reporter stay out of the story.

In the previous examples, the writers reported the sights, sounds and smells they observed. Those observations were factual—evidence of conditions that anyone on the scene could have observed. The writers let the readers form their own opinions.

The left-hand column that follows is an example of description from a story about a plane crash. Most of this story is detail based on observation. The second paragraph contains a vivid description of the crash site. Note that an opinion is expressed in the last paragraph, although it is attributed to someone on the scene, not to the reporter. In contrast, the right-hand column shows how not to write the story. Note the improper use of the first person (inserting the reporter in the story). Opinion that is not attributed to someone else is printed in italics.

Appropriate	**Inappropriate**
A US Air jetliner landing at Los Angeles International Airport collided on the ground with a SkyWest commuter plane Friday night, creating a fiery tangle of wreckage. At least 12 people were killed, 24 were injured and 21 were missing, officials said.	A US Air jetliner landing at Los Angeles International Airport collided on the ground with a SkyWest commuter plane Friday night, creating a fiery tangle of wreckage *that was horrifying to behold.*
Orange flames boiled up from the fuselage, and a huge column of smoke towered over the airport. Spotlights and the lights from police, fire and other rescue vehicles silhouetted the smoldering wreckage against the darkened sky.	*I saw* orange flames that boiled up from the fuselage, and a huge column of smoke towered over the airport. *It was eery to see* the spotlights from police and other rescue vehicles silhouetting the smoldering wreckage against the darkened sky.
"It was a sight beyond belief," said Brett Lyles, 23, of San Francisco. . . .	*It was a frightening sight.*

Los Angeles Times

Observation to Find Questions

Use observation as a reporting tool, not just as a writing tool. When you observe action or details at a scene, what questions occur to you?

When Martha Miller observed the blood spots, she wondered not only how big they were but also how many there were and how long it took the man to get to the convenience store after he was shot. Details make a difference in your reporting and writing.

Observation for Visual Presentation

When you are at the scene of an accident or look at a photograph, many of the basic reporting questions are likely to come to mind. Just as important are ideas for a good photograph or graphic illustration. Does the story need a diagram to explain how something works? Would a photo or graphic eliminate the need for lengthy explanation in your story? What do you see that you would want the reader to see as well? Don't forget to observe locations and pinpoint them by proximity to major streets or specific distances from a site that the artist can interpret and the reader can understand. You need to see your story as well as hear it when you collect information.

Exercises

1 Role-playing for curiosity training: You have lent your car to a friend. You find out that your friend has had an accident with your car. Write a list of questions that come to your mind. Now add any questions you might need to answer to make the incident a news story. Write a list of the sources you would contact as a reporter.

2 Observation for curiosity training: You are gathering information for a graphic about a fire at your apartment, home or residence hall. What information do you need so the artist can draw a map pinpointing the location of the fire? Try to draw a location map.

3 Sequence for curiosity training: Write directions for a recipe for any food you know how to prepare. Be specific. First give the ingredients. Then give the directions for preparation in the proper sequence.

4 Detective role for curiosity training: Interview a detective, or invite a member of the police force to class. Ask how the officer investigates a crime, what kinds of questions he or she asks, what reports must be filled out and what information they contain. What information must police release to the public, and what can they withhold?

5 Description for observation training: Describe in detail some statue, painting or special landmark at your school.

6 More description for observation training: Without looking at the person next to you, write a brief paragraph describing what he or she is wearing and everything else you can remember about the person's appearance.

7   Show-in-action technique for observation training: Write a descriptive paragraph about a professor, a relative or a good friend. Use the show-in-action technique to describe the person's mannerisms, characteristic expressions and other details.

8   Observation: Describe the office of a source you have interviewed or of a professor you confer with frequently. List at least 10 items that are memorable. Do not include such standard items as desk and bookcase.

9   Blindfold experiment for observation training: This exercise is designed to help you increase your awareness through your senses of hearing, smell and touch. Pair up with a classmate, and cover your eyes with a blindfold. Your partner will be your guide. As you walk around your campus together, tell your partner what you hear, smell and feel. Try to be as specific as possible. Your partner should take notes on your observations. Then let your partner put on the blindfold and describe his or her observations to you. When you return to class, write a descriptive paragraph about your experience.

10   Graphic exercise for observation training: Imagine that a rare painting was stolen from a museum on your campus or in your city but was discovered the next day in a recycling bin or large trash receptacle on your campus. Go to that site (choose any area containing a large bin), and collect all the information you can for a location map or graphic illustration describing exactly where the painting was found. Write a list of information that you would give to an artist so he or she could draw a location map. Make sure you include nearby streets, the number of feet or yards from a recognizable spot, dimensions of the garbage bin, and other details you think would be helpful to the artist. Then, using your own directions, draw a location map to test whether you have gathered good information.

11   Create a mood piece or scene: Go to some favorite or interesting place on campus or in your community (a park bench, for example), and observe the surroundings and people. Use all your senses. Write a few paragraphs or a brief essay creating mood as though you were describing the scene for a feature news story or a short story. Include dialogue if you overhear people speaking or any other details that might help create the mood. If you use a demonstration or rally for your observation exercise, write a feature story about the event.

COACHING

TIPS

Use the matchmaking technique: Ask one source to recommend another one who is knowledgeable about the subject you are researching.

Check newspaper clips or data bases before you begin your reporting.

Check any records or documents related to your story.

Sources of Information

6

M ark Potter calls his source book his "bible." He takes it with him everywhere. It is a 7-by-9-inch address book, so worn that it is held together by sturdy strips of packing tape. Potter, an investigative reporter for the ABC television network, says he couldn't function without his source book. It is so crucial to his job that he keeps a duplicate in his home.

Potter cross-indexes his source book three ways: by name of the source, occupation and location. If he wants to contact an FBI agent he once interviewed in Detroit but whose name he may have forgotten, Potter looks it up under *FBI* or *Detroit.* Under each listing, Potter records the source's address and telephone numbers for work and home.

Getting the home phone numbers is not always easy, especially for police officers who keep their numbers unlisted. So Potter asks for the information this way: "How can I reach you in the off-hours?" That way, if the source does not want to reveal a home number, he or she can give you an option of another way to be contacted, Potter said. It avoids placing a negative tone on the interview.

Potter and many other reporters also note in their source books some personal information, such as sources' birthdays, favorite pastimes or anything else that would be helpful to remember.

It's not too early in your career for you to start a source book, either in an address book or in your computer and saved on a floppy disk. The people you interview in college, such as professors who are experts on foreign policy or the economy, may be good sources for stories later in your career.

If you are looking for authoritative sources on anything, there are people of all nationalities. . . . The feedback from readers—whites and minorities—about the use of multicultural sources has been good. It's not only the right thing from a standpoint of fairness and equality, it's smart. The opportunities are there, and anyone who fails to exploit them is stupid.

Taylor Buckley, senior editor,

USA Today

But how do you get sources, and how do you know which ones to use for a given story?

Where to Find Sources

A good reporter needs human sources, namely people to interview, and written sources, such as records and library materials. Scott Thurm used both types of sources to write a story that won the Pulitzer Prize when he was part of a *Courier-Journal* team in Louisville, Ky., investigating a school bus crash caused by a drunken driver. Thurm's editor asked him to investigate whether the structure of the bus had contributed to the deaths of the 27 people on the bus.

Thurm said that within a few hours he and his partner, Hunt Helm, had more sources than he could imagine. At a conference of the Investigative Reporters and Editors, he described how he developed them. "We began with nothing," he said. "We drew up a list of possible factors: Was the bus too crowded? We looked at seat belts, regulation of school buses and maintenance. Then we got lucky. A former school superintendent called and said, 'You ought to look at the seats.' They were highly flammable."

That tip led to many others. "For every issue, I'm convinced there is a group of people crying in the wilderness about the issue," Thurm said. "You've got to find them. In this case the people were school transportation directors."

One way he acquired those sources was through data bases of articles from newspapers, magazines and trade journals. He asked the newspaper librarian to find articles in the data base about school buses. He called up the author of one article, interviewed him and then asked the author to recommend other people who knew about school bus safety. "One guy had a bad bus fire so he was working on research about seats," Thurm said. "Another was worrying about exits. Another was worrying about gas tanks. By the end of the first morning, I had more avenues than I could pursue in a month just by going from one person to another."

Other sources were survivors of the bus crash, whom he was reluctant to interview at first. "I can hardly explain how traumatized they were. A lot of them had lost siblings, best friends. I would say, 'Look, I understand what you've been through. We're trying to do some stories that can prevent this from happening to other people.' I was shocked by the amount of cooperation we got. We did a detailed reconstruction of the accident based on survivors."

He also relied heavily on records of the National Transportation Safety Board. As a result of his investigation and other stories in the *Courier-Journal* series, the state of Kentucky changed regulations for school buses.

Human Sources

News writing needs human sources to make the story credible and readable. Information from eyewitnesses and participants lends immediacy to a story, and direct quotes make a story interesting. You can find human sources in a number of ways.

Newspaper files: All newspapers have reference libraries, which used to be called "morgues," where clips of stories that have been published in the paper are stored. At many newspapers, these clips are now filed in a computer data base. You can also find human sources through on-line data bases, such as news groups and bulletin board services, which are discussed later in this chapter.

Before you begin reporting for any assignment, your first step is to check the clips. There you can find the names of people cited in previous stories about the subject. If you are writing a story about a topic but have no idea whom to contact, check magazine articles as well as other clips on the subject.

When you are assigned to a breaking-news event, such as a fire or accident, you may not have time to check the clips before you leave the office. But you should check them before you begin writing. The building that burned may have had problems with sprinkler systems or previous fires in the past.

The same recommendation applies to crime stories. A suspect arrested on charges may have been arrested previously for the same or other charges. Caution: Newspaper library files may not be up-to-date, and follow-up stories may not have been written about crime suspects. If you find a clip about a suspect's previous arrest, make sure you find out if the charges were dropped or what happened in the case.

Plagiarism, using information from published or broadcast material and passing it off as your own work, was mentioned in Chapter 3 but is worth mentioning again here because it is such a serious offense. If you are using information from other newspapers, magazines, broadcasts or other published sources, you must attribute the publication where the material appeared.

Sponsorship: Suppose you find a source who is reluctant to talk to you, such as a police official. You can use a technique that Mark Potter calls "sponsorship," getting someone who knows and trusts you to recommend you to the new source.

For example, when Potter was working on a story about the problems of Haitians in Miami, the Haitian refugees were reluctant to talk to him. Many of them were illegal aliens. Potter said they thought he was an immigration official who was seeking to deport them. So he asked a community social worker who had gained the trust of several Haitians to recommend him to one of the Haitians. The social worker introduced him to a Haitian named Pierre, but Pierre didn't have the information

Potter wanted. However, Pierre said his brother-in-law might help, and
Pierre introduced Potter to him. After establishing trust with the brother-
in-law, Potter asked him to get other Haitians to talk to him. And that's
how he got the sources he needed for his story.

You also can use sponsorship as a self-introduction technique when
you set up an interview. Give your name and say, "Chief Joe Smith suggested I call you" or "Chief Joe Smith gave me your name." Then explain the purpose for your call.

Self-sponsorship: Nancy Tracy, a former reporter for *The Hartford* (Conn.) *Courant,* was in trouble. She was working on a follow-up story about three people who survived when the Mianus River Bridge collapsed and their vehicles plunged into the river. But a key source, Eileen Weldon, wouldn't talk to her or anyone else in the media. Weldon had severe injuries and was tired of press coverage.

So Tracy tried self-sponsorship, a way of recommending herself. "I'm going to send you some clips of other stories I have done to show you that I am a very sensitive reporter," she told Weldon. "Please read them. I'll call you in a few days. If you don't think I can be fair, I won't ever bother you again."

Tracy got the interview. Her clips "sponsored" her.

Matchmaking: You have found a source, and you are interviewing her or him. But you want the names of other sources for the story. Try "matchmaking," a form of sponsorship. Ask the source who else might know something about the subject or have an opposing point of view. Who else is involved in the issue? Ask how you can reach those people. Your source may even provide telephone numbers of others who are close to the subject.

Primary and secondary sources: When you are conducting an interview, if your source says something about another person, particularly if it is derogatory or controversial, make sure you check with that second person. The first source's statements not only could be wrong, they could also be libelous. You should éven check out written information about sources to make sure it is accurate.

In most cases, except when your secondary sources are famous people, such as the president or celebrities who cannot be contacted, do not use someone's name in a story without making an attempt to check with that person.

The up/down principle: If you want to learn how to sweep floors, talk to a janitor, not to the corporation president. The same principle is involved in reporting a story. If you want to get the most accurate and vivid information about a story, talk to the people who were directly involved. Go down the organizational ladder. Contact the police officer who wrote the report (the name is listed on a police report), the researcher who conducted the study or the source closest to an incident.

Another version of the down-the-ladder principle is to be kind to secretaries. Remember their names, and be genuinely friendly. A good secretary can be like a pit bull guarding the boss. If you want to interview an official, your first source is the person who schedules that official's time.

After you have interviewed people down the ladder, go up the ladder of the organization. Who is the next supervisor with responsibility? Who is the official with ultimate responsibility for the department or organization?

You can proceed either way. You can start with a top official and then go to the primary people or the reverse. In many cases, police officers and people in corporations, government and other bureaucratic organizations will refuse to talk to you until they have authorization from their supervisors. As a result, you may often have no choice but to start with the top officials.

Anonymous Sources

Many people will be willing to talk to you if you promise not to use their names. An anonymous source is one who remains unnamed. But should you make this promise? Most editors today would say no, unless there is no other way to get the information. And even then, many editors would refuse to grant that immunity from identification. The more you rely on unnamed sources, the less credibility your story has.

If you must use anonymous sources because you have no other alternative, you should check the information with other sources, preferably ones who will allow use of their names, and check documents.

When using unnamed sources, you may identify the person with a vague reference, such as "according to one official." Or you might give the person a pseudonym, a false name. Although most editors discourage pseudonyms, they are sometimes allowed in feature stories about sensitive subjects such as rape. But they are rarely used in hard-news stories. It is preferable to use no name or a first name only. If you use a full-name pseudonym, which is not preferred, you should check your local telephone directories to make sure you aren't using the name of someone in your community. And in all cases, you must tell the reader that this is a false name to protect the identity of the source.

Janet Cooke didn't do that. And she touched off a furor in the newspaper industry that persists, years after the incident. Cooke, then a reporter for *The Washington Post,* won the Pulitzer Prize in 1981 for a story called "Jimmy's world," about an 8-year-old heroin addict. There was only one problem. Jimmy didn't exist. When she first discussed the story with her editors, she said she had located the child's mother, who was reluctant to talk. Her editors said she could grant the mother anonymity. Cooke turned in a compelling story about the child and his mother. But when Cooke won the Pulitzer and was profiled in newspapers, some discrepancies in her resume were discovered. That led to questions about her story. She ultimately admitted that she had made up the story about Jimmy and his mother. The *Post* returned the Pulitzer, and Cooke resigned in disgrace.

Cooke's story wasn't based on an anonymous source; it was a false source. But the impact was a crisis of credibility for the press. Newspapers throughout the country began developing policies against using pseudonyms, and many editors banned the use of anonymous sources altogether. But the policy is difficult to enforce, especially since many people, such as officials in Washington, refuse to be quoted by name for fear of revealing information their supervisors might not like. *The Washington Post* relied heavily on anonymous sources for its investigative stories in the early 1970s about the Watergate scandal, which led to the resignation of President Nixon. The *Post* still uses many unnamed sources. But most reporters, especially investigative reporters, use anonymous sources primarily for tips that can be confirmed with documents and other on-the-record sources.

Many sources, named or unnamed, have their own agenda and want to manipulate reporters so the sources can promote their cause. For fairness and balance, it is crucial for reporters to check with other sources to confirm, deny or provide other points of view.

Promises   Dan Cohen had an agenda, and he made the issue of anonymous sources even more complicated. He was a public relations executive. In 1982 he gave reporters from the Minneapolis *Star Tribune* and the *St. Paul* (Minn.) *Pioneer Press* damaging information about a candidate for lieutenant governor in Minnesota on the condition that they would not reveal him as the source. The information was a record of the candidate's shoplifting conviction that was no longer available in court records because it had been expunged (erased by court order). Reporters agreed to grant Cohen anonymity. But editors of the two newspapers overruled the reporters and insisted on printing Cohen's name in the story. The editors decided that since Cohen was working for the opposing political party, the readers had a right to know the source of the information.

Cohen sued. He claimed that the newspapers had violated an oral contract of confidentiality and that, as a result, he had suffered harm by losing his job. A jury at the first trial level agreed that a reporter's promise of confidentiality is as legally binding as an oral contract. The newspaper appealed and lost. The case went all the way to the U.S. Supreme Court, which ruled in 1991 that the First Amendment does not protect journalists from being sued if they break promises of confidentiality. The high court sent the case back to the Minnesota Supreme Court for a ruling on damages, and Cohen was awarded $200,000.

If you promise a source anonymity, you are bound by your promise. Before you agree to anything, however, you should check with your editors to determine the policies of your organization.

The *Star Tribune* established policies regarding anonymity and other relationships with sources as a result of Dan Cohen's lawsuit. In the policy, the newspaper says: "Always review the ground rules of a promise with the source before you receive the information, so that both persons completely understand the conditions. Do not make vague statements, such as 'I probably won't use your name,' and don't rely on a term such as 'off the record,' which means different things to different people."

The terms "anonymous source" and "confidential source" are used interchangeably by most people. *The Wall Street Journal,* however, makes a distinction. The newspaper considers an anonymous source a person whose name is not used in the story "but whose identity we may later need to disclose—in the event of a libel suit, for example." The newspaper defines a confidential source as one whose name will not be published and whose identity will not be revealed in court, even if the reporter has to go to jail to protect the source. Sources, however, may not recognize such distinctions.

Even when sources agree to be identified, they often ask for anonymity for portions of the interview. They'll say, "This is off the record." Sometimes they aren't even aware of what the term means.

On and off the record   Here are some definitions of the terms used most often to establish ground rules in an interview:

On the record: The source agrees that all information can be used in a news story and that he or she can be identified as the source of it. The easiest way to establish this understanding is to identify yourself as a reporter immediately and state your purpose for the interview. For example, "I am a reporter for *The Campus Review,* and I'm calling to interview you about . . ." If you are interviewing people who are not accustomed to dealing with the media, you may need to remind the source during the interview that you are quoting him or her about the material, especially if you are writing about controversial issues. Such a reminder may jeopardize your chances of using some of the material, but it is better to take that chance during the interview than later in a courtroom after you have been sued.

Off the record: The information from this source may not be used at all. If you can get the same information from another source, you may use it, but you may not attribute it to the source who told it to you off the record.

Not for attribution: You may use the information as background, but you may not identify the source.

Background: This is similar to the term "not for attribution." Generally, it means that you may use the information but can't attribute it. Some reporters define background as the ability to use the information with a general attribution, such as "a city official said." If you are in doubt during the interview, ask the source how you can identify her or him, and give the specific wording you intend to use.

Deep background: This term is rarely used or understood by most sources except for officials in Washington, D.C. It means you may use the material for your information only but may not attribute it at all, not even with a general term, such as "government official."

Multicultural Sources

How you deal with sources is one problem. Which sources you choose is another important factor in gathering news. For example, can you imagine a modern newsroom without women? Today, when 60 percent of the journalism students are female, it may be difficult for you to conceive of a newspaper without the opinions of women. But in many newsrooms, women don't have key managerial positions, and several studies show that women are not quoted or featured in news stories as often as men. Do women have different views from men about how news should be covered? Perhaps not, in some cases. But you and your readers will never know if you don't seek women's views.

The same is true for minority groups. The overwhelming amount of news about minorities is negative and promotes stereotypes, according to a series of articles on the subject by David Shaw, media critic for the *Los Angeles Times.* "If all one knew about real-life blacks and Latinos in particular was what one read in the newspaper or saw on television news . . . one would scarcely be aware that there is a large and growing middle class in both cultures, going to work, getting married, having children, paying taxes, going on vacation, and buying books and VCRs and microwave ovens," Shaw wrote.

And that's the problem. If a racial disturbance were to occur in your community, you would seek opinions of community leaders representing the groups involved. But would you seek opinions of African-Americans (the term preferred by many blacks), Latinos and Asian-Americans who are experts in various fields for other stories?

Reporters from *USA Today* do. The newspaper's editorial page features a standing quote by the founder, Allen H. Neuharth, which says, "*USA Today* hopes to serve as a forum for better understanding and unity to help make the USA truly one nation." To do that, the newspaper urges reporters to make an effort to get views in all news stories from people of both sexes and various ethnic and racial groups.

"It comes up in every story conference or in every photo/graphic assignment," says J. Taylor Buckley Jr., senior editor at *USA Today.* "If you are doing a story on the new techniques of orthodontia, it's just as easy to find a black kid with braces as a white kid. The feedback from readers—whites and minorities—about the use of multicultural sources has been good. It's not only the right thing from a standpoint of fairness and equality, it's smart. The opportunities are there, and anyone who fails to exploit them is stupid.

"In the early days of the newspaper in our effort to just get gender diversity, the editor would tear up pages if they didn't feature women," Buckley says. "If you are looking for authoritative sources on anything, there are people of all nationalities. Over the years we have accumulated those kinds of sources. We have a committee on diversity that is consolidating a source book."

Like reporters from *USA Today,* if you start your source book now and accumulate multicultural sources, you will have them when you need them for future stories.

A related issue is the identification of people in newspaper stories as black or some other ethnicity. Almost all newspapers have policies against mentioning a person's race or ethnic background unless it is relevant to the story. To show that it uses multicultural sources, *USA Today* prints pictures, especially in columns containing readers' points of view.

You can find many multicultural sources for stories about racial and ethnic issues in a data base called Ethnic Newswatch, a comprehensive collection of newspapers and periodicals published by the ethnic and minority press in the United States. Although it is not widely available in libraries, you might inquire about this service, which is produced by Dataware Technologies, Inc.

Written Sources

As mentioned earlier, the search for human sources starts in the newspaper library. You can find many additional clues for human sources and other information from a variety of written sources.

Telephone Directories

The white and yellow pages of telephone books are primary places to locate sources. Most local telephone books also contain information about city and county government agencies, utilities, and other frequently used services.

Cross-directories

These directories, also called "city directories," list residents of a community three ways: by name, address and telephone number. Imagine that you are on deadline and have the address of a woman whose house is on fire and that you want to reach her neighbors for comments. How can you do this if you don't know the neighbors' names? You can look in the cross-directory under the address you have. The adjacent homes will be listed first by address, with names and telephone numbers of the occupants beside the address (unless they have unlisted telephone numbers). If you have a phone number but not the name, check the section for phone numbers.

The cross-directory is one of the most useful ways of locating people for comment when you can't go to the scene. These directories are published by realtors in most major communities and are kept in most newsrooms. If you don't have access to one, your local library should; you can ask the reference librarian to look up the information you need.

Libraries

Your local public library and your college library contain a wealth of source material to help you find background about a story. Some of the most useful reference works are The Reader's Guide to Periodical Literature, encyclopedias, almanacs and other books of facts, population data, and financial records of major corporations.

Most college and university libraries also have a section devoted to federal and state documents and publications. In this section you can find transcripts of congressional hearings, publications from federal and state agencies, and reports from all sorts of government offices.

Electronic Sources

Many types of references are now available through computer data bases and on-line services, which make it easy for you to find information.

Data Bases

A data base is a collection of information. The term now generally refers to massive collections of information stored in computers. Many newspapers subscribe to data bases containing newspaper and magazine stories compiled by a commercial company.

For daily news stories such as meetings, local events and other breaking news, checking a data base is too time-consuming. But when you are seeking background for an in-depth story or feature, data bases are worth checking. For instance, if you are working on an in-depth story about date rape on college campuses, a data base check would be helpful. By reading other stories, you can get ideas for an angle on your story or find expert sources to contact.

The best way to learn how to use a data base is to go to the library and ask for assistance. Each data base has a different set of instructions; many include charges for use.

One of the most popular data bases for newspaper and magazine writers is NEXIS, a collection of newspaper, business and trade sources. It is available in some libraries but often with restrictions for users. LEXIS, the other part of this service, contains the text of court decisions, legislative records and legal resources. It is available in most law libraries.

Many other data bases contain only an abstract (a summary) of the article in a journal, newspaper or magazine. You still have to look up the paper or microfilm version to see the entire article.

Public Records

Many government records, such as data from the U.S. Census Bureau and documents from state and local agencies, may be obtained from data bases consisting of public records.

Access to such records has spurred a type of reporting called "computer-assisted journalism." Using software programs that have sophisticated mathematical tools, reporters have been able to do complicated searches and analyses of huge banks of data that they would not be able to do with paper records. For example, if you want to find out who earns the highest salaries in each department at your university or college, you could spend days sifting through a printed version of the budget and trying to compare salaries. But if the budget is available on a data base, you can use a computer program to analyze this information for you in minutes. However, a large data base can still be time-consuming to interpret, which is a deterrent to computer-assisted reporting at some publications.

The hardest part of using such data bases may be convincing public officials to release the computer-taped records. You may have to file a request under the Freedom of Information Act (which is explained later in the chapter). That is what Mike McGraw and Jeff Taylor did to receive 8.2 million records about farm programs from the U.S. Department of Agriculture. With the help of their newspaper's data base expert, Gregory Reeves, they spent 16 months analyzing those records and conducting hundreds of interviews, which resulted in a seven-part series about abuses in the USDA. They won the Pulitzer Prize for their efforts.

For example, McGraw and Taylor analyzed all records of USDA meat inspection sites, which are responsible for the nation's 7,000 meat-packing plants:

Poor sanitation and failure to control rodents and insects remain major problems in the meat-packing industry nationwide, a computer survey by the Kansas City Star shows. . . . Of the 137 problem plants chosen for government review, 133—or 97 percent—were cited for sanitation problems.

Mike McGraw and Jeff Taylor, *Kansas City* (Mo.) *Star*

They also analyzed the data base of taxpayer-assisted subsidies to farmers, which are supposed to be limited to $50,000 per farmer:

The Kansas City Star reviewed all farm payments and refunds last year in all 50 states and U.S. territories. But the newspaper's study found that nearly 8,000 farms last year exceeded the $50,000 in payments. Of those, nearly 1,300 collected $100,000 or more; some collected more than half a million dollars. . . .

Stevens County, Kan., has exactly 300 farms, at least according to the U.S. farm census. But last year the Agriculture Department sent checks to 1,342 "farmers" there.

That's four times as many farmers as farms. It appears that phantom farmers must be working the prairie.

Jeff Taylor (left) and Mike McGraw (center) on the day the Kansas City (Mo.) Star *won the Pulitzer Prize for national reporting, for a series about the U.S. Department of Agriculture*
Courtesy of Tim Janicke/
The Kansas City Star

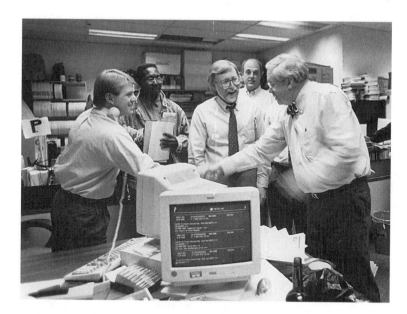

Exhibit 6-1 is an infographic illustrating some of the abuses McGraw and Taylor described in their series.

Although the statistical results were dramatic, McGraw stresses that computer-assisted reporting is only one tool in gathering information for a good story. He says it is crucial for reporters to do old-fashioned, face-to-face interviewing as well. For his series, he traveled to meat plants for on-site observation and personally interviewed scores of inspectors and other officials.

On-line Sources

You can also get many public records and documents on the Internet, a massive international network of data bases that you can access through academic or commercial services. Electronic data bases are often referred to as on-line sources because you can access them through telecommunications lines. (See the appendix for a list of on-line sources useful to journalists.)

But records are only one source of information through computer networks. You can also reach human sources through electronic mail and through bulletin board services called BBSs. A bulletin board is a service coordinated by a person or organization. It is an interactive, electronic discussion forum where people express their opinions about a topic by sending their messages to the list. By reading the forum, you can get the e-mail address of a person who has written something you wish to explore further and send a message directly to that person. Or you can send a message to the entire list.

For example, if you want to learn more about computer-assisted journalism, you could read a bulletin board about the subject by

Exhibit 6-1

Infographic accompanying McGraw and Taylor's series

Courtesy of Dave Eames/ *Kansas City Star*

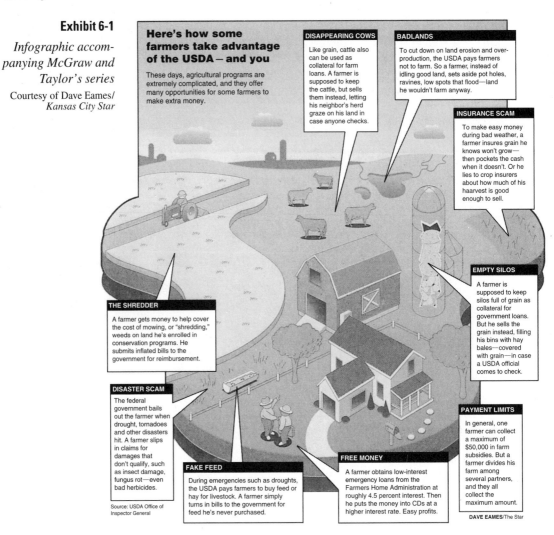

Here's how some farmers take advantage of the USDA — and you

These days, agricultural programs are extremely complicated, and they offer many opportunities for some farmers to make extra money.

DISAPPEARING COWS

Like grain, cattle also can be used as collateral for farm loans. A farmer is supposed to keep the cattle, but sells them instead, letting his neighbor's herd graze on his land in case anyone checks.

BADLANDS

To cut down on land erosion and over-production, the USDA pays farmers not to farm. So a farmer, instead of idling good land, sets aside pot holes, ravines, low spots that flood—land he wouldn't farm anyway.

INSURANCE SCAM

To make easy money during bad weather, a farmer insures grain he knows won't grow— then pockets the cash when it doesn't. Or he lies to crop insurers about how much of his haarvest is good enough to sell.

EMPTY SILOS

A farmer is supposed to keep silos full of grain as collateral for government loans. But he sells the grain instead, filling his bins with hay bales—covered with grain—in case a USDA official comes to check.

THE SHREDDER

A farmer gets money to help cover the cost of mowing, or "shredding," weeds on land he's enrolled in conservation programs. He submits inflated bills to the government for reimbursement.

DISASTER SCAM

The federal government bails out the farmer when drought, tornadoes and other disasters hit. A farmer slips in claims for damages that don't qualify, such as insect damage, fungus rot—even bad herbicides.

Source: USDA Office of Inspector General

FAKE FEED

During emergencies such as droughts, the USDA pays farmers to buy feed or hay for livestock. A farmer simply turns in bills to the government for feed he's never purchased.

FREE MONEY

A farmer obtains low-interest emergency loans from the Farmers Home Administration at roughly 4.5 percent interest. Then he puts the money into CDs at a higher interest rate. Easy profits.

PAYMENT LIMITS

In general, one farmer can collect a maximum of $50,000 in farm subsidies. But a farmer divides his farm among several partners, and they all collect the maximum amount.

DAVE EAMES/The Star

contacting carr-l@ulkyvm.louisville.edu, the e-mail address for a BBS operated at the University of Louisville in Kentucky. If you subscribe to the commercial on-line service CompuServe, you could discuss job opportunities and other topics with media professionals in broadcast, print and public relations on a bulletin board called JForum, the journalism forum.

In some cases you cannot read the list until you join by giving your name and requesting membership in the news group. In other cases you may just read the list anonymously.

Suppose you want to reach an expert in Haitian politics or any other academic or scientific subject but have no idea who might be doing research in that area. You could contact Profnet (Professors Network), a bulletin board operated by a cooperative of university public information officers. You can send your request for information to profnet@sunysb.edu, operated at the State University of New York at Stony Brook. Your request will be sent to public information officers at more than 700 colleges, universities, research laboratories and scientific institutions represented by this group. Within a few days, you should receive a response without charge. You could also contact this network by telephone at 800-PROF-NET.

The advantage of these electronic sources is that you can contact people all over the world in minutes and often get very prompt responses. The disadvantages are that without personal contact or voice contact, you may not be able to determine nuances or context. You may not even be getting the person's real name. You should always verify the information you get from electronic sources, because anyone can send inaccurate information on these networks.

You should also be cautious about reading a bulletin board and using a person's comments for publication without his or her knowledge. Copyright of comments posted to on-line bulletin boards remains a gray area. Regardless of the legal issues, to be ethical you should ask people if you may use their comments.

Other Public Records

An official at your university tells you that there are no serious fire safety violations on campus. But you want to be sure, so you decide to check the state fire marshal's report on the last fire safety inspection of campus buildings. The report may list many violations that the official might not have deemed serious. Records on paper or in computer form are valuable information sources.

Not only do such records as fire and police reports provide detail about investigations, they also give names of people to contact. When police investigate an accident or a crime, they fill out reports with details of the scene and crucial information about the people involved, including names, addresses, birth dates, physical descriptions and other material. Most of the records are public.

The most complete listing of where and how to find records is *The Reporter's Handbook: An Investigator's Guide to Documents and Techniques,* written by Steve Weinberg and published by St. Martin's Press.

The following list mentions just a few of the public records that should be available to you locally. In addition, government offices in your state capital contain records from all state agencies, including your university if it is state-owned. Federal offices in a state capital contain many records of federal agencies and of federally funded programs in your locale. The location of these records may vary from city to city, and access may also vary.

Real estate records: Mortgages, deeds (which record the property owners, purchase date and sale price in some states), the legal property description, indexes listing previous property owners, and commercial property inventories (lists of everything the commercial property owner has, such as trucks, supplies, equipment, etc.) are available in the Register of Deeds office. This office also has maps showing all the property in the county and individual maps called "plats," which show the zoning of each piece of property. Records for tax rates and assessed value of the property are located in the county assessor's office. If you don't have a property description or know what property your subject owns, the county clerk's office has a listing of who owns what.

Voter registration records: These records, located in the county clerk's office, list the person's political party if he or she is a registered voter, as well as the person's address and date of birth. They also list telephone numbers. In some cases, people who have unlisted telephone numbers may have listed their numbers on these records.

Fish and game licenses: These are also recorded in the county clerk's office.

Salaries of county employees: The salaries are listed by position only (not by employees' names) in the county clerk's office. In some counties or cities, names may be included.

County government expenses: These can also be found in the county clerk's office.

Corporate records: Articles of incorporation, which list the officers of the corporation and the date the company registered with the state, are very useful if you are trying to find out who the company officers are. Articles of incorporation are located in the Register of Deeds office or in the state office that regulates corporations.

Court records: Filings in all civil and criminal court cases except juvenile cases are open to the public. They are located in your county courthouse.

Military records: You can find out the details of individuals' military service in the Register of Deeds office in some municipalities, but only for people who registered for the service in that county. Otherwise, you have to file a request under the Freedom of Information Act to the individual branch of the service.

Personal property loans: If a person has taken out a loan over $1,000 or bought something on time, such as a stereo, worth more than $1,000, the information could be on file under the Uniform Commercial Code listings kept in your county courthouse.

Tax payments or delinquent tax records: These records are kept in the county treasurer's office.

Motor vehicle registrations: These records and the personal property tax are on file in the county treasurer's office.

Building inspection records and housing permits: These are available in the city's building inspection and housing department. Also available there are all the complaints that have been filed against a property owner, which are useful for stories on substandard housing. This office also has records on all permits issued for construction or building improvements.

City commission meeting records, local ordinances and resolutions: The city clerk's office keeps these records.

City expenses: Information about purchase orders, accounts payable, the inventory of city agencies, budgets, expenditures and the like are available in the city's finance department. Records of purchase orders and accounts payable are extremely useful if you are investigating the expenditures of any city department or the actions involving any contract the city has with a vendor or builder.

Public works records: Plans for public works projects—such as sewers, traffic signals and traffic counts—should be available in the public works department of your municipality.

Fire department records: These include records of all fire alarms, calls (including response times), fire inspections, and firearms owners and registration (which may be in a different location in some cities). Also on file, but not available to the public, are personnel records, including pension records and other items of a personal nature. Salaries, however, are public record. These are in the fire department or in your city or county clerk's office.

Police records: Criminal offense reports, statistics of crime, accident reports and driving records are in the local police department and the sheriff's department. Records of ongoing investigations generally are not available to the public.

Utility records: Water records—such as bacterial counts, water production, chemical usage, and other items pertaining to the city's water and sewage operations—are available in the city utilities department.

School district records: Almost all information pertaining to the expenditure of public school funds—including purchase orders, payroll records, audits, bids and contracts—is available from the school district. Personnel records of employees are also available in limited form. Names, addresses, home phone numbers, locations of employment, social security numbers, birth dates, dates hired and work records are available, but information about employee work performance and other personal information is not public. Information about students, other than confirmation that they are enrolled, is not public.

The Freedom of Information Act

The Freedom of Information Act was established by Congress in 1966 to make federal records available to the public. It applies only to federal documents. In addition, the act allows for several exemptions that prohibit the release of documents. Records classified by the government because their release would endanger national defense or foreign policy are exempted. So are certain internal policies and personnel matters in federal agencies, as well as a number of records involving law enforcement investigations. If an agency refuses to release documents you have requested through the FOIA, you may appeal the decision.

In many cases, the document you request comes with information blacked out or cut out. Some documents look like paper doll cutouts by the time they are released.

Another drawback to using the FOIA is that it is time-consuming. Although an agency is required by law to respond to your request within 10 working days, delays are common.

However, many reporters have found the FOIA invaluable. The documents they have received have led to major investigative stories, such as the series by Mike McGraw and Jeff Taylor discussed earlier.

Before you file an FOIA request, try the direct approach: Ask the agency for the records. You might get them. If you must file a formal FOIA request, it is a good idea to check first and make sure you are contacting the appropriate agency for your request. For questions or more advice, you can call the libel and FOI hotline, 24 hours a day, seven days a week: 800-F-FOI-AID. You can also access a complete on-line guide to the FOIA through the Internet (see the appendix for specifics).

When you file your request, be sure to write "Freedom of Information Request" on the envelope and on the letter. You do not have to explain your reason for the request. The agency may charge copying and processing fees, but if you are not using the material for commercial purposes and the material is likely to contribute to an understanding of government operations, you may be entitled to a fee waiver.

You can use a form letter for your request. The sample on the facing page is recommended by the Society of Professional Journalists. If you prefer to be contacted by mail, omit your telephone number.

[Date]

[Agency head or Freedom of Information Officer]
[Agency]
[City, State, Zip Code]

Freedom of Information Act Request

Dear [FOI Officer]:

This is a request under the federal Freedom of Information Act.

I request that a copy of the following documents [or documents containing the following information] be provided to me. [Identify the documents or information as specifically as possible.]

In order to help determine my status to assess fees, you should know that I am [insert a suitable description of the requester and the purpose of the request, such as

- A representative of the news media affiliated with the newspaper (magazine, television station, etc.), and this request is made as part of news gathering and not for a commercial use

- Affiliated with an educational or noncommercial scientific institution, and this request is made for a scholarly or scientific purpose and not for a commercial use

- An individual seeking information for personal use and not for a commercial use

- Affiliated with a private corporation and seeking information for use in the company's business]

[Optional] I am willing to pay fees for this request up to a maximum of [dollar amount]. If you estimate that the fees will exceed this limit, please inform me first.

[Optional] I request a waiver of all fees for this request. Disclosure of the requested information is in the public interest because it is likely to contribute significantly to public understanding of the operations or activities of government and is not primarily in my commercial interest. [Include a specific explanation.]

Thank you for your consideration of this request.

Sincerely,

[Your name]
[Address]
[Optional telephone number]

Exercises

1 **Cross-directory:** Imagine that the mayor of your town, another city official or a university official has disappeared. You want to talk to members of his or her family and to the neighbors. Find the missing person's telephone number in the cross-directory. Now find three neighbors you could interview.

2 **Data bases:** Select a topic for a feature story about an issue on your campus, such as date rape, racial tensions on college campuses, alcohol bans, political activism or such health issues as sexually transmitted diseases among college students. Now go to your library and use a data base to find stories about your topic. Make note of any national experts on the subject and any statistical material or reports you would find helpful in your story.

3 Get copies of a police report, a university study, or any other report that has been released at your school or in your community. Make note of the primary sources (officers, investigators or researchers) you would contact.

4 Make a list of multicultural sources at your college or university who are experts in a field such as foreign policy, Mideast relations, the environment or any other subject.

5 **Sponsorship:** Select a topic that would require you to interview sources in your community who might be reluctant to talk to you. Or just choose a topic for any story that would require several sources. Whom would you contact as a primary source to sponsor you to other people you need to interview? Where would you start your reporting? Make a list of sources who could help introduce you to others knowledgeable about your topic.

6 Conduct a record search of a person, preferably a politician or other person in your community who owns property. Your task is to construct a paper-trail profile. Try to find out all you can about the person without ever talking to him or her. However, you could drive by the person's home to observe the property and include that information in your report. Write the profile based only on records and observation. You may be surprised how much you can write. Here are some suggestions for records that should be available to you:

- Land records, which should include a complete description of the person's house
- Court records of criminal and civil suits, possible marriage or divorce, or even birth records
- Delinquent tax records
- Corporation records for ownership of personal property or corporation papers (if applicable)
- Records of voter registration, auto registration and tax liens
- Educational background, including curriculum vitae for university employees
- Financial disclosure (for politicians)

7   Write a Freedom of Information Act request for some information from a federal agency that funds a program in your school or community.

8   Enterprise: Write a story about the people for whom buildings or landmarks on your campus are named. Using your campus library, check the archives to find the background of these people. Then conduct interviews with students who use these buildings, or live in them if they are residence halls, and find out how much or how little the students know about these people. In the clips, try to find interesting anecdotes about the namesakes and reasons for naming the buildings for them.

COACHING

TIPS

Write your observations in your notes; include specific details.

Write questions in notebook margins or on notebook covers as they occur to you during the interview.

Mark the information in your notes, such as quotes and facts, that you plan to use when you write the story.

7

Listening and Note-taking Skills

Truman Capote knew how to be a good listener. He didn't take notes during his interviews for his book *In Cold Blood.* Nor did he use a tape recorder. He was convinced that a notebook or a tape recorder would inhibit his sources. "People would reveal themselves, he maintained, only in seemingly casual conversations," wrote his biographer, Gerald Clark.

With his childhood friend, Nelle Harper Lee, Capote conducted scores of in-depth interviews for the book, a nonfiction story recounting how two men murdered a family in rural Kansas. Each night Capote and Lee would return to their hotel and write notes about the interviews they had conducted that day. "Each wrote a separate version of the day's interviews; then they compared notes over drinks and dinner. . . . When their combined memory failed, as it sometimes did, they went back and asked their questions in a slightly different way. On occasion they talked to the same person three times in one day," Clark wrote in his book *Capote: A Biography.*

That technique is impractical for a reporter on a daily newspaper. And in these days, when the credibility of newspapers is under attack, trying to reconstruct interviews and direct quotes from memory is downright dangerous. When free-lance writer Janet Malcolm reconstructed quotes, she got sued for libel, as Chapter 3 explained. Even though the U.S. Supreme Court ruled that it's all right to reconstruct quotes as long as the meaning isn't changed, if you don't have Capote's memory, it's better to take good notes.

Capote said he trained himself to be a good listener. "I have a fantastic memory to begin with," he said in an interview with

It is the disease of not listening,

the malady of not marking, that

I am troubled withal.

William Shakespeare, *King Henry IV*

Charles Ruas, author of *Conversations With American Writers.* "I can repeat almost verbatim any conversation up to as long as eight hours. I could never have written *In Cold Blood* if I had ever produced a pencil, much less a tape recorder."

The Pros and Cons of Tape Recorders

Capote's objections to using tape recorders are well-founded. A tape recorder is not a substitute for good notes. Tapes can break, and machines can fail you when you need them most. They can inhibit a source. They can also prevent you from taking good notes if you rely on them too much. And tape recorders can't pick up observations—a smile, a nervous tic, a source's appearance or mannerisms. But they can be useful.

If you want to get the exact wording of quotes, or if you are interviewing a source about a controversial subject, a tape recorder is beneficial. But you shouldn't play back the entire tape and transcribe it before you write your story. That is too time-consuming. If you use a tape recorder, scan the tape until you get to the quotes you need.

Before you begin taping your interview, follow some etiquette. Start your interview with basic introductions—who you are and why you are there—and some opening conversation. To put the source at ease, you might even ask a question or two before you ask the source if he or she would object to the recorder. Then, if the source agrees to allow the recorder, don't place the machine directly in her or his face. Put it off to the side of the desk or table, where it is not so intrusive.

If you want to record a telephone interview, be aware of the laws in your state. Eleven states prohibit tape-recorded conversations without the consent of the person being taped: California, Florida, Georgia, Illinois, Maryland, Massachusetts, Montana, New Hampshire, Oregon, Pennsylvania and Washington. Other states mandate that only one person must be aware of the taping, either the reporter or the person being interviewed.

But you can't secretly tape any conversation between two other people when you are not a part of the discourse. For example, if you are on an extension phone and neither party knows you are taping the conversation, you are violating a federal law against wiretapping. The Federal Wiretap Statute provides for penalties of up to $10,000 in fines and up to five years in prison.

The most ethical approach is to let your source know you are taping the interview, except in a very few situations. For example, if you are conducting an undercover investigation in a state where the one-party rule applies, you could tape a conversation without knowledge of the source. However, most editors consider the use of deception or other undercover techniques a last resort.

Listening Tips

Before you write notes or record conversations, you should follow Capote's example and develop good listening skills. Here are some tips:

Focus on the "hear" and now: Concentrate on what the source is saying now, not on what you will ask next. One of the major obstacles to good listening is poor concentration caused by worrying about what you will say instead of focusing on what the source is saying. Your next question will be better if you have heard the answer to your last one.

Practice conversational listening: Base your next question on the last sentence or thought the source expressed, as though you were having a conversation with your friend. If you want to move to another topic, you can do so either with a transition—"on another subject"—or by just asking the question. But if you are really paying attention, the order of your questions will be more compatible with the source's trend of thought.

Practice critical listening: Evaluate what the source is saying as you hear it. Listen on one level for facts, on another for good quotes and on a third level for elaboration and substantiation. Is the source making a point clearly and supporting it? Do you understand the point? If not, ask the source to repeat, elaborate or define the meaning. If you listen for meaning, you can direct the interview instead of letting the source control it.

Be quiet: Whose interview is this anyway? Do not try to impress the source with what you know. You can't quote yourself. Let the source explain a point, even if you understand it, so you can get information in the source's words.

Be responsive: Make eye contact frequently so your source knows you are listening. Nod, smile, say yes, mumble "uh-huh" or look confused. Just let the source know you are paying attention. If you don't understand something, say so. "Why? How? I don't understand" and "Please explain" are good follow-up reporting questions based on good listening. Conversely, if the source makes a strong point or gives you a great quote, you might smile or nod affirmatively, encouraging the source to continue.

Listen for what isn't said: Is the source avoiding a topic? Who or what isn't the source talking about—a family member (in a personal profile), a close official, a crucial part of his or her background? Sometimes what is omitted from a conversation is more revealing than what is included.

Listen with your eyes: What kind of body language is the source displaying? Is the source fidgeting or showing signs of nervousness at some point in the interview? Is the source smiling, frowning or exhibiting discomfort when you ask certain questions? Does his or her mood change during the interview? Are these telltale signs that the source may be lying or withholding information? Observation can be a good listening tool.

Be polite: If the source starts to ramble or give you irrelevant information, don't interrupt. Wait for the source to pause briefly, and then you can change the subject.

Block out personal intrusions: You've had a bad day, your car broke down, you failed a test, or you have some emotional concerns. Make a willful effort to block out these personal thoughts. They intrude on your concentration while you are trying to listen. Your problems will still be there when the interview is over. The source will not.

Develop listening curiosity: Don't go to your interview with a rigid agenda of questions. Although you may start with prepared questions, allow yourself to be surprised when the interview goes in another direction, and follow that course if it is interesting. Listen for what you want to know and what you didn't expect to know.

Note-taking Tips

When Foster Davis was a writing coach at *The Charlotte* (N.C.) *Observer,* he checked reporters' notes to determine if problems in the stories originated in the reporting process. "The quality of stories has something to do with the quality of notes," says Davis, now managing editor of the *St. Louis* (Mo.) *Post-Dispatch.* "Writing is the least important part of it; everything that leads up to it is what matters."

Davis says he looked at notes to see if they were legible and if they included names and dates as well as reporters' observations. "When the notes said 'trees,' were they specific trees? Were the notebooks dated? Were exact titles spelled out? Detail is what makes the difference between good and bad notes," he says.

Davis learned from personal experience. He used to take very brief notes, but one day he noticed another reporter taking voluminous notes. Davis started doing the same thing, mostly out of embarrassment, he says. Then he noticed that his stories had become much more vivid.

Detailed notes give you this advantage: When you begin writing your story, you may need more information than you anticipated during the reporting process.

When you take notes can be as important as how you take them. Note taking can make some sources nervous. If you are dealing with people who are not accustomed to being interviewed, start your interview slowly by asking a few nonthreatening questions. After you have established some rapport with the source, take out your notebook.

Here are some tips to help you take good notes:

Be prepared: Bring extra pens or pencils. You can run out of ink, or your pencils can break. You can't take notes without the right tools. In addition, take *both* pens and pencils. If you do an interview in the rain, you'll want to keep pencils handy.

Concentrate: When you hear a good quote or the start of one, write rapidly. Then concentrate on what you have just heard and block out everything else until you have written the quote. Even if you are concentrating on a previous thought, you will still hear what is being said. So if the person says something better than the last quote, you can switch your concentration to the new information. Thinking of your next question while you are trying to write down a complete quote will interfere with your concentration.

Use key words: When you are not trying to get a direct quote, jot down key words to remind you of facts and statements. The better your memory, the fewer full sentences you will need in your notes.

Develop a shorthand: Abbreviate as many words as possible. Don't waste time writing unimportant words, such as conjunctions. The word *government* might become *gov,* and *you* could be abbreviated as *u.* Some type of shorthand is especially important when you are trying to write complete quotes.

Slow the pace: When you are taking notes for a quote, slow the pace of the interview by pausing before your next question until you write the quote. If you think you are pausing too long, ask a question that will not require a crucial answer. You could ask the source to elaborate about the last statement. If your source is speaking too fast, politely ask him or her to slow down.

Request repetition: Don't be afraid to ask your source to repeat a quote or fact you missed. Although the quote may not be worded exactly as before, it will be close enough. In fact, the repeated statement may be even better. When people have had a chance to think, they often state things more clearly.

Make eye contact: Don't glue your eyes to your notes. Make sure you look at your source during the questioning and while you are taking notes. Practice taking notes without looking at your notebook.

Give praise: If your source gets nervous as you take notes, you can ease his or her concern with sincere praise. You can say, "That was interesting" or ask the source to tell you more about the point. That's one way of gaining some time as you take your notes.

Mark your margins or notebook covers: When you hear something that prompts another question in your mind—a fact you want to check or the name of another source you want to contact—jot it in the margin as soon as you think of it. Don't depend on your memory to think of it later. Some reporters use the covers of their notebooks to write questions that come to mind during the interview so they can find them easily without flipping through notebook pages. And don't forget to take notes on your observations, either in the margins or elsewhere.

Verify vital information: Make sure you get the exact spelling of your source's name and his or her title during or at the end of the interview. Don't go by a nameplate on a door or desk. That could be a nickname. Ask the source the name he or she prefers to use, and ask for the spelling even if you are sure of it. A simple name like John Smith could be spelled *Jon Smythe.* If you get this information at the end of your interview, you also could ask for a home telephone number at this time.

Double-check: If your source says he or she has three main points or reasons for running for office, make sure you get all three. Write *3 reasons* in the margin, number them as you hear them, and check before you conclude the interview.

Be open-minded: You may have one idea for the story when you begin taking notes. But don't limit your notes to one concept. Your story angle could change any time during the interview. You can't always envision how you will write the story. When you do, you may be sorry you didn't take better notes, especially if you decide to change the focus during the writing process.

Use a symbol system: To save time writing your story, while you are taking notes, put a star or some symbol next to the information or quotes you think will be important. Develop your own system. Some reporters put one or two stars next to quotes they want or a note next to information that will work for a lead. Other reporters use highlight pens to mark the notes they will use in their stories; most do this after the interview, while they are planning to write the story.

Stand and deliver: Practice taking notes while you are standing. You will not have the luxury of sit-down reporting, especially at the scene of fires, accidents, disasters and most other breaking-news stories. And practice taking notes and getting full quotes everywhere else you get the chance—in your lecture classes, when you are watching television news and in any meetings you attend. The best way to become a fast note taker is to gain experience.

Save your notes: You should save your notes before and after the story is published. How long you should save them is debatable. Lawyers disagree whether notes are helpful or harmful in court cases if you are sued for libel or any other reasons. But most editors advise saving the notes at least for a few weeks after the story in case any questions about it arise. For this reason it is helpful to date your notebooks.

Transcribe notes only for major stories: Should you transcribe your notes in your computer before you write a story? Definitely not if you are on deadline. Some reporters find it helpful to rewrite their notes before they write a major story because it refreshes their memory, especially if a story will involve many sources and be written over a period of days. If you haven't mastered the art of writing clear notes, it may also help you to transcribe your notes immediately after your interviews.

Exercises

1 **Listening:** This exercise is designed to test your ability to listen and follow up with related conversation or questions. The technique is to concentrate on a key word or thought that was expressed by the person who precedes you and follow with a related thought.

To do this exercise, one person should begin a conversation. It can be based on a controversy on campus, or it can be a fictional story. The instructor will call on students at random, stopping the speaker at any point. When you are called on, you should pick up one word from the last thought that was spoken and develop the story from that point. For example, if the person before you starts a story with "Jack and Jill went up the hill to fetch a pail of water," you might pick up on the key word *water* and elaborate: "And when they got the water, they discovered it was polluted." The point is to test your conversational listening ability, which will lead to better follow-up questions during interviews.

2 **Note taking:** The object of this exercise is to see how accurately you can quote sources. Tape an interview from any television news show. Use a VCR or regular tape recorder. As you are watching the show, write down some direct quotes. If you use videotape, watch the screen periodically as though you were making eye contact with a source. Then play the tape and test your accuracy. If you do this in a classroom, you can compare your notes with classmates' notes. Analyze what caused you to be inaccurate—if you were—and how you can improve your note taking.

3 **Notes:** Submit your notes for the last story you wrote. Share your notes with another student, and critique each other's notes for the points Foster Davis recommends. Are your notes legible? Do they have names, dates, titles and details? Compare your rating of your notes with another student's evaluation of them. Discuss improvements in your note taking that might have helped your story.

COACHING
TIPS

Brainstorm: Ask a friend to listen to your story idea. Discuss questions and points of interest to pursue.

When interviewing athletes or people who have been interviewed frequently, try to find a new angle or a question they haven't been asked.

Always check spelling of the source's name and wording of job titles.

Ask the follow-up questions "why" and "how," and ask sources to give you an example.

Gather details for graphics; ask questions as though you had to describe the scene to a blind person. Get information an artist would need to draw a map or other illustration. Details will make your writing more vivid as well.

Interviewing Techniques 8

B arbara Walsh had tried for months to get an interview with convicted murderer William R. Horton Jr. Finally his lawyer gave her
permission. She walked into the jail, met Horton and learned a
painful lesson.

"Willie" Horton was serving two life sentences plus 85 years
in a Massachusetts prison for the murder of a gas station attendant
and a subsequent crime he committed while out of prison on a furlough (a brief stay in the community). He broke into the home of
a Maryland man, slashed him repeatedly and raped his fiancee
twice. That crime made him infamous in advertisements that the
Republican Party used in 1987 to criticize former Massachusetts
Gov. Michael Dukakis, the unsuccessful Democratic presidential
candidate. Republicans blamed Dukakis for operating a system in
Massachusetts that allowed murderers to leave jail on furloughs.

Walsh, then a reporter for the *Lawrence* (Mass.) *Eagle-
Tribune,* faced Horton through the window that separated them.
"The first question I asked was 'How the heck did you get out on
furlough?' It was the stupidest thing I've ever done," she says.

Horton wanted to terminate the interview. Walsh salvaged the
interview with Horton by switching to something he wanted to
discuss. "I asked him, 'What do you want to tell me?' And he said,
'I'm not a monster. You people (the press) have made me out to be
a monster,'" Walsh says.

The interview then went on for two hours, and eventually
Walsh returned to the tough questions she wanted to ask Horton.

The story was one of a series about the Massachusetts furlough program that earned Walsh the Pulitzer Prize. Walsh, who

*Being a reporter is great because
you can ask people questions no
one in their right mind would ask
a complete stranger.*

Diana Griego Erwin, columnist

Barbara Walsh, reporter

later became a reporter for the *Sun-Sentinel* in Fort Lauderdale, Fla., says she was lucky that Horton talked to her, but she learned a valuable lesson about interviewing techniques: "Save your tough questions for last."

She still covers prisons, and she still asks tough questions—but at the end of the interview. "I've learned to be real slow and real patient," she says. "I'm more inclined to let people talk longer. You may not use all the information, but you can offend them if you rush."

Walsh says the key to good interviewing is good listening. "In interviewing, if you are sincere and the sources know that you have compassion, they're going to talk. A lot of the skill is just being open to what they have to say."

But when sources are reluctant to answer her questions, she rephrases the questions and asks them again—sometimes three or four times—as in the following story about women in a Florida prison. "I asked one of the female inmates on death row, 'What's it like to sit there and know the state wants to electrocute you?' She skirted the question the first time. I asked it three times during the interview." Eventually Walsh got the answer. "If you ask—not in a cold way, but sincerely ask what was it like for you—they'll answer." The result was this revealing portrait (also notice how Walsh weaves in her own observations):

Kaysie Dudley spent two years on Death Row meditating and learning more about how the state was going to kill her.

"I did a lot of research on what they were going to do to me," Dudley says. "It was very morbid, but I wanted to know."

Dudley, 28, was sent to Death Row at Broward Correctional Institution in 1987 after she was convicted with her boyfriend of strangling and slicing the throat of an elderly Clearwater woman.

"My boyfriend killed her," Dudley says. "I held the woman in my arms as she took her last breath. It was a terrible experience."

As she talks, Dudley sits in the cafeteria of the women's prison, nervously rubbing her fingers together, her nails raw and bitten to the quick. From her neck hangs a small silver cross.

It is cool, and Dudley wears a black sweater over her state-issued aqua dress.

"I wasn't afraid of dying," Dudley says. "But I didn't like to think about electricity running through my body. . . ."

After spending two years on Death Row, Dudley says, she feels she has suffered more than enough.

"I was 22 when they locked me up in there," she says. "I feel like in a way they've already killed me. It took me almost a year to get my facial expressions back, my emotions, my ability to laugh.

"I was a zombie when I came out of there," she says, absently twisting her hair with her constantly moving fingers.

Barbara Walsh, *Sun-Sentinel*

Walsh is a master interviewer once she meets her sources, but getting the interview is sometimes the major hurdle. Walsh recounts an experience she had when she went to interview the parents of a child who allegedly had been molested by a teacher. The parents refused to be interviewed. So Walsh tried this technique: "I said, 'Let's just talk about doing an interview. Here is the kind of story I want to do and these are some of my questions.' I ended up spending three hours with the parents, and I never wrote down a word. Then they said I could use what they said."

She wrote the story from memory. "It was easy," she says. "I would never forget some of the mother's quotes. I did call back and check quotes, however."

Although Walsh usually takes notes, she says a notebook can be threatening. She waits until she has established rapport with her source before she opens her notebook. And she rarely uses a tape recorder—too unreliable and threatening, she says.

Her advice to student reporters? Don't overlook anyone as a source. "When I go to the courthouse, I consider anybody who talks as a source—from the janitor to the people who sell coffee. These are real people who may not be high-priced attorneys, but they know what is going on. Reporters narrow their sources too much."

Sensitivity

The way you deal with sources can differ, depending on whether they are public or private individuals. Because public officials are accustomed to dealing with the media, you have a right to expect them to talk to you. Private individuals do not have to deal with the media, and you need to exert even more sensitivity when interviewing them. If a public official utters an outrageous quote, it's fair game. When a private individual does, you could remind the person that it will be published and make sure the source will stand by the comment. Although many reporters believe that once they have identified themselves as members of the media, anything in an interview is fair game, reporters who display extra sensitivity usually end up with more information.

All sources, public and private, want to be portrayed well in the media. Many sources, especially public officials, will manipulate reporters by revealing only information that furthers their cause. As a result, reporters need to be aware of the source's bias and ask probing questions that go beyond what the source wants to reveal. It is also crucial to check the information and seek alternative points of view.

Tips for Interviewers

The following sections present some other tips to help you become a good interviewer. But before you even start, consider your mission. You are a reporter, not a stenographer who just receives information and transcribes it. A reporter evaluates information for its accuracy, fairness, newsworthiness and potential to make a readable story. During the reporting process, you will look for facts, good quotes, substantiation and answers to the five W's—who, what, when, where, why—and also "how" and "so what." One question should lead to another until you have the information you need.

An interview with one source is just the beginning of reporting for most stories. For credibility and fairness, you need other sources—human and written—for differing points of view and accuracy checks.

Planning the Interview

If you are sent to cover a breaking-news story, you should get to the scene quickly and find sources there or start calling sources on the telephone. The planning stages described here apply only to interviews that you need to set up in advance. Most of the other reporting techniques apply to both kinds of stories.

Research the background   Check news clippings and available documents—court records, campaign records or other relevant written and electronic sources—to familiarize yourself with the topic and the source. Check with secondary sources—friends and opponents—before or after you interview the subject of a story. Ask the source's friends, secretaries or co-workers to give you anecdotes and tell you about the person's idiosyncracies.

Plan an interesting question to start your interview. Try to find a question or approach that would interest the source, especially if the person is a celebrity, an athlete or an official who has been interviewed often. These people often give standard answers to questions they consider boring because they have been asked the same questions so many times. If you research well, you will find some tidbit or angle to a story that might lead to an unusual question—and an interesting answer.

Identify your goals. What kind of information are you hoping to get from this source? Is it primarily factual, as in an interview with a police officer for a story about an accident? Or do you want reaction from the source to an issue or to something someone else said?

Is the source going to be the central focus of the story, as in a profile, or just one of several people cited in the story? Get a general idea of why you need this source so you can explain briefly when you call for an interview.

Plan your questions. This step may seem premature, considering that you haven't even been granted an interview. However, if the person refuses to see you when you call for an interview, you might be able to ask a few questions while you have the source on the phone. If you are a good interviewer, you can prolong the conversation and wind up with a good interview.

To plan your questions, try the mapping technique: Make a list of questions, or draw a circle or tree, with the main topic in the center or on the tree trunk, and jot down related issues. Then narrow the list to important questions.

Prepare your list of questions two ways: Write all the questions you want to ask, preferably in an abbreviated form. Then mark the questions you must ask to get the most crucial information for your story. If your source refuses to grant you the time you need, you can switch to the crucial list during your interview.

Request the interview. Now you are ready to call for an appointment. The most important point is to plan ahead. Officials, educators and many other sources are busy people. They may not be able to see you on brief notice.

When you make the call, first state your name and purpose. If you are a reporter for your campus newspaper, make that part of your identification: "I'm Joe Smith, and I'm a reporter for the *University Daily Tribune.* I'd like to interview you for a story I'm writing about the increase in tuition." Or better yet, try the sponsorship technique: "I'm working on a story about date rape on campus, and Officer John Brown suggested that I call you. I understand that you have some information about a survey the university conducted on this subject." Try to convince the source that her or his opinions are important to you.

Then ask what time would be convenient. Negotiate the length of time you need. If you want an hour but the source can't spare the time, settle for a half hour.

If you are calling an official, you probably will have to negotiate through a secretary. Be courteous and persuasive. First ask to speak to the source. If that's not possible, tell the secretary that you would like to interview her or his boss about a story you are writing. You don't need to elaborate unless you are asked to do so.

Dress appropriately. If you are interviewing a source on a farm, don't wear a three-piece suit. On the other hand, show your source respect by dressing neatly. Avoid wearing tattered jeans and sloppy shirts. However, if you are interviewing corporate officials or people in more formal business settings, you should dress as though you worked there—tie and jacket for men, a dress for women.

Arrive on time. You could arrive 10 to 15 minutes early, but don't arrive too early, because you could inconvenience people who are busy. And never come late.

Conducting the Interview

Interview questions can be classified as two types: closed-ended and open-ended. You need both types.

Closed-ended questions are designed to elicit brief, specific answers that are factual. They are good for getting basic information, such as name and title, yes or no answers, and answers to some of the who, where, when questions. For example, these are closed-ended questions: How long have you worked here? Who was at the meeting? How many people were at the rally? When did the accident occur?

Open-ended questions are designed to elicit quotes, elaboration or longer responses. Follow up your closed-ended questions with open-ended ones, such as why and how. Some others: What is the purpose of your program? What are your goals in starting this organization? What is your reaction to . . . ? When you want anecdotes, ask questions like these: Could you give me an example? Can you recall a specific incident when this happened to you? To clarify anything you don't understand, just ask the source to explain further.

Keep your questions brief. A long lead-in to a question can confuse the source. Slow the pace between questions so you can take notes. Ask unimportant questions or ask for elaboration while you are writing down quotes.

Remember to be responsive—smile, nod or react appropriately—and make eye contact frequently during the interview.

Beginning reporters often worry that they will appear dumb to sources. Don't worry about what you don't know. You are there to listen and learn, not to be the expert. The whole point is to get information from the source. In fact, acting dumb can give you an advantage. Even if you know the answer to a question, you should ask it anyway, so you can get the information in the source's words. If you think a question is too simple, you might apologize for not knowing more about the subject. You might say, "I'm sorry I don't understand this. Could you explain so I can write it clearly for my readers?" Most sources enjoy the teaching role or showing off what they know.

Acting dumb does not mean forgetting about preliminary background work. It is dumb if you can't tell your readers something because you were afraid to ask. It's better to feel dumb during the interview than afterward, when you turn your story in to an editor or when you read it in the newspaper.

Here are some ways to conduct the interview and some types of questions to ask. Not all of these techniques and questions apply to every story.

Start out by using icebreakers. Introduce yourself and briefly state your purpose. Be friendly. Establish rapport with some general conversation. Don't pull out your notebook immediately. Try to sit at an angle to your source so you are not staring directly at her or him in a confrontational manner. A desk might serve as a barrier and provide enough distance so you don't appear threatening.

Observe the surroundings. Do you notice something you can mention as an icebreaker, a way to establish rapport? Barbara Walsh says that during one interview she noticed a map of Ireland on the wall and commented that she had lived in Ireland. That comment broke the ice.

Don't be artificial. If an official has a picture on his desk of his family, don't get overly familiar. Use good judgment. Then explain a little more about what you are seeking in your story.

Put your questions in nonthreatening order. In most cases you will want to follow Walsh's advice and start with nonthreatening questions. However, if you have only five minutes with a source, you may have to ask your toughest question first or whichever one will yield you the most crucial information for your story.

Ask the basic questions. Who, what, when, where, why and how are the most basic. Then add the "so what" factor: Ask the significance. Who will be affected and how? This question will give you information for your impact and scope paragraphs.

Ask follow-up questions. These are the questions that will give you quotes and anecdotes. Use a conversational technique. Let the interview flow naturally. When a source answers one question, follow the trend of thought by asking why and how and asking the source to explain or give examples. Frame your next question on the information you have just heard by focusing on key words in the last answer. When you want to change the subject, ask an unrelated question or use a transition: "On another topic . . ." or "I'd like to go back to something you said earlier. Could you explain why you were at the scene where the murder occurred?" Use follow-up questions to go from the general to the specific. If the source makes a vague statement, ask for specific examples.

You may have a long list of questions, but don't let your source see them. A long list can make the source watch the clock. Write your questions on the front or back of your notebook so you can refer to them easily without turning pages frequently. One student reporter took out a press release during the interview. When the source saw it, he told the student to use the comments in the release and terminated the interview.

Control the interview. If your source rambles or prolongs an answer and you want to move the interview in another direction, don't interrupt. Wait for a natural pause and ask your next question, using follow-up question techniques.

Repeat questions. You've asked an important or sensitive question, and the source has given you an evasive or incomplete answer. Even a request to elaborate does not produce a satisfactory response. What should you do? The best tactic is to drop the question and continue the interview. After you have discussed a few other points, repeat the question you want answered, but state it in a slightly different way. Sometimes a source will recall more the second time the question is raised.

Ask background questions. Get the history of the issue, if applicable. How and when did the problem or program start? Why?

Ask about developments. Go from the present to the past and to the future. What are the current concerns and developments? How did the issue evolve? What is likely to happen in the future? The answer to the future developments question may provide you with a good ending for your story. In some cases, it may give you a lead and a new focus for your story. The next step is often the most newsworthy angle. Many newspapers prefer this approach, which is called "advancing the story."

Construct a chronology. This tip is somewhat related to the previous point. When appropriate, ask questions to establish a sequence of events. You don't need to write the story in chronological order, but you need to understand the order in which events occurred.

Role-play. If you were in the reader's place, how would you use the information? For example, if you needed to apply for a loan, what steps would you have to take, and where would you go? What does the reader need and want to know? Ask the source questions that will meet the reader's needs.

Ask about pros and cons. Ask your source to discuss both sides of an issue, when relevant. Who agrees and disagrees with her or his point of view? What are her or his responses to the opposition?

Ask for definition. Your job is to translate jargon for readers. So always get your source to define any bureaucratic or technical terms in language that you and your readers will understand. Don't accept or write any information that you can't explain. To clarify, you might restate the information in your own words and ask the source if you have the correct interpretation. For example, you might ask "Do you mean that . . . ?" or "Are you saying that . . . ?"

Verify. Ask questions even if you know the answers. You need to quote or attribute information to your source, not yourself.

Always check the spelling of your source's name—first and last names and middle initial. Check the person's title and the dates of crucial events. Check the accuracy of information on a resume or press release. You don't have to repeat everything, but you should ask the source if the information released is correct. Then ask some questions that expand on the basic information. For example, if you are interviewing the president of MADD (Mothers Against Drunk Driving), you might ask, "Have you ever been involved in an accident involving a drunken driver or were you ever arrested for drunken driving?" Such a question may not be as insensitive as it seems, because many people get involved with causes after they have had a personal experience with the problem.

Also, remember that if the source tells you something about another person, you must check it out with that person.

Use the "lie detector test." Bill Marimow, a two-time winner of the Pulitzer Prize, assumes that his sources might lie to him. When he interviewed sources for his prize-winning series about police brutality, he warned sources who were accusing police that if he found out they were not telling him the whole truth, he wouldn't print a word they said. He got their police records before he interviewed them.

In one case, Marimow asked a source if he had ever been arrested, and the source said no. "I took out the file and said, 'What about this attempted rape?' I knew then that I wouldn't write anything about that source," he said at a conference of investigative reporters. "I believe in laying 51 of 52 cards on the table. But I want to keep one card. The arrest report was that one card."

Use the silent treatment. Pause for a few seconds between questions to let the source elaborate. If the pause seems uncomfortable, the source may break the silence first. One reporter was writing a profile of a nun. He asked her if she missed having a sex life and how she coped without one. She gave a brief, expected answer that she had made a conscious choice of abstinence when she took vows of celibacy. The reporter was disappointed with the answer. He said nothing. She said nothing. For several seconds they just sat in silence. Both were slightly uncomfortable. Then she broke the silence and began elaborating about how difficult celibacy was for her at times. Sometimes the best follow-up question is no question.

Use the "blame others" technique. When you have to ask tough questions, blame someone else: "Your opponent says you cheated on your income taxes. How would you respond to that?"

Reporters and editors have mixed feelings about warning the source that a tough question is coming. Don't do it, they say, in confrontational interviews when you are trying to get a source to reveal information that could be damaging. It puts the source on notice and gives him or her a few seconds to become defensive and evasive. But do warn the source or apologize if it's going to be a tough, emotional question, especially if you are interviewing grieving people, says Jacqui Banaszynski, who won a Pulitzer Prize for a series about a man with AIDS. She tells sources that she will ask tough questions but they don't have to answer them. "But I'll try to convince them to do so," she says.

Handle emotional questions with tact. Emotional questions can be difficult. Ask your source to recall how he or she was thinking or feeling at the time of an incident. "Were you frightened when the train lost power? What were you thinking at the time?"

Avoid insensitive questions. There's a saying in journalism that there are no stupid questions, only stupid answers. That's not exactly true.

"How do you feel about the death of your three children?" is not only a stupid question, it's insensitive. Instead of asking such an emotionally loaded question, ask the person to recall specific memories about his or her children, or ask how the source is coping with the tragedy.

Ask summary questions. Restate information, or ask the source to clarify the key points he or she is making. For example: "Of all the goals you have expressed, which would you say are the most important to you? What do you think are the three major issues you face?"

Use the "matchmaker" technique. Ask your source to suggest other sources for your story. Ask if anyone else is involved in the issue or if there are other people the source would suggest you contact. Remember that you will want more than one source for your story so you can strive for fairness and balance.

Ask free-choice questions. Ask the source if there is anything he or she would like to add.

End on a positive note. When you have finished the interview, thank your source. Ask if you can call back if you have any further questions. At this point, you also could ask for a home telephone number or another way to reach the source.

Reporting for Graphics

If you had to draw your story instead of write it, how would it look? You may have gathered enough information through an interview for a verbal presentation. But you still have to think about visual presentation.

Whenever you go on an assignment—especially a breaking news story involving an accident, a disaster such as a flood or explosion, or a crime—gather information for the graphic artist. Even if you don't use all these details for a graphic, you can use many of them to make your writing more vivid. Get maps, brochures or any other written materials that might be available to help the graphics department pinpoint the location of the crime or disaster scene.

And ask questions as though you had to describe the scene to a blind person. How many feet or yards away from the landfill is the nearest house? What buildings are in the area? When the gas pipe exploded, how many feet from the gas line was the nearest building? What are the names and exact locations of the businesses in the area? Detail, detail, detail!

Here are some types of information to gather for a graphic that could accompany your story:

Locations: Get the names of streets and major intersections nearest to the site of the incident. Ask details about specific measurements: yards, feet, number of city blocks or whatever else would help pinpoint locations.

Chronology of events: Get specific times or dates and other information to recount the sequence of events. For example, suppose a terrorist takes a hostage. When did the incident occur? At what time did each development occur before the hostage was released or killed?

Weather data: Suppose your community has had a drought. How many days or months have gone by since the last rainfall? What were the temperatures in the last 30 days of a heat wave or cold spell? How many inches of rain fell during each day or week in a period of flooding?

Statistics: Think of charts. If your city council has raised taxes, what have taxes been during the past five years? How much has tuition increased during the past several years? How many students have dropped out of college? How does this year's enrollment compare with enrollments in previous years? Statistics like these can be boring to read. But they are easy to understand in chart form.

Highlights: Gather information for a facts box, such as important dates or highlights of someone's career. Suppose you are doing a profile. Instead of listing key dates and incidents in your story, could you place them more effectively in a box? Ask about interesting hobbies, favorite books, favorite movies, marital status or other personal information that might help the graphic artist—and the reader.

Think of yourself as part of a team and the graphic artist as one of the key players. The better your story looks, the better chance you have of attracting the reader to those words you have worked so hard to report and write. In the past, when a reporter turned in a story that was reported and written well, editors used to say, "Your story looks good." It's up to you to make sure it does—verbally and visually.

The GOAL Method of Interviewing

The "GOAL method" is a concept to help you frame questions for a variety of stories, especially profiles, features, and stories about programs and issues. It is a variation of a technique devised by LaRue W. Gilleland, a former journalism educator. It does not work with all stories, nor should you limit your questions to these concepts. But it is a starting framework. Here's what the letters stand for:

G = goals

O = obstacles

A = achievements

L = logistics

Many interviews can be designed around this GOAL concept, especially for profiles and features about new programs. If you structure your questions around these ideas, you will get answers to the questions of why, how and what. Here are some ideas for specific questions using this method:

Goals: What are or were some of your goals in this program (or in your career)? What are you trying to accomplish? Why do you want to do this? Try to discern the person's motivation for his or her actions.

Obstacles: What were some of the obstacles you faced (or are facing)? Get specific examples or anecdotes. What is one example of a difficult problem you experienced? Try not to qualify your question by asking for the most difficult problem or the funniest or happiest moment. People have difficulty deciding what is best, worst, hardest, easiest, happiest or saddest. They need clues, such as a specific period during their life.

Achievements: How did you overcome these obstacles? How did you achieve your goal (or how do you plan to achieve it)? Again, get specifics.

Logistics: How did the source or the program get to this point? This is the background, past, present and future. How did the source's background affect his or her goals, obstacles and achievements? What factors in the person's background relate to the focus of your story? Is there a chronology of events you need to get so the reader can understand the story? Weave in the background where it will be interesting and relevant.

Telephone Interviewing

Edna Buchanan was persistent. The former *Miami Herald* police reporter spent much of her life making difficult phone calls to people who were grieving. If a source hung up on her, Buchanan waited a minute or two. Then she called back. The second time she identified herself again and said, "We were cut off." Sometimes her sources changed their minds, or someone else who was willing to talk answered the phone. But if they hung up again, she didn't call a third time.

More often than not, people are willing to talk to reporters, especially on the telephone. For many sources, talking about a loved one who died is cathartic.

Not all telephone interviews involve difficult situations. Reporters on a daily newspaper get many of their stories by telephone—from daily checks with police about crime stories to interviews with politicians, government officials and community leaders for reaction stories, issue stories and a wide range of features.

Nancy Tracy, a former *Hartford* (Conn.) *Courant* reporter, had a way of almost seeing through the telephone. She would ask her sources for details. She asked what they were wearing, what they were doing, what they were thinking, how they were coping and reacting. She was always empathetic. Sometimes she would apologize for asking difficult questions; sometimes she would sympathize. Then she would ask more questions. And rarely did anyone refuse to answer her.

Here is an excerpt from a story Tracy did about a Georgia couple who survived when their truck plunged into the Mianus River in Connecticut when the bridge collapsed. In her telephone interview with David Pace, Tracy asked such questions as "Where are you sitting now? What is your daily routine? What do you think about and dream about?" and even "What is the weather today?"

Some days when the pain isn't too bad, he stands by the front door, watching trucks roll by on Highway 41 on their way to Macon. Then the memories come flooding back, the crash, the pain.

Inside the small mobile home, his wife also remembers the day their world fell apart, when a metal and concrete span that was the Mianus Bridge split, sending them and four others tumbling 70 feet to the Mianus River in Greenwich.

It is a year today since the bridge collapsed, but for David and Helen Pace of Perry, Ga., it's as if it happened yesterday. It still figures in their nightmares, still limits their days.

A living hell, 27-year-old David Pace calls the past year.

It is raining. Helen Pace has taken to her bed. On damp or rainy days, her back hurts more than usual.

On the days she is up, she wears dark stockings to cover the scars on her legs. She used to be proud of those legs, her husband says.

They had been married six months, and he'd gotten into the habit of bringing her with him on the long-distance runs. The night the bridge fell down, they were on their way to New Hampshire with 26,000 pounds of empty beer bottles in their semi-trailer.

He loved trucking—the good money it brought, the chance to see the country. Now, David Pace says, his and his wife's injuries are so severe that his parents are afraid to leave them alone.

"I've had to turn to my mother-in-law, my father-in-law, my mom and dad," he says. "It kind of takes a part of my manhood away from me. It hurts. It hurts bad."

Nancy Tracy, *The Hartford Courant*

Tracy got all that information by telephone.

Although interviewing people in person is preferable, it is often not practical, especially if you are on deadline. You won't be able to observe facial reactions, gestures and surroundings when you conduct telephone interviews, but you still can gather information accurately and thoroughly.

The techniques of telephone interviewing are very similar to methods of interviewing in person. The major difference is that you need to work harder at keeping the source's attention and focusing your questions. Researchers suggest that the average telephone interview should be limited to 20 minutes. After that, the attention span of the person responding wanes. If you call a source at home, he or she may be further distracted by children or other family concerns.

Here are some guidelines for telephone interviewing:

Identification: Immediately state your name and affiliation and the purpose for the call.

Icebreakers: These may not be necessary. Get to the point quickly. If you use any icebreaker to establish rapport, keep it very brief.

Length of questions: Keep them very short. Phrase each question clearly and simply. Limit questions to no more than two sentences; one is better.

Clarification: Make sure you understand the information you receive. It may be harder to understand information in a telephone interview, so clarify anything that is confusing. Repeat any confusing terms or information in your own words, and ask your source to verify your interpretation.

Specifics: Ask for details and examples. If you want to describe the scene, ask your source to give you the descriptive details.

Chronology: A chronology is especially important in police and fire stories you receive by telephone. Make sure you understand the sequence of events so you can write the story clearly. If you do not understand how an event occurred, try restating the chronology: "Let me understand, is this how it happened?" Or after a source tells you the high points of what happened, you could ask him or her to explain the order in which events unfolded.

Limits: Because your time may be limited by many events beyond your control, limit the number of questions in a telephone interview. Plan two lists: all the questions you want to ask and crucial questions. If you have time for only a few questions, switch to the crucial list. You may also want to ask your questions in a different order. Don't wait too long to ask the crucial ones. You never can tell when the source will be interrupted and will terminate the interview.

Control: Changing the subject to get to the questions you need to have answered is even more crucial in a telephone interview than in person. You can't spare too much time establishing rapport or engaging in nonproductive conversation. Be mindful of the information you must get for your story.

Verification: Double-check the spelling of the name, title and other basic information. If you haven't heard it clearly, spell it back to the source. This basic information is crucial when dealing with police officers. They usually do not identify themselves by their full names when they answer the phone on duty, so make sure you get first and last names and the proper rank, such as lieutenant, sergeant or captain.

At the end of the interview, thank the source and ask if you may call back if you have more questions. Use judgment here. Don't ask this of police or reluctant sources; just call back if you must have more information.

Exercises   **1**   Interview a reporter from your local newspaper about his or her reporting techniques. Or choose a reporter whose stories you like, and interview him or her about techniques.

2   Make a list of questions you would use as icebreakers to interview a professor or a source whose office you have visited.

3   Interview a local police officer about a crime or accident. In addition to getting basic information, ask questions to establish the chronology of events. If possible, get a copy of the police report. If the class is not doing this exercise as a group, check to make sure several people will not be interviewing the same officer.

4   **Technical clarity:** This exercise was suggested by Jacqui Banaszynski, senior editor at *The* (Portland) *Oregonian*. Interview a source about some technical information you don't understand. The source could be anyone from an auto mechanic to a scientist. Work on clarifying jargon and other information you don't understand. Then write the results of your interview in a brief story or several paragraphs explaining the technical information clearly.

5   Plan 10 questions to ask a community leader, college official or other person you might interview about an issue in your community. Or, if you prefer, take any issue in the news and imagine that you are a reporter covering that story. Plan 10 questions you would ask.

6   **Graphics:** Check your local newspaper or another newspaper that uses graphic illustrations. Study a graphic, and write a list of questions you would have asked to gather the information that the artist used to design it.

7   **Enterprise:** Conduct an interview in order to write a news story about an issue on your campus or in your community. Here are some suggestions:

  • Write a reaction story based on interviews with students or local residents about any controversial topic in the news.

  • Attend a demonstration, rally, meeting or other public event on your campus or in your community.

  • Check the psychology department for studies being conducted with classes or other studies professors are doing.

  • Check your college or university's office of institutional research for studies.

  • Check your campus and local newspapers for clubs and support groups in your community.

  • Write a story about the economic or psychological impact any unusual weather in your area may have had on businesses, agriculture or people.

THREE

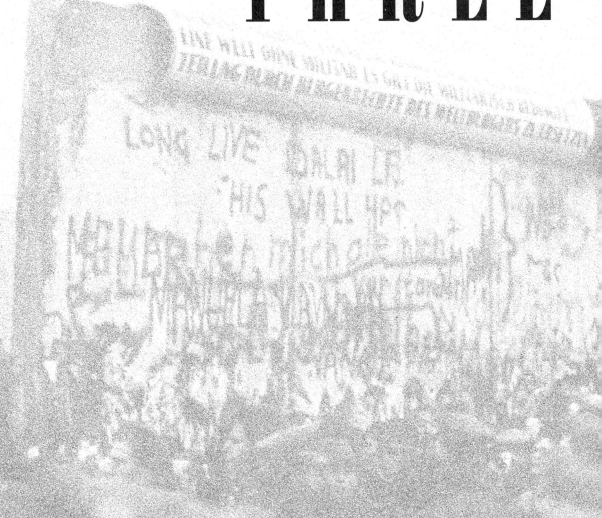

Constructing Stories

COACHING

TIPS

Find your focus by writing one sentence explaining what the story is about.

Plan an order for your story using key words for the ideas and quotes from your notes. If graphics will accompany your story, consider what you should leave out of the text.

Write a highlights box to find key points; use the box as a guide for your organization.

Write a first draft quickly; then revise it. Cut all extraneous words, unnecessary quotes and repetitive transitions.

Read your story aloud to catch typos, cumbersome phrases and poor rhythm.

Write your story as a brief before you write the full text.

The Writing Process

9

Bill Ryan wrote stories for newspapers and magazines for more than 40 years, and his process was always the same. When he returned from his assignments, he didn't start writing with a pencil, typewriter or computer. He started with his mind.

"If you start writing right away, you're wasting a lot of time because you'll have to keep backtracking through your notes," says Ryan, a former writer for *The Hartford* (Conn.) *Courant* and *Parade* magazine. "If you do nothing for five minutes except think about it, you'll have a better story."

Ryan says he started thinking about his stories in the car as he drove back to the office from interviews. He never wrote formal outlines: "I'm not a super organized person." Occasionally he sketched some notes to indicate the order of his story. He organized his stories by using what interested him first, and then he thought about all the other material readers needed to know. "I think you should write a story in the order in which it interests you," he says.

Writers work in many different ways. Some writers pace around the newsroom before they write. Others outline their stories or write a rough draft first. And many writers just stare at their computer waiting for a muse to inspire them to create the perfect lead. They insist that they can't write the rest of the story until they find their lead. Deadline approaches, and the rest of the story gets short shrift because the writer is almost out of time. But the writing process doesn't have to be that painful; you can use several techniques to develop a writing process that works for you.

There's nothing to writing.

All you do is sit down at the

typewriter and open a vein.

Red Smith, sportswriter,

The New York Times

Don Fry, writing coach
Courtesy of Don Fry

Ways to Approach the Writing Process

Don Fry almost never worries about what he is going to say first. He writes his leads last. Fry, one of the foremost writing experts in the country, takes less time to write an entire story than most writers spend on their leads.

Fry says he begins the writing process long before he sits down at his computer. "I'm imagining the story while I'm reporting it," he says.

After Fry gathers his information, he thinks about his story, "rehearsing" it in his head. Then he plans an order for his story. He codes his notes, marking just the material he intends to use—usually only 5 percent of the notes he took.

Then he puts his notes aside and writes a plan for his story, a rough order with just a few words for each point he wants to make. "I ask myself what are the parts and in what order do I want to put them," he says. Other questions he asks in the planning stage: What questions does the reader need answered and in what order?

Fry concentrates on what he calls the "point statement," also known as a focus graph or nut graph. He asks himself what the story is about and what the point of the story is. Any information that doesn't relate to the point statement isn't included in the story.

And then he starts writing. Not at the beginning, but at the paragraph containing the point statement. He continues writing until he gets to his ending, which he calls the "kicker." Then he writes his lead. After that he revises.

Fry has a five-step writing system: Conceive the idea, report, organize (plan an order), draft and revise. The four-step coaching process used in this book—conceive, collect, construct and correct—is adapted from Fry. But no single writing process will work for everyone. Good writers develop their own methods.

The FORK Method

In the coming chapters, you will study many ways of writing leads and organizing stories. But before you get to those specific methods, try the following writing process—called the FORK method of organization—to help you organize stories before and while you write:

F = focus

O = order

R = repetition of key words

K = "kiss off"

Focus   This is the main point of your story. In a hard-news story, the focal point could be in your lead. In a soft-news story, it is your nut graph. But it is also a crucial organizing tool; once you find it you have to keep it. Your lead should lead to the focal point, and all other infor-

PEANUTS®   BY CHARLES SCHULZ

The agony of writing a lead
Reprinted by permission of United Features Syndicate, Inc.

mation should relate to it. Information in your notes that does not relate to this focus should not go in the story. If you don't know the focus of your story, your story will ramble.

Here are some tips for finding your focus:

Headline technique: Try writing a headline for your story. If you had only a few words to express the main point, what would they be?

Tell-a-friend technique: If you were telling someone about your story, how would you describe it? How would you answer the question "What's it about?" Explain your story in one or two sentences.

Even Pulitzer Prize–winning writers and editors use the tell-a-friend technique to find their focus. For example, Laura Sessions Stepp, a writer at *The Washington Post,* tells a story about when she was the editor of a Pulitzer Prize–winning series at *The Charlotte* (N.C.) *Observer.* For nearly a year, she had worked on a series about brown lung disease, which cotton pickers were getting from inhaling the dust of the cotton. After all the editing was completed, she sat down to write a brief introduction explaining what the series was about. And she sat. And she sat. The city editor, noticing her agony, came over and asked what the problem was. "I'm stuck. I can't write a lead for this," she said.

"What's it about?" he said.

"Cotton dust is killing people, and farmers are . . ."

"Stop!" he said, as she was about to drone on.

Cotton dust is killing people. That was the lead. And the focus of the series.

Steve Lovelady, an editor at *The Philadelphia Inquirer,* uses a slightly different version of the tell-a-friend technique, the "challenge technique," which forces the writer to justify the "so what," "who cares" aspect of the story. Lovelady, who edited many of the *Inquirer's* Pulitzer Prize–winning stories, uses the following scenario to bait writers into finding their focus. He envisions himself at a party, where he meets a reporter who works for another editor at his newspaper. "Hi, Charlie, what are you working on?" he says.

"I'm working on a story about how toxic waste is seeping into the underground water supply in the suburbs," Charlie says.

"Sounds boring," Steve replies.

"Boring! Are you kidding? Kids are deformed for life, the trees have died, houses are worth nothing . . ."

"Thanks, Charlie."

Jacqui Banaszynski, winner of a Pulitzer Prize for feature writing, uses the "stoplight technique." Imagine that you are at a stoplight and have 30 seconds to tell your story before the light changes. Chances are in 30 seconds you'll express the focus—or the lead. This technique is the supercharged version of "What's it about?"

Order   Look through your notes, and mark information you want to use. On a separate piece of paper or in your computer, write key words or phrases to remind you of the items you want to use. Then put them in the order you will use them in your story. You can change the order when you start writing if you don't like your initial plan.

Some writers need a very complete outline; others need only a few words to plan their stories. Decide what works for you.

Susan Ager, writing coach for the *Detroit Free Press,* calls the "order" step a road map. Envision a story as though you were planning a trip. You need a map to tell you where you are going, she says.

Graphics also affect your story content and order. Consider whether some statistics or other material to be presented in a graphic would be redundant in the text. However, if the information is crucial to understanding the story, leave it in both places.

Here are some suggestions to help you decide an order:

Topics: List all the main points you want to cover. Decide which are the most important and which point naturally follows another. Then put them in that order. Arrange information from the most important to the least important. Then group together all the information—quotes, supporting facts—related to a specific point or topic.

Graphics: If you were writing a highlights box, what would your main points be? Use the highlights as a guide for organization, giving clues about what to include and in what order.

A test: If you had to test the reader on the most important points of your story, what questions would you write? Put the questions in natural order, with answers for one question leading to another question.

Question/answer: Jot down an idea for your lead (you don't need the exact wording at this point). What questions does it raise that need to be answered and backed up in the story? After you answer those questions, continue asking what additional questions need to be answered and in what order of importance or interest.

Ending: Decide how you want to end the story. Do you have a quote that summarizes the main point or refers back to the lead? Is there a future angle? After you have a lead and an ending, figure out what kind of information you need to get from the beginning to the end. Many writers consider the ending just as important as the lead, and they want to know where they are going when they organize their stories.

Time sequence: Does the story have distinct time elements? Consider arranging the story in some chronology. You could start with what is happening now, go to background (the past action), then return to the present and end with the future. You may decide that only a part of your story should be in a chronological order.

Quotes: Mark the quotes that are most important, and design your story by sources, starting with the ones who have the most important points to make and proceeding to the lesser quotes. Vary the pace. Mix quotations with paraphrased information, facts and anecdotes. If you have a very good quote, you might base your lead on the concept and use the quote for backup to the lead.

Free-writing: If you are stuck, put away your notes and just write what you remember. Then review what you have written, and arrange it in an order that seems logical. Plug in quotes and facts later.

Tell-a-friend technique: The method of telling a friend may also give you an order.

Repetition of key words   This is a technique that provides smooth transitions during the writing process or serves as a thought bridge to get you from one concept to the next. The technique also is known as "stitching," because it helps stitch one paragraph to the other.

As you write, look at the last sentence in each paragraph and find a key word that will lead you to the next paragraph. That key word can trigger a question you can answer in the next paragraph or can serve as a bridge for the next thought. You may either repeat the word in the next sentence as a transitional device or just use the concept of the word as a bridge to the idea in your next paragraph. Don't overuse the exact repetition of key words for transitions, because your writing may become boring.

In the following example, the underlined key words serve as transitions to the next thought. In some cases the writer repeats the key word, and in others he uses it as a thought bridge.

What we need are some mandatory classes that you would attend before you attempted to move your household. These would be much more useful than those classes you go to before you have a baby.

When you have a baby, you are surrounded by skilled professionals, who, if things get really bad, give you drugs, whereas nobody performs any such service when you move. This is wrong.

The first thing the burly men should do when they get off the moving van is seize you and forcibly inject you with a two-week supply of sedatives, because moving, to judge from its effect on my wife, is far more stressful than childbirth.

Even in the worst throes of labor, even when she had become totally irrational and was making voices like the ones Linda Blair made in "The Exorcist," only without the aid of special effects, my wife never once suggested that we should put wet, filthy scum-encrusted rags, which I had been cleaning toilets with, into a box and have paid professionals to transport them 1,200 miles so we could have them in our new home.

Dave Barry, syndicated columnist

Key word **drugs** *serves as a bridge to the next thought.*

Key word **childbirth** *serves as a bridge to elaborate the idea.*

The kiss off Do you get annoyed when a person's last name is mentioned in a story on a second reference but you have forgotten who the person is? The kiss-off technique helps eliminate such confusion. It is a way of organizing information by using sources in blocks instead of sporadically throughout a story. After a person is identified by full name once, newspapers use only the last name if the person is mentioned again in the story. If only one or two people are mentioned in a story, this device isn't confusing. But the reader will have trouble remembering many sources by their last names.

Here is how the kiss-off technique works to avoid this problem: When you have three or more sources in a story, use each source once or in consecutive paragraphs, blocking all his or her comments in one place, and then kiss off that source. Do not weave back and forth with sources, unless you have fewer than three. If you must use a source again in another part of the story, reintroduce the person by title or some reference to remind the reader of the person's identity. The exception is a well-known source, such as the mayor, the governor, the president, a celebrity or the central character in a story. The name of such a source may be placed anywhere in the story without confusing the reader.

The kiss-off concept also may be used for a story that has several different supporting concepts. After you have determined your main focus, plan an order for each supporting point. Block all the backup material related to that point, and then kiss it off. If you have several people discussing several ideas, as in a meeting, you will have to be selective about which comments to include. Even in a story arranged by topics, you still should try to block information from each source—if you have more than three—in one place, so you don't confuse the reader by weaving too many people throughout the story.

In this example of the kiss-off technique, notice how the sources are organized in blocks:

Focus

Beginning next spring, smokers at Lansing Community College will have to take their habit outside.

The LCC Board of Trustees has approved a smoke-free campus at the end of the next spring term. It is expected to make LCC the first campus with totally smoke-free facilities in the state.

1 (first speaker)

"It gives a year for the thing to settle in and for people to accept it and adjust to it," said Erik Furseth, chairman of the board.

Under its current policy, smoking is permitted only in designated areas, such as portions of cafeterias. When the new policy takes effect, smoking will be banned in all parts of all buildings.

Key word buildings *leads* to next thought.
2 (second speaker)
3 (third speaker)

"We do have a smoking area. It's outside the building," said Trustee Judith Hollister.

Karen Krzanowski, assistant executive director of the American Lung Association of Michigan, said she believes that LCC is the first community college in the state to adopt a smoke-free policy.

3
Key word others *leads to* next thought.

"We're delighted," she said. "I think they are taking the lead and others will follow."

A growing number of employers statewide are banning smoking, Krzanowski said. Those include Michigan Bell, Comerica and the state Public Health Department.

3

LCC trustees adopted the policy after holding hearings and developing a comprehensive report on smoking. The one-year delay in implementation is designed to give employees and students a chance to prepare.

The college will offer assistance to people trying to quit, perhaps by offering smoking cessation sessions, said Jacqueline Taylor, vice president for college and community relations.

4 (fourth speaker)

LCC also will develop an education program to explain the policy and encourage people not to smoke.

"I think it's great," said Elizabeth Saettler, a non-smoker from Owosso. "I certainly think it benefits the majority of people."

5 (fifth speaker)

Sherry Brettin of East Lansing said she could accept the new policy. "I smoke, but I'll go outside. It doesn't bother me," she said.

6 (sixth speaker)

"I plan to stop smoking anyway," said Geoff Waun of East Lansing. "I still think there should be a place for people to smoke."

7 (seventh speaker)

Chris Andrews, *Lansing* (Mich.) *State Journal*

The kiss-off technique is only a guideline and should not be adhered to strictly when the story order would be more logical if sources were repeated in different places throughout the story. Plan your story first by topics and natural order of one concept following another; then decide if the kiss-off technique for sources will be effective.

Briefs

Another technique to help you organize your story is to write it as a brief. A "brief" is an abbreviated story, usually ranging from one to four paragraphs. Even if you are writing a long story, if you can compress your thoughts into a few paragraphs, you will be able to determine your focus and some of the essential information. But that may be harder than it sounds.

If you are a good reporter, you will take far more notes than you need. In these days, however, the more you know, the less you may have to write about it. One of the hardest tasks for writers is to decide what to leave out of a story. Richard Aregood, two-time Pulitzer Prize winner, gives this advice: "Resist the temptation to tell everything you've learned; much of it doesn't matter."

Writing briefly is not only an art, it is often a requirement in newspapers and is essential in broadcast news. Newspapers use briefs as teasers to full stories inside the paper or as substitutes for long stories. Magazines also feature many briefs, and on-line news stories also are often preceded by summary lines or briefs.

Here is a brief that substituted for a full story in the Life section of *USA Today:*

UNTOLD TWAIN TALE: Scholars poring over the recently discovered first half of Mark Twain's *Adventures of Huckleberry Finn* manuscript have found a lost passage about Jim's encounter with a cadaver. Twain deleted it, probably because it was too gruesome. The 2,000-word episode takes place after Huck escapes his father and flees to Jackson Island, where he meets Jim. While the two wait out a rainstorm, Jim describes his disastrous efforts at trying to warm up a cadaver for a medical student who was to dissect it. Publication of the new section is prohibited because a New York City foundation owns the rights to unpublished Twain material.

USA Today

Try using briefs as a writing tool in this manner:

• Write a one-line brief as a summary line. This brief would be the same as your focus sentence, and it can serve as your lead or nut graph.

• Condense your story into a brief of one to four paragraphs. Decide what is your most crucial information. Then, using the brief as an organizing tool, expand and elaborate on the main points you selected for your brief.

How to Revise Stories

Mark Twain not only wrote stories, he wrote about writing: "The difference between the right word and the nearly right word is same as that between lightning and the lightning bug."

Choosing the right words isn't easy. Revising your story doesn't mean just going back and cleaning up the grammar and style. Do what a writing coach does when working with a reporter to discover the problems in a story: Ask questions to reveal where the problems originated. They could be at any point in the process, from the conception to collection to construction. A coach would ask questions like these: What did you like about the story? Where did you struggle? What were you trying to say?

When you revise your story, ask yourself some of these coaching questions as well:

Conceive: Is the idea well-focused? Should the story be developed around another angle?

Collect: Does the story need more information?

Construct: Does the order work? Is it logical and interesting? Is the focus clear?

Correct: Did any problems occur in the earlier steps? Are any minor corrections necessary to improve grammar or spelling or to tighten sentences?

Although you may need additional information, more often you will need to cut the story. *USA Today,* which is known for brevity, offers these guidelines to its writers for focusing, tightening and revising stories:

Squeeze a fact on every line: Allow one idea per sentence.

Focus tightly: Think about what the real story is, and choose a slice of it. Emphasize what's new, what's coming and what it means to readers. Tell them the impact, how they can act on or use this information.

Use impact leads: Don't ignore the news just to be different, but avoid rehashing what readers already know. Think forward spin. Instead of writing "A jet crashed Tuesday, killing 534 people," write "Airline takeoff procedures might be overhauled after Tuesday's crash that killed 534 people."

Make the story move: Make your point early. Use only the information that helps make that point.

Keep it tight: Propel the story with punctuation. Colons, semicolons and bullets can replace some words and help the reader move faster.

Use specific details instead of adjectives: Instead of writing "the ancient windmill," refer to "the 100-year-old windmill."

Don't overattribute: You don't need a "he said" after every sentence, although it should be clear where the information came from.

Use strong, lively verbs: Instead of writing "There were hundreds of people in the streets to see the pope," write "Hundreds of people lined the streets to see the pope" (or jammed, crowded or thronged the streets). Sentences that start with *there* force you to use a weak "to be" verb.

Avoid weak transitions: A well-organized story needs only a few transitions.

Choose quotes that advance the story: Avoid quotes that merely illustrate the last point made. And don't paraphrase if you have a good quote. Be selective. Don't repeat.

Writing Process Tips

Here are some other tips to help you during the writing process:

Remember your focus: Put your focus graph (the "so what" paragraph) at the top of your story as a reminder to choose only material related to the focus for the body of the story. Then remember to place the focus within your story.

Write many leads: Instead of struggling to get the perfect lead, try writing several leads. Then write the rest of the story. Choose one lead when you've finished.

Fix later: As you are writing, when you get to a sentence or paragraph that doesn't sound right, write *fix* next to it or follow it with question marks to indicate that you want to return and polish it. Don't get slowed down by perfectionism as you draft your story.

Use the question/answer technique: As you are writing, does one paragraph raise a question or point that should be answered or explained in the next? Try to anticipate the reader's questions and answer them.

Read aloud: If you are struggling with a sentence that doesn't sound right, read it aloud. Also read your story aloud after you finish writing it. You'll hear the cumbersome parts that your eye didn't catch. Find them and fix them. This technique is especially helpful for broadcast journalists.

Check accuracy: Go back and check names, titles and quotes. Make sure you have the right person's name attached to the quote you have used. Check for typos and spelling.

Use active voice whenever possible: Here's an example of passive voice:

> Her first story always will be remembered by her.

The active voice has more impact:

> She always will remember her first story.

Write short sentences: On average, your sentences should have fewer than 25 words.

Write simple sentences: Keep the subject and verb close together. This example shows what happens when you don't. It is from a story about school board approval of remodeling and construction projects at the city's two schools.

> Those two projects—calling for construction of classrooms, office area and media center at Wakefield and construction of a new district-wide kitchen and computer lab plus remodeling projects at the high school—will be paid for by using approximately $800,000 of the district's special capital outlay fund.

Whew! That's a long sentence. The subject is *projects,* and the verb is *will be paid.* They are separated by too many words. Split it into three sentences:

> One project will involve construction of classrooms, an office area and a media center at Wakefield. The other includes building a new district-wide kitchen, a computer lab and remodeling projects at the high school. The $800,000 approximate cost of the projects will be paid from the district's special capital outlay fund.

Vary the pace: Follow long sentences with short ones. If you use complex sentences, follow them with short, punchy ones:

> Pamela Lewiston thought she was leading a normal life as the daughter of Dr. Normal Lewiston, a respected Stanford University physician, and his wife, Diana.
>
>   She thought wrong.
>
>   Her father had been married to—and lived with—two women besides her mother, all at the same time. His carefully managed deception ended in a cascading series of revelations after his death from a heart attack in August.
>
> S. L. Wykes, *San Jose* (Calif.) *Mercury News*

Avoid jargon: Translate bureaucratic terms into simple ones; define technical terms. Here's advice from writer George Orwell:

> Never use a metaphor, simile or other figure of speech which you are used to seeing in print. Never use a long word when a short one will do. If it is possible to cut a word out, always cut it out. Never use the passive when you can use the active. Never use a foreign phrase, a scientific word or a jargon word if you can think of an everyday English equivalent. Break any of these rules sooner than say anything outright barbarous.

Here's an example of garbled writing from the U.S. federal budget:

> Funds obligated for military assistance as of September 30, 1979, may, if deobligated, be reobligated.

Write the way you speak: Unless you speak like the bureaucrat who wrote that budget item.

Exercises

1 Using information for any story you have gathered, write a plan for organizing it. Then write a draft and revise.

2 Try free-writing a story you have reported. Then write your first and final versions.

3 **Revision:** Take any full-length story from your campus or local newspaper, and tighten it or rewrite it, using the guidelines of *USA Today.*

4 **FORK exercise:** Organize this story using a feature lead and the kiss-off technique. Consider repeating key words to make transitions. Make sure you have a clear nut graph (focus paragraph). Put it at the top of your story to guide you and in the body of your story where you think it is appropriate.

This story is about the resurgence of blind dating in New York City. You have interviewed several authorities, as well as people who have had blind dates. Feel free to paraphrase when appropriate; you do not have to use all these quotes or even all these sources. Do not just string quotes together. This information and these quotes, based on a story from *The New York Times,* are not in good order:

Nathaniel Branden, a Los Angeles psychologist and author of *The Psychology of Romantic Love and How to Raise Your Self-Esteem:* "Today, when people find it so hard to meet other people and when there is so much fear of different diseases, it's predictable and inevitable that we would see a resurgence of blind dating."

Amy Jaffee, 29, a journalist from New York who considers herself a matchmaker: "There's a Jewish legend that if you fix up two people and they get married and have children, you're guaranteed a place in heaven. I have three marriages under my belt, so I guess I'm in good shape." She says most romances that are arranged fizzle after the second or third date. "Usually, people try to fix others up on the basis that they both like to ski or they both like Islamic art. But I find those things don't make any difference. Instead, I ask friends to describe the last person they were in love with."

Herbert J. Freudenberger, a New York City psychologist: "Not long ago, a person willing to go on a blind date was perceived as a poor nebbish who had to rely on someone else to meet people. There's a complete shift in attitude now. It's a subtle swing back to a more conservative time."

Steven Veer, 28, a Manhattan attorney who has been on dozens of blind dates: "Personals are a last resort. A blind date is much better. It's a screen. You know the person hasn't 'overcirculated' in this time of caution" (referring to AIDS).

Melissa Mack, 24, a public relations writer: "New York can be a really lonely place. Everyone acquires an anonymous character. On the subway, the same people kicking and shoving and ignoring you might be loving and caring in a relationship." She is discouraged by the club scene. "What's so disenchanting about the club scene is that being cool and detached is the order of the day."

Morris Panner, 25, in his last semester at Harvard Law School: "In law school, my friends and I live on blind dates. Five years ago I would have thought it was really crass."

Barbara Wasserman, a New Yorker who met her husband, Bob Goldman, on a blind date: They had arranged to meet for their blind date by the Dumpster in front of Jeremy's Ale House, a popular hangout at Manhattan's South Street Seaport. They had low expectations that it would work out. Goldman had already had five unsuccessful blind dates.

Wasserman said that she was turned off when her date said on the telephone that he would be the good-looking guy in the blue suit. "I found the Dumpster, put down my briefcase and saw a sea of blue suits. All of a sudden, a truly good-looking guy in a blue suit came out of the crowd, smiling, and kissed me on the cheek."

They walked to Chinatown, ate dinner and shared a pitcher of beer. They spoke in French and discussed work, politics, travel, mutual friends and college experiences.

Goldman proposed 14 months later by tucking a diamond ring inside a fortune cookie.

Part of the reason for the popularity of the blind date is the AIDS epidemic. Another reason is dissatisfaction with the club scene and the overall loneliness of living in a big city like New York.

Pamela Harris, 26, a New York associate art director: "Someone you trust says there's this guy who's really great. There's a sense of safety. You feel like you're not being thrown to the wolves. A friend has insight into me and knows the kind of men I like, so basically, she's just cropped out 80 percent of the male population."

Sharon Lependorf, a consultant at People Resources, a New York singles club: "I've had at least three friends who got married in the last year and a half who met on blind dates."

5   Briefs: Condense a story you are writing for class into a brief of one to four paragraphs. If you are not working on a story, write a column of briefs for stories on the front page of your local newspaper.

6   Enterprise: Interview a writer you admire in your field (newspaper, magazine, public relations, broadcast, advertising) about his or her writing process. Ask specific questions about how the writer gets the idea, gathers information and organizes it. Ask the source for tips, such as the ones offered in this chapter by writers and editors.

COACHING

TIPS

Keep leads short—preferably fewer than 35 words.

Points of emphasis: Place the key words at the beginning or the end of the sentence for emphasis.

Write a focus sentence at the top of your story.

Write a "so what" (impact) line at the top of your story.

Avoid suffering: If you can't devise your lead, start with your nut graph and write your lead later, or write several leads and choose one later.

Don't invent your lead. Base it on the backup in your notes.

Leads and Nut Graphs 10

The lead is crucial. It's the beginning of your story, a promise to the reader of what is to come. "Three seconds and the reader decides to read or turn to the next story. That's all the time you have to catch a reader's glance and hold it; all the time have to entice and inform," says Donald Murray in his book *Writing for Your Readers*. No wonder writers are paranoid about their leads.

The Eye Trac study, which monitored the movement of readers' eyes as they read newspapers, revealed that readers scan headlines. Many of them don't even read the story. And if they start reading, many of them don't finish the story.

The study also revealed some startling facts about how people read a news story: They often skip the lead and go to the third or fourth paragraph to find the nut graph, an interesting quote or an impact statement, because they are so conditioned to reading leads that reiterate headlines.

It's up to you to write leads that are enticing enough to make readers continue. There are many ways to do that.

The best day is the one when I can write a lead that will cause the reader at his breakfast the next morning to spit up his coffee, clutch at his heart and shout, "My God! Martha, did you read this?"

Edna Buchanan, former police reporter, *The Miami Herald*

Hard-news Leads, Soft Leads and Nut Graphs

The lead (originally spelled *lede* to differentiate it from "lead" type) tells the reader what the story is about. Think of the lead as a teaser or foreshadowing of what will come in the story. No matter what type of lead you write, you must back it up with information that substantiates it. If you haven't got material to support your lead, you have the wrong lead.

If you have been writing focus statements above your stories, you have a head start on writing leads. To write a focus statement, you asked yourself: What is the story about? What is the most important information? What is the point of this story? Those are the same questions you need to ask yourself to write a lead or a nut graph.

Sometimes nut graphs and leads are the same; sometimes they aren't. Here's how to tell the difference:

Hard-news leads: Also called a "direct lead" or a "summary lead," a hard-news lead summarizes in the first sentence what the story is about. A hard-news lead usually is only one sentence or two at most. It gets directly to the point. In this example, the first sentence is a summary lead. It tells who, what, when, where, and why.

> HUDSON, Fla.—A 13-year-old girl shot and slightly wounded her stepfather with a BB gun after he hit her mother on the head with a frying pan Saturday afternoon, according to the Pasco County Sheriff's Office.
>
> Larry Dougherty, *St. Petersburg* (Fla). *Times*

Nut Graphs: Also called the "focus graph," the nut graph is a paragraph that explains the point of the story—what the story is about. A summary lead often tells that information and takes the place of a nut graph.

Soft leads: Also called a "feature lead" or a "delayed lead," a soft lead, which can be several paragraphs, takes a little longer to get to the main point of the story. It delays telling the reader what the story is about by teasing the reader with description or a storytelling approach. With a soft lead, you must tell the reader the point of the story in the nut graph. In these days of impatient readers, the nut graph should be early in the story—usually by the third to fifth paragraph. Here is an example of a soft lead and the nut graph:

SAN JOSE, Calif.—A nervous flight attendant was having trouble taking a urine drug test. So she drank a glass of water—and another—and another.

Soft lead: who, what

After guzzling three liters in three hours, she still couldn't urinate. But hours later, the 40-year-old woman staggered into a Burlingame, Calif., hospital, her speech slurred, her thinking fuzzy.

More what

Where

The diagnosis: She was drunk—on water.

The unidentified San Mateo County resident is the first drug-test taker known to suffer from "water intoxication," doctors reported yesterday in the *Journal of the American Medical Association.* There have been only seven other reported cases of healthy people with the dangerous condition, which causes water-logged brain cells and a dilution of body minerals. One died.

Nut graph: The focus tells "so what." The story is about the dangers of water intoxication in connection with drug testing.

Knight-Ridder/Tribune News Service

Many editors object to soft leads because they take too long to get to the point of the story. New York University journalism professors Gerald Lanson and Mitchell Stephens fueled that concern, blasting the soft lead as "Jell-O journalism" in a journalism magazine article. The professors provided alarming examples of ineffective soft leads. Consider this one:

Emma and Alfred Mitchell are surrounded by broken beer bottles, crumbling cigarette packages and other rubbish. But even when trespassers start grass fires, the couple never complains.

They can't. They're dead. This story was about deterioration in local cemeteries. That lead isn't just soft; it's deceptive.

How do you decide whether to use a hard or soft lead? The choice depends on several factors: the significance of the news, the timing, proximity (interest to your local readers), subject matter and, in many cases, your editor's preference. If the subject is serious—death, disaster, a major change in the law—consider a hard-news approach. Breaking news that happened yesterday or today also lends itself to a hard-news lead.

The next two examples are about the same subject. Consider why one was written with a soft lead and the other with a hard lead. (Note that these examples begin with a location in capital letters, called a "dateline." It indicates that the news occurred in a location outside the newspaper's circulation area. Newspapers have their own guidelines about when to use datelines.)

Soft lead

SAN MATEO, Calif.—The dog in her arms was shaking, its rheumy eyes wide with fear.

"Just relax, sweetheart, it's OK," crooned Chris Powell, the manager of the Peninsula Humane Society animal shelter, where 10,000 unwanted pets are put to death each year.

The dog settled into Ms. Powell's embrace, making it easier for a veterinarian to inject a lethal dose of sodium pentobarbital.

In seconds, the dog was dead, carried to a can, atop a mound of puppies and kittens, all awaiting pickup by a rendering company that would turn the animals into fertilizer.

"There's not a day when you don't think about walking away from this misery," Ms. Powell said.

Tired of carrying out the daily killings, officials at the Humane Society in San Mateo, on San Francisco Bay, have proposed a novel solution to the pet overpopulation problem: a moratorium on breeding cats and dogs that will be considered by the San Mateo County Board of Supervisors on Nov. 13.

The ordinance, thought to be the first of its kind in the nation and opposed by professional breeders, would fine animal owners who allow their pets to reproduce and would prohibit transporting cats and dogs outside the county for that purpose.

Nut graph

Jane Gross, *The New York Times*

Hard-news lead and nut graph

REDWOOD CITY, Calif.—In an effort to reduce the number of unwanted pets put to death each year, the San Mateo County Board of Supervisors on Tuesday passed the nation's first law requiring owners of dogs and cats to buy a breeding license or get their pets sterilized.

The action, which affects pet owners in the unincorporated area of San Mateo County, culminates a heated and emotional two-month effort by local humane society officials to educate the public about the problems of pet overpopulation.

Fed up with putting more than 10,000 unwanted cats and dogs to death each year, the Peninsula Hu-

mane Society launched a grisly campaign to generate support for the ordinance. First, the group bought advertising inserts in local newspapers and subjected readers throughout the Bay Area to pictures of trash barrels full of dead cats.

Then the society held a public pet execution at a press conference, injecting five cats and three dogs with poison from a bottle marked "Fatal Plus" as cameras whirred and reporters jotted notes.

Miles Corwin, *Los Angeles Times*

Timing and proximity were factors in the choice of lead. The story in *The New York Times* was written before the law passed and for a national audience not directly affected by the law. The hard-news version in the *Los Angeles Times* was written immediately after the law passed, and it affected people in the newspaper's circulation area.

The Wow Test

There is no set rule to determine whether you should use a hard-news lead or a soft lead. The choice is really a matter of judgment.

One guideline is the Wow test. If the subject is very important, sensational or urgent enough to elicit a "Wow" or other exclamation when you tell a friend what the story is about in one sentence, consider a hard-news lead. Here is an example of a "Wow" lead:

> A gay St. Cloud State University student who announced this spring he was running for mayor was arrested Tuesday, accused of molesting a 9-year-old boy.
>
> *St. Cloud* (Minn.) *Times*

The Impact of Graphics on Leads

It's a catch-22 situation. The reporter writes a summary lead. The copy editor writes a headline and a deck headline (the secondary headline) to hook the reader. The reporter doesn't know what the copy editor will write. And the copy editor needs to summarize the story in the headline. By the time readers get to the lead, they have read the same information three times. Consider this example:

Headline	**MU fraternity punished for hazing**
Deck headline	*Hitting was alleged*
Second deck headline	This was the 2nd group suspended this year
Summary lead	A University of Missouri fraternity has been suspended after a pledge complained he was hit so hard during initiation rites it made his head ring.

The fraternity, Phi Beta Sigma, became the second MU fraternity suspended this year for hazing. Earlier Phi Kappa Theta was suspended.

The Associated Press

The increasing use of graphics compounds the dilemma for the reporter. Studies show that readers are drawn first to pictures, then to headlines, briefs and other graphic devices. Highlights boxes, pull quotes and subheads (miniheadlines within the story to break up paragraphs) all vie for readers' attention.

Copy editors strive to avoid repetition, but they still need to summarize the story. Much of the burden is on the reporter to devise more creative leads that still get to the point quickly. To be a good writer, you need to know how to do many types of leads.

Hard-news Leads

Sometimes the lead on a hard-news story doesn't get right to the point in the first sentence. But most breaking stories use hard-news leads, also known as summary leads.

Summary Leads

A summary lead should answer several, but not all, of the basic questions: who, what, when, where and why, plus how and so what. If you cram all of them into the lead, it could be cumbersome.

Choose the most important factors for the lead. Save the others for the second or third paragraph. This example stresses who and what, the most common type of summary lead:

TALLAHASSEE, Fla.—A Florida law student was held Tuesday on a charge she hired a hitman to kill a secretary who found out the student had stolen an exam, police said.	*Who, what, when, why*

This example stresses why:

Brown University has expelled a student for shouting racial epithets, violating an anti-harassment rule enacted in 1989 as part of an effort by the university to combat racism on campus.	*Who, what, why*
It is the first time that a Brown student has been expelled for such a violation and is thought to be the first such expulsion in the country.	*So what (impact)*

The New York Times

In the next example, what happened is stressed. It is also an example of cramming; the lead has 68 words! Try reading this aloud:

NEW YORK—Police scuba divers inspecting the hull of an oil tanker in New York Harbor made an unusual discovery Thursday, and it was not only 366 pounds of cocaine hidden under water in the rudder compartments, but also the people who were guarding it: two shivering and louse-infested Colombians who had survived five stormy days in a 10-foot square compartment, virtual prisoners of the sea, authorities said.	*Who, what, when, where*

The New York Times

Summary leads are most effective when they follow subject-verb-object order. Avoid writing long summary leads that begin with clauses, as in this example:

> Declaring that property owners must be protected from an arrogant government, House Republicans are nearing approval of legislation that would weaken federal efforts to protect wetlands and endangered species.
>
> The Associated Press

That lead would have been clearer if it had begun by explaining who is doing what: "House Republicans are nearing approval. . . ."

Here's another example of a summary lead so flooded with clauses that it is hard to discern the news:

> Saying that a New Jersey law that requires law enforcement authorities to notify the public when a convicted sex offender is released into a community amounts to additional punishment for sex offenders who have done their time, according to U.S. District Judge Nicholas H. Politan, who yesterday ruled the law, known as Megan's Law, named after 7-year-old Megan Kanka, who was slain by a sex offender who lived across the street from her home in Hamilton Township, unconstitutional.

Order of information   When you write a summary lead, how do you decide which basics to include and in what order? The points of emphasis should be the first or last words in the lead. Decide which elements are the most important—who, what, where, when, why, how or so what. Usually it is safe to use a subject-verb-object format: who did the action, what happened, to whom. But sometimes the how or why is most important.

Here are some facts presented in a story:

Who: three boaters

What happened: two killed, the third injured when the boat capsized

When: Sunday

Where: Lake Harney near the Volusia-Seminole county line in Florida

Why: high winds and waves

How: explained later in story

The lead that appeared in the newspaper stresses who first, followed by what:

> Two boaters were killed and a third was injured Sunday when their small boat capsized in high winds and waves on Lake Harney near the Volusia-Seminole county line.
>
> *The Orlando* (Fla.) *Sentinel*

Now look at the way the lead would read with different elements placed first:

What | A small boat that capsized in high winds and waves on Lake Harney near the Volusia-Seminole county line caused the death of two boaters and injuries to a third Sunday.

Where | On Lake Harney near the Volusia-Seminole county line, a small boat capsized Sunday in high winds and waves, causing the death of two boaters and injuries to a third.

When | On Sunday two boaters were killed and a third was injured when their small boat capsized in high winds and waves on Lake Harney near the Volusia-Seminole county line.

Why | High winds and waves on Lake Harney near the Volusia-Seminole county line caused a small boat to capsize Sunday, killing two boaters and injuring a third.

The actual lead from the newspaper seems the most logical because the point of emphasis—the important news (boaters died)—is first. The last lead, focusing on why, is the next best option; the point of emphasis (boaters died) is at the end.

Most of the time when you write a hard-news lead, you will put the most important information first. Or you might want the point of emphasis at the end of the sentence, as in this example:

> A consumer group said Thursday that some sunscreens and cosmetics contain an ingredient that can promote cancerous skin tumors, and it called on the government to <u>halt their sale.</u>
>
> The Associated Press

Active versus passive voice   Active voice is generally preferable to passive. Active voices stresses who is doing the action; passive voice stresses those to whom the action is done. But you may need to use passive voice when the emphasis is on what happened instead of who caused it to happen, especially in police or court stories.

Active voice is stronger for the following example, because it emphasizes the iguana as the subject:

Active	**Passive**
A pet iguana started a fire in a split-level house in Hillsmere Shores by knocking over a heat lamp with its tail, fire officials said.	A fire in a split-level house in Hillsmere Shores <u>was started</u> by a pet iguana that knocked over a heat lamp with its tail, fire officials said.

In the next example, however, passive voice is preferable because it gets to the point faster:

Passive   A former employee of the University of Pennsylvania's Van Pelt Library was sentenced to seven years of psychiatric probation yesterday for the theft of $1,798,310 worth of rare books and documents.

The Philadelphia Inquirer

The sentence was imposed by Philadelphia Common Pleas Court Judge Russell M. Nigro, as the story later explains. The emphasis in the lead is on the employee who was sentenced. Here is how the lead would sound in active voice:

Active   Philadelphia Common Pleas Court Judge Russell M. Nigro yesterday sentenced a former employee of the University of Pennsylvania's Van Pelt Library to seven years of psychiatric probation for the theft of $1,798,310 worth of rare books and documents.

In the active version, it takes longer to get to the point of the story, and the emphasis is on the judge, not the employee.

Where to say when   The time element can be confusing in a lead. In breaking news, when something happened yesterday, the time element usually does not come first in the sentence. But you need to place it where it is accurate, even if it sounds awkward.

Here is an example of a confusing time element:

University officials agreed to raise tuition by $100 <u>Monday.</u>

As written, the lead indicates the tuition will increase on Monday. Wrong. Tuition won't go up until next fall. Here's what really happened:

University officials agreed <u>Monday</u> to raise tuition by $100.

Delayed identification When the who in your lead is not a well-known person in your community or in the nation, you can identify the person by age, location, occupation or another modifier in the first paragraph. Then identify the person by name in the second paragraph. When you use delayed identification, even if your story involves several people, the first name you use should be the one you referred to in your lead.

All states have laws restricting the release of juvenile offenders' names, and several states prohibit the release of names of rape victims. In addition, many newspapers have policies to withhold names of criminal suspects until they are formally charged with crimes. Therefore, you need to use alternative forms of identification in these situations as well.

The following examples show how to say who in the lead and delay identification:

Age

An 18-year-old Tampa man was shot and killed Wednesday after he and two friends confronted a gunman who had beaten a friend of theirs, Tampa police said.

Warren Smith III, of 3524 E. 26th Ave., was shot behind his right ear at 6:40 p.m. and was pronounced dead shortly after arriving at Tampa General Hospital, police said.

St. Petersburg Times

Occupation

Two Minneapolis meter monitors have been charged with stealing an estimated $35,000 worth of nickels, dimes and quarters from parking meters.

Dale Timinskis, 42, and Leroy Siner, 40, both of Minneapolis, were arrested Tuesday after police watched their activities.

Minneapolis *Star Tribune*

Location

A Joliet man who got up to change the channel on a TV set was hit in the forehead by a stray bullet and critically wounded, Joliet police said Monday.

Jimmie Anderson, 28, of 211 S. Chicago St., was being kept alive Monday by life-support machines in St. Joseph's Medical Center, said Detective Thomas Stein of the Joliet Police Department.

Chicago Tribune

Other identifier

A former Duke University student who posed as a wealthy French baron was a con artist with lavish desires, said a judge who sentenced the imposter to three years in prison for fraud.

Maurice Jeffrey Locke Rothschild, 38, who changed his name from Mauro Cortex Jr., was sentenced in Greensboro, N.C. for bilking two banks by posing as a nobleman from France's wealthy Rothschild family. The charges involved $12,000 Rothschild received after submitting false information on credit card applications.

Newsday

If you are writing a story about a person who has been in the news frequently, such as a suspect in a trial, you may use the name, but add a phrase or clause to identify the person, as in this example:

Lisa Fox, the Ames (Ia.) woman convicted of shooting an Iowa State University professor, has asked for a new trial, saying her daughter, who wasn't allowed to testify, can prove she is innocent.

Fox, 34, was found guilty March 15 of attempted murder for shooting poultry science professor Robert Hasiak a year ago in the home they shared. Her daughter, Sonya, 17, also charged with the shooting, pleaded guilty the week before.

The Des Moines (Iowa) *Register*

Second-day Leads

The summary lead usually stresses basic facts about the news in the immediate past, and it is usually written in past tense. This type of breaking-news lead often is referred to as a "first-day lead," as if readers were hearing the news for the first time.

Because television provides more immediate news, newspapers often try to use a "second-day lead" that moves the story to the next step. This is especially important for afternoon newspapers reporting a story that occurred the previous day. This technique is also called giving the lead a "forward spin," an approach often used by broadcast journalists to give stories immediacy even when the event happened earlier the same day as the broadcast.

In the following examples, the first version is a standard summary lead that appeared in a morning paper. It stresses what happened yesterday in the search for a missing University of Arizona professor.

Rescue workers combed a rugged area in the Tucson Mountains yesterday evening in search of a UA music professor who has been missing since Tuesday night.

The (Tucson) *Arizona Daily Star*

The second lead appeared in a competing afternoon newspaper. It gives the story a forward spin, stressing what will happen today even though there is no new information.

Deputies planned to resume a search this morning in rocky terrain in the Gates Pass area for missing University of Arizona music Professor Roy Andres Johnson, 58, who they fear was killed.

Tucson (Ariz.) *Citizen*

A few days later the professor's body was found; he had been murdered.

Impact Leads

The "impact lead" explains how the readers and viewers will be affected by an issue. It is an excellent tool to make a story seem fresh and relevant. The impact lead is especially helpful on bureaucratic stories. It answers the questions "So what? What does this news mean to a reader?"

Heath Meriwether, executive editor of the *Detroit Free Press,* is committed to making sure that stories at his paper contain the impact—within the story if not in the lead. He insists that writers place an impact statement explaining "so what" at the top of their story, as a guide to editors. That's a good idea you can use to coach yourself: Add an impact statement after your focus sentence at the top of your story.

Impact leads can be written in a hard-news summary form or in a more creative form, like a soft lead. However, the story is still hard news, not a feature. The information you give must be factual, not your interpretation. And if you use an indirect lead, you must write a clear nut graph early in the story.

This impact lead uses a direct summary approach:

Summary lead with impact

Southwest Missouri State University must release its campus crime reports to the public, a federal judge ruled Wednesday in a case that could affect colleges across the nation.

U.S. District Judge Russell G. Clark called the withholding of those reports unconstitutional and ordered university officials to provide the public and media access to them.

The ruling, thought to be the first of its kind in the nation, has prompted the U.S. Department of Education to begin re-evaluating its stand on the release of campus reports.

Backup with more impact

The Kansas City (Mo.) *Star*

Here is a creative impact lead that directly addresses readers; the nut graph is in the second paragraph:

If the state commission says OK, you might never have to talk to an obnoxious salesman, harassing caller—or for that matter your whiny brother-in-law—over the phone again.

Pacific Bell, GTE California and Contel are seeking approval of a controversial service that allows subscribers to see the phone number of an incoming call before answering.

The Orange County (Calif.) *Register*

Attribution in Leads

Attribution tells the reader where you got your information. Too much attribution can clutter a lead. Too little can get you in trouble. So when should you use it?

• If you know the information is factual and you witnessed it or have firsthand knowledge that it is true, you may eliminate the attribution. If you received the information by telephone, as in police or fire stories, attribute it to your source.

• Whenever you are saying anything accusatory, as in police or political stories, you must attribute the information.

• You also must attribute the quotes or partial quotes you use in a lead.

To keep attribution clutter to a minimum, you may give a general reference to some sources—such as "police said" or "experts say"—if their titles are long. Then, as in delayed identification, give the specific name and title in the second reference.

Fact versus opinion   Here are some examples that demonstrate when to use attribution:

An 88-year-old man died Monday afternoon when fire spread through his second-floor apartment at the Wellington Arms Apartments in north St. Louis County.	*Fact: No attribution is needed.*
An 88-year-old man died in north St. Louis County Monday afternoon, apparently after he started a fire while smoking in bed, authorities said.	*Opinion: Speculation about the cause needs to be attributed.*
The body of a man who had been fatally stabbed was discovered Monday morning in a city trash bin in the Lewis Place neighborhood, police said.	*Attributed fact: Attribution for fact is needed because the reporter got the information secondhand (by telephone).*

St. Louis (Mo.) *Post-Dispatch*

Accusations   A person is innocent until proved guilty in court. In crime stories, attribute any accusatory statements to police or other authorities, especially when you are using a suspect's name. If the person has been charged with a crime, you may state that without attribution. The word *allegedly* can be used when the charges have not been proved, but direct attribution to the police is preferable. Here are some examples:

A University of North Florida chemistry major has been charged with building a 35-pound "megabomb" powerful enough to destroy everything within a radius of 150 yards.	*No attribution is needed.*

The Associated Press

David Roger Flint killed 16-month-old Brittany K. Boyer on Monday by dangling her by the arms, swinging her side to side and beating her head against the floor and wooden furniture, police say. The 23-year-old Flint was arrested about 10:30 p.m. Tuesday and accused of murder.

Jane Meinhardt, *St. Petersburg Times*

An attribution is needed for an accusatory statement.

A 38-year-old paroled murderer has been arrested in St. Croix County, Wis., for allegedly kidnapping and raping two 16-year-old girls in Minneapolis last month. . . .

He was charged with two counts of first-degree criminal sexual conduct and two counts of kidnapping.

St. Paul (Minn.) *Pioneer Press*

The word allegedly *is used because it has not yet been proved that the kidnap and rape occurred.*

Later, the lead is backed up this way.

A 38-year-old paroled murderer has been charged with kidnapping and raping two 16-year-old girls in Minneapolis last month.

This lead would be a safer alternative.

Quotes   Whenever you quote someone directly, indirectly or partially, you need to attribute the statement. Full quotes are difficult in leads and can be awkward. Reading a story that starts with a full quote is like coming into the middle of a conversation; it's hard to tell the context and meaning of the quote. "Quote leads" are more common in feature stories than hard news but may be effective in some hard-news stories like speeches or court cases.

A more effective technique is the use of partial quotes, especially when the speaker says something controversial or dramatic. Leads also may contain reference quotes, just a few words referring to something controversial. These do not need immediate attribution. Both partial and reference quotes should be backed up later in the story with the full quote or with the context in which the statement was made.

Here are some examples of how quotes are used and attributed in leads:

Clarence Thomas, defiant in the face of allegations of sexual harassment, told senators Saturday that he would not give up his nomination to the Supreme Court, saying, "I'd rather die than withdraw."

Knight-Ridder/Tribune News Service

A full quote is used in the lead.

"I've done everything out there," 31-year-old Gilbert Franco told his wife Thursday. "All that's left to do is learn the Bible and to die."

The next day, San Jose police say, Franco entered the C&S Market at East Julian and 26th streets and shot to death Katherine Young Suk Choe, 40, whose family owns the store.

Seconds later, 50 yards away, Franco fatally shot himself in the head.

San Jose (Calif.) *Mercury News*

A full quote is used in this lead because it is dramatic, but it is still confusing.

The University of Pennsylvania announced yesterday that it was penalizing a senior scientist for "lapses of judgment" in an experiment last April in which more than 120 people may have been exposed to a virus that can cause a fatal form of leukemia. . . .

The committee concluded that the professor was not guilty of research misconduct as defined in a school policy. However, the committee concluded that there were "lapses of judgment and failures of communication" in the experiment.

The Philadelphia Inquirer

A reference quote is used in the lead.

The backup puts the partial quote in context.

Amid charges of "smelly politics," Gov. Terry Branstad and key legislators sparred Monday over the state's obligation to finance a pay raise for state employees. . . .

"Smelly politics is what it amounts to, and we're not going to stand for it," said Sen. Mike Connolly.

The Des Moines Register

A reference quote is used in the lead.

The backup uses the full quote.

Attribution first or last   The rule of thumb in the lead is to put the most important information first. If the attribution is cumbersome and will slow the lead, put it at the end. If it is brief, you can put it first.

Casual drug use has dropped sharply during the last five years, but the number of addicts using cocaine daily has not changed significantly, the federal government reported yesterday.

The Philadelphia Inquirer

Attribution last

The federal government reported yesterday that casual drug use has dropped sharply during the last five years, but the number of addicts using cocaine daily has not changed significantly.

Attribution first (acceptable but not as strong)

Women who work full time earn about two-thirds the annual income of men, according to a report on the status of American women.

The report by the nonprofit Women's Research and Education Institute also said female college graduates normally make less than males who have finished only high school—$25,444 in 1987, compared with $27,293 for the men.

The Washington Post

Attribution last (because name is cumbersome and not as important as conclusions)

Cluttered attribution   In the example that follows, note how a long attribution at the start of the sentence clutters the lead:

Cluttered

Uncluttered (identification in second paragraph)

Karen Davisson, child protection worker with the Kansas Department of Social Rehabilitation Services district office in Emporia, said Tuesday that only rarely are neglected or abused children removed from their parents' care and placed in foster homes or put up for adoption.

Neglected or abused children are rarely removed from their parents' care and placed in foster homes or put up for adoption, a state social worker said Tuesday.

One of the most common causes of clutter in leads is too much information about where and when something was said. Put some of this material in the second paragraph. Put the location of the meeting much further down in the story, or eliminate it altogether unless it is important to the reader.

Cluttered	Uncluttered
Fort Riley is being considered as a possible host for the proposed joint landfill for Geary and Riley counties, Riley County Director of Public Works Dan Harden said during an informational meeting Tuesday night at the Geary County 4-H Senior Citizens Center.	Fort Riley is being considered as a possible site for a landfill, a Riley County official said Tuesday. Dan Harden, director of public works said. . .

Soft Leads

Coaching Tips

Try writing many different leads instead of struggling to find the perfect one. Don't wait for a creative muse.

Make sure your lead is related to your focus and can be backed up in your story.

Do not strain to "create" a lead from your head. Pull from the story, not from your head, for inspiration.

Soft leads can be fun to write and fun to read. They can also be painful. If you don't get to the point quickly, they can be tedious.

Although soft leads are also called delayed leads, the lead is still first. Only the nut graph is delayed. Remember that all leads, especially soft leads, must be backed up in the story and must lead to a nut graph. In some cases, if the lead is very compelling, you may delay the nut graph until the 10th paragraph or more. But it is still better to place the nut graph higher in the story, preferably by the third to fifth paragraph.

There are many types of soft leads. They can be used on news or feature stories. Most of them follow a simple concept: specific to general. Use a specific example at the beginning to illustrate the main point of the story.

People like to read about other people. As a result, many soft leads start with something about a person who is one of many people sharing the same problem. The idea behind these soft leads—called "anecdotal leads"—is that readers can relate better to one person's problem than to a general statement of a problem.

Other common types of soft leads are descriptive and narrative. "Descriptive leads" describe a person or a scene. "Narrative leads" are storytelling leads that recount the event in a dramatic way, like the plot in a novel, to put the reader on the scene as the action occurs.

And then there are leads that are just clever or catchy.

It's not what you call soft leads that matters. It's how you write them. The important point is to tell a good story. When writers struggle with soft leads, it is often because they think they must create something clever. All too often, the result is a cliche. It is best to look at your notes and build a lead based on something interesting in the story, instead of waiting for the creative muse.

The sections that follow show a variety of ways to structure a soft lead. The basic techniques are descriptive, anecdotal and narrative. The others are applications of these three.

Descriptive Leads

This type of lead describes a person, place or event. It is like the descriptive focus-on-a-person lead, but it doesn't have to focus on a person who is one of many. It can be used for news or feature stories.

In this example, the story focuses on the man who is causing the problem:

> Skippack farmer John W. Hasson stood ankle-deep in mud, pumping milk into a wooden trough as his pigs, squealing and grunting, snouts quivering, climbed over each other to get to their feed.
>
> Hasson inhaled deeply.
>
> "Does that smell sour to you? That's what they call noxious fumes," he said with a sniff toward his new neighbors, Ironbridge Estates, a subdivision of two-story colonial houses costing $200,000 plus.
>
> Ironbridge's developers say Hasson's farm smells.
>
> And his 250 pigs squeal too much.
>
> So they have filed suit in Montgomery County to force him to clean up his act. The case is scheduled to be heard May 8.   ***Nut graph***

Erin Kennedy, *The Philadelphia Inquirer*

Anecdotal Leads

This type of lead starts with a story about a person or an event. In a sense, all soft leads are anecdotal, because they are all storytelling approaches. Many combine descriptive and anecdotal techniques.

This lead is an anecdote—the story behind a woman's court case:

Late one spring night in 1981, after drinks at a bar and a bit of protest, Elaine Hollis agreed to her boyfriend's desire to capture their passion on videotape.

Inside Edward Bayliss' apartment, the video camera rolled at the foot of his bed.

He promised to erase the tape.

Seven years later, Hollis, who has a son with Bayliss, was in Delaware County Court accusing him of contriving to bring her into disrepute by exhibiting the tape.

Bayliss, president of Philadelphia Suburban Electrical Service in Upper Darby, admitted showing the tape to one of his friends.

Hollis contended he showed and distributed the tape in Delaware County and surrounding areas, as well as gave copies of it to two bar owners in Darby, who played it for customers.

Last week, after three years of litigation, a county judge upheld an Oct. 15 Common Pleas Court order that mandated Bayliss pay Hollis $125,000 to settle her lawsuit.

Nut graph

Patrick Scott, *The Philadelphia Inquirer*

This lead uses both anecdotal and descriptive techniques:

Dawn Clark's cat walked carefully across the lawn, then stopped suddenly, looking bewildered.

The cat sniffed tentatively, then bolted off the grass and spent the next few minutes licking its paws—trying to clean the paint flecks from them.

The lawn had recently been mowed and was green as a billiard table, because it had just been painted with a vegetable dye.

Nut graph   Santa Barbara residents have devised innovative ways to keep their yards green since the city, faced with

an expected water shortfall of nearly 50 percent for the year, declared a "drought emergency" in late February and banned lawn watering.

Clark's cat had just experienced one: Several landscape companies now offer painting and local nurseries are stocking their shelves with green paint and pump sprayers.

Extension of nut graph

Miles Corwin, *Los Angeles Times*

Narrative Leads

Like an anecdotal lead, a narrative lead tells a story with enough dramatic action so readers can feel as if they are witnessing the event. Narrative writing uses all the techniques of fiction, including dialogue, scene setting and foreshadowing—giving the reader clues to what will happen. It takes longer to set up the nut graph for this kind of lead, but if the story is dramatic enough, the narrative approach may work.

Police Officer Juan Cabrera felt the barrel of the gun press against his head.

"I'm gonna kill you," a voice from behind said.

"I didn't see who it was. I didn't know what was happening," Cabrera said. "I just thought someone was going to kill me."

Cabrera instinctively knocked the gun away, wrestled the suspect to the ground and handcuffed him.

The suspect was a 12-year-old boy.

The gun was a toy.

"It looked like a .38-caliber short-barrel revolver," said Cabrera, a five-year veteran of the force. "It was a cap gun."

The incident was no joke for the boy. He was arrested on a charge of battery on a law enforcement officer.

Kevin Davis, (Fort Lauderdale, Fla.) *Sun-Sentinel*

Focus-on-a-person Leads

You can focus on a person in two ways: use an anecdotal approach, telling a little story about the person, or use a descriptive approach that describes the person or shows the person in action. This type of lead can be used in profile stories about the person or in news stories about issues, where the person is one of many affected by the point of your story. This example uses the descriptive approach:

Nita walked slowly down the narrow hall, deftly guiding her tottering 11-month-old son around the abandoned baby walkers, strollers and toys.

Inside her tiny bedroom, the 17-year-old mother pointed to photographs of her son's father and some of her friends. Cards congratulating her on her recent high school graduation were nearby. The baby's crib was crammed into an area near the door.

Nita, one of 85 residents at Florence Crittenton Services in Fullerton, is one of a growing number of teenagers having babies in Orange County—a figure that has increased 36 percent in five years.

Janine Anderson, *The Orange County Register*

Nut graph— points out that person is one of many

Contrast Leads

This type of lead can be used to set up stories about conflicts or unusual circumstances. The two most common ways to write contrast leads revolve around circumstances and time.

But-guess-what contrast   Contrast leads that revolve around circumstances can be used to explain something unusual:

William Pearce, known to his patients as Dr. William J. Rick, was charming and slick, say his former associates and police detectives.

He came to town with medical degrees, numerous national board certificates and myriad other qualifications.

But the real Dr. Rick died in 1986, police say.

And now William John Pearce, 57, is in jail on charges of impersonating a doctor.

Sharon McBreen, *The Orlando* (Fla.) *Sentinel*

Nut graph

Here is a descriptive lead setting up contrast without the "but":

DENVER—Above a pond labeled "Industrial Waste," two bald eagles perch on a tree limb. Down the road from workers in white protective suits, scores of prairie dogs scurry across a field. Around the corner from hundreds of barrels containing remnants of mustard gas, a dozen mule deer stand in a thicket.

It's a paradox that some view as almost poetic: The Army's Rocky Mountain Arsenal—a shut-down war factory, a boarded-up lesson in how not to treat the environment, one of the most poisoned pieces of land in the United States—has become a haven for wildlife.

John Woestendiek, *The Philadelphia Inquirer*

Nut graph

Then-and-now contrast   Time contrasts— then and now— are useful ways to show change. This type of lead also can be used when the background is interesting or important and is relevant to the focus.

It was March 1964 when Lewis "Hackie" Wilson, the 7-year-old son of a St. Petersburg firefighter, disappeared after stopping to pick up flowers on his way home from school.

His case received national attention a month later when a sheriff's posse on horseback, flushing out rattlesnakes ahead of a line of

80 searchers, found the child's bones in a field south of Venice.

Now, nearly 27 years later, the case may be revived. Prosecuters in Sarasota County have realized that Joseph Francis Bryan, a convicted child kidnapper indicted for Hackie's murder in 1965, has never been brought to trial.

Karen Datko, *St. Petersburg Times*

Nut graph

Teaser Leads   These leads use the element of surprise to tease the reader into the story. The nut graph may also be a contrast, but the first sentence sets it up as a tease into something unusual.

BURLINGTON, Vt.— This is no ordinary public library.

For one thing, there are only four books on the shelves. For another, you won't find any of these works, or the many that are expected to join them soon, at other libraries or bookstores.

You probably never will.

That's because the Brautigan Library, which opened here last weekend, has a unique policy—it only accepts books that have never been published.

Steve Stecklow, *The Philadelphia Inquirer*

Nut graph

Motorists heading north on U.S. 101 customarily slow down when they see Officer Gregory—with his radar gun—sitting in his patrol car.

But he's never pulled anyone over and never will.

Officer Gregory is a dummy.

The mannequin is not meant to be a trick, but Police Chief A.C. "Andy" Anderson just wants people traveling through Fold Beach to wonder: Is it live or is it Gregory?

The department obtained Gregory three weeks ago on the premise that drivers invariably slow down when they see a policeman with a radar gun.

The Associated Press

Nut graph

Mystery Leads

Like teasers, these leads promise the reader a surprise or a treat for reading on. They set up the story like a mystery novel. They're fun to write and fun to read, but they won't work unless the subject matter lends itself to this approach.

One technique for writing mystery leads is to start with a vague pronoun, "it" or "they," and to delay naming the noun to which the pronoun refers: "It began at midnight." Later you specify what "it" was. Here are other examples of mystery leads:

They know who you are, what you eat, how you procreate—and where to find you.

Do you like ice cream? The U.S. government has used that information to track down draft-dodging 18-year-olds who signed up for ice cream parlor "birthday clubs."

Can't have kids? Georgetown University Medical Center last year got a mailing list of upscale, childless couples and sent them a letter reading: ". . . with proper treatment, nearly 75 percent of infertile couples can go on to conceive and successfully deliver a child."

Been turned down for a Master-Card or Visa? List Brokerage and Management, a New York list marketer, may have your name. It rents a list of 1.6 million people rejected for bank cards—obtained, the company says, from the very banks that turned you down. "All kinds of businesses" use the mailing list, "because some- one turned down for credit is looking for opportunity," says Phil Hurowitz, a broker at List Brokerage.

No fact, it seems, is too private to market. From your belt size to your Playboy subscription, details about your life are routinely traded, rented or sold. And thanks to modern technology, it's only going to get worse—or better, if you like getting lots of direct mail that's sent to you specifically because of those personal details.

For the first time, computer companies are hooking up with credit bureaus and massive data banks to allow people with only a desktop computer to single you out by income, age, neighborhood, car model or waist size.

Nut graph

Stephen Koff, *St. Petersburg Times*

This next lead uses not only the mystery approach but also the format of the novel as part of the lead:

The case has all the elements of a 1950s film noir mystery.

The characters: the scheming husband, the trusting wife, the other woman.

The story: The husband, Ray Valois, buys a lottery ticket, scratches it and finds three "Spin, Spin, Spin" symbols. That makes him eligible to win up to $2 million in the California "Big Spin" lottery, but he does not want to tell his wife, Monica, according to his statement in San Luis Obispo County Superior Court records. So he gives the ticket to another woman, waitress Stephanie Martin. She agrees to cash in the ticket, according to court records, and secretly give him half.

The inevitable plot twist: Valois and Martin turn on each other. He claims that he owns the ticket. She claims that she owns the ticket.

The conclusion: Martin spins and wins $100,000. But the wife finds out and sues both of them for fraud.

Now neither Martin nor Valois has the $100,000. His wife's attorney, Gary Dunlap, obtained a temporary restraining order, restricting lottery officials from awarding the winnings until a court hearing today.

Nut graph

Miles Corwin, *Los Angeles Times*

Build-on-a-quote Leads

If you have a great quote, build your lead around the quote that will back up your first sentence. But be careful not to repeat too much of the quote in your lead; that's boring and repetitious. Building on a quote is an easy and effective way to find a lead, providing the quote is related to the focus of the story. This technique works equally well for hard-news leads.

ANDOVER, Kan.—Melinda Easterbrook knows exactly how long it took for a tornado to blast apart her comfortable home while she and her husband huddled in the basement.

"It lasted five Hail Marys and two Our Fathers, but you have to say them quickly," she said yesterday.

While she was praying, the concrete basement rumbled and shook. When she and her husband, Bryan, came upstairs, they were hardly prepared for the scope of the destruction that had swept through this small town about five miles east of Wichita.

Nut graph

Larry Fish, *The Philadelphia Inquirer*

The next example is the kind of build-on-a-quote lead to avoid. The backup quote says the same thing as the lead, and it's right after the lead, so it's boring.

A commitment to high-tech learning and small classes taught by professors has made Fort Hays State University the fastest-growing university in the state Board of Regents system, FHSU's president said today.

FHSU had the largest 1994 spring semester enrollment increase among the six regents' universities—2.4 percent compared with spring 1993.

"We've been the fastest growing of the regents' institutions over the last five years," FHSU President Edward Hammond said.

List Leads

If you have a few brief examples to lead into your focus, you may list them in parallel sentences—making sure your sentences have the same construction, such as subject-verb-object order. Three seems to be a magic number; more than three can be awkward and tedious.

Boston College has an assistant dean for alcohol and drug education. Rutgers University sets aside dorm rooms for recovering student alcoholics. The University of Nevada bars students from leaving school sports events to make alcohol runs.

Increasingly, colleges are confronting problem drinking by providing education and rehabilitation programs, alternatives to the campus bar scene and stricter regulation of on-campus parties.

The Associated Press

Nut graph

Question Leads

These can be effective if the reader is interested in finding the answer to the question you pose. If not, you could lose the reader. One way to test question leads is to determine if the answer would be yes or no. Those are the dangerous ones. A question that raises a more thoughtful, and more interesting, answer is preferable.

What are the odds of finding your true love by placing an ad with a telephone dating service?

About one in 40, according to Terry Ehlbert.

On April 13, Ehlbert is planning to marry Scott Anderson, who was the last of 40 guys she agreed to meet after placing a voice-mail ad with the 1-976-DATE service she saw advertised on TV. . . .

The phone services work in much the same way published personal ads do.

Rich Shefchik, *St. Paul Pioneer Press*

Nut graph

The next example is a little dangerous. What if you don't want to buy cigarettes at all? Will you read on?

Nut graph

Want to buy cigarettes while at the gas station? Or while sipping a cocktail at your favorite bar?

Not in Lower Merion, if township officials have their way.

Officials there, concerned about the availability of cigarettes to minors, have proposed a municipal law prohibiting cigarette vending machines in the township. The law would be the first of its kind in Pennsylvania.

The Philadelphia Inquirer

Cliche Leads

In general, avoid cliches. But occasionally, a play on words will work as a clever lead. Consider this:

Nick Agid's workshop is just a stone's throw from the Torrance post office. Good thing, too. When Agid drops a post card into the mail, it lands with a five-pound thud.

Nut graph   Agid is a sculptor who carves messages on leftover chunks of marble and granite. They become postcards when he adds scratched-on addresses and slaps stamps on the slabs.

Bob Pool, Los Angeles Times

Leads to Avoid

The leads in this section are strained, obtuse, rambling or just plain awful. They don't work for a variety of reasons.

Good news/bad news leads

The bad news is this type of lead. They're cliches, and they're used so often that they're boring. They're also judgmental.

Some good news for city workers: The Dinkins administration has been giving signals that it might not have to give out any pink slips, at least for now.

Some bad news for city taxpayers: The Dinkins administration has shown no signs of scaling back its proposal to raise taxes for the next several years.

Newsday

Crystal ball leads

These are dream-sequence leads that foretell the future. If you were writing about psychics, perhaps you could write this kind of lead. But most people can't predict the future. "John Jones never imagined when he boarded the plane that it was going to crash." Would he have been stupid enough to board it if he had known? Leads that emphasize "if only they had known" are farfetched. Consider the following. It's unlikely that a child who is choking is thinking about the future—much less about what he can do for someone else.

When 10-year-old Jason Finser of Clermont was saved from choking to death at a family dinner two years ago, he never dreamed he would be able to return the favor.

Nut graph   But luckily for his classmate, 9-year-old Abby Muick, Jason knew exactly what to do when she choked on a chocolate-and-Rice Krispies treat in the lunchroom at Minneola Elementary School.

The Orlando Sentinel

Nightmare leads   These are also dream leads, usually relating to a past experience. The nightmare analogy is overused: "The past three days were like a nightmare for John Jones." For the reader, too. Every bad experience someone has does not have to be compared to a nightmare. Nightmare leads appear in both hard and soft leads.

> The laughter and frivolity of lunchtime recess turned into a horrifying nightmare of terror and death Tuesday when a heavily armed gunman shot and killed five children and wounded 30 others at Stockton's Cleveland Elementary School.
>
> *The Stockton* (Calif.) *Record*

> The nightmare became reality for local police on Dec. 5, 1985 when a Niagara Falls drug dealer was arrested at the Greater Buffalo International Airport. Hidden in his baggage were $50,000 worth of heroin, some PCP, and a sampling of a new drug he referred to as "smokable cocaine."
>
> *Niagara* (N.Y.) *Gazette*

Chair-sitter leads   This type of lead is a pet peeve of Jane Harrigan, a journalism professor at the University of New Hampshire, who coined the term. Setting the scene is fine, she says, but if sitting in a chair is the most unusual thing that the subject of the story does, can you blame a reader for turning the page? Harrigan makes a good point.

Consider this lead from a story about a very famous author. Is sitting in a chair the most interesting thing the writer could find about this world-renowned man? This example is a poor use of the but-guess-what lead because the reader may be too bored to get to the twist.

> ST. PETERSBURG, Fla.—He sits behind his desk in a yellow nylon jacket, blue shirt and khaki pants. With his thin face, glasses and fringe of white hair, he could be any winter visitor.
>
> But he is not. He's author James Michener, who is about to end his first winter in St. Petersburg.   ***Nut graph***
>
> *St. Petersburg Times*

Plop-a-person leads   This type of lead is a misuse of the focus-on-a-person lead. When the writer just tops the story with a sketch of a person and does not back it up in the text, that's plopping. It's also misleading. The reader starts the story thinking that the person has something to say or do in the story. But after the lead, the person disappears.

Tuesday was a good day for psychology professor Carnot Nelson.

He spent most of it helping an honors student work on her thesis. He read another student's doctoral dissertation and two master's thesis proposals. Then he went to a meeting, which he left after an hour and a half so he could do some reading of his own.

This is the last time we hear about Nelson, despite his being a good example.

Nelson, a senior professor at the University of South Florida, who also teaches large undergraduate classes and small graduate seminars, is a good example of the range of activity involved in teaching Florida university students.

"Education is a one-at-a-time, hand-made business," said state university spokesman Pat Riordan. "You can't mechanize it, you can't computerize it and you can't put it on an assembly line."

Nut graph

But college professors in Florida are under increasing pressure to do exactly that. Recurring state budget cuts have made some classes larger and eliminated many others. And a political climate that says there can be no new taxes until a state government becomes "more productive" has fueled a drive to force professors to spend more time in the classroom.

St. Petersburg Times

Strained leads   The lead must relate clearly to the nut graph. When you try too hard to be clever, you may miss the point.

This story is about a farm show featuring sheep and other animals. Although the lead is backed up, it doesn't really relate to the focus of the story:

Men with discriminating taste read GQ and women in the know read Cosmo.

For sheep, there's just one place to learn what's cool in wool—the Pennsylvania Farm Show, the yearly agricultural exhibition that opens for the 75th time today.

Nut graph

Unless you were raised by shepherds, you may not realize that the way sheep are sheared for shows changes year after year, just as, well, haircuts and clothing styles for people.

The Philadelphia Inquirer

Suitcase leads   These are leads written as though you were packing for a trip, squeezing everything you can in your suitcase and then sitting on the lid to close it. They're cluttered.

> Tens of thousands of children with no identifiable physical or neurological defects are being shunted into expensive programs for the handicapped, programs established with the best of intentions for children with specific disabilities but now often used for children who simply need counseling and smaller classes.
>
> *The New York Times*

Weather-report leads   These leads set the scene by describing the weather: "It was a dark and stormy night." Avoid using the weather as a lead when it isn't related to the story.

> It was hot and humid the day the city council decided to ban smoking from all public buildings.
>
> The ordinance, passed unanimously, will go into effect immediately.

Stereotype leads   These are most common in features about older people, women and groups with special interests. The writer tries hard to be complimentary but instead only reinforces stereotypes.

This is the lead for a story about Senior Olympics, games for people over age 60:

> At the age when most of their contemporaries are in rocking chairs, these athletes will be competing in swimming, archery, badminton, bicycle racing—just about every imaginable sport, through the long jump and shot put.
>
> *The Baltimore Sun*

If you look around your college campus, you're likely to see many professors in their 60s, and most of them don't spend much time in rocking chairs.

Unsolved Mysteries   This type of lead teases the reader, but the mystery is that the story is about something else. These leads must relate to the focus and be backed up with the answer to the mystery. If they don't, they're misleading.

The man couldn't believe what he was hearing.

"You mean I could go to jail for this?" he asked Detective Bob Ankenbauer.

Only minutes before, the man had been arguing vigorously with officials from the state Department of Environmental Regulation (DER), claiming that what he had done wasn't that bad.

Then Ankenbauer explained he was doing a criminal investigation for the Pinellas County Sheriff's Department and the man's mouth dropped open. Ankenbauer has become accustomed to that kind of reaction in the past 10 months. As the Sheriff's Department's first full-time investigator of environmental crimes, Ankenbauer is treading unexplored ground.

St. Petersburg Times

So is the reader. What was the man's crime? The reader never finds out. The rest of the story is about Ankenbauer's new job. Remember to back up your leads.

Soft leads can be enticing and creative, but they must be accurate. Remember that the lead must lead to the focus. If it doesn't, the reader may never wade through it.

How to Find Your Lead

To find a lead that will work for you in your story, first find your nut graph. Ask yourself what the main point of the story is. Then ask some of these questions to find your lead:

Reader interest: What did you or would the reader find most interesting about this subject?

Memorable item: What was the most memorable impression or fact?

Focus on a person: Is there someone who exemplifies the problem or issue? If you tell a story about this person or show the person in action, will it lead to the point in the nut graph?

Descriptive approach: Will a description of the scene relate to the focus?

Mystery approach: Can you tease the reader with a surprise that leads to the nut graph?

Build on a quote: Is there a great quote to back up the lead? If so, write the lead so it refers to the quote without repeating it.

Contrast: Would a then-and-now approach work?

Problem/solution: Can you set up a problem so the reader wants to discover the solution?

Narrative storytelling: If you were just telling a good story, how would you start? Can you reconstruct the events to put the reader on the scene?

Exercises

1 **Hard-news leads:** Write summary leads from the following information. For the time element, use the day of the week instead of yesterday or today.

a A study was released Monday by the University of Colorado. The study was funded by the Alfred P. Sloan Foundation. The study said that 60 percent of college students who begin studying science, mathematics or engineering switch to another major. The study cited poor teaching and an aloof faculty as the cause.

b There was a fire yesterday at a pizza restaurant. It is located at 2035 Main St. Two firefighters were injured when the roof fell in. They were treated at St. Luke's Medical Center for minor injuries. The fire started in the basement of the building. The cause is under investigation. The roof collapsed and the inside of the restaurant was destroyed. Damages are estimated at $100,000. The information comes from fire officials in your community.

c The Centers for Disease Control today released the results of a survey of nutritional supplements. Nutritional supplements include vitamins, protein supplements and products promising muscle growth. Only supplements in powder, capsule or tablet form were surveyed. "It turned out that at least half of the ingredients have no documented medical effect," said Rossane Philen, a medical epidemiologist at the National Center for Environmental Health and Injury Control. She was part of the surveying team. The survey said many nutritional supplements have no medical support for their advertised claims.

2 **Active/passive voice:** Change this lead to active voice:

> A 29-year-old Phoenix man was killed Tuesday when his motorcycle was struck by a car on East Ina Road.

Write a lead in passive voice from this information:

> Jones County Circuit Court Judge Billy Landrum yesterday sentenced a 17-year-old high school sophomore to two consecutive life terms for the murder of two men in a convenience store.

3 **Delayed identification:** Write a lead using delayed identification from this information:

Background provided by the police: Michael Stephens, who lives in the 3700 block of North Camino Street in Tucson, was driving a flatbed truck in central Tucson early yesterday morning. He lost control of his truck, and it overturned on East 15th Street near South Kino Parkway. He died of head injuries at the scene of the accident at 2:30 a.m. He was 44 years old.

4   Write a second-day lead from this information, giving it a forward spin for Tuesday's paper:

> **Background:** Vandals broke into the Midtown Magnet Middle School at 300 Fifth Ave. just before 7 p.m. on Sunday. They broke windows and damaged 11 classrooms and an office area. They damaged computers and other equipment. The cost of the damages has not yet been estimated. Classes are scheduled to resume today. School was closed Monday while school district employees spent the day cleaning up damage to the school.

5   Write impact leads from this information:

> **a**   The Board of Regents (or the governing body of universities in your state) has approved an increase in rates for campus housing at your university. The biggest increase will be in residence halls, where rates will increase 14.8 percent for double-room occupancy. The current rate is $2,684, and it will increase to $3,080 next fall.

> **b**   The Rockville City Council will meet at 7 p.m. Tuesday. The council will consider adopting an ordinance that would impose penalties for false alarms that are sent to the police department from faulty or improperly operated electronic security systems. Under the proposed ordinance, an alarm system owner would be allowed six free false alarms. The owner would have to pay a $30 penalty for each additional false alarm.

6   Attribution: Write a summary lead from this information. Decide whether you need to include attribution.

> **Capt. J. Randall Ogden, a spokesman for the Tucson Fire Department (or use your local fire department spokesperson):** A fire destroyed a home on East 17th Street. It was started by a cigarette that was discarded in a sofa. The fire left the husband, his wife and their four children homeless. The fire started at 1 a.m. and caused $30,000 in damages.

7   **Anecdotal, focus-on-a-person lead:** Write an anecdotal lead with a person focus from the following information; include a nut graph. Your focus is about the frustrations students experience trying to park on campus because the parking department has sold too many permits. Nancy Pauw is a graduate student. One morning, she circled the parking lot east of the computer center three times before she found a parking space. Last year there were 7,565 student parking permits sold for 3,930 spaces. "I have to get here an hour early so I can get to class on time," Pauw says. She is one of many students (on your campus) who experience the daily frustration not finding a parking space even though they have purchased $30 and $50 permits.

8   Write a soft lead, including a nut graph, that uses the specific-to-general technique to convey the following information.

> **Background:** The General Accounting Office, the investigative arm for Congress, issued a report yesterday that said record keeping at the National

Park Service is defective. The report said information in the Park Service's financial statements is inaccurate and filled with accounting errors. Property owned by the Park Service is overstated by more than $90 million, the report stated. Examples of inaccurate data in the Park Service records include a vacuum cleaner that is really worth $150 but is listed in records as worth $800,000; a dishwasher worth $350 but valued at over $700,000; and a fire truck worth $133,000 but undervalued at 1 cent.

9 Write a descriptive lead for a story about apartments that violate city codes and are considered hazardous but that are often rented to students anyway. You interviewed a student who lives in an attic apartment. His story is similar to the stories of many other students in this neighborhood, known as the Oread neighborhood. As you climbed the steps to his apartment, you noticed that duct tape keeps the banister in place on the stairs. You saw that the kitchen is infested with mice and roaches. The student, Ted Flis, took you to the bathroom and said it has no electricity. "It's a dump," said Flis, a senior majoring in architecture. "But it was the cheapest thing I could find." This apartment is located at 1032 Main St.

10 Change this lead into a narrative lead:

A man threatening suicide kept police at bay for more than nine hours Sunday before he was pulled back from the ledge of a parking garage rooftop.

The man, a 36-year-old Topeka State Hospital patient and Wichita resident whose name wasn't released, threatened to jump from the south ledge of St. Francis Hospital and Medical Center's three-story parking garage at S.W. 6th St. and Mulvane.

Louis Cortez, St. Francis public safety officer, spotted the patient walking toward the ledge on the roof of the garage about 8:40 a.m. Sunday. Cortez stopped his vehicle and told the man to move away from the ledge.

The patient shook his head, "No."

"I stepped out and asked him, 'Can I help you, sir?' and he said, 'I'm going to jump,'" Cortez said.

Shortly before 6 p.m., several teenagers in front of St. Francis House, 701 S.W. Mulvane, began shouting, "Don't jump!" and "It's not worth it." The patient shouted back, "You want to see me jump?"

But the teens distracted the patient just long enough for Cortez to grab him around his waist and pull him from the ledge.

11 **Leads analysis:** Use two or three different newspapers so you can see if they have different writing styles. Find leads as directed, and attach copies of the leads to your paper.

    a Find an example of a descriptive lead, an anecdotal lead and a narrative lead. Label each type. Analyze whether your examples are effective, and explain why or why not.

    b Find three feature news leads you like. Explain what techniques the writers used and why you like them.

    c Find three feature leads you do not like, and explain why.

COACHING

TIPS

Write a first draft; mark "fix later" if you get stuck. Don't perfect every line during the drafting process.

Read your story aloud when you finish. You will hear the pacing and catch errors.

Use lists to move the reader quickly through the story.

Use parallel structure: a few sentences (three is the magic number) in identical structure with some repetitive beginnings.

Test your endings to see if you have overwritten or strained your last paragraph. Put your hand over your last paragraph and see if the previous paragraph or the one before that is a better ending.

Lead reversal: Would your ending work as well as a lead? Sometimes the lead and ending can be reversed.

Body Building

11

When Ken Fuson was in high school, he played the drums. He still hears the beat of the drums when he writes his stories for *The Des Moines* (Iowa) *Register.* "I think a lot about rhythm," he says. "I work at getting the tap, tap, tap. I want to make sure every paragraph doesn't sound the same." To achieve that musical quality, Fuson reads all his stories out loud.

Rhythm, also called pacing, helps readers move through the middle of a story. And Fuson wants to make sure they read to the end. "I probably spend as much time on the ending as I do on the beginning," he says. He thinks a good ending makes a story memorable. "If readers remember a story I wrote, that's better than money." One time, after he won a prestigious award from the Gannett Co., which owns *The Des Moines Register,* he told company executives that editors who cut the ending of a story should be executed.

Getting from the beginning to the end of a story isn't a haphazard process for Fuson. He carefully plans the parts of his stories. First he thinks. "I look for ways to show conflict and to describe the mood. I think a lot about what is the right tone and the personality of the story." Then he starts organizing his material. "I type up all my notes. I select what I want to use. Then I put that information in an order. I need to know where I'm going and what the ending will be. Once you know what you're going to say and the way you're going to say it, then you can worry about what goes first."

And worry he does. "The first paragraph has to be perfect," he says. "And the second paragraph has to be perfect. I wish I had

Ken Fuson
Courtesy of Ken Fuson

learned a better way of writing instead of worrying about what I'm going to say first."

It may not be the best writing process, but it works well for Fuson, who consistently wins awards. This chapter explains some other ways you can construct the body of your story.

Middles of Stories

Journalists need to be optimists. They have to believe people will read stories all the way through, even though research says otherwise. The trick is to keep the middle moving.

If you have followed the advice presented in Chapter 9, you are planning an order for your stories before you write. In most cases, you map that order by topics that support your focus or by chronological order for all or a part of your story. However, good organization is only part of what makes a story readable. You can use other writing techniques as well.

Transition Techniques

Getting smoothly from one paragraph to the next may require a transition. But the best transition is no transition—a story so well organized that one thought flows naturally into the other. The information in one paragraph should raise a question that needs to be answered in the next. Or it can present information that can be backed up with a supporting quote or facts in the next. If it does that, you don't need any special transitions. But when you do, you can try some of these techniques to pave the way for the next paragraph:

• Use cause and effect. If one paragraph raises a question, answer it in the next paragraph or elaborate with an example or quote. Try to anticipate questions the reader might have.

• To introduce a new speaker after a previous speaker, use a statement about or from the new person. Then lead into the quote or paraphrased material. For example:

A controversial proposal that would require all Temple University undergraduates to take a course related to racism drew strong support yesterday from a racially mixed group of students and faculty members who testified at a campus hearing.

Anika Trahan, a junior, said the proposed requirement would encourage more dialogue among students who come to the university from largely segregated neighborhoods. "They (white students) come from communities where they are never able to interact with black people," she said.

But opinion was sharply divided on whether the course should focus on black-white relations in America or include racism against Asian Americans and other groups.

Transition to new speaker

Molefi K. Asante, chairman of Temple's African American studies department, contended that the requirement should focus on the white racism toward African Americans because that has been "the funda-mental pattern of racism" in the United States.

A white student, sophomore Amy Dixon, agreed. "Our predominant problem on campus is black-white relations," she said.

Transition to new speaker

Huntly Collins, *The Philadelphia Inquirer*

• To insert background, you can use words and phrases, such as *Previously* or *In the past,* or specific time elements, such as *Two months ago.* If you are going to recount part of the story chronologically, you can set it up with a phrase like *The incident began this way.*

• To get from one point to another, especially in stories about meetings where several issues are discussed, you can use transitional phrases: *In another matter, On a related issue, Other items discussed included.*

• A word or phrase from one paragraph can be repeated in the next. Here is an example that uses repetition of key words:

With a relentless sun beating on him as he cut through fields, swamps and shaggy forests, Earl Davis always looked ahead to the next <u>leg</u> of the project.

The <u>legs</u> were long and stretched interminably. The crews made slow progress. Mosquitoes whined about their heads, and snakes thrashed away when the right-of-way crews stumbled across them. . . .

Davis, who had lived in Pinellas County for almost 50 years, sympathized and <u>suffered</u> with them (the road builders).

The <u>suffering</u> wouldn't be over for a long time.

Mark Davis, *Tampa* (Fla.) *Tribune*

Techniques for Maintaining Interest

There are many other ways a writer can keep the middle moving. Here are some of them.

Parallelism   Parallel sentences help the reader move quickly through the story. Parallel construction means the sentences are worded in the same grammatical order. Some of the words can be repeated for effect, especially those at the beginning of sentences. In this example, the writer uses parallelism at the beginning of the story, but you can use it anywhere:

Rudolph Almaraz kept his battle with AIDS his personal business, even though his professional business was surgery.

He didn't tell his patients. He didn't tell officials at Baltimore Johns Hopkins Hospital, where he was a cancer surgeon. He didn't tell the doctor who bought his medical practice earlier this year.

But now the case of Dr. Almaraz, who died of AIDS on Nov. 16 at the age of 41, has frightened his patients.

Matthew Purdy, *The Philadelphia Inquirer*

Pacing Vary the length of sentences. Follow long ones with short, punchy ones.

> On New Years Eve Lisa Botzum visited the emergency room of the Hospital of the University of Pennsylvania, complaining of nausea and vomiting. She was given a pregnancy test. She was elated by the result.
>
> Few others were.

Loretta Tofani, *The Philadelphia Inquirer*

Read the following example aloud so you can hear the rhythm of mixing long and short sentences and fragments. You can use fragments (incomplete sentences) for emphasis, but do so sparingly. This example is from a story about why one inmate in a Connecticut prison killed one prisoner and beat another.

> At 4:30 a.m., in the red wash of a prison dormitory night, Ernest John Miller was having a hard time finding the man he was about to kill.
>
> Miller could barely see him, lying face down on a bunk. Crouching closer, he saw a gray, woolen blanket pulled almost over the man's head. Miller had to be sure.
>
> He put his face about a foot from the bed. As his eyes adjusted to the darkness, he saw some hair. Long, black curly hair.
>
> If I don't do this, Miller was thinking, I'll never be safe in here.
>
> He pulled an industrial can opener from the waistband of his uniform. It weighed 5 pounds and felt slippery through his white cotton gloves.
>
> He raised it and swung it hard onto the man's skull.
>
> The man didn't move. Miller thought he had missed. He grabbed the man's prison gown and hit him again.
>
> Somewhere, a guard started yelling. But Miller was already running through the dark, past footlockers and rows of bunks of inmates who were beginning to sit up. There was another man he had to get.

Alan Cullison, *The Hartford* (Conn.) *Courant*

Anecdotes You often use anecdotes in your leads; consider them for the middle of your story as well. An interesting little story or experience can brighten a long story or a bureaucratic one.

This example is from a story about a law that allows federal agents to confiscate the property of suspected drug dealers. But many of the people mentioned in the story were not drug dealers. Throughout the story, anecdotes help keep the reader's interest. Here is one:

Ethel Hylton of New York City has yet to regain her financial independence after losing $39,110 in a search nearly three years ago in Hobby Airport in Houston.

Shortly after she arrived from New York, a Houston officer and Drug Enforcement Administration agent stopped the 46-year-old woman in the baggage area and told her she was under arrest because a drug dog had scratched at her luggage. The dog wasn't with them, and when Miss Hylton asked to see it, the officers refused to bring it out.

The agents searched her bags, and ordered a strip search of Miss Hylton, but found no contraband.

In her purse, they found the cash Miss Hylton carried because she planned to buy a house to escape the New York winters which exacerbated her diabetes. It was the settlement from an insurance claim and her life's savings, gathered through more than 20 years of work as a hotel housekeeper and hospital night janitor.

The police seized all but $10 of the cash and sent Miss Hylton on her way, keeping the money because of its alleged drug connection. But they never charged her with a crime.

Andrew Schneider and Mary Pat Flaherty,
The Pittsburgh Press

Dialogue   When possible and appropriate, use dialogue in your story. It works well in feature stories, news stories about council meetings and especially stories about court cases. Note that in this example the attribution is not given every time the speaker changes, because in dialogue the speakers sometimes are understood. This excerpt is from a story about a child-abuse murder trial:

"This is a photo of the belt you used to strike Keith, isn't it?" asks Assistant State's Attorney Tom Gibbons, who is cross-examining defendant Edward Thirston.

"Looks like it," answers Thirston, who is on trial for murdering 22-month-old Keith Jones.

"Is that where you struck the baby with the belt?"

"No," the defendant says.

Linnet Myers, *Chicago Tribune*

BBI: Boring but important stuff   Many stories, especially government stories, need explanation or background that could be boring. Don't put all the boring information in a long block. Break it up into small paragraphs and place it where it will fit, but not in one long, continuous section. Also consider graphics as a way to present statistics and other information that could clog a story.

In their Pulitzer Prize–winning series about the U.S. Department of Agriculture, reporters Mike McGraw and Jeff Taylor used charts for many of their statistics (see Exhibit 11-1). But in the body of this story, called "Deadly meat," they broke up much of the potentially boring but important factual material with quotes, anecdotes and lists. (They also used shorter sentences for complex material, as suggested in the next section.)

Exhibit 11-1

Graphic illustration from McGraw and Taylor's "Deadly meat" series

Dave Eames, *Kansas City* (Mo.) *Star,* December 10, 1991

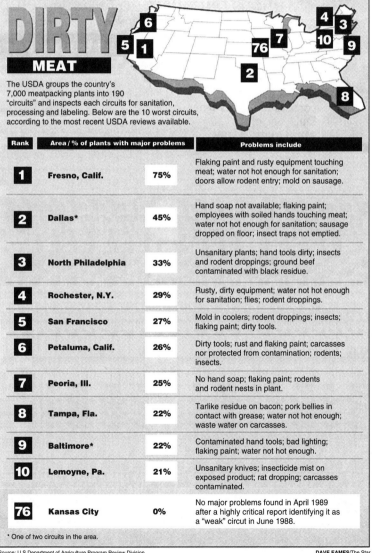

DIRTY MEAT

The USDA groups the country's 7,000 meatpacking plants into 190 "circuits" and inspects each circuits for sanitation, processing and labeling. Below are the 10 worst circuits, according to the most recent USDA reviews available.

Rank	Area / % of plants with major problems		Problems include
1	Fresno, Calif.	75%	Flaking paint and rusty equipment touching meat; water not hot enough for sanitation; doors allow rodent entry; mold on sausage.
2	Dallas*	45%	Hand soap not available; flaking paint; employees with soiled hands touching meat; water not hot enough for sanitation; sausage dropped on floor; insect traps not emptied.
3	North Philadelphia	33%	Unsanitary plants; hand tools dirty; insects and rodent droppings; ground beef contaminated with black residue.
4	Rochester, N.Y.	29%	Rusty, dirty equipment; water not hot enough for sanitation; flies; rodent droppings.
5	San Francisco	27%	Mold in coolers; rodent droppings; insects; flaking paint; dirty tools.
6	Petaluma, Calif.	26%	Dirty tools; rust and flaking paint; carcasses nor protected from contamination; rodents; insects.
7	Peoria, Ill.	25%	No hand soap; flaking paint; rodents and rodent nests in plant.
8	Tampa, Fla.	22%	Tarlike residue on bacon; pork bellies in contact with grease; water not hot enough; waste water on carcasses.
9	Baltimore*	22%	Contaminated hand tools; bad lighting; flaking paint; water not hot enough.
10	Lemoyne, Pa.	21%	Unsanitary knives; insecticide mist on exposed product; rat dropping; carcasses contaminated.
76	Kansas City	0%	No major problems found in April 1989 after a highly critical report identifying it as a "weak" circuit in June 1988.

* One of two circuits in the area.

Source: U.S Department of Agriculture Program Review Division   **DAVE EAMES**/The Star

Each year tainted food kills up to 9,000 Americans. And it makes anywhere from 24 million to 81 million people sick, according to estimates gathered by the Centers for Disease Control. At least a third of the cases, according to congressional research, can be traced to meat and poultry.

Why is this happening? Agriculture Department officials typically blame consumers for the outbreaks. Families undercook their dinner, they say, or food service workers don't wash their hands. . . .

For consumers, one of the most crucial breakdowns may be in the warning system designed to keep those problems from ending up in the meat drawers of their refrigerators.

In its simplest form, it's supposed to work this way: In about 7,000 federally checked meat plants across the country, 7,000 USDA meat inspectors ensure that only wholesome meat comes off the assembly line. Slaughter plants must always have an inspector on duty, but processing plants operate under a system in which one inspector can check several plants each day.

If those inspections fail, and hazardous meat gets to consumers, the Washington-based "emergency programs staff" is supposed to recall it and issue a public warning.

Sometimes both systems fail. Indeed, sometimes even the watchdogs don't feel safe.

Earlier this year, after a day of classes at the USDA's training center in College Station, Texas, six veterinarians told a reporter they don't order rare beef for dinner. Too big a chance of getting sick, they say.

Halfway across the country in suburban Virginia, Carl Telleen serves reporters a vegetarian dinner. After working 30 years for the inspection service—including several years on an inspection review team—the retired veterinarian won't eat poultry and eats little red meat. He doesn't trust the process.

Mike McGraw and Jeff Taylor,
The Kansas City (Mo.) *Star*

Simple sentences for complex information   The more difficult the information is, the simpler your sentences should be. Use short sentences with simple construction especially for bureaucratic information that would be hard for the reader to comprehend.

This excerpt is from a story explaining how the judiciary committee of the Connecticut legislature works:

The judiciary is one of the legislature's busiest. By the end of the five-month session in June, the committee will have drafted, amended, approved, or killed about 500 bills— about 14 percent of the 3,649 bills filed with the Senate and House clerks.

Judiciary's 14 percent will touch nearly everyone. The committee considers matters of life and death, marriage and divorce, freedom and imprisonment.

This year's issues include surrogate parenting, birth certificates, and adoption. The death penalty and letting the terminally ill die. Longer prison sentences and home release. Committing the mentally ill to hospitals.

Mark Pazniokas, *The Hartford Courant*

Lists Itemizing information, especially results of studies or the main points in governmental actions, is an excellent way to keep the flow going through the middle of your story. You may use lists in a couple of ways:

- To itemize a group of statistics or any other cumbersome information
- To highlight key points within a story

Lists are usually preceded by a dot called a "bullet" or by some other graphic device.

This example from a story about budget cuts at California State University is a very common way to use lists:

Despite an outcry from students, California State University on Wednesday increased academic fees 20 percent to $936 a year. . . .
Meeting at Cal State Long Beach, the trustees reduced the budget from $2.1 million to $1.65 billion and called for:

- Eliminating 420 faculty positions and leaving vacant an additional 330.

- Not replacing 229 professors when they go on sabbatical.
- Reducing other staff by 856 positions.

"None of these is a happy solution."

Steven Silberman, *The Orange County* (Calif.) *Register*

Cliffhangers: Mystery middles Every day millions of Americans watch soap operas. They are so popular that the *Iowa City Press-Citizen* and other newspapers even print weekly summaries of the shows for viewers who missed some episodes.

The concept is a simple one: Give readers or viewers a mystery and make them want to find out what happens next. In writing, this kind of suspense ending is called a "cliffhanger." It is usually reserved for the endings of stories arranged in sections or in series, when another part appears the next day.

But why wait for the ending? Why not use the same technique to make readers continue reading? Edgar Allan Poe used cliffhangers throughout his stories. In "The Pit and the Pendulum," he described a prisoner of the Inquisition in Paris. The story, told in first person, described the prisoner in a dungeon with a pit. One more step and he would have fallen into the chasm. But then he looks up and sees a glittering steel pendulum, "the under edge evidently as keen as that of a razor." It is descending slowly. Will he be sliced by the sharp crescent blade?

Down—certainly, relentless down! It vibrated within three inches of my bosom. . . . I gasped and struggled at each vibration. I shrunk convulsively at its every sweep. My eyes followed its outward or upward whirls with the eagerness of the most unmeaning despair; they closed themselves spasmodically at every descent, although death would have been a relief.

Cliffhanger, or suspense ending

Can the reader dare stop now before finding out if the prisoner will live or die? The prisoner is spared in the last four sentences:

> An out-stretched arm caught my own as I fell, fainting, into the abyss. It was that of General LaSalle. The French army had entered Toledo. The Inquisition was in the hands of its enemies.

Not all newspaper stories lend themselves to cliffhangers. But many could be structured that way by putting the key points of the story on the front page and stopping with a question or suspenseful point in the last sentence before the story continues or "jumps" to another page. Of course, reporters, editors and the copy desk, which lays out the pages, would have to cooperate. However, even without placing the cliffhanger at a jump point, the technique works to keep the reader moving through the story.

This method is much more conducive to narrative storytelling, especially in a long feature, but it can be applied to hard news if the story stops at a crucial point. The headline also is crucial. It can give a clue to the story, but it shouldn't give away the punch line.

This is only the beginning of a story that uses cliffhangers. Would you want to turn the page to continue reading?

In Fort Myers: Money, mercy and murder

Patricia Rosier's death was supposed to be peaceful and dignified.

She had made all the arrangements. Ordered food for the wake. Said a final goodbye to friends and family. Put the children to sleep.

On the nightstand rested a bottle of Seconals, powerful sedatives prescribed by her husband, Dr. Peter Rosier. Suicide would finally free Pat, 43, from the pain of invading cancer.

When the time came, she downed Seconals like "jellybeans," one witness recalled.

Cliffhanger

But something went wrong in the Rosier's stylish Fort Myers home that January night in 1985.

Pat wouldn't die.

Peter frantically began injecting doses of morphine to finish the job. Pat's breathing slowed to a rasp.

But after 12 hours of the grim ritual, Pat would not die.

Finally, Pat's stepfather, Vincent Delman, decided something had to be done. Pat, he would later tell prosecutors, was suffering too much.

He took Pat's two half brothers into the bedroom and closed the door.

Twenty minutes later, the door opened. The Delmans walked out, their faces sullen. Peter was waiting in the living room, calming his ravaged nerves with a beer.

"Patty is dead," Vincent said.

After the funeral, the Delmans left Fort Myers. They carried with them the dark secret of what happened behind the bedroom door.

Another cliffhanger

On Monday, Peter Rosier, 47, is scheduled to go on trial for the first-degree murder of his wife of 22 years.

The Rosier story has it all—sex, love, wealth, murder and a major mystery: Who really killed Pat Rosier?

And another cliffhanger

Mark Stephens and William Sabo, *Fort Myers* (Fla.) *News-Press*

On the jump page you would find out why Peter is on trial and what kind of evidence exists to try him. You also would find out why this is an unusual case: There's no body and no autopsy report. Pat's body was cremated. There are no morphine syringes; they were thrown away when she died. And there is one other unusual twist: Peter wasn't even in the room when Pat was killed.

Court stories lend themselves to this kind of dramatic structure. But so do many others.

Endings

Call them lasting impressions. To many writers, the ending is as important as the beginning of the story. Unfortunately, many readers don't get that far. But if they do, you should reward them with a memorable ending.

The ending also is called the "kicker." Think of it as a clincher. It should give a summary feeling to your story without repeating any information you have stated previously.

For columnists, the ending is more important than the beginning. The twist or main point the writer is trying to make is at the end of the column. Roger Simon, an award-winning columnist for *The Sun* of Baltimore, once said he sometimes switches his leads and endings. He uses whichever is strongest. In many cases the lead could be an ending. And returning to your lead as a way to find your ending is an excellent technique.

The following sections describe some ways to form your endings.

Circle Kickers

When you return to your lead for an idea to end your story in a full circle, you are using a circle kicker. Ken Fuson frequently uses this technique to devise his endings. In this example from a story about how families cope with Alzheimer's disease, Fuson repeats phrases from the lead—but ends with a twist:

"Mother, mother, mother, other, other, other. . . ."

The sound comes in short, grating bursts, like a children's record played at too high a speed.

Every day, relentlessly, another small slice of the person that once was Betty Jennings disappears. The brand of hell called Alzheimer's disease has reduced the 58-year-old woman to a stoop-shouldered, hand-wringing blabber of meaningless words and phrases.

She must be fed, bathed and diapered. Some mornings, after a particularly brutal night, Gordon Hanchett will look in the living room and see that his sister has attacked her plastic diaper, ripping it apart with her fingers and leaving small pieces littering the floor.

"It looks like a miniature snow-storm," he says.

The limits of devotion are stretched thinnest in the homes of Alzheimer's victims. Often operating on little or no sleep and frequently ruining their own physical health, family members witness the disintegration of a loved one's mind with the understanding that no matter what they do today, tomorrow will be worse.

Circle kicker, which ties together the lead and the ending

The story continues with more about the family in particular and the disease in general. Here's how it ends:

> "Mother, this mother, this other . . . Daddy, daddy, daddy."
>
> The chatter is loud, constant and haunting. His sister's voice fills the house.
>
> "Oh that," says Hanchett, waving his hand. "I don't even hear that anymore."
>
> Ken Fuson, *The Des Moines Register*

Quote Kickers

The most common type of ending for features and hard-news stories is the quote kicker. Look for a quote that sums up the mood or main idea of the story. When you end with a quote, put the attribution before the quote or, in a two-quote ending, after the first sentence. Do not let the last words the reader remembers be "he said."

> Employment counselors often advise job seekers to treat the interviewing process as a time for personal enrichment. But Eugene Roscoe may have gotten a bit carried away.
>
> According to Houston Police Sgt. Roy House, Mr. Roscoe was pulling in $100,000 to $150,000 a year—not from jobs, just from interviews. In an indictment returned last month by a state grand jury in Houston, Mr. Roscoe is accused of bamboozling interviewers into reimbursing him for travel expenses that were never incurred or that had already been covered by another interviewer, if not three or four.
>
> "He was making very good money doing job interviews as a career," says Sgt. House.

The story continues with details and ends with this kicker quote:

> Mr. Roscoe was arrested earlier this week when he showed up for his last interview—the interviewer was Sgt. House. "We let him fill out a voucher for his travel expenses," the sergeant says. "Then we told him we had just the position for him. It was down at the county jail."
>
> Christi Harlan, *The Wall Street Journal*

Future-action Kickers

Many stories end with the next step in the development of an issue. But this technique works only if the story lends itself to a future element. If the next step is crucial to the story, it should be higher in the body. But if it works as a natural conclusion, then it can be the ending. It can be in the form of a statement or a quote.

HERRING BAY, Alaska—World attention focused Friday on the attempt to rescue birds and animals from the oil spilled in Prince William Sound. Cameras in Valdez focused on the few animals saved— fewer than 20 birds and four sea otters by evening Friday. The birds on the evening news were expensive symbols for Exxon, costing more than $1,000 apiece to rescue.

But on the water, the rescue efforts getting all the attention stumbled along with the air of a Sunday outing. In this bay at the north end of Knight Island, a diverse and committed group of people tried to learn to perform a futile task.

The story continues with detail about the rescue operation. Here is the ending:

By Friday afternoon, about two miles of the shore of Herring Bay had been thoroughly searched.

Only a few thousand left to go.

Charles Wohlforth, *Anchorage* (Alaska) *Daily News*

Climaxes

This type of ending works on stories written like fiction, where the reader is kept in suspense until the end. It is more suited to features in narrative style or short news stories that tease the reader in the beginning and compel the reader to find out what happens. It can be used on stories structured in the pyramid style (described in Chapter 12). Here is an example:

Scott T. Grabowski sat Tuesday in the courtroom where a federal judge would determine his future, hoping that when the words were pronounced he would hear probation and not prison.

But Grabowski, 27, of Greenfield, is an admitted drug dealer.

Early last summer, he pleaded guilty to a charge of possessing 3 ounces of cocaine on June 5, 1988, that he intended to sell on behalf of an international drug network.

The story continues with the arguments from Grabowski's defense lawyer and the prosecutor. But what sentence did he receive? The reader doesn't find out until the end.

Finally, after a 2½ hour hearing, Curran (the judge) sentenced Grabowski to 30 months in prison, to be followed by three years of parole.

And with a nod to the parents, Curran told Grabowski: "I'm sure their hearts are aching as they sit here today."

Jill Zuckman, *The Milwaukee Journal*

Cliffhangers

Cliffhangers were described earlier in regard to mystery middles. But cliffhangers are more commonly used as endings, particularly in series that will continue to another day. This technique can also be used in stories written in sections, with the cliffhanger at the end of a section so the reader is compelled to continue. The concept is "What will happen next?"

This example is an excerpt from a series about an FBI undercover operation to catch Colombian drug dealers. In this segment, the FBI undercover agent Robert Paquette has convinced the Colombians that he is a Wall Street financier who can launder money for them. But will the drug dealers believe him? The section ends on a suspenseful note:

One day Paquette scored big. Juan Restrepo, who ranked at the top of the laundering operation (of the Colombian drug dealers) made a rare visit from Medellin and decided to deliver some cash in person.

"You know," Paquette remembers saying, "I've got this special solution in this bottle. You know dogs can be trained to smell money that comes from an area where there are narcotics."

Dropping to his hands and knees, Paquette clambered over the scattered bills, blasting them with his blue pepper spray.

"This throws the dogs' scent off," he said.

Restrepo's expression became earnest. He, too, dropped to the pile and meticulously shifted the cash to ensure Paquette's miracle spray was liberally and thoroughly applied.

He also tasted it. But he didn't say anything about its distinctly unpeppery flavor. He just looked at Paquette, quizzically.

In another section, the ending also is a cliffhanger:

There was an odd kind of trust between Paquette and the Colombians. . . .

By following the dealer and money couriers, the agents believed they had enough evidence to crack the ring. On Sept. 4, 1986, they struck in a series of coordinated raids.

Paquette spent Sept. 4 in his Greenwich office, wondering whether the Colombians would realize he had set them up. Was his cover blown?

Edmund Mahony, *The Hartford Courant*

Factual Kickers

These are strong factual statements that could sometimes substitute as leads. They are statements that summarize the mood, tone or general character of the story. They are harder to write than quote kickers, but if done well, they give the reader a powerful punch. They are truly kickers. Strive for a very short, simple sentence that states a fact. But choose a meaningful fact that will leave a lasting impression.

Julie Sullivan is a master of the factual kicker. One of hers appears in the introduction to this book. In the following example, she is writing about a man who lives in a run-down hotel in Spokane. (The full story will appear in Chapter 25.) This ending is a simple statement that is circular in its reference to the lead.

Here is the lead:

Joe Peak's smile has no teeth.

His dentures were stolen at the Norman Hotel, the last place he lived in downtown Spokane before moving to the Merlin two years ago.

Gumming food and fighting diabetes have shrunk the 54-year-old man's frame by 80 pounds. He is thin and weak and his mouth is sore.

But that doesn't stop him from frying hamburgers and onions for a friend at midnight or keeping an extra bed made up permanently in his two-room place.

"I try to make a little nest here for myself," he says.

The story continues with detail about the difficulties Peak encounters living in the Merlin. It ends with factual statements. Here are the last few paragraphs:

When conditions at the Merlin began worsening three months ago, junkies and gray mice the size of baby rats moved in next door. He hated to see it, but he isn't worried about being homeless.

He's worried about his diabetes. He's frightened by blood in his stool and sores on his gums. He wonders whether the white-staffed hospitals on the hill above him will treat a poor black man with no teeth.

Julie Sullivan, *The* (Spokane, Wash.) *Spokesman-Review*

Out-of-gas Endings

Just end when you have no more to say. This method is appropriate for hard-news stories, particularly those structured with a summary lead and arranged with supporting points in descending order of importance. You can end on a quote, future action or another fact in the story.

Here is a story with a factual out-of-gas ending:

TAMPA, Fla.—For the first time, a shrimper has been imprisoned for failing to use a federally mandated turtle protection device on his boat, the National Marine Fisheries Service said.

The story continues with the basic who, what, why, when, where and ends with this fact:

The government estimates more than 11,000 sea turtles drown in shrimp nets in U.S. waters each year.

The Associated Press

Body Building From Start to Finish

Here is a short story that could have been written as a routine police story. The writer makes it interesting by using many of the techniques described in this chapter. Note how the writer uses good pacing, parellelism and a circle kicker:

Mystery call has police barking up wrong tree

Mystery lead

The following nail-biting police drama probably won't find its way onto the "Rescue: 911" TV show, but it's had some folks around Eldridge talking about it since it happened at the end of last week:

Short sentences

A call comes to the Eldridge police dispatcher over the 911 emergency line. The dispatcher answers and asks what the problem is.

Fragments for emphasis and drama

No response. Silence. The dispatcher can hear very heavy breathing. That's all. Pretty obvious somebody's in trouble.

Pacing: long sentence followed by short ones

Police Chief Martin Stolmeier, on patrol in the area, takes 20 seconds to get to the Frank and Paula Griggs residence, where the dispatcher's computer says the call is originating.

Key word: **still** *for parallelism*

The caller is still on the line. Still breathing heavily. Still needing help.

Short, choppy sentences to build drama

Stolmeier arrives. Announces loudly that the police are there, begins a room-by-room search. Stolmeier knows somebody needs help. He enters the situation assuming someone may have broken into the house. Maybe some sort of struggle.

Stolmeier nears a downstairs bedroom. The dispatcher hears him over the phone getting closer. On the other side of the door is the situation—the burglar, killer or heart attack victim.

Foreshadowing

Right about now, if this were a movie, the camera would zoom in very close on Stolmeier's perspiring face and the music would be building to a crescendo of tension and you would be going crazy as Stolmeier at last comes face to face with . . . with . . .

Cliffhanger

Blaze. A 6-month-old black Labrador who seemed very energetic and very happy to see Stolmeier. In a fit of rambunctious puppyness, Blaze had knocked the phone off the wall and somehow dialed 911.

Paragraph could also work as a climax kicker

No word on whether Blaze's phone privileges have been restricted since the incident. But they'd better not tell him about 900 numbers or the Home Shopping Network.

Circle kicker (returns to concept in lead)

Patrick Beach, *The Des Moines* (Iowa) *Register*

Body-building Checklist

For middles:

• Read aloud to check your pacing. Do short sentences follow long ones? Do your paragraphs start different ways? Do you have too many sentences with clauses?

• Would lists of short sentences itemizing findings or material substitute for lengthy paragraphs?

• Could you eliminate any transitions? Would some quotes naturally follow the previous point without needing a transition?

For endings:

• Have you overwritten or strained the ending? Try the hand test. Put your hand over the last paragraph and see if the previous one or two paragraphs would make a better ending. Does your ending repeat previous points?

• Have you avoided ending with the attribution?

• Is your ending memorable? Could it even be a lead?

• Is your ending too repetitious? Does it summarize the story like a term paper? If you are repeating information, cut the story to the last important point or last good quote.

Exercises

1   This is an exercise for awareness of pacing. Listen to classical music or other music of your choice. With your eyes closed, draw lines on a piece of paper to express the rhythm or movements of the music. Then find a story that you think has good pacing and compare it to the rhythm of music.

2   Watch a mystery television show, a movie or even a soap opera and note the foreshadowing elements and the cliffhangers. Analyze whether these elements keep you interested, and consider how you can apply the concepts to writing.

3   Read aloud a story you have written. Note where you can improve the pacing or how you can make the middle flow better.

4   Take any story you have already written and try a different ending, using a circle kicker, quote kicker or factual kicker.

5   Take any news story from your local or campus newspaper and rewrite it to improve the middle and ending. Analyze which stories have quote endings, circle kickers or factual endings.

COACHING

TIPS

Envision your story order as a blueprint for designing a building. What shape will the story take?

Consider a model for your story during and after the reporting process. Some forms require more anecdotal material. Always gather more information than you need so you can be flexible during the design process.

Write subheads for your story to organize it topically.

Story Structures

12

J ack Hart tells writers to think logically when they organize their stories. He calls the process "sequencing." Hart, writing coach at *The* (Portland) *Oregonian,* says writers should organize the information in a sequence that helps readers understand how one item leads to another.

Hart also says sequencing helps writers visualize a shape for their story. When he coaches writers, he uses models of organization and gives the models names so writers will remember them.

"I think we are lexicon impoverished," Hart says. "We haven't had many names for story structures. I am a firm believer that if you walk through the woods and you know the names of all the plants, you'll see a lot more. A lot of writers get halfway through a story and don't realize that they are writing in a particular structure."

Although many other writing coaches don't stress names and shapes of stories as much as Hart does, almost all coaches talk about order and logic and storytelling. They ask writers to envision what the reader needs to know and in what order. And they often tell writers to let the story flow naturally, as though they were telling it to a friend.

All stories should help readers understand the focus, the conflict, the background and solutions to the central topic. Most stories can be arranged by a topical order, points of view or chronological order for all or part of the story. Models of story structures can help you plan the organization. Your choice of

An effective story has a shape that both contains and expresses the story. . . . The writer must find a form that gives the reader a satisfying sense of completion, a feeling that everything in the story flows toward an inevitable conclusion.

Donald Murray,

Writing for Your Readers

Jack Hart, writing coach

structure depends on the type of material you have. Although there are many structures, the following six structures are the most common:

Inverted pyramid: This is one of the most basic story forms. It is used most often for hard-news stories. The structure is a summary lead that gives the focus, followed by supporting points in descending order of importance.

***Wall Street Journal* formula:** This structure is based on the principle of specific to general. The formula is to start with an anecdotal lead, usually focusing on a person or event that exemplifies the main issue, which is expressed in a nut graph. The body of the story is arranged topically, with one point leading to another. The ending usually comes full circle, referring back to the lead. This structure is useful for stories about trends, major issues, features, news sidebars and news events that lend themselves to a feature approach. Although it is used in newspapers throughout the country for many news and feature stories, it is named after *The Wall Street Journal* because that newspaper became famous for using it in its front-page trend stories every day.

Hourglass: The hourglass form starts with the hard news and then proceeds in a chronological order for part or the rest of the story. It ends with comments or the outcome of the news. It is useful for police and court stories and other stories that lend themselves to some storytelling. It also is a good technique for avoiding attribution in every sentence, because the writer can use an overview attribution before the chronological portion—for example: "Police gave this account" or "Neighbors describe the incident this way."

List: This structure, used most often by *USA Today,* starts with a lead and a few paragraphs of backup information and then includes lists of supporting points. The list items are usually presented in brief form with a large dot, square, check or other graphic item to set them off. This technique is useful when you want to give many facts in short form. Lists can be used anywhere in the story.

Pyramid: This structure is chronological storytelling from beginning to end. It works well on shorter stories or those with enough suspenseful action to carry the reader to the end. You still need a nut graph high in the story and some foreshadowing to keep the reader's interest.

Sections: This is a technique of dividing a story into sections, like book chapters, and separating them by a graphic device such as a large dot or a large capital letter. Each section can present a different point of view or a different time element (present, past and future). It works best for in-depth stories such as investigations or long features. The most effective section stories have good leads and good endings for each section. This form lends itself to cliffhanger endings for each section or for each day's installment if the story is presented as a series. Think of the sections as separate chapters, complete in themselves but tied together by the overall focus and story plot.

Understanding these basic structures will help you plan the lead and the order of your story. Regardless of the structure you use, you still can organize your information by topics, points of view, chronology or a combination of these factors.

Inverted Pyramid

Summary lead

Backup (quotes or facts)

Supporting points

Ending

Exhibit 12-1

Inverted pyramid structure

This structure organizes the story from the most important information to the least important (see Exhibit 12-1). It usually starts with a summary lead that gives some of the basics: who, what, when, where, why. The elements that can't fit in the lead are in the backup. This is one of the most common forms for hard-news stories.

How do you decide what is most important and what should follow in descending order of importance? Use your judgment. Some questions to ask: What will affect the reader most? What questions does the lead raise that need to be answered immediately? What supporting quotes are strongest?

The advantage of this form is that the reader gets the crucial information quickly. The disadvantage: The reader may not read past the crucial information.

This form is the primary structure for breaking news, and it is an important form for on-line journalism, where readers have unlimited choices and more control over their story selections. Because of the volume of material available on-line, the inverted pyramid is a useful way to let readers determine immediately whether they are interested in the story. On-line journalism does not have the space limitations of newspapers, so readers who are really interested in a topic may read more of the story and even pursue additional information that might be offered through links to other stories.

Regardless of the medium, stories still must be well written to entice readers. Adding an impact paragraph—explaining how the story affects readers—is one way to strengthen the inverted pyramid. Here is an example of a basic inverted pyramid story:

Headline	# Teen sentenced to read book about Holocaust
Summary headline	*He must write report on "Diary of Anne Frank" for his role in cross burning on black family's lawn*
Summary lead: who (delayed identification), what, why	SEATTLE—Instead of being sent to jail, a teen-ager was sent to the library to read the grim Holocaust tale, *The Diary of Anne Frank,* for his part in a cross burning on a black family's lawn.
Backup: who, when	Matthew Ryan Tole, 18, was sentenced Friday to read the famous story by a young Jewish girl of her family's failed attempt to escape Nazi persecution during World War II.
Supporting facts: why	King County Superior Court Judge Anthony Wartnik said Tole received a light sentence because he was not one of the leaders in the

April 16 cross burning in Bothell, a suburb north of Seattle.

"The Anne Frank book is great for someone to get a picture of the most extreme thing that can happen if people aren't willing to step forward and say this is wrong," Wartnik said. "I'm hoping it will make him more sensitive." *Supporting quote*

Wartnik told him to write a book report on *The Diary of Anne Frank* within three months. *More explanation*

Tole pleaded guilty to rendering criminal assistance in the cross burning, which involved at least a dozen Bothell High School students. The cross was built during a party at Tole's home. *Background*

Tole did not help build or light the cross, but some of the materials belonged to him. *Factual ending*

The Associated Press

Soft lead

Nut Graph

Backup for lead and nut graph

Supporting points: quotes, facts, anecdotes

Developments: cause/effect, explanations, points of view

Circle kicker: anecdote, description, future action related to lead

Exhibit 12-2

Wall Street Journal *formula*

Wall Street Journal *Formula*

This structure starts with a soft lead, focusing on a person, scene or event (see Exhibit 12-2). The idea is to go from the specific to the general, starting with a person, place or event that illustrates the main point of the story. The concept, whether stated or implied, is that this person or scene is one of many affected by the issue in the nut graph. The lead can be anecdotal, descriptive or narrative.

It is followed by a focus graph—nut graph—that gives the main point of the story. This paragraph should explain what the story is about and why it is important ("so what").

The story then presents backup for the lead and supporting points. The body of the story may be organized by different points of view or developments related to the focus.

The ending is often a circle kicker, using a quote or anecdote from the person in the lead or a future development of something mentioned in the beginning of the story.

This is a very versatile formula that can be applied to many news and feature stories. It is very useful for brightening bureaucratic stories. While you are reporting, consider this writing form and seek out a person who is one of many exemplifying your point or try to find an anecdote that illustrates the main point of your story.

If you had written a news story about a government hearing in inverted pyramid style, the lead might sound like this:

> About 350 people attended a federal hearing yesterday by the bipartisan Commission on Comprehensive Health Care to discuss problems of long-term health care.

This is how the lead sounded using the *Wall Street Journal* formula:

Terry Idleson of South Philadelphia never sleeps more than three hours at a stretch a night. It's the only way she can tend to her brain-damaged 2-year-old daughter, Stephanie, who needs round-the-clock attention.

Miriam Burnett of West Philadelphia used to be a schoolteacher. But she quit her job to care for her 76-year-old mother, who has Alzheimer's disease.

Joyce Singer of York, Pa., could think of only one thing to do when her husband, Michael, had a stroke at age 38, incurring medical expenses that threatened to bankrupt her family. She divorced him.

These three caregivers—mother, daughter, wife—were among a dozen witnesses who testified yesterday at a federal hearing on long-term care and its often devastating impact on the family. *Nut graph*

The hearing before the bipartisan Commission on Comprehensive Health Care—called the Pepper Commission for its original chairman, the late U.S. Rep. Claude Pepper (D.-Fla.)—drew an overflow crowd of about 350 to the ceremonial courtroom in the U.S. Courthouse at 601 Market Street.

Beth Gillin, *The Philadelphia Inquirer*

In this example, the formula is used in a feature story about a program:

Nearly a year ago, Rebecca Antholz was in despair.

She had a stack of medical bills she could not pay, no health insurance and nowhere to turn if her children became sick.

"I was between a rock and a hard place," she said.

Nut graph Then she heard about the Caring Program for Children, which raises money to provide free health care to families who can't afford health insurance for their children.

"I was just frantic trying to figure out how to get coverage for my kids," Antholz, 313 W. Sixth, said. "It was a tremendous blessing." ***Secondary nut graph***

Her family was one of the first in Ellis County to join the program, which began last March in Ellis and Shawnee counties and will begin in Sedgwick County in February.

Merry Hayes, *The Hays* (Kan.) *Daily News*

The next example is a complete version of the *Wall Street Journal* formula, from the paper for which it is named. This is a trend story about the dangers of farming. Note that it also illustrates how the FORK method works:

Focus: Farming is the most dangerous occupation.

Order: The story is arranged by topics that substantiate the focus: (1) extent of the problem, (2) government role, (3) effect on children, (4) illnesses of farmers.

Repetition of key words: In the last sentence of several paragraphs are key words that serve as thought bridges to the next paragraph. In some cases, the key words are repeated to make a smooth transition.

Kiss off: Each new source is blocked; the source's comments are in one place, and then the source is not mentioned again, except for the central character introduced in the lead. He is used in the circular ending.

Farming Is Dangerous, but Fatalistic Farmers Oppose Safety Laws

By Bruce Ingersoll
The Wall Street Journal

Soft lead: focus on a person who illustrates main point of story

BATAVIA, N.Y.—Behind the barn, in a swale of sweet clover, Leo Bolas lost part of his right leg. The 69-year-old farmer had been funneling fodder into a silo when his tattered overalls caught in a spinning power-attachment on his tractor. In an instant he was yanked into the whirring drive shaft, and in a bloody blur his leg was nearly severed below the knee. To free himself he finished the amputation with a jackknife. Otherwise, he says, "it could have dragged me in further and finished me off."

First person quoted

Nut graph

Farm life belies its tranquil image. Farming is America's most dangerous line of work.

Backup: elaboration for nut graph

Agriculture has eclipsed mining as the occupation with the highest death rate. More precisely, while mining has reduced the number of fatalities substantially over the past decade, farming hazards continue for the most part unabated. Agriculture's accidental-death rate—48 per 100,000 workers—is five times higher than the national average for all industries.

About 1,500 farmers and farmhands are killed each year, according to the National Safety Council. Many die in tractor accidents, are electrocuted, suffocate under tons of grain or are killed by bulls and cows and sows. Some 160,000 people suffer serious injuries. Still others fall victim to farm-related illnesses.

Foreshadowing: gives clues of information later in story

Hardly a farming community is untouched. An Iowa farmer, over morning coffee, counts 20 neighbors he knows by name who have been killed or crippled in farm accidents since 1980. Three of them were children. Each year, 300 youngsters under the age of 16 die in farm-related accidents, and 23,500 more are hurt.

More specifics

Farming is inevitably hazardous. But accidents also reflect economic pressures that have farmers taking dangerous shortcuts, and they reflect meager safety initiatives at all levels of government.

For the most part, agriculture is exempt from federal regulation by the Occupational Safety and Health Administration. Unlike nations such as West Germany and Britain, "We (the U.S.) really have no policy whatsoever," says Kelley Donham, a University of Iowa associate professor of agricultural medicine.

Supporting topic: government role (government is key word to next thought) Second source quoted, then kissed off

Regulation is fiercely resisted, notably by farmers themselves, who fear the loss of independence and aren't sanguine about the possibilities.

Third source blocked

Second supporting topic: children injured

Fourth source blocked

Key word (kids) repeated for transition

Fifth source blocked

Third supporting topic: farmers' illnesses

Nor do farm policy makers or Farm Belt politicians seem prepared to confront a problem that costs the U.S. economy more than $3 billion a year. "You start talking farm safety, and you're unpopular," says Rep. David Nagle, an Iowa Democrat. "But we can't continue to lose 300 kids a year; we can't continue to have farmers maimed and killed. These injuries are predictable and preventable."

Marilyn Adams of Earlham, Iowa, agrees that more needs to be done. Her 11-year-old son Keith was helping his stepfather in 1986 when the boy fell into a wagonload of corn and suffocated. "They call it drowning in grain," says Mrs. Adams. "It works like quicksand. Within 8 to 10 seconds an adult can be completely submerged in grain. It takes less time for kids."

The risk is especially acute if grain is being unloaded through a chute at the bottom, creating a current that can suck a person in. In her grief, Mrs. Adams organized a group called Farm Safety for Just Kids. She is urging rural women to curb child labor on the farm. "Dads are building up tractor pedals so eight-year-olds can drive," she says. "Moms and kids have to learn to say no to dads."

Unless agriculture solves its "kids problem," lawmakers may ban child labor, predicts John Pollack, a Cornell University farm-safety specialist. "They could call it a form of child abuse." He favors setting a minimum age of 12 for driving tractors. Tractor rollovers are the No. 1 killer on farms. Some groups seek federal requirements for roll bars on new tractors.

Farmers also have the highest hospitalization rate and, oddly, the lowest rate of doctor visits of any occupation. Farmers have more serious illness but tend not to seek medical attention for the little things. The good life of the farm—the sunshine and the fresh air—is something of a bill of goods. Of all occupational groups, farmers have the highest rate of skin disorders, including skin cancer resulting from too much sun, and eczema from handling detergents and chemicals. Farmers, sometimes insouciant about wearing face masks, inhale clouds of dust, animal dander, even deadly fumes. Many suffer hearing loss from the clatter of machinery.

The contradictions of rural life strike home here on Leo Bolas's farm in the dairy belt of upstate New York. As cows graze on a lush hillside, lowing in the twilight, Mr. Bolas re-enacts how he became entangled in the power-takeoff attachment to his tractor three years ago. Scattering chickens with his cane, he retraces the path he crawled—through standing corn across the barnyard into a machine shed—to reach a telephone and call for help. "It took four phone calls," he says. "I never thought of 911."

But like many farm-accident victims, he blames himself. He should have replaced the broken shield on his tractor; he ought to have discarded the torn overalls before they could get caught in the works. "You get careless," he says, hobbling along on his artificial leg. "I ain't the only one. Farmers are the most dangerous people there is."

Ending: back to beginning source

Circular wrap-up

Quote ending

Hourglass Structure

Exhibit 12-3

Hourglass structure

The hourglass form can start like the inverted pyramid, giving the most important hard-news information in the top of the story (see Exhibit 12-3). Then it contains chronological storytelling for a part or for the rest of the story. Use the hourglass structure when the story has dramatic action that lends itself to chronological order for part of the story. The technique is useful in crime or disaster stories to recount the event.

To set up the chronological narrative, an overview attribution often is used, such as "Police gave the following account" or "Witnesses described the accident this way," and then followed by a colon. However, this type of attribution should be used only for a few paragraphs so the reader does not forget who is speaking. All quotes still need attribution. If the speaker changes, the new source also must be attributed.

Advantage: The narrative storytelling in the chronological portion adds drama to the story. Disadvantage: The chronological portion of the story may repeat some of the key information in the top of the story, making it longer than a basic inverted pyramid.

Boy, 3, shoots 16-month-old

Summary lead

TAMPA, Fla.—A 3-year-old boy shot and seriously wounded his 16-month-old half brother Thursday after he found a .32-caliber pistol under a chair cushion in the family's apartment, Hillsborough sheriff's deputies said.

Attribution Backup for lead

Melvin Hamilton, shot once in the chest about 9:30 a.m., was flown by helicopter to Tampa General Hospital, where he was in serious but stable condition late Thursday after surgery, hospital officials said.

Attribution Basic inverted pyramid structure with attribution for each point

Otis Neal, who pulled the trigger, did it accidentally, authorities said.

Sheriff's officials said they did not know who owned the handgun but were still investigating. Under state law, the gun's owner could be criminally liable for leaving the gun in a place where a child could get it.

The state Department of Health and Rehabilitative Services (HRS) was contacted by authorities, and it too is investigating the incident.

HRS spokesman Tom Jones said the agency has no prior involvement with the family but gave no further details.

Observation: no attribution needed

Hours after the accident, Otis sat bewildered on a curb outside his family's apartment as television camera crews and reporters jockeyed around him.

"He is saying very little. I don't think he really knows what is going on," sheriff's spokeswoman Debbie Carter said.

Facts

Otis and Melvin live with their mother, Dina Varnes, in the Terrace Oaks Apartment complex at 6611 50th St.

Relatives and sheriff's officials gave this account:

Overview attribution: chronological narrative begins and continues to the end

The two youngsters were downstairs in the living room playing Thursday morning, while a 15-year-old friend of the family slept on the couch. Ms. Varnes was upstairs.

Melvin was walking around the living room when Otis found the gun under the seat cushion. He pulled the gun out and fired one shot.

Arabell Ricks, Ms. Varnes' aunt and neighbor, said she was walking to the store when her niece ran out of the apartment screaming.

"She said, 'Melvin is shot.' She said the oldest shot Melvin," Ms. Ricks said. "I went in and looked at him, and then I just ran out of the house and started praying."

She said she flagged down a sheriff's deputy who was patrolling the area.

"I said, 'Lord, please don't let him die,'" Ms. Ricks said.

Ending reaction quote

Heddy Murphy, *St. Petersburg* (Fla.) *Times*

List Technique

Lists can be useful in stories when you have several important points to stress. Think of a list as a highlights box within the story or at the end of the story. This technique works well for stories about studies, government stories such as meetings, and even features about people or programs if there are several key points to list. *USA Today* uses this structure in most of its stories.

When using a list for the body and ending of a story, you can start with a summary lead or a soft lead followed by a nut graph (see Exhibit 12-4). Give some backup for the lead in quotes or facts or both. Then itemize the main points until the ending. Investigative reporters often use the list high in the story to itemize the findings of their investigation.

Limit lists in the beginnings and middles of stories to five items or fewer; lists at the end can be longer. Parallel sentence structure is most effective, but not essential, for lists. Each item should be in a separate paragraph. Lists often are used in stories about meetings to itemize actions not related to the lead. The list is preceded by "In other business" or a similar transition. The following example uses two sets of lists:

Exhibit 12-4 *List technique*

Summary lead

Campus crime records must be open to the public, a judge in Springfield, Mo., ruled Wednesday in a case with far-reaching implications.

Backup: reaction quote

"The gentlemen who wrote the Constitution would be proud," says Traci Bauer, 22, editor of the Southwest Missouri State University newspaper.

Background

Bauer sued the school, saying it concealed crime reports to protect its image. Federal Judge Russell Clark ruled:

- Withholding crime investigation and incident reports is unconstitutional.
- Campus crime records aren't exempt from Missouri's open-records law or protected as educational records.

Media-law experts say the ruling could set a precedent.

Testimony showed:

- A rape allegedly committed by a star athlete was not disclosed and no charges were filed.
- Springfield police were not told of several crimes.
- Drugs were seized and destroyed without disclosure.

University spokesman Paul Kincaid says regents will meet Friday to consider an appeal.

Future action kicker

Claude Burgett, *USA Today*

Here is an example of how the list technique can be used in the middle of a story:

Finally, some facts to justify cursing at people with car phones.

A recent study of car phoning showed that drivers involved in car-phone conversations were 30 percent more likely to overlook potential hazards, such as your rear bumper.

"They were so engrossed in the phone call that they were oblivious to what was going on," said James McKnight, whose experiments with 51 drivers were the basis for the findings.

What McKnight found through controlled tests on driving simulators was this:

- Even casual chitchat or just dialing a car phone distracted drivers enough so that they failed to respond to hazards nearly 7 percent more often.

- When talk turned to solving simple math problems—designed to simulate business conversations—drivers failed to respond to hazards nearly 30 percent more often.

- When engaged in casual or businesslike conversations, drivers 50 or older failed to respond to hazards 38 percent more often than younger drivers.

- Drivers who had experience with car phones were as easily distracted as drivers who were using the phones for the first time.

And his No. 1 finding:

"If there is any group that should not be using cellular phones while driving, it is those in the older age group," McKnight reported.

Failing to notice hazards was even more common among drivers 50 years old or older. They were twice as likely to overlook your bumper.

McKnight, a researcher with the National Public Services Research Institute in Landover, Md., conducted the study for the Automobile Association of America Foundation for Traffic Safety.

Mark Vosburgh, *The Orlando* (Fla.) *Sentinel*

Pyramid Structure

Once upon a time, storytellers began at the beginning and continued to the end, saving the climax for last. Chronological storytelling is still the popular form used by fiction writers. It can be used in some news stories as well—with one difference. You still need to give the nut graph, telling the reader what the story is about, high in the story. You also should use some foreshadowing, a clue that something exciting or mysterious will happen later in the story—for example, "The worst was yet to come" or "But something went wrong."

This structure is similar to the hourglass, but with the pyramid, the chronology begins almost immediately and continues until the end (see Exhibit 12-5).

This structure works best in brief stories so the reader doesn't have to wait too long to find out what happened. It also can be used in longer stories with a dramatic plot, providing you have a nut graph, some foreshadowing and a story compelling enough to keep the reader interested.

Advantage: The suspense can compel the reader to finish the story. Disadvantage: An impatient reader won't bother waiting to find out what happens.

Lead

Foreshadowing

Chronological storytelling

Climax at end

Exhibit 12-5

Pyramid structure

In the following example about a fire, the last three paragraphs would be the top of the story in inverted pyramid form. In this story, the lead tells the reader what the story is about and provides some mystery, which serves as foreshadowing. From that point on, the story is told in chronological order. In more dramatic, suspenseful stories, the climax of the chronology would be at the end.

Hard-news lead

NEW PORT RICHEY, Fla.—Help came to the Knight family in the form of a stranger and a cat named Gizmo when their house caught on fire early Sunday.

Chronological storytelling begins.

Family members were sleeping in their rented home at 4633 Gazania St. when fire broke out shortly after midnight. Susan Knight awoke when Gizmo, a 6-month-old white cat, ran across her face.

Mrs. Knight sat up and saw smoke and flames. She woke her husband, Thomas, and got their three children out of the house.

"The smoke was so bad we just had to get out," Mrs. Knight, 30, said Sunday afternoon. "He tried to call 911, but the smoke was so bad he couldn't give the address."

Outside, Thomas Knight, 33, dragged a hose toward the front door. But it wasn't long enough to reach the flames.

That's when the "mystery guy," as Mrs. Knight called him, appeared. The man took the hose from her husband and told him to call for help. The stranger carried the hose around the house and sprayed water through a window into a bedroom where the fire had started.

The man helped slow the flames until Pasco County firefighters arrived, Fire Rescue Chief Mike Morgan said. Ten minutes later, the fire was out.

The stranger spoke to Mrs. Knight before he left.

"I hope I've helped you in some way. I've done everything I could," Mrs. Knight recalls him saying. She had never seen him before and with the confusion, couldn't remember what he looked like.

Chronology ends.

The fire began with a short circuit in a cord leading to a lamp and a fan, Morgan said. The house received more than $15,000 in damage.

Basic news summary information

Smoke and heat damaged all the family's belongings, Mrs. Knight said. "The little girls lost everything they had."

(In more dramatic stories with suspense, the climax is at the end.)

None of the children—11-year-old Michael, 6-year-old Ashley and 3-year-old Jenna—was injured. Their father was treated for smoke inhalation.

Larry Dougherty, *St. Petersburg Times*

Section Technique

The technique of separating the story into sections is very useful for in-depth stories. It can be used with many kinds of feature and news stories. The key to the section technique is to treat each section like a separate chapter, with a lead and an ending that will compel readers to continue (see Exhibit 12-6).

Exhibit 12-6

Section technique

One common way to organize section stories is by points of view. For example, in a story about a controversial government issue, such as a new landfill, you could arrange the story by different points of view—a section for each group affected by the proposal.

The other way frequently used to organize section stories is by time frames—starting with the present, then moving to the past for background and back to present developments, and ending with the future. Although the order can be flexible, the opening section must contain a nut graph explaining why you are telling the reader this story now.

This technique is very effective for stories written in narrative style. To determine whether your story is suitable for sections, envision subheads for it. Then decide if you have enough information in each subheaded group to warrant a separate section.

The following story uses a combination of points of view and time sequences to organize the sections. This is a story about a drunken driver who killed a teenager. It is a story that can occur in any town like this small town in Connecticut; it is the type of story you could do. This one is written in dramatic narrative form, storytelling that reconstructs the event. All the information was taken from court records or interviews, so attribution is limited. The newspaper used a combination of bullets and subheads to separate the sections. Outlining a long story with subheads is also a good organizational technique. The time sequence of this story is past and present in the first section, past in the second section, back to present in the third section, and future at the end. Notice how the sections are structured as separate chapters with kicker endings.

This section explains the past—what happened—to establish the reason for the story and to identify the first character. It also uses foreshadowing, clues to let the reader know something mysterious has happened.

A life in shambles ends a life full of promise

A late summer Saturday afternoon fades into twilight as Patricia Nurmi drives south on I-91, straining to focus on the highway rushing under her gray Ford Granada. Empty vodka bottles and beer cans rattle in the back.

She's drunk at the wheel again, trying to get home. Her 7-year-old daughter, Trisha, sits beside her on the front seat.

Nurmi takes the Exit 47W and looks into the setting sun for the nearby ramp to Enfield Street. A car passes her on the left, and she drifts right. There's a thud. A body flies up over Nurmi's hood, shatters her windshield and disappears.

"I hurt somebody," Nurmi says aloud as she drives away, leaving pieces of her broken headlight on the road.

■

Earlier that day in 1992, two 15-year-olds in love sip non-alcoholic pina coladas at the Ground Round restaurant in Enfield. Cartoons flicker on a screen behind Malissa McCauley and Ryan Reale as they sit at their table for two.

Malissa had arranged a day of surprises for Ryan to celebrate their first anniversary as a couple. They captured the occasion with a portrait at Sears.

After dinner, they leave for Malissa's family's apartment on Pearl Street, where they plan to watch his favorite videotape, "Dream a Little Dream."

This section identifies the other main characters and sets up the plot with past time sequence.

They hold hands as they walk along busy Hazard Avenue. There's no sidewalk, so Ryan tells Malissa to walk on the inside, out of harm's way.

Malissa glances over her shoulder and sees a gray car coming down the exit from I-91. Suddenly, the car weaves toward them, scooping Ryan up from behind. His hand is torn from Malissa's grasp.

The force propels Ryan across the hood and into the windshield, then throws him almost 9 feet into a light post. He falls to the ground on his back, unconscious beside Malissa. Blood gushes from his head.

■

This section brings the characters together and sets up the present—why this story is being told now.

Ryan Reale and Patricia Nurmi were neighbors on different paths.

For about three years, they lived a few doors from each other in Green Valley–Laurel Park, a cluster of rent-subsidized duplexes in Enfield where some families strive to get ahead while others struggle with alcoholism and domestic violence.

After nine years in the neighborhood, Ryan and his family moved out and were on their way up. Nurmi was falling deeper into darkness.

That September evening in 1992, the forces that Nurmi succumbed to claimed them both.

Ryan lies in a grave at St. Adalbert's Cemetery in Enfield. Nurmi, who was sentenced Monday, is in prison after five arrests on drunken driving charges.

This section uses past time sequence to establish the background of the characters. Subheads take the place of bullets to separate the sections.

Their stories were told by their friends and relatives, and in court, motor vehicle and police records.

Nurmi's Story

Ten years earlier, in 1982, Nurmi was a 23-year-old bartender at The Point in East Windsor. She knew all the regulars who came to wash away the day's tensions with a shot or a beer.

A petite 5-foot-2, Nurmi was just four years out of Enfield High School. She was already divorced from her first husband and struggling with an alcohol problem rooted in a lifelong exposure to heavy drinking in her family.

The Point, now closed, was a tough place where women sometimes lifted wallets from drunks who stumbled into the parking lot at closing time. Some nights, Nurmi slipped free drinks to her roommate, Sharon Dabrowski.

At work, Nurmi mostly stayed sober and kept a friendly eye on Dabrowski.

"You don't need another beer," Nurmi would say. "It's 12 o'clock. I'm shutting you off."

Nurmi caught the attention of Jose Gonzales, a 43-year-old highway laborer for the town of East Windsor who often stopped in after work.

In Nurmi, Gonzales saw youth and companionship. In Gonzales, Nurmi saw stability.

The two were married in 1982 by a justice of the peace, in the Simon Road apartment in Enfield where they had moved in together. About a dozen family members watched as Gonzales exchanged vows with his bride.

The couple soon had children, T.J. in 1984 and Trisha in 1985. Nurmi quit bartending to stay home with the kids.

But her time as a housewife was short. At 26, she became restless and began tending bar again in East Windsor. She began to drink more frequently and stay out late with a former high school friend, Scott Fletcher, a convicted burglar with a tattoo of a devil on his chest.

After her binges with Fletcher, Nurmi would come home late and fight with Gonzales.

"Get out of the house," she yelled in frustration over their failing marriage.

Sometimes Nurmi would come home at daybreak and load the kids into the school bus she drove for the town of East Windsor.

Some mornings she didn't come home at all; Gonzales stayed home from work to watch the children.

Nurmi's first drunken-driving arrest was in 1986, the same year she and Gonzales agreed to divorce. She was allowed to participate in a state program for first-time drunken-driving offenders. After completing an educational program, the charge was dropped and her record cleared.

By 1988, Nurmi and Fletcher were living together in a violent relationship centered on alcohol and drugs.

At 5:24 a.m. one July morning, Nurmi sped past an East Windsor police officer at 70 mph in a 45 mph zone on North Street. T.J. and Trisha were in the car with her. She scored 0.211 percent on a blood-alcohol test, more than twice the 0.10 percent legal limit for intoxication.

In December, Nurmi got a 90-day suspended sentence, a year's probation and 100 hours of community service. Her driver's license was suspended for a year.

Shortly after the arrest, Nurmi complained to the police that Fletcher threw her down a flight of stairs.

Fletcher and Nurmi had one daughter together—Nicky, born May 4, 1989. A few months later, in November 1989, East Windsor police again charged Nurmi with drunken driving. This time, she could have been sentenced to a year in prison.

On Dec. 15, the state dropped the charge. In exchange, Nurmi pleaded guilty to a lesser charge of violating probation by failing to perform her community service. She was sentenced to 48 hours in prison and the state took away her license for another year.

"I'll let this one go in light of the fact that she is pleading out," then-Assistant State's Attorney T.R. Paulding told the judge. "She, more than anyone in the courtroom, knows what she has to do to take care of her problem with alcohol."

By December 1990, Fletcher was barred from Nurmi's house by a court order to stop him from beating her. But on Dec. 19, he broke in through a cellar window and woke Nurmi at about 3 a.m. She frantically dialed 911, but Fletcher unplugged the telephone and turned his drunken fury on Nurmi.

He beat her with his fists and with the telephone receiver, splitting her lip. Nurmi managed to plug in the telephone and call police while T.J., Trisha and Nicky cried in fear. Police found Fletcher hiding in the basement.

"He told me he would kill me," Nurmi said in a statement to police. "I fear for my life and feel the system isn't helping me." Fletcher was convicted of assault.

East Windsor police caught Nurmi again in May 1991 as she drove out of JR's Cafe and weaved along Bridge Street at 2 a.m. Her car jumped the curb as she pulled over. She refused a breath test.

In slurred speech, Nurmi told the police officer she'd had "quite a few."

"You got me—I'm drunk," she said.

When Nurmi went to court in October, she could have been sent to prison for up to two years. She was given a 45-day jail sentence. She served 14 days.

Nurmi returned to her apartment in Green Valley–Laurel Park on Oct. 24, 1991. There was nothing to stop her from getting behind the wheel again except her suspended license.

Ryan's Story

This section uses Ryan's point of view and past time sequence, also to establish background and character. The structure is parallel to that of the previous section.

Ryan lived most of his life in a two-story duplex in Green Valley–Laurel Park. It's the kind of neighborhood where children play in a patchwork of small back yards, where people know their neighbors, even though some stay only a short time.

Ryan was a careful child, the sort of kid who listened when his parents told him to look three times before crossing the street. He couldn't bring himself to get on roller coasters or ride on the handlebars of his friends' bicycles. But he was also a dreamer who wanted to be a pilot.

He was 7 when his friend, Andrew Welk, also 7, died after being struck by a car in Enfield. For the rest of his life, Ryan carried a photograph of Andrew in his wallet.

Soon after Andrew died, Ryan's grandmother also passed away. Ryan had a question for his mother.

"Why do all good people die?"

Ryan made other friends, such as Paul Paquette. The two would hang out with another buddy and call themselves The Three Stooges.

Once, a few of the boys were playing baseball in Paul's back yard, which bordered the back yard of the house where Patricia Nurmi lived with Scott Fletcher. Paul's mother remembers looking out the window to check on the boys and seeing Nurmi and some friends drinking and smoking on the back porch.

For nine years, Ryan's mother and his father, a warehouse worker, had been working hard to find some-place better. In August 1991, the family moved across town to a house on Hazard Avenue.

That September, Ryan attended Enrico Fermi High School. He stayed close to his old friends, who went to Enfield High, but made new ones quickly. He was a charmer who liked to spend time with people, not schoolbooks. He was a computer whiz, and his mother thought he might make a good accountant or programmer someday. He earned mostly B's and C's on his report cards, A's in math.

Ryan worked hard on assignments that interested him. For one assignment, he put together a list of dreams:

I want my feet to shrink (he wrote about his size 14's).

I want to travel cross-country.

I want no disease in the world.

I want no racism.

I want no hunger in the world.

I want people to die only from old age.

At 15, Ryan already had decided who he wanted to spend his life with.

He found Malissa McCauley, a neighborhood girl with long red hair and soft blue eyes.

"Will you go out with me?" Ryan asked Malissa, getting onto his knees. "Please, will you go out with me?"

Malissa's family lived a few houses down from the Reales' new home. They came from the Bronx to escape the guns and drugs outside their door. In Enfield, Malissa's mother thought, her children could ride bicycles and walk safely on the streets.

"I'm getting married to Malissa McCauley," Ryan wrote on the blue three-ring binder he carried at school. "I love Malissa always and forever."

Ryan and Malissa wanted to go to college, maybe in California. Then they'd get married. They'd have kids at age 26. Eventually, they could both become counselors. He could learn to fly.

Malissa was already signing her last name 'Reale' when she wrote notes to Ryan.

Malissa and Ryan gave each other lots of presents. One was a diamond pre-engagement ring for Malissa.

But the couple's favorite gift came from Ryan's parents—necklaces brought back from California. Each held a silver pendant shaped like half a broken heart with pieces of the words, "Best Friends."

Today, Malissa's piece of the heart dangles near her own.

Ryan wears his half in his grave.

The Fatal Day

This section is still using past time sequence, establishing the plot and points of view of both main characters— Ryan and Nurmi. Smaller subheads divide the section as the focus shifts from one character to another.

While Ryan and Malissa celebrated their anniversary, Nurmi spent the day arguing with Fletcher and drinking.

Nurmi went to the home of her friend, Sharon Dabrowski, where she downed a Budweiser. She drank some more after she drove her children to Booth Road, where another boyfriend, Jim Nisbet, lived.

Near dinnertime, Nurmi called Dabrowski. Nisbet had taken Nicky and T.J. to the store. Nurmi was alone with Trisha, looking for a friend to talk with.

"I'm going to come over to your house in Laurel Park," Nurmi said, slurring her words.

"No, don't. You can't drive with the kids," Dabrowski begged. "Stay there."

"Help Me! Help Me!" At 6:19 p.m., Ryan lay bleeding on Hazard Avenue as Nurmi drove away at about 35 mph, never slowing down.

"Help me! Help me!" Malissa screamed.

One driver chased Nurmi's gray car, another stopped to call 911 on his cellular telephone.

Malissa climbed into a passing couple's car and went down New King Street toward her aunt's house. She jumped from the moving car and ran to tell her aunt what had happened. Then she sat outside rocking back and forth, as her mother, Jackie Wyman, arrived.

"Mommy, Mommy," Malissa sobbed. "Ryan got hit."

Wyman drove Malissa back to the accident scene. Malissa ran to where Ryan lay. Paramedics held her back.

The next time Malissa saw Ryan was in a hospital bed at Baystate Medical Center in Springfield. He was already dead.

"I love you," she whispered at his bedside. "Good bye."

"Mommy Hit Something."
Nurmi pulled her car deep into her driveway, less than 2 miles from the scene of the accident, and parked near a large oak tree that concealed the shattered windshield and dented front fender. She stumbled into the house.

Seven minutes after the accident, for reasons that are not clear, Nurmi telephoned police to complain that Fletcher had threatened her.

Police officers entered Nurmi's house unaware that she was the driver in the hit-and-run. They found her face down on the couch, her eyes glassy and bloodshot. She was having trouble staying awake.

The officers found no evidence of violence, but told Nurmi she was in no condition to take care of Trisha. They left after Fletcher agreed to take the girl to the nearby house of her father, Jose Gonzales.

Shortly after Fletcher and Trisha left, Nurmi walked out the door. She stumbled down the street, weaving from the sidewalk to the grass and back. She thumbed a ride back to Nisbet's house on Booth Road.

As Fletcher and Trisha walked to Gonzales' house, the girl felt a pain in her left foot. She took off her shoe and pulled out a piece of windshield glass. Fletcher saw more glass in the girl's shoes and hair as they started off again.

"What happened?" he asked.

"Mommy hit something," Trisha replied.

The Arrest

About three hours after the accident, Fletcher directed police to Nisbet's house, where they clamped handcuffs on Nurmi's wrists.

An officer drove her to the station and she was read her rights at about 10 p.m. She wrote a statement for police: "I was in the right travel lane and I saw a car passing me on the left and I swerved to the right. I then heard a loud noise and my windshield on the passenger's side shattered. I kept going because I was not thinking."

Almost four hours after the accident, Nurmi's blood-alcohol level was measured at 0.177 percent—close to twice the legal definition of intoxication.

Nurmi stayed overnight in the police lockup. The next morning, her father put up his house to post $25,000 bond and free his daughter.

'Wasn't Ryan Enough?'

Children who knew Ryan waited for justice.

A few of the younger ones sought a symbolic revenge by throwing rocks at Nurmi's empty house. Nurmi was driven from the neighborhood shortly after the accident by a barrage of taunts, epithets and threats.

Some of Ryan's classmates wrote letters to the judge asking for the maximum sentence.

"As far as I am concerned, Ryan's death was not justifiable and will never be," wrote Shannon Crowley. "The woman who hit him, Patricia Nurmi, had no excuse for her actions. . . . Please let justice be served before she harms someone else. Wasn't Ryan enough?"

The Sentence

Last Monday, Nurmi was sentenced in Enfield Superior Court.

Prosecutor Keith B. Duboff, who did not handle Nurmi's previous cases, said the state did everything to stop Nurmi but "shake her by the head and shoulders and scream at her to do something."

"Ms. Nurmi could have done something to prevent this tragedy," Duboff said. "The choices she made led to this."

Her defense attorney, Gerald M. Klein, portrayed her as a woman who had come to comprehend the terrible damage she'd caused. In fact, in the weeks after the accident Nurmi became so remorseful she needed anti-depression medication.

In court, she apologized to Ryan's family.

"I know what I did to these people," she said to the judge tearfully. "I just want to say that I'm sorry."

And she cried when she heard her punishment: eight years in jail and five years' probation. She was sent to the women's prison in Niantic. Her two older children went to live with their father, and Nurmi's sister agreed to take care of Nicky, almost 4.

This last section brings the reader back to the present, and it ends on the future. The point of view shifts from Nurmi to Ryan's family and friends.

Life Without Ryan   Ryan's family hasn't moved many of his things. His bedroom is much as he left it. A deflated helium balloon Malissa gave him for his birthday hangs on the wall above his bed carrying the words "I Love You."

"You come in here and you can feel Ryan," his mother said as she looked around the room.

Malissa has put together a scrapbook of some of the things she shared with Ryan. It includes a ragged piece of Ryan's blue jeans and a toothpick he chewed.

"Now," Malissa says, "I have to plan my whole future over by myself."

At the Reale house, there's an empty seat at the dinner table.

His parents only recently persuaded their other sons to venture to the basement recreation room, which was Ryan's place.

On the top of a bookcase down there, in a spot only Ryan could reach, there are words scrawled in the dust:

"I love Malissa."

Tom Puleo and Laura Ungar, The Hartford (Conn.) *Courant*

Exercises

1   Inverted pyramid exercise: Organize the information for this story in the inverted pyramid order. Here are your notes, based on a story from The Associated Press:

Who: Connecticut State Police

What: Ordered ban of hand-held radar guns

When: Yesterday

Where: Meriden, Conn.

Why: Because of concerns that troopers could develop cancer from long-term exposure to the radiation waves emitted by the devices. The ban was ordered as a precaution while studies are conducted into the possible links between cancer and use of the devices.

How: The ban affects 70 radar guns that will be withdrawn from service. State troopers will continue to use radar units with transmitters mounted on the outside of their cruisers.

Source: Adam Berluti, a state police spokesman

Backup information: "The feeling here is to err on the side of caution until more is known about the issue," Berluti said. "The whole situation is under review."

The move is considered to be the first of its kind by a state police agency. It comes two months after three municipal police officers in Connecticut filed workers' compensation claims, saying they developed cancer from using hand-held radar guns.

2   *Wall Street Journal* formula exercise: Organize this story according to the *Wall Street Journal* formula. The information is taken from a *Los Angeles Times* story by Barry M. Horstman and Jennifer Toth. Use an anecdotal lead, and label your nut graph. There is no one right order. Write the story so it reads smoothly. To give you a clue, here are the headline and summary lines that appeared above the story:

Answer to Idealism or Joblessness

Volunteer agencies are seeing a surge of interest from college seniors. For some students it's a shift away from the Me Decade. For others, it's mostly the path to a paycheck.

The flood of young applicants eager for public service contradicts common assumptions about the supposed apathy of the twenty-something generation.

Volunteerism, seen at best in recent years as a well-intentioned diversion from the fast track, is being increasingly viewed by college students as a logical entry point into the workplace instead of postponement of a career.

College students already account for a growing share of the 3,300-member volunteer force of VISTA (Volunteers in Service to America)—about 240 of whom work in California. People 55 and older make up another 20 percent, as do people without college degrees between 18 and 27. The remainder of the volunteers are widely distributed among other age groups.

"I'm basically very, very conservative, so I'm skeptical about a lot of government programs," said Douglas May, a VISTA volunteer working in Los Angeles' Chrysalis project in a job-development program for the unemployed. "But I like the idea of putting a federally paid volunteer in the hands of a private nonprofit organization. That's much more effective."

Teach for America also has struck a responsive chord on college campuses. When news of its establishment hit campuses in 1990, the organization received 2,500 applications for 500 positions. Last year it had 3,100 applications and accepted 700 people, about 90 percent of them recent college graduates.

A stagnant economy, changing attitudes toward volunteer work and heightened interest in world affairs have given organizations such as the Peace Corps, VISTA and Teach for America a higher profile on college campuses, generating applications at an unparalleled rate.

In the first week of January, for example, the Peace Corps' Washington telephone lines were jammed with so many calls—nearly 900 a day at one point—that the system broke down, according to Mike Berning, the agency's director of recruitment. At the same time last year, the Peace Corps' information hot line drew 150 to 200 calls a day, he added.

Recent visits to campuses in Los Angeles, Claremont and San Diego produced recruiting dividends, as VISTA staffers had no difficulty luring applicants for low-paying positions in programs that deal with homelessness, drug abuse, hunger and unemployment.

At the Peace Corps, the pendulum's swing back toward volunteerism has been fueled by enthusiasm over serving in former communist bloc nations. Over the next year, the Peace Corps plans to open 250 to 500 field positions in the Commonwealth of Independent States, formerly the Soviet Union.

From the perspective of some top federal administrators, the volunteer agencies' resurgence on campus is seen as a return to the 1960s style of idealism after the self-absorption of the Me Decade of the 1980s, when college graduates felt compelled to land high-paying jobs and quickly move up career ladders.

William Baldwin, a University of Southern California senior contemplating several volunteer options, said many students are "learning that there's more to being satisfied than making $50,000, $60,000 a year."

"The '80s showed us that those values may be satisfying in the short run," Baldwin said. "But eventually they go belly up. These programs have a lasting value that isn't going to disappear."

In contrast to the subsistence allowances received by VISTA and Peace Corps volunteers, Teach for America volunteers are paid normal starting salaries by local schools, ranging from $15,000 in rural Arkansas to $29,000 in Los Angeles.

For many volunteers, altruistic motivations override economic concerns.

Some even bypass lucrative private-sector alternatives, as did Jameson Hill, a 27-year-old Teach for America instructor in rural Louisiana. He passed up a job in international banking.

"College students are a lot more idealistic than the media give them credit for," said Teach for America founder Wendy Kopp, whose program recruits graduates who majored in fields other than education to spend two years teaching in needy school districts.

"This isn't a '60s thing for me—I'm not a neo-hippy," said USC senior Beth Lipton, a journalism major whose bleak job prospects have led her to consider joining VISTA. "I'm interested in doing something about literacy, but I'm also interested in finding a job. I know people with master's degrees who are driving taxis, so I'm trying to be flexible."

When he graduated from Northwestern University and fulfilled his Navy ROTC obligation, Marty Siewart did not anticipate that he would spend seven months unemployed, soberly pondering the real-world value of his college degree and military experience.

Discouraged and "just about to get panicky" over his job search, Siewart finally landed with a federal poverty-fighting program in Hollywood where, paradoxically, he tries to help others find employment.

"I've always been interested in social service, so this is a good opportunity to get a better feel for it," said Siewart, sitting in the small, cluttered office from which he finds temporary jobs for teen-age runaways and homeless youths. "Plus with the economy the way it is, I feel lucky to be working here—or anywhere."

Emblematic of a rise in volunteerism among college-age individuals that blends idealism with economic realities, Siewart recently began a one-year enlistment in VISTA, the Great Society—era federal agency dedicated to alleviating poverty.

Anita Fuchslocher, a Teach for America kindergarten teacher in Los Angeles, admits being relieved when she was accepted by the program and no longer had to worry about overcoming difficult economic conditions in New England, where she went to college and where her family lives.

"I saw so many friends having trouble finding good jobs that I was really scared," Fuchslocher said. "So I was happy when this came along."

3   Hourglass structure exercise: Arrange these facts in hourglass order, placing attribution where it is needed. (This story is taken from the *St. Louis Post-Dispatch.*) Attribute information to Capt. Ed Kemp of the Jefferson County Sheriff's Department, unless otherwise noted.

Who: Two bank couriers

What: Helped police capture four suspects in a robbery

When: Last night

Where: At the Boatman's Bank of Pevely, Mo.

How: One courier, Dennis Boushie, who lives near Festus, chased a suspect on foot. The other courier, Willie Moore of St. Louis, drove a bank van, chasing a getaway car.

Police have booked three people on suspicion of drug possession. The three, who were found in the getaway car, are being held in the jail at Pevely.

Backup information: "This is beyond the call of duty. They acted more like police officers than private citizens or bank couriers," said Capt. Ed Kemp.

Boushie said he had asked the teller who was robbed if the robber had a weapon, and she said he did not. He said his pursuit of the robber had been "just common sense."

A man entered the bank shortly after it opened Tuesday morning and shouted, "Give me the money or else!" The teller gave the man an envelope containing the money, and the man ran out the front door.

Boushie chased the man on foot, and when the suspect jumped into a car, Boushie pointed the car out to Moore, who pursued it in a bank van. A few minutes later, Boushie got in a police patrol car and helped police track the getaway car.

The getaway car pulled off the highway and let out a man, who ran into the woods. Police arrested a man near Barnhart after a 10-minute search.

Police broadcast a description of the getaway car, which had continued north on I-55 carrying two men and a woman. Police spotted the car, stopped it and arrested three suspects.

Police said they had found several thousand dollars in the car. The female suspect had stuffed money down her pants, police said.

Police were seeking federal warrants for bank robbery.

4   List technique exercise: Write this story (based on a story from the United Press International wire service) using the list technique:

Who: Report of a study by the National Institute for Occupational Safety and Health

When: Report issued in today's *New England Journal of Medicine*

What: Findings that working at a video display terminal (VDT) does not increase the risk of miscarriage

Why: No significant difference in miscarriage rates between the two groups of women studied

How: Survey conducted among 2,430 telephone operators over a four-year period

Background and elaboration: From Teresa Schnorr, government epidemiologist: "We looked at the question every which way and could find nothing. The answer is clear—there's nothing about the VDTs that causes spontaneous abortions."

The study included some of these details: Half of the women worked at terminals and half did not. Of the women in the study, 730 got pregnant during the study period, some more than once, for a total of 876 pregnancies. Over the four-year study period, there was no significant difference in miscarriage rates between the two groups (those who did and did not work at terminals). The results held true no matter how many hours a week the women sat at terminals and during the entire pregnancy.

From Karen Nussbaum, executive director of 9 to 5, National Association of Working Women, who was critical of the study: "We continue to get reports from VDT users having fertility problems."

"We are pleased with these findings," says David Legrande, health and safety director, Communications Workers of America.

5   Pyramid structure exercise: Write this story using pyramid form. Here are your notes, based on information from a story by the McClatchy News Service:

Who: Burglars who broke into a shoe warehouse twice in one week

What: They ransacked the place, causing about $5,000 in damage.

When: This week

Why: Because they were infuriated. Among the 50,000 shoes, no two pieces matched.

Background: Attribute to Georgia Hehr, a Sacramento nurse who founded One Shoe Crew, the owners of the shoe warehouse. One Shoe Crew is a nonprofit group that supplies new footwear to amputees and people who have different size feet. Hehr founded the organization about five years ago. Her feet aren't the same size. She was forced to buy two pairs of shoes to get one that fit before she founded this organization.

"Apparently, when all (the burglars) found was one-sies, they got so mad they destroyed our desk equipment."

One Shoe Crew gets the shoes free from manufacturers. It distributes them to customers who pay only the postage, a one-time registration fee and, if they can afford it, a small handling charge.

6 **Sections technique exercise:** Find a long story or project in a newspaper, and organize it in section form. Mark where it could be divided into sections, and rewrite the kickers if needed.

COACHING

Gather as many specific details as possible while you are reporting. Take notes of your observations as well as information from sources.

Use show-in-action techniques. Describe what people are doing.

Use vivid action verbs.

For narrative writing, try to envision yourself at the scene. Gather details and chronology to reconstruct events as they occurred.

Think of your story as a plot with a beginning, middle and climax. Envision your sources as characters in a book; make your reader see, hear and care about them.

To write well, read well. Read as much fiction and nonfiction as you can, and study the writing styles.

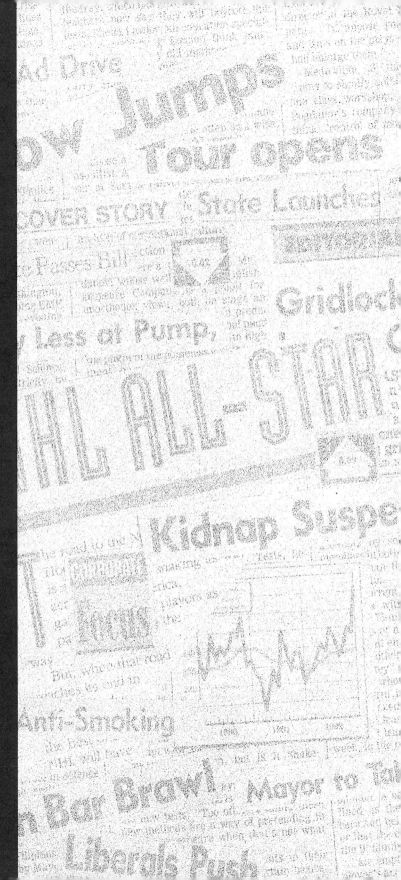

13

Storytelling and Feature Techniques

> The victim wasn't rich. She wasn't the daughter of anyone powerful. She was simply a 36-year-old woman trying to make a life for herself. Her name was Karen Gregory. The night she died, Karen became part of a numbing statistic. . . . It was what people sometimes casually refer to as "a little murder."
>
> Tom French, *St. Petersburg* (Fla.) *Times*

Tom French was fascinated by Karen Gregory's case. He wrote a 10-part series about her murder and the man on trial for it. It was called "A Cry in the Night."

Something very unusual happened when the series began. Readers ran out to greet the newspaper delivery trucks each day to get the next chapter in the series. Why were they so eager to read these stories?

You decide. The previous passage was an introduction to the series. The first story began with this description of the trial of George Lewis, a firefighter who lived across the street from Karen Gregory and was charged with her murder:

We're supposed to be tellers of tales as well as purveyors of facts. When we don't live up to that responsibility, we don't get read.

Bill Blundell, The Art and Craft of Feature Writing

His lawyer called out his name. He stood up, put his hand on a Bible and swore to tell the truth and nothing but. He sat down in the witness box and looked toward the jurors so they could see his face and study it and decide for themselves what kind of man he was.

"Did you rape Karen Gregory?" asked his lawyer.

"No sir, I did not."

"Did you murder Karen Gregory?"

"No sir."

He heard a scream that night, he said. He heard it, and he went out to the street to look around. He saw a man he did not know, standing over in Karen's yard. The man said to go away, to not tell anyone what he'd seen. He waited for the man to leave—watched him walk away into the darkness—and then he went up to Karen's house. There was broken glass on the front walk. He knocked on the front door. There was no answer. He found an open window. He called out to ask whether anyone needed help. There was still no answer. He looked through the window and saw someone lying on the floor. He decided he had to go in. He climbed inside, and there was Karen. Blood was everywhere.

He was afraid. He ran to the bathroom and threw up. He knew no one would believe how he had ended up standing inside that house with her body. He had to get out of there. He was running toward the window to climb out when he saw something moving in the dark. He thought someone was jumping toward him. Then he realized he was looking at a mirror, and the only person moving was him. It was his own reflection that had startled him. It was George.

Tom French, *St. Petersburg Times*

The entire series was written like a mystery novel. But it was all true, based on interviews with more than 50 people and 6,000 pages of court documents. The writing style, called narrative writing, is a form of dramatic storytelling that reconstructs the events as though the reader were witnessing them as they happened. French later turned the series into a book called *Unanswered Cries.*

French says he never believed his series would be so popular. "The way the readers responded was so gratifying," he says.

French relied heavily on dialogue throughout the series, even from the dead woman. Although most of the dialogue and description are based on interviews and his own observations, Karen's dialogue was second-hand information, based on recollections about her.

"After I wrote it, I spent three weeks checking everything with all the participants," French says. "I read it to them word for word to make sure it was accurate."

Narrative storytelling requires very detailed reporting. The writing is equally difficult, especially if you have interviewed more than 50 people and used thousands of documents to gather the information.

Although less dramatic than a murder mystery, a series on life in a Florida high school became compelling reading when French used dialogue and show-in-action description for storytelling.

Those two types of writing—narrative and descriptive—are the basic writing tools of storytelling.

Tom French
Photo by Todd Richardson, courtesy of Tom French

In this passage about a history teacher's first day in school, you can see how French uses descriptive writing. The teacher, Mr. Samsel, has given his homeroom students some forms to fill out.

The future leaders of America sit silently, some of them slumped forward, staring into space through half-closed eyes. Over to the side sits a boy. He is wearing a crucifix, blue jeans and a T-shirt. On the front of the shirt is a big smiley face. In the center of the face's forehead is a bullet hole, dripping blood. . . .

Around the room, students begin writing.

"Isn't this great?" says Samsel. "Just like real life—forms and everything."

Smiley Face looks at one of the sheets in front of him. He reads aloud as he fills it out.

"Please list medical problems."

He stops.

"Brain dead," he says.

Tom French, *St. Petersburg Times*

Once again readers lined up at the delivery trucks every morning to get the next chapter in the seven-part series. They were fascinated with the stories about the lives of the students and the troubling picture they revealed about education. As a result, French also turned the school series into a nonfiction book, *South of Heaven.*

French did not become a compelling storyteller without effort. Good writers are good readers, and French said he was inspired to do narrative writing after he read a book by a Latin American writer, Gabriel Garcia Marquez. *The Story of a Shipwrecked Sailor* is a riveting story about a man who survived 10 days at sea without food and water.

French also was influenced by the literary journalists, a group of writers who, in the 1960s and 1970s, used the storytelling techniques of fiction for nonfiction newspaper and magazine stories. These journalists—Joan Didion, John McPhee, Tracy Kidder and Tom Wolfe—were influenced by Truman Capote's nonfiction book, *In Cold Blood.* The literary journalists immersed themselves in a subject and wrote their stories with characters, scene, dialogue and plot. They were factual stories written like fiction.

Storytelling still includes the basic factual elements of news, but the presentation differs. Jeff Klinkenberg, another *St. Petersburg Times* writer, views the five W's this way: *Who* is character, *what* is plot, *when* is chronology, *why* is motive, and *where* is place or scene.

Journalists often think storytelling techniques are limited to feature stories, but as you will see, you can apply this kind of writing to news about crime, courts and many other daily news stories. But first you need to understand the mind-set of a storyteller.

Storytelling Concepts

Christopher Scanlan was on his first job at a small newspaper in Connecticut. He was sent to cover a drowning in a park. As Scanlan watched, divers surfaced with the body of the boy, clad only in his jeans. Nearby the boy's mother had been chain smoking and beating "a tattoo in the dust" with her feet as she waited for news of her son. Scanlan wanted to describe the scene and the mother's anguish. But when he returned to the newsroom, his attempts at storytelling were futile. He tried many leads, but none of them worked. In frustration and faced with the deadline, he settled on a summary lead that said something like this: "A 17-year-old Milford youth drowned yesterday in the lake at the park."

Scanlan says he knew he had a good story to tell, but he didn't have the storytelling tools. He describes the incident to working journalists, whom he trains in storytelling techniques at the Poynter Institute for Media Studies, where he is director of writing programs.

One of those storytelling tools is finding your focus, as recommended many times in this book. Scanlan tells writers to ask themselves these two questions: What's the news, and what's the point? Then he advises them to look for pivotal moments that make a story dramatic, such as

When things change

When things will never be the same

When things begin to fall apart

When we learn lessons

When you don't know how things will turn out

He also suggests that you change your point of view. Instead of writing the story from your point of view as the uninvolved observer, consider writing the story through the eyes of someone on the scene, especially someone affected by the incident.

That is precisely what Suzanne Sataline did to convey the drama from a news event like the one Scanlan covered on his first job. Sataline told the story through the eyes of the man who rescued a woman from an icy river, also in Connecticut. Like Tom French, she used the narrative writing technique of reconstructing the event through the character's eyes and the descriptive technique of showing the rescuer in action so readers feel as if they are witnessing the event.

When Ian J. O'Brien started out Friday morning, he was a commuter. Along the way he became a hero.

Waiting in a line of cars on Hartford Avenue about 7:30 a.m., he saw a woman pull her Chevy Blazer out onto Route 9 and hit an icy patch, and go into a spin. The Blazer slid over an embankment of trees and into the Connecticut River.

"As soon as I realized she was going over the bank, I realized *somebody* has to go in," said O'Brien, 26, of East Hampton. "Who else was going to do it?"

He parked his car and ran down the slope and stripped his jacket off. He jumped in the icy water. As the front end of the Blazer sank, he heard the screams of Mary K. Kokoszka, 61, of Middlefield.

He swam to the closest door, the passenger side, and noticed the window was slightly open. "As soon as she saw me, she calmed down," he said. "I told her to open the window, but she said she couldn't."

He struggled to get the door open, but it wouldn't budge. With the nose of the car submerged, he went around the back, seeking frantically for a way to get Kokoszka out.

"The truck was sinking more and more, and I told her to hold her breath," said O'Brien, a technician at Raymond Engineering in Middletown.

The Blazer went under rapidly, hitting bottom in about 10 to 12 feet of water. O'Brien lost sight of Kokoszka, so he dived down into the murky water.

He started kicking at the back window. It wouldn't give.

"I didn't have the feeling she was OK. I was really, really scared that she wasn't. For a minute there, I was at a loss for something to do."

Then, someone in the small crowd along the shore yelled "Driver's door!"

O'Brien swam around. The door was locked, but the window was open. He reached inside, trying to work the door handle. It wouldn't budge. He surfaced, gasping for air, then went under again.

Seeing something dark inside, he reached inside the window. It was her purse. He took another breath and returned.

"I saw something again and just grabbed it," he said. It was her arm, and he pulled her through the opened window.

When they came to the surface—about five minutes after the car first went in—Kokoszka was still holding her breath, her lips tinged a faint blue. She was clutching her glasses. "Everyone on shore told her to breathe," O'Brien said.

The two were treated for exposure at Middlesex Hospital and released. Meanwhile, teams of divers

from the police and fire departments worked until after noon to remove the car, submerged about 65 feet from shore.

Kokoszka rested in bed Friday afternoon. Her grown children, William and Carole, said she was having trouble remembering much of anything, except being at the traffic light in the Blazer she had borrowed that day from her son. Her children took a message to O'Brien, from her, to thank him "from the bottom of her heart."

O'Brien, staying home from work, tried to keep warm in his heated waterbed.

Nothing like this had ever happened to him, he admitted. He had pulled a friend from a stream when he was 6 or 7, but "it was no big deal," O'Brien said. "I'm a good swimmer."

Suzanne Sataline, *The Hartford* (Conn.) *Courant*

Compare that story with this hard-news version written from the point of view of the uninvolved reporter/observer:

A 61-year-old Middlefield woman was rescued yesterday after her vehicle slid over an embankment and into the Connecticut River.

Mary K. Kokoszka was driving onto Route 9 from Hartford Avenue about 7:30 a.m. when her vehicle, a Chevy Blazer, hit an icy patch, police said. She was trapped inside the Blazer, which sank rapidly in about 10 to 12 feet of water in the freezing river.

A commuter who was driving on Hartford Avenue saw the accident and stopped to help, police said. Ian J. O'Brien, 26, of East Hampton, dived into the river and pulled Kokoszka through an open window of the submerged car, police said.

The two were treated for exposure at Middlesex Hospital and released. Teams of divers from the police and fire departments worked until after noon to remove the car, submerged about 65 feet from shore.

Kokoszka was resting at home. Her children said she didn't remember much of anything, except being at the traffic light in the Blazer she had borrowed that day from her son. They took a message to O'Brien, from her, to thank him "from the bottom of her heart."

O'Brien, reached at his home, said, "It was no big deal. I'm a good swimmer."

Which do you prefer? The differences between the two versions are the point of view, the human element and the style—narrative and descriptive writing filled with detail and dramatic action. As you can see in the first version, the writer used storytelling in a basic news story. You can use the same techniques in feature stories.

What's the difference between hard-news and feature stories? Sometimes not much. Hard news is often defined as timely stories about events that happened or are about to happen. Likewise, feature stories can be timely stories about events or people, but they can also be stories about general topics, profiles or a certain angle on the news, particularly human interest. By dictionary definition, *to feature* means "to give special prominence to"—in other words, to focus on one aspect of an issue and give that special attention.

Although both types of stories can be enhanced by storytelling techniques, before you can do this type of writing, you need to develop the reporting tools of a storyteller.

Reporting Tools

Mary Ann Lickteig has a storyteller's instincts. A feature writer and columnist for *The Des Moines* (Iowa) *Register,* she knows how to find extraordinary angles in ordinary events.

It is summer, and Lickteig is covering the annual Iowa State Fair. She is strolling from one booth to another in search of a good feature story. A pitchman is hawking a Robo-Cut slicing machine. Space-age plastic, he bellows. Lickteig laughs. Great angle for a story, she thinks.

Backstage at the pageant to choose the state fair queen, 77 girls are primping and practicing to compete for the crown. Lickteig decides that will be a good angle for another story.

Now it is midnight. The fairgoers have gone home. Lickteig has not. In the center of the midway, a Catholic priest is baptizing four children. Lickteig listens. She can hear pool balls cracking in the background, where carnival workers may be playing.

The next day *Des Moines Register* readers will hear them, too, when Lickteig writes about the baptism and describes the empty paths in the midway—quiet "except for the hum of a giant generator and the occasional crack of pool balls." Or when she describes these sights and smells in this excerpt:

Mary Ann Lickteig, feature writer and columnist

The day before the fair opened to the public, hot dogs spit as they turned on roasters; tattooed midway workers smeared with grease hauled pieces of steel out of the back of trucks and turned them into carnival rides; brand new pig feeders stood waiting to be admired under a sign that pronounced them non-rusting, non-caking and non-corrosive.

Odors emanating from the horse barn indicated the exhibits had arrived.

Mary Ann Lickteig, *The Des Moines Register*

These are the kinds of stories that you probably will do when you get started at a newspaper. Even with almost 10 years of experience, Lickteig said she still loves writing features about the state fair and other routine kinds of stories.

Lickteig always looks for a good angle or theme for her features. The focus is the reason for the story, which should be stated in a nut graph, but the theme is a literary device of an angle or unifying approach.

"You hope the theme will present itself," Lickteig says. "Usually, if you see something that fascinates you, it probably will fascinate the readers."

That's one way to find either the theme or just an idea for a story, she says. "I don't think about covering the whole Iowa State Fair. You need to break it down—show the fair through one family, one idea, one theme."

The key to good feature writing is gathering good details and then selecting the ones that will work in your story.

"You want people to be able to see your story," Lickteig says. "Choose the details that stick out in your mind, the ones you remember when you run back to the office and tell somebody what you've found."

Like the last 83 steps of a man's life. Lickteig was writing a story about a man who had murdered three women and had spent 17 years on death row. He was scheduled to be executed. Lickteig wanted to convey what steps were involved in execution—figuratively and literally. So she walked from the inmate's cell to the electric chair, in 83 steps.

These kinds of observation techniques are crucial tools for a storyteller.

William Ruehlmann, author of *Stalking the Feature Story,* says writers must concentrate when they observe and then analyze what they observe. He gives this example: "Flies take off backward. So in order to swat one, you must strike slightly behind him. An interesting detail, and certainly one a writer would be able to pick up on. Other people see flies; a writer sees how they move."

During the reporting process, you don't always know what details you will need when you write your story. So gather all the details you can—from how many steps to the electric chair to what the inmate had for his last meal. Ask what were people thinking, saying, hearing, smelling, wearing and feeling. Be precise.

To help you gather specific details, envision a ladder with rungs leading from general to specific. Start with the broadest noun, and take it to the most specific level. For example:

A dog

A Lhasa apso

A tan and white Lhasa apso

A tan and white Lhasa apso named Joe

A tan and white Lhasa apso named Joe after Joe DiMaggio

Ladder of Details

A tan and white Lhasa apso named Joe ran onto the baseball field and interrupted the game when he stole the ball. It was only natural. After all, his namesake was Joe DiMaggio.

Writing Tools

You've gathered all those details. Now what do you do with them? The better you are as a reporter, the more you will struggle as a writer deciding what information to use. The two basic tools of storytelling are descriptive and narrative writing techniques.

Descriptive Techniques

Too much description will clutter a story. Too little will leave the reader blank. How much is enough? First decide if the story lends itself to description of the scene or person. Then take the advice of Bruce DeSilva, a writing coach and editor of enterprise stories for The Associated Press.

> Description, like every element in either fiction or nonfiction, should advance the meaning of your story. It would be a good idea to describe the brown house in more detail only if those details are important. Description never should be there for decoration. It never should be there because you are showing off. And when you do describe, you should never use more words than you need to trigger that mental image readers already have in their minds.

> Some techniques for good descriptive writing include the following.

Avoid adjectives   Write specific detail with vivid nouns and verbs, but avoid modifiers. When you use adjectives, you run the risk of inserting your opinions into the story. Author Norman Mailer put it this way:

> The adjective is the author's opinion of what is going on, no more. If I write, "A strong man came into the room," that only means he is strong in relation to me. Unless I've established myself for the reader, I might be the only fellow in the bar who is impressed by the guy who just came in. It is better to say: "A man entered. He was holding a walking stick, and for some reason, he now broke it in two like a twig." Of course, this takes more time to narrate. So adjectives bring on quick tell-you-how-to-live writing. Advertising thrives on it. "A super-efficient, silent, sensuous, five-speed shift." Put 20 adjectives before a noun and no one will know you are describing a turd.

Use analogies   A good analogy compares a vague concept to something familiar to readers. For example, what is a "fat" man? David Finkel leaves no doubt in his story about a circus performer. How do you visualize the "World's Biggest Man" at 891 pounds? Finkel uses familiar items to help the reader see.

> Now: 891 and climbing. That's more than twice as much as Sears' best refrigerator-freezer—a 26-cubic-footer with automatic ice and water dispensers on side-by-side doors. That's almost as much as a Steinway grand piano.

David Finkel, *St. Petersburg Times*

Limit physical descriptions   Use physical descriptions only when they are relevant to the content. They work well in profiles, in stories about crime, courts and disasters, and whenever they fit with the context. They don't work when they are tacked onto impersonal quotes.

Avoid stage directions, descriptions of people's gestures, facial expressions and physical characteristics inserted artificially as though you were directing a play. You don't need to describe what city commissioners are wearing at a meeting or how they gesture unless their clothing and movements enhance what they are saying and doing.

Effective	**Ineffective**
A Florida jury needed only 77 minutes to find that William Kennedy Smith was not guilty of raping a woman at his family's estate in March, bringing to a swift end the most highly publicized trial of its kind in recent times. Smith first closed his eyes, then broke into a small smile when the verdict was read. And clearly jubilant, he bounded to his feet and embraced his main lawyer, Roy Black, in a clumsy bearhug.	The study shows college students are becoming more conservative, the researcher said, blinking her blue eyes and clasping her carefully manicured hands.

Paul Richter, *Los Angeles Times*

The color of the researcher's eyes and her hand motions have nothing to do with her comments about the study.

Avoid sexist/racist descriptions   When you decide to include descriptions of people, beware of sexism, racism or other biased writing. Writers often describe men with action verbs showing what they are doing and women with adjectives showing what they are wearing and how they look. One way to avoid bias is to ask yourself if you would use a similar description for both men and women or equal treatment for all racial and ethnic groups.

Consider this example:

Ineffective

> Even Chandra Smith, busy being adorable in her perky non-runner's running outfit, actually looked at the track. A minute later, she was jumping around and yelling, along with most of the other 41,600 people on the old wooden benches at Franklin Field.
>
> *The Philadelphia Inquirer*

The story about the Penn Relay Carnival, a track meet in Philadelphia, also mentions a few men among those 41,600 people, including some volunteers who wear gray trousers and red caps. But they aren't adorable or perky.

Show people in action   One of the most effective ways to describe people or places is to show action. Cheryl Lavin, a feature writer, always uses description to let the reader see her subjects, from what they are wearing to how they sound. But her description relates to the story. Here is an excerpt from a profile about George Burns when he was 90:

> From stage right walks a little old man, stooped over, wearing a tuxedo in a size that would fit a bar mitzvah boy. There's a neat little gray toupee on his suntanned head, shiny black shoes on his tiny feet, a perky red silk hanky in his breast pocket. His eyes are sparkling behind his round black-rimmed glasses; his ears are huge. He looks like an organ grinder's monkey.
>
> When he gets to center stage—he's taking his time about it—he turns to the audience and says what they're all thinking: "Look at that! And he walks, too!" Then he carefully flicks the ashes off his big, smelly El Producto, waits for the laugh, gets it, and rolls right on to the next bit. His timing, as ever, is impeccable.
>
> "Usually a performer gets a standing ovation at the end of his act," he says, his head engulfed in a cloud of smoke. "I get mine at the beginning. You're afraid I won't make it."
>
> Cheryl Lavin, *Chicago Tribune*

Chapter 18 will deal with racist and sexist writing in more detail.

Use lively verbs   News is action, says Jack Hart, *The* (Portland) *Oregonian's* writing coach. But writers often "squeeze the life out of an action-filled world," he says. "We write that thousands of bullet holes were in the hotel, instead of noting that the holes pocked the hotel. We report that a jumper died Monday when his parachute failed, instead of turning to action verbs such as *plummeted* or *plunged* or *streamed*."

Mitch Albom, a sportswriter, knows the value of action verbs. Notice the ones he uses in this story about the day Detroit Tigers baseball player Cecil Fielder hit his 50th home run. Also notice the analogies and the show-in-action description.

He swung the bat and he heard that smack! and the ball screamed into the dark blue sky, higher, higher, until it threatened to bring a few stars down with it. His teammates knew; they leaped off the bench. The fans knew; they roared like animals. And finally, the man who all year refused to watch his home runs, the man who said this 50 thing was "no big deal"—finally even he couldn't help himself. He stopped halfway to first base and watched the ball bang into the facing of the upper deck in Yankee Stadium, waking up the ghosts of Maris and Ruth and Gehrig.

And then, for the first time in this miraculous season, Cecil Fielder jumped. He jumped like a man sprung from prison, he jumped like a kid on the last day of school, he jumped, all 250 pounds of Detroit Bambino, his arms over his head, his huge smile a beacon of celebration and relief.

The Big Five-O.

Mitch Albom, *Detroit Free Press*

Set the scene   You need to set the scene by establishing where and when. Although it is common to establish the time and weather, often in a lead, beware of using that technique unless time and weather factors are relevant to your story. "It was 2 a.m. and the wind was blowing" is akin to the cliche "It was a dark and stormy night." In this story from the California State University student newspaper, the time and weather conditions are relevant to the story:

TIJUANA, Mexico—Shivering in the mud under a 2-foot high chaparral, Jose carefully lifts his head into the cold night mist to monitor the movements of the U.S. Border Patrol.

On a ridge above a small ravine, patrol trucks scurry back and forth while a helicopter above provides the only light, turning spots of the nighttime terrain into day.

In the distance, guard dogs growl, bark and yelp.

At one point a patrol truck speeds toward Jose and his group of six Mexican farm laborers. Squatting in the brush, they quickly slide flat into the mud like reptiles seeking shelter.

Within seconds the helicopter hovers above them as its search light passes nearby, then at once directly over them. All their faces are turned downward to avoid detection by the brightness of the light that illuminates every detail of the soil, roots and insects that lie inches under them.

Soon, the truck and helicopter make a slow retreat. Jose and his group, safe for the moment, will remain motionless in that same muddy spot for the next three hours as the mist turns to rain and the rain turns back to mist.

To those who have never passed this way before, the sights and sounds are of another world. But to the expert scouts called "coyotes," this alien land between Mexico and the United States is home.

Every weekday evening, approximately 2,000 people attempt to illegally cross the border from Mexico to the United States. On weekends the numbers can climb to between 5,000 and 10,000, said Victor Clark, director of the Binational Center for Human Rights in Tijuana, Mexico.

Brett C. Sporich, (Long Beach, Calif.) *Daily Forty Niner*

Nut graphs

In the next example, the story is about a reading program. Although the lead about the weather is backed up by a quote, the weather has nothing to do with the focus or the rest of the story.

It was a beautiful springlike Sunday, and the heat on the first floor of the Kansas City Public Library Downtown was on full-blast. But that didn't stop about 400 people from crowding inside to read and hear their favorite selections from African-American authors.

The crowd, people of all ages and races, was there to take part in the national Read-In sponsored by the Black Caucus of the National Teachers of English.

"That is true commitment," said Mamie Isler, program director for Genesis School, which helped coordinate the event in Kansas City.

The second annual Kansas City Read-In opened with a performance by 30 students from the Genesis School choir and a word from Mayor Emanuel Cleaver.

The Kansas City (Mo.) *Star*

Narrative Techniques

Narrative writing combines show-in-action description, dialogue, plot and reconstruction of an event as it occurred. It puts the reader on the scene as though he or she were witnessing it. This type of writing requires a bond of faith with the reader, because attribution is limited. You need to make it clear where you got the information, but you don't need to attribute repeatedly. You also can use an overview attribution for portions of the story and then attribute periodically, especially when you are quoting sources.

Before you can do narrative writing, you need to do thorough reporting. It takes a different kind of questioning to gather the information you will need to reconstruct a scene with dialogue and detail. Narrative writing is not fiction. You must stick to the facts even though the story may read like a novel. You need to ask questions like these: What were you thinking at the time? What were you feeling? What did you say? What were you wearing? What were you doing? You need to get details about colors, sounds, sights, smells, sizes, shapes, times, places.

If you were witnessing the event, you would see, hear, smell and feel—perhaps even taste—the experiences of your subject. Since you are reconstructing the event, you need to ask the questions that will evoke all those images.

Those are the kinds of questions Jane Schorer asked when she wrote this Pulitzer Prize–winning story about a woman who had been raped. In this opening part of her series, Schorer sets the scene (with relevant weather and time references) and reconstructs the woman's experience so the reader is a witness to the event:

She would have to allow extra driving time because of the fog.

A heavy gray veil had enveloped Grinnell overnight, and Nancy Ziegenmeyer—always methodical, always in control—decided to leave home early for her 7:30 a.m. appointment at Grand View College in Des Moines.

It was Nov. 19, 1988, a day Ziegenmeyer had awaited eagerly, because she knew that whatever happened during those morning hours in Des Moines would determine her future. If she passed the state real-estate licensing exam that Saturday morning, she would begin a new career. If she failed the test, she would continue the child-care service she provided in her home.

At 6 a.m. Ziegenmeyer unlocked the door of her 1988 Pontiac Grand Am and tossed her long denim jacket in the back seat. The weather was mild for mid-November, and her Gloria Vanderbilt denim jumper, red turtleneck sweater and red wool tights would keep her warm enough without a coat.

The fog lifted as Ziegenmeyer drove west on Interstate Highway 80 and she made good time after all. The digital clock on the dashboard read 7:05 as she pulled into a parking lot near Grand View's Science Building. She had 25 minutes to sit in the car and review her notes before test time.

Suddenly the driver's door opened. She turned to see a man, probably in his late 20s, wearing a navy pin-striped suit. He smelled of alcohol.

"Move over," the man ordered, grabbing her neck. She instinctively reached up to scratch him, but he was stronger than she was. He pushed a white dish towel into her face and shoved her into the front passenger seat, reclining it to a nearly horizontal position. Then he took her denim jacket from the back seat and covered her head.

He wasn't going to hurt her, the man said; he wanted money. She reached toward the console for the only cash she had with her—$3 or $4—and gave it to him. He slid the driver's seat back to make room for his long legs, started the car and drove out of the parking lot.

"Is this guy going to kill me?" Ziegenmeyer wondered. "Is he going to rape me? Does he just want my money? Does he want my car?" She thought about her three children—ages 4, 5, and 7—and realized she might never see them again.

Jane Schorer, *The Des Moines Register*

Use foreshadowing   When you give a clue about something that will happen later in the story, you are using foreshadowing. It is a way of providing mystery and teasing the reader to continue. In this example, the writer teases the reader by indicating that more ghostly experiences are coming:

SULLIVAN HARBOR, Maine— Gail Stamp was doing the dishes when she heard a noise in the hall stairway. Her husband was away, and she thought she was alone in the living quarters over the store here.

Stamp doesn't scare easily, so she went to investigate. She entered the hallway, and there, at the top of the stairs, she saw the gray form of a man.

"I stopped dead in my tracks," she said. "We both kind of froze for a second." Then the form turned and went down the stairs.

"It shook me up a little bit," she said. "But I knew right away who he was."

It was the ghost of Cling Clang, she said, a man whose life, marred by tragedy, ended about 130 years ago, next to the building the Stamps now own.

It was September 1978, and that was the first encounter she had with a ghost.

But it wouldn't be the last.

Now she and Jim, her husband, are convinced they are not alone. They believe the ghost of Cling Clang inhabits their home with them.

And therein begins this story of spirits of the dead.

Foreshadowing

Tom Shields, *Bangor* (Maine) *Daily News*

Create tone Hard-news stories often have an objective, factual tone, mostly an absence of mood. But in storytelling, you should create a "tone," or "mood," such as happiness, sadness, mystery, excitement or some other emotion.

You don't need to tell the reader that the mood of the place was festive or mournful. You can show it by the images you select for your story.

Another way of creating tone is by your writing style. Mary Ann Lickteig creates a lighthearted tone by writing this profile of a hypnotist as though the reader were undergoing hypnosis:

You will read this story.

You will hang on its every word, and you will not get sleepy.

As you proceed, you will learn about hypnosis and a Clive hypnotherapist whose work has led her to the International Hypnosis Hall of Fame.

You are ready to begin. Shari Patton is sitting on the couch in her home telling you that she first went for hypnosis "like a doubting Thomas." She was a student at the University of Minnesota when a friend was going to be hypnotized and wanted Patton to come along. Listen, now, to what she has to say:

"My friend had said, 'Go with me.' And I had said no, and after several requests begging me, I said 'All right. I'll go.' And I went to stop smoking, not believing that it would work, but very much wanting to stop smoking, and I was so amazed and delighted that it worked for me that I went back and started using hypnosis for weight control and lost 90 pounds."

That's how she got started.

Mary Ann Lickteig, *The Des Moines Register*

In contrast, Saul Pett wanted to create a somber tone to reflect the mood of the nation when President John F. Kennedy was killed. Pett chose vivid details that showed what people were feeling, and he did something else that was quite unusual. He established the reverent tone of his story by emulating biblical style.

You can also create tone by the length of your sentences. Short, choppy sentences can reflect fear, excitement, anxiety or stabbing pain. Long sentences can project suffering, thoughtfulness or a quiet mood. That is another way Pett created the mournful tone of his story. He broke many traditional journalistic rules: His sentences were long, he used the first-person *we*, and he made no attempt to write objectively. Yet his story is one of the great feature articles of the 20th century. The article describes the four days after Kennedy was shot. Here is an excerpt:

And the word went out from that time and place and cut the heart of a nation. In streets and offices and homes and stores, in lunchrooms and showrooms and schoolrooms and board rooms, on highways and prairies and beaches and mountaintops, in endless places crowded and sparse, near and far, white and black, Republican and Democrat, management and labor, the word went out and cut the heart of a nation.

And husbands called wives and wives called friends and teachers told students and motorists stopped to listen on car radios and stranger told stranger. Oh, no! we cried from hearts stopped by shock, from minds fighting the word, but the word came roaring back, true, true, true, and disbelief dissolved in tears.

Incredibly, in a time of great

numbers, in a time of repeated reminders that millions would die in a nuclear war, in a time when experts feared we were being numbed by numbers and immunized against tragedy, the death of a single man crowded into our souls and flooded our hearts and filled all the paths of our lives.

A great shadow fell on the land and the farmer summoned to the house did not find the will to return to the field, nor the secretary to the typewriter, nor the machinist to the lathe.

There was a great slowing down and a great stopping and the big bronze gong sounded as a man shouted the market is closed and the New York Stock Exchange stopped, just stopped. The Boston Symphony Orchestra stopped a Handel concerto and started a Beethoven funeral march and the Canadian House of Commons stopped and a dramatic play in Berlin stopped and the United Nations in New York stopped and Congress and courts and schools and race tracks stopped, just stopped. And football games were canceled and theaters were closed and in Dallas a nightclub called the Carousel was closed by a mourner named Jack Ruby.

In Washington, along Pennsylvania Avenue, they had waited all that Friday night outside the iron picket fence, their eyes scarcely leaving the lovely old house. Early in the morning the guards had kept them moving and so they walked slowly down the street, eyes right, and at the corner they turned and came back on the street side of the sidewalk, eyes left. They looked like a strange silent group of mournful pickets demonstrating love, not protest.

In the chill darkness before dawn they were still there, now motionless, standing, staring across the broad lawn and through the bare elms at the house, at the softly lighted windows in the family quarters, at the black crepe lately hung over the door under the north portico.

They saw the blinking red lights of the police cars up Pennsylvania Avenue and they knew this was the moment. The president was coming home. No sirens, no police whistles, no barking of orders that usually accompanied his return. At 4:22 a.m., Saturday, Nov. 23, 1963, there seemed to be no sound on the street or in the land.

The gray Navy ambulance and the six black cars behind it paused at the northwest gate and turned in. And along the fence, men removed their hats and teen-agers removed their hands from the pockets of their jeans and women tightened their fingers around the pickets of the fence. Tears stained their faces, their young and their old faces, their white and their black faces.

At the gate the procession was met by a squad of Marines and led in along the gracefully curving drive between the elms. In days to come there would be larger and more majestic processions, but none so slow, none so geared to the rhythm of tears, as the cadence of the Marines this Saturday morning. In two straight lines, glistening bayoneted rifles held across their chests at port arms, they marched oh so slowly up the drive and all that could be heard was the sound of their shoes sliding on the macadam.

Under the portico, under the handsome hanging lantern, they stopped and divided and lined up with the soldiers and sailors and airmen on the sides of the steps, at the stiffest, straightest attention of their lives. Jacqueline Kennedy emerged first from the ambulance, still wearing the same pink suit stained through eternity the afternoon before.

With her husband's brother, the attorney general of the United States, with his other brother, the youngest member of the United States Senate, with his sisters and his friends and aides whom he had led to this house, this far and now no farther, Jacqueline Kennedy waited in motionless silence while the flag-covered casket was removed from the ambulance. Then she and they turned in behind it and walked up the steps and through the glass doors and into the lobby and down the long corridor lined with stiff, silent men in uniform and finally came to a stop in the East Room.

There the casket was laid gently onto the black catafalque that held Mr. Lincoln on another dark incredible night almost 100 years ago. There, the kneeling priests began praying as they and others would through the long day and night by the flickering light of the candles which silhouetted the honor guard riveted to the floor.

It was now 10 o'clock in the morning of a Saturday and Jacqueline Kennedy, still sleepless, returned to the silent East Room. She kissed her husband for the last time and the casket was sealed. A few moments later, she returned with her children and spoke to them quietly, trying to tell them something of the fact and the meaning of death. A fact and a meaning for which millions groped that day.

Saul Pett, The Associated Press

Storytelling Structure

Up to this point in the book, even though you have had many story structures to choose from, you probably have been organizing your stories by focus and supporting topics or in chronological order. Even with a storytelling approach, you still need to get the focus first. A narrative story can then be arranged topically or chronologically, or it can follow a literary plot form—with a beginning, a middle and an ending called a "climax."

"Most news stories are endings without beginnings attached," says Jon Franklin, a Pulitzer Prize–winning writer and author of *Writing for Story*. Reporters miss the dramatic point of view when they concentrate only on the end result instead of on the actions leading up to the event. Franklin says stories should be built around a complication and a resolution. In the middle is the development, how the central character gets from the problem to the solution.

If you have a story that lends itself to this kind of plot, your focus would be the complication the main character has to overcome. The organization could be chronological, starting with the inception of the problem. The middle would be how the character wrestles with the problem, and the climax would be the resolution of the problem.

Or you can start in the middle of the action, as long as you explain to the reader why you are telling this story now (the "so what" factor). This approach is somewhat like using the time frame organization—starting with the present, going to the past, back to the present and on to the future. The technique of developing the story in sections, perhaps arranged by points of view, can also work in a narrative story. You can even use storytelling with a topical organization or any of the methods suggested in Chapter 12.

Regardless of the technique you choose, you should plan your order before you write.

William Blundell, who spent years writing features and profiles for *The Wall Street Journal,* suggests in his book, *The Art and Craft of Feature Writing,* that features should be organized around "The Laws of Progressive Reader Involvement":

Stage one: Tease me, you devil. (Give the reader a reason to continue reading.)

Stage two: Tell me what you're up to. What is the story really about?

Stage three: Oh yeah? Prove what you said. (Include the evidence to support your theme.)

Stage four: Help me remember it. (Make it clear and forceful, and give it a memorable ending.)

Blundell says features should include the following elements, but not necessarily in this order:

Focus: What is the central theme?

Lead and nut graph: What is the point of the story? (Often it is introduced anecdotally or descriptively.)

History: How did the problem develop?

Scope: How widespread is the development?

Reasons: Why is this problem or conflict happening now?

Impacts: Who is affected and how?

Moves and countermoves: Who is acting to promote or oppose the development, and what are they doing?

Future: What could happen as a result of the situation and developments?

Blundell also suggests blocking material from any one source in one place in the story, especially if the story has many sources—which is basically the kiss-off technique. The organization is not as rigid as the list implies. If the material lends itself to narrative storytelling, it can be told in chronological order or natural story order: beginning, middle, climax, end.

Applications

On the following pages you will see how writers use a combination of storytelling techniques. As you read, consider the basic techniques for storytelling:

- Use concrete details rather than vague adjectives.

- Use dialogue when possible and appropriate.

- Set a scene.

- Use action verbs.

- Observe or ask questions involving all your senses.

- Use show-in-action description.

- Tell a story like a plot, with a beginning, middle and climax. Get a chronology or sequence of events. You may want to use the chronology in all or part of your story. Even if you don't use chronological order, you need to understand the sequence.

- Follow Mark Twain's advice: "Don't say the old lady screamed— bring her on and let her scream."

Descriptive Writing Example

This story is an example of descriptive writing with portions of narrative writing. The story is a follow-up feature about a child who was murdered. The parents were not granting interviews. Reporter David Silverman used the sponsorship technique, asking the family's rabbi, whom Silverman knew, to intervene for him. The rabbi did. Then Silverman called the family, and they agreed to the interview. He convinced them that Nicky's story needed to be told.

The story reflects the reporting skills of observing and gathering detail. Even Nicky's parents couldn't remember his exact time of birth, but Silverman noticed it on a hospital record in a stack of materials the parents showed him. He wrote it in his notebook without knowing if he would need it. When he began to write his story, he discovered that the detail about the birth was exactly what he needed for the emotion he was trying to convey. (Remember to gather more information than you think you might need.)

Silverman also used the feature technique of weaving portions of the child's journal into the story to reveal Nicky's thoughts and to show the passage of time. He gathered anecdotes by asking the parents for specific memories of their child—a good technique when covering grief. After the story ran, Silverman received scores of complimentary letters and phone calls. But the one that meant the most, he said, was from Nicky's father, Joel Corwin.

Reporting techniques: Observation, establishment of chronologies, sponsorship, narrative reconstruction of events, anecdotes.

Writing techniques: Weaving of time frames—past and present—with a journal, descriptive detail without adjectives, chronological storytelling in parts, narrative and anecdotal writing, use of contrast, pacing (mixing short and long sentences).

Nicky's story

By David Silverman
Chicago Tribune

Journal quote lead to introduce Nicky in his own words: establishes Nicky as focus of story

"Hi, I would like to tell you about myself. I'll start with my hobbies. I like sports a lot. My favorite one is baseball and then football. Oh, I forgot, my name is Nick. Nick Corwin, really. My initials are N.B.C., Nicholas Brent Corwin. My birthday is April 9th. I am 7 years old."

It was September 1987, the first week of school in Mrs. Amy Deuble's 2d grade class at the Hubbard Woods School, and all the students in Room 7 were writing about themselves on sheets of wide-lined paper.

"I have two brothers, one older, one younger. They are 5 and 10. My dad's name is Joel. His job is a lawyer. My mom's name is Linda. She takes care of us as her job. My favorite color is blue. My favorite letter is N. My favorite number is 3."

It was the first entry in a journal each student would keep throughout the year. On special occasions, they would write about how they felt, and Mrs. Deuble would take a picture of each of them, to be glued at the top of the page.

In September, Nicky Corwin had a suntan. He leaned toward the cam-

Other key characters introduced through journal device (note use of italics)

Descriptive detail with strong verb (advertised)	era with his hands on his legs, just above his knees. A broad smile advertised the gap between his new front teeth.

Scene: journal used as transition from past to present

The small handwritten booklet now sits unfinished on a coffee table in the bright living room of Joel and Linda Corwin's Winnetka home. It is among a stack of stories, drawings and dreams they found in Nicky's small school desk, just a few feet from where he was murdered.

Descriptive detail based on observation

Photographs of him are everywhere in the whitewashed living room. On the piano against the wall. On the mantle above the fireplace. On the bookshelves. Linda and Joel

Show-in-action technique

sit close to each other on an overstuffed couch near the center of the room, surrounded by memories of their son and the horror of what happened at 10:25 a.m. on May 20.

Foreshadowing and nut graph: reason for story

They remember it was the first day Nicky was allowed to ride his bicycle to school. He was late, but his older brother waited for him anyway.

Narrative device: quote reconstruction based on recollection

"It's okay, Mom. I want to ride with Nicky," he shouted from the edge of the driveway.

After two weeks spent learning the rules of the road, Nicky had earned this privilege.

Background leading up to murder: scene setting

If he passed the written bicycle safety test at school that day, he could ride with his brother until the end of the year.

Linda Corwin had watched as her two sons rode off.

Quote establishes source for previous information.

"They had one and only one day to ride their bikes to school together," she said. "And that was it."

Key background to set up story: narrative style based on fact; no attribution needed

The nation knows what happened during Nicky Corwin's bicycle safety test that morning. Around 10:15, just as he began the test, a ragged, dark-haired woman wearing shorts entered the 2d grade classroom and sat down. She said nothing and soon left. She returned at 10:25 with two guns and opened fire.

Five children were wounded. Eight-year-old Nicholas Brent Corwin was killed. He was shot once in the heart.

On a hazy Sunday morning almost two months later, the Corwin house is quiet. No more national magazine coverage or live television interviews. The flood of thousands of letters has slowed to a trickle. The new phone number is unlisted.

What remains are the stack of papers from school, the photographs and daily reminders of a boy whose name meant "giver of gifts."

"There is a void," Joel says. "It's like a picture, and there's a blank there. We'll always have the feeling that he's there, but he's not."

"We're just left with the grim reality," Linda said, continuing her husband's thought. "I've been experiencing a kind of sensory deprivation. I can't see him or touch him. It's very painful.

"Our world view has been permanently altered. All the rules were broken with this incident."

The elementary rule in Winnetka used to be: Our children are safe—safe from the crime and violence the Corwins thought they left behind when they abandoned the city for Winnetka 11 years ago.

They had met at Yale University and graduated as part of the first co-educational class there. They were married and went on to the University of Minnesota to earn advanced degrees: his in law, hers in public affairs. They moved to Chicago and began to climb. The urban lifestyle suited the new corporate lawyer and his wife, a city planner. But when Linda became pregnant, she willingly gave up her career, and the couple prepared for a change.

"I could have done a lot of things, but there wasn't anything I could have done that was more important,"

Short sentences for drama

Contrast through description

Transition through repetition of key word (rule)

Transition to background of couple through time device (11 years ago) she said. "Anybody can be a lawyer or city planner, but there was one job no one else could do, and that was to be a mother to my own kids."

They sought refuge in the heart of the North Shore, where the homes were expensive and large, and the schools were the best. They chose a red brick and white stucco house on a street lined with close-cut lawns and 50-foot-tall oaks. It reminded Linda of her childhood home in Waterloo, Ia., which she remembers as being "a suburb without a city."

"We sought the peace of mind, the perceived peace of mind, that we thought we would have for our children—not having to worry about anything happening to them," Joel explained, shaking his head.

The house was too big for the couple and their only child, a newborn son. But they were planning ahead. They were going to fill the rooms with a family.

Three years later, son No. 2 practically jumped into the world.

Joel had little time to spare when he rushed Linda to Highland Park Hospital on April 9, 1980. They arrived at 12:45 p.m. Nicky Corwin was born in the emergency room at 12:48.

"I got there just in the nick of time," Joel said, displaying a brief smile as he recounted the hospital dash. "That was part of the reason for his name. He was in a hurry to get into life."

A third son followed three years later, and the family was complete. Joel and Linda Corwin had created the suburban dream. They had a Volvo station wagon in the driveway, a beautiful family and success.

But all the rules would be broken.

Laurie Wasserman Dann, a troubled 30-year-old with a history of bizarre behavior, shattered the

Corwin's lives before ending her own during a brief but violent rampage. Her story and those of the five children and the young man she wounded are well known. But somehow, Nicky Corwin was lost in the crush of publicity.

Aside from a brief statement the Corwins released the day of his death, and a funeral sermon two days later, the story of Nicky's short life was left to the memory of the neighbors, classmates and friends.

"A friend told us her daughter asked: 'Why are there so many pictures of the bad lady in the paper and hardly any pictures of Nicky?'" Linda said. "There was a little bit of that feeling on our part. But I guess bad guys always make the headlines."

The papers the Corwins brought home from the Hubbard Woods School show life through Nicky's eyes. It's a collection of stories, drawings and journal entries that reveal a creative young boy who passionately loved sports and learning.

"If I could study anything I wanted, I would choose math," Nicky wrote to his teacher on one of the sheets.

"That's the cruel irony," Linda says. "Normally he wouldn't have been in that room at that time; he would have been in an older [kids'] class for math. But they had the bicycle test that day. That's why he was in that room."

She picks up the journal Nicky kept and begins to leaf through it. It's loosely bound in green construction paper, the handwriting is large and neat, and the words are descriptive. After the first day of school, the next entry was added at Halloween.

The picture shows Nicky and Linda in the classroom, mugging for the camera. The words tell of a party and candy.

The next page is from Thanksgiving, and a brightly colored turkey fills the page instead of the usual entry. In its giant feathers, Nicky wrote of the things he was most thankful for.

"Mom, Dad, little brother, older brother, house, bed, money, doctor, grandma, school, my friends, my life, and me."

In January, the assignment was to write about three important strengths.

"I'm kind of nice. I am smart. I have good athletic ability."

Linda Corwin laughs as she rereads the entry aloud.

"Only kind of nice?" she asks. Her eyes begin to glisten as she stares at the picture on the top of the page. Nicky was growing. He was taller, and his dark brown hair was longer. The teeth in the smile were bigger, but the gap remained.

The final entry came after the Spring Sing, a class performance in April in which Nicky had a speaking part between songs.

"I had a really good time. Afterward we went to Peter's for dinner and played Nintendo [video] games."

He looked grown up, dressed in a coat and tie, head cocked a little to the left. And there was the smile.

Nicky Corwin had just turned 8.

"He played soccer, hockey, tennis, baseball and football," Linda said. "He was very much a natural athlete. He had a natural grace about him. I think he learned early on that to be cocky wasn't going to get him anywhere. So he was very supportive of the other kids on his teams. He was very aware of the talents he had been blessed with."

One of those talents happened to be climbing. Anything upright was fair game, especially the tallest trees. Acting the part of a monkey, he would climb to the top before calling his mother to see his accomplishment.

"I had to call the fire department because I was so petrified," she says, laughing outright. "He loved to climb high. He loved to scare us with his daredevil climbing feats."

Joel remembers the autumn football. Nicky teamed with his older brother, against his dad and younger brother, for backyard games that would last past dark. When the snows came, it moved to the living room. Linda played quarterback, sending Nicky deep to the fireplace while rock blared on the stereo.

The floor in front of the fireplace now is covered with baskets of condolence letters. Some have been answered. Others wait. Linda has promised herself she'll get to them all. The signatures are those of parents, strangers mostly, compelled to let the Corwins know they weren't alone in their anguish.

"I've gotten so many beautiful letters," Linda said. "It means a lot to us to know that so many other people care, and it means a lot to know that he touched so many people, even though he was only around for such a short time."

On the mantle above the baskets, a display of pictures depicts family trips to Arizona and Walt Disney World. Joel plucks a favorite from the bunch. Nicky, wearing a comically too-large cowboy hat, is tucked snugly under his father's arm as they sit perched on the edge of the Grand Canyon.

"We were really on top of the world," he says, absorbed in the memory.

"He wanted to go to Maine," Linda says. "I don't know how he even knew about Maine, but he kept asking if we could go. One of these days I may be brave enough to get there."

Repetition of key word for transition (talents)

Key word (fireplace)

Pictures used as recurring theme to set up quotes and recollections

Foreshadowing for ending

There's a knock at the door. One of their oldest son's friends appears in the hall, dressed in a Little League uniform, carrying a glove and bat. Linda and Joel remember there's a game in an hour, and they have to stop for juice boxes on the way.

Natural progression from past to present to future

"In the beginning, they asked, 'Why?'" Linda said. "They don't ask about it anymore. Partly because they know there really is no answer. Partly because I think they are trying to protect our feelings, too."

On the day of the funeral, Rabbi Robert Schriebman had the family write notes to Nicky, to be placed in the casket with him.

"Our youngest just wrote, 'I love you, Nicky,'" Joel said. "He understands what happened."

After the funeral, Joel took his sons back to the cemetery. Together they walked the grounds near Nicky's grave, looking at the other names. He wanted to make them understand.

"All the graves near his are of much older people," Joel said. "There's one nearby where the person was 88. And I told the boys that's how long a person should live—88, not 8."

Frustration. Anger. Fear. Grief. Linda and Joel Corwin are left with these emotions, and a million more, every time they replay the events of May 20. All the activity has left them little time for each other, and the emotions.

"We've probably not done very well with that," Linda said. "One does not feel a whole lot like giving in this situation. I don't know, I don't feel I have a lot to give right now. I used to enjoy living life to the fullest. Now it's a struggle.

"I think a loss is a loss. If you lose a child through an illness or a car accident, it's a terrible loss and no less painful than this. But the horror of the way this happened is really too difficult for us to contemplate."

And what about the anger? Anger at a woman who can never stand trial for her crime. At a legal system that neglected, or couldn't act on, repeated calls to remove her from the streets before she lashed out.

"It goes beyond that," Joel says, almost in a whisper. "There aren't words to express that.

"But there are a couple of primary feelings. We miss hugging him . . . basking in his radiance. At the same time, there is a frustration that is difficult for me to deal with. He is missing everything life had to offer."

Even harder, perhaps, were the things that had to be done shortly after Nicky's death. There were necessary and painful things such as retrieving his bicycle from a deserted rack after all the other kids had gone home, cleaning out his desk and carefully removing his name tag so as not to rip it.

"There is no way to put closure on this kind of loss," Linda said. "All we can ever hope to do is come to terms with it. This is the kind of pain that will always be there. There may be some layers of protection over it, but it will always be there.

"Every day I see him smiling at me with a twinkle in his eye. That keeps me going."

Sets up mood for ending

"Nicky would have wanted us to go on. He would have said, 'Don't fold,'" Joel says.

The Corwins have to go. The kids are shooting baskets in the driveway, and Little League waits for no parent. They are gracious and say they would love to talk about Nicky all day, but it is time to pile everyone into the station wagon. It is time to move on.

Ends on future note with simple sentence: intentional understatement for highly emotional story

Narrative Writing Example

Martha Miller interviewed Dan Vickroy several times before she wrote this story. Each time he remembered more. She asked him to recall what he was thinking, feeling, saying and experiencing when he was injured, 25 years earlier.

Miller also reconstructed dialogue, based on Vickroy's recollections. The technique is acceptable but not preferable. If you can't confirm the dialogue with the original source, you can attribute it to the source who related it. If it is not controversial and you are sure it is accurate, you can reconstruct it as Miller has done.

After she finished all her interviews and filled several notebooks, Miller sat down to write the story. She was overwhelmed. She planned the story and organized it by different periods of Vickroy's life. Then she tried free-writing, just writing what she remembered to get it out of her head. After that she began refining the story, and before she revised her final draft, she read the story aloud.

This part of the story, the second section, contains almost no direct attribution. It is all based on Vickroy's recollections. Do you need attribution? Is the story believable?

Reporting techniques: Establishing chronology, gathering detail, asking questions to get source to reconstruct specific events using all senses.

Writing techniques: Organized by section technique in time sequences; although most of the story takes place in the past, each section deals with a different part of the character's life. Primarily follows chronological order, with cliffhanger endings for each section. Other techniques: short sentences, pacing, dialogue, definitions, description, narration.

A soldier's story

By Martha Miller
Iowa City Press-Citizen

Descriptive beginning for section: sets scene
Reconstructed dialogue

Two hands lifted the sheet that covered what was left of Dan Vickroy's body.

"You're one tough son of a bitch," the surgeon said from behind a green mask.

"I'm a Vickroy," Dan said. "Take me in and sew me up."

They did.

Narrative chronological storytelling through Vickroy

Vickroy regained consciousness. He figured he was in the base hospital at Cam Ranh Bay. He could see nothing through the bandages over his eyes, but he could hear the squeaks of rubber soles in the hallway and hushed conversations between doctors as they hurried from bed to bed. It sounded like a busy place.

He was scared, scared to death he was blind.

His ears wanted to believe what he heard, but his eyes would believe what they saw.

The nurses told him they were bandages and that he was strapped down. They told him he had been in bed for almost two weeks. And they told him he had a 104-degree temperature. He knew that. He couldn't stop shivering.

As he lay there, his memory returned. He knew the mine had exploded and that he was badly hurt. He remembered waking up twice in

Clues of attribution without direct attribution (he remembered)

Scene

surgery. The last time, he felt a surge of pain. He saw a surgeon cutting off his leg with a bone saw.

The days and nights came and went. All the same. Dark.

This time, it was night. Someone shut off all the lights in his hospital room. The doctors were back. Slowly, they unraveled the gauze around his eyes.

Vickroy held his breath. He opened his eyes and saw a faint light. It burned, but this time it was a good sign. Doctors had worked through the night cleaning his eyes. What he saw made him want to put the bandages back on.

There were wire stitches in his stomach and his right hip. There were tubes in his nose and left arm. Instead of legs, he saw blood-soaked gauze wrapped around two stumps.

The doctors told him what happened: His right leg was blown away by the explosion and his left leg was amputated in surgery; his right arm was amputated below the elbow; and he had lost part of his stomach. Being so close to the mine saved his life; the blast threw him up and out of the way.

His face was intact, saved by that last glance back to camp.

Vickroy took the news better than most.

"Psychologically, I was pretty positive."

He had no legs, but he did have a wife and new baby. He had married Sharon Kay in 1968 in Tulsa. She was 8½ months pregnant when he left for Vietnam. Danny Ray was born March 28, 1969.

Baby pictures were taped, one under the other, on the side of his bed so Vickroy could look at Danny Ray while laying on his back.

Those pictures and thoughts of heading back to the United States kept Vickroy's hopes up. But back home, his family wasn't so positive.

Dan's mother, Louise, was waiting tables in a Cedar Rapids restaurant when an Army officer handed her a telegram. She cried.

Louise had never wanted her youngest to join the service. She wouldn't sign his enlistment papers and couldn't see him off.

Vickroy had started to believe he could live without legs until the day a nurse read him a letter. It had arrived at Cam Ranh Bay several days earlier, but nobody wanted to read it to him.

It was from his wife. She wanted a divorce.

"She told me she didn't want half a man."

*Direct quote,
no attribution;
speaker understood*

*Short sentences
and pacing*

*Punch ending
to this section;
short sentences*

Exercises

1 Scene: Go to a busy place on campus or to the cafeteria and listen to people talking. Gather information about the scene. Then write a few paragraphs setting the scene and weaving in dialogue.

2 Analogies: Study some objects on your campus. Write similes and metaphors to describe the objects.

3 Narrative writing exercise: Interview a classmate about any experience he or she has had, preferably a traumatic or emotional one. If your subject can't think of one, ask him or her to describe the morning routine from today or yesterday. Imagine that the nut graph is "And then (your subject) disappeared and hasn't been seen since."

You will need to ask specific questions, such as what was the person wearing, what color and kind of car was he or she driving (if a car is involved), what time of day did the events occur, what was he or she thinking, feeling, doing, saying. Get the person to reconstruct the event exactly as it happened by asking questions about sequence of events and details.

Then write the information in narrative style in a few paragraphs or a brief story.

4   Timed free writing: This exercise, borrowed from Lucille deView, writing coach for *The Orange County* (Calif.) *Register,* requires you to write very quickly—in 10 to 15 minutes. Write a story about a personal experience and let your mind ramble, or write your thoughts about a topic. Remember you are just getting your thoughts on paper. You can take any words that trigger thoughts—*soup, pizza, cars*—or a topic the instructor gives the class. Some topic suggestions from deView include:

The happiest day of my childhood

My favorite assignment

My worst assignment

The most interesting person I interviewed (or know)

A turning point in my life

5   Narrative and descriptive writing exercise: The following information is taken from a *Chicago Tribune* story by Paul Weingarten. This story lends itself to either a narrative or a descriptive lead. First write a descriptive lead and then a narrative one, up to the nut graph. Then choose the lead you prefer and finish organizing the story.

The story is about a Holocaust memorial in Euless, Texas. The memorial features an exhibit called The Hiding Place, a high-tech exhibit that takes visitors into a boxcar that disgorges its "prisoners" into a simulated concentration camp. The camp is a large room decorated with tattered prison garments and a hangman's noose. There a graphic presentation, filled with special lighting and visual effects, tells the story of Corrie ten Boom, a Dutch woman who was banished to the Ravensbruck concentration camp for helping to hide hundreds of Jews in her home during World War II.

> Against a collage of photos of cadaverous concentration camp victims and naked bodies being fed into ovens come the voices of Nazi guards who are joking about extracting gold fillings from the teeth of Jews.
>
> The exhibit is located at the Mike Evans Ministry, a fundamentalist Christian church in a town of 24,000 just outside of Fort Worth, Texas.
>
> Evans, 40, a born-again Christian evangelist whose mother was a Jew, says he created the exhibit "because this was the story of a Christian family that was willing to lay down their lives for the Jewish people, which in our opinion is a great way of combating anti-Semitism."

During the war, the ten Booms constructed a false wall to create a 2½-foot-wide space behind a full-length bookshelf in Corrie ten Boom's third-floor bedroom.

In the end of the presentation, Corrie ten Boom, who died in 1983, explains why she risked her life for the Jews: "Because my savior and Lord is Jewish. I do it for his sake."

In the stark room cold and dim, a red Nazi flag hangs above a small wooden desk. A glaring portrait of Adolf Hitler adorns another wall.

"Achtung! Achtung!" a voice barks from loudspeakers. "All Jews must be identified. Step forward."

A grim-faced Nazi soldier emerges from the shadows and directs a group of wide-eyed eighth graders from the Brandon Street Christian Academy to step through a railing and stand behind a yellow line.

Suddenly, lights glare in their eyes. Each is handed a yellow cloth Star of David.

"According to our records, all who are in this room are Jews," the voice booms. "This yellow patch must be worn on your chest in plain sight at all times. No exceptions. No exceptions."

Immediately another door swings open, and the new "Jews" are herded down a hall amid a cacophony of angry voices and screams.

"All of you vermin move into the car," a voice snarls.

The students clamber into a wood-slatted railroad boxcar. The Nazi soldier shoves the laggards from behind, and the door clangs shut.

Inside, the boxcar begins to pitch as if in motion, and two lanterns clatter against the iron ceiling. There are voices in here, too.

"Mama, mama," a child calls.

"I wonder where we are going."

And then there is a woman's voice, which identifies itself as that of Corrie ten Boom. She is asked by another passenger if she is Jewish, and she says no.

"But why should you be taken with us? What crime have you committed?" the other passenger persists.

"For obeying God, for loving his chosen people . . . for hiding them in our home," ten Boom replies.

Later, the visitors crowd into a narrow "hiding place," listening to the muffled voices of Nazi troops searching the house. The real hiding place is now a museum in the ten Boom home and clock shop in Haarlem, Netherlands.

COACHING
TIPS

Study your audience. Find out if the editors you want to reach prefer hard-news or soft-news style, short or in-depth releases, and single releases or media kits.

Find your focus. Use the focus statement as a headline or guideline for your lead.

Consider graphics—charts, illustrations, photographs, diagrams—to make your package more appealing.

Write a fact sheet. Even if you don't include a separate fact sheet with your release or media kit, use it as a writing tool to make sure you have provided crucial facts about the organization in your story.

Always include the name and telephone number of a person to contact, the date information can be released, an address and the date the release was written.

Public Relations Writing 14

W hen Evie Lazzarino studied journalism in college, she didn't think it would lead to an all-expense-paid trip to China. But just a few years after she graduated from college, she wound up in front of the Great Wall of China with a bunch of dolls called Cabbage Patch Kids. She was coordinating part of a world tour featuring children from America who went to seven foreign countries as "ambassadors" for the dolls, then among the most popular toys in the United States.

"The Chinese people had never seen a Cabbage Patch doll. It was fun to see people's first reaction to them," says Lazzarino, who was then working for a Los Angeles public relations agency that handled the Cabbage Patch Kids account. "My job was like an advance job for a politician. I went to China to set up a party, places we could visit, and I met with all the Western press such as bureaus of *The New York Times* and *Los Angeles Times*. I tried to get them to cover what we were doing. We did a photo shoot on the Great Wall and the photo moved worldwide."

The trip to China was one of the high points in a varied career that has been somewhat circular. Lazzarino began her career working as a reporter and editor for her local newspaper. Now she works for the country's largest metropolitan newspaper, the *Los Angeles Times*. But she isn't a reporter or an editor. She is the manager of its community affairs department. In this job she supervises many public relations programs the *Times* sponsors, such as a summer camp for underprivileged children, the newspaper's speakers bureau, its scholarship fund and other events in the community.

You have to write as professionally in public relations as if you were writing in a newspaper. Avoid hype and be realistic about what you are selling.

Evie Lazzarino, manager of community affairs, *Los Angeles Times*

*Evie Lazzarino,
community affairs
manager,*
Los Angeles Times
Courtesy of Evie Lazzarino

Lazzarino's experience reflects the wide range of jobs in the public relations field. In addition to working with the media, she has been responsible for developing products, writing speeches for corporate officials, coordinating trade shows and promoting plans for several major accounts, including Polaroid and Mercedes-Benz of North America.

Although Lazzarino has a newspaper background, other people featured in this chapter started directly in public relations work after college. "I hadn't really thought about going into public relations," Lazzarino says. "But I found the transition delightful. It blended a growing interest I had in business with my interest in journalism."

Whether you work for one client or an agency that serves many, in public relations you are serving several masters at once, Lazzarino says. If you are writing a press release, you are not only trying to please your client, you also have to please an editor at a newspaper, magazine or television station. So in a sense, you are working for several people.

She says her journalism background helped her understand the kind of writing the media wanted. "You have to write as professionally in public relations as if you were writing in a newspaper. Avoid hype and be realistic about what you are selling."

Students going into public relations may think deadlines in public relations are not as strenuous as they are in newspapers. But you have many deadlines because you may have five or 10 clients you are trying to serve at one time, Lazzarino says. "People are paying a lot of money for your services," Lazzarino says. "When it's someone else's money, there's a real sense of risk that you could lose clients."

*Cabbage Patch doll at
the Great Wall of China*
Courtesy of Evie Lazzarino

One of her main suggestions is to know your audience. "You have to know different styles. Some magazines may prefer something clever, but if you are pitching something to *The Wall Street Journal,* you should have a great news story. You have to study your market. Go out and meet editors and find out what they want."

Media Resistance

Sending press releases to the media doesn't guarantee that your material will be used. A California marketing communications agency conducted an unscientific survey of 30 print and broadcast media organizations to find out how many of the press releases they received were actually read. Then the company sent out this press release about its findings:

Paper Waste Irresponsible
PR Agency Surveys Media, Adopts Green Policies

NEWPORT BEACH, Calif.—The public-relations division of InterCommunicationsInc, a marketing communications agency here, is making an effort to reduce the amount of paper it sends to newsrooms for clients and thus minimize the agency's impact upon the environment.

The company has changed its media relations policies and practices after reviewing the amount of paper it distributes to working journalists and conducting a telephone survey of Los Angeles-area newsrooms.

Survey Confirms Need

InterCom surveyed assignment editors June 3–14 to determine the impact of unsolicited public-relations material upon newsrooms' waste streams. A total of 30 newspapers, magazines, radio and television stations, and wire services were contacted.

Major findings: (1) the 30 newsrooms received an average of 122 press releases every day (from a minimum of 20 to a maximum of 600), (2) less than 10 percent of the press releases received were "actually read," (3) of those, assignment editors considered less than 20 percent "useful," (4) most assignment editors (27) indicated that press releases and other media materials printed on both sides of paper wouldn't hinder readability, (5) 28 assignment editors indicated that press kits contained "too much" paper, and (6) two thirds (20) subscribe to services such as BusinessWire and PR NewsWire and prefer to read company announcements via those rather than receive hard copy in the mail.

All assignment editors indicated a desire to reduce their individual newsroom's waste stream. . . .

# # #

The press release went on to explain that the company would counsel clients on what is newsworthy so the company could avoid "useless, newsless paper."

Although the point of the release was to promote the company's attitude toward environmental responsibility, the only part *The Wall Street Journal* and other newspapers printed was the information that fewer than 10 percent of the press releases were read.

Judy Brower, account supervisor in charge of media relations for InterCommunicationsInc, says the press release was sent by her former boss against her wishes. "I knew the media would be interested in it, partly in fun and partly in a serious manner. The public relations and journalism people are on two sides of a fence. I felt the results of the survey were negative toward an industry in which I've invested 10 years of my life." Little came of the release, except that the company began conserving paper within the office. Brower says editors and clients prefer releases printed on one side of the paper, despite the survey's findings.

Media's Needs

There is some validity to the survey's findings that many press releases are not read all the way through. But most editors at least skim the releases to find out if there is some newsworthy information. Community newspapers and local television stations rely heavily on news releases about events in their area. And a good public relations practitioner can be an invaluable source to a reporter.

Newsworthiness

Brower, whose company specializes in serving clients in real estate and shopping center development, says the test of newsworthiness is the same for a public relations release as it is for a newspaper, magazine or television station. The basic principles of timeliness, local interest and unusual nature apply. With magazines, especially trade magazines, information that imparts new knowledge or something that will help readers is especially helpful, she says.

"If you are looking to place something in the media, take your subject and envision the headline the newspaper might print. Use that as an angle to force yourself to determine what is newsworthy about your information," Brower says.

She also stresses the importance of visuals—charts, graphs and photos. "Magazines and newspapers have become much more graphic," she says. "Although many of the larger newspapers prefer to use their own photographers, the weeklies and small community newspapers prefer something they can just grab."

Writing Ability

There is no substitute for good writing. "The more we can write the way journalists want the information to come out, the more chance it has of being published," Brower says. "You must have the basic skills for news writing." She has even implemented a writing test for people she wants to hire.

Although Brower works extensively with the media, she didn't learn her basic skills on a newspaper. She graduated from the University of California with a communications degree. She says the most valuable training she received was through internships at public relations firms while she was in college. "Even if you don't get paid for it, an internship is worth the experience," she says. She also strongly advises students to gain experience on the college newspaper.

Despite the similarities between public relations and newspaper writing, there is a major difference in approach, Brower says. Public relations practitioners are advocates for their clients.

Credibility

Charles W. Hucker, former division vice president for public affairs and communication, Hallmark Cards, Inc.

Courtesy of Charles W. Hucker

"Journalists sometimes claim p.r. people don't tell the truth," Brower says. "That isn't the case. I look at my clients as family. I prefer to think we always tell the truth, but just like comments about our family, we don't bring up negative qualities. If you are asked a negative question, you would probably try to soften the answer. But it is important to be honest. If the media find you are dishonest, you're done. They won't ever believe you again."

Honesty is stressed in the code of ethics for the Public Relations Society of America, cited in the chapter on ethics: "A member shall adhere to truth and accuracy and to generally accepted standards of good taste," the code states.

Charles W. Hucker is also concerned about the image that public relations practitioners have with the media. Hucker, former division vice president in charge of public affairs and communication for Hallmark Cards, Inc., in Kansas City, Mo., says he doesn't even like the term *public relations*. "In some respects it is a term lacking in credibility, so why use it?" Hucker says. "To me the term has too much connotation of flim-flam connected to it. The word I use is *communication*. We are in the communication business."

Hucker prefers to think of corporate communications as writing from a point of view rather than advocacy journalism. "We are not trying to be investigative journalists within the confines of these walls," he says. "We are writing from the point of view of the corporation. We are not trying to tell everything."

Media Kits

Although Hallmark sometimes sends out just a press release, more often it sends "media kits." Media kits are usually decorative folders containing a variety of press releases, fact sheets about the company and its products, and samples of the company's products.

Hucker says he favors media kits because they leave more of an impression than just a press release and tend to be kept around. "The objective is to plant enough seeds or hooks so an editor can go through the material and find an angle and develop an idea into a fuller story," he says.

Planning a media kit can be a very creative experience. You should design a striking cover or package for your media kit and include information that will be useful for different kinds of stories. A brief sheet of facts about the company is usually helpful. If you have a product sample that is suitable for enclosure, consider it part of your media kit. For example, Hallmark usually includes greeting cards.

The cover letter for your media kit should briefly state what is included. Here is a cover letter for a media kit from Hallmark:

Dear Editor:

The latest in Easter card and gift-giving trends from Hallmark Cards is tucked inside. We hope you find this information helpful as you prepare your springtime holiday stories.

Hallmark offers about 250 gift and party items. The Easter gift line includes wicker baskets, stuffed animals, activity products for children (such as washable markers, stickers and coloring books), decorations and partyware.

In addition to Hallmark's regular line of Easter products, selected Hallmark Crown stores will be offering exclusive Easter items, such as Hallmark Keepsake Easter ornaments and fresh-cut flower bouquets.

Writing Skills for Press Releases

With the exception of the difference in point of view, Hucker says there are more similarities between corporate communications and newspaper or broadcast writing than there are differences. He says he isn't impressed when job applicants tell him they are good with people. "When I hire people here, I want good writers," he says.

"People don't want a lot of breathless prose; they want the ideas and facts," he says. He also wants writers to have good analytical skills, especially for corporate proposals. "We're paying a lot more attention to critical thinking, the ability to sort through a mass of stuff."

He likens writing a press release or proposal to organizing a hard-news story: "Figure out what is the most important point for the lead.

Then organize it by key points explained and argued in such a way that the audience understands. Never forget who the audience is."

A Direct Approach

Mark O'Brien offers the same advice. As media communications representative for Binney & Smith, makers of Crayola products, he favors a brief approach. He targets newspaper editors as his first audience.

"You have to listen to the editors out there," O'Brien says. "They get a lot of material across their desks each day. If you have to read a page before you get to the meat of the subject, that's too much. Very few newspapers are going to print your story exactly. The release is just to pique their curiosity."

O'Brien, who began work in public relations for General Foods after graduating from the University of South Florida, says he studied what worked by comparing releases and newsletters that got published and those that didn't. Now his news releases rarely exceed two double-spaced, typewritten pages; most are just a few paragraphs on one page. (Double spacing is another requirement for press releases, because it is easier to read.) But he also includes fact sheets in a media kit with product samples, all enclosed in a folder with a bold graphic of smiling crayons or a cover similar to the familiar gold and green Crayola box of crayons.

And his releases get results. In one year *USA Today* printed six front-page stories based on his releases. Scores of newspapers throughout the country—including The Associated Press, with its national distribution—wrote stories based on the following release. O'Brien included these essential elements:

- The company address
- A contact (himself, in this case) with telephone number
- The date of the release
- When the release can be published (for immediate release, in this case)

O'Brien sent this release out a week earlier than the date on it so editors could publish it the day the news supposedly was announced. That's another quality of a good publicist. Editors want timely information. Unless special arrangements are made to hold the news, they usually will print it as soon as possible. As a result, "for immediate release" is a good way to write the release date.

Compare O'Brien's release and the story, which also included information (underlined) from fact sheets in the media kit and a phone call to the company. (Note that because Crayola is a trademark name, it should be capitalized in all news stories.)

Illustration from media kit
Courtesy of Binney & Smith Inc.

Press release

Binney & Smith Inc.

1100 Church Lane

P.O. Box 431

Easton, Pennsylvania 18044-0431

[Company telephone number]

For Immediate Release

Contact: Mark J. O'Brien

Media Communications

[Telephone number plus direct extension]

[Date]

Crayola Introduces New Crayons That Are Literally "Off the Wall"

1992, EASTON, Pa.—Parents can put away the scrub brushes and stain remover thanks to Binney & Smith. The maker of Crayola products has introduced a totally off-the-wall product—washable crayons.

Unlike the billions of crayons produced before them, Crayola washable crayons are made from a patented formula that washes from most surfaces, including walls and fabric.

"Washable crayons address our number one consumer complaint—getting crayon marks off different surfaces," says Mark O'Brien, Binney & Smith spokesperson. "Each year we receive thousands of calls and letters regarding crayon stains, mainly from parents of preschool children. With the introduction of washable crayons, parents can breathe a little easier when it comes to crayon mishaps."

The difference between traditional and washable crayons is in their formulas. Washable crayons contain special water soluble polymers found in many health and beauty aids. This allows them to be

Front-page story

Crayola cleans up kids' act

Parents can now offer junior artists a crayon that won't leave permanent impressions of childhood—on walls, draperies and floors.

Binney & Smith, maker of Crayola brand, is introducing a crayon made from a formula that can be cleaned with soap and water.

"Washable crayons address our number-one consumer complaint," says company official Mark O'Brien.

That's good news for parents: According to Binney & Smith, the USA's kids spend almost 6.3 billion hours a year with crayons in hand.

Unlike traditional crayons, washable ones aren't made of the waxy substance paraffin. The substitutes are water-soluble compounds found in cosmetics.

Grown men and women colored on walls coated with a variety of paints and wallpapers to test formulas.

"They are truly Mom-friendly," says Binney & Smith's Brad Drexler.

So your toddler's wayward works of art can be cleaned off most walls and other surfaces up to two months after they're made.

One rub: Washable crayons are being marketed for preschoolers only in Crayola's large and "So Big" sizes.

But they come in the same eight colors—red, green, orange, blue, black, brown and violet—as the first Crayolas in 1903.

USA Today

Press release (continued)

removed from most surfaces by simply using soap and water. Tests have shown
washable crayon marks can even be removed from walls and fabric one to two
months after being stained. However,
crayon marks are easiest to remove if
washed soon after they happen.

Crayola washable crayons are non-
toxic and available in two sizes. The So
Big size, for younger children, comes six
to a box and has a suggested retail price
of $2.99. Boxes of eight, large size wash-
able crayons will sell for approximately
$2.59.

# # #

O'Brien says part of the release's success was due to the product, one that is "ingrained in our society as part of our culture." The other reason was some relief from depressing news, he says. "It's nice to put something on the front page that's not devastating."

Here's an excerpt from a 15-inch feature story based on the same release. It is based on more extensive interviews with O'Brien.

The folks at Crayola finally have seen the handwriting on the wall.

And they're going to wash it off.

Yes, the company that since 1903 has brought you rainbows inside a gold-and-green box is offering washable crayons—many years and paint jobs too late for thousands of American families but just right for what the company quite politely refers to as "crayon mishaps."

For years, says company spokesman Mark O'Brien, parents' No. 1 complaint has been that Crayola stains don't wash off walls or out of clothes. So, he says, Crayola scientists have been working in their Pennsylvania offices for those years—"night and day" for the past three—to develop a washable crayon that also meets Crayola's standards for vibrancy.

The Wichita (Kan.) *Eagle*

The Structure of Press Releases

Press releases differ very little from basic news stories. Some have a feature approach; others are organized the same as a hard-news story, with a summary lead. As with any news story, you need to get to the point quickly in a press release. If you have a soft lead, put the nut graph high in the release, preferably by the second paragraph.

Headings: At the top of the release, preferably on the left side, write the date of the release, a release date and the author of the release. On the other side give a contact.

Date: [month, day, year]   FOR MORE INFORMATION CONTACT:

Release Date: Immediately   [name]

Story By: (optional)   [phone number]

Headline: Leave about 2 inches below the previous information, and then write a headline all in capital letters.

Lead: If you have a strong news angle, use a summary or impact lead. Get to the point quickly. If the story is geared to a feature section of the newspaper or a magazine, use any of the soft-lead techniques. Many companies begin the lead with a dateline, the location of the story in all capital letters, (such as DALLAS), followed by a dash. Here's an example of a press release that is hard to read because the lead starts with too many phrases and is too long:

Offering 15-second transmission speed, an easy-to-read liquid crystal display, and a five-page automatic document feeder, Sharp Electronics Corporation recently introduced two new low-end facsimile models which boast a number of features not usually found in comparable priced units. The UX-101 and UX-111 facsimiles have now joined Sharp's successful lineup of personal home office facsimiles.

Focus: Write a sentence explaining the main point and the "so what" factor above your story. This could be your headline or your lead, just as in a news story. The following example, also a hard-news approach, is much clearer than the first one. Note how the headline is the focus and the basis for the lead as well.

JC PENNEY TO STUDY SITE FOR DISTRIBUTION CENTER

DALLAS, June 22—J.C. Penney Company, Inc. has acquired an option on a 150-acre site in Rockingham County, Virginia, near Harrisonburg, and will study the feasibility of locating the company's seventh catalog distribution center there.

Backup   Rodney M. Birkins, president of JCPenney Catalog, says the company acquired the option on a portion of the Jordan farm, which is located at the northeast corner of Route 682 and I-81. He emphasized that the action was merely exploratory at this time.

Backup: Just as you would in a news story, you should back up the lead with a quote or supporting facts. Before you write, jot down the crucial information a reader needs—who, what, where, when, why and how. If you are promoting an event, make sure you have the date, time and location—or rain-date possibilities. Think of your list as an empowerment box. Use the basic role-playing technique: If you were buying the product, attending the event or seeking information about the company, what questions would you have? Answer them quickly.

Ending: You often can end press releases with a fact or basic information about price or other sales information. Keep it simple; don't strain. End the release with —*30*— or —*End*— set off by dashes or a row of three number symbols: *# # #.*

Revision: Use the basic coaching method: conceive, collect, construct, correct. In the final step, strike out every superfluous word. If you had to limit your release to one page, what would you delete? Revise your release, checking for spelling and factual accuracy, and try to limit it to one or two pages. If you must use a second page, write —*MORE*— at the end of the first.

Corporate Publications

When you are writing press releases for the media, use newspaper style. If you are writing a company magazine with news and features about people and events in the organization, newspaper style still applies. But when you are writing a memo or proposal to the company president or other corporate officials, you need to state your position in an analytical way.

That's where many business writers have difficulty, says Anne Baber, a writing coach who conducts seminars in corporations to improve communication techniques. She has also conducted seminars for the International Association of Business Communicators and has written books and many articles about career topics.

The key factor is to know the audience, she says. "There are some psychological problems people have when they write for folks up the ladder in management. One of my theories is that power warps communication. When people are writing for a boss, it's like a teenager talking to a parent. The parent says, 'Where are you going?' The teenager answers, 'Out.' The teen isn't saying everything he or she knows because of the power structure. In corporations, the power structure also affects communication. The writing becomes very formal, very passive. The writers don't want to put themselves forward as being initiators of action. They hide behind the third person. They write *the employee* rather than the word *you*."

Baber bases her theories on many years of experience in corporate communications. A former director of communications for United Telecom (now called Sprint), she heads her own consulting firm, Baber and Associates, in Kansas City, Mo.

Many of the coaching techniques she uses are similar to those described earlier in the book. But the outcome is different. "News writing operates on the idea that if you give the public enough information, they will inform themselves," she says. "We're not doing that in an organization. We want to create attitudes or actions. It's much more like advertising."

Here are Baber's tips for writing proposals and company plans:

Reporting steps

Make a list: Ask what the audience—in this case management—really wants to know. Then itemize all the points you can. (This is the same as brainstorming for a news story.)

Envision the result: Ask yourself, what kind of action is the reader expected to take as a result of this information?

Make a checklist of what and why: Write a sentence beginning "I want to tell you that . . . ," and then answer why. Then add this teaser to support the why factor: "This is necessary because . . ." (This teaser is similar to the focus—"so what"—sentence at the top of your news stories.)

Writing steps

Draw a "mind spill": Get all the research together. Draw a circle in the center of a large piece of paper. Put the main topic in the center circle. Then draw circles, filling each circle with an idea. Take a colored pencil or highlighter, and mark the key components related to the main idea. Draw a line to connect one related idea to another so that all like information is grouped together. Then number the points, preferably in the order you will write them in the proposal. (This is the same technique as mapping for ideas or reporting.)

Organize the order: Write a topic sentence (the same as a focus sentence) that completes this thought: "I believe that . . ." For example, "I believe that we should market Mother's Day cards a different way." Then write the word *because* followed by point one, point two, point three—like the list technique. The most persuasive structure is three in parallel order.

Use inverted pyramid style: Put the strongest point of the proposal in the lead, and then plan your proposal with supporting points.

Put information in perspective: Ask yourself: What does the reader know already, and what is new? If this is one of a series of proposals, you may need just a summary sentence referring to past information the reader already knows. The reader is going to read this proposal quickly and will get irritated if he or she has to wade through previously known material.

Write a strong conclusion: Summarize, but do not repeat, your lead. If you have written a proposal about marketing Mother's Day cards and you have given the supporting points that answer why you should change the method, the ending could be a strong statement like "We should start marketing these new cards in six months." If that time frame is part of your proposal, you could just end with a statement telling why it is a good idea.

Check your verbs: After you have written your draft, go back and circle the verbs and see if they are strong action words. If not, revise.

Press Release Checklist

Editors expect press releases to follow a fairly standard format:

• Include the name of a contact person, preferably two people, and phone numbers.

• Include a date when the release was written, and indicate "For immediate release" or another date for publication.

• Write a headline that states the focus of your release.

• Double- or triple-space the type.

• Try to limit the release to one or two pages.

• Write on one side of the paper. (This preference could change as environmental awareness increases.)

• Write *More* at the end of the page if the release continues; mark the end with the symbol # # # or the word *END,* set off by dashes.

Certain writing conventions are expected as well:

• Cover all the basics: who, what, when, where, why, how and so what.

• Use simple sentences, strong verbs, short sentences and short paragraphs. Try to limit a paragraph to four or five lines of type.

• Consider your audience, and write in the style most suited to that medium.

• Favor the inverted pyramid or a simple style that gets to the point quickly, even if you start with a creative lead.

• Use the list technique if you have several points to make, preferably in parallel construction.

• For a proposal, write a strong lead and support it with clear points. Again, consider the list technique for clarity.

• Consider whether a media kit would work better than a single release. If so, include one or several releases to provide different ideas, a fact sheet, graphics and perhaps a sample or other teaser.

Exercises

1 Gather information from an organization for an event on your campus or in your city. Write a press release announcing the event.

2 Study a company in your community. Devise a media kit to promote some product or aspect of the company. This activity may require some coordination so many students do not bother the same firm. If a team of students or the whole class is studying a large company, divide the responsibilities and have students study different aspects of the company.

3 Do your own survey of the media. Find out what editors read and what newspapers, magazines, and radio or television stations in your area prefer in the way of press releases.

4 Here is some information from PUMA USA, a company based in Massachusetts. Write a press release geared to newspapers' business sections. Use your name and phone number as the contact. Give yourself the title director of public relations. Put this address on your release: PUMA USA, 492 Old Connecticut Path, Framingham, MA 01701. Use your phone number again as the company's phone number. Write a headline and text from the following material:

Who: Christopher H. Smith, company president and chief executive officer

What: Announced a new policy about sales. PUMA products will no longer be sold through discount merchants.

When: For immediate release

Where: At company headquarters

Why: The policy is an outgrowth of the company's recently announced termination of the so-called "White Box" special product and marketing program. In the future, PUMA will target trade customers including athletic footwear specialists, sporting goods stores, and national retailers of quality footwear and apparel.

Backup information: New policy states that the company will not sell to dealers or retailers whose regular business practices include the frequent and aggressive discounting and advertising of quality national brands of athletic footwear, apparel and accessories.

From Smith: "This is a serious promise by PUMA and it will result in a significant drop in current volume that we've got to scramble to make up. We want sporting goods dealers and athletic equipment retailers to know that once current shoes are out of the pipeline, they will not see PUMA shoes being sold at mass merchant discounters."

Facts about the company: PUMA USA designs, produces and markets high-quality performance athletic footwear, apparel and sporting goods in the United States through a national network of sporting goods stores, specialty shops and department stores.

5 Convert a news story from your newspaper into a press release.

COACHING

TIPS

Use conversational, tell-a-friend style.

Use short sentences, one idea per sentence.

Use active voice.

Give attribution first—who said what before what was said.

Read your copy aloud.

Broadcast Writing

15

I t's a slow news day at KSNT-TV, and John Rinkenbaugh is worried. It's 9 a.m. and Rinkenbaugh, news director of the Topeka, Kan., station, is conducting the first news meeting of the day. Only three stories have been scheduled so far. A typical broadcast has a minimum of six stories, more often 10 to 12.

He looks in the planning file for this day. Not much going on. A community meeting about crime fighting is scheduled tonight. One reporter is working on a story about new management of the Expocentre, an entertainment and sports arena. Another is covering teachers' negotiations with the school board. And another reporter is checking out a few news tips.

Rinkenbaugh looks through the local newspaper. "We will not do any stories out of the paper as a given rule," he says. "We should beat the newspapers most of the time. I just look to see if there is a story we should do better."

But the newspaper offers little help today. "I don't start to panic until 1:30," he says. He'll need to know what will air on the 6 p.m. newscast by 2:15, when he conducts his next news meeting. "When you're desperate, you can pull off the network," he says.

The station is an affiliate of NBC. Not all of the 1,497 television stations in the United States are affiliated with a national network, but they are all ranked by market size. With 152,000 viewers, KSNT is ranked 141st out of 210 markets for television stations. It is one of three television stations in Topeka, and it is the kind of station where reporters get their start. All but two of the 17 employees in the news department have less than two years of experience.

In broadcast writing one of the most important decisions you have to make is not what you can put into your story but what you have to leave out.

Leona Hood, news producer,

KUSA-TV, Denver

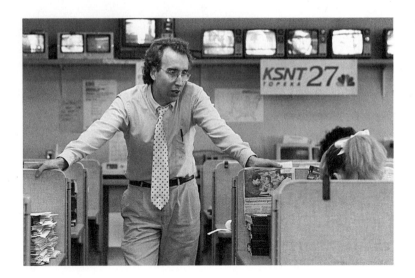

Rinkenbaugh has 14 years of experience in broadcast journalism. He started as a reporter in Kansas City. Then he worked in Minneapolis, Little Rock and Phoenix as a "producer," the person who writes the script that the newscaster, called an "anchor," reads.

At KSNT and many local television stations, two anchors share the newscast. Sometimes anchors rewrite their portions of the newscast to suit their own style. Reporters write their own stories and submit the copy to the producer, who incorporates it into the newscast. And at a small station like KSNT, reporters double as photographers and shoot the video for their stories or for another reporter.

Although print journalism is enhanced by photos and graphics, broadcast journalism depends on visuals. "A good TV reporter will let the pictures tell the story," Rinkenbaugh says. "You strive for more visual than verbal. A newspaper reporter can write a story without ever leaving the building. A TV reporter almost always has to be where it is happening."

The writing style also differs in some ways. Although the conversational, tell-a-friend style is suggested throughout this book for newspaper writing, it is essential for television. Clarity is crucial. A newspaper reader can reread a sentence or paragraph that may not be clear; a television viewer doesn't get a second chance to hear an unclear sentence.

Brevity is also more critical in television. The typical story a television reporter writes seldom runs longer than a minute and a half (written as *1:30* in broadcast copy). That includes the "sound bites," segments of the story showing the source in direct speech (called "actualities" in radio).

Reporter Mary Elbow setting up an interview with a source
Courtesy of Philip Meiring

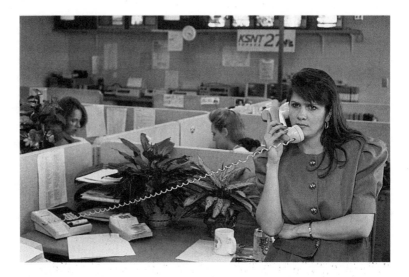

Here is the breakdown of a 30-minute newscast at KSNT:

- 10 minutes total for news
- 3:50 minutes (three minutes and 50 seconds) for weather
- 4:30 minutes for sports
- 1:20 total for introductions to the stories, called "lead-ins"—each running about 15 seconds
- 11 minutes of advertisements

At this point in the day, Rinkenbaugh can only count on stories to fill about five minutes of air time. A couple of reporters are working at their desks when reporter Rick Blum comes into the office. Two story ideas he was pursuing have fallen through. But he says he is pursuing a phone tip about a government red tape story. "I know I've got a story; I don't know how good it is," Blum says.

Reporter Janie Peterson says she's working on a story about neighbors' reaction to a recent police search in an apartment complex.

The day is getting better. Leigh Anne Stout, the assignment editor, checks the wire services—one from NBC and the other from The Associated Press. Nothing important to localize. But she's beginning to get a story budget together for the nightly newscast. She's also checking press releases and planning assignments for tonight's 10 p.m. newscast and for the next day. In addition, Stout is listening to the police scanner. If a major news story breaks, she will send the reporter and photographer closest to the scene. But on this day, nothing major happens.

Planning a Newscast

It's 2:15, time for the afternoon meeting to plan the 6 p.m. newscast. The two anchors and the producer have arrived; they'll stay through the 10 p.m. newscast. The assignment editor gives a rundown of the stories in the works. Rinkenbaugh and his staff discuss the stories and the order in which they will appear on the newscast.

Stories can be arranged in various order:

• By topics, blocking similar stories about crime, government, education and so on, starting with the most significant story (the most common order)

• By importance, from the most significant stories to the least

• By location, such as local, regional, state and national stories

• By some combination of these factors

In most cases, the producer will look for a theme that ties several of the stories together so that transitions between them are natural.

On this day, producer Tami Hale decides there is a topical theme: trouble. She uses a combination of significance and topical order. The lead story will be about new management at the Expocentre, a convention and sports center that has had financial troubles. Then she plans to run the story about trouble between teachers and the school district. With two months left before school starts, the contract impasse is important but not critical. She'll follow with two briefs about Kansas banks in trouble and the state's wheat crop in trouble because of too much rain.

News director
John Rinkenbaugh
conducting the afternoon
news meeting
Courtesy of Philip Meiring

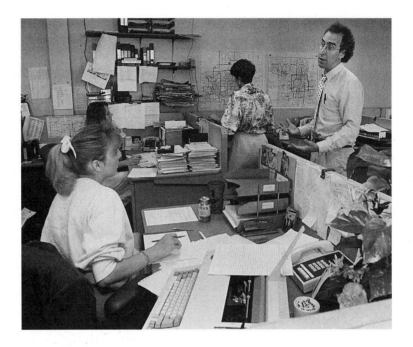

After a commercial break, Hale plans to run two stories about crime, one local and the other regional. After a few more stories, she'll end the newscast with a kicker, a story on the light side that she calls a "feel good" story.

Next to each story on the budget, Hale marks the minutes and seconds it will take in the newscast, including the time for an introduction.

By 3:30 p.m. several of the reporters have returned to write and edit their stories.

Nancy Mandell is editing the tape of her story about the Expocentre. She views the tape for sound bites, the segments that show the source speaking. When she finds the quotes she wants, she writes down the number indicated on the tape counter where the source's quotes start and stop and marks how many seconds the sound bite takes. In her written script, called "copy," she'll write the first few words of the direct quote—preceded by the word *IN*—and the last few words—marked *OUT*—to let the producer, anchors and broadcast director know when the source will speak and when the reporter will resume narration.

Here is one of the sound bites from Mandell's story. At KSNT all copy is typed in capital letters, and sound bites are set off by lines. The left side gives instructions for the "director," who coordinates the technical operations; the right side is for the copy. (In this example, explanations of terms are in italics.)

Reporter Janie Peterson editing videotape while compiling her story
Courtesy of Philip Meiring

SUPER *(superimpose name of source, which follows, on video):*
JOSEPH BRIGLIA
V.P. SALES/SPECTACOR
MANAGEMENT GROUP

BITE: (:12) *(sound bite will take 12 seconds)*
IN: 8:18 "ABOVE ALL I . . . *(first three words of quote, which are at 8:18 on tape counter)*
OUT: 8:30 . . . IN THIS AREA" *(last three words of quote, located at 8:30 on tape counter)*

After Mandell chooses her sound bites, she combines them with her own recorded comments and records it all on another tape for the final version. She also writes a "lead-in," the introduction to her story that the anchor will read. The complete story with sound bites is called a "package."

Reporter Rick Blum returns with his government red tape story. He writes his copy first and then views the tape to choose sound bites. He took thorough notes of the quotes during the reporting process, so when he views the tape, he spots the strongest sound bites quickly. "I try to use less of me and more of the sources," he says. "The story has a lot more meaning when it comes from them."

It's 4 p.m. The reporters check in with producer Hale. She begins writing the newscast. She writes the script that the anchors will read and decides the order in which the reporters' packages will be aired. For the 6 p.m. newscast Hale doesn't include much national news, because it will be covered by the network newscast that precedes this local one. But for the 10 p.m. show, she'll write briefs of national news for viewers who missed the network newscast. She pulls some wire stories and rewrites them. The news director does not permit "rip-and-read," or direct reading of wire copy.

Since this is a small station that does not have computers, Hale still types all her copy on special forms with six carbon duplicates. She types directions on the left side of the page and copy on the right. The pages are then fed into a TelePrompTer, a machine that projects the copy onto a video screen from which the anchors read. At stations that have computers, the copy can be sent directly via computer into the TelePrompTer. But even computerized stations still provide printouts of the newscast to the anchors, the director (who coordinates the technical production) and the producer.

At this station, all copy is typed in capital letters and double-spaced. Some news directors prefer to have the instructions typed in capital letters and the story copy typed in uppercase and lowercase letters.

About 30 minutes before the newscast, Hale gives her copy to the anchors. Art Navarro, one of the anchors, rewrites some of the copy to suit his own style. Today he has time. On a busy news day, he may not. "I try to write as much copy as possible. I want a very conversational style with simple sentences," he says.

It's almost air time. The anchors take their place behind a semicircular desk. The cameras are in place. In the control room, technicians are ready to coordinate the tapes from reporters with the anchors' lead-ins and stories. Hale has marked each page with a number to indicate the order of the newscast.

The red light goes on; the news program is on the air. Anchor Helen Neill reads from the script on the TelePrompTer, although both she and co-anchor Navarro have printed copies as well. Their cues and words are on the right side; the directions on the left are for the control room. Script directions for Navarro and Neill are marked with their first names. Here is the beginning of the script:

EXPOCENTRE MANAGER [Date] PM

PKG Lead-in	**ART**	AFTER SIX MONTHS OF NEGOTIATIONS, THE KANSAS EXPOCENTRE FINALLY HAS A NEW MANAGEMENT.
		GOOD EVENING AND WELCOME TO THE KSNT NEWS AT SIX.
	HELEN	SHAWNEE COUNTY COMMISSIONERS HAVE AGREED TO SIGN A FIVE-YEAR CONTRACT

KSNT anchor Helen Neill
Photo courtesy of Philip Meiring

WITH PHILADELPHIA-BASED
SPECTACOR MANAGEMENT
GROUP.

ART KSNT'S NANCY MANDELL
TELLS US THE NEW COMPANY
HOPES TO PUT THE EXPOCENTRE
UP IN LIGHTS.

Nancy Mandell's package follows this lead-in. The newscast continues with nine more stories and ends with a "feel good" feature story about a Big Brothers and Big Sisters program. Somehow the staff managed to come up with enough stories to fill both programs. News director John Rinkenbaugh has gone home. Maybe tomorrow will be a better news day.

Writing for Broadcast

When Leona Hood writes a newscast for her television station, she uses the "WIFM principle"—What's in It For Me. The *me,* in this case, is the viewer. Hood is news producer for KUSA-TV in Denver, an affiliate of the ABC network. She says you need to make people understand how the story affects them and why it is important.

"The big thing in broadcasting is that people only get one chance to hear what you say. If they miss something, they have so many other choices in these days of channel clickers," Hood says. "Every sentence has to contain something that interests them. Tell them something about this story that will make them care."

KUSA-TV is a large station, ranked 21st out of 210 in market size. But every viewer sees the broadcast as one person, Hood says. "Even though you are reaching hundreds of thousands of viewers, you try to talk to them on an individual level. These people are looking at you talking to them. The illusion you are trying to create, is 'Gee, did you hear what happened in your neighborhood today?'" The concept is the same as the tell-a-friend technique used throughout the book. Except that Hood uses tell-a-neighbor.

"When you write, think to yourself, 'How am I going to say this?' Think like you talk and then write like you think," Hood says. "That way you can imagine yourself telling someone a story. For every sentence you write, ask yourself: 'Would I say it this way to my neighbor?'"

One way to write conversationally is to write simple sentences. Keep the subject and verb close together, and avoid extra clauses and phrases. "That doesn't mean 'See Jane, See Dick, See Spot run,'" Hood says. "It means write so people can understand it the first go-'round. Don't make the viewer try to figure it out."

Making things simple for the viewer isn't so simple for the writer, however. You gather much more information than you can use. "In broadcast writing one of the most important decisions you can make is not what you can put into your story, but what you have to leave out," Hood says. "A lot of facts in a newspaper story are not important to a TV story. What you end up doing is just giving a nugget of the most important information."

For example, the names, ages and addresses that you would include in a newspaper story might bog down a TV story. In one KUSA story, suspects in a kidnapping case were caught because neighbors videotaped the kidnapping attempt. "We decided that in the context of the story, the names of the suspects were not important. The important information was that neighbors videotaped it. If you use the names of all the people involved, by the end of the 25 seconds for the story, you have completely lost the viewer."

To judge how much they can say in seconds or minutes, KUSA-TV writers get some help from a sophisticated computer system. The computer has a timer that converts the number of words into the length of time it would take an average reader to say them.

But it doesn't help writers coordinate their stories with the video sound bites. That's another skill that newspaper writers don't have to contend with. However, there are some similarities between using sound bites and using quotes in a print story. Broadcast writers must avoid repeating what the source will say in a sound bite. That's like avoiding a stutter quote in a print story—giving a transition that repeats the quote.

"Parroting what the subject will say is a cardinal sin," Hood says. "You enhance the pictures, not narrate them. You don't want to be a play-by-play announcer."

However, you do want to repeat some information in the story. Unlike a newspaper or magazine reader, who may stop reading and resume later, a broadcast viewer has to be listening. But the phone may ring, the kids may cry, and the dog may bark, says Hood. So when you write for broadcast, you need to repeat some information—the location of the story or the name of a key person—if that is crucial to the story.

For example, suppose a plane crashes. You tell where in the beginning of the story. But perhaps the viewer wasn't paying attention. Then, as you start talking about the crash or showing the scene, the viewer perks up. So you need to repeat the information in a different way. If you said in the lead that the plane crashed in Denver, in the middle you could make a reference to Denver police. If location isn't important, but a person or situation is, refer to those facts again in a subtle but clear way. Repetition is particularly important in stories about tragedy, Hood says. "Never leave the viewer wondering where it happened."

Here are some other basic writing tips:

Write in active voice: For example:

Active   Teachers in the Topeka School District are declaring an impasse tonight.

Passive   An impasse was declared by teachers in the Topeka school district tonight.

Use present tense whenever possible: Present tense gives the story a sense of immediacy. For example:

Present tense   Democratic leaders in Congress are vowing quick action to guarantee a woman's right to abortion.

Past tense   Democratic leaders in Congress have vowed quick action to guarantee a woman's right to abortion.

But don't strain to convert a sentence to present tense. Use the tense that fits the story naturally. In the next example (with verbs underlined), the present tense is awkward because it is mixed with the past tense:

72 people <u>go</u> to jail after an abortion protest in Milwaukee <u>turned</u> disorderly.

It's better to use the past tense (or present tense) consistently:

72 people <u>went</u> to jail after an abortion protest in Milwaukee <u>turned</u> disorderly.

Avoid long introductory clauses: Favor simple sentences with subject-verb-object order, instead of using complex sentences.

Subject-verb order

43-thousand General Motors workers will be returning to work. A nine-day strike at a G-M assembly plant in Ohio ended a few hours ago. Members of a United Auto Workers local in Lordstown, Ohio, overwhelmingly approved a new contract. The local plant produced parts for nine other G-M assembly plants.

Introductory clause

After a nine-day strike at a General Motors assembly plant in Lordstown, Ohio, that idled 43-thousand workers nationwide, members of a United Auto Workers local overwhelmingly approved a new contract a few hours ago. The Ohio plant produced parts for nine other G-M assembly plants.

Put a human face on the story whenever possible: Try to find someone personally affected by the issue. You can start with the specific, using a person first and then going to the nut graph:

Iris Duncan woke up one morning and said she thought someone had put waxed paper over her eyes.

 SOUND BITE: It was all fuzzy and cloudy and I couldn't see. I had no idea what was wrong.

 She went to her doctor that afternoon. She learned she had glaucoma. The disease strikes one of every 200-thousand people.

Starting with a general statement and going to a specific person is less effective:

Glaucoma strikes one of every 200-thousand people.

 Iris Duncan is one of them. She woke up one morning and said she thought someone had put waxed paper over her eyes.

Tell who said something before telling what was said: If the attribution is delayed until the end of the sentence, the statement may sound as if it is the reporter's opinion.

Say

Police say a 42-year-old woman whose body was found in a Kansas City motel early this morning may be the latest victim of a serial killer.

Do not say

A 42-year-old woman whose body was found in a Kansas City motel early this morning may be the latest victim of a serial killer, police say.

Use contractions with caution: Write them out. Let the anchors contract them if they want to. Avoid *can't*. It may sound too much like *can*.

Use action verbs: Avoid sentences starting with "There is." Those are wasted words with a weak verb.

Weak verb There is a new type of brain surgery that can cure epilepsy, a disease suffered by two-and-a-half-million Americans.

Stronger verb (and two simple sentences) A new type of brain surgery can cure epilepsy. The disease affects two-and-a-half-million Americans.

Omit needless words: Words like *that, which* and *who is* aren't always needed.

Wordy Investigators from Houston, Texas, are on their way to Tuscaloosa at this hour to help in the search for two Alabama men who are wanted in a mass killing.

Tighter (with action verb) Investigators from Houston, Texas, <u>flew</u> to Tuscaloosa this morning to help search for two Alabama men wanted in a mass killing.

Limit the use of numbers: They can be numbing, especially to the ear. Use percentages to give comparisons, when possible. If you must use numbers, round them off. Say "320-million dollars," not "320-million-122-thousand-three-hundred-44 dollars." The style for writing numbers is explained later in the chapter.

In general, remember to keep your writing short and simple. Follow this advice from KSNT news director John Rinkenbaugh: "The shorter the message, the greater the impact."

Broadcast Versus Newspaper Writing

A broadcast package ends up being quite different from a newspaper story on the same issue. The following example compares treatment of the Supreme Court ruling on an abortion case. The day of the court's decision, KSNT reporter Rick Blum localized the story for the evening newscast. The story appeared in the newspaper the next morning. In the broadcast version, note the dashes in place of commas to indicate pauses and the minimal use of punctuation. The explanations in italics are not part of the script.

ABORTION [Date]

PKG LEAD-IN	**HELEN**	THE SUPREME COURT HAS RULED MOST OF A RESTRICTIVE PENNSYLVANIA ABORTION LAW PASSES CONSTITUTIONAL MUSTER.
		GOOD EVENING AND THANK YOU FOR JOINING US.
	ART	THE PANEL STOPPED JUST SHORT TODAY—OF

OVERTURNING ROE VERSUS
WADE—THE 19-73 DECISION
LEGALIZING ABORTION.

HELEN

KSNT'S RICK BLUM REPORTS
TODAY'S RULING CARRIES
STRONG IMPLICATIONS
NATIONALLY—BUT MAY NOT
HAVE MUCH OF AN EFFECT IN
THE SUNFLOWER STATE.

TAKE PKG *(start reporter package)*

TODAY'S FIVE-FOUR SUPREME
COURT DECISION COULD MAKE
ABORTION TOUGHER TO GET
AROUND THE NATION.

YET LOCAL WOMEN'S
ORGANIZATIONS SEE HOPE
IN TODAY'S RULING.

SUPER *(sometimes labeled CG
for character generator, the
machine that creates the super):*

BITE: (:09)

**SARAH WOOD-CLARK
PRESIDENT CAP CITY NOW**

IN: 28:04 "IT IS A SURPRISE . . .
OUT: 28:13 . . . AS WE THOUGHT."

**SUPER: RICK BLUM
KSNT TOPEKA**

BOTH SIDES IN THE ABORTION
BATTLE AT THE CAPITOL SAY THE
RULING WILL SUPPORT BOTH
THE RECENTLY PASSED BILL AND
THE REASONS THEY WORKED
FOR IT.

SUPER: GOVERNOR JOAN FINNEY

BITE: (:10)
IN: 32:01 "I BELIEVE THIS IS . . .
OUT: 32:11 . . . LAST SPRING."

**SUPER: REP. KATHLEEN
SEBELIUS (D) TOPEKA**

BITE: (:12)
IN: 23:17 "I AM PLEASED . . .
OUT: 23:29 . . . PARTNERS."

THE PENNSYLVANIA LAW
UPHELD BY THE SUPREME COURT
HAS SOME PROVISIONS JUST LIKE

THE KANSAS LAW. THEY INCLUDE INFORMED CONSENT OF THE PATIENT, A WAITING PERIOD AND PARENTAL CONSENT FOR MINORS. BUT PRO-LIFE GROUPS SAY SINCE ROE VERSUS WADE WAS NOT OVERTURNED, THE POLITICAL RAMIFICATIONS ARE MINIMAL.

SUPER: CYNTHIA PATTON
KANSANS FOR LIFE

BITE: (:10)
IN: 9:31 "I THINK THESE . . .
OUT: 9:41 . . . GOING TO HAPPEN NOW."

BUT EVEN THOUGH ABORTION MAY NOT HAVE SO MUCH POLITICAL FIREPOWER THIS YEAR—BOTH SIDES MAY NOT HAVE LONG TO WAIT.

A DECISION ON WHETHER ROE VERSUS WADE IS CONSTITUTIONAL COULD COME BY THIS TIME NEXT YEAR.

RICK BLUM, KSNT NEWS, TOPEKA *(standard out cue, SOC, or reporter signing off with the name of the station)*

# # #

The next morning, the *Topeka* (Kan.) *Capital-Journal* published on the front page one national story on the ruling, with a graphic outlining the way the Supreme Court justices voted, and another story of local reaction. Four more stories covered past decisions on abortion, future legislative battles, and ways the ruling reflects the conservative and moderate views of Supreme Court justices. The newspaper stories would have taken about 30 minutes to read aloud, compared to Blum's package of 1:30 minutes. Compare Blum's lead-in with the beginning of The Associated Press version and of the *Capital-Journal* reaction story:

A divided Supreme Court ruled Monday that states can't ban abortions, upholding the core of its Roe vs. Wade decision. But the court said the states may raise new hurdles for women seeking to end their pregnancies.

The court, by a 5-4 vote, said women have a constitutional right to abortion. But a separate 7-2 coalition of justices substantially weakened the right as defined by the 1973 landmark ruling.

Dramatically concluding its 1992 term, the court upheld most provisions of a restrictive Pennsylvania abortion law.

Crowds of abortion-rights advocates and foes filled the plaza of the Supreme Court building for the court's latest, but surely not its last, word on this most divisive and emotional of national issues.

The decision not to abandon Roe vs. Wade was written by three conservative justices—Sandra Day O'Connor, Anthony M. Kennedy and, in his first vote on abortion since he was appointed by President Bush, David H. Souter.

The other Bush appointee, Justice Clarence Thomas, was one of the four who voted to let states outlaw virtually all abortions.

The decision lets states, among other things, instruct women seeking abortions on the available alternatives, and to make them wait 24 hours after receiving such information.

The Associated Press

The story continues with more detail. Note the use of clauses and specifics in the newspaper version, compared to the short, clipped broadcast version.

Here is the local reaction story:

Gov. Joan Finney said Monday she knows of no facet of the state's new abortion law, which goes into effect Wednesday, that would be altered by a U.S. Supreme Court decision on a much stricter Pennsylvania law.

"I have some information on the decision, and from what I can tell now, there is apparently no effect on our law," Finney said.

Attorney General Bob Stephan, anti-abortion and pro-choice activists, and several state lawmakers instrumental in passage of the Kansas law said it is apparently untouched by the high court decision.

The court upheld the basic premise of Roe vs. Wade but created some new areas in which states can move to restrict access to abortion.

"This issue isn't over," Finney said. "I don't know what the Legislature will propose next year in terms of abortion legislation, but I have said and I'll stick to my promise that I will not initiate any abortion legislation myself."

Stephan said he will have to study the full opinion on the Pennsylvania case, but "from its highlights, I don't see any real changes, except for a section that is somewhat troubling about the reporting of abortions."

Martin Hawver, *Topeka Capital-Journal*

The story continues with reactions from pro-choice and anti-abortion advocates and Kansas legislators. As you can see, the writing styles differ considerably.

The Writing Process

The coaching process used for newspaper writing can apply to broadcast writing as well. And although television writing is stressed here, most of these tips also apply to radio writing:

1 Conceive: In addition to planning a story for its verbal content, you must consider its visual impact. Will your story contain sound bites from sources on camera, action at the scene or graphics to superimpose on the screen? Will the story contain a reporter "standup" (talking on camera)?

2 Collect: Just as with reporting for a print story, you need to gather more information than you can use. You don't need to describe a source or scene that will be shown on the screen, but you should gather other details about the scene of an accident, disaster or breaking news event. Make sure you get the correct spelling and titles of your sources so their names can be superimposed on the screen.

3 Construct: For broadcast writing, as in newspaper or magazine writing, you need to plan your story like a road map. But with only 30 to 90 seconds to tell the story, it isn't a long-distance trip. Selectivity is even more important in broadcast writing because you have so little time to tell the story. Start with a focus sentence to guide you. Jot down the most important idea you want to express. Then review your notes and select only a few other key points to include in an average 90-second story. As Hood suggests, consider what you can leave out. You can eliminate much of the detail you would write for a newspaper. Pictures and sound bites will take their place.

4 Correct: After you have written your story, edit it to remove unnecessary words, and then read it aloud.

Story Structure

Like a newspaper story, a broadcast story has a lead, a body, and an ending. In many respects, they are the same in both media. But the differences are important.

Lead Every story needs its own lead. Max Utsler, a broadcast journalism professor at the University of Kansas, said the No. 1 consideration for a lead is that it must fit the pictures the viewer sees. "Good television writing is not the craftsmanship of words; it is the presentation of the words and pictures fitting together," he said.

Once you have decided which pictures to use at the beginning of your package, you can decide whether the story needs a hard or soft lead. That decision will also depend on the content of your story. Feature stories may take softer leads; a breaking-news story calls for a very direct approach. In all cases, you must get to the nut graph—the main reason for the story—very quickly, generally by the second or third sentence.

Regardless of the type of lead, most of the basic news elements—who, what, when, where, why, how, so what—must be included in the story. But you can't include all of them in a simple, coherent sentence for the lead. So select the ones that are most important to your story.

In broadcast writing, the placement of points of emphasis for these elements often differs from print journalism. The most common elements to stress in a broadcast lead are where, when and who; why and how often take too long to explain in a simple sentence. Here are some ways to use these elements in hard-news leads:

Where: Because most radio and television stations reach such a broad audience, the location of a story is even more important in broadcast than in print. Newspapers can use datelines to indicate location. Broadcast reports can superimpose the name of the location on the screen, but you also need to say it in the story. If the story follows a series of other stories from different regions, you might start it this way:

In Pawtucket, Rhode Island, police are looking into the suspicious death of a 15-month-old baby.

When: Almost all broadcast stories, except features, have a "today" element. Avoid using *a.m.* or *p.m.* If the specific time element is important, say something like "An earthquake struck Southern California at 7:15 this morning." In most cases, a general reference, such as "this morning" or "earlier today," is sufficient. Place your time element after the verb, which is more natural, conversational order:

Awkward	At least five people <u>today</u> were arrested in an anti-abortion protest outside a Milwaukee clinic.
Preferred	At least five people were arrested <u>today</u> in an anti-abortion protest outside a Milwaukee clinic.

Who: Identify a speaker by title before the name:

Say	Broward County Sheriff Ron Cochran said today he would not seek re-election when his term ends next year.
Do not say	Ron Cochran, sheriff of Broward County, said today . . .

Avoid using unfamiliar names in a lead and too many names in a story. When you have video sound bites, you may not even need the name in the story. The person can be identified by a superimposed title under his or her image in the taped segment. For a delayed identification, follow the same guidelines as for print journalism. Identify the person by an age, a location, an occupation or some other generic identifier. Then follow with the person's name:

One of two suspects in the fatal kidnapping of Exxon executive Sidney Reso (Ree-Soh) has pleaded guilty.

Irene Seale entered the plea to charges of extortion and conspiracy to commit extortion.

She appeared in court in Newark, New Jersey.

The Associated Press

Not all stories directly affect viewers' lives. But when possible, try to stress the impact within the first few sentences. Use an element that will make viewers care or understand why this story is important, unusual or of human interest. Don't be afraid to use the pronoun *you,* especially in consumer stories, to heighten impact. Instead of writing a story about a drought in California that will cause lettuce prices to increase, try this approach:

You're about to pay more for your salad. A drought in California is raising the price of lettuce.

When you can, "advance the lead"—that is, stress the next step—to gain immediacy.

Immediacy   Two people remain in serious condition following a car accident this afternoon.

No immediacy   Two people were injured in a car accident today.

The focus-on-a-person lead works as well in broadcast as in print, especially for a feature or a news story that the anchor introduces with a hard-news lead-in. Like the *Wall Street Journal* formula, this type of lead goes from the specific to the general. The person is one of many affected by the problem.

Judy and Joe Westbrook spent the morning cleaning up the furniture in their front yard. The Blue River had overflowed its banks and forced its way into their Independence home.

More than 25 families share their predicament. Late this afternoon all of those families were awaiting word about their flood insurance claims.

The mystery-teaser lead is another effective soft-lead technique, as long as you don't keep the viewer wondering what the story is about for too long. You must get to the point within the first few sentences.

In some ways it looks like an ordinary camp. It has hiking trails, a swimming pool and tennis courts.

But you don't have to worry about what clothes to wear. In fact, this is one of the few places where you'll feel out of place wearing clothes.

At this camp near Denver men and women of all ages frolic in the nude.

SOUND BITE: Nudism is about the only recreation that anybody can do whether they're rich or poor. We all share in the same satisfaction, so it's a very great equalizer.

Adapted from NBC News Channel

Body   As with all story structures, you first identify your focus. Then jot down the order of your supporting points—facts or quotes from sources in sound bites.

Limit transitions. One point should follow another one naturally. You have little time for wasted words or redundant transitions that parrot what the source will say in a sound bite. If you need transitions from the present to the past in your story, you can start the sentence with the time element—"yesterday" or "earlier today," for example.

One common transition device in broadcast news is the "key-word technique," picking up on a word in the last sentence and repeating it in the next. It's also a useful technique for bridging thought from one story to the next in the newscast. In this example, the reporter uses the word *shoes* as a transition device for the next paragraph:

The Nike commercial touts Michael Jordan's basketball prowess. Spike Lee says it's gotta be the shoes.

But Mike and his buddies wouldn't even have to wear shoes to waltz to the Olympic gold.

Some of the story structures described in Chapter 12 can apply to broadcast writing as well as print. However, because of the need for simplicity and brevity, the structure of broadcast news stories should be guided more by conversational storytelling than by rigid form. Here are some ways of organizing broadcast stories:

Problem/solution: The most common structure starts with a statement of the problem, provides support in sound bites and facts, offers background, and discusses the solutions if any exist. It often ends with the next step in the action.

Statement of problem   Three-hundred Korean-American merchants demonstrated for the sixth straight day in Los Angeles. They're demanding they be reimbursed for their losses resulting from the L-A riots.

Background   The merchants held up signs and chanted outside L-A's City Hall. They're particularly upset about a rebuilding ordinance passed by the City Council. The law allows stores destroyed in the riots to skip the usual 75-day process to obtain a building permit. But the law does not apply to liquor stores and gun shops.

Future tag: next step

The merchants are also considering a hunger strike.

NBC News Channel

The next example starts with an impact lead, offering the solution to a problem that has been resolved. Then it provides support for the lead, followed by background.

Impact: solution to a problem

If you took your car to Sears for repairs in the past two years, you may get a refund.

Support for lead

The company agreed to settle charges that it cheated customers by doing shoddy or unnecessary car repair work.

An estimated 12-thousand-500 Missourians will be eligible to receive 50-dollar credit coupons for any Sears merchandise.

Background

The alleged problems took place between August of 1990 and January 31st of this year.

Time sequence: A story may lend itself to order by time. Since broadcast stories need immediacy, the time sequence is usually a reverse chronology that starts with the present action, goes to the past (background) and ends with a future element. Here is an example of reverse chronology:

Present

Animal-rights activists are protesting this morning outside the Pittsburgh hospital where doctors transplanted a liver from a baboon to save a man's life.

Past (background)

About 15 protesters carried signs and chanted at the entrance to the University of Pittsburgh Medical Center. One member of the Pittsburgh Animal Activists says they don't believe one species should be sacrificed for another.

Pickets are holding signs saying, "There are no lesser creatures" and "Animals are not expendable."

Future

Doctors say if their patient continues to recover for the next month or more, they'll do three more of the same transplants.

The Associated Press

Hourglass: This structure is a type of time sequence. However, you start with a hard-news summary lead and then rebuild the story chronologically:

Summary lead

A toxic chemical spill near Superior, Wisconsin, forced hundreds of residents from two cities to flee their homes. At least two children received hospital treatment. A hospital official says more people will need treatment.

Beginning of chronology

The problems began this morning when 13 freight cars derailed just outside Superior. One Burlington Northern car fell into the Nemadji (Neh-Ma'-Jee) River, spilling some of its cargo of benzene. Benzene is a flammable solvent, and its fumes can cause hallucinations, dizziness and coughing.

In Superior and neighboring Duluth, Minnesota, officials ordered the evacuation of hundreds of homes within a mile of the river. And the Coast Guard says it's placed a boom across Superior Bay to prevent the benzene from spreading.

The Associated Press

Circle: Envision your story as a circle. The main point is the lead. All supporting points should relate to the focus in the lead. Unlike an inverted pyramid, where points are placed in descending order of importance, in a circular construction, each part of the story is equally important. Your ending can refer back to a point in the lead, as in this example about a water problem in a Kansas community:

Lead

Supporting points

If you live near Baldwin City, you may want to avoid drinking the water tonight.

The Kansas Department of Health and Environment is warning folks in Water District No. 2 in Douglas County about the water. Officials found bacteria in the water which may be harmful.

SOUND BITE (from Greg Crawford, an official with the Kansas Department of Health and Environment): These are indicator bacteria which may indicate the presence of more serious bacteria. Bacteria can cause a number of gastro-intestinal problems. And we would like people to prevent those problems by boiling their water or using bottled water or perhaps treating their water with Clorox or other liquid bleach.

Ending referring

back to lead

Crawford says bacteria come from dead animals. Until officials can clear up the problems, people in the area should take precautions.

KSNT-TV

Ending In broadcast writing, endings are called "tags" or "wrap-ups." Newspaper stories often end with a quote from a source, but in broadcast writing, the reporter has the last word in a package, followed by her or his name and the station identification. Often the only time the viewer sees the reporter is at the end of the story. However, many news directors now prefer using reporter standups within the story rather than at the end.

The most common endings:

Summary: A fact that reinforces the main idea without repeating previous points.

Future: The next step in some action.

Factual: A background statement or just another fact.

Consumer: Helpful items, such as where to call or go for additional information. If this information is important to the viewer, avoid giving it only one time. Warn the viewer that you will be repeating telephone numbers or locations later in the program.

Teasers and Lead-ins

A "teaser" is a few sentences to entice the viewer to stay tuned for the story that will come on the next newscast or after the commercial. (A teaser before a commercial is also called a "bump" or "bumper" at some stations.) A "lead-in" is the anchor's introduction to a story that a reporter will present.

Although teasers and lead-ins precede the story, they are written by the producer or anchor after the reporter turns in the story.

The concept behind all these promotional briefs is "Stay tuned, you'll want to hear this." Use the tell-a-friend technique, as though you were saying "Guess what?" or "You won't believe what happened." Write one to three brief sentences that are enticing enough to arouse curiosity.

Here is a teaser for a 10 p.m. newscast:

Coming up on the KSNT news at ten . . .

Diedra Davis will tell us about a group of city leaders coming together to fight crime in Topeka . . .

And . . .

You're never too young to learn the dangers of smoking . . .

We'll show you how one program is teaching pre-school children how to stay smoke-free . . .

These stories and more coming up on the KSNT news at ten.
KSNT-TV

A teaser before the commercial break can be preceded by such phrases as "Just ahead," "Still to come," "When we continue," "Stay tuned." Or you can end the bump with the statement "We'll have that story for you when we come back." Sometimes stations do a teaser and end with "But first . . ." Here are two examples of a teaser before a break:

A battle over the French abortion pill heads to the U.S. Supreme Court. Stay tuned.

Earthquake aftershocks rattle Southern California. We'll have the details on the damage and the cleanup when we come back.

Sometimes fragments can get the point across better than complete sentences. Teasers especially lend themselves to phrases without verbs:

In a moment . . . sex behind bars. A scandal brewing in Georgia.
CNN

Lead-ins immediately precede the story package by a reporter. They are written more like a lead to a story, but they should not repeat the reporter's lead. The lead-in gives the essence of the story, like a focus line, and ends with a statement that the reporter, usually cited by name, has more:

Many women exercise hard to get in shape. But a new study says too much exercise can often lead to serious health problems for women. Ileana Bravo tells us how some female college athletes could suffer from eating disorders as a result . . .
NBC News Channel

Here is how one NBC promo would vary depending on how it was used:

Teaser for next newscast

Patients of a dentist who died recently are very concerned over the news that his death was due to AIDS. Phones are ringing off the hook at the local health department in Bowling Green concerning Dr. Donald Hewitt. We'll have that story and more for you on our 6 o'clock newscast.

Teaser before commercial

Patients of a dentist who died recently are very concerned over the news that his death was due to AIDS. Phones are ringing off the hook at the local health depart-ment in Bowling Green concerning Dr. Donald Hewitt. We'll have that story when we come back.

Lead-in

Patients of a dentist who died recently are very concerned over the news that his death was due to AIDS. Phones are ringing off the hook at the local health department in Bowling Green concerning Dr. Donald Hewitt. Reporter Mike O'Connell has more.

Just ahead you'll learn how to write a reporter package with direc-tions for a newscast. But first . . .

Copy Preparation and Style

Broadcast copy differs considerably from newspaper copy. When writ-ing copy to be read aloud, punctuation changes. Everything should be written so the anchors or reporters can read it easily. The less punctua-tion, the easier it is to read. Although many producers use points of ellipsis (three dots) to indicate pauses, broadcast professor Max Utsler says the comma, semicolon or dash is preferable. "Ellipses tend to lead to run-on sentences," he says. "If you want a short pause, use a comma; for a longer pause, use a dash. Even better, write short sentences and use periods."

Some of the rules for copy preparation differ from station to station. For example, although many stations use capital letters for both text and directions, others use lowercase and uppercase letters for story text or just for the sound bites. You will have to adapt to the news director's preferences.

Here are some general guidelines:

• Give the story a "slug" (a one- or two-word title), and write it at the top left-hand corner of each page. Follow it with the date and the name or initials of the writer. Put a slug on every page. If the same story continues for several pages, use that title. When the story changes, use a new slug for that story.

• Double- or triple-space all copy. Write on only one side of the paper.

• Number every page. If a story continues to another page, you may prefer to number it 1A, 1B, and so on until the next story, which would start with the number 2.

• Use a separate page for each story, including briefs or teasers. If a story continues on another page, write *More* in parentheses or set off by dashes at the bottom of the page. Mark the end of the story with a # # # symbol or *(End)* or *-30-*.

• Use capital letters for instructions to the director; type them on the left side of the page. For computer copy, you will need a two-column format.

• Type the story on the right side of the page in a column approximately 3 inches wide. Capital letters are preferred by many news directors and producers for this copy also, but not universally.

• Indent paragraphs.

• Do not split and hyphenate words at the end of a sentence. Let the anchor see the whole word.

• Use dashes for pauses.

• If you have a typo or need to change a word, cross out the mistake completely by typing X's over it or blacking it out with pencil. Write the correct word next to it. Do not cross out part of a word for a correction. That makes the copy difficult to read. Strive for clean copy.

• Set off sound bites with double lines above and below the bite.

Punctuation   Avoid quotation marks. Generally, sound bites take the place of quotations. But if you want to quote someone, write out the word *quote* in this way: "She said . . . quote . . . this situation is impossible" or "and these are her exact words. . . ." Don't bother with *unquote* or end marks. The reader's emphasis should make the end of the quote clear.

Limit punctuation to the comma, period, question mark and dash.

Numbers   Write out the numbers one through nine; use numerals for numbers over 10. Write out *hundred, thousand, million, billion* and *trillion.* Round off numbers when possible.

Write numbers to be read, as follows: "13-hundred, two-thousand, 14-thousand, one-million, 17-million." More complicated numbers would be written this way: "320-thousand," not "320,000"; "15-million-230-thousand," not "15,230,000."

For decimals, write out the word *point:* "It comes to 17-point-two-million dollars." Write out the word *dollars* also, instead of using the symbol.

There are some exceptions. Addresses, telephone numbers and time of day are written in numerals, even if the figures are lower than 10: "She lives at 5 Westbrooke Avenue"; "The accident occurred at 10:30 this morning" (avoid *a.m.* and *p.m.*); "The telephone number to call for information is 5-5-5-1-2-3-4" (separate the numerals with dashes so they are easier to read).

Names and titles   Spell difficult pronunciations of names and locations phonetically. Some anchors prefer only the phonetic spelling instead of the real name followed by the phonetic pronunciation. For example, KUSA producer Leona Hood's name would be pronounced *Lee-Ahna Hood,* and KSNT reporter Rick Blum's name would be written *Rick Bloom.*

Identify a person's title before the name: "State Attorney General John Lawmaker is pleased with the results of a crackdown on fraudulent coal dust testing," not "John Lawmaker, state attorney general, is pleased with the results. . . ."

Using Broadcast Terms

Before you can write your own story or newscast, you need to understand some basic terms. Some of these have already been mentioned.

Anchor: Reads the news.

Backtiming: Exact time in the newscast that a segment will air. For example, a story that will air 12 minutes and 15 seconds into the newscast will be labeled 12:15. If the last segment in a 30-minute newscast is one minute, the backtiming will be 29, alerting the anchor that the segment must start at precisely that time or it will have to be cut.

Brief: Abbreviated news story, from 10 to 20 seconds.

Bump: "Stay-tuned" teaser before a commercial, to entice viewers to continue watching the broadcast for stories that will follow after the break.

Character generator: Computer-type machine that produces the letters, numbers or words superimposed on the screen to label a visual image, such as a person or place.

IN: Indicates the first few words of the source's quote to start a sound bite.

News director: Oversees all news operations at the station.

OUT: Indicates the last few words of the source's quote, ending the sound bite.

Package: Reporter's story that includes narration, visual images and interviews with sources.

Producer: Writes the copy that anchors read for the newscast.

Reader: Story the anchor reads without visuals or sound bites.

Rip-and-read: Copy from the wire services that is read exactly as it was written instead of being rewritten.

Seg time: Length of time for a news segment. Brief may be :10, or 10 seconds; reporter's package, including the lead-in by an anchor, may be 1:45.

SOC (standard out cue): Reporter's sign-off comments at the end of the story. For example, "This is Rick Blum for KSNT TOPEKA."

SOT (sound on tape): Similar to a sound bite; indicated in copy along with the amount of time the taped comments will take. For example, *SOT:15* means the comments on the tape will take 15 seconds.

Sound bite: Video segment showing the source speaking.

Super: Letters, numbers or words produced by the character generator and superimposed over visual images; often used to identify the person appearing on the tape. At some stations, the letters *CG*—for character generator—are used to indicate the super.

Teaser: Introduction to a story on the next newscast, to tease viewers to tune in.

TelePrompTer: Video terminal that displays the script for the anchor to read.

VO (voice over): Anchor's voice over video images. Words and images should coincide.

VOB (voice over bite): Anchor's voice over video images with a sound bite from a source.

Writing a Package

The example in this section is a reporter's package from KUSA-TV in Denver. The story is slugged *POW*—for "Person of the Week," a regular feature at the station. It focuses on a person who had a great impact in the community that week.

Note that the directions for the anchor and technical crew are on the left and the story text is on the right. The story text is in capital letters. The explanations in italics were not in the package.

This story is about a teen-ager who died trying to save his mother and sister. The shooting happened on a Monday; the package aired on Friday during the regular POW segment. It ran 2:35 minutes, which is longer than the normal 1:30 minutes.

KUSA writes out sound bites for close-captioned television so hearing-impaired people can see the words. Generally, you would just introduce the sound bites in copy with the first three words and last three words.

The story is labeled *G* because it comes in the G segment of this broadcast. At KUSA, segments A through C are for news, D for weather, F for sports and G for a special feature. The last story is H.

Ed is Ed Sardella, the anchor who is reading this package.

The word *BOX* indicates that a super with the name and picture of the person of the week, Kevin Woodson, will appear over Sardella's shoulder, even though the story does not mention Woodson's last name until the end.

This story was introduced by a teaser saying, "Coming up, we'll introduce you to our person of the week."

ED ON BOX ——————— G-1 ———————

POW *(graphic called box appears over Sardella's shoulder, containing name of Kevin Woodson and slug* Person of the Week; *anchor's introduction to story)*

DOMESTIC VIOLENCE TOO OFTEN CHOOSES THE INNOCENT TO BE ITS VICTIM. TOO OFTEN, IT DESTROYS FAMILIES—THIS WEEK, IT TOOK ANOTHER.

A MOTHER IS DEAD. HER 15-YEAR-OLD SON DID WHAT HE COULD TO PROTECT HIS MOTHER AND HIS SISTER. BUT HE LOST HIS LIFE TOO.

HE IS OUR 9 NEWS PERSON OF THE WEEK.

TAKE PKG *(start taped package)* ——— ——————— **TAKE PKG** ———————
(NAT—BEST FRIEND) ——————— G-2 ———————
(FRIENDS ARRIVING)
(anchor reading all words in capital letters; **NAT** *means natural sound, in this case of friends arriving at house;* **G-2** *means next part of this segment)*

SHOCK AND HORROR SHATTERED A QUIET MONDAY MORNING. FRIENDS WERE OVERWHELMED WITH GRIEF. TRACY STUART AND HER SON KEVIN WERE DEAD. POLICE SAY TRACY'S

HUSBAND RAY STUART BROKE INTO THEIR HOME AND KILLED HER FIRST. KEVIN GRABBED A GUN AND TRIED TO STOP HIM; TRYING TO PROTECT HIS MOTHER AND SISTER. HE DIDN'T KNOW HIS MOTHER MIGHT ALREADY BE DEAD.

KEVIN SHOT HIS STEP-FATHER. BUT STUART FIRED BACK, AND KILLED KEVIN. A TRAGIC LOSS OF LIFE.

FUNERAL TAPE #1 *(file tape)*

CG KAREN SCOTT
KEVIN'S TEACHER
5:13 – 5:18

(CG means character generator, to super-impose name under person speaking in sound bite; numbers are location of sound bite on tape; bite is 5 seconds long)
TAPE TOWN SHOTS *(anchor resumes reading)*

Teachers work and work and work and they find some students coming to leadership, and zap they're gone.

Why do we have to lose young people of youth like this, this is what we need for our country, for our little town.

IN THIS LITTLE TOWN, KEVIN WAS A TYPICAL TEENAGER. HE LOVED SPORTS, ESPECIALLY BASKETBALL AND BASEBALL.

FUNERAL TAPE #2
CG SHAWN LOTTMAN
KEVIN'S BEST FRIEND

He was always playing first, and I was over at 3rd, and I threw at the ground in practice and hit him in the nose, and he's always been giving me heck about that all the time.

CG MIKE GRANDSTAFF
SCHOOL PRINCIPAL

Pretty solid athlete, he made a turn around from an average student to an honor roll student.

A lot of growth in the last couple of years from Kevin, he really tried to take care of his mom and sister.

BYERS SHOOTING #2 *(anchor resumes over tape of shooting in Byers, Colo.)*

HIS FRIENDS SAY HE NEVER LET ANYONE TEASE HIS SISTER TRISHIA. THEY STUCK TOGETHER. SHE CRIED OUT FOR HIM, WHEN THE SHOTS WERE FIRED MONDAY.

CG BARBARA ALEXANDER
VICTIM'S ASSISTANCE COUNSELOR

Her brother was her protector. She felt like her brother was there for her. She has a feeling her brother may have saved her life.

FUNERAL TAPE #2 (*anchor resumes over pictures of funeral tape*)

BUT HE WAS UNABLE TO SAVE HIS OWN. AND WHILE FRIENDS MOURN HIS DEATH, THEY ALSO REMEMBER KEVIN THEIR FRIEND.

CG KEN LOTTMAN
KEVIN'S BASEBALL COACH

Always a person with a smile on his face, and always there for anybody.

The smile, and his energy, the leadership.

They will remember him as an athlete and friend. We'll still have tournament games and as of now, we'll go on with that, I think they will handle it, and play for Kevin—that's what they'll do.

BYERS TAPE
(FLOWERS IN FRONT OF HOUSE)
ED SINGLE (*anchor finishes package, with camera on him*)

THEY WILL REMEMBER KEVIN, A YOUNG MAN WHO HAD SO MUCH LIFE AHEAD. BUT RISKED IT ALL FOR HIS MOTHER AND SISTER. KEVIN WOODSON IS OUR 9 NEWS PERSON OF THE WEEK.

KEVIN'S SISTER, TRISHIA, IS 13. SHE IS GOING TO LIVE WITH HER AUNT IN LONGMONT. A FUND HAS BEEN SET UP FOR HER AT THE BYERS STATE BANK.

# # #

Exercises

1 Write a broadcast brief, about 15 seconds, based on this information from an NBC News Channel story:

Who: A consumer group, the Florida Consumer's Federation

What: Filed a suit charging the Publix Grocery Store chain with discrimination

Why: Group claims that the grocery chain failed to put enough women, blacks and Hispanics in management jobs and that the company doesn't have enough stores in minority neighborhoods.

When: Today

Backup information: Publix management agrees with some of the complaints but says it is working to overcome them, according to Publix president Mark Hollis.

2   Write a broadcast package based on the following newspaper story. Write the quotes you want to use in sound bite form; estimate the time of the sound bites.

A 16-year-old boy, driving without a license, led Louisville police on a 13-minute chase yesterday afternoon, driving at up to 80 mph on streets in the Highlands sections where the sidewalks were crowded with pedestrians.

The pursuit ended at 5:05 p.m., when the boy—whose name police did not release because of his age—rammed his father's 1991 Honda Accord into the rear of Officer Bob Arnold's patrol car on Trevilian Way just east of Valley Vista.

No one was injured, and the police car suffered only a minor scrape on the rear bumper. The other car was damaged more.

Officer John Butts said the chase started near Cherokee Park when he tried to stop the boy for running over a stop sign, and the boy refused to pull over. Butts radioed for help and Arnold joined the chase.

"I was concerned, because he came close to hitting several pedestrians who were out walking because of the nice weather," Butts said last night.

"Anxiety sets in when a chase continues on for this amount of time," he added. "It's longer than any officer would prefer to be in a high-speed vehicle pursuit."

Butts said the boy forced several cars off the road during the chase, which came to an end when Arnold managed to get in front of the boy and slowed down.

He said the boy will be charged with numerous felonies and traffic violations; among the charges are wanton endangerment and resisting arrest. The boy was taken to the Jefferson County Youth Center.

Butts said he did not know why the boy refused to stop, but added, "He has no license, and he was not supposed to be driving his father's car."

The (Louisville, Ky.) *Courier-Journal*

3   Design a newscast from your local newspaper. Choose 10 to 12 stories for your newscast. Decide which ones should be briefs and which should be longer packages. List the stories in the order you would present them: by topics, location, significance or a combination.

4   Cover an event on campus, and write it up as a broadcast package. Write your quotes as sound bites.

5   Write a teaser for the "Person in the News" story in this chapter.

6   Write lead-ins for the stories in this chapter in the "Body" section.

7   Choose three stories from your local newspaper and write teasers, leads and lead-ins for them.

FOUR

Understanding Media Issues

Accuracy and Libel

Media Ethics

Multicultural Sensitivity

COACHING

TIPS

Seek documents to substantiate source's claims.

Check resumes and other materials from sources.

Seek other sources with alternate points of view.

Role-play: If you were the source or the source's attorney, what would you find libelous or objectionable in the story?

Accuracy and Libel

16

Miami Herald reporter Paul Shannon thought the tip he received from a teacher would make a good story. A 10-year-old child in Fort Lauderdale, Fla., was dying from sickle-cell anemia. Her mother, a Bahamian citizen, wanted to be by her side when she died. But the mother's visa had expired, and U.S. immigration officials were trying to deport her.

Shannon began to check out the story. He visited the mother and her daughter at their apartment. The mother showed him documents, including a letter from a doctor confirming that the child had this incurable disease and a letter from a university clinic. The child talked about her blood transfusions and the trances during severe attacks of the disease when she would almost lose consciousness.

Shannon returned to the newsroom and called the doctor, who confirmed that the child had sickle-cell anemia. Then the doctor's beeper sounded and he had to hang up, but he promised to call back later.

Shannon checked with the child's school principal and a woman in the mother's prayer group. "It is a sad story," the woman said. Then he called some local medical experts.

If the trancelike seizures are coming often, her life expectancy is very short, one expert said.

Deadline was approaching. Shannon began drafting his lead:

There is no such thing as a minor mistake, not even just one or two little errors in a lengthy manuscript.

Steve Weinberg, former director, Investigative Reporters and Editors, Inc.

> In the clinical jargon of doctors, 10-year-old Celestial Jones has a short life expectancy.
>
> She will change in the matter of a few months from a giggling little girl to one bent over and bedridden like a very old woman. The trance-like seizures have already begun. As her immune system is slowly sapped, the infections will start, one after another. Then comes the crippling stroke.
>
> Finally, unless the crisis mysteriously fades, Celestial will die. Her mother wants to be at her bedside.
>
> Paul Shannon, *The IRE Journal*

He told his editors he would have the rest of the story in 15 minutes.

Shannon had talked to immigration officials. One promised to re-open the case so the mother could have a hearing.

Then the child's doctor returned his call. Shannon read his lead to the doctor to check its accuracy. "I don't believe that is correct," the doctor said. The disease was in remission, he said. It might not return until the child was in her forties. He added: The child fakes her trances; she has major psychological problems.

Shannon spiked the story. Three weeks later, the local competition ran a story with this lead:

> Sometimes, when the pain becomes too much for her to bear, Celestial Jones loses consciousness.

Nowhere in the story was the doctor quoted. Apparently he could not be reached for comment.

Shannon, who recounted the experience in an article in *The IRE Journal,* a publication of the Investigative Reporters and Editors organization, said one of his editors had suggested writing a story about how the mother was trying to deceive immigration officials, but the idea was discarded.

How do you know when a story is inaccurate? You don't unless you check it out. It's easy to be fooled, especially when you're dealing with emotional stories. Make one more phone call. Check one more document. And when you can't reach someone for comment, try and try again.

Deadline pressure, especially for breaking news, may force you to run the story when some key source can't be reached for comment. You should say that in the story so the reader knows you tried. But one try isn't enough.

The Importance of Accuracy

Accuracy is paramount for a good journalist. Every mistake you make jeopardizes the newspaper's credibility with readers. Because of that credibility factor, newspapers throughout the country print corrections every day, many for the incorrect spelling of names. That's another reason why you should always double-check the names in your stories.

Checking Information

ABC television reporter Mark Potter found out the hard way how important it is to check not only names but also information on resumes. He was reporting a story about a drug rehabilitation counselor in Detroit who said he was an All-American football player in college. Potter and his camera crew completed the interviewing and taping for the story. Then Potter returned to his home base in Miami and called the university to get some tape of the former football star in college. The university had never heard of the man. Potter killed the story. He said he could have kicked himself for not checking the man's resume before he and the camera crew went to Detroit.

Some sources falsify their resumes to make themselves look better; other sources use the media to serve their own purposes.

Reporters at *The Arizona Republic/Phoenix Gazette* learned both lessons in a rather startling way. Darrow "Duke" Tully, the newspaper's publisher during the 1980s, had bragged for many years about his impressive record as a U.S. Air Force fighter pilot and lieutenant colonel in the reserves. He said he had been shot down during the Korean War in 1952, had flown 100 missions in Vietnam and had earned innumerable medals, including the Purple Heart and Vietnam Gallantry Cross. He was often photographed in his medal-studded Air Force uniform at various functions.

But the county attorney serving the Phoenix area had some doubts. The newspaper had been publishing a series of stories criticizing the attorney, Tom Collins, for his "free-spending" use of his government expense account. Collins claimed the newspaper was conducting a smear campaign. So he investigated the publisher's background.

On Dec. 26, 1986, Collins announced at a press conference that Tully had never served in the military. Tully, aware of the forthcoming revelations, had resigned as publisher shortly before the press conference. He later confessed that he had fabricated his military record nearly 30 years earlier to help him gain promotions, and over the years the lies just mushroomed. The medals and uniform that he wore so proudly were purchased in a San Francisco uniform shop.

Tully had his motives for lying; Collins had his motives for exposing the lies. To its chagrin, the newspaper got caught in the middle.

You don't have to suspect everyone of lying, including your own publisher. However, you should make an effort to check documents and seek balance in your stories. And you should realize that many sources, especially politicians, try to use the media to promote their own agendas.

However, most problems with inaccuracy result not from sources but from carelessness.

Showing Copy to Sources

Paul Shannon checked the accuracy of his information by reading the lead of his would-be story to the doctor. Should you show your story to sources or read it to them before you print it? Many of your sources will ask you to do that.

And many editors will say you shouldn't. They claim the risks are too great that sources will recant what they have told you or ask you to delete any information that puts them in a bad light.

Steve Weinberg, former director of Investigative Reporters and Editors and a leading authority on researching records, says it's time to change that traditional way of thinking. "I am convinced that my practice of pre-publication readbacks and manuscript submission has led to more accurate, fair and thorough newspaper pieces, magazine articles, and books," he wrote in *Quill* magazine.

While working on an unauthorized biography of industrialist Armand Hammer, Weinberg asked about 300 of his sources to check the accuracy of portions of the manuscript in which they were quoted or cited. As a result of his checks, he identified two errors in his 1,000-page manuscript. "There is no such thing as a minor mistake, not even just one or two little errors in a lengthy manuscript," he wrote.

Weinberg makes it clear that the source who is checking the story has the right only to check for accuracy, not to make any changes.

If you don't show the entire story to your source, it is considered acceptable—even wise—to check with a source any technical information you may not fully understand. You can read what you have written and, like Weinberg, ask the source to check its accuracy.

If you are sure your information is accurate and you don't want to read the information to sources before publication, you could try this suggestion from Bill Marimow, two-time winner of the Pulitzer Prize. Marimow, an editor at *The Baltimore Sun,* suggests calling a source the day after the story is published and asking if the story was accurate and fair. He claims that call will deepen the source's respect for you, and the source may even give you information for a follow-up story.

Several newspapers also check reporters' accuracy by contacting sources after the stories have been published. But that system usually antagonizes reporters.

Libel

The First Amendment to the U.S. Constitution provides the media with protection against censorship, and it is often referred to during the defense of libel suits:

Congress shall make no law respecting an establishment of religion or prohibiting the free exercise thereof; or abridging the freedom of speech, or of the press; or the right of people peaceably to assemble, and to petition the Government for a redress of grievances.

"Libel" is publication of a falsity that causes injury to someone's reputation. Anyone can sue or threaten to sue for libel, claiming injury to his or her reputation. The real concern is whether the person has grounds enough to win.

"Libel is essentially a false and defamatory attack in written form on a person's reputation or character. Broadcast defamation is libel because there is usually a written script. Oral or spoken defamation is slander," according to Donald Gillmor and his co-authors in *Mass Communication Law: Cases and Comment.* The "script" is not limited to a news story, the authors explain; it can take the form of headlines, photos, cartoons, film, tape, records, signs, bumper stickers and advertisements.

The key factors for a writer to consider are whether you published untrue information that hurt the reputation of an identifiable person and whether you were either negligent or reckless in failing to check the information.

• Are you publishing something you aren't sure is truthful?

• Are you carelessly publishing something that is inaccurate?

• Are you publishing something accusatory that you haven't checked out?

If your answer is yes to any of those questions, you could be in trouble for libel.

Times v. Sullivan

Those standards were the ones the U.S. Supreme Court applied in 1964 in a landmark libel case, *New York Times Co. v. Sullivan,* and the standards have been applied since then.

The *New York Times* case stemmed from an advertisement the newspaper accepted in 1960 from a group of people in the civil rights movement. The group was trying to raise money for the Committee to Defend Martin Luther King. The ad claimed that King had been arrested seven times and that his home had been bombed. It also claimed that black students who had staged a nonviolent civil rights demonstration at Alabama State University had been the target of police brutality. The advertisement accused the Montgomery, Ala., police department of being armed with shotguns and using tear gas to subdue students.

Even though the police commissioner, L.B. Sullivan, had not been named in the advertisement, he sued for libel. He claimed that the ad contained factual errors concerning the police and damaged his reputation. He claimed that the police did not ring the college campus or padlock the college dining hall, as the ad had claimed. Furthermore,

Dr. King had been arrested four times, not seven, and three of the four arrests had occurred before Sullivan was commissioner.

Sullivan won in the lower courts and the Alabama Supreme Court. But the U.S. Supreme Court reversed the decision in its landmark ruling about "actual malice." Malice, in this context, does not mean intent to harm someone; it means that you published something knowing it was false or not bothering to check its truth or falsity. The justices said:

> The constitutional guarantees require, we think, a federal rule that prohibits a public official from recovering damages for defamatory falsehood relating to his official conduct unless he proves that the statement was made with "actual malice"—that is knowledge that it was false or with reckless disregard of whether it was false or not.

The court placed the burden of proving libel on the plaintiff, the person who is suing. The justices made this a constitutional issue, applying the First Amendment right of a free press to publish matters of public concern. In the ruling, Justice William Brennan wrote:

> Thus we consider this case against the background of a profound national commitment to the principle that debate on public issues should be uninhibited, robust, and wide-open, and that it may well include vehement, caustic, and sometimes unpleasantly sharp attacks on government and public officials.

The *Times v. Sullivan* ruling applied only to people who are public officials. The application was later broadened to include "public figures."

Public Officials

Who is a public official for purposes of libel law? Elected officials and candidates for office are definitely considered public officials. Appointed officials may or may not be. Here are the criteria: Do they have authority to set policy in the government, and are they under enough public scrutiny to have easy access to the media?

The Supreme Court defined public officials this way in *Rosenblatt v. Baer,* a case about the status of appointed officials:

> It is clear, therefore, that the "public official" designation applies at the very least to those among the hierarchy of government employees who have, or appear to the public to have, substantial responsibility for or control over the conduct of government affairs.

Is a police officer a public official? Courts in Pennsylvania are split on that decision, but most courts have ruled that law enforcement officers are public officials because they have the power to make arrests, a form of control in government. Teachers, professors and other employees in a public education system, however, are not usually defined as public officials, because they are carrying out policies set by other

officials of the school district or university. If they achieve fame or notoriety, however, they may become public figures.

Public Figures

Who is a public figure, and why is the distinction between public
officials and public figures important? People may be considered public
figures if their achievements or notoriety place them in the public eye or
if they seek attention by voluntarily thrusting themselves into a public
controversy. But if they are brought into the public spotlight involuntar-
ily, they may not be public figures. A court usually will determine
whether the person qualifies as a public figure.

Just as with public officials, if a person suing is considered a public
figure, he or she has the burden of proving that alleged libelous information is false. The person or organization being sued does not have to
prove libel.

The courts identify three types of public figures: pervasive, vortex
and involuntary public figures.

A "pervasive" public figure is a person who has gained prominence
in society or great power and influence. Well-known entertainers and
athletes and people who voluntarily seek public attention are in this
category.

A "vortex" or "limited" public figure is a person who has voluntarily
thrust himself or herself into a public controversy to influence the outcome. The Supreme Court has stated that people in this category are not
public figures for all aspects of their lives but only for the aspects that relate to their role in a particular public controversy. A key point is the
"voluntary" concept. An individual does not automatically become a
public figure if he or she is thrust into a newsworthy situation; the involvement in the controversy must be the person's choice. Access to the
media is another factor in determining whether someone is a public
figure. The person must have enough regular and continuing access to
the media to counter criticism and expose falsehoods.

Consider the case of *Hutchinson v. Proxmire.* In 1975 when Sen.
William Proxmire issued his annual "Golden Fleece" awards, which sat-
irize some government-funded research projects as wasteful, he issued a
press release targeting a researcher who was using monkeys to study
stress. The scientist, Ronald Hutchinson, sued Proxmire for damaging
his reputation and subjecting him to public ridicule by falsely claiming Hutchinson's research was wasteful. Key to the case was determining whether Hutchinson was a public figure

Proxmire claimed the scientist was a public figure because he had received federal grants and had access to the media when they contacted
him about receiving the Golden Fleece award. A federal district court
agreed with Proxmire and dismissed the suit. But Hutchinson appealed.
The U.S. Supreme Court ruled that Hutchinson was not a public figure

because he was not willingly involved in a public controversy until Proxmire caused it. The court said Hutchinson could not automatically become a public figure by being thrust into a newsworthy situation. Also, the court determined that Hutchinson did not have regular and continuing access to the media. He was only sought out by reporters to respond to Proxmire's criticism. Hutchinson ultimately received $10,000 from Proxmire.

The third type of public figure, "involuntary," is someone who does nothing voluntary to garner attention or to get involved in a public issue but finds himself or herself in the middle of a public controversy anyway. Courts have found that this category rarely fits an individual in a libel suit.

Private Figures

The difference between being a public or private figure is crucial because the standards for proving libel can differ. Many states have made it easier for private persons to prove libel than for public figures. The Supreme Court has left it up to the states to determine their own standards of liability for private figures:

> We hold that, so long as they do not impose liability without fault, the States may define for themselves the appropriate standard of liability for a publisher or a broadcaster of defamatory falsehood injurious to a private individual.

The court made this ruling in a 1974 case, *Gertz v. Welch.* Elmer Gertz was a Chicago lawyer who claimed he had been libeled when a John Birch Society magazine, *American Opinion,* published an article labeling him a Communist. He sued the publisher, Robert Welch.

Even though Gertz was a prominent lawyer, the Supreme Court ruled that he was a private person under the circumstances of this case. The court also declared that, because private people don't have the same access to the media to defend themselves as public officials, they shouldn't be held to the same strict standards in proving libel.

In *Gertz v. Welch* the court decided that a private individual only needs to show that the material was published with carelessness or negligence instead of proving actual malice, which means publishing with knowledge or reckless disregard of falsity. But all libel plaintiffs, public and private, have to prove the material is false and damaging to their reputation.

Even though the Supreme Court left it up to states to determine their own libel standards in cases involving private figures, the *Gertz* case paved the way for allowing private people to abide by less rigid standards than public officials and figures. Many states have followed the "simple negligence" standard in the *Gertz* case. Others require private individuals to abide by the same "actual malice" standard as public individuals. Negligence in this context means you failed to exercise reasonable care in doing your job as a journalist.

Corrections

The most common cause of lawsuits is carelessness. Most news media don't publish material they know or suspect is false.

Although newspapers get sued by people targeted in major investigative projects, the majority of libel suits stem from much less important stories. Incorrect captions, defamatory headlines, an inaccuracy in a police story or a feature can result in a libel suit.

Printed corrections don't prevent libel suits. They may assuage an angered source enough to forestall a lawsuit or they may be evidence of the newspaper's good faith, but corrections do not undo the harm of inaccurate published material. It's up to a jury to decide if you were negligent, careless or reckless in your disregard for the truth.

A printed correction by the *National Enquirer* didn't stop entertainer Carol Burnett from suing the tabloid in 1976 for insinuating that she was drunk. The article said that she had an argument with Henry Kissinger at a Washington restaurant and then "accidentally knocked a glass of wine over on one diner—and started giggling." Burnett denied the incident occurred, and even though the *Enquirer* apologized in a retraction, Burnett pressed her lawsuit. She was awarded a total of $1.6 million by a Los Angeles jury and ultimately settled for an undisclosed amount.

It may become more difficult for people to collect damages for libel from newspapers and other publications in states that pass the Uniform Correction Act. This legislation would not prevent people from suing for libel, but it would limit the amount of money they can receive if the publication runs a full, fair and timely correction. The purpose of the act is to provide a consistent law throughout the country, but legislatures in individual states must approve it before it becomes law.

Even when you use the word *alleged,* meaning that the accusation is a charge without proof, you are on dangerous ground. This word, although widely used by reporters in police cases, does not save you from libel. It is better to attribute the information to official sources or records.

If you don't name the person against whom the accusation is made, you still can be sued for libel. A person who can claim he or she was identified—either by enough information to describe the person physically or by position—could sue.

Nor does attribution save you. Say that a candidate for mayor tells you his or her opponent is a crook. You print the statement and attribute it to the candidate. The opponent could sue you and your newspaper. Just because you named the source of the statement, you cannot avoid responsibility for it. And if it isn't true and you haven't documented it as true, you could be considered guilty of reckless disregard for the truth.

If you are going to print any accusations that could be defamatory, you should always check with the person being accused and ask for a response. Cross-checking may not save you from libel, but it at least gives you a chance to prove you were not reckless.

There are times when you can print accusatory or damaging information, especially when you are writing about crime. You have certain privileges as a member of the press, and so do some of the officials who deal with you.

Privilege

Privilege—in a legal sense—comes in two forms: absolute and qualified.

"Absolute privilege" means that public officials, including law enforcement officials, can make statements in the course of their official duties without fear of being sued for libel. This form of privilege extends to court proceedings, legislative proceedings, public and official meetings, and contents of public records. For example, if Senator Proxmire had announced his Golden Fleece awards on the floor of the Senate instead of in a press release, he would have had absolute privilege and could not have been sued by Hutchinson, the researcher who claimed he was libeled.

As a member of the media, you have "qualified privilege." You may print defamatory statements made by people who are absolutely privileged as long as you are being fair and accurate and the information is from a public proceeding or public record. But if your report contains errors, you could lose that qualified protection.

If a city council member calls another member a crook during a public meeting, you may print the accusation. If the same city official makes the same comment to you during a telephone interview or after the meeting, you can't print it without risking libel. The key is that the defamatory statement must be made in an official capacity during an official proceeding. Or you may use, with attribution, something stated in court records. But make it clear that the accusations were made by other people in records or meetings and are not proven fact.

Suppose that a police officer tells you something about a suspect. You may print that information if the officer is acting in an official capacity and if the information is documented in a public record, such as a police report or court files. However, you still should be careful about how you word accusations in crime stories. (More detail will follow in Chapter 23.) The police officer may say the man stabbed his wife, but you may not say the same thing without attribution. If the information is not stated in a public record, such as a police report or court record, it can be libelous. Generally, statements made outside of the court by police are not privileged, but some states may extend privilege to these comments.

Never call anyone a murderer unless he or she has been convicted of murder in court. Don't call suspects robbers or use any other accusatory term before they are convicted. Use terms such as "the suspect," "the man accused of murder," "the woman charged with the robbery."

Suppose a man has been murdered and you go to the neighborhood for reaction. A neighbor says the man's wife killed him. The neighbor isn't an official acting in an official capacity, and the wife hasn't been convicted. The neighbor's comments could be libelous, and you could be sued for printing them.

Neutral Reportage

Another type of privilege called "neutral reportage" has been recognized in about 10 states. It gives the news media First Amendment protection in writing accusations about a public official or figure in a public controversy as long as the reporter states them accurately and neutrally. If one official or person considered responsible and newsworthy accuses another public figure of wrongdoing, you may print the information as long as you get reactions of the accused or other participants.

Under neutral reportage you aren't responsible for determining whether the accusations are true. However, many states don't extend this type of privilege to the media, so it's always safer to beware of printing unsubstantiated accusations.

The best defense for a reporter is the "truth" defense, proving that what you wrote is true.

What you can do and what you ought to do may differ. You may have the right to print statements from court records or meetings, but if you think they could be untrue or unfair, should you print them? Those are the kinds of ethical decisions journalists must make. Most editors advise: When in doubt, leave it out.

Fair Comment and Criticism

Suppose you are writing a review of a play, concert or book and your review is very negative. Can you be sued? Yes. You can always be sued. But you are protected under the right of fair comment.

Writers of editorials, analysis stories, reviews and other criticism may express opinions, but they may not state inaccurate facts. A factual error can be grounds for libel; an opinion is protected.

To qualify as fair comment, a comment must generally be on a matter of public interest, it must be based on facts known or believed to be true, and it may not be malicious, or made with reckless disregard for the truth. In this case also, truth is considered a good defense.

Invasion of Privacy

Issues of privacy involve ethical decisions, not matters of accuracy. However, with the proliferation of invasion of privacy lawsuits, a journalist should understand the legal issues.

In privacy cases, damage is usually considered the mental anguish that results from wrongfully revealing to the public some part of the plaintiff's life. Truth may not be enough of a defense in privacy cases.

Suppose that a child drowns and a mother stands on the dock as her son's body is dragged from the river. She is hysterical. A photographer takes her picture without her consent. Has the photographer invaded her privacy? Perhaps, if the photographer was on private property. The photographer could be considered an intruder. It is not an invasion of privacy, however, if the photographer was on public property. Even if a scene on private property is visible from public property, the photographer would be within his or her rights to take pictures.

The courts have acknowledged four grounds for invasion of privacy lawsuits, which are described in the following sections.

Intrusion Into a Person's Solitude

Eavesdropping, harassing someone and trespassing on private property can be considered intrusion. So can using a telephoto lens, listening behind doors and using any device to enhance what the unaided eye can see or the unaided ear can hear on private property. In other words, a journalist who uses subterfuge to obtain and publish confidential material could be risking a suit for invasion of privacy. The intrusion can be either physical or mental.

In *Dietemann v. Time Inc.*, two *Life* magazine reporters were sued for going undercover as husband and wife to do a story on a plumber, A. S. Dietemann. The plumber was believed to be practicing medicine with herbs. The so-called healer told the female reporter she had cancer and prescribed an herbal cure. The female reporter taped Dietemann's comments, and her partner took pictures with a concealed camera. Even though the plumber later pleaded no contest to a charge of practicing medicine without a license, he sued the magazine company for invasion of privacy. A California court awarded him $1,000. An appeals court upheld the award and said that the undercover methods, used without Dietemann's consent, were an invasion of his privacy. "The First Amendment is not a license to trespass, to steal, or to intrude by electronic means into the precincts of another's home or office," the court opinion said.

Unlike libel suits, publication isn't required for someone to claim invasion of privacy in this type of case.

Public Disclosure of Private Facts

Publishing such facts as information about a person's sex life or medical history that the public considers offensive could be considered invasion of privacy, even if it's true. But if the facts are taken from the public record, such as court documents, they probably will be considered privileged.

In 1975 the Supreme Court ruled in *Cox Broadcasting Co. v. Cohn* that a television station in Atlanta was within its First Amendment rights to publish the name of a rape victim even though state law prohibited doing so. The victim's family had sued for invasion of privacy, claiming a private fact had been disclosed. The family had won, but Cox appealed the decision to the U.S. Supreme Court. The court said the news media had the right to report matters on the public record.

Information not on the public record is more susceptible to lawsuits. The courts have ruled that the media may be invading privacy if the private facts in question would be offensive and objectionable to a reasonable person and would not be of legitimate public concern. Community standards of what is "offensive" may vary from one place to another. That's why these are difficult cases for courts to decide.

Regarding the public concern standard, the case often cited is *Sidis v. F-R Publishing Corp.,* which involved a profile in *New Yorker* magazine of James Sidis, a genius who had graduated from Harvard at age 16. Twenty years later the magazine wrote a profile about his life as a recluse. Sidis sued for invasion of privacy, but the courts ruled that he was a public figure who had lost his right to privacy and that his life was, therefore, newsworthy or of legitimate public concern.

Publicity That Puts a Person in a False Light

If a published story or picture gives the wrong impression and is embarrassing to the person, the possibility exists that the court will consider a "false light" verdict. For example, in one case a television station doing a story about teen-age pregnancy took pictures of a young woman walking down the street. The television station did not say she was pregnant, nor did the station identify her. However, she claimed the picture put her in a false light—indicating that she was a pregnant teen-ager—and she won her lawsuit against the station.

False light is related to defamation, but the story or picture does not have to defame a person to be considered false light. It does have to portray the person inaccurately.

Truth is a defense in these cases. Generally the plaintiff has to prove the media showed actual malice by knowingly publishing false information.

The case often cited here is *Time Inc. v. Hill,* because it was the first false light case to reach the Supreme Court. James Hill, his wife and five children were held hostage in their suburban Philadelphia home by three escaped convicts in 1952. After the incident, the Hills moved to

Connecticut. A few years later, *Life* magazine was planning to publish a review of a play partially based on the incident. The magazine took the cast of the play to the Hills' old home and photographed the actors in some scenes from the play. Hill sued, saying the pictures in *Life* gave readers the impression that the scenes portrayed the family's real experiences. Hill initially won his suit. But it eventually went to the Supreme Court, which ruled that Hill would have to prove actual malice on the part of *Life* magazine. The court sent the case back for retrial to a lower court, but Hill dropped the suit.

Another Supreme Court decision (*Cantrell v. Forest City Publishing Co.*) also upheld the standard of proving actual malice in a false light case. In this case, Margaret Cantrell sued for false light and invasion of privacy, claiming that *The* (Cleveland) *Plain Dealer* had inaccurately portrayed her as living in poverty several months after her husband died in a bridge collapse. In a follow-up story to the bridge disaster, the reporter described Cantrell as wearing the same "mask of nonexpression" she wore at her husband's funeral and living in abject poverty. But the reporter only talked to Cantrell's children; he never talked to her. She won the case because she proved that some information was untrue and that it was damaging to her reputation.

Use of a Person's Name or Picture Without Permission

This doctrine applies when the picture is used for commercial purposes, such as advertising or promotion. For example, use of an athlete's photograph to promote a product without her or his consent could be grounds for a lawsuit. The easiest way to avoid this kind of lawsuit is to have the person sign a consent form.

Television personality Vanna White sued Samsung Electronics when an advertisement the firm used featured a robot that resembled White as she appeared on the game show "Wheel of Fortune." White claimed her image was appropriated without her permission, and a court agreed.

A Guideline for Avoiding Lawsuits

Grounds for a lawsuit vary, so the best guideline for reporters is to be careful. If you are accurate and fair, you can defend your actions.

If you aren't sure whether something is libelous or invades privacy, check with an editor. In many cases, newspapers retain lawyers to review information that could be considered grounds for a lawsuit. You can't be expected to know all the legal angles; you can be expected to be careful.

Exercises

1   For a week, check the corrections in *The New York Times,* your local newspaper or any other newspaper that prints daily corrections. Analyze the nature of the corrections: Are they for names, facts, photo captions or other errors?

2   Interview a classmate for biographical information as though you were writing a profile or an obituary. Ask questions that will elicit quotes, such as why the person chose this college or what memorable experiences the person has had in college or high school. Write a brief paragraph containing the factual material: date and place of birth, information about high school, college major, hobbies, other interests. After you have written it, ask your classmate to check its accuracy.

3   **Actual malice:** Write a paragraph explaining "actual malice" and "reckless disregard for the truth" as defined by the U.S. Supreme Court in *Times v. Sullivan.*

4   Discuss this scenario for libel potential: You are the editor of your campus newspaper. A female student at your university says that last semester a male professor asked her for sex in return for a good grade. She says she dropped the class and filed a complaint of sexual harassment a few months ago with the university's Office of Affirmative Action. She gives you the professor's name. However, the student insists that you not use her name. She says she doesn't think the university will do anything, so she wants the press to know about it.

The Office of Affirmative Action keeps all records confidential and will not confirm or deny the existence of the complaint, but the student has provided you with a copy. The professor refuses to speak to you, and officials in his department and in the university refuse to comment.

You publish news that a complaint has been filed, and you name the professor. In addition, you print the unnamed complainant's side of the story, including her sexually explicit version of the professor's comments to her, which are not in the complaint.

Discuss whether you should have printed the professor's name and the steps you would have taken before doing so. Discuss what information in the story, if any, could be considered libelous. Would the professor be considered a public or private figure?

Would the situation be any different if you substituted a politician for the professor? This time, you are the editor of your local newspaper. A U.S. senator has decided to seek re-election. Five women who worked for him several years ago say he sexually harassed and abused them while they were in his office. The women refuse to be named. Their allegations range from stories that he plied them with drugs and alcohol and then sexually abused them to accusations of rape. All the women are reputable, including a political lobbyist and a former secretary to the senator, but none have gone to the police. As a result, you have no record of formal complaints about their allegations. However, three years ago a formal complaint by a former employee charged him with sexual molestation, but the charges were dropped. Will you print these women's allegations and use his name? Does the senator have grounds for a libel lawsuit?

5 Privacy issue 1: A candidate for city council in your community had a nervous breakdown 10 years ago. The candidate's opponent has slipped you a hospital document confirming this fact. Should you print the story? Why or why not? If you do, does the candidate have any grounds to sue you for invasion of privacy?

6 Privacy issue 2: You are a photographer who went on assignment to the county fair. You snapped a picture of a woman whose skirt blew up to her shoulders, exposing her underwear, as she emerged from the fun house. Your editor decided that this picture captured the fun mood of the fair and used it. The woman is now furious and sues the paper for invasion of privacy—disclosure of a private fact. Discuss whether she has grounds for a lawsuit and whether you think you should have taken the picture.

7 Privacy issue 3: A couple is having a divorce ceremony to which they have invited friends and relatives. Their "unwedding ceremony" is on a hillside on private property. During the ceremony, the bridegroom removes bonds from his ankles and the bride removes a noose from her neck. A reporter and a photographer from the local newspaper had learned about the event and, although uninvited, witnessed it from a public place. They subsequently published a story and pictures. The couple sued for invasion of privacy. Explain whether the reporter and the photographer were legally within their rights to report this story.

8 Libel concerns: Discuss any concerns about libel that you have or that you have had in relation to any of the stories you have covered or have read recently in your campus or local newspaper.

COACHING

TIPS

Examine all your alternatives.

Consider all the parties who will be affected. Do you need other points of view?

Weigh the benefits and harms of your decision.

Justify why you are making this decision.

Media Ethics

17

I magine that you are a reporter for your local newspaper. A drunken driver almost kills a young girl in an accident in your town. You call the hospital for information about her condition, but officials will not release it except to family members. So you ask a fellow reporter to call the hospital and identify himself as the girl's uncle. He gets the information.

Would you do that? Is it ethical?

This was one of 30 cases presented to 819 journalists in a survey conducted by Ohio University journalism professor Ralph S. Izard for the Society of Professional Journalists. Eighty-two percent of the journalists who responded said they would not ask their colleague to lie to gain information.

If someone is going to be hurt by what gets printed or broadcast about them, then journalists need to provide a reason—a good reason—for going with it. "That's my job," doesn't cut it. Nor do appeals to First Amendment freedoms.

Deni Elliott, ethics professor,
University of Montana .

Ethical Dilemmas

Test yourself. Would you go along with the actions of journalists in the following case, which was presented in the survey?

Agree   Disagree   Reporters investigating alleged racial discrimination by real estate agents were getting nowhere. They had interviewed officials of the local realtors' association and scores of realtors, all of whom denied that they steer black buyers away from houses for sale in white neighborhoods. The city editor sent two white reporters, posing as potential buyers, to see what houses several real estate firms showed them when they expressed interest in a new house of a certain size and price range. Then she sent two black reporters to the same firms with the same requests.

Now consider these situations, all of them real ethical dilemmas faced by reporters and editors:

    Yes   No   You have heard rumors that a politician has had extramarital affairs. You stake out his townhouse and confirm that he has spent the night with a woman who is not his wife. Will you write the story?

    Yes   No   A woman has accused the nephew of a prominent U.S. senator of raping her. Your newspaper has had a policy of not printing the names of alleged rape victims. The paper also withholds names of suspects in criminal cases until they are formally charged with the crime. In this case, police have acknowledged that the nephew is a suspect, but he has not been charged yet. Will you print the name of the woman who claimed she was raped? Will you print the name of the senator's nephew?

Deception

The cases about the accident victim and about racial discrimination both deal with deception. Did you decide that it is all right to use deception to get a story? Is it OK in some cases but not in others?

In the case about the accident victim, 82 percent criticized the deception. But in the case involving racial discrimination, 95 percent of the journalists in the survey agreed that they would use deception.

A classic case of deception occurred in 1978 when investigative reporters at the *Chicago Sun Times* set up a bar called The Mirage and posed as bartenders and waiters. With hidden cameras and tape recorders, they provided evidence that building inspectors, police officers and other city officials were soliciting bribes to allow them to operate the bar. Although the series won several awards, the Pulitzer Prize board ruled that the reporting methods were unethical and rejected it for the media's highest award. The case renewed debate about deception, and today this type of reporting is considered a last resort by many editors.

Although print and broadcast media have used hidden cameras for many years, use of them proliferated in television news magazine shows during the 1990s. One reason was the improved technology of cameras, which could be small enough to be hidden in tie clips. But media critics charged that a more common reason for using hidden cameras was sensationalism.

Deception can take different forms, from posing as someone else to using hidden tape recorders and cameras. Before using any form of deception, ask yourself if there is any other way to get the story. Louis Hodges, an ethics professor at Washington and Lee University, suggests that you apply three tests: importance, accuracy and safety. Ask yourself: Is the information of such overriding public importance that it can help people avoid harm? Is there any way you could obtain the information through conventional reporting methods, such as standard interviews or public records? Are you placing innocent people at risk? For example, you should not pose as a nurse, law enforcement officer or employee in a job for which you might not be trained.

Deceptive reporting techniques are fraught with risks, such as lawsuits for invasion of privacy, as discussed in Chapter 16. On the other hand, deception may be the only way to reveal matters of great public concern. Even with such reasoning, using deception may still be unethical.

Privacy Issues

Some of the most wrenching ethical dilemmas the media face involve people's privacy. You may have the legal right to publish certain information, but do you have the moral right?

To understand the ethical concerns, it may help to define "ethics." Ethics is the study of moral choices, what we should or should not do, whereas morality is concerned with behavior. So ethics can be considered the process of making decisions about the way a person behaves.

Some of the thorniest ethical dilemmas facing journalists concern public officials, celebrities, rape victims and photo subjects.

Public officials
Would you print information about the sex life of a politician? When is the private life of a public figure relevant? When does it serve the public interest to publish such details?

Reporters and editors at *The Miami Herald* decided the private life of a politician was relevant in the summer of 1987. Former Sen. Gary Hart was seeking the Democratic nomination for the presidency. Rumors of Hart's infidelity to his wife had circulated for months, and during the campaign the rumors called into question his character and credibility. When asked about the rumors, Hart challenged reporters to "follow me around. . . . They'd be very bored." Acting on a tip that Hart had a relationship with a Florida model, *Herald* reporters staked out his townhouse. They revealed that Hart spent the night with the woman, Donna Rice. Hart never admitted that the relationship with Rice was sexual. Nevertheless, he withdrew his candidacy the day before *The Washington Post* was set to reveal evidence about his involvement in another affair.

Four and a half years later, during Bill Clinton's campaign for the presidency, rumors of his infidelity surfaced as well. But the circumstances differed from the Hart coverage. The *Star,* a tabloid newspaper, broke the story. It printed allegations by former television reporter Gennifer Flowers that she had had a long-term affair with Clinton; the *Star* paid Flowers for her story. The mainstream press, which had not been able to verify the allegations, then picked up the story. Their justification was that it had become news, especially after Clinton appeared on the CBS "60 Minutes" show to respond to the allegations. He admitted that he and his wife had had marital problems over the years but denied Flowers' claim of a 12-year affair with him. The American public didn't decry his behavior; the public blasted the press instead.

During Clinton's presidency, an Arkansas woman, Paula Corbin Jones, filed a lawsuit accusing Clinton of sexual harassment when he was Arkansas governor. The stories received limited coverage in most of the mainstream press. Many editors said they questioned the woman's motives and her veracity. And polls showed the American public didn't care very much about the story.

The ethical dilemma of when to publish information about the private lives of public officials surfaced in another political campaign in 1992. *The Seattle Times* published a story of eight unidentified women who had accused U.S. Sen. Brock Adams of sexual harassment and physical molestation. The senator dropped his re-election campaign the next day. This case also involved the ethical dilemma of using anonymous sources, which diminish credibility of a story. In a sidebar to the story, editor Michael Fancher told readers he felt the story was in the public interest because it reflected on the senator's fitness for office.

Is it in the public interest to reveal the criminal background of a candidate if he withdraws from the race before you can print the story? Editors at the campus newspaper of the University of Kansas faced this dilemma after they found out that a candidate for student government had been convicted of indecent solicitation of a child six years earlier. But when the candidate learned that the newspaper was planning to print the information, he held a press conference to resign his candidacy. He claimed it was because he had just learned he was HIV-positive. At the same time, he resigned as director of the organization representing gays and lesbians on campus. He never referred to his criminal record, nor would he answer reporters' questions.

Was his criminal record relevant to the public now that he was no longer a candidate for office or leader of the gay rights group? What

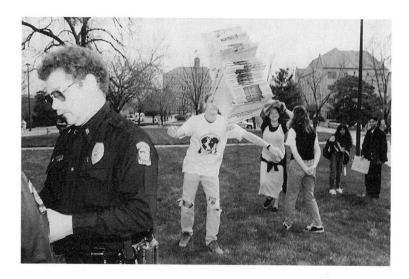

University of Kansas students dumping the campus newspaper to protest a story
Photo by Brian Vandervliet

harm would the publication of his record cause him? The student's friends pressured the editor not to run the story, saying it would cause their friend immense personal suffering when he was already suffering from the HIV-positive news. In addition, they said, he had already paid his debt to society by serving time in prison.

Stephen Martino, editor of *The University Daily Kansan* at the time, said the decision was the most difficult one he ever had to make as an editor. He said he decided to run the information because it was relevant; it was why the candidate resigned. Martino said the candidate had learned about his HIV-positive status three weeks earlier and had made no attempt to resign then. "To my way of thinking, omitting the truth is the same thing as lying. Had *The Kansan* not reported the full story as it knew it, it would have been accused of a cover-up, and its credibility would have been destroyed," Martino wrote in an editorial page column the day the story ran on the front page.

Angry students protested the next day by dumping copies of *The Kansan* on the lawn in front of the newspaper offices in the journalism school.

Celebrities   A privacy case that caused even more media backlash was the disclosure a year before he died that tennis star Arthur Ashe had AIDS. And it posed even greater ethical hand-wringing, because Ashe was not running for public office and was no longer playing on the professional circuit. Is the private life of a public figure always fair game for disclosure in the media?

Ashe didn't think so. When *USA Today* received an anonymous tip that Ashe had acquired the disease from a blood transfusion many years earlier, a sportswriter from the newspaper interviewed Ashe to check it out. Ashe didn't confirm or deny anything. But he called the paper's managing editor for sports to find out the status of the story. The editor, Gene Policinski, said that the newspaper would not print the story without confirmation from a credible, named source but that the paper would pursue it. Ashe still did not confirm the story. Instead, he called a press conference the next day and reluctantly told the world. He said he was sure some newspaper eventually would publish the story, and he wanted to be able to tell the story on his terms. Although he acknowledged that he was a public figure and that the story was newsworthy, he said his privacy had been invaded.

Public opinion polls seemed to agree. The day the story was published in *USA Today,* the newspaper received 481 phone calls. Most calls were from readers critical of the coverage, even though the newspaper published the story only after Ashe announced he was going to have a press conference.

Policinski, in a sidebar to the press conference story, explained his reason for pursuing the story: "There was no question that this was a significant news story. A great U.S. athlete could be critically ill. If he had cancer or a heart attack—as he did in 1979—it was and is news."

Privacy issues like these are among the most difficult ethical dilemmas for the media. Is the story fair? Is it in the public interest to know? What harm or benefit will result? Those are questions reporters and editors often ask before they publish such stories. And rarely is there unanimous agreement on the decision.

Rape victims Whether to name rape victims is another continuing ethical debate in the media. Because of the stigma associated with rape, most newspapers withhold the names of people who claim they have been raped.

Geneva Overholser, former editor of *The Des Moines* (Iowa) *Register,* wrote a column saying the stigma of rape would be reduced if it were treated like any other crime and the names of rape victims were used. As a result, Nancy Ziegenmeyer agreed to let the newspaper use her name in a story relating her ordeal as a rape victim. Reporter Jane Schorer, who won a Pulitzer Prize for the story, said she received scores of calls from rape victims who expressed gratitude that the story had been told.

The Register still has a policy of printing the names of alleged and confirmed rape victims only with their permission. *The New York Times* didn't ask for permission before it decided to use the name of a woman who accused a nephew of Sen. Edward Kennedy of raping her. And the story raised a firestorm of controversy.

In addition to withholding names of alleged rape victims, the majority of newspapers, including *The Times,* usually withhold the names of suspects before they are formally charged with a crime. But newspapers throughout the country printed the name of William Kennedy Smith before he was charged with the crime, justifying their action by saying the prominence of his uncle warranted it.

The *Times* editors said they made the decision to name the woman in a profile about her because the woman had been named in a supermarket tabloid, *The Globe,* and on NBC television. Therefore, her name was already in the public domain. Media critics blasted *The Times* for weak justification. But naming rape accusers (the term *victim* implies that the suspected attacker is guilty) is gaining more favor at many newspapers.

The *Times* profile of the woman raised other objections as well. It included public records about her traffic tickets, her family history, her dating habits and the illegitimacy of her 3-year-old daughter. Were these facts relevant to a story about a crime? Would a profile about a man who was the victim of a crime include information about his traffic tickets or his dating habits? These are the kinds of questions ethical reporters should ask.

Ultimately William Kennedy Smith was judged not guilty. After the trial, his accuser, Patricia Bowman, revealed her identity in press conferences and television interviews. Bowman said she felt the media coverage of her had been another assault on her.

Columbia University professor Helen Benedict says the media promote myths and stereotypes of rape in the way they portray women in sex crimes. In her book *Virgin or Vamp: How the Press Covers Sex Crimes,* she says the media characterize rape victims in one of two ways: "She is either pure and innocent, a true victim attacked by monsters— the 'virgin'. . . or she is a wanton female who provoked the assailant with her sexuality—the 'vamp.'" Benedict says one solution is to stop publishing profiles of rape victims.

Photo subjects Many privacy issues involve photographs. Should a photographer take a picture of a grieving mother whose son has drowned, even if she doesn't want the picture taken? At what point is a photograph an invasion of privacy?

Another concern for photo editors is taste: what the reader needs to see versus what the reader wants to see. For example, should newspapers print pictures that depict gore and tragedy even if they would upset readers? In 1987, Pennsylvania state treasurer R. Bud Dwyer convened a press conference the day before he was scheduled to be sentenced for conviction of mail fraud, perjury and racketeering. At the end of the conference, he took a gun from his briefcase, put the barrel in his mouth and pulled the trigger, killing himself instantly. Stunned photographers for television stations and newspapers shot vivid pictures of the event.

Many television stations did not air the footage of him with blood gushing from his head, and several newspapers did not publish that picture. But other newspapers published three photos, including a gory one of his head as the bullet pierced it. Readers in several locations protested loudly.

A guideline for privacy issues   Such ethical dilemmas arise daily at newspapers and television stations. And editors agonize over the decisions. But how do they make those decisions, and how can you decide what is ethical?

Whether it is a photo or a story, ethicist Louis Hodges suggests this guideline for privacy issues: Publish private information about public officials or public figures if it affects their public duties. But for victims of crime, publish private information only if they give their permission, because these are people with special needs and vulnerability.

Political Correctness

The term "political correctness," which was created during the 1960s and 1970s to foster diversity, has since taken on negative connotations associated with censorship of free speech and controversial ideas. As a result, ethical dilemmas involving political correctness have proliferated in the 1990s, particularly for campus newspapers. Consider:

• DePaul University students staged a sit-in at the school newspaper to protest a reference to African-American students in a story about a fight at a student dance. They claimed that race was not relevant and that mentioning it perpetuated negative stereotypes.

• The University of Denver student media board withdrew funds from the campus newspaper, forcing it to fold, after it ran jokes considered offensive to women.

• University of Kansas African-American students picketed the newsroom because they felt a photograph of African-American students dancing at one event during a three-day government leadership convention promoted stereotypes of them as entertainers or athletes instead of as future political leaders.

Innumerable incidents of this type have occurred throughout the country. The problem in many cases was simply a lack of sensitivity or a lack of awareness that certain language or photographs could be considered offensive.

Monica Hill and Bonnie Thrasher, University of Alabama graduate students who won an ethics competition with their paper on political correctness, devised a "Model of Respect." It poses two questions to ask yourself: "If I were a member of the minority/cultural group involved with this information, what might my reaction to publishing this material be? Does my professional obligation to publish this material outweigh the fact that it may offend members of a particular minority or cultural group?"

The questions can help prevent some insensitivity, but they have an inherent danger: If you are not a member of the minority group being discussed, you may not even realize what might be offensive. Whenever possible, go a step further and seek the advice of a member of the minority group affected by the story.

The Unabomber Case

In 1995 the media faced another kind of dilemma: manipulation by a terrorist. A serial killer known as the Unabomber had killed three people and injured 23 others with mail bombs he had sent over a 17-year period. In all those years, the FBI and other agencies had not been able to identify him. In the summer of 1995, the Unabomber declared that he would stop the killings if within three months *The New York Times* and *The Washington Post* would print the entire text of a 35,000-word "manifesto" he wrote, assailing industrialized society. In his letters to *The Times* and *The Post,* the Unabomber also demanded that the newspapers print three follow-up messages over the next three years. However, he did not agree to stop bombings that would cause property damage.

The U.S. attorney general and the director of the FBI urged the newspapers to print the manifesto. Five days before the Unabomber's deadline, *The Post*—in an agreement with *The Times*—printed the manifesto in an eight-page broadsheet supplement. The newspapers shared the publication costs. In a joint statement, *Post* publisher Donald E. Graham and *Times* publisher Arthur O. Sulzberger Jr. said they acted in the interest of public safety. However, the two publishers made no commitment to printing subsequent messages.

"Whether you like it or not, we're turning our pages over to a man who has murdered people," Sulzberger said in an interview with *The Times.* "I'm convinced we're making the right choice between bad options." A suspect was arrested seven months later, but the manifesto decision still raises strong ethical questions.

Most people in the media agree that the options were bad either way, but many editors denounced the decision to publish the material. They said that it set a bad precedent and that the media were being held hostage. Critics asked what would happen the next time anyone threatened to kill people if his or her message was not printed. Many journalists also expressed concern that *The Times'* and *The Post's* cooperation with government officials jeopardized the media's independence.

In his statement explaining the reasons for publishing, *Post* publisher Graham said, "Newspapers always listen [to law enforcement] in cases where the safety of citizens is involved. . . . The editors of *The Post* and *The Times* made their evaluations as journalists that there was no reason to print the Unabomber's document. But we could not ignore the fact that there was a threat."

Shortly after the manifesto was published in *The Post,* it was distributed on the Internet by Time Inc. at its Pathfinder site. *The Oakland*

(Calif.) *Tribune* downloaded the file from that site and published it in response to overwhelming requests from readers.

What would you have done if you had been an editor of *The Post* or *The Times?* Do you think it was ethical to put the Unabomber's manifesto on the Internet? If you were the publisher of the Oakland paper, would you have published it? What are your ethical concerns, and what are the harms and benefits of your decision? To help you make such difficult ethical decisions, you can use some of the following principles of moral reasoning.

Moral Reasoning

Journalists use several methods to justify their decisions. In most ethical dilemmas, editors and reporters discuss the issue and the consequences of publication before making the decision. They consider how newsworthy the story is and whether the public really needs this information.

The process of moral reasoning can be broken into three steps:

1   Define the dilemma. Consider all the problems the story or photograph will pose.

2   Examine all your alternatives. You can publish, not publish, wait for a while until you get more information before publishing, display the story or photo prominently or in a lesser position, or choose other options.

3   Justify your decision. Weigh the harms and the benefits of publication, or weigh such factors as relevance and importance of the story to the public.

The Poynter Institute Model

Robert M. Steele, associate director in charge of ethics at the Poynter Institute for Media Studies, suggests that journalists ask these questions before making decisions in ethical dilemmas:

• Why am I concerned about this story, photo or graphic?

• What is the news? What good would publication do?

• Is the information complete and accurate, to the best of my knowledge?

• Am I missing an important point of view?

• What does my reader need to know?

• How would I feel if the story or photo were about me or a member of my family?

• What are the likely consequences of publication? What good or harm could result?

- What are my alternatives?
- Will I be able to clearly and honestly explain my decision to anyone who challenges it?

People using the same moral reasoning methods may emerge with different decisions. There is rarely one right decision. In the cases presented at the start of this chapter, you may have made a decision different from that of your classmate. But it is your reasoning process that matters.

Philosophical Approaches

The harms-versus-benefits concept is one of several derived from philosophers. Their reasoning forms a framework for many moral decisions. Jay Black, a media ethics professor at the University of South Florida, and Deni Elliott, ethics professor at the University of Montana's Mansfield Center, apply the reasoning of philosophers this way:

John Stuart Mill: His philosophy is based on a principle known as "utilitarianism." Ethical decisions should seek the greatest amount of happiness or benefit to the greatest number of people while at the same time seeking to harm the least number of people. If Mill were editor, he would ask his staff to (1) list all persons likely to be affected; (2) decide the likely consequences of each option; (3) weigh the benefit or harm that would result, giving added weight to the major benefit or harm; and (4) choose the consequence that provides the most benefit to the largest number of people or the least harm to the smallest number of people.

Aristotle: If Aristotle were editor, he would tell his staff to act as "virtuous journalists," arguing that moral virtue lies somewhere between the extremes of excess and deficiency. In other words, he would seek a "golden mean," a middle ground between the two extremes.

John Rawls: He would ask his reporters to pull on a "veil of ignorance" as they grapple with ethical dilemmas—basically, to consider the points of view of all people involved. The steps would be to (1) make a list of all people who will be affected by the decisions, including readers, sources, co-workers, yourself; (2) put yourself behind a veil of ignorance, giving up your identity and assuming the identities of the other people affected by the decision; and (3) assume that a discussion takes place among the various players, with none of the participants knowing what their ultimate identities will turn out to be when the veils of ignorance are removed.

Although many journalists tend to rely on Mill's harms-versus-benefits approach, a single philosophical approach will not apply to every ethical dilemma. But you should ask the questions. You may not please your readers. You may not even please yourself. But you should at least believe that you have made the best decision you could under the circumstances at hand.

"If you don't act in accordance with moral rules, you are blame-worthy," Elliott says. "If you act in accordance, you are not praise-worthy. No one congratulates you for not lying."

Codes of Ethics

In addition to making decisions about what to report and write and how to present stories, journalists must consider whether their behavior is ethical as they perform their professional duties.

Many newspapers have devised codes of ethics that govern the behavior of employees. These include policies about accepting gifts or free-lance assignments, as well as guidelines about conflicts of interest. Staff members who violate these policies at newspapers can be fired, and many have been. In some cases reporters have been fired for entering into business relationships with a source or for using for personal gain information they get from sources. Journalism societies, such as the Radio-Television News Directors' Association and the Public Relations Society of America, also have basic codes of ethics to guide members.

One industry standard that all journalists are expected to comply with is a prohibition against plagiarism—passing off the materials of another source as your own without giving any credit to the original source. If you are copying information from another publication, you must attribute the source.

The Society of Professional Journalists

This prohibition against plagiarism is one of many declarations in a code of ethics adopted by The Society of Professional Journalists in 1926. The code, meant to serve as a guideline for the broadcast and print media, has been revised several times. A new code of ethics has been proposed by the society but was not adopted at the time of this book's publication. You can access the latest code of ethics on the Internet at http://town.hall.org/places/spj/ Here is the society's 1987 code of ethics:

> The Society of Professional Journalists, Sigma Delta Chi, believes the duty of journalists is to serve the truth.

> ### I Responsibility

> The public's right to know of events of public importance and interest is the overriding mission of the mass media. The purpose of distributing news and enlightened opinion is to serve the general welfare. Journalists who use their professional status as representatives of the public for selfish or other unworthy motives violate a high trust.

II Freedom of the Press

Freedom of the press is to be guarded as an inalienable right of people in a free society. It carries with it the freedom and the responsibility to discuss, question, and challenge actions and utterances of our government and of our public and private institutions. Journalists uphold the right to speak unpopular opinions and the privilege to agree with the majority.

III Ethics

Journalists must be free of obligation to any interest other than the public's right to know the truth.

1 Gifts, favors, free travel, special treatment or privileges can compromise the integrity of journalists and their employers. Nothing of value should be accepted.

2 Secondary employment, political involvement, holding public office, and service in community organizations should be avoided if it compromises the integrity of journalists and their employers. Journalists and their employers should conduct their personal lives in a manner that protects them from conflict of interest, real or apparent. Their responsibilities to the public are paramount. That is the nature of their profession.

3 So-called news communications from private sources should not be published or broadcast without substantiation of their claims to news value.

4 Journalists will seek news that serves the public interest, despite the obstacles. They will make constant efforts to assure that the public's business in conducted in public and that public records are open to public inspection.

5 Journalists acknowledge the newsman's ethic of protecting confidential sources of information.

6 Plagiarism is dishonest and unacceptable.

IV Accuracy and Objectivity

Good faith with the public is the foundation of all worthy journalism.

1 Truth is our ultimate goal.

2 Objectivity in reporting the news is another goal that serves as the mark of an experienced professional. It is a standard of performance toward which we strive. We honor those who achieve it.

3 There is no excuse for inaccuracies or lack of thoroughness.

4 Newspaper headlines should be fully warranted by the contents of the articles they accompany. Photographs and telecasts should give an accurate picture of an event and not highlight an incident out of context.

5 Sound practice makes clear distinction between news reports and expressions of opinion. News reports should be free of opinion or bias and represent all sides of an issue.

6 Partisanship in editorial comment that knowingly departs from the truth violates the spirit of American journalism.

7 Journalists recognize their responsibility for offering informed analysis, comment, and editorial opinion on public events and issues. They accept the obligation to represent such material by individuals whose competence, experience, and judgment qualify them for it.

8 Special articles or presentation devoted to advocacy or the writer's own conclusions and interpretations should be labeled as such.

V   Fair Play

Journalists at all times will show respect for the dignity, privacy, rights, and well-being of people encountered in the course of gathering and presenting the news.

1 The news media should not communicate unofficial charges affecting reputation or moral character without giving the accused a chance to reply.

2 The news media must guard against invading a person's right to privacy.

3 The media should not pander to morbid curiosity about details of vice and crime.

4 It is the duty of news media to make prompt and complete correction of their errors.

5 Journalists should be accountable to the public for their reports, and the public should be encouraged to voice its grievances against the media. Open dialogue with our readers, viewers, and listeners should be fostered.

Public Relations Society of America

The code of ethics of the Public Relations Society of America adheres to the same basic principles of truth, accuracy and fairness. However, since public relations practitioners are advocates for clients, the code includes these principles specifically applying to the industry:

- A member shall deal fairly with clients or employers, . . . with fellow practitioners and with the general public.

- A member shall conduct his or her professional life in accord with the public interest.

- A member shall adhere to truth and accuracy and to generally accepted standards of good taste.

- A member shall not represent conflicting or competing interests without the express consent of those involved, given after a full disclosure of the facts; nor place himself or herself in a position where the member's interest is or may be in conflict with a duty to a client, or others, without full disclosure of such interests to all involved.

- A member shall safeguard the confidences of present and former clients.

• A member shall not engage in any practice that tends to corrupt the integrity of channels of communication or the processes of government.

• A member shall not intentionally communicate false or misleading information.

• A member shall be prepared to identify publicly the name of the client or employer on whose behalf any public communication is made.

• A member shall not make use of any individual or organization purporting to serve or represent an unannounced cause, or purporting to be independent or unbiased, but actually serving an undisclosed special or private interest of a member, client or employer.

• A member shall not intentionally injure the professional reputation of another practitioner. (If the member has evidence that another member has been guilty of unethical, illegal or unfair practices, the member shall present the information to the authorities of the Society for action.)

• A member called as a witness in a proceeding for the enforcement of this code shall be bound to appear, unless excused for sufficient reason by the judicial panel.

• A member, in performing services for a client or employer, shall not accept fees, commissions or any other valuable consideration from anyone other than the client or employer in connection with those services without the express consent of the client or employer, given after a full disclosure of the facts.

• A member shall not guarantee the achievement of specified results beyond the member's direct control.

• A member shall, as soon as possible, sever relations with any organization or individual if such relationship requires conduct contrary to the articles of this code.

On-line Ethics

Most ethics codes deal with the behavior of journalists and the publication of materials in printed or broadcast form. But with the increasing use of on-line technology, such as electronic mail, journalists are facing new dilemmas. Is it OK to print someone's comments you read from a news group even though those comments were not specifically meant for publication? Can you publish information from a source's electronic correspondence or from a news group without his or her knowledge? When a person sends you an e-mail message, chances are she or he doesn't expect to find the message printed in your newspaper or magazine.

Many legal and copyright issues involving electronic postings remain untested, although some on-line ethics codes are being devised. Until journalists can agree about the proper way of handling on-line correspondence, let good journalistic practice be your guide. If you are planning to quote someone by name, ask the person for permission to use the correspondence unless the information is public. Ask yourself how you would feel if you were the source.

Methods of delivering the news may change, but you can apply good ethical reasoning to any medium.

Exercises

1 Apply moral reasoning, using the Poynter guidelines, to the following cases (or to other cases described in this chapter):

a An anonymous source tells you that a U.S. senator for your state has voted against many gay rights issues even though he is gay. You have heard other rumors that the senator is homosexual, but the senator has denied that the rumors are true. What will you do about this story?

b Would you have pursued the story about Arthur Ashe? If you had been able to confirm the report that he had AIDS, even if he had not admitted it, would you have printed the story?

c You have heard rumors that your local nursing home is abusing its clients. However, no complaints have been filed with state regulatory agencies or with the police. You have contacted some of the clients' family members, who say they are concerned but have no proof. Will you go undercover as a volunteer aide at the nursing home (no special training required) to investigate?

2 Discuss the ethical dilemma described in the chapter about revealing the criminal record of the student government candidate who resigned before the story could be published. What would you do if you were the editor of your campus publication or broadcast station? Do you agree or disagree with the decision made by the editor of *The University Daily Kansan?*

3 Students at DePaul University demanded that the student newspaper, *The DePaulia,* apologize for using the police term "M-B" ("males black") to refer to the people involved in a fight at a student dance. They claimed that race was not relevant and that mentioning it perpetuated negative stereotypes of African-Americans. In response to a sit-in, the university administration suspended publication of the newspaper for a few issues and promised to increase recruiting of minority students and faculty. If you were one of the editors of the newspaper, would you apologize? Discuss whether you would have printed a reference to race in the story. Discuss incidents of political correctness and the media at your school.

4 Your campus newspaper has received an anti-Holocaust advertisement that promotes a revisionist point of view, stating that the Nazi Holocaust of World War II never occurred. The ad, accompanied by a $125 check, was sent by the Committee for Open Debate on the Holocaust, an organization run by Bradley R. Smith from his home in Visalia, Calif. He sent the advertisement to colleges all over the United States. In a cover letter he urges campus editors to run the ad to promote dialogue and to support the First Amendment.

You are aware that, when the University of Miami campus newspaper, *The Miami Hurricane,* ran the ad, nearly 400 students demonstrated outside the newspaper. A wealthy alumnus threatened to withdraw a $2 million gift but later recanted when the school promised to offer courses on the Holocaust.

Other school newspapers have refused to print the ad. You know that this ad will offend many people on your campus and in your community, but you do want to uphold the First Amendment. Will you run this ad or reject it and return the check? Justify your decision.

COACHING

TIPS

Seek sources from different racial and ethnic backgrounds for all kinds of stories, not just stories about minorities.

Ask your sources how they prefer to be addressed.

Ask yourself if you would write the same type of description for a man as for a woman, for a white source as for a person of color, for a disabled person or member of any other ethnic or special group.

Multicultural Sensitivity 18

on't call him articulate. You might be tempted to do that if you meet Tim Gallimore. A lot of people who wrote letters of recommendation for him after he got his doctorate from Indiana University called him articulate. They meant well. But Gallimore says the term is really an insult.

Gallimore is an African-American. And he says when the term *articulate* is used to compliment him, it presumes that most African-Americans can't express themselves well. So in reality it is a slur.

Gallimore, an assistant professor of journalism at the University of Missouri, teaches multicultural sensitivity in his journalism courses.

In a study he conducted about the interpretation of mass media messages, he asked students to define a number of words, including *majority, ghetto* and *inner city*. He concluded that it is hard, if not impossible, to get people to agree on one meaning for a word. Gender, race, and geographical and ethnic background influence interpretation. Consider, for example, the word *majority*. "It is remarkable that women view themselves as minorities although they are a majority of the population in every society," he says. "This can be explained only through the connotation of majority as possession of power—the white male–dominated majority."

Other loaded words are *ghetto* and *inner city,* which Gallimore's students tended to define as an area with drugs, poverty, crime and gangs rather than as an urban geographical location. On television, when a news anchor says "inner-city youth," the phrase is almost always followed by descriptions and visuals of young

We need to be aware of how we communicate—of our built-in biases. Language is not a neutral thing.

Tim Gallimore, assistant professor,

University of Missouri

School of Journalism

Tim Gallimore, assistant professor of journalism
Courtesy of Tim Gallimore

blacks killing one another for crack or high-priced athletic shoes, Gallimore says. "Language is not a neutral thing," he says.

The Language of Multiculturalism

Language changes, too. *African-American* is the term now preferred by many blacks, but it is not accepted at all newspapers. *Chicano* is preferred by Mexican-Americans in some parts of the country, yet it is offensive to many older members of the group.

How can a journalist know the proper term to use? The University of Missouri's Multicultural Management Program tried to address that problem by producing a booklet, *Dictionary of Cautionary Words and Phrases.* It was highly controversial: Some journalists blasted it for "sanitizing the language," and others labeled it "hypersensitive newspeak."

Any terms that might be acceptable today could be out of vogue tomorrow. In fact, the whole concept of political correctness has become unpopular. But sensitivity to other people—regardless of gender, race or ethnic background—will always be an important tenet of journalism.

Instead of memorizing the popular term of the day, Gallimore suggests that reporters ask people of different ethnic or special interest groups how they prefer to be addressed. "The newspaper can demonstrate sensitivity with the words the person uses to define himself or herself," he says. "That gets the newspaper off the hook. If someone objects, you could say that is the person's term."

Jose D. McMurray, former executive director of the National Association of Hispanic Journalists, also stresses dealing with people as individuals, especially before using labels. "*Hispanic* is a generic term created in Washington so bureaucrats can conglomerate an ethnic group," he says. "In California, second and third generation Hispanics prefer to be called *Latinos;* some second and third generation Mexican-Americans prefer *Chicano.* It is very much an individual decision. I'm Irish Basque. I prefer to be called Latino. But I'd rather be called Jose."

McMurray says it is also a misnomer to refer to Latinos as a minority in some areas of the country. "We are not a minority in El Paso, San Antonio or Los Angeles. *Ethnic* is a better term."

Minorities in the News

Gallimore recommends gathering a list of advocacy sources for different groups: by race, age, disability, gender and so on. If you choose a person from that group to check things out that might be insensitive or controversial, you have a better chance of being sensitive, he says. "We make most of our mistakes in the information gathering," Gallimore says. "No amount of expert wordsmanship can overcome faulty materials. Go to a variety of sources. Be more aware of different points of view. If the story involves some statement about a group, go to members of that group."

Mervin Aubespin, associate editor and director of staff development at *The* (Louisville, Ky.) *Courier-Journal,* says one way the media can become more sensitive to the needs of minorities is to hire more minorities. Although the employment of minorities in newsrooms nearly doubled from 1982 to 1992 (see Exhibit 18-1), there's still room for improvement.

Minorities made up 10.49 percent of the work force at newspapers in the mid-90s, but less than 8 percent were supervisors, according to a survey by the American Society of Newspaper Editors. Although the numbers are improving, 45 percent of the newspapers in the country still have no minorities on their staff. Other sources show that in broadcast news organizations, minorities made up about 13 percent of the work force.

The need for minority representation in the media work force and in media coverage is only going to increase. By the year 2010, 87 percent of the growth in the United States will be in minority communities, and the media must reflect the concerns of this significant population.

Aubespin says hiring minorities is only the first step; editors have to encourage minority reporters to express their diversity. One of the problems is that white editors "really want black faces that write like whites," he says.

Exhibit 18-1

Employment of minorities in newsrooms
Bob Laird/*USA Today*

USA SNAPSHOTS®

A look at statistics that shape your finances

Minorities at newspapers

More than 5,100 minorities work at U.S. daily newspapers, vs. 2,800 in 1982. Percentage of newsroom employees:

9.4%

5.5%

8%

6%

4%

Top 50 U.S. newspapers, **5B**   2%

'82   '92   0

Source: American Society of Newspaper Editors   By Bob Laird, USA TODAY

A board member of the National Association of Black Journalists and recipient of numerous awards for his contributions to journalism, Aubespin says he doesn't believe there is a specific set of guidelines to give journalists sensitivity. "There is no formula, no one way to write about a minority group," he says. "The best guideline is to treat each person as an individual. We are as different as you are."

As for Hispanics, McMurray is also concerned about stereotypes. "I would like to say there is a stereotype of Latinos as hard working, family oriented, loyal people but I seldom see that," McMurray says. "Instead I get the sense there is this group of people—Lord knows where they come from—that are not trustworthy, that point guns."

Representatives of Asian groups say they are also victims of stereotypes, such as conclusions that Asian students are either mathematical geniuses or gang members. Joann Lee, co-director of the journalism department at Queens College in New York, examined more than 2,000 stories about Asians. "By far the largest number of stories on Asian-Americans was reported in connection to aspects of immigration, crime and gang violence," she wrote in an article in *Editor & Publisher*. "In education and work ethics, Asians are often linked with phrases such as 'model minority.' . . . But in the area of crime, it's a different story. The stereotype of Asians as members of gangs/tongs/organized crime grows, as attested to by the types of stories reported."

McMurray says some gains are being made to portray ethnic sources in a positive light, especially by *USA Today*. "If they have five front-page pictures, two or three will be of people of color who are not involved in crime," he says. "We need to praise the positive changes and use them for inspiration." *USA Today* newspaper uses multicultural sources in as many stories as possible.

Multicultural sensitivity involves not only the sources you use but also the kinds of stories you choose. Innumerable studies have been conducted to show how women and minorities are portrayed in biased or stereotypical fashion. Minorities often are featured in stories about crime but excluded as sources in general stories about lifestyles, the economy and other stories where experts are cited. Conversely, women and minorities often are portrayed as unusual if they have operated a successful business or accomplished some of the same newsworthy feats as white males.

Adrienne Rivers, a journalism professor at the University of Kansas, conducted a study to determine if there was bias in the Kansas City, Mo., print and broadcast media. She found that news sources thought coverage was biased, showing African-Americans in a negative light or not at all. News managers and editors thought the coverage at their stations and newspapers was very fair.

Although bias was not pervasive, Rivers found many examples of insensitivity. In one case, two city councilmen had an argument at a meeting. The headline said two black councilmen argued. "What difference did race make in that case?" Rivers says. In another story, a writer reviewing a musical performance of a group from England mentioned that one of the band members was Chinese, yet the ethnicity of the other members was not mentioned. "Are Chinese people not supposed to live in England? What was the significance of that?"

Rivers says the most pervasive stereotype is the picture of the black suspect in handcuffs, often on the front page, whereas stories and pictures of white crime suspects often are played inside the paper. "I suggest a reality check," she says. "Ask yourself, if you are going to use a picture or a phrase, would you do the same for people of other categories?"

Rivers stresses the need for a variety of multicultural sources in all kinds of stories. She says reporters tend to go to the same ethnic sources over and over. "They anoint people as leaders of the community and get their voices. There may be other people of that race or ethnic origin with other points of view."

The Ethnic Beat

Murray Dubin understands the need to be sensitive to racial and ethnic groups. He created the ethnic beat at *The Philadelphia Inquirer.* "I decided that the only stories on racial and ethnic issues were stories about violence. It was clear to me that the nation was changing in terms of its color and ethnicity. But we weren't doing stories about their lives and what was going on. It seemed to me that *The Inquirer* and newspapers in general were missing that story," he says.

Dubin writes stories about Ethiopians, African-Americans, Puerto Ricans, Vietnamese, and every other racial or ethnic group in Philadelphia. He doesn't speak their language. He hasn't had their background. He describes himself as "a white, Jewish boy from South Philadelphia." But he doesn't have any trouble getting people to talk to him.

"When I first started the beat, I called people and said, 'Help me out. This is who I am and what I do.' People like to be asked questions about what they know and where they feel smart. They like to share information. I don't care whether you are a plumber or a Cambodian asked about a ritual. When I'm done, I ask, 'Is there anyone you know who is even smarter than you?' They laugh and give me two names. Now I have a list of hundreds of names of people around the country."

Here is an unusual news story by Dubin:

It's official

They're American Indian, so they can get married

The Indian war is over.

The Indians and true love won; the bureaucrats lost.

On Thursday, Brenda Lynch and William Dimalanta, Native American Indians who live in Kensington, were refused a marriage license.

Neither the clerks nor their supervisors in the Marriage License Bureau would permit them to write "Native American Indian" as their race on the application form.

"I don't know if Indian is a race. I'm not an anthropologist," said Thomas F. Gehret, attorney for the bureau in City Hall Room 413. "We don't put down Afro-American or Italian-American. Is Indian equal to Italian-American or is it closer to Caucasian?"

Gehret said the marriage bureau had never faced a problem like this.

"We don't want to prevent them from getting married," he said. "Have someone show us it's a race and we'll do it. Saying it doesn't make it a race. Show me something."

How about the U.S. Census, which lists "American Indian" as an acceptable answer to its question on race?

Or talk to Temple University anthropology professor Judith Goode.

"Native American is a racial designation," she said.

The state marriage license form is dated 1969. Under the designation of "Color or Race," it says: "White, Negro, Other, Specify."

So there appears to be room, intellectually at least, to have replies other than white or Negro. Gehret said acceptable answers in Room 413 are "white, black and brown."

How do the clerks designate race for Asian brides and grooms-to-be?

He said "yellow" was an acceptable answer.

After complaints from Lynch's employer, United American Indians of Delaware County, Gehret yesterday scheduled a meeting with Orphans Court Administrative Judge Edward Pawelec. Orphans Court oversees the bureau.

"The judge had done some research," Gehret said after the meeting. "Native American Indian" was a race, the judge said, and will now be an acceptable response to clerks and supervisors in the marriage bureau.

Shortly after the 11:30 a.m. meeting with the judge, Lynch and Dimalanta went into Room 413, sat on the molded plastic chairs, gazed at the red cupids and hearts and cuddly bears on the walls, and filled their forms anew.

No problems.

Lynch and Dimalanta are from North Carolina. She is a Haliwa-Saponi; he is from the Lumbee tribe.

"I'm relieved that we got the license and I'm happy we're going to get married, but everything is not all right," Lynch said.

"Things have to be changed. The applications should be changed. And those people's attitudes should be changed."

The wedding date is April 11.

Murray Dubin, *The Philadelphia Inquirer*

Dubin says that when dealing with ethnic groups, especially with people who are not accustomed to being interviewed by the media or whose language skills are different, face-to-face interviews are preferable. "I try to chat with people on their own territory," he says.

He also believes in cleaning up quotes when his sources don't speak English well. Or he limits the quotes in his stories. "If I'm not doing a story about language difficulties, I don't feel you should be faithful to the way they speak, because you don't want to embarrass them."

Dubin says this beat is crucial for the future. "I think newspapers and the media in general ought to be devoting more energy to how people with brown skins and yellow skins and whatever color are changing the way America looks and America works and America plays and America eats," he says. "Sometimes it's just a little story about the way things are changing. If there's more bok choy in the market than there used to be, we ought to tell people that. I think we miss too many stories because no one wrote a press release. We ought to tell people what is going on."

Gender Differences

One of the ways America is changing involves women's roles. Women make up 52 percent of the population, but studies show they don't get nearly that much media coverage.

An annual study conducted by the Women, Men and Media Project at Columbia University since 1989 examined gender in photos, bylines and story sources at 20 major metropolitan newspapers and three broadcast networks. The 1995 study, called "Slipping from the Scene," showed that women's progress as sources in broadcast and print news and as reporters is declining. "The drop in news coverage is part of a backlash against women across the country," says Betty Friedan, co-chairperson of the study.

References to women on the front page of newspapers slid from an average of 25 percent in 1994 to 19 percent in 1995. However, that figure is an improvement from 11 percent in 1989, the first year of the study. Female bylines on the front page remained at 34 percent, the same percentage every year since 1992.

In the broadcast media, the average percentage of stories reported by female correspondents on the nightly news shows of ABC, CBS and NBC dropped from 21 percent in 1994 to 20 percent in 1995. The average percentage of women interviewed on the three major network news programs was 24 percent, the same as it had been the previous year. However, that figure is nearly double the coverage of the early '90s, so coverage of women has improved—although not nearly enough to reflect the percentage of women in the population.

As Exhibit 18-2 shows, the coverage of women in news magazines is also far less than proportionate to their numbers.

Like many other studies, the report from the Women, Men and Media Project blamed many of the problems for story sources and story selection on the male-dominated power structure in the media. At the beginning of the 1990s, only 6 percent of the top media bosses were female. "The messages the American people receive pass through a male filter," the report said.

By the mid-1990s, the percentage of women in top management hadn't increased. But coverage of issues about women had—although not necessarily because of sensitivity. At newspapers, for example, female readership declined 26 percent in the mid-1980s.

Studies show that an increasing number of women are working, and they have little time to read newspapers. In focus groups with women, media executives have discovered that women would read newspapers if there were more stories of interest to them, such as stories about education, women in business and women in general.

Many newspapers have begun focusing more on such stories. In the 1970s, partially because the feminist movement was stressing equal

Exhibit 18-2

*Coverage of women
in news magazines*
Marcy E. Mullins/*USA Today*

USA SNAPSHOTS®

A look at statistics that shape the nation

Equal writes

Women make up 52% of the U.S. population but receive relatively little coverage in the news magazines. Percentages of people mentioned in the magazines that are women:

	Newsweek			Time			U.S. News & World Report		
	'89	'90	'91	'89	'90	'91	'89	'90	'91
	17%	13%	18%	13%	14%	11%	7%	8%	10%

Source: Women in Communications study of August issues

By Marcy E. Mullins, USA TODAY

rights, newspaper sections devoted primarily to women's issues gave way to the more generic "lifestyles" sections. But by the '90s, women's sections began reappearing. The *Chicago Tribune,* for example, created a women's section called Womanews. Television news also featured more stories about health, parenting, education, day care and other issues believed to be of interest to women.

A danger accompanies this well-meaning attention. The result can be an overemphasis on "gee whiz" stories that stress how amazing it is for a woman to succeed. Instead, the focus should be the newsworthiness of women's achievements.

Just as women are victims of stereotypes, so are men. Women are supposed to be emotional; men are supposed to be strong. More often the men featured in the news have no feelings at all. Women have an agenda of child support and social issues; men want to read about sports.

Nonsense, says Jack Kammer, a free-lance writer about gender issues. In an article in *Editor & Publisher,* he says it is a mistake to conclude that women have no interest in sports or business sections and that men have no interest in lifestyle sections. In fact, he says, one study showed that 84 percent of the men surveyed said family mattered most to them. Men also want a say about child care, sexual harassment and social issues.

Shifts in treatment of women and men are apparent in advertising as well. To reach the huge female buying market, advertisers have overcompensated, particularly in several television ads, by portraying men as stupid or incompetent. The use of women as sex symbols in many beer and automobile ads has also declined. But despite some progress, examples of sexism—mostly against women—persist in all areas of the media.

The principles for coverage of gender are the same as they are for coverage of minorities. Make an effort to include female sources as experts, as well as males and multicultural sources, in general stories, not just stories geared to women. Seek diversity of opinion, but write about people as being all equal. When you write about a woman, don't include descriptive details about her appearance unless you would also include descriptive details about a man's appearance.

Consider the following story about Dolly Parton, for example. The writer says the focus of the story is Parton's new movie, a point the writer makes in the 18th paragraph. The writer also acknowledges that Parton (the writer doesn't call her anything but Dolly) has achieved great success—a $100 million fortune—from records, movies, TV shows and her Dollywood amusement park in Tennessee. Read the selection and decide for yourself if the story, despite its tongue-in-cheek tone, is offensive:

NEW YORK—No way they're real, not *that* big.

Women would kill to have them. Men would kill to somehow get them off Dolly Parton and onto their wives. They are just so . . . so . . . what, titanic?

Ooooo, the way they sit right *up there,* so prominently, so, so, so openly.

And up close, they look different from each other. The one on the left is almost square. The other's got a kind of pear shape to it. No wonder two security guards, with guns and walkie-talkies, are right outside the fancy hotel room.

But it just seems far too crass to mention them, to come right out and ask: "Dolly, are those *real* diamond rings?"

And so you don't.

Instead, you just sit there and stare at this tiny little woman, talking and giggling, giggling and talking, just as she does with Johnny Carson or Phil Donahue.

You've got to hand it to her—she's no different right there on the couch than she is on the teevee. Just as bubbly, just as self-deprecating. And talk about *looks.*

No lie. She is sitting there in these spike-heeled, knee-high black leather boots, jeans that must've pinched her when she was 12. And for a top, she's got on some kind of black frilly, lacy thing. Whew. It's all topped off by a silver-gray leather jacket that's got Lawrence Taylor shoulder pads and surely cost about what Lee Iacocca has made in all his years with Chrysler.

Lord have mercy, why doesn't this woman just spontaneously combust?

Of course, it's a look that Dolly Parton, now 46, has cultivated for years.

"I *l-o-v-e* all this gaud," she squeals. "It's like a kid with paints and crayons. I think it has to do with me growing up poor and wanting more. I lived in fairy tales with stories about kings and queens with their robes and diamonds. And that's what I always wanted to be."

Dolly giggles.

"I patterned myself after the trash in my home town. There was this woman, I swear." She giggles again, and leans in a bit to share a story.

"You know how every small town has a trollop or a tramp or a slut or whatever. Well, there was this woman when I was growing up. Every Saturday she'd walk the streets until somebody would pick her up. Men would be driving around, tooting the horn. She had long, blond hair that was peroxided. She wore bright red lipstick. She had long, bright-red fingernails, and tight skirts in these bright colors, and high heels.

"I thought, THAT IS HOW I WANT TO LOOK WHEN I GROW UP. I didn't know she was the town tramp. I didn't even know what that meant. So, sure enough, when I grew up, I looked like trash. But I don't feel like trash."

The giggle.

Oh, this woman is fun. Of course, she's not here just to explain her lifetime fashion philosophy. She is here because she's got a new movie out: Straight Talk, which opened Friday.

In ST, Dolly—sorry, but it just doesn't feel right calling her Parton—plays Shirlee Kenyon, a small-town Arkansas dance instructor, thrice divorced and stuck in a nowhere relationship.

The Philadelphia Inquirer

Most sexism is not so blatant. But the writer of the article said he had excellent rapport with Parton and she was not offended by the article. Parton does enjoy discussing her figure and her style and refers to herself in terms that might well be considered sexist by the politically correct.

In an Associated Press story about a biography of Parton, the writer also discusses her physical traits but in a different tone. Compare the two excerpts and decide if you think one is more offensive than the other.

Look beyond the trademark big hair and, well, the other obvious big traits of Dolly Parton, and you marvel at the heart of a big-time star who emerged from the humblest of backwoods roots.

She holds back nothing. She likes herself, likes life. With a candor rarely found in show business or anywhere else, she bares her soul's joys and sorrows and scars with an earthiness that can bring laughter, tears and blushes.

She is raw and round and perky and personal, but as genuine and distinctive as the high-pitched Smoky Mountains twang that launched her career as a country singer.

In short, she's someone you just like being around.

"This outrageous look fits my outrageous personality," said Parton, wearing a black leather short skirt and low cut V-neck leather blouse adorned with white, loopy, lacy decorations on the sleeves.

Her autobiography, "Dolly: My Life and Other Unfinished Business," hit the book shelves Sept. 27.

The story continues with more details about her life and ends with these four paragraphs.

And, oh yes, she candidly admits to plastic surgery but won't say exactly what was nipped and what was tucked. Suffice it to say her face and her prominent chest were both lifted. In a chapter on her figure, she credits a surgeon with doing "uplifting" work.

"I'd be much more ashamed to be tripping over them than to have them perked up a little bit," Parton laughed during the interview. "I told him to just perk them up and make them stand at attention. They're brave little soldiers."

For Parton, that's just a warmup.

"I always had big boobs. I was proud of them, too. I figured if it was growing on me, I was going to show these little nuggets," Parton said. "That was the first sign I was going to be a woman, and not only that, I was going to be a hell of a woman. When I die, I'll probably have a special coffin made for my boobs and my hair."

Robert Dvorchak, The Associated Press

How can you avoid sexism and gender stereotypes? Here are some tips published in *The Gannetteer,* a magazine for employees of Gannett newspapers:

- Avoid using masculine pronouns such as he or his. Instead of "Everyone should eat his own biscuit," say, "everyone should eat a biscuit." (If you must use a pronoun, use his and her together.)

- Avoid words that, by definition, refer to one sex or the other but not both. Instead of governess, use tutor.

- Avoid words starting or ending with man. Instead of mailman, use mail carrier. Instead of fireman, use firefighter; police officer in place of policeman.

- Avoid stereotypes in illustrations and graphics. Not all quarterbacks are white. Not all basketball players are black. Not all single parents are women. Not all newspaper editors are men. Not all pro golfers are men.

- Avoid calling groups of people men, unless they are all male. A congressional group should be called lawmakers or members of Congress, not Congressmen.

- Avoid the stereotype of a mother. Don't say "chicken soup like your mother used to make." Maybe father made the soup once in a while. Avoid phrases like "old wives' tale," "tied to her apron strings" or "Dutch uncle."

- Avoid referring to women by their first names in stories. This is almost always patronizing, and not usually done to men.

- Avoid describing women with adjectives that dwell on sexual attributes. Ask yourself whether you would describe the walk of an IBM executive as "suggestive" if you were profiling a man, or would the walk just seem "confident." Ditto for "feisty." When is the last time you saw a man described as "feisty?"

- Be careful with "first" stories: the first woman to pick up the garbage for a living, fly into space or run for the school board. *(However, if it is a first, it may be worth mentioning, but it does not have to be the focus of the story.)*

- Avoid phrases that carry an element of surprise such as "smart and dedicated woman." Is it unusual that someone who is smart and dedicated is a woman, too?

- Beware of approaching any story with the subconscious idea that it is more of a man's story or a woman's. Almost always we quote women in stories about child care. Why not men? A lack of child care is just as big a problem to them—or should be.

Guidelines for Writing About Special Groups

During baseball's 1991 World Series between the Atlanta Braves and the Minnesota Twins, Native Americans protested the use of team names that they considered degrading to their heritage. They wanted the teams with names like Redskins, Braves and Indians to change their names, and they wanted the media to stop using the old names.

William Hilliard, former editor of *The* (Portland) *Oregonian,* took the request seriously. He instituted a policy requiring the newspaper staff to use the names of the cities (such as Atlanta played Cincinnati) in place of the names of the teams. Hilliard said many people didn't understand his decision (his mail was 60-40 against the policy). But until Native Americans raised the issue, he hadn't thought the names could be offensive. "I, too, am a product of a white male–dominated environment," he wrote in an article for the American Society of Newspaper Editors. And Hilliard is an African-American. He continued:

> Very few, if any, of my coworkers have any understanding of what I, and other persons of color, endure on an almost daily basis because of an indignity—a racial slur here, a slight there, even a show of surprise. . . . This is a color question, and whites in America have not had to deal with that one. Our society is multicultural and multiracial. If we are to make all Americans feel free and equal, then we must find innovative ways to solve problems associated with race.

Every group has some special needs and concerns about language. A man who uses a wheelchair probably doesn't consider himself handicapped (a derogatory term). He may, however, have a disability that requires him to use a wheelchair. A person who has AIDS is not a victim but rather an AIDS patient or a person living with AIDS. And not all people over age 65 are ready for the stereotypical rocking chair.

You cannot be expected to memorize dictionaries for each special interest group. However, if your beat is a specialty that frequently deals with aging, disabled people, AIDS or some other minority interest, you could call an umbrella organization and ask for guidelines. Most organizations have these printed.

Your first source, however, should be the people you interview. Ask them how they prefer to be addressed. Next, consult the *Associated Press Stylebook,* which includes guidelines under such listings as *handicapped* and *AIDS.* You'll minimize trouble by avoiding the use of adjectives to describe people.

People With Disabilities

Do not characterize someone as disabled unless that condition is crucial to the story. Avoid the word *handicapped,* unless the person uses it to describe himself or herself. If the disability is a factor, don't say "disabled people." Instead, use "people with disabilities." Avoid such terms as *crippled* and *deformed.*

Many euphemisms—such as "physically challenged," "partially sighted" and "physically inconvenienced"—have come into vogue. However, disability groups object to such euphemisms, because they are considered condescending.

Heather Kirkwood, a journalism student at the University of Kansas, is legally blind but can see with the use of various aids. She doesn't like being called visually challenged or partially sighted. She prefers the term "blind." But she says organizations representing blind people disagree with her and insist that the distinction between partially and fully blind should be made.

"As far as political correctness, my own feelings are that it isn't the word, it is what the word means," Kirkwood says. "Saying 'visually impaired' instead of 'blind' doesn't really change the way the blind are viewed in society. What matters is what comes to mind when you say the word 'blind.' Progress is changing what it means to be blind, not changing the word for it."

Kirkwood is an A student, an aggressive reporter and a talented writer. She regularly writes columns and news stories for the university newspaper. She uses computer aids and other equipment to help her take notes and read, but she expects no special treatment. Other people call her "amazing," but she prefers to be treated the same as sighted people.

Kirkwood acknowledges that many stories about people with disabilities have that same "gee whiz" factor as stories about successful women. "As far as the 'amazing factor,' that must really confuse people," she says. "Many blind people truly believe they are amazing. That is because we are taught to think that from a very early age.

"While we can expect journalists to try to understand all of this, we know the general public probably won't," Kirkwood says. "We also expect journalists to understand that we are not all representative of an entire group of people, yet we know the general public won't be as fair. The biggest problem we face is not blindness, but rather the public's perception of blindness."

The Research and Training Center for Independent Living at the University of Kansas, which offers guidelines for writing about people with disabilities, says euphemisms "reinforce the idea that disabilities cannot be dealt with up front." When in doubt, ask your sources how they prefer to be addressed.

Here are some more tips:

• When interviewing people with disabilities, do not speak louder unless the person has a hearing impairment. A common complaint of people who have disabilities unrelated to their hearing is that everyone treats them as though they were hearing impaired. Treat people with disabilities exactly as you would any other source.

• Avoid overcompensating by writing about people with disabilities as though they were superhuman. The hidden implication is that all people with disabilities are without talent and that your source is unusual. The same principle says to avoid calling an African-American articulate or qualified, implying that other African-Americans are not.

• Avoid writing about people with disabilities as though they don't have any fallibilities.

• Avoid using adjectives as nouns to describe people with disabilities in a group, such as "the deaf" or "the retarded." Say "people who are deaf" or "people with mental retardation." For people who are blind, "visually impaired" is a preferred term.

• For mental illness, avoid such terms as *crazy* and *demented. Psychotic* and *schizophrenic* should be used in context—and only if they are the proper medical terms. Preferred terms are "people with emotional disorders" or psychiatric illness, mental problems or mental disabilities.

• Avoid "gee whiz" stories that stress how amazing it is that this person could accomplish anything special, given his or her disability.

Stories About Aging

If there were ever a group subject to "gee whiz" stories, it would have to be people over age 65. Most newspaper feature stories treat people in this age group as absolutely amazing just because they walk, run, dance or accomplish anything. People over 65 are usually described as spry, sometimes feisty, but always remarkable.

Consider this feature:

This place hops.

The food's tame, the dance steps slower than they used to be, the stiffest drink comes from the water fountain.

Still the Gray Crowd jams the Armory Park Senior Citizens Center.

Typically, 1,200 men and women gather daily for gossip, games, and yes—even to cast some plain old-fashioned goo-goo eyes.

The (Tucson) *Arizona Daily Star*

Or the story will feature a twist—surprise, surprise, they're old!

The teams, each with two rows of participants, face one another. As the blue balloon floats through the air, the two seemingly docile teams transform into aggressive competitors.

You'd think they were teenagers. They were . . . perhaps 50 or more years ago.

Tulsa (Okla.) *World*

Make age a factor, not the focus of a person's accomplishments. Readers can decide for themselves if the person's accomplishments are surprising because of the person's age. Especially avoid the astonishment factor: Isn't it amazing this person can accomplish such and such at this age?

At this point in American society, people over age 65 are often classified as older Americans entitled to certain privileges. The *Associated Press Stylebook* also uses age 65 as a delineator. Here are some general guidelines for dealing with people of this age:

- When writing about people over age 65, avoid such adjectives as *gray-haired* or other terms unless you would use the same type of description if the story were about a younger person with blond or brown hair.

- Avoid stereotypes. Don't introduce rocking chairs or similar stereotypical images if the people in the story aren't using them.

- Avoid "the graying population," "senior citizens" and other group designations unless you are writing a trend story. And then use such a term only if it is relevant, necessary and appropriate—for example, if a group uses the term in its own name, as in Gray Power.

- Avoid saying such things as "She doesn't consider herself old," unless she says it. Even though you are meaning to extend a compliment, by writing such denials you are introducing a stereotype.

AIDS Stories

Feb. 16, 1989, started out as a good day. Carolyn Warmbold was working on the final stages of her dissertation for her doctorate in English at the University of Texas, Austin.

At 1:40 that afternoon, her husband, Ted, called. He had the worst headache he had ever had. Nine days later he died at age 45.

The doctors attributed his death to cryptococcal meningitis. The *San Antonio Light,* the newspaper of which Ted Warmbold was editor, attributed it to AIDS.

"On Sunday (a week before Ted died), when the doctors told me of his meningitis, they did not tell me of his AIDS," Carolyn Warmbold says. "The managing editor of the newspaper told me. The paper was going to mention it in his obituary. My first reaction was to get a gun and shoot both Ted and myself because he would not survive the disease, and I would not survive the stigma."

The story of how Ted Warmbold died from an AIDS-related illness got into the newspaper. This is the story that didn't. It is the story of Carolyn Warmbold, an editor at the *Atlanta Journal and Constitution,* and her crusade to make journalists sensitive to the needs of people living with AIDS.

At first she worried about why the newspaper insisted on printing the cause of her husband's death from an AIDS-related disease. "How could it help the community? My privacy would be invaded," she says. "I foresaw what the disclosure would mean. People would speculate that I, too, had AIDS. The announcement would make us unpeople—unemployable, uninsurable. I swore while he was dying that I would try to keep it out of the paper. But the newspaper editors said it was likely to be rumored anyway, and if they covered it up, how could they deal with others."

The *Light* announced it only locally. The note that went to The Associated Press didn't say AIDS, but the Texas AP revised it and included the term.

When her husband died, Carolyn Warmbold had resolved that he could not be just another AIDS statistic. She decided to give the eulogy at his funeral. "His death had to count for something."

For the first time Warmbold, a former reporter, was on both sides of the news. It was the last "gloriously free moment" she would experience in two years. She gave speeches and became an advocate for AIDS patients. But she suffered from the stigma.

"The doctors said I was free of the AIDS virus. But after my husband's death, the pest control man came for his regular visit and wore rubber gloves for the first time. He pointed a sprayer at me as though I were some giant cockroach. I was stuck with a scarlet letter *A* for *AIDS* on my breast."

Warmbold and her husband of 22 years had experienced sexual difficulties throughout their marriage. But it was only in the two years prior to his death that she suspected he was gay. However, the couple had not discussed her suspicions. She says during one period when they had separated, her husband was sexually promiscuous and could have contracted the disease at that time.

She admits it is hard for people to understand why she did not suspect her husband was gay long before his death. She dismisses such concern. She was busy getting her doctorate, he was busy running a newspaper, and they hadn't engaged in sex for years anyway.

Today Warmbold is committed to trying to make people sensitive to the needs of people living with AIDS (not dying with AIDS, she stresses). She says the media need to write more personal narratives about people with AIDS so they are not statistics and so the stigma of having AIDS ultimately will be reduced. "We must have stories with names," she says. "What is more effective than the Vietnam Memorial when you see all those names? That shows the numbers more than anything."

The writer's task   Writing about AIDS is different from writing other stories, Carolyn Warmbold insists. The biggest problem is the public perception, she says. "The public views people with AIDS as innocent victims—those who get it by transfusions, wives who are infected—and guilty victims—the gays and drug users. The very acronym implies guilt—Acquired Immune Deficiency Syndrome, as something you go out and acquire like a car. But you need to persuade people that there is no such thing as a guilty or innocent victim. You are just dealing with people. Nobody asks to get AIDS. It happens."

Warmbold admits her attitude borders on advocacy journalism. But she says it is not possible to be objective about such stories. "It's not like covering city council. You are dealing with death. I don't think it's wrong to feel emotion."

Asking questions about death is difficult. But Warmbold says reporters shouldn't go into the story with a hopeless attitude. "People with AIDS are going to die, but at the same time the quality and quantity of their life depends on having a positive attitude," she says. "When you are interviewing, you want to keep that in mind. Most will talk about death. Take the cue from them. Most of them are going to accept the fact that their life is going to be short. Talk about it matter-of-factly." Warmbold suggests these kinds of questions: "Are you frightened by it? Do you think about the pain?"

Warmbold also suggests that before publication, reporters check parts of the story with the people who are affected. You don't have to read them the story, but check the facts and tell them what you are going to say. Make sure they are comfortable about using names. "You have to take the whole family into consideration," she says.

There is no formula for covering AIDS stories. Just be a compassionate human being, Warmbold says.

A Pulitzer Prize AIDS story   There was no formula to prepare Jacqui Banaszynski, a former reporter at the *St. Paul* (Minn.) *Pioneer Press,* for the emotional toll that AIDS can take on the patients and on the reporter who writes about them. Her stories about the life and death of a Minnesota farmer and his partner won her the 1988 Pulitzer Prize for feature writing. She spent 15 months reporting how Dick Hanson and Bert Henningson lived and died with AIDS.

She became as close to them as a family member—actually, closer than some of their family members. When Henningson was dying, his family even asked her to help decide whether they should pull the plug (she refused).

The rules change for this kind of story, Banaszynski says. "You have to be empathetic. On the other hand, you have to be honest and true to the reader who may be hostile to the subject. You walk a fine line between not blaming and not whitewashing."

The idea for the series was to find an AIDS patient who was willing to be chronicled throughout the disease. She found Hanson. He was willing to talk about his disease, but he couldn't face the thought of dying.

"I'll never forget the day I had to confront him with the prospect of dying," Banaszynski says. "It was the hardest thing I've ever done as a journalist, knowing I was going to ask if I could watch him die. I said I want to do the whole story, that means to the end. But he was in denial (about death). He kept saying, 'I want you to do a story about life.' I told him, 'If you beat this, you'll be the first man to do this. But if you die— and everybody dies from AIDS—I want to be there at the end.' I was hoping he would say no.

"He got very quiet. And then he got very angry. I said I'm going to leave. I allowed him some time to think. He cried and realized he was dying. Then we made our pact to do the story."

For the next 15 months, she became attached to these two men. "You can steel yourself emotionally if it's just one story, but they became a beat for me."

The series appeared as three stories on different dates, the first chapter on June 21, 1987, when Hanson was still alive. He died on July 25, and the third chapter appeared two weeks later. When Henningson died a year later, she wrote an epilogue to the series that was not part of the Pulitzer package.

Banaszynski says there is no question that the story took an emotional toll on her. "I allowed myself a limited time to be emotional, never during the interviews." And then she forced herself into her role as journalist and wrote the stories.

Banaszynski says one of the reasons AIDS stories differ from other stories is the social stigma. "The disease is one story, the social context of the disease becomes another story. If you ignore the opportunity to deal with the societal revulsion, you miss the whole crux."

Readers don't want to read about AIDS or deal with it, she says. So she decided that the best approach was to portray these two men as two ordinary Minnesotans who had a commonality with readers. "If Joe and Suzy Reader could not relate to two gay pig farmers, they could relate to two men who plant impatiens, feed kittens and tend a vegetable garden, because that's what all Minnesotans do."

In her introduction, she stresses that this is a story about people living—as well as dying—with AIDS:

Death is no stranger to the heartland. It is as natural as the seasons, as inevitable as farm machinery breaking down and farmers' bodies giving out after too many years of too much work.

But when death comes in the guise of AIDS, it is a disturbingly unfamiliar visitor, one better known in the gay districts and drug houses of the big cities, one that shows no respect for the usual order of life in the country.

The visitor has come to rural Glenwood, Minn.

Dick Hanson, a well-known liberal political activist who homesteads his family's century-old farm south of Glenwood, was diagnosed last summer with acquired immune deficiency syndrome. His partner of five years, Bert Henningson, carries the AIDS virus.

In the year that Hanson has been living—and dying—with AIDS, he has hosted some cruel companions: blinding headaches and failing vision, relentless nausea and deep fatigue, falling blood counts and worrisome coughs and sleepless, sweat-soaked nights.

He has watched as his strong body, toughened by 37 years on the farm, shrinks and stoops like that of an old man. He has weathered the family shame and community fear, the prejudice and whispered condemnations. He has read the reality in his partner's eyes, heard the death sentence from doctors and seen the hopelessness confirmed by the statistics.

But the statistics tell only half the story—the half about dying.

Statistics fail to tell much about the people they represent. About the people like Hanson—a farmer who has nourished life in the fields, a peace activist who has marched for a safer planet, an idealist and a gay activist who has campaigned for social justice, and now an AIDS patient who refuses to abandon his own future, however long it lasts.

The statistics say nothing of the joys of a carefully tended vegetable garden and new kittens under the shed, of tender teasing and magic hugs. Of flowers that bloom brighter and birds that sing sweeter and simple pleasures grown profound against the backdrop of a terminal illness. Of the powerful bond between two people who pledged for better or worse and meant it.

"Who is to judge the value of life, whether it's one day or one week or one year," Hanson said. "I find the quality of life more important than the length of life."

Much has been written about the death that comes from AIDS, but little has been said about the living. Hanson and Henningson want to change that. They have opened their homes and their hearts to tell the whole story—beginning to end.

Jacqui Banaszynski, *St. Paul Pioneer Press*

Ground rules for sensitive questions   When you write about AIDS, you have to ask about dying and you have to ask about sex. How do you approach either of these sensitive questions?

"The only thing to do is to set it in context," Banaszynski says. "When I get to it, I ask as directly as I can: How many men did you sleep with? I don't warn them that this is a hard question. I set that up in the ground rules. I say, 'We're going to talk about a lot of personal things, and a lot may be embarrassing. You don't have to answer, but I'll try to get you to answer.' If you ask honestly and directly with no judgment in your voice so there is no shame involved, they will answer. If you are embarrassed, they will pick it up. I ask the question as matter-of-factly as I would about the weather."

Banaszynski says people are really very eager to tell their stories. "I think you can ask anybody any question if you are non-judgmental and a good listener. Nobody listens anymore."

She also used another interviewing technique in her many visits with Hanson and Henningson. "I did something I don't normally do," she says. "I reminded them of my mission. They got to like me so much. My job was to be responsible and remind them that I was there as a reporter. I broke rules and invented new ones. I said when the notebook was down they could talk freely. Nothing was fair game until the notebook was out. And then I would remind them again that it was now on the record."

When she wrote the stories, she also did something that is not general practice in journalism. "I called each person involved in the story and read them their quotes, and I told them the context. For example, in one case I said, 'I set you in the context of a fight with your family.' Then I told them, if you can convince me that I have erred or been insensitive, I'll consider changing it."

Only one person complained. She didn't take out any of his comments, but she added a sentence that appeased him.

She also took the newspaper to Hanson and Henningson the night before it hit the morning newspaper stands so they could see it first. "They couldn't change anything, but that's just courtesy. If they allow me to invade their privacy, I owe them that courtesy."

Banaszynski says the ground rules are different when you are writing about people who are not accustomed to dealing with the media. "I do a lot of real-people stories," she says. "These people don't know the rules. I have more responsibility to tell them what I'm going to be writing, the general thrust, and what I'm trying to do."

Sometimes in stories about AIDS, family members don't know about the diagnosis or are not willing to have the information made public. Banaszynski tells AIDS patients that she must use their name and picture. She gives them time to tell their family.

For her Pulitzer series, "AIDS in the Heartland," the family knew the stories would be public, but not all the members were cooperative. In fact, she got threats from some people who were upset that she was doing the story. The turmoil is part of doing the whole story, Banaszynski says, and she thinks the statements from family members may have been one of the most powerful parts of the series.

Here is an excerpt from the second chapter, where Banaszynski writes about a family quarrel she witnessed:

Tom Hanson is angry at Dick Hanson for making news of such a shameful disease, at his sister, Mary, for siding with Dick, at his brother Grant because "he's not man enough" to say that homosexuality is wrong, at a local minister for refusing to denounce homosexuality from the pulpit, at the media for exploiting his family.

"I feel Dickie is helping the public by talking about this," he said. "But he could have done it without bringing his name into it or his picture or the town. This is not fair what he's doing to the family. . . . It's not easy being single trying to go through this, having girls come up and say, 'His brother's gay and he has AIDS. Is he gay, too?'. . .

"He never stopped to think of the innocent people who would be suffering for his glory."

Jacqui Banaszynski, *St. Paul Pioneer Press*

Some things she heard that night with the family were so powerful, but so private, that Banaszynski worried about using them, even though they were said "on the record."

She uses this method to determine whether a revealing quote that could hurt someone is really necessary: First she writes it in the story. Then she takes it out and shows the story to several people at her newspaper. If they can get the meaning and emotion from the story without the sensitive quote, she leaves it out. If they aren't moved by what she is writing, then she considers that the quote might be necessary. She also uses ethical reasoning: Is it for the greater good? Will more people be helped by this information than harmed?

Terminology The language of AIDS is changing, as it is for many special interest groups. The best advice is to ask the people you are covering how they preferred to be addressed.

People with AIDS do not like to be called "victims." They prefer to be called "AIDS patients" or "people *living* with AIDS."

The *Associated Press Stylebook* says the scientific name for the AIDS virus is the human immunodeficiency virus. People who test positive for it are referred to as HIV-positive. That doesn't mean they have AIDS; it means they are carrying the virus. To have AIDS means they have developed the symptoms of the disease and have been diagnosed with the disease, not merely with the virus.

Banaszynski isn't always willing to use the technical term, such as "HIV-positive," if it won't be readily understood by readers. She often writes about the "AIDS virus." Banaszynski says what she writes must pass "the Ethel test," in honor of her mother, Ethel. "My mother is very bright, but she lives in a small town and is not very worldly. She is the common reader. If I don't think Ethel will understand a term, I won't use it." But the terms you use will depend on your newspaper's policy.

Banaszynski predicts that it will get increasingly difficult to interest the public in AIDS stories. "The one thing you always have to remember about AIDS is that it has an overlay of homosexuality," she says. "It is a stigmatized disease that the public doesn't want to read about. You have to get past a big barrier of rejection.

"You have to focus on the common denominator. This could be your brother or neighbor or your doctor. AIDS serves as an extreme example of all the challenges in reporting more than other stories. You have got to find ways to have it connect to everyone's life."

Exercises

1 Interview members of various ethnic and racial groups in your community or on your campus about their concerns and the kinds of stories they think newspapers are not writing about them. Devise 10 story ideas based on your interviews.

2 Write a trend story based on one of the story ideas you developed in Exercise 1.

3 Sexism, ageism and racism: Look for examples of language, description or other elements of stories that you think are sexist, racist or ageist.

4 Using highlighters of two different colors, read the news sections of your newspaper for a few days. Use one color to mark the female sources quoted and the other color for the male sources. Analyze the types of stories that feature women more than men and vice versa. Also try to determine if multicultural sources are used in the news stories.

5 Multicultural profile: Interview a person on campus who is a member of a minority group—whether because of the person's race, ethnic background or sexual orientation. The focus should be this person's feelings about how the media treat members of his or her minority. Get some background about the person. Then ask questions related to the focus. Some questions to include might be

- How do you prefer to be addressed? How do you think the media portray people in your minority group? Are the portrayals positive or negative? (Ask for specific examples.) Have you ever experienced insensitivity or prejudice because of your race, ethnic background, disability or special interests? (Please specify.)

- Have you ever been interviewed by the media? Was your experience good or bad? (Please specify.) What advice would you give to reporters about coverage of minorities such as yourself? (Again, ask for specifics.)

Write your findings in the form of a miniprofile.

FIVE

Applying the Techniques

COACHING

TIPS

Ask one source to recommend others.

Ask people you meet what stories they would like to read in your field.

Keep a tickler file of story ideas and follow-up stories.

Contact sources regularly.

Check records on your beat.

Make stories relevant to readers.

Seek human elements in stories.

Translate jargon in technical stories or specialized fields.

Beat Reporting

19

When Mark McCormick began covering the religion beat for the *Courier-Journal* in Louisville, Ky., he had no sources and few story ideas. But within a few weeks he had more sources and story tips than he could cover.

"I asked each person I interviewed two things: 'If you could name five or 10 people that I would need to know to do this beat well, who would they be? If there were five stories about religion that you would like to read, what would they be?' Between those two things, I amassed a large calling list," McCormick says.

McCormick kept names of all his sources in his computer. "If five people said I needed to talk to the same people, I put a star next to that person's name," he says. "I made it a point to cultivate a relationship with those people by going to lunch with them and trying to win their confidence."

He also used the matchmaker technique, asking one source to introduce him to people who might be skeptical about dealing him or with the media in general. "I'd say, 'Would you mind telling this person I'm not a hatchet man.' That is how I made a breakthrough in the Jewish community and the Muslim community."

In the past, religion news was relegated to a page on Saturdays to announce church services and other information. But it is becoming a significant beat because newspaper studies have shown that religion affects people's lives as much as or more than any other news in the paper.

The religion beat was a new challenge to McCormick, who had covered police and community beats in the past. "I was a little intimidated because I am not theologically trained," he says. As he

To be a good beat reporter, you have to love what you're doing.

Sevil Omer, reporter,

Reno (Nev.) Gazette-Journal

Mark McCormick, beat reporter

soon discovered, however, the religion beat is like any other beat. The content of the news differs, but the techniques of reporting and writing do not.

A "beat" is a specific area of coverage. It can be an entire municipality or parts of the government, such as the police department, the school board or the city officials. It can be a topical beat, such as environment, business, minorities or religion.

The skills you have studied so far can be applied to all beats. Some of the following chapters will be devoted to specific beats, such as police, courts and government, but the tips from McCormick and other writers in this chapter will help you get started covering any beat.

Developing Story Ideas

Although McCormick received many tips for story ideas by asking people what they wanted to read, he also used his natural curiosity to develop ideas. One day he was covering the funeral of a 15-year-old boy who had been shot. The boy's friends showed up wearing T-shirts with the boy's picture and the words "Rest in Peace." McCormick says the shirts struck him as odd, but then he noticed similar markings on T-shirts and baseball caps after another young man died. Although it may not seem like a story for the religion beat, McCormick says this social phenomenon is, in fact, a very spiritual story.

The front of the shirts that Thomas Cooper made after the death of his friend, Tony Sullivan, read "R.I.P. T LUV" in artful script and colorful airbrushed design.

On the back was an enlarged, equally artistic design featuring "T LUV"—Sullivan's nickname.

"He's my homey; you've got to remember him," Cooper, 19, said of Sullivan, who was shot by a police officer in Lexington's Bluegrass-Aspendale housing area last month in an incident that sparked civil unrest in the city.

On Friday, Cooper was wearing a baseball cap with "T LUV" across the front. "I just got this to have something to remember him by. He was my boy." And at Sullivan's funeral the previous week, many young people were wearing their "T LUV" T-shirts. Such shirts—with the deceased's picture or name emblazoned across them—are becoming a common sight at services for teen-age victims of violence.

Some youths say wearing the shirts has nothing to do with being cool and everything to do with respecting the memory of fallen friends. Other teens and school counselors argue that many who wear the shirts don't even know the victims and are not grieving but trying to connect with a culture they see as alluring.

Mark McCormick, *The* (Louisville, Ky.) *Courier-Journal*

One story can lead to many others, as when McCormick wrote about a hospital chapel that was closing. "I went there and talked to people about their memories," he says. "I found a woman who had spent many hours praying in the chapel 20 years ago because her husband had cancer and was supposed to die. He is still alive today." McCormick says 135 people called him or left voice mail messages to comment about the story, and many people told him similar touching stories about how faith had affected their lives. As a result, he had many sources for another story about the power of faith.

McCormick also checks newspaper clips, journals, newsletters, press releases and national research organizations that cover religion to keep abreast of his field. "I keep tabs of polls about young people in church, single people, why men don't go to church as much as women. I also keep everything I write in a notebook so I don't have to go to the library and look things up for follow-up stories," he says.

Many beat reporters also check the Internet to read interactive news groups, where people express their opinions. Although this source doesn't always lead to local stories, it gives reporters an idea of what people are discussing in their field and provides sources for stories on national trends.

But to do a good job on any beat, you still need to use the traditional reporting skills of meeting people and developing sources in person.

Cultivating and Keeping Sources

Once you find sources, you need to get them to trust you. McCormick, who has since become a reporter for *The Wichita* (Kan.) *Eagle,* says when you start any beat, it's always better to write a positive story the first time you cover a group if you can. "I never want my first contact to be negative."

That is especially true with groups that haven't had much coverage in the past, such as the Muslims and the African-American churches on McCormick's beat. Unlike sources on police and government beats, sources in religious organizations don't expect controversy or negative coverage in the media.

But that's what they got when McCormick covered the General Association of Baptists, an organization of more than 500 black churches. The group hadn't been covered by the newspaper in the past. At the first meeting McCormick attended, the association ousted churches that had licensed women to preach. To McCormick, the association's action was a good story. The leaders of the association didn't agree. "They still won't speak to me," he says.

Sevil Omer, beat reporter

McCormick says he always tries to give all sources a chance to comment or to do a follow-up story that explains the issue in depth. That approach didn't work with the General Association of Baptists. Most times, however, sources will be cooperative if you give them a chance to explain their views and if your story is accurate and fair, he says.

Sevil Omer, who covers the police and courts beat for the *Reno* (Nev.) *Gazette-Journal,* recommends contacting sources regularly. She calls her sources even when she has no specific story in mind. "I think you need to let them know you are taking an interest in them," she says. "When you run into them, it's important to say 'Hi, how are you.' You have to make sure they know who you are and what you look like. Meet people on the scene."

Omer says regular contact is particularly important on her beat because many times police, lawyers and other sources are reluctant to give information about crimes and court cases. "A lot of times people are a bit skeptical of you; they haven't sized you up yet. In my case, some of the police who read my stories were surprised when they met me because my name confused them. They said, 'We thought you were a man.'"

Because beat reporters deal with the same sources repeatedly, it is easy to become friendly with them. But Omer says she draws the line at socializing with sources because it can cause conflicts of interest. On the other hand, if you know that a good source has a birthday or some important event in his or her life or has been ill, you can make a phone call or send a card. Many good beat reporters keep such notations about the source in their card file or in a computer source file.

Checking Records and Human Sources

Omer doesn't depend exclusively on police and attorneys for information. She says all good reporters should check records, especially on her beat. "Check the police files, public documents in courts and go to the sources. Then do what detectives do. Knock on doors and do your homework. Ask family members and victims."

A typical day for Omer starts at 8 a.m., when she calls 18 police departments in the Reno area to check on crime that occurred overnight. If something important is happening, she might go to the scene. She usually writes one main story a day and several briefs about police news. She also checks court schedules for the next day to know what cases she will go to cover. She may end up spending the entire day covering a trial.

In addition to covering stories as they occur, Omer watches for trends on her beat. For example, she noticed that the crime statistics revealed an increase in the number of young women arrested for violent crimes. She wondered what was causing this trend. Her investigation led to a package of stories, including a mainbar about why the trend was occurring and sidebars profiling women who were involved with gangs and in other crimes.

When the Bloods headed into Truckee Meadows from Southern California to organize a narcotics ring last year, they sought the toughest and brightest gang member to head the effort.

They found her in Reno.

When Harrah's officials and police reviewed a recent video of purse snatchings inside the downtown casino, they were surprised to see the suspect's young, female face.

When metal flashed at Sparks Middle School in March, security guards took two girls into custody on charges of carrying a concealed weapon on school grounds.

More and more young women are mirroring men, especially their rebelliousness, law-enforcement officials say. Increasingly, girls are committing violent crimes.

Now they call the shots and elicit fear from rivals.

"There's a large, solid group of females in gang activity," Reno Police Chief Jim Weston said about increases in the past two years.

Sevil Omer, *Reno Gazette-Journal*

The story was accompanied by charts of statistics.

"There's a lot of mechanical work to this beat that any clerk could do. But you have to keep checking police and court files so you know the pulse and the trends," Omer says. "And despite the blood and gore, there's always a human element. You can put compassion into any story." In this example, Omer portrays the human side of a young girl who is in Wittenberg Detention Center:

Her thin arms are folded tightly across her purple T-shirt. She has a ready smile and gentle eyes peering from underneath a curtain of light brown bangs.

She is 14. When she grows up, she wants to be a police officer. She was raised among sisters and brothers "too many to even count."

She's in Wittenberg as a result of a domestic dispute. She says she was trying to protect herself from an older sibling's beatings. She's no stranger to violence.

"I've become violent because I was brought up in violence and have been abused," she said.

"It cuts deep.

"And on the streets, it's kill or be killed," she said.

She wants help. She begs for counseling and recreational programs for herself and other girls from troubled homes.

"If you stuff your feelings in, one day you're going to explode."

She will be sent later this week to Willow Springs adolescent treatment center.

Later, she hopes to graduate from a police academy. Motherhood is out of the question, she said.

"I won't have children. If I did, I will give them up for adoption. I just wouldn't trust myself with them."

Sevil Omer, *Reno Gazette-Journal*

Beginning a Beat

The tips suggested by Mark McCormick and Sevil Omer will help you get started in any beat. If you are beginning a job or internship in an area that is unfamiliar to you or if you are assigned to cover a municipality, here are some other tips for starting your beat:

Use shoe leather: Get to know your community or the agency you cover. Meet its members in person. Take a walking tour of the community. Talk to people. Eat where the politicians and the city employees eat or socialize after work. Get your hair cut by the barber or beautician who has been in town a long time. Ask people what they are interested in and what they want to read in their newspaper. Get a map. Cruise the streets. See where the rich and poor, the famous and infamous live. If you have a campus beat, introduce yourself to the officials, department heads, or leaders of a department or an organization. Tell them that you are interested in what they do and are seeking story ideas on a regular basis. In many cases, the people on your beat will want the coverage.

Check clips: The newspaper library or resource room is a starting place for your beat and for every story you write. When you find clips about major issues on your beat, consider an update story.

Let your fingers do the walking: Read the classified pages of your telephone book. How many churches are there of each denomination? Are massage parlors, astrologers or other unusual services advertised? Check the municipal services, sometimes listed in a separate section. Is there a poison control center or a government agency that sounds interesting? A quick scan of the classified section of your telephone book can give you some sense of your community and story ideas for a municipal beat. If you have a campus or city beat, check the directories of your school or city. Are there agencies or departments you don't know anything about? Find out what people in these jobs do, what they like and don't like about their jobs. Check campus directories for clubs and student organizations that might be worth a feature.

Study the classifieds: Check newspaper classified sections, such as the real estate section. What is for sale? What prices are the houses? This information will give you some idea of the economic climate of the community. Maybe you can write a story about why a particular area of town has many homes for sale. Sometimes you'll find a touching story in the personal ads. Check the rewards for lost dogs, cats, birds, snakes or unusual pets. And check the legal notices. They'll tell you what the city must advertise, as in notices for meetings or of items the city wants to buy. For campus beats, check classifieds and other advertisements in the college newspaper for unusual job opportunities, new organizations and other items that could be of interest to students.

Plan for the future: Read the news. Are interesting people who are worth profiles mentioned in news stories? Are briefs in the newspaper worth features? Are ideas tucked into a news story that need exploring or follow-up? Start your own idea file.

Visit the library: The local librarian is often a good source for information about the community.

Check bulletin boards: Visit the offices or agencies you cover, and read the notices on the bulletin boards. You will find notices for job openings and other interesting information that could lead to news and feature stories.

Check with your predecessor: If the person who previously covered your beat is still at the newspaper, ask for a briefing about the beat and for key sources.

Be a tourist: Visit the historical society, the chamber of commerce and other community agencies. Find the places of interest, and investigate what they were like years ago. You might develop angles for features. At the very least, you will gain some understanding of your community.

Press for press releases: Get on mailing lists. Call the city or town clerk, and get the releases from your city and county government or from the agency you cover. Call the public relations officers of agencies and businesses in your community. Introduce yourself. Tell them you are interested in ideas for stories. It's their job to provide them. You don't have to use their handouts, but having them will give you ideas about what is happening in your community. Call agencies like senior citizen organizations, the Red Cross, churches and social service organizations, and make sure you are on their mailing lists for announcements, reports and news.

Find out who's in charge: Be kind to the folks who prepare the memos for officials. Get to know them, and use their names when you see them or call their offices. Talk to the janitors, the security guards, the people behind the scenes. They know what is going on, and they can be sources for tips. Meet the officials, of course, and then find out who heads the unions and professional organizations in the schools and government. The leaders of these organizations know what is going on behind the scenes. They also have stories from the workers' point of view. Use the up/down reporting principle: Go up and down the organizational ladder.

Hit records: Know how and where to find records. Start with the city or county clerk, who will direct you to municipal offices where records are available. Visit the courthouse, and familiarize yourself with the filing system there by asking the clerks for help. These are public records, and it's the clerks' job to serve the public. If your university is part of a state system, check records on campus or at the state level for fire inspection reports, police statistics or reports on environmental hazards.

Write a source book: Record names and telephone numbers for everyone you interview, call or meet on your beat. Develop a filing system and a cross-listing system. Put a memo after each name. If a source tells you something personal about a child or a family member who is ill, make a note and call in a few weeks to find out how the person is doing. Or mention the ill person the next time you talk to your source. Be thoughtful. Your source will appreciate your interest and be more receptive when dealing with you.

Covering Specialty Beats

You don't have to be a doctor to cover medicine or a scientist to cover the environment, but you do need to acquire knowledge of the subject in your beat. The challenge for writers of specialized subjects is to make the stories clear and to define the jargon so the average reader can understand the story.

The Education Beat

Peter Lundquist faces that challenge every day as the education reporter for the *Lawrence* (Kan.) *Journal-World*. Educators often use so many acronyms that their language in print looks like alphabet soup. It's up to the reporter to avoid such terms and make the information meaningful to readers.

"When I write a story, I think about who's reading it," Lundquist says. "You've got to tell the readers why they should care before you put them to sleep." Lundquist inserts an impact paragraph in most of his stories so readers can see how they or their children might be affected by the information, as in this story about school test scores:

Prairie Park School children have a better handle on mathematics than they did four years ago. Children with disabilities have a better chance of classroom participation at Central Junior High than they did four years ago.

How do the schools know? Data says so—data collected as part of the state's embattled accreditation system.

The results are trickling in about how pilot schools are performing four years after they began seeking accreditation under the newest set of state rules, known as Quality Performance Accreditation, or QPA.

What the results mean for children and teachers in Lawrence remains a point of debate, however.

Vicki Weseman, principal at Prairie Park, said QPA forced the whole school to evaluate how math was being taught. Before QPA, individual teachers would evaluate how they were doing for their individual classes, she said.

"In our case, specifically with math, we saw an improvement. What did it do for the kids?" she asked. "Their scores went up."

Put three official-sounding words together, make it an acronym, and you have a new educational buzzword and a new line in the sand for reformers and conservatives to battle over. Such has been the case for QPA. Regardless of what principals in Lawrence are calling good news, the accreditation system remains under fire.

Peter Lundquist, *Lawrence Journal-World*

Peter Lundquist,
education reporter

Before covering education, Lundquist covered city government, a municipality, the general assignment beat and even the boxing beat. On the education beat Lundquist uses all his skills, covering meetings, press conferences and budgets and using many of the other techniques you will learn in the following chapters. But one of his biggest challenges is finding time to write about what is really happening in the schools, because so much of the news on his beat involves school administration and budget problems.

"People want to know what's going on in their kids' schools, especially now because parents don't have as much time to check personally, he says. "I get at least two calls daily from parents and teachers wanting stories about what their kids are doing. The challenge is to weed out the ideas and choose what would be of general interest."

When he does get into the schools, Lundquist is often overwhelmed by the number of story ideas he encounters. "The hardest thing to do is to focus when you get into a classroom," he says. "There is so much going on. I'll get two or three story ideas in one hour, and I'll be tempted to include all that information in one story, but I've learned to stick to one focus and save the rest for another time:

Some additional tips:

• Check educational journals for trends and national comparisons of school performance.

• When writing about test scores or other school statistics, explain what they mean and how they affect students.

• Translate jargon.

• Make sure you get into the schools to write stories about education.

Medical and Environmental Writing

Jonathan Bor, a medical writer for *The Baltimore Sun,* covered crime, courts, politics and education before writing medical stories. "I learned how to convert the blather of educators, bureaucrats and cops into plain English before tackling doctor-speak," he says in an article in *Coaches' Corner,* a publication devoted to techniques for coaching writers. "And I learned to look first for stories about real people. I believe the hallmark of good medical writing is clear, colorful prose that takes the lay reader inside a world whose inhabitants—doctors, scientists and insurers— speak a secret language."

Good medical writing, in many ways, is simply good reporting and writing, Bor says. "It is thoroughly researched. It is written cleanly, and when possible, with a human touch. Bad medical writing, among other things, is written for insiders."

Here is an excerpt from a story about a heart transplant operation that Bor wrote for his previous newspaper. He witnessed the operation and wrote the story on deadline after going without sleep for 48 hours.

He used the basic techniques of descriptive writing: show in action and details. Note how clearly he explains a complex procedure.

A healthy 17-year-old heart pumped the gift of life through 34-year-old Bruce Murray Friday, following a four-hour transplant operation that doctors said went without a hitch. . . .

The team—consisting of a surgeon, a physician's assistant and a nurse—removed the donor's heart at about 1:30 p.m. They placed it inside a plastic bag filled with an iced-saline solution, and they laced that bag inside three outer bags. The package was placed inside a blue beer cooler that bore the stamp "Transplant."

By the time their jet landed at Teterboro at 3 a.m., Murray was in the operating room where he was being prepped for surgery. Anesthesia put the patient into a deep sleep. A respirator breathed air into Murray's lungs via a tube inserted in his throat. Doctors cut a slit the length of Murray's chest. As many as a dozen doctors, nurses and technical assistants hovered over the patient, passing instruments, attending to heart monitors and swabbing the patient's bleeding chest.

Meanwhile, a state police escort ensured swift passage from Teterboro, over the George Washington Bridge and to the hospital for the vehicle carrying the transplant team and beer cooler. Within 10 minutes after landing, the transplant team was rushing the beer cooler through the hospital emergency room and up an elevator 18 floors.

By the time the heart arrived in the operating room, Murray's chest was wide open. Doctors had used a power saw to cut through his sternum, and a clamp-like retractor spread his chest apart. Murray's diseased heart, about half-again larger than normal, was fluttering inside the exposed chest cavity.

Surgeons swiftly turned the task of pumping blood over to the heart-lung machine. Their hands moving with quick deliberation, surgeons inserted tubes inside the heart's major blood vessels and severed the vessels from the heart.

The tangle of tubes carried the blood to a cylinder that supplied it with oxygen. From there, the blood traveled to a large console, which performs the job of the heart. Three spinning disks pumped the blood through the clear, plastic tubes back to the patient's body.

In one careful, spectacular moment, the surgical team made the exchange.

At 4:33 a.m., doctors lifted the diseased heart—milky but purple—out of Murray's chest cavity and handed it to attendants. They, in turn, placed it in the steel bowl. On a platform at the foot of the operating table, the spent heart rested for the duration. . . .

The beer cooler was opened, and the donor heart was placed inside the patient's chest. The new heart, about as large as a relaxed fist, was attached to the blood vessels.

It jerked and fluttered and became Bruce Murray's.

Jonathan Bor, *The* (Syracuse, N.Y.) *Post-Standard*

Bor offers these tips, which apply to all beats but are particularly useful for medical and environmental stories:

• Challenge the source to speak to laymen. If that fails, allow the scientist to speak his language, but constantly challenge him with your version of the facts—"Are you saying that . . . ?"

• Never forget to ask your source the cosmic questions. What does the new treatment mean for the AIDS sufferer? Will this prolong life for days, months or more? Will the patient live longer but just as miserably, or what? Does a new medical finding represent an incremental advance or a true "breakthrough" that will change the lives of many people?

• Don't forget to give your story a sense of true proportion. If health inspectors have closed down an inner-city nursing home because of rodent infestation, it doesn't hurt to say that inspectors observed mice chewing on patients' feeding tubes and lapping the IV fluids that oozed out. If it's that bad, say it and say it vividly. Reporters need to say, however, whether the horror was an isolated finding or a condition observed throughout the nursing home.

• Anecdotes can be wonderful or tedious. At best, they bring to life the suffering of the afflicted, the benefits of new treatments or the breadth and social costs of an epidemic. At their worst, they turn a story into a tear-jerking soap opera worthy of a tacky TV-movie.

When do anecdotes work? Perhaps they work when they vividly show the human side—the joy and suffering—of an issue. They also show the practical dimensions of a problem better than some doctor or bureaucrat spouting generalities.

• Metaphors can be nice, but they also can trivialize. I don't like stories that describe antibodies as little foot-soldiers engaged in hand-to-hand combat with disease-carrying bugs. I have seen this. Lacking something less trivial, I'd state the obvious: antibodies are substances produced by the body to fight infection.

Business Writing

The Wall Street Journal, a newspaper devoted to business writing, is famous for its features. They just happen to be about business, financial and social trends. But the newspaper's style of writing has been emulated by newspapers all over the country for all types of stories.

In the early 1950s, *The Wall Street Journal* issued a memo to its writers about how features for the newspaper should be written. Many of the style guidelines in that memo are still applied today at this newspaper and at many others that have adopted the *Wall Street Journal* formula.

Gina Henderson, assistant business editor of The Kansas City (*Mo.*) Star, *where the* Wall Street Journal *formula is applied to business stories as well as other types of stories*
Courtesy of Brian Crites, *The Kansas City Star*

Our aim is to do very complete, very thorough research-type stories—but to avoid the obvious danger in such work of becoming dull and dry. To achieve maximum readability, we try to carry the reader along with a liberal sprinkling of color, examples and other illustrative gadgets. We try to keep our stories factually complete and correct enough to interest the banker, economist or other authority on the subject—yet always bearing in mind that it must be intriguing enough and simple enough to appeal to our average reader, who might be a retailer in Des Moines, a gas station owner in Dallas, a grain merchant in Oklahoma City or someone else with no familiarity with our subject.

With the current emphasis at newspapers to make stories more relevant to readers, the following *Wall Street Journal* guidelines are as applicable to stories for today and the future as they were in the 1950s:

- These page one "leaders," as we call them, are interpretive stories. They most often report *trends*—what they mean and what they portend.

- The stories generally have one theme or point. This is usually put into a one- or two-paragraph nutshell summary high up in the story. Then the rest of the piece is made to hang together by harking back to this central theme. The story should be *clearly organized* or compartmentalized along the central thread of this theme—it should not meander around without a perceptible organization.

- We want to tell the story in terms of the *specific,* not in generalized or vague terms. One way we do this is to pack the story with lots of *detail.* For example, it isn't enough to make a general statement that there was inflation in X country until 1950 and then prices began to level off. We would want this nailed down with the official price index figures (specifying wholesale or retail, of course) showing the rise to 1950 and then the more recent leveling off. It would also be desirable—besides these concrete figures on the overall situation—to illustrate the trend with the prices of a few typical goods—such as shirts or soap—in 1946, 1950 and now, for example.

  Another way we reduce the general situation to the specific is to give lots of colorful examples, anecdotes or small case histories to *illustrate* the overall situation we are describing.

  We also lean heavily on illustrative *quotes*—attributable if possible though not necessarily so. The quotes need not be from government officials only; they could be from businessmen, shopkeepers, men-in-the-street, anyone who can shed some *color* on the situation or who can illustrate the general in specific, *individual terms.*

- Be sure to include all *background* the reader might need. We can assume no prior knowledge by our readers of the subject or of financial lingo. We try to spell out all situations *with super-simplicity and clarity*—from how France's inflation has been brought about over the years to the recent economic history of Australia and what led up to its present economic situation. Please explain everything in clear-cut fashion.

- We try to achieve very tight writing—short, punchy sentences and all essential information on the subject conveyed *concisely.*

- At the same time, these leaders aim at being pretty *thorough* studies of the particular subject or trend. This means the inclusion of all detail and background and interpretation mentioned above. It also means we take pains to make sure the story contains the answers to every question that the story and its statements are likely to raise in the reader's mind. We can't use a story that raises questions it does not answer, so please re-check copy for this possible pitfall—and again, be sure all points are fully and *clearly explained,* and solidly *nailed down with fact.*

Here is how that memo translates into stories currently being published by the newspaper. This lead is from a trend story used as a leader.

ATLANTA—Ollie Smith's third-graders are willing.

"The number is 2,427," says Mrs. Smith, a teacher at Cleveland Avenue Elementary School here. An eager volunteer, one of 17 blacks in a class of 18, walks to the blackboard beneath the U.S. flag in a scene familiar to anyone—until the chalk moves.

Instead of the numeral 2, the girl draws two lotus flowers, followed by four coiled ropes, two oxen yokes and seven vertical strokes.

"Very good, Jeannette," says Mrs. Smith, praising a perfect rendition of 2,427 in ancient Egyptian hieroglyphics. "You can take your seat."

Mrs. Smith's arithmetic lesson is part of a new Africa-centered curriculum that is fast spreading in urban schools. Atlanta, Baltimore, Detroit, Indianapolis, Portland, Ore., and Washington, D.C., are in various stages of similar course-content changes that stress, to a high degree, the history and culture of black people.

Gary Putka, *The Wall Street Journal*

Sportswriting

Sportswriters have always had to rely on feature techniques of descriptive and interpretive writing, even more than other writers at a newspaper. Their readers may have seen the game, but they still want to read about it. Others who haven't seen the game want to know what happened. So sportswriters face the challenge of providing readers something more than the basic facts.

Unlike most news stories, where reporters rely on information from sources, sportswriters covering a game are witnessing the action firsthand. They have the responsibility for interpreting what they saw through interviews with coaches and players and their own analysis. They need to stress angles: why and how the game was won or lost or what the strategy was. How was this game different from or similar to others?

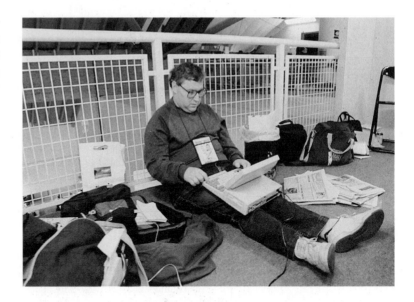

But sports stories are not limited to game coverage. The range of topics on sports pages—profiles, trend stories and general sports features—is as broad as in any other section of the paper.

Years ago, sportswriters could rely on knowing their craft and writing primarily about games and the athletes. Today they need to be as well-versed in court reporting and other fields as the reporters who cover the news, because many stories involve athletes in legal contract disputes and court cases about drugs, violence and other criminal charges.

Sportswriting also requires knowledge about games, leagues and style of sports scores. Check the *Associated Press Stylebook* for this information.

Some of the best writing in the newspaper—as well as some of the worst—can be found on the sports pages. Karen Brown, a director at the Poynter Institute for Media Studies, says all writers, especially those facing tight deadlines, could take some tips from sportswriters. She offers this advice:

• First, writers must see the same old story in different ways. . . . The characters and events in sports stories aren't necessarily more interesting than those in news stories. But in sports, more attention is paid to the people and the action. Personalities, motives and mannerisms are fleshed out to add color and meaning to stories.

• A second message from sportswriters is to keep your eyes on the story. "You can't look away when you're covering a sports story," said Merlissa Lawrence, a sportswriter for *The Pittsburgh Press.* "In that one moment something dramatic could happen."

*The game itself, no
longer the sole focus
of sportswriters*
Courtesy of Philip Meiring,
The University Daily Kansan

• A third strategy is to write background information ahead of time and plan for likely eventualities. . . . It is a method commonly used by journalists covering major sports events on deadline.

• A fourth message is to give some thought to the best format for telling the story. Some games are worth only a box score. So are some meetings. Some stories require a brief; others need a long story or several textual and graphic elements.

• Finally, sportswriters write in ways that draw readers into stories. Often the readers know the score and have seen the event. The task for the writer then is to elucidate, analyze, amplify and soothe the reader with the pleasure of the words that recapture the event.

Many of the writing techniques sportswriters use to accomplish those tasks are the same ones you have studied for other basic news, feature and specialty stories. The major difference is that sportswriters must stress interpretation, how and why, more than in basic news stories. Good sportswriters try to do that by setting a tone and developing their stories with a theme.

In this example, notice how the writer weaves the story around a theme of surrender, incorporates statistics and puts the coach's comments in perspective:

CHESTNUT HILL, Mass.—Villanova surrendered last night.

Rollie Massimino didn't have to wave a white flag. Putting in walkons and sitting down starters with nearly 13 minutes left against Boston College served the same purpose.

The defeat was stunning in its totality. The Eagles, only a year ago a hapless 1–15 in the Big East, pounded Villanova, 82–46, at Conte Forum. Winning meant Boston College (14–7 overall, 6–6 in the Big East) took over sole possession of seventh place in the conference from Villanova (8–13, 5–7).

Afterward, Massimino was almost eerily calm. Of the Wildcats' 14 percent shooting in the first half, he said: "I think we've climbed into a little bit of an offensive rut." But when you make 16 of 61 shots, as Villanova did, it might seem the rut is more like a chasm.

The Villanova coach even found something about his team to praise. "I thought, when it was 11–2, we defended extremely well to keep it 11–3 after six straight possessions," he said.

That's what this season has come to. Proudly proclaiming the times when the bad score doesn't get worse.

Diane Pucin, *The Philadelphia Inquirer*

Here are some of the basic facts to include in game stories:

- Who played, where (stadium and city), when
- Score (placed high in the story)
- Major plays and players
- Turning points
- Injuries
- Important statistics (conference standing, records for season)
- Weather, if it had an effect on the game
- Crowd count, if relevant (fully packed stadium or sparse attendance)
- Outcome of previous games between these two teams, if relevant
- Comments from coaches and players to explain the how and why of the game

Notice how many of the important elements are high in the next story—theme, names of teams, score, location of game, crowd size, conference records, analysis, perspective and "injury" (the flu) to the key player. Notice, too, the circular ending: a return to the flu theme.

Rolando Blackman had the flu and was home Friday night. At least he had an excuse.

Most of the other Mavericks were no-shows in a 97–91 defeat to the expansion-like New Jersey Nets before a crowd of 16,121 at Reunion Arena.

The flu wasn't the only bug to hit the Mavericks (6–8). They suffered from turnovers, bad defense and poor rebounding in losing to a team that had dropped 11 of its last 12 games, and had won only one road game before Friday.

Doug Smith almost provided the cure with the best game of his rookie season, a 14-point, eight-rebound effort. But after leading the rally from a 14-point deficit, he gave way with five minutes left for veteran Rodney McCray.

"I could not put Doug out on the floor because he doesn't know what we're doing, and we have six or seven late-game plays that we run," said coach Richie Adubato. "So we went with the guys we think will perform under pressure."

On this night, they didn't deliver. Playing without Blackman, their leading scorer and only true go-to player for clutch baskets, the Mavericks conked out on offense. In the final 3:29, they scored on only two of five possessions. . . .

The Mavericks' shooting was poor, also. Some of that can be attributed to Blackman's absence. Besides leading the team with a 21.8-point scoring average, he is their only regular making at least 50 percent of his shots from the field.

Blackman's bug is just one the Mavericks have to find the cure for. Fast.

Mitch Lawrence, *The Dallas Morning News*

Exercises

1　Using the *Wall Street Journal* formula, write a business feature about a trend in your community. For example, is business in your downtown area suffering or improving? Are stores closing or opening? Has a new business catering to students or other people opened in your community?

2　Choose a specialty subject of your choice—medicine, education, religion, sports, environment—and write a feature about a topic or program in this category.

3　Interview a beat reporter in the field that interests you. Write a story about the skills, tips, and reporting and writing techniques this reporter uses and recommends to other reporters in the field. Include specifics about problems the reporter faces on the job.

4　Choose a field of interest, and write a list of sources and government records available in this field on the Internet. Check the appendix in this book for some possible sources.

5　List the beats covered by your campus newspaper, and then list at least five beats that aren't covered but might be of interest to readers. Write a story from one of those beats.

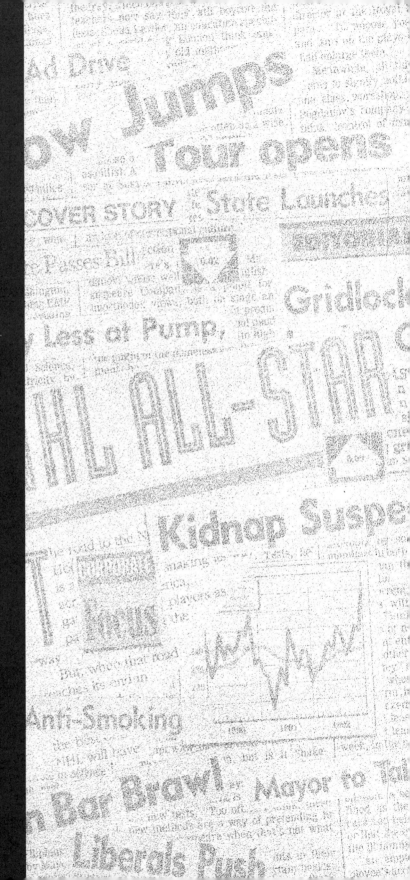

COACHING
TIPS

Ask yourself: What made this person memorable?

Have you written this obituary well enough for it to be saved in someone's family Bible?

Check the accuracy of spellings and information. Also, make sure you call a funeral home or family member to confirm that the person really died.

Obituaries

20

He is known as "Dr. Death." Years ago, when he was an investigative reporter for the now-defunct *Philadelphia Bulletin,* he risked death; the Pagan motorcycle gang members he investigated threatened to firebomb his home. Now he writes about death. And he does it so well that he has won awards for a type of writing rarely honored. He's Jim Nicholson, whose obituaries for the *Philadelphia Daily News* are being used as models by newspapers around the country.

They read more like profiles. Nicholson says that's what they are—stories about the lives of people, not about their deaths. Like the obituary for Lawrence Pompie "Mr. Buddy" Ellis, a retired maintenance man who was a leader in his church:

> He came to be known affectionately among friends as "Dial-A-Prayer" for his unceasing availability to those who wanted him to pray with them. If he couldn't meet personally with someone, he would pray with them on the telephone, said his wife, Fannie, who shared 38 years with him. . . . At 5-foot-7 and 205 pounds, Ellis loved to eat. "He loved everything about a pig," said his wife, "and if he didn't watch out, he'd catch his grunt."

Jim Nicholson, *Philadelphia Daily News*

Remember that you are not writing about death. You are writing about life.

Jim "Dr. Death" Nicholson, obituary writer, *Philadelphia Daily News*

*Jim Nicholson
("Dr. Death"), obituary
writer for the* Philadelphia
Daily News

And for Ella Hurst, a homemaker:

> She could cook, quiet babies, protect small children, pass down religion, boss people around, give advice, listen to problems, have patience, be tough or be soft, and had all the other attributes of an authentic grandmother. . . . She enjoyed reading magazines and watching soaps, especially "The Young and the Restless," which she liked to say was filled with love, sex and trash.
>
> Jim Nicholson, *Philadelphia Daily News*

Custodians, homemakers, sanitation workers—they don't have to be rich and famous to make Nicholson's list of special people for an obituary. To Nicholson, all people are special.

Nicholson makes them memorable by the questions he asks family members and friends. He wants to write character portraits, warts and all, he says. "Cleaning up someone's act after he or she has died does not serve the cause of the deceased or loved ones," Nicholson says. "A sanitized portrait is indistinguishable from any other. It is the irregularities that give us identity. A person described as being a strict parent, impatient with unprofessional conduct, becomes real people to the reader. The ultimate acclaim may be when a reader thinks, 'I wish I had known this man or woman.'"

Although Nicholson has won acclaim for investigative reporting, writing obituaries is more rewarding, he says. His investigative stories are saved in dusty library archives; his obituaries are saved in family Bibles. Nicholson's own file cabinets at the *Daily News* bulge with letters from grateful relatives of people he has profiled in obituaries. Most reporters don't consider obituaries their most important stories. But they are among the most well-read items in the paper, and their significance to relatives and friends of the deceased cannot be overstated.

The Importance of Facts

A misspelled name or a factual error is a major problem in any story; in an obituary it is disastrous. So you should check every fact, every name, every reference. And you should check with the funeral director and the family to make sure the person you are writing about is dead.

Someone from the *Detroit Free Press* didn't do that. And the death of Dr. Rogers Fair turned out to be greatly exaggerated, as Mark Twain would say. Fair, a Detroit physician, woke up one morning to read in the newspaper that he had died of cancer. The newspaper had received the obituary information by telephone from a woman who claimed she was Fair's aunt. And the reporter didn't call back to check with family members or a funeral home.

Fair, 40, claimed the "aunt" was a 21-year-old woman who was infatuated with him. She had wooed him with flowers and love notes, but when he rejected her and began dating another woman, he began receiving harassing telephone calls, bomb threats and vandalism to his home. "She is obviously an obsessed person," Fair told the *Free Press*. "She has stated that if she can't have me, nobody else can."

The follow-up story was an embarrassment to the paper:

The obituary for Dr. Rogers Fair in Tuesday's Free Press took a lot of people—especially Fair—by surprise.

"My beeper was just jumping off the hook," the 40-year-old physician said Tuesday. "My secretary called me. She was in tears. . . ."

The erroneous report of Fair's demise was the second phony obituary published by the Free Press in recent years. The first, in July 1985, prompted a revision of reporting practices, requiring all obituary information phoned in by friends and relatives to be confirmed either by a funeral home or law enforcement officials.

But Fair's obituary wasn't properly double-checked, and a woman identifying herself as Fair's aunt was able to hoodwink the Free Press with details of his death.

Detroit Free Press

An obituary, by general definition, is just a notice of someone's death, but in a newspaper it is defined as a news story about the person. Most newspapers have free or paid death notices—announcements from the family about the deceased. In addition, funeral directors and families call the newspaper to request an obituary. How do you decide who deserves one?

Almost all newspapers will publish an obituary about anyone prominent in the community. Some newspapers, especially those in large cities, have policies to determine who else should be profiled on the obituary page. Generally, reporters scan the paid death notices to look for interesting people, long-term residents or those active in community service.

Nicholson sometimes just picks a name at random or focuses on a person whose family calls him to request an obituary.

Then you make the phone calls—or double-check the validity of the ones you have received by calling a funeral home, checking the phone book, and calling the family back or calling other relatives and friends. And, as in any other newspaper story, you check newspaper clips.

Calling people about death isn't easy. But it isn't as difficult as you might expect, especially for obituaries. Most families are grateful, because this is the last story—and more often the only story—printed about their loved ones. Usually someone in the family is prepared to deal with the media. And for many grieving people, talking about their loved one is cathartic. You're not going to be asking them how they feel that someone in the family died; you're asking them how that person lived and what was special about the loved one.

If the obituary is for a person who died under tragic circumstances that might have and probably did result in a news story, you can call and ask if a family member or friend can give you information.

The easiest way to start is with the funeral director, if one has been selected. The funeral director should have the basic information and should be able to tell you which family members to call and their phone numbers.

Bare Essentials

Obituary writing follows some basic forms, even when you are writing a special profile. All obituaries, no matter how long or short, must contain the same crucial information:

Name: Use full name, middle initial and nickname if it was commonly used. Enclose the nickname in quotation marks.

Identification: Usually people are identified by occupation or community service. Always try to find something special to use following the name, such as "John Doe, a retired salesman" or "Jane Doe, a homemaker who was active in her church."

Age: In some cases, a family will request that you withhold the age. You should confer with an editor about honoring this request.

Date and place of death: Use the day of the week if the death occurred that week, the date if it was more than a week prior to the obituary. State the name of a hospital, if applicable, or other location where the death occurred.

Cause of death: This fact is not required at all newspapers, especially if the cause of death was suicide or AIDS-related or when the family requests that the cause be withheld. This item has become especially controversial because of the stigma attached to AIDS-related deaths. Other newspapers require the cause of death, regardless of stigma or family wishes. So check your newspaper's policy before you gather the information. You may have to inform family members of the policy.

Address: Tell where the person lived when he or she died and previous areas of residence for any major length of time. Some newspapers use specific addresses; others just require the town. Generally, the smaller the newspaper, the more specific the address reference.

Background: Specify major accomplishments, organizations, educational background, military background, and any other highlights. When people are very active in their church, mosque or synagogue, this fact should be mentioned in the obituary.

Survivors: Use the names of immediate family members (husband or wife, with her maiden name, children, brothers and sisters). Grandchildren are usually mentioned only by number: "He is survived by five grandchildren." New complications are arising these days because of changes in family relationships. Most newspapers still do not list unmarried partners as survivors, or "bonded" partners (homosexual couples united in a marital ceremony), but that rule is changing. In the future, these relationships also may be part of obituaries.

Services: Specify the time, date and location.

Burial: Name the place, and provide memorial information when available.

Obituary writing follows a pattern. Most obituaries, except special feature stories, start with the person's name, identification, a statement that he or she died, and a cause of death. Follow with the age. Then add the other information. When the death occurred a week or more ago, it is customary to start with information about the service or a memorial if that has not yet been conducted.

Some style tips:

Terminology: A funeral is not held; it is scheduled. The term *funeral services* is acceptable but redundant because a funeral is a service or ceremony. Just write "Services will be Saturday" with the time and location.

Names of services: Mass is celebrated, not said. The word is capitalized when referring to the specific ceremony, such as Mass of Christian Burial, but in lowercase letters for a generic mass. Find out the exact wording you should use for the particular mass. Likewise, ask for the proper wording of a service for other denominations.

Courtesy titles: Although many newspapers have eliminated courtesy titles (*Mrs., Mr., Ms., Miss*) for news stories, several keep them for obituaries. Again, you must check your newspaper's policy.

Titles for religious leaders: Check the proper title for a rabbi, minister or priest. When writing about a priest, do not use *Father* or *Pastor* for the title. Use *the Rev.* (the reverend) followed by the priest's name: "the Rev. Vince Krische." For a rabbi, use *Rabbi* before the name on first reference: "Rabbi Jacob Katz." On second reference for clergy, including priests, use only the last name. But for second reference to high-ranking clergy, use "the cardinal," "the archbishop" and so on. Check the *Associated Press Stylebook* for specific religious titles.

Basic Obituary Examples

This example about the death of a local citizen follows all the basic guidelines; it also includes information about contributions:

Lucy Davis Burnett, a Dallas native and longtime civic leader, died of cancer Saturday at her home. She was 79.

A graduate of Woodrow Wilson High School in Dallas and Mary Baldwin College in Staunton, Va., Mrs. Burnett was active in numerous cultural and civic affairs.

She was past president of the Southern Methodist University Lecture Series, vice president of the Dallas Junior League and president of the Junior League Garden Club.

She was a founding member of the Dallas Slipper Club and also held memberships in the Dallas Women's Club, the Dallas Arts Museum League, the women's division of United Way of Dallas and Highland Park United Methodist.

She is survived by her husband, F.W. Burnett of Dallas; a daughter, Lucy Chambers of Vancouver, British Columbia; a son, F.W. Burnett Jr. of Dallas; and six grandchildren.

Services for Mrs. Burnett will be at 2 p.m. Tuesday at Highland Park United Methodist Church.

Memorials may be made to Children's Medical Center of Dallas, the Dallas Chapter of the American Cancer Society or a charity of the donor's choice.

The Dallas Morning News

This next obituary is an example of how to "advance" the story by starting with the services. Note the use of courtesy titles.

Services are scheduled Saturday for Hulda Kettler Stoner, who was believed to be the oldest living native Californian. She died Jan. 21 at the age of 109.

Mrs. Stoner, who lived in Santa Monica, was born on her pioneer German immigrant family's ranch in the Wilmington area. The 240-acre ranch had been purchased from the holder of a Mexican land grant.

While visiting a cousin in 1906, Mrs. Stoner personally experienced the San Francisco earthquake.

Her granddaughter, Laurie Merryfield, said Mrs. Stoner often recalled other events in her long life—including arduous family vacation trips to Calabasas by horse and wagon, and the first automobile, radio and phonograph in Los Angeles County. She had been equally intrigued, the granddaughter said, with television coverage of the 1969 moon landing.

Mrs. Stoner, a former teacher who maintained an apartment until she was 103, attributed her longevity to a moderate lifestyle and good luck.

Survivors in addition to her granddaughter include a sister, Lucy Marshall of Newport Beach, a daughter, Eileen Abel of Santa Monica, two great-granddaughters and two great-great grandsons.

The memorial service will be at 11 a.m. in the First United Methodist Church, Santa Monica.

Los Angeles Times

This next example also advances the story by starting with the service. *The* (Portland) *Oregonian* always prints the cause of death. Notice in this case that the person died of complications from AIDS, not from AIDS. That is the proper way of writing about death related to this disease. Also notice the use of courtesy titles. Many newspapers, including this one, pass along the family's requests of donations to a specific organization.

A memorial service for William Frank Peterson of South Carolina, a former resident of the Portland area, will be at 2 p.m. Friday in the Damascus home of his parents, Clinton and Nancy Peterson.

Mr. Peterson died Sunday in a Charleston, S.C. hospital of complications arising from AIDS. He was 32.

Born in Corvallis, Mr. Peterson lived in a number of cities in Oregon. He was a graduate of Sam Barlow High School in Gresham and served in the U.S. Navy for three years. Mr. Peterson had owned a landscaping business in South Carolina for a number of years.

Survivors besides his parents include his sisters, Karen Southard of Damascus, Marsha Peterson-Tengwall of Hood River and Sonja of Portland; and his brothers, Dwight of Portland and Jerry of Chicago.

The family suggests remembrances be contributions to Cascade AIDS Project or to the Ronald McDonald House.

The Oregonian

Feature Obituaries

More extensive obituaries, written like feature personality profiles, are the specialty of Jim Nicholson. When you begin working on an obituary, he recommends starting with the funeral director. Then when you call the family, start with known facts that the source can remember easily.

"You may know facts about the services, but the object is to get the source talking," Nicholson says. "You might start with the professional background of the deceased—'Why did your father choose to become a tree surgeon?' The interview can progress as any feature profile interview would. The fact that the subject is dead is almost incidental, although how some people face death can be an important part of an obituary because it may reveal how they handled the previous 70 or 80 years of their life."

Nicholson also suggests asking for a photo. The family will probably be happy to furnish it, and it can add a great deal to your story.

Obituary Guidelines

A feature obituary, like any good story, needs quotes. Quote people the way they talk, Nicholson says, including fragmented sentences and slang expressions. Even though many editors permit writers to correct the grammar in quotes, Nicholson says the exact quotes give a better portrait of people.

He also believes someone's bad habits and criminal background, if there is any, should be part of an obituary. This view also is controversial; obituaries tend to be flattering portraits. But Nicholson says they should be true portraits. Many editors would disagree. And families are not likely to be happy with unflattering material. Generally, news editors weigh whether criminal background was a crucial part of the person's life and if the crime was highly publicized. If a person was arrested at one time for shoplifting or for another misdemeanor, most editors would recommend omitting such information. When you are faced with such decisions, it is wise to confer with an editor.

Less disputable is Nicholson's recommendation to include vivid details. Some of the items, such as the type of liquor a person drank or the jewelry he or she wore, may seem unimportant, but Nicholson says those are the details that make the obituary special. And he adds another type of question rarely considered in an obit: historical notes. "Sometimes in a few sentences or graphs, you can put the subject in his youth or childhood and thus place the reader in another era of the city or town's history," he says. "For example, 'Bob Smith was raised in the east end of town in the early 1920s, when Zeke Clayton's blacksmith barn was still standing only a few hundred yards from the Smith family's clapboard house. Years later, Bob would tell his grandchildren how he would wake up most mornings to the hard ping of a hammer bouncing against an anvil.'"

In addition to the basics previously listed, here are some less traditional items that Nicholson includes in his obituary information checklist:

- Physical description (height, weight and build, hair color and style)
- Dress (favorite type of clothes or item of clothing)
- Occupation (how long, what previous jobs)
- Speech (tone of voice, gestures, description of smile, method of eye contact, favorite expressions and sayings)
- Temperament
- Habits (favorite easy chair, places, preferences, mannerisms)
- Scene indicators (for example, orange sofa with threadbare cushions)
- Weather/lighting ("In warm weather she would sit on her porch in her favorite chair with an ever-present Pepsi")
- Historical notes

Feature Obituary Examples

Here is an example of how detailed information translates into the kind of obituary that won Nicholson the Distinguished Writing Award from the American Society of Newspaper Editors. Notice how many of his guidelines he follows in this story:

Edward E. 'Ace' Clark, 85

Richmond ice & coal dealer

Edward E. "Ace" Clark, who hauled ice through Port Richmond by horse-drawn wagon and by truck for nearly 40 years, died Saturday. He was 85 and lived in Port Richmond.

Clark also had been active in church activities and local sports teams since the mid-1930s.

"Ace," who got his nickname as a kid from the gang that hung out at Tucker and Cedar streets, quit school in the sixth grade because life on his father's ice wagon seemed more interesting than books. He took over the business—Pastime Ice & Coal Co.—when he was 17.

His favorite among his horses, which he stabled at Seltzer Street below Somerset, was one named "Major." He could go into a house with ice, through the back door, across the alley and out the front door of the house in the next street, and Major, who knew the route, would walk himself around the block and be there waiting on the next street.

"We used to say that if us kids had of been horses, we'd have been the best-raised kids in the neighborhood because Dad knew more about horses than he did kids," said his son, Bob Clark, with a laugh.

Powerful arms and shoulders atop spindly legs, Ace Clark was a man of many friends who had a zest for life and would toss out the old icemen's line: "Every man has a wife, but an iceman has his pick."

Bob Clark said his father had keys to many of the homes; if someone wasn't home, he would bring in the ice, empty the refrigerator and then repack the food around the ice.

"Can you imagine someone doing that today for a quarter?" said Clark, adding that the only day's work he ever knew his father to miss was when he got loaded the night of VJ Day and couldn't get up the next morning.

In the winter, when the ice business dropped off by as much as 75 percent, Ace delivered coal.

Though he loved horses, getting a Ford truck in 1937 meant he didn't have to feed the horses on Sundays. And Sundays for Ace Clark were for the church.

He was a past president of St. Anne's Holy Name Society and the St. Anne's Men's Club. He also was one of the organizers and first president of the Icemen's Union in Philadelphia in 1933.

"We had the first telephone in the neighborhood," said his son. "I think it was a fringe he got for being president, to do union business. But I don't think he did much business on it."

Ace Clark loved sports. He was manager of St. Anne's softball team in the 1930s and '40s and the basketball team in the 1940s and '50s.

Normally an easy-going sort, Ace Clark turned rogue elephant when his team was on the court or field.

"People used to go to the games just to watch him," said Bob Clark. "He'd throw his cigar down and get over the referee's case. He al- ways thought his team was getting short-changed."

By 1950, the ice delivery business itself was going the way of the iceman's horse a decade before, and Clark went to work for A&M Beer Distributors in Frankford. His son said he believes his father enjoyed that job even more than delivering ice, because he could pause for a "boilermaker"—a shot of whiskey chased by a glass of beer—to get him on his way.

After six years delivering beer, he went to work for Highway Express and was still loading and unloading trucks when he retired at age 68.

After retiring, he became involved with senior citizens' organizations.

His late wife was the former Agnes M. Bannon.

In addition to his son, Robert J., he is survived by two other sons, Edward A. and Francis X.; two daughters, Anna M. McMenamin and Agnes M. Conahan; 29 grandchildren; and 27 great-grandchildren.

Mass of Christian Burial will be celebrated at 10 a.m. tomorrow at St. Anne's Church, E. Lehigh Avenue and Memphis Street. Burial will be in Resurrection Cemetery, Hulmeville Road below Bristol Road, Cornwells Heights, Bucks County.

Friends may call from 7 to 9 tomorrow night at the Hubert M. McBride Funeral Home, 2357 E. Cumberland St.

Jim Nicholson, *Philadelphia Daily News*

For more prominent people, obituaries are like profiles. They can contain more reactions from other people and more quotes from the person when he or she was living. In cases of famous people who are ill or elderly, many newspapers write advance obituaries and keep them on file, because the research takes time.

When Theodor Seuss Geisel, "Dr. Seuss," died in 1991, many newspapers ran an obituary and separate reaction stories. Others wrapped the reaction in the obituary. Here's the beginning of an obituary that took the traditional form:

> Theodor Seuss Geisel, "Dr. Seuss," perhaps the most popular children's author of all time, died at his home near San Diego Tuesday night. He was 87.

The Philadelphia Inquirer

Here is a feature obituary for Dr. Seuss. The story begins with the writer's death, some basic information about his accomplishments and then a chronology of his life. It ends with information about survivors. No information was available about services, but if it had been, it would have been included at the end.

Theodor Seuss Geisel, alias Dr. Seuss, whose rhymed writing and fanciful drawings were loved worldwide and helped teach generations to read, died Tuesday night at his home in La Jolla.

Geisel's stepdaughter, Lea Dimond, told reporters the world-famous author died with his family around him. No other information was released regarding the cause of death, but Dimond said Geisel, 87, had been ill for several months.

In the 1950s and '60s, Geisel's books gave millions of children relief from the drab textbook adventures of Dick and Jane. His 48 children's books were translated into 18 languages and sold more than 100 million copies.

Geisel also drew most of the fanciful illustrations in his books, creating a menagerie of Whos, grinches, ziffs and zuffs, talking goldfish and loyal, sweet elephants. He was awarded a special Pulitzer Prize in 1984 for his contribution to children's literature.

Geisel's tales were filled with his own moral concerns, particularly for the environment and world peace. "The Lorax" warns against polluting the environment, while "The Butter Battle Book" tells of an arms race between creatures who disagree about whether it is better to eat bread with the butter side down or up.

When asked recently whether he had any final message, Geisel told a reporter from the San Diego Union: "Whenever things go a bit sour in a job I'm doing, I always tell myself, 'You can do better than this.' The best slogan I can think of to leave with the USA would be 'We can do this and we've got to do better than this.'"

Geisel was born in Springfield, Mass., on March 2, 1903. His father was a brewer and superintendent of parks, which included the zoo, where Geisel said he started drawing animals.

He graduated from Dartmouth College in 1925, having drawn cartoons for the school humor magazine. He went to England to study literature at Oxford University, but dropped out, in part, after receiving encouragement in his artistic ambitions from another American student, Helen Palmer. She became his first wife a few years later.

Geisel spent a year in Paris, where he got to know Ernest Hemingway, James Joyce and other expatriate US writers. He returned to the United States in 1927, hoping to become a novelist.

He wrote humor for the magazines "Judge" and "Life," adopting his now-famous pen name, Dr. Seuss, as a spoof of scientific developments.

His first children's book was released in 1937, the same year as his first novel for adults. But the former, ". . . And to Think That I Saw It on Mulberry Street," which initially had been rejected by 27 publishers, became a smashing success. His career was off.

Among his most famous books are "The Cat in the Hat," "Green Eggs and Ham" and "Horton Hears a Who!" which was made into a popular TV special, as was "How the Grinch Stole Christmas!"

He moved to La Jolla soon after the end of World War II. During the latter part of the war he served in the Army, helping director Frank Capra make training and documentary films. Two Geisel documentaries, "Hitler Lives?" and "Design for Death," co-written with his wife, won Academy Awards for their producers in 1946 and 1947.

After the war, Geisel's work continued to be translated to movies, with his cartoon short "Gerald McBoing Boing" winning an Oscar in 1951. He turned his attention to television in the 1950s, designing and producing cartoons, including the Peabody Award-winning "How the Grinch Stole Christmas!" and "Horton Hears a Who!"

Michael Watenpaugh, a former teacher and administrator in the Capistrano Unified School District, used to dress up as the Cat in the Hat each year to celebrate Dr. Seuss Day on Geisel's birthday. Reached at Hill Middle School in Novato, where he is now a principal, Watenpaugh said children understand Dr. Seuss' message.

"Kids get it and it's enjoyable to them," Watenpaugh said. "It was a real avenue for me to encourage kids to read, encourage kids to write. I consider his books to be children's literature."

Geisel did not have any children of his own. His first wife died in 1967. He later married Audrey Dimond, who has two daughters from a previous marriage. He also is survived by his niece, Peggy Owens, and her son, Theodore Owens, of Los Angeles.

Laura Bleiberg, *The Orange County* (Calif.) *Register*

Exercises

1 Gather information from news clips or magazines about a celebrity or otherwise prominent person in your community who is still alive. Write an obituary, and include comments the person has made and comments about the person.

2 Using the following facts, write a basic obituary. If you want to write a feature obituary, you may do library research to add to this information.

Facts: Jim Henson. Age 53. Died May 17, 1990 (but use yesterday as your time factor). Creator of the Muppets, puppets that became famous on the "Sesame Street" television program. Some famous creations: Kermit the Frog, Miss Piggy, Big Bird, the Cookie Monster. Considered one of the most famous puppeteers in the world. Entertained millions of children and their parents who watched "Sesame Street," the public television program now seen in more than 80 countries.

Circumstances of death: Died at New York Hospital 20 hours after entering with a bacterial infection, streptococcus pneumonia. He was given a high dose of antibiotics, but his kidneys and heart failed. He died at 1:21 a.m.

Residence: He lived in Manhattan. He also had homes in California, Connecticut and London.

Funeral plans: The family is planning a memorial service but has not yet announced details.

Background: Born in Greenville, Miss. Grew up in Washington, D.C.
Henson was a theater arts major at the University of Maryland. He first appeared on television with his own show, called "Sam and Friends," when

394 Applying the Techniques

he was a freshman in college. In 1959 he married Jane Nebel, a woman he met in college and who helped him operate the puppets in his first television show.

In 1956 he built a hand puppet called Kermit. "I suppose that he's an alter ego," Henson once said. "But he's a little snarkier than I am—slightly wise. Kermit says things I hold myself back from saying."

In the 1960s, Henson began appearing with his puppets on "The Ed Sullivan Show."

In 1969, the creators of Children's Television Workshop began "Sesame Street," which featured Henson's puppets.

In 1976, he gained fame with his own show, "The Muppet Show," which featured Kermit and Miss Piggy. The show was seen in more than 100 countries by an estimated 235 million viewers.

When Henson died he was in the midst of concluding a deal with the Walt Disney Co. to sell Henson Associates, Inc., which owns the Muppets, for a price estimated at $100 million to $150 million.

Henson coined the name Muppet to describe a combination of marionette and foam-rubber hand puppet. The Muppets' heads are hand puppets, but other parts of their bodies may be controlled by strings and rods.

Survivors: Henson's wife and five children (whose names were not included in this obituary).

From Peggy Charren, founder of Action for Children's Television: "He could make you laugh while you were crying."

From Erwin Okun, spokesman for Walt Disney Co.: "I never met a kinder, gentler wonderful soul in the entertainment industry or anywhere."

From Joan Ganz Cooney, chief executive of Children's Television Workshop: "Jim was dedicated to children's education, and with all his commercial success, he never lost his idealism."

Prepared statement from officials of the Public Broadcasting Service: "His legacy is the lesson that one can both laugh and learn."

COACHING

TIPS

Do your homework. Check clips and other sources for background about the speaker or issue at a conference or meeting.

Listen for what the speaker doesn't discuss. Then ask questions to find the answers that the readers (or viewers) will want.

Ask yourself what the most interesting information was—whether it came during a speaker's prepared comments or afterward. Then lead with that information.

Try to get as many good direct quotes as possible. Favor full quotes over partial ones.

Use graphics as a writing tool. Write a highlights box—to accompany your story or to organize your story.

21

Speeches, Press Conferences and Meetings

Mark Fagan gets most of his news stories at meetings. But he gets most of his best quotes when the meetings end. Fagan, a city government reporter for the *Lawrence* (Kan.) *Journal-World*, says the most important part of a meeting story is what you cover before and after it.

One night the city commission was debating a zoning change. A business owner wanted to expand his electrical shop in a residential neighborhood. Commissioner Jo Andersen was angry. More business would bring traffic and crime to the neighborhood, she said.

Fagan headed straight for Andersen after the meeting. "Why were you so upset?" he asked.

"What I really wanted to say was that even if Jesus Christ himself wanted to expand his carpenter's shop in East Lawrence, we would respectfully request that he find another area that is more appropriate," she said.

"You can still say that," Fagan said. This is the beginning of the story he wrote the next day:

Most press officers at the Pentagon wouldn't tell you if your coat was on fire.

Don Campbell, former director, Paul Miller Fellowships, The Freedom Forum

Not even divine intervention could help a proposal to expand an East Lawrence electric shop onto vacant lots next door.

During their meeting Tuesday night, Lawrence city commissioners denied a request from Patchen Electric & Industrial Supply Inc. to expand its 47-year-old business at 602 E. Ninth onto two lots zoned for apartments.

In the end, the request never had a prayer.

"If Jesus Christ himself wanted to expand his carpenter's shop in East Lawrence, we would respect-fully request that he find another area that is more appropriate," Commissioner Jo Andersen said after the meeting. "It has nothing to do with a person's personality. It has everything to do with zoning."

Mark Fagan, *Lawrence Journal-World*

Mark Fagan (right) interviewing City Commissioner John Nalbandian

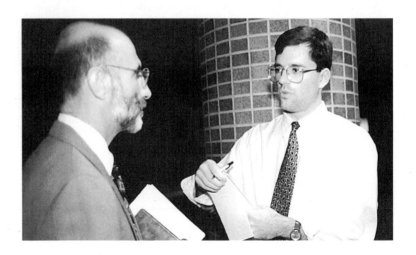

The story continued with explanations of how zoning had changed from commercial to residential use since the business was built and why residents objected to its expansion.

"The comments officials make during a meeting are for public posturing," Fagan says. "Some of the best quotes you get are after the meeting when you ask them to explain why they did or said something."

That advice also applies to someone from the public who speaks at a meeting. "A person may speak for 30 seconds and afterward she'll tell you, 'My kid needs a safe place to walk because he was attacked two years ago,'" Fagan says. "Don't just sit in the meeting if the person leaves; follow him or her out and get those additional comments."

What you write before the meeting is even more important, Fagan says. He writes at least one story, called an advance, to tell readers what officials will discuss at their next meeting. If people don't know what officials plan to do, they won't get a chance to participate in government.

Although many newspapers are curtailing meeting coverage because the news is sometimes dull, Fagan thinks that's a mistake. Meetings are where officials make decisions that affect the public.

Fagan goes to at least three meetings a week: the commission's public meeting; its study meetings, where officials decide what they will discuss at public meetings; and neighborhood group meetings to learn what people are really concerned about.

"I'll write stories sometimes and no one (from the public) will show up at a meeting, and I wonder if what I do makes a difference. Then a city commissioner will say, 'I got about 20 phone calls after your article.' So I know people are reading them."

Even if people don't read his stories or attend the meetings, Fagan thinks it's important for reporters to be there as watchdogs for the public. He says the officials know he is really there for 20,000 other people: his readers.

"I put the commissioners' comments in the paper, and everyone knows where they stand," Fagan says. "That's a great power of the press."

Whenever you are covering a meeting, it's important to look beyond what officials say publicly. Fagan says reporters should ask questions before and after the public event to find out how the story affects readers. "An item on a meeting agenda may say they are going to award bids for highway improvements on North Second Street," he says. "I look at that and say, 'What does that mean?' Are they going to widen the street? This is the only artery that connects downtown and an old neighborhood. Are they going to close the road to traffic for eight months? This is how officials plan to spend taxpayers' money. You need to find out how it affects readers."

Fagan has also covered plenty of speeches and press conferences on his beat, especially when he is writing about elections. Many of the reporting and writing principles for those events are the same as they are for meetings. Don't just write what the officials say; find out why they are making certain comments or decisions and what the impact is on readers.

Media Manipulation

Sources who give speeches or conduct press conferences are often using the media to further their own causes. There's nothing wrong with that. It's a way of presenting news. But a responsible reporter should ask good questions after the speech or press conference and add points of view from opposing sources when possible.

For example, in the summer of 1991 Operation Rescue, an anti-abortion group, waged massive demonstrations to close an abortion clinic in Wichita, Kan. The sources from that group had a definite agenda; they clearly were trying to manipulate the press, says Steven A. Smith, former managing editor of *The Wichita* (Kan.) *Eagle.* One of the leaders of Operation Rescue conducted a press conference during which he held up a fully developed fetus, which supposedly had been aborted at about seven or eight months. Smith says the situation posed a difficult ethical dilemma for the *Eagle* staff. The leader's actions were news. But there was no evidence that the fetus had been aborted at the Wichita clinic. The result: *The Eagle* published news about the protest and the leader's actions, including the statement that there was no proof the fetus came from the Wichita clinic. But the paper did not publish a picture of the fetus. Smith says he was convinced the situation was staged to manipulate the press. Television stations also refused to show the fetus.

Throughout the summer, protesters on both sides of the abortion issue came from around the nation to converge on Wichita, and 2,600 of

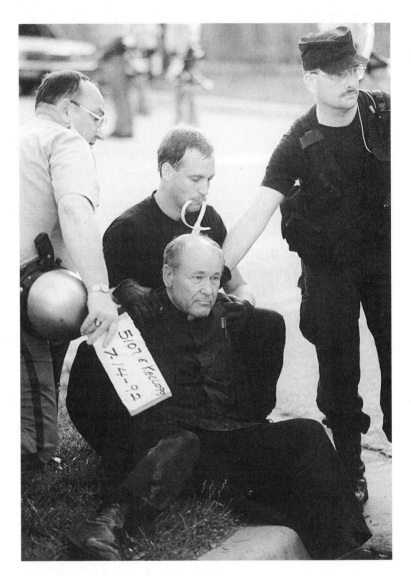

A Roman Catholic priest, leader of the pro-life group called the Lambs of Christ, being arrested after attempting to block the entrance to the Women's Health Care Center in Wichita, Kan.
Courtesy of Richard Hernandez, *The Wichita Eagle*

them were arrested for violating city laws and defying court orders prohibiting them from blocking the abortion clinic. Both sides sought to manipulate the press. Smith says the newspaper tried so hard to give balanced coverage that some of the editors actually measured the number of inches of type given to the pro-choice and anti-abortion sources to make sure they had equal treatment.

The problems of manipulation were even greater for the three local television stations. Operation Rescue leaders staged their press conferences shortly before the 5 p.m. newscasts in hopes of receiving live coverage from television. News directors, concerned about issues of accuracy and fairness, limited the live coverage. They edited the tape to be shown at the end of the 5 p.m. newscasts or only on the 10 p.m. programs, so they could have more control and present balanced viewpoints.

Preparation

Most speeches, press conferences and meetings do not pose such severe problems. Still, reporters always need to do more than listen and repeat what they hear. As Mark Fagan suggests, reporters need to ask good questions after the event as well.

To ask good questions, however, you must prepare for the event. You need to find out all you can about the speaker and the issue. Be sure to check the clips and data bases.

With a prominent speaker, you can often get the text of the speech in advance. But be careful not to rely on it. The speaker may depart from the prepared text. However, you can still use the prepared text. Just say, "The speaker said in prepared remarks" or "in a written text." Reporters sometimes have to rely on the written version, especially if their deadlines come before the speech or press conference is over.

During the speech, try to get full quotes of the important points (especially if they vary from the written text), and jot down reactions of the speaker and the audience. Note when and if the speaker shows emotion and how the audience responds. Write follow-up questions to ask the speaker after the speech or press conference.

Try to get an aisle seat. If someone asks a good question after the speech or meeting and then leaves, you should follow that person out of the room quickly so you can check the name and get more information.

Stories About Speeches

Your story should always include some basic information:

• Size of the audience

• Location of the speech

• Reason for the speech

• Highlights of the speech, including good quotes

• Reaction of the audience, especially at dramatic points during the speech

Although you need to include this basic information, don't clutter the top of your story with it—unless it is crucial to the event. Write the story just as you would any other good story.

You can lead with a hard-news approach emphasizing a main point the speaker made or a soft-news approach describing the person or using an anecdote from the speech. Just don't lead with a no-news approach: Someone made a speech. Tell the reader what the speaker said.

For example, here is the kind of lead to avoid; this one appeared on a story in a campus newspaper:

> Students from Gay and Lesbian Services spoke yesterday to a psychology class about their lives and experiences.

What did they say? It's better to focus on some interesting point they made.

Speakers usually don't make their strongest points first and follow in chronological order, so your story shouldn't be written in that order. Put the most emotional or newsworthy information first. Then back it up with quotes and supporting points.

Sometimes the most interesting information isn't what happens during the speech. It can be what happens after the speech or outside the place while the person is speaking, especially if there is a protest or other major reaction to the speech. Reaction can also be important to the story.

In most cases, the audience is a minor part of a speech story. But in the next example, the people who came to protest the speech were more newsworthy than the speech itself:

> Five gay-rights activists were arrested Saturday after disrupting a speech by U.S. Rep. William Dannemeyer at a seminar on "The Preservation of the Heterosexual Ethic."
>
> While the five were handcuffed with plastic restraints after entering Power Community Church, 1026 S. East St., to disrupt the seminar, about 100 other activists picketed on the sidewalk shouting "bigot" and "hatemonger."
>
> Dannemeyer, R-Fullerton, who announced his candidacy for the U.S. Senate, shrugged off the protest, saying, "I've reached the point in my political career that if I'm not picketed, I really haven't had a good day."
>
> Before the interruption, Dannemeyer urged an audience of about 120 people to support laws requiring doctors to notify health officials of patients who test positive for AIDS.
>
> Scott Thomsen, *The Orange County* (Calif.) *Register*

You can use storytelling techniques for speeches, too. In the next example a journalism student used narrative and descriptive writing to convey the drama of a speech by a survivor of the Holocaust. Notice where the writer put the basic information: when, where and how many people attended the speech.

Zev Kedem huddled in silence with his grandparents in a pigeon coop above his family's apartment while soldiers searched for them. His grandparents were prepared to swallow vials of poison as the soldiers tried the metal door they hid behind. The door held. And the soldiers went on.

The year was 1942, and so begins Zev Kedem's story of survival that began over 50 years ago as Adolph Hitler orchestrated the Holocaust.

A "Schindler's List" survivor, Kedem spoke for over an hour as he told the story of his childhood in a Nazi concentration camp to 750 people in the Union Ballroom last night.

Gail Johnson

Here is another example of a feature approach to a controversial speech:

Leonard Jeffries holds up two pictures. One is actor Al Jolson, a white man in blackface. The other is a lynching. A black man has been hanged, his body burned.

"This is our history," says the professor from New York City. "This is what we cannot allow to happen again."

To some who listen to Jeffries' impassioned call for equality for African-Americans and the need to make American education inclusive of many peoples, he is a cultural hero.

But to others, who hear in his speeches vicious attacks on Jews and other groups, he is as racist as those he tars as bigots.

The controversial chairman of the Black Studies Department at City College of the City University of New York spoke Tuesday night to about 800 people at the University of South Florida. He said his message had been mangled by a "hysterical conspiracy" of Jewish leaders and "rich white men with property and power."

Jeffries says his message "is not anti-white, not anti-gay, not anti-Semitic, not anti-Jewish."

Rather, he said he is trying to reverse a systematic attempt by whites to enforce a stereotype of people of color that keeps them second-class citizens.

A "white supremacist" education that focuses on the contributions of whites and Europeans leaves young blacks and whites "ill-equipped to deal with the realities of the human experience," Jeffries said.

The controversy around the 55-year-old professor has increased since last summer when he gave a speech in Albany, N.Y., that led many people to label him a bigot and call for his resignation. Jeffries says that he receives death threats regularly and that universities across the country where he is invited to speak have been pressured to cancel his appearances.

But that didn't temper his words Tuesday, when he attacked the "Jewish moguls" in Hollywood who, he says, are responsible for generations of systemic stereotyping of blacks, like the Al Jolson character in his photograph.

On Tuesday, he talked of some of his most controversial statements, the ones that say European whites are "ice people," aggressive and individualistic, and African blacks "sun people," warm and communal.

Jeffries said that the geography of the Ice Age shaped Europeans, making them "aggressive and progressive" to survive. And life in the climate of Africa's sun shaped blacks, he said.

"The Europeans are very proud of their ice experience. So why are they raising hell about me?" Jeffries said.

Although protesters attended some of Jeffries' appearances, his speech at USF was unmarked by dissent and met with warm applause.

Jennifer Orsi, *St. Petersburg* (Fla.) *Times*

Stories About Press Conferences

Press conferences are like speeches, except that the questions reporters ask after a press conference are often more important than the prepared comments the speaker makes. The answers to those questions are an important part of the story—and sometimes are the story. Consider news reports after the U.S. president conducts a press conference. His prepared remarks often are less interesting than his answers to the press corps. (Texts of the president's press conferences are available on the Internet; see the appendix for site addresses.)

Stories about press conferences must include certain pieces of information:

Who conducted the press conference

Reason for the press conference

Highlights of the news, including responses to questions

Location, if relevant

Reaction from sources with similar and opposing points of view

One of the following stories includes information the reporter got by calling an official who wasn't at the press conference—but who might have an opposing view—for a reaction. The reporter also included related background and perspective. The other story concentrated only on the report presented at the press conference. It lacks perspective and balance from other points of view. See if you can tell which is which.

Ronald Reagan, former president of the United States, at a press conference
Courtesy of Bill Snead/
The Washington Post

Version 1

The surgeon general said yesterday that alcohol is leading the nation's youth into emergency rooms and jails, and she cited statistics ranging from date rape to drownings to make her case.

It's part of a crusade that Surgeon General Antonia Novello has been on for months, and the alcohol industry was clearly irritated after her news conference.

Jeff Becker, a spokesman for the Beer Institute, said the industry has been trying to get Novello to discuss the issue quietly.

Novello cited figures to show the problems caused by young people abusing alcohol, including accidents, deaths, assaults, rapes, bad grades and dropping out of school.

She didn't offer much that was new; even the statistics that she released were drawn from reports already published in newspapers, magazines and medical journals during the past 10 years.

Among the statistics:

- About a third of the youths committing serious crimes consumed alcohol just before them.

- More than 70 percent of teen suicides involved frequent use of alcohol or drugs.

- Alcohol figures in more than half the rapes among college students.

- Nearly 40 percent of drownings and 75 percent of fatal accidents with all-terrain vehicles involved use of alcohol.

Just last month she called on the alcohol industry to change its advertising, which she said glamorized drinking and played down its risks by showing people climbing mountains, racing cars or steering boats.

Her attacks on alcohol and

Version 2

Risky sexual behavior, crime, suicide and bad grades are overlooked repercussions of teen-age drinking, a government report out Monday says.

"Alcohol is not consumed in a void; there are consequences," says Surgeon General Antonia Novello.

Among those cited in *Youth and Alcohol: Dangerous and Deadly Consequences,* the report reviewing research:

- Sexual assault—55% of perpetrators, 53% of victims said they were under the influence during the assault. In a high school student survey, 40% of the boys and 18% of the girls said it was OK to force sex if a girl was drunk.

- Risky sex—One survey found half of 16- to 19-year-olds were more likely to have sex if they and their partner had been drinking. Also, 17% said they were less likely to use a condom when drinking.

- Suicide—70% of youths trying suicide were frequent drug and/ or alcohol users.

- Grades—Among 1,991 high school seniors, twice as many binge drinkers (five or more drinks in one sitting) had grades of "C" or lower.

Novello wants clearer warning labels, better enforcement of drinking laws, voluntary advertising reform and education. A teen rarely realizes, she says, that after he or she "takes a drink, then another, (that) finally the drink takes the teenager . . . and according to these reports, where it leads him or her is not a pretty sight."

Another report out Monday says a fourth of U.S. teens are at serious health risk from alcohol and drugs,

Version 1 (continued)

tobacco have not been warmly embraced by the White House. Presidential spokesman Marlin Fitzwater
said last month that "we generally
stay away from intrusion in market-
place decisions."

Richard L. Vernaci, The Associated Press

Version 2 (continued)

sexually transmitted diseases, poor
nutrition, depression and violence.

Fateful Choices, written by Fred
M. Hechinger for the Carnegie Council on Adolescent Development,
calls for more school-related health
centers, federal gun control laws and
health insurance for all teens.

Mike Snider, *USA Today*

The Associated Press version is the one enriched by reaction, background and perspective.

Stories About Meetings

The decisions that affect readers' daily lives—such as where they take
their trash, get their water and send their children to school—are made
by local government officials at meetings. Yet meeting stories often are
written without explaining their real impact on the reader.

Countless surveys conducted by newspapers and news organizations
reveal that local news is near or at the top of the list of the kinds of stories readers want. They just don't read them all the way to the end.
Sometimes they don't read past the lead, especially when the lead is dull.

The stories don't have to be boring. They may not be as compelling
as a story about a murder trial. But they can be written with flair and
with an emphasis on the meeting's significance to readers.

All states have open-meeting laws requiring officials who have the
authority to spend public funds to conduct their business in public.
These boards may conduct executive sessions behind closed doors for
certain discussions, such as personnel matters or collective bargaining,
but all decisions must be made in a public meeting. Although open-
meeting laws vary from state to state, most of them require public agencies to give advance notice—usually 48 hours—of their meetings and to
conduct public hearings.

Understanding the System

When a board makes a decision at a meeting, you need to understand
what kind of authority that board has. Suppose you are covering a zoning board meeting. The board is discussing a zoning application from a
developer for a major shopping center. If the board approves a zoning
change, is that the final decision? Probably not. Most zoning boards are
advisory and must submit their recommendations to a city or county
board of officials for final approval. When you write the story, that is essential information to include.

If you are covering meetings of your university administration, find out who can make the decisions and which boards are advisory. Who can raise the tuition—school officials or a board of regents? Is the action taken at a meeting a recommendation or a ruling? You need to explain the system as well as the next step in an action, as in this story:

A little spray paint would go a long way—about 1,000 hours long—for those who scrawl graffiti on walls and fences in Chicago, under an ordinance amendment before City Council.

Vandals who take a few seconds to paint their "tags" and then are caught could be forced to scrub off their unsightly work—and someone else's, as well.

With no debate and little discussion, the Police and Fire Committee Tuesday unanimously approved the ordinance change, which would increase the maximum number of mandatory hours of community service work for vandalism convictions from the current 120 hours to 1,000 hours.

"I think this is a step in the right direction," said Ald. William Beavers (7th), the committee chairman, who said he would ask the full City Council to approve the change at Wednesday's meeting.

Robert Davis, *Chicago Tribune*

Writing the Advance

Many times, knowing what is going to happen at a meeting is more important to readers than knowing what did happen. A story that tells readers what is being proposed can alert residents to make their concerns known before a measure is adopted by local officials. A pre-meeting story is called an "advance."

An advance is especially crucial if local officials are planning to conduct a public hearing about an issue. If the public doesn't know about it, how can the public be heard?

City and school boards usually publish an agenda in advance of their meetings. This agenda lists the items to be discussed, although new items can and will be presented.

When you receive an agenda, look through it for items that might be of special interest to readers. Call board members and ask for comments or ask them to pick out the items they expect to be most interesting or controversial. If the issue has been in the news previously, check clips and call other interested parties.

The point of your advance is to inform readers about items that they may want to discuss during the public comment part of a meeting or just to let readers know what their officials are proposing. If you are writing an advance for a public hearing, make sure you give the time and location of the hearing.

Here is an example of an advance with an impact lead:

For the first time in its 107-year history, Temple University may require all undergraduates to take a course related to race and racism.

The proposal, which grew out of black students' demonstrations at Temple in spring 1990, is to be debated by the school's faculty senate on Friday.

Among the faculty, however, the proposal has already sparked intense discussion. The debate mirrors that of other campuses—including Stanford, Wisconsin, Michigan and Berkeley—where courses related to race are required.

Huntly Collins, *The Philadelphia Inquirer*

The following excerpt from an advance includes the time and location of the meeting:

> The stage is set for changing the city's human relations ordinance to include protections for homosexuals.
>
> Lawrence city commissioners agreed to set ground rules for public comment on a proposal to add the words "sexual orientation" to the city's anti-discrimination ordinance.
>
> The ground rules—such as how long people will be allowed to speak—will be determined during next week's meeting, which begins at 6:35 p.m. Tuesday at City Hall, Sixth and Massachusetts streets. A draft form of the ordinance is planned for a vote one week later on April 25.
>
> Mark Fagan, *Lawrence Journal-World*

Covering the Meeting

Arrive early. Find out the names of board members (usually they have nameplates), and find out who is in charge.

Ask board members, especially the head of the board, if you could talk to them after the meeting. If you know people in the audience who are leaders of a group favoring or opposing a controversial issue, greet them and tell them you would like to get comments after the meeting.

Check items on the agenda, and get any background that you need.

Check the consent agenda, a list of items on the agenda that the board will approve without discussion. They may include bids for approval or other points the board may have discussed in work sessions. A "gem" of a story may be buried in the consent agenda.

One reporter wondered why the school board had approved $30,000 in "token losses." That's a lot of money to be considered "token" losses. She discovered that it represented losses of bus tokens that the school board sold to students who had to ride public buses because there were no school buses in the city. Why $30,000 in losses? The school district had no system of monitoring the sales, and the money had been stolen at several schools. By school officials! The board didn't want to discuss this item publicly, so it was buried in the consent agenda. But the reporter wanted to discuss it. In a front-page story.

Don't remain glued to a seat at a press table. When members of the audience give public comments, get their names and more comments. Many times they will leave immediately after their testimony. Follow them out of the meeting. You can catch up with the action inside later. Or sit in the audience. Sometimes the comments of people attending the meeting are more interesting than the ones the board members make.

Stay until the end, unless your deadline prohibits staying. The most important issue could emerge at the end of a meeting when the board asks for new business or public comments. Or something dramatic could happen. The mayor could resign. Violence could erupt. You never can tell, especially if you're not there.

Writing the Story

First, how not to write it: Do not say the city council met and discussed something. Tell what they discussed or enacted. This is the kind of lead to avoid:

> The 41st Annual Environmental Engineering Conference met yesterday at the Kansas Union to discuss solutions to environmental problems.
>
> Representatives of the Kansas Department of Health and Environment, the Environmental Protection Agency and other organizations spoke to about 180 people who attended the conference.

So what did they say? This lead reveals nothing.

Some meetings are long. They can be boring. Avoid telling the reader how much you suffered listening to board members drone on and accomplish nothing in a long meeting. The reader doesn't care how much you suffer. The reader wants the news. If the length of the debate is crucial to the story, you should include it. But if the meetings are usually long and the time element is not a major factor related to the focus, don't mention it.

Here are some points to include in your story:

Type of meeting and location: But if the city council or school board meets all the time in the same building, don't mention the location.

The vote on any major issue: For instance, say "in a 4-1 vote . . ." If the issue is particularly controversial, say who voted against it—or for it, if an affirmative vote was more controversial. If the measure was approved unanimously, say so. Don't give the vote for every minor item, however.

The next step: If a major issue or ordinance cannot be adopted until a public hearing is conducted, tell readers when a hearing is scheduled or what the next step is before the action is final.

Impact on readers: Explain how the decision will affect them.

Quotes: But use only quotes that are dramatic, interesting or crucial to the story.

Background of the issues: What do readers need to know to understand what has happened?

To write the story, select one key issue for the focus. If the board approved several other measures, add them at the end: "In other business." If several important actions occurred, consider breaking another key issue into a separate story, if possible. If not, try a lead mentioning both items, or put the second key point in the second paragraph and give supporting background later, after you have developed the first point. For example: "City commissioners yesterday approved plans for the city's first shopping mall but rejected plans for a new public golf course." Then proceed with the discussion about the shopping mall.

Consider advancing the story with a second-day lead. This kind of advance tells readers what the next step is or how the story will affect them. In most newspapers, this type of lead is becoming more popular because it makes the news more timely. However, it is optional, and a first-day lead may be acceptable.

Although many meeting stories are written with summary leads, especially if the news is significant, they do not have to follow that form. If you think a softer lead is appropriate for the type of news that occurred, you can use it.

Here are some more writing tips:

• Use the tell-a-friend technique to make the story readable. This technique is especially helpful with stories about meetings.

• Remember the kiss-off technique if you have three or more sources: Block comments from a single speaker in one place, and don't use the source again. However, the mayor or another well-known official may be used as a source intermittently.

A few matters of style:

• *Board* is a collective noun and therefore takes a singular verb: The board discussed the issue at *its* meeting, not *their* meeting. If this approach seems awkward in your story, say that the board *members* said *their* next meeting would be Tuesday.

• Capitalize *city council, city commission* and *school board* when they are part of a proper name—such as the Rockville City Commission—and when the reference is to a specific commission in your town—the City Commission. If you are referring to a city commission in any city, use lowercase letters.

• Capitalize the titles of board members or other officials when they come before the name, as in *Mayor John Corrupt.* If the title follows the name—*John Corrupt, the mayor*—use lowercase letters.

• For votes, use *3-1,* not *3 to 1.*

Stories about meetings can take a hard, soft or advance-impact approach. Whichever one you use, make the story relevant to readers. Here's how:

Basic hard-news meeting story

LAGUNA BEACH, Calif.—Despite neighbors' objections, a North Laguna Beach couple were given per-	*Summary lead: what happened*

mission Tuesday to adorn their home with a 17-foot-high outdoor sculpture of 30 water heaters and two house trailers.

The City Council, after viewing a scale model of the artwork, voted 3-1 to endorse the sculpture. It will climb around a pine tree in the back courtyard of Arnold and Marie Forde's home.

Vote

Mayor Neil Fitzpatrick dissented, saying the sculpture infringed on neighbors' views. Councilwoman Martha Collison was absent.

Dissenting vote

"It's a victory for the freedom of expression," said Los Angeles artist Nancy Rubins, who will craft the sculpture. "It would have been a sad day if a community that sees itself as supporting the arts struck down an artwork in a private yard."

Reaction

The sculpture had been the focus of an intense neighborhood battle.

Impact: so what

Residents who live near the Fordes have called the sculpture junk and complained that the artwork would block their view and spoil the neighborhood character.

David DeLo, who lives across Cliff Drive from the Fordes, said he was considering challenging the council's action in court.

More reaction

Next step

"If the council wants to place a piece of junk in a residential neighborhood, that's their prerogative, but this council has been overturned before," he said.

To appease neighbors, the council approved the sculpture on the condition that the Fordes place it as low as possible in the yard and landscape the area with another tree and a hedge. The additional plants should hide the sculpture from neighbors, officials said.

Backup: conditions of council action

The $5,000 sculpture will take a week to build. Rubins said she did not know when it will be finished.

Future kicker

Harrison Fletcher, *The Orange County Register*

Meeting stories may also be written with a creative lead—if the news lends itself to a soft approach:

Conversational style

Life used to be so simple.

Whenever families were discussed, the couple was assumed to consist of one male and one female: one mom, one pop.

The City Council's Public Safety Committee entered the 1990s Tuesday night. Members noted that couples now come in three configurations: male-female, male-male and female-female.

"Let's face reality. You can't get around homosexuality," said Alderman Eugene Thompson. "If we said, 'two adults,' that should cover everything."

The matter came before the committee as it approved the sale of family passes for the use of the swimming pool in Garfield Park. To play it safe, "family" was defined as any two adults and up to four dependents.

Kevin Cullen, (Danville, Ill.) *Commercial-News*

Exercises

1 Speech story: These are excerpts from a speech by Burl Osborne, editor and publisher of *The Dallas Morning News.* He made this speech at a convention of the American Society of Newspaper Editors when he was president of the organization. Write a news story based on this speech as though Osborne gave it at your journalism school to an audience of 100 journalism students and teachers. Write it for tomorrow's campus newspaper, using yesterday (use the day of the week) as your time frame. Tailor your angle to your campus audience.

On college campuses all across the country there are growing restraints on free speech and academic freedom.

It is troubling that the attacks are coming from those who once defended the right to free expression—and who achieved their own status by exercising it.

Trying to squelch unpopular speech isn't a new idea, of course. In the era of Sen. Joseph McCarthy in the 1950s, supposed Communists and their sympathizers were the targets and the security of the United States was the excuse.

More recently, proposed laws would have imprisoned those who burn the American flag as a form of political protest. Congress made such a law, which the Supreme Court struck down. There was talk of a constitutional amendment but that also was beaten back—at least for the moment.

Most people don't want to endanger democracy or burn the flag. But it is just plain wrong to try to protect democracy by denying its principles or to try to protect the flag by denying the rights that it stands for.

In these, and most, cases, the urge to censor is the reaction of well-intentioned people to the expression of views they find repugnant.

Censors are always certain they are acting for the common good. The current wave of censorship has all these characteristics. The common good for which the censors would supersede the Constitution is protection from being offended, insulted or ridiculed.

The goal is to eliminate prejudice, particularly that based on race, gender or sexual orientation. That is an admirable goal. Using censorship as a tool to achieve that goal is not an admirable strategy. Yet censorship has become the strategy of choice.

A growing number of campuses now forbid offensive speech or expression, with penalties ranging from censure to expulsion to thought-remedial visits to a psychologist. Behavior that complies with what is deemed to be proper is politically correct. Censorship is the discipline imposed on the politically incorrect.

The core activities of a university, the competition of ideas and the pursuit of academic inquiry, can flourish only with the right to express any opinion or ask any questions without regard to the correctness of the premise. It is one thing to disagree with an opinion and defeat it with logic. To deny the mere expression of a bad idea is quite another. We find ourselves accepting intolerance of disagreeable or offensive speech in order to fight intolerance of other kinds.

Here are some examples culled from journals and magazines during the last several months. I disagree with many of the views that are expressed, but I disagree more with the notion that one shouldn't be permitted to express them at all.

• At the University of California at Berkeley, a professor wrote in a magazine that he believed the school's affirmative action program discriminated against white and Asian applicants. Students who disagreed disrupted his class and the university gave him to wonder whether or not he would be permitted to continue teaching.

• In the New York University law school, the moot court board assigned a case concerning the custody rights of a lesbian mother. Students temporarily forced withdrawal of the case on grounds that arguments against the mother would be hurtful to a particular group.

• The University of Connecticut prohibited "inappropriately directed laughter" and "conspicuous exclusion of students from conversations." A woman student was banned from campus for posting a sign on her dormitory door that was judged to be offensive and thus in violation of the student code.

• The student senate at the University of Wisconsin in Madison protested an "All-American Halloween Ball," on the grounds that masked students might anonymously insult others.

• At San Francisco State University, 30 students disrupted a class in black politics. They were not protesting anything the professor said; they objected because the course was listed in the catalog under Political Science rather than Black Studies.

- A University of Michigan student read a limerick containing joking references to homosexuality. He was required to publish a written self-criticism, "Learned My Lesson," in the student newspaper.

- At the University of Minnesota, an entire department, including one woman, was charged with sexual harassment. One charge was based on a professor's negative comment about a woman student's paper; another was that a professor failed to return a greeting before class.

- At Harvard, a student displayed a Confederate flag to demonstrate what she described as a surge of Southern pride stimulated by the war in the Persian Gulf. An African-American student was offended and displayed a swastika to demonstrate his view that the Confederate flag is a hateful sign. Jewish students were offended because of the swastika's Nazi symbolism. The first student was offended because the Confederate flag didn't mean to others what it means to her.

- At Smith College, students were given a list of terms of oppression, including, with appropriate references to racism and sexism, some others that required new words because the victims, as the handbook took note, may not yet know they are oppressed.

- Ableism, for example, is defined as the oppression of the differently abled by the temporarily abled. Classism is the oppression of the working class and non-propertied by the upper and middle classes. Lookism, is, in part, the construction of a standard for beauty or attractiveness.

In the course of collecting written material on this subject, I ran across a tongue-in-cheek forecast of particular interest to me. It predicted that the next ism might be heightism, whose victims would no longer be called short, but instead would be known as the vertically challenged.

Gotcha. Some of you were guilty of inappropriately directed laughter. Even though the story didn't offend me, it might offend someone. For the benefit of the thought police, I need to point out that I was trying not to poke fun at their good intentions but to point out the complexity of deciding exactly what speech is permissible and what isn't.

I take the entire subject very seriously. But I have to say that if we hope to make good on this country's promises of freedom to speak one's mind, then we are not going about it in a very productive way.

What we should be doing is defending and promoting the right of free speech; that is the best way to persuade each other of the moral validity of the civil treatment of everyone.

These concerns are especially important to journalists because censorship on the campus today will be censorship in the newsroom tomorrow. Campus newspapers are speaking out on this subject in places like the University of Colorado in Boulder. In others, I suspect the fear of offending has kept them quiet; they need First Amendment protection, too.

I am pleased that the ASNE will intensify efforts to strengthen First Amendment values. I hope that ASNE will study what is happening on the campuses. We need to know whether what we are seeing is a fad or a permanent change on the university scene.

Last night several editors met for dinner at the Cafe Budapest. The group was met by an elegant, silver-haired woman in a flowing white gown. She was the owner of the restaurant, Dr. Livia Hedda Rev-Kury. As she welcomed the party, Dr. Rev-Kury asked about the "Celebrate the First" button that editor Frank Sutherland was wearing.

"It celebrates the First Amendment," he said. "Would you like to have it?" he asked. "Oh, yes," she responded.

As she took the button, she said, "I know a little about the First Amendment," and she paused.

"You know, I love America more than you do."

"Why is that," the editor asked.

She rolled up her sleeve and extended her arm. "You see, I have these numbers . . ."

That was one more First Amendment minute given to us by a survivor of Dachau and Auschwitz and citizen of the United States. The tattoo she carries is a permanent reminder of the value of the First Amendment. We need to somehow tattoo that value on our souls. We need to figure out how to reduce prejudice without sacrificing individual liberties and freedom of thought and expression.

2 Press conference: Write a story based on excerpts from the following press conference as though you were covering it; use today or yesterday for your time frame. Include material from the prepared remarks, the questions and answers, and the facts boxes or the background. (You also should consider the graphics and facts boxes you would include.) Although Magic Johnson resumed his career a few years later, ignore that fact for purposes of this exercise.

Background: Earvin "Magic" Johnson Jr., a basketball superstar who played for the Los Angeles Lakers, stunned the nation in 1991 when he announced that he was retiring from the game because he had contracted the HIV virus, meaning he had tested positive for AIDS (acquired immune deficiency syndrome). The 32-year-old player ended his 12-year career with the National Basketball Association in a press conference at the Forum in Inglewood, Calif., the Lakers' home court (see Exhibit 21-1). Johnson, who is 6 feet 9 inches tall, was drafted by the National Basketball Association in 1979 after playing basketball for two years at Michigan State University in his original hometown of East Lansing, Mich.

He announced his retirement in November 1991. He had been married a few months earlier, on Sept. 14, to Earletha "Cookie" Kelly, who was seven weeks pregnant at the time of his press conference. He said his wife did not have the AIDS virus.

RENO GAZETTE-JOURNAL

35¢

FRIDAY, NOVEMBER 8, 1991

SPORTS SHOCKER

Basketball loses its Magic

PERSONAL VIEW

Johnson shared delight for life

Sports Editor Jamie Turner has covered Earvin Johnson since "Magic" was a high school star in Michigan.

By Jamie Turner
GAZETTE-JOURNAL

Until today, I believed the days of Lou Gehrig and John Kennedy had passed into American mythology. Not the men, particularly, but the country they represented.

A country that believed in heroes. A country that picked out a man or woman and imbued him or her with stature and dignity grown from a national faith in their essential decency.

The Iron Horse. "I consider myself the luckiest man on the face of the earth." Utter strength against impossible odds.

Camelot. "Ask not what your country can do for you, but what you can do for your country." Profiles in Courage.

And then a man whom I have watched from his teens stepped up to a national audience Thursday and smiled before a personal abyss. In 10 minutes, Earvin Johnson confronted a deadly ailment and a national stigma as professionally as he would have a National Basketball Association championship series.

See **MAGIC** on page **8A**

"It can happen to anybody — even me, Magic Johnson."
Revealing he has AIDS virus on Thursday

- **Earvin Johnson retires:** Lakers star has AIDS virus
- **Cause:** Uncertain
- **Outlook:** 'I'm going to go on'; NBA champ promotes safe sex
- **Reaction:** Fans, players sad

Complete report, 1,2E

- **In Reno:** News strikes high school, UNR basketball players and bettors at sports books like a thunderbolt.
- **How do you feel:** Call the Gazette-Journal TalkLine, 324-0225, ext. 3267.
- **Telling kids:** Be sympathetic, non-judgmental, experts advise.
- **Praise from ex-coach:** Pat Riley shaken.

HIV AND AIDS
KNOWING THE DIFFERENCE
- **HIV:** The virus that causes AIDS.
- **AIDS:** A result of HIV infection. The AIDS virus attacks the immune system so a person can no longer fight off other infections, which become fatal.
- **How AIDS is spread:** AIDS is caused by a virus that spreads through sex (vaginal, oral or anal) and blood-to-blood contact (such as sharing needles or syringes with someone infected with the virus). HIV cannot spread by ordinary social contact.
Source: American Red Cross HIV-AIDS Instructor's Manual.

Here is a career highlights box that appeared in *The Orange County Register:*

- Holds the NBA career assist record at 9,921.

- Named the NBA's Most Valuable Player in 1987.

- Led the Lakers to championships in 1980, 1982, 1985, 1987 and 1988. The Lakers also made the league finals in 1983, 1984, 1989 and 1991.

- Selected MVP of the regular season and the NBA finals in 1987. One of only four players so honored.

- Raised more than $9 million for the United Negro College Fund and other charities.

The *Reno* (Nev.) *Gazette-Journal* added this information box on its front page:

HIV and AIDS

Knowing the difference

• **HIV:** The virus that causes AIDS.

• **AIDS:** A result of HIV infection. The AIDS virus attacks the immune system so a person can no longer fight other infections, which become fatal.

• **How AIDS is spread:** AIDS is caused by a virus that spreads through sex (vaginal, oral or anal) and blood-to-blood contact (such as sharing needles or syringes with someone infected with the virus.) HIV cannot spread by ordinary social contact.

Here are excerpts from the press conference (from The Associated Press). The wording is exactly as Johnson expressed it.

First of all, let me say good after—good late afternoon. Because of the HIV virus I have attained, I will have to announce my retirement from the Lakers today.

I want to make clear, first of all, that I do not have the AIDS disease, because I know a lot of you want to know that, but the HIV virus.

My wife is fine, she's negative, so no problem with her.

I plan on going on, living for a long time, bugging you guys like I always have. So you'll see me around. I plan on being with the Lakers and the league—hopefully David (Stern) will have me for a while—and going on with my life. I guess now I get to enjoy some of the other sides of living—that because of the season and the long practices and so on.

I just want to say that I'm going to miss playing. And I will now become a spokesman for the HIV virus because I want people, young people, to realize they can practice safe sex. And, you know, sometimes you're a little naive about it and you think it could never happen to you. You only thought it could happen to, you know, other people and so on and on. And it has happened.

But I'm going to deal with it and my life will go on. And I will be here enjoying the Laker games and all the other NBA games around the country. So life is going to go on for me, and I'm going to be a happy man.

Now, medical questions that you have, you have to direct them to Dr. (Michael) Mellman and he can answer all those questions for you. Anything concerning the Lakers and so on, we have Jerry West (Lakers general manager) here, I'm sure—of course, the league, we have our commissioner, who I want to thank. I want to thank everybody up here, as well as my teammates because they've been behind me all the way.

I want to thank Kareem (Abdul Jabbar) for coming out here. Man, cool, cool. We stood side by side and won a lot of battles. Larry Drew, another good friend of mine who I played with. But the commissioner, David Stern, has been great in support of me and I will go on and hopefully work with the league and help in any way that I can.

I want to thank also Jerry West for all he's done. Dr. (Robert) Kerlan, Dr. Mellman who—he will tell you who my other doctors are that will help me through this—as well as, like I said, my father in a sense, Dr. Jerry Buss for, you know, just drafting me and me being here.

Now, of course, I will miss the battles and the wars and I will miss you guys. But life goes on.

Now any other questions medical-wise you can ask, like I said, Dr. Mellman. Anything with the Lakers, Jerry West. Or anything with the league. I'll take a few questions about myself and my plans.

Stop here and write a list of questions; then compare your questions with the excerpts from the question/answer period following Magic Johnson's press conference (also from The Associated Press):

Q: Can you please describe for us, this has been your life, Michigan State, the Lakers. Emotionally for you right now, knowing this part of your life is over, how do you feel, how do you deal with mortality?

Johnson: Well, I think mortality is—I always wanted to be, after it was over, just live a normal life anyway. And now my life will change, no question about it, but I think I'll still be a part of the game—with working with the Lakers, working with the league—and as I do that then I'm hopefully still on a team. Basketball will still be a part of my life. I told (Michael) Cooper and Kareem, both of them a while ago, that I'll be calling them to play them one-on-one. And we'll have some fun that way. I just won't be a part of the Lakers.

Q: Can you give us a special message for your biggest fans, the kids?

A: Well, no question—for the kids, that's why I am going to be a spokesman for this HIV virus, because I want them to understand that safe sex is the way to go. I think sometimes we think, well, only gay people can get it, only—it's not going to happen to me. And here I am saying that it can happen to anybody. Even me, Magic Johnson, it could happen to.

So yes, I will be going out, telling them. I'll be speaking around the country about this.

Q: When did you know?

A: Well, Wednesday, so that's yesterday.

Q: How did you get HIV? How did you acquire the virus?

A: We'll get into that medically through the doctors, OK.

Q: How do you feel right now?

A: I feel really good. I feel great. A part of my life is gone. But my wife is healthy, that's great. And we're going to go on.

Q: Magic, when did you take the test?

A: Well, I took the test only because of a life insurance policy. And that's what happened. And they kind of thought something was wrong. They didn't know quite what it was, so they—that's why we've been going through all these tests and then, finally yesterday.

Q: What will be people's response regarding your statement on AIDS?

A: Well, I think that everybody will be more careful. That's what I want to preach—and for everybody to understand that they just have to be more careful.

Q: Do you have something to say to your fans?

A: Well, I'm going to miss them. I'm going to miss them. I'm going to miss coming in at 5 o'clock. I'm going to miss saying hello to the security people when I first get there. Then the ushers. Then I get to see most of you about 6 o'clock. Oh, man. "Magic, what about this? What about that? What about the team?" I'll miss that. I'll miss the battles and the wars. But most of all, what I'll miss is the camaraderie that I had with the guys, being one of the fellows.

Q: This is such a tough illness to deal with. Are you scared right now?

A: No. No. You know, what you have to do—it's another challenge, another chapter in my life. It's like being—your back is against the wall. And I think that you just have to come out swinging. And I'm swinging. You know the only thing I can do is have a bright side. If I slip, then it might be over. If I'm down and out—you know, I can't be like that. I never have been, that's why I'm telling you now, today, you know that's why I'm here right now. And that's why I'm going to be a spokesman for the virus, because I want other players to be tested. . . . Just the everyday person, the same thing. Also practice safe sex. The whole thing.

But I am going to go on. I'm going to beat it. And I'm going to have fun, OK? So thank you again, and I'll see you soon.

Questions for others:

Q: What, exactly, has happened to Johnson and how does it affect his life?

Dr. Michael Mellman: Earvin Johnson has been infected with the HIV virus. He does not have AIDS. The HIV virus is something that over years can and does impair an individual's immune system, which is what we all have to defend against other illnesses. So there's no immediate effect on his life other than we have advised him to avoid those activities which can further impair his immune system, which is playing professional basketball.

Q: What is the prognosis for a complete recovery?

A: . . . Some people last a decade or longer before they get ill, some people get ill very quickly. We have Earvin at one point in time in a very healthy state. There is no way to give you a prognosis that is accurate at this point other than to say that he is healthy now, we expect him to remain healthy and we expect to have him around for a long time.

Q: What type of medication is available for AIDS?

Dr. Esther Hayes: In treatment of HIV disease, the medications that we have are very important in prolonging life and making quality of life better at the stage when someone is HIV positive. Dr. Mellman is his physician, but we—so I don't know whether he will be taking any medication immediately. But I can say for someone who is HIV positive like Mr. Johnson, there are a lot of options for treatment and help to prolong life.

Q: Dr. Mellman, has Magic authorized you to discuss how he contracted the AIDS disease?

Dr. Mellman: No. The answer is that I don't believe we know at this point specifically.

Q: Could you speculate on the impact that a player coming forward like Magic Johnson who is saying he has HIV could have on public perception of the disease?

A: I think what we have witnessed today is a courageous act by a very special man. He is not compelled by any legal, um, legal descriptions or legal requirements to disclose what he has disclosed today. He is not a person who is invisible. And because of his presence, because of his potential impact on society with a situation that is not only serious, but for which we are all at risk, I think that he should not only be commended, but held as a modern-day hero. And I hope that we in our activities, and the impact that it has on us, reflect that. This is a very, very special person and a very, very special admission.

3   Cover a speech or press conference on your campus or in your community.

4   Cover a meeting of your local city or county commission, school board, or student government on campus.

COACHING

TIPS

Write an impact, "so what" sentence on top of your story.

Try impact leads; your impact sentence could be a lead.

The more complex the information, the simpler your sentences should be.

Avoid jargon.

Write for your readers, not your sources.

Use quotes that advance the story, not the egos of the bureaucrats.

Use analogies to help readers understand numbers.

Think about graphics before you write your story. Use boxes and charts for numbers and concepts in a proposal and empowerment boxes for information to help the reader.

Government and

Statistical Stories

22

Robert Zausner is walking through a hall in the Pennsylvania capitol complex in Harrisburg when he sees two men changing a light bulb in a ceiling fixture. Zausner stops, observes and takes a few notes. Is this a story for a reporter who covers the legislature?

It is if you have Zausner's eye for news. It is if you want to show taxpayers how their money is spent:

How many state employees does it take to change a light bulb?

Only two.

But they also need a $9,447 machine to reach the socket, at least in part of the east wing of the Capitol complex. . . .

Although the massive building has been opened for more than two years, there was not until recently any way to reach some of the light fixtures, particularly those situated in the middle of the expansive glass ceilings and far away from any walls.

"With the new wing, there isn't anything to lean a ladder against,"

explained Pamela DeSalvo, press secretary for the Department of General Services.

To help shed light, the department bought a "hijacker," a device that is able to straddle obstacles on the ground—like the Senate's granite-encased fountains—and hoist a bulb changer to heights up to 40 feet.

How did the state change those bulbs before it got the machine?

It didn't.

It takes two workers to change a light bulb using the hijacker, one to screw in the bulb and the other to watch.

Robert Zausner, *The Philadelphia Inquirer*

Zausner, a reporter for *The Philadelphia Inquirer,* says he tries to let readers know how government works and how it affects them, especially because their money is involved. "I think you

There are no boring government stories, but there are a lot of boring reporters and editors.

James Steele, investigative reporter,

The Philadelphia Inquirer

**Robert Zausner, reporter,
The Philadelphia Inquirer**
Courtesy of Robert Zausner

have to keep your eyes open on this kind of beat. Some of the stuff that happens around here is unbelievable.

"Every Monday I ride the elevator to the fourth floor of the Senate offices and just visit people. Usually by the time I hit the ground floor again, I've got something. I think you need to do the legwork to know what's really going on. If you write from a press release, you may have the story, but you won't have more than a surface understanding of something."

Stories about government often involve money and statistics. Although these are hard stories to write, Zausner says he tries to make his stories readable by using simple terms that people can understand. "You have to make them read it," he says. "Spit it back in simple terms that people can understand. It's safer to use the bureaucrats' terminology. It's easy. It's lazy. Someone introduces a bill, you get three quotes, and you have a story. But if you just regurgitate the stuff in the bureaucratic language, you lose everyone."

Another way of making stories readable and relevant is to focus on the people affected, as in this one about the impact of Gov. Robert Casey's order to fire 2,450 state employees:

> For the last 20 years, Mark Holmes has worked for the state. He has enjoyed his $45,000-a-year job as a telecommunications expert and the other major benefit that came with government employment—security.
>
> But now Holmes is wondering how he will support his wife and nine children, how he will keep his oldest in college. He is pondering food stamps. He thinks about the sudden predicament he finds himself in at the age of 43. And then, offering an apology, he starts to cry.
>
> Holmes is one of the 2,450 people behind the numbers. He will be out of work by month's end under a dismissal plan being put into effect to reduce a deficit approaching $1 billion. The firings, ordered by Gov. Casey, are estimated to save $154 million this fiscal year.
>
> Robert Zausner, *The Philadelphia Inquirer*

Zausner also believes in interpreting an issue for readers. Consider this story with an impact lead about the Pennsylvania governor's proposed budget cuts:

It's not that Gov. Casey is a kill-joy, but if he gets his way it will cost more in Pennsylvania to go to a state museum or enjoy a Sunday picnic. Even the price of driving around with a cutesy license plate will go up.

It will cost more to be born, and more to die.

For buried amid the big news of Casey's proposed budget, with its whopping business and cigarette taxes, is the governor's plan to raise an extra $80.1 million in new and increased fees for seemingly everything.

Boating and billboards, state museums and learners' permits, camping and coal mining would all be affected. Even state employees, who are already being hit with firings and pay cuts, would have to start paying $5 biweekly for their parking spots at the Capitol.

Casey officials made little noise about the proposed fee increases on Wednesday, when they presented the budget for fiscal 1992, which begins July 1.

Robert Zausner, *The Philadelphia Inquirer*

The reporter has a responsibility to interpret government for the reader, Zausner says. "If a guy announces that he's introducing a bill, but he's only trying to score some political points and you know the bill is not going anywhere, you have to say that. If you write that story and you don't say what he really wants, you are doing people a disservice. You'd be better off not to write it. I don't think it's editorializing. I think it's serving the reader."

Reporting Tips

Zausner's advice is not limited to coverage of state government. His emphasis on making government relevant to readers applies as well to stories about local government, school districts and campus administrations.

Although much government news may come from press releases and meetings, you should also try to find stories that reveal how the government operates or fails to operate in the interests of citizens. Don't just rely on officials to give you news; find it yourself.

Here are some basic tips for covering local government, some of which were mentioned in Chapter 19:

Human interest: Make government relevant to readers by finding people who are affected by the actions of government agencies.

Bulletin boards: Check them for job offerings and other announcements that could result in stories.

Memos and letters to and from city officials: Check with the city clerk or secretaries for access to files about any issue involving public funds. Most of these—except for personnel and labor matters—are public record.

Planning commission: Check agendas for meetings, and develop sources in planning offices. Seek information not only about future plans but also about the past. Some great stories can result from plans gone awry.

Consultants: Check who gets consulting contracts and fees, and investigate previous studies on the same subject. Sometimes government agencies hire consultants to write studies on subjects that have already been studied frequently.

Zoning meetings: They can be full of human interest. People care about what is going up or down in their neighborhood.

Legal notices: Check them for bids and other notices. Government agencies must advertise for any major purchases. Check with disgruntled bidders for major contracts. Many good stories lurk behind these seemingly boring subjects.

Audits: Read them carefully. They can reveal misuse of public funds.

Union leaders: Cultivate heads of unions in school districts and cities as sources. They know what is going on behind the scenes.

Non-officials: Talk to the people who do the work. In school districts, get into the schools and write about what teachers and students are doing. In cities, talk to people on the job. Spend some time learning about what they do, how they do it and whether they do it. Many good stories can result from finding out how lower level employees work in government.

The system: Learn how it works. Are officials in your town following the laws? If you don't know how government is supposed to operate, you won't be able to find out if it is working properly.

Records: Check expense accounts, purchasing vouchers and other records pertaining to issues or officials you are covering.

Offices: Check all the offices in your government building, and find out what kind of work the people in them do. For example, do you know the function of every office in your campus administration building? You could find features or great news stories just by checking what the people in these offices do.

Graphics

Before you write your story, think not about what you can put in it; think about what you can pull out of it, especially when you are writing stories with statistics. Use highlights boxes, facts boxes and charts to break out key concepts of a proposal or budget. Then you don't need to clutter the story with the same information. Consider empowerment boxes: information that tells readers what the story means to them and what they can do. These boxes should contain information about where they can call for help, more information or other facts that would be useful. Once you have decided what can be displayed visually, you can present the remaining information verbally. Here's an empowerment box from the *Reno* (Nev.) *Gazette-Journal* that accompanied a story about overdue parking tickets. The city adopted late fees that would add $30 to tickets not paid within a month.

TO PAY

• Pay at the city clerk's cashier office, using cash, check or Visa or Mastercard.

TO PROTEST

• Make an appointment. The hearing officer is setting aside time in Room 204 at City Hall. Call 334-2293.

• Hearing times are: From 5–8 p.m. on Nov. 4 and Nov. 6; 1–4 p.m. on Nov. 8; 5–8 p.m. on Nov. 13 and Nov. 14.

Writing Tips

Presuming you have found good stories, how can you make them readable?

One way is to avoid jargon, stilted or technical words and phrases that officials use but readers don't. Writing coaches call this artificial language "journalese," long words or phrases instead of short ones that would be clearer. Examples: *medication* for *medicine, restructuring* for *changing, funds* for *money.* When you need a loan from a friend, do you ask to borrow "funds"?

"Reading journalese is like having a series of small strokes," says Jack Cappon, writing coach for The Associated Press. "Unless you start writing the way your neighbors talk, you're not going to go anywhere."

Cliches are another common form of journalese in government stories. Journalists love to use words related to heat and cold: "heated debate," "hotly contested," "blasted," "chilling effect," "cooling-off period." In this example, the reporter strained the lead by picking a holiday that had nothing to do with the story just so she could use these "heated" terms:

The Fourth of July is four months away, but insults and accusations exploded like fireworks at the tumultuous Board of Supervisors meeting yesterday.	The firecracker was Republican Supervisor John Hanson, who blasted his colleagues by calling them "crooks."

Here are some other tips:

Use short, simple sentences: The more complex the information, the simpler and shorter the sentences should be:

Complex	**Simpler**
The City Commission last night approved a resolution to authorize the city staff to apply for funding through the systems enhancement program of the state Department of Transportation for a $3.6 million project for the expansion of U.S. Highway 77 from two to four lanes for 2.2 miles between Interstate 70 and Kansas Highway 18.	The City Commission last night agreed to apply for $3.6 million from the state Department of Transportation to expand a portion of U.S. Highway 77 from two to four lanes. The project would widen the highway for 2.2 miles between Interstate 70 and Kansas Highway 18.

Avoid clause leads: Use subject-verb-object order, which is the way you normally speak. If you were telling a friend about the government's efforts to save the school lunch program, would you say, "Arguing that the government food purchases support farm prices while feeding youngsters, the administration has taken its fight to save the school lunch program to the nation's farmers"?

Keep the subject and verb close together: Long clauses and phrases before the verb make it hard for the reader to remember what the subject is—who said or did what:

Complex	**Simpler**
Rather than having government inspectors sweep through businesses, finding violations and imposing fines, in Maine, officials at the federal Occupational Safety and Health Administration, in an effort to improve work conditions and save the government money, are urging employers to identify health and safety problems and then to work with the agency to correct them.	A federal agency is urging employers in Maine to find and correct health and safety problems in their businesses instead of having government inspectors seek violations and impose fines. The move is an attempt by the federal Occupational Safety and Health Administration to improve work conditions in businesses and save the government money.

Vary the pace: Avoid writing huge blocks of complicated concepts and complex sentences. In the following story about problems with air traffic control, the first paragraph is cumbersome. The next one is even more dense—that is, if the reader gets that far. For simplicity and clarity, the long sentences could be broken into sentences of varying lengths.

For thousands of travelers who fly in and out of the three major New York airports every day, the air traffic control system is a vital but unknown reality—heavily reliant on technology and on controllers who say they are underpaid and overworked, and it is a system burdened with 1.74 million flights last year, a volume undreamed of a generation ago.

Despite personnel shortages, wobbly morale, budget problems and modernization delays—and the recent crash of a Colombian jetliner approaching Kennedy International Airport—the almost unanimous view of government and airline officials, controllers and other experts is that the region's air traffic control system is essentially safe.

The New York Times

Focus on a person to explain impact: The way an issue affects one person makes it clear to many. That's the concept of *The Wall Street Journal's* formula, and it can be used effectively in government stories. Lead with an anecdote about a person, then go from the specific to the general. It's the "one of many" technique.

Linda Green paid $42,000 in 1982 for a house on a half-acre lot in Fontana, banking on the equity that would build over the years.

But if Fontana's new general plan is approved, Green is fearful her property may be worth no more than the day she bought it.

The proposed plan would change the zoning on her half-acre so no additional homes could be built on it, making the site less attractive to buyers.

Green is not alone in her fears. She was among several landowners complaining Monday that the revised general plan—a blueprint for Fontana's growth—will put their properties in less profitable zoning areas.

"I bought my land as an investment. If they zone it down, I will lose my money, and I worked hard to put my money into it," Green told the planning commission during the first public hearing on the new 20-year plan.

More than 130 people attended the hearing.

Tony Saavedra, *The* (San Bernardino, Calif.) *Sun*

Use an impact lead or explain impact in the story: Tell how the reader will be affected by a bureaucratic action or proposal.

A $10,000 car would cost $25 more in taxes, a $40 power saw an extra dime and a $4 six-pack of imported beer a penny extra in Rockford if Alderman Ernst Shafer, R-3rd, gets his way.

Shafer wants Rockford to join the push in Springfield for a 0.25 percent increase in the sales tax. Locally the sales tax would rise from 6.25 to 6.5 percent under the proposal.

Brian Leaf, *Rockford* (Ill.) *Register Star*

Avoid boring quotes: You don't have to quote an official to prove you talked to her or him. If you can express the official's point better in your own words, do so. You could say that park repairs included cutting trees, removing sand, adding soil for a seed bed and repairing a shelter. But one reporter quoted an official instead:

> "The total project involved tree take-downs, removal of some of the sand and replacement with some soil that would actually provide a seed bed," he said. "We also had to make some repairs on a shelter."

Use conversational style: Write the story as though you were having a conversation with a friend. Here is how one reporter used the conversational style in the lead of a government story:

> How'd you like an airport for a neighbor? Or maybe a landfill or an incinerator?
>
> Probably about as much as government officials like trying to find a site for these things.
>
> But what if you could negotiate noise insulation for your airport-area home? Or an agreement requiring the incinerator to douse its fires if it didn't burn hot enough to eliminate most pollutants?
>
> Those alternatives were offered Wednesday to a roomful of Twin Cities area public officials frustrated by their protracted and often doomed efforts to make people accept controversial facilities they don't want.
>
> In an area where officials are looking for places for new landfills, a new airport, light-rail transit routes and other public works projects, the Metropolitan Council sponsored yesterday's conference in an effort to see if there's a better way.
>
> There is, they were told by a specialist in how to make the risks of such facilities more acceptable to their neighbors.
>
> Steve Brandt, *The* (Minneapolis) *Star Tribune*

Use lists: Use them in the middle or at the end of the story, especially to explain key points of an issue. Lists are particularly helpful in stories with numbers or explanations of proposals.

Avoid the city-dump syndrome: Be selective. Use only quotes and facts that you need. Don't dump your notebook into the story.

Use the kiss-off technique: If you have more than three speakers, block the comments from each one, and then do not use the sources again unless you reintroduce them. The reader can't remember all the officials by second reference only.

Statistical Stories

Numbers can be numbing for readers. But statistics are the basis of many of the stories you will write, such as campus or community crime reports, enrollment stories, monthly or annual weather reports, and budget stories.

Whenever you are writing about numbers, you must analyze what they mean. Most reports list numbers in comparison to a previous year or time frame. Always put numbers in perspective in two ways:

• Explain change. Do the numbers show an increase or decrease from a previous period?

• State the significance. What do the numbers mean, and why are they important? Explain what is interesting or important about these statistics in a way that will make readers care.

All of the previous writing tips apply to stories with numbers. But here are a few more that are particularly important for statistical stories:

Use charts and graphs: Try to get the numbers out of your story. You need to mention some of them, but always consider whether a chart or graphic could convey the information better.

Use analogies: Whenever you are referring to large numbers, comparisons with something familiar to readers are especially helpful. This is an analogy from a story about pollution in Alabama's rivers:

> Each minute, about 30 million gallons of Alabama river water, or the equivalent of what it would take to fill 60 Olympic-sized swimming pools, flush into Mobile Bay, washing over oyster beds in the northern part of the bay closed to harvesting.
>
> Dan Morse, *The* (Montgomery) *Alabama Journal*

In this analogy, the writer compares the concept behind the federal deficit to the kind of credit most readers would understand:

> Picture a family hooked on credit cards living beyond its means.
>
> New clothes? Charge it. More medicine? Charge it. A night on the town? Charge it.
>
> Pretty soon the situation is out of hand. The parents have to borrow money just to pay the monthly interest. The balance owed on their credit cards keeps rising, faster and faster.
>
> Some restraint is attempted, but results are mixed. The parents can't stop whipping out the plastic.
>
> That is the situation of the federal government as it closes the borrow-and-spend decade of the 1980s.
>
> It took two centuries for the government's debt to reach $1 trillion, but only four years—from 1982 to 1986—for it to balloon to $2 trillion.
>
> Now the Treasury Department says the government cannot operate past Nov. 8 if Congress does not raise the limit on the government's debt to nearly $3 trillion. That's $3,000,000,000,000.
>
> Charles Green, *The Philadelphia Inquirer*

Round off numbers: In the previous example, the writer included all the zeroes in $3 trillion for emphasis. But in most cases it is better to round off numbers, for instance to $3 million or $3.5 million instead of $3,499,590. Make it easy for the reader to grasp large numbers.

Avoid bunching numbers in one paragraph: Spread numbers out over a few paragraphs, rather than glutting one sentence or paragraph with them. For example:

A survey by the American Bar Association has found an "astonishing rise" in reported alcohol consumption by lawyers—with 13 percent of them admitting to having six more drinks a day.

That compares with less than one-half of 1 percent of lawyers who said they drank that much in the last survey, in 1984.

Women lawyers reported even greater dissatisfaction and alcohol consumption than men. Twenty percent of the women lawyers surveyed reported having six more drinks per day, compared with 11 percent of the men.

The findings link the apparent rise in drinking by lawyers to greater dissatisfaction and stress among them.

The Associated Press

Interpret numbers: Show the impact on readers in terms they can understand.

A 10-year analysis of enrollment patterns at Kansas University and five other state universities revealed two dating tips for college students:

- Men hoping to improve dating prospects might consider attending Emporia State University, where 60 percent of students are women.

- Women interested in more dating opportunities should look to Kansas State University, the only state university in the area with more men than women.

Tim Carpenter, *Lawrence* (Kan.) *Journal-World*

Use storytelling techniques: Even statistical stories can lend themselves to storytelling. In this example, the writer uses an anecdotal-narrative approach to a story about statistics:

In the early morning of Jan. 25, a woman left a friend's Northwest Portland house and began walking home. As she neared Northwest Flanders Street and 21st Avenue about 3:30 a.m., a man grabbed her arm, forced her to the ground and threatened her with a handgun. Then he raped her.

She was one of 32 persons who told Portland police they were raped in the first four weeks of January. Police have not yet tallied the reports from the last five days of the month. But even so, the count already ex- ceeds the 20 rapes that were reported for January 1990. In Oregon, rape is defined as forcible sexual inter- course.

That increase bears out a trend that rape victim advocates and law enforcement officials began seeing last year: The number of reported sexual assaults in Portland is on a slight rise. Police statistics show 427 rapes in 1990, compared with 412 in 1989, or a 4 percent increase, said Steve Beedle, a public safety analyst for Portland police.

Diane Dulken, *The* (Portland) *Oregonian*

Weather Stories

People enjoy reading about the weather. Oddly enough, even though they know if it has rained or snowed, they like reading the next day about the amount that fell.

Although weather stories may have many human interest angles, they always include some statistics. Here are a few other elements you should include in weather stories:

Forecast: Always include the forecast for the next day or for an extended period, especially when you are writing about floods, droughts, or hot or cold spells.

Unusual angles: Look for any unusual weather patterns as an angle for your story. If the weather is unusual, include explanations from weather forecasters.

Human interest: Tell how people are coping with the weather if it is very unusual. Use the focus-on-a-person technique for a weather feature.

Warnings: Explain how extremely hot or cold weather affects people, especially old people. For example, when the weather is over 100 degrees, older people may suffer from heat-related illnesses. Tell how to cope with or prevent problems. Also include warnings about keeping animals safe in extremely hot or cold weather. Include any road or traffic information, such as road or bridge closings and alternate routes.

Records: Explain if the weather has broken any records or come near to breaking records, especially if you are doing a roundup of statistics or a story about unusual weather. Even if no records have been broken, put the weather statistics in perspective by comparing them to other months or years.

Terms: Check your *Associated Press Stylebook* for definitions of weather terms. If you use such words as *blizzard,* or *hurricane,* define them by explaining how high the winds must be. In any flood story, explain what the flood stages of a river are and how far above or below flood stage the river is.

Here is a typical statistical roundup weather story. Note the forecast, explanations of unusual weather and perspective for statistics.

Rainfall total is inching to record

The unseasonable Pacific storm that washed across the West Coast the past couple of days dropped enough rain Monday to make this the ninth-wettest rainfall season in 120 years of official record keeping in San Jose.

By 4 p.m. Monday, 21.94 inches of rain—about 150 percent of normal—had fallen at San Jose Civic Center since last July 1.

The storm also left everyone wondering why the weather seems to be ignoring the calendar.

Well, first some good news: Skies are supposed to start clearing today, forecasters say. The downside: Rain may return later in the week.

As for why winter seems to be with us still, no one can pin down an exact reason.

Forecasters say the atmospheric high pressure that normally starts building off the coast in late spring to block weather systems, shunting them to the Pacific Northwest, hasn't developed fully yet. And the jet stream that guides storms across the Pacific is taking a straight shot at California.

However, no one's going beyond that in trying to explain the weather, other than to say it's not really that unusual.

"The whole pattern has slowed up, and winter has progressed into May," said meteorologist Jeff Millard at the National Weather Service center in Monterey. "The high will build; it will just take a little longer."

With the jet stream coming out of the Pacific instead of the Gulf of Alaska, tropical moisture is flowing into California from south of the Hawaiian Islands, Millard said. The jet stream is expected to bring another storm Friday, but it won't be as strong, he said.

Some records have been set this year, said Robyn Joseph, who monitors the official weather station at the San Jose Office of Emergency Services at Civic Center. The all-time record—30.30 inches in 1889–'90—seems safe, however.

It rained a record 24 of 31 days in January, and the 8.66 inches measured for that month was exceeded only twice before. In March, another month of floods, we had 16 days of rain, short of the record 18. The 6.85 inches of rain that month made it the second-wettest March on record.

Despite the month's start, the odds for a wet May are slim. The average rainfall for the month is only 0.26 inches, Joseph said.

Frank Sweeney, *San Jose* (Calif.) *Mercury News*

Budget Stories

Readers want to know how the government spends money—their money. To tell them, first you need to understand the budget process of the agency you cover. Then you need to make it relevant to readers.

Budget planning starts several months before the budget is approved. Learn how to interpret the proposed budget by asking a financial officer of the city, school or agency to explain it to you before the budget is released. If he or she can't brief you on this year's proposal, use last year's budget to learn the system. In most cases, officials will be willing to cooperate, because they want you to present the facts accurately.

Basically, budgets have two sections:

Revenues: The income, usually derived from taxes—primarily property taxes in municipalities. But there also are sales taxes, income taxes and fees. Look for clues about how the revenue will be raised. Will property taxes increase? If you are covering a university budget, will tuition be increased? Find out how the revenue source will affect your readers.

Expenditures: Where most of the money will be spent. Will some departments be increasing expenses more than others, such as police or fire departments? If so, why? Will salaries be increased or more people be hired? How do the expenditures for this year compare with those of the past few years?

Generally, budgets include figures from the previous year or past few years. Look for major increases and decreases in revenues and expenditures.

Before a government agency can adopt a budget, it must conduct public hearings, where the public can comment about the budget. If the budget proposal is at the hearing stage, be sure to include the dates of the hearings in your story. Taxpayers often want to attend to protest cutbacks or request money for programs they support.

Budget and Tax Terms

If you want to explain budgets, you must know what these terms mean:

Assessments and property taxes: Common in municipal budgets, where taxes are based on real estate. Homeowners pay taxes based on an assessment, or estimated value, of their property. This value is determined by a city property appraiser based on a number of factors: size of the property, number of bedrooms, construction and so on. For example, suppose you decide to buy a condominium or a house selling for $80,000. That is its "market value," the price it sells for on the market. Some communities base their tax on the full market value, but most use only a percentage of the total value. The property is given an "assessed value," a value for tax purposes. If your community bases its tax on half the market value, your house would be assessed for $40,000. Your annual property taxes equal some percentage of the assessed value.

Capital budget: Money used to pay for major improvements, such as the construction of highways or new buildings. Capital is often raised by selling bonds, and people who buy the bonds receive interest. The government then uses the money and repays the bonds, plus interest, over a period of years in what is called "debt service." The process is much like buying a house: The bank lends you money; you live in the house and repay the loan plus interest on a long-term basis, often over 30 years.

Deficit: When government spends more money than it receives. Most municipalities and states require a balanced budget: The expenses must be the same as the income. The difference between the expenditures and the income is the deficit, or debt.

Fiscal year: Year in which budgeted funds will be spent. In government, the budget term often starts on July 1 and goes to June 30, instead of the calendar year beginning in January. So if you use a fiscal year, give the dates: "in this fiscal year, which starts July 1." Or if you are writing about when the money will run out: "in this fiscal year, which ends June 30."

Mill: Unit equal to $1 for every $1,000 that a house is assessed (or 0.1 cent for each $1 of assessed valuation). Local school and city taxes are based on mills. Explain the impact of these taxes clearly. If the school tax rate is 25 mills, your story should say, "The tax rate is 25 mills, which equals $25 for every $1,000 of assessed property valuation." Or you could insert a definition: "A mill equals $1 for every $1,000 of assessed value on a property." Then give an example: "Under this tax rate, a homeowner whose property is valued at $40,000 (multiplied by 0.025) would pay $1,000 in school taxes." Try to avoid using the term *mills;* just say the tax rate will be $25 for every $1,000 of assessed property value. Follow with a specific example so residents can figure out how much their tax will be.

Operating budget: Money used to provide services (police, fire, garbage removal and so on) and to pay for the operation of government. Most of the money for this budget comes from taxes.

Other taxes: Wage tax, income tax and sales tax. Cities and states often charge these additional taxes. Check when you write your budget stories to determine whether they will be increased or decreased. If they will stay the same, say so.

Reappraisal: State or local decision to re-evaluate properties in the community, usually to increase their values. This action almost always generates good stories because it affects people dramatically. For example, Kansas had not reappraised properties for 20 years. When the state decided to do it, property values soared and a tax revolt resulted. People who had been paying $200 in taxes on their homes suddenly were paying $1,000. A similar situation occurred in Atlanta:

A groundswell of protest over the mass reappraisal of Atlanta and Fulton County property is threatening to become a wholesale tax revolt.

Thousands of homeowners have turned out at meetings throughout the city and county to express displeasure with their new assessments, in some cases more than double last year's.

At the South Fulton County Annex, more than one thousand people gathered Monday to talk about fighting the assessments.

"My assessment went up 190 percent and I'll gladly sell my home to the county for what they think it's worth," said Mitch Skandalakis, a leader of the Task Force for Good Government, as the crowd roared.

Mark Sherman, *Atlanta Constitution*

Writing Techniques

Impact is crucial in budget stories. So are graphics. A chart or list of key numbers can make a story more presentable. Also get reactions from city officials, residents at public hearings or the people most affected by budget cuts. If you are writing about university budgets, get reactions from administrators, students, professors and the officials whose departments will be affected most.

Here are some key points to include in a budget story, not necessarily in this order:

• Total amount of the budget (rounded off when possible: $44.6 million instead of $44,552,379; most budgets are supposed to be balanced, so the figure applies to both revenues and expenditures)

• Amount of increase or decrease

• Tax or tuition levy, or how funds will be raised (impact on reader, comparison to current tax)

• Major expenditures (major increases and decreases in department funds)

• Consequences (impact on the government or agency—cuts in personnel, services, and so on)

• Historical comparisons (how budget compares to previous year and past few years)

• Reactions from officials and people affected by increases or decreases

• Definitions and explanations of technical terms

Here is an example of the kind of budget story you should avoid writing. It is flooded with statistics but doesn't clarify how the budget will affect the reader.

The recommended 1997 Rockville city budget would require a 2.56-mill property tax increase.

City Manager Joan Weinman recommended to Rockville City Commission a budget of $55,672,309, which would require a local levy of 42.59 mills. Last year's budget of $50,322,409 required a levy of 42.03 mills.

A mill is $1 of tax for every $1,000 of assessed property valuation.

Weinman is recommending a 3 percent across-the-board salary increase for city employees. She is also recommending an addition of five police officers to the public safety department.

Here is the lead on another budget story, but this one explains the impact on homeowners:

HACKENSACK, N.J.—A $39.2 million budget that offers residents their first property-tax break in 20 years has been adopted by the City Council.

The budget, which includes $4 million in new state aid, was approved by a 4-1 vote following a public hearing Monday. No residents commented.

Despite a 6 percent increase in spending, the boost in state aid means that total property taxes for the owner of a home assessed at $180,000, the borough average, will drop $54 a year.

Tom Topousis, *The* (Hackensack, N.J.) *Record*

Here is another way of explaining impact in a lead that is not cluttered with statistics:

Pinellas School Superintendent Howard Hinesley has proposed a list of budget cuts for the next school year that will mean fewer textbooks, fewer teachers and fewer administrators if School Board members approve them next Wednesday.

Patty Curtin Jones, *St. Petersburg* (Fla.) *Times*

The next story was a sidebar, but it contains the kind of information that should be included in a story about a city budget—the effect on residents:

Mayor Goode said last night that under his budget plan one of two things was certain—death or taxes. He said city residents needed to pay new and increased taxes to avert the fiscal demise of the city.

Goode proposed raising an additional $142 million for next year's budget by increasing the wage, net-profits and property taxes and by

adding a 1 percent city sales tax to the state's 6 percent sales tax.

The Goode administration estimated that for someone earning $25,000 a year, the wage tax increases—to 5.36 percent—would add $100 to his or her current tax payment of $1,240.

The real estate tax increase of 2 mills, from the current 37.45 mills of assessed value, would add $32 to the current tax bill of $1,322 paid by the owner of a home with a market value of $50,000.

Dianne E. Reed, the executive director of the local chapter of the Pennsylvania Economy League, estimated that the average citizen would pay $80 more a year if the local sales tax were approved.

Matthew Purdy, *The Philadelphia Inquirer*

Don't forget that budgets affect people. So when you are writing advances and reaction stories, you can use feature techniques. Here is an example of an anecdotal-narrative approach to an advance on the city budget:

It was 8:05 on a Monday in August, Rosemary Farnon remembers, when her husband, Tony, called the police to report that their rowhouse in the Juniata Park section had been ransacked.

Amid a shambles of overturned furniture, scattered papers and food taken from the fridge, the Farnons nervously and angrily waited nearly five hours before an officer appeared. He explained apologetically that the local police district had no cops to spare.

Theirs is one story, from one neighborhood, but it typifies what is happening across Philadelphia:

Taxes are up and services are down—and residents are unhappy about it.

So Rosemary Farnon and hundreds of thousands of taxpayers will be listening closely Thursday when Mayor Goode proposes the budget for the coming fiscal year, which begins July 1.

Dan Myers and Idris M. Diaz,
The Philadelphia Inquirer

University budget stories can use the same techniques. Here is a first-day budget story stressing the impact on students and reaction. Comparative statistics were given in graphic form (see Exhibit 22-1).

LONG BEACH, Calif.—Despite an outcry from students, California State University on Wednesday increased academic fees 20 percent, to $936 a year.

Fees at all 20 campuses could climb even higher if the state budget crisis, which has left CSU with a $402.5 million shortfall, worsens this spring, Chancellor Ellis E. McCune warned the Board of Trustees.

Students will not only pay more in the fall, they will get less. They will have fewer professors to teach them, a smaller array of courses from which to choose, and bigger classes to attend.

Meeting at Cal State Long Beach, the trustees reduced the budget from $2.1 million to $1.65 million and called for:

- Eliminating 420 faculty positions and leaving vacant an additional 330.

- Not replacing 229 professors when they go on sabbatical.

- Reducing other staff by 856 positions.

"None of these is a happy solution," McCune said.

Steven Silberman,
The Orange County (Calif.) *Register*

Exhibit 22-1

Graphics accompanying a story on a university's budget

The Orange County
(Calif.) *Register*

Student fee comparison

Tuition and miscellaneous costs for a resident undergraduate at
California State University and comparable public universities, 1990-91

	Total
Rutgers, NJ	$3,281
Virginia Polytechnic Inst.	2,840
Cleveland State U.	2,397
U. of Maryland, Baltimore	2,390
Illinois State U.	2,272
U. of Wisconsin, Milwaukee	2,258
Georgia State U.	1,812
Arizona State U.	1,640
SUNY, Albany	1,485
U. of Colorado, Denver	1,458
U. of Nevada, Reno	1,380
N. Carolina State U.	1,109
CSU	911

20% increase

Sources:
California State
University and
California
Postsecondary
Education
Commission

CSU academic fees

Annual fee for full-time undergraduates who are state
residents. Individual campuses might add some charges.

Source: California
State University

'79-'80	'80-'81	'81-'82	'82-'83	'83-'84	'84-'85	'85-'86	'86-'87	'87-'88	'88-'89	'89-'90	'90-'91	'91-'92
$144	$160	$252	$430	$612	$573	$573	$573	$630	$684	$708	$780	$936

The Orange County Register

Exercises   **1**   Figure your taxes using the following method:

a   You own a home that is worth $100,000 on the market. The city appraises residential property for tax purposes at 11.5 percent of its market value. What is the assessed value of your property?

b   Using your assessed value as calculated in **a,** figure your tax rate as follows:

1   Write your assessed value:

2   Divide the assessed value by 1,000, because a mill is $1 tax on every $1,000 of assessed property value. Write that figure:

3   The tax levy in your community is 125 mills. Multiply the amount in **2** times the tax levy to figure your tax bill. Write the result.

c   Last year your taxes were $1,250. Using the answer from **3** for this year's taxes, figure your tax percentage increase.

d   The city had a tax rate of 125 mills last year and is raising it to 137.5 mills this year. What is the percentage increase?

2   **Your dream home:** Envision the home you would like to own. How much will it cost? If you want a swimming pool, sauna and other amenities, make sure you figure them into the price along with the land value in your community or wherever you want to live. When you figure the selling price, that's the market value.

Now figure your taxes. Your community assesses property at 30 percent of its market value for tax purposes. The tax rate for city and schools combined will be 75 mills. How much will you pay in taxes?

3   **Statistics:** Analyze the following information, and write a story about which sandwiches are healthiest (lowest in fat and sodium). These statistics are based on a study by the Center for Science in the Public Interest, a consumer, nonprofit nutrition organization. The organization analyzed 12 sandwiches for fat, saturated fat and sodium. Daily limits of fat recommended by the Food and Drug Administration for adults are 65 grams of total fat, 20 grams of saturated fat and 2,400 milligrams of sodium.

Turkey with mustard: 6 grams fat, 2 grams saturated fat, 1,407 milligrams sodium

Roast beef with mustard: 12 grams fat, 4 grams saturated fat, 993 milligrams sodium

Chicken salad: 32 grams fat, 6 grams saturated fat, 1,136 milligrams sodium

Corned beef with mustard: 20 grams fat, 8 grams saturated fat, 1,924 milligrams sodium

Tuna salad: 43 grams fat, 8 grams saturated fat, 1,319 milligrams sodium

Ham with mustard: 27 grams fat, 10 grams saturated fat, 2,344 milligrams sodium

Egg salad: 31 grams fat, 10 grams saturated fat, 1,110 milligrams sodium

Turkey club: 34 grams fat, 10 grams saturated fat, 1,843 milligrams sodium

Bacon, lettuce and tomato: 37 grams fat, 12 grams saturated fat, 1,555 milligrams sodium

Vegetarian (cucumbers, sprouts, avocado and cheese): 40 grams fat, 14 grams saturated fat, 1,276 milligrams sodium

Grilled cheese: 33 grams fat, 17 grams saturated fat, 1,543 milligrams sodium

Reuben: 50 grams fat, 20 grams saturated fat, 3,268 milligrams sodium

Background: Interview with Jane Hurley, nutritionist for the center. She analyzed 170 sandwiches from Washington, New York, Los Angeles and Chicago delicatessens. "People tend to think of a sandwich as just a bite to eat, but many shops are giving you a dinner's worth of fat and calories. Tuna itself is fat free, but in sandwiches, it's drowning in one-third cup of mayonnaise. That's the equivalent of three McDonald's Quarter Pounders, fat-wise."

The center also did studies showing fat in Mexican, Italian and Chinese food. One of its most controversial studies showed that one bag of popcorn popped in coconut oil, as it was served in movie theaters, had as much saturated fat as six Big Macs.

4 Jargon and journalese: Identify the cliches and journalese in this paragraph:

Affirmative action has become a political football causing a firestorm of protest among lawmakers in various parts of the country. In California there have been cries of protest, heated debate and widespread resistance to affirmative action. The president remains cautiously optimistic that measures to retain affirmative action will succeed, but he is keeping a low profile about the matter because the issue has become a hot potato. The last election sent a very clear message to politicians that any efforts to support affirmative action would have a chilling effect on their political futures. The worst-case scenario for the president is if California passes laws abolishing affirmative action, but he has fired a warning shot to Congress and has vowed to take a hard line and veto any attempts to ban affirmative action measures at the federal level.

5 Get a copy of portions of your most recent campus administration budget or a budget for some department. Each student may choose a different department. The budget should list figures for the previous year. Discuss story ideas based on major increases or decreases in the budget, particularly emphasizing any impact on students, faculty or staff. Check clips from the previous year when this budget was passed, and write a follow-up story on the impact of budget cuts or increases.

COACHING

Use graphic reporting skills. Gather enough detail and specifics so you could draw a diagram or write a chronology of the crime as though you were designing a graphic.

Role-play: Ask yourself what you would want to know if you were affected by this crime.

Use the tell-a-friend technique.

Avoid the jargon of police or other legal authorities. If you don't understand a term, chances are the reader may not know it either.

Always include the background of the case, no matter how many days a police story or trial continues. Never take it for granted that the reader has read previous stories.

Be careful. Double-check your accuracy, and make sure you don't convict someone of a crime before a judge or jury does.

Crime and Punishment

23

The police beat, which often includes the fire department, is considered an entry-level job. Most reporters move on to other beats after a few years of covering crime stories. Edna Buchanan did not. She covered the police beat at *The Miami Herald* for more than 20 years before resigning to write books. But while she was at *The Herald,* she turned police reporting into an art form. The most famous police reporter in the United States, Buchanan won the Pulitzer Prize for a collection of her stories in 1986.

A soft-spoken woman, she writes with a strong punch. One Pulitzer Prize juror said, "She writes drop-dead sentences for drop-dead victims. She is never dull." Consider:

> There was music and sunlight as the paddle wheeler Dixie Bell churned north on Indian Creek Thursday. The water shimmered and the wind was brisk. And then the passengers noticed that the people in the next boat were dead.

Buchanan is most famous for the lead she wrote on a story about a man who shoved his way to the front of a line at a fried chicken restaurant. The counter clerk told the man to go to the end of the line and wait his turn. He did. But when he reached the head of the line again, the restaurant had run out of fried chicken. He battered the clerk fiercely, and he was shot fatally by a guard in the restaurant. Her lead: "Gary Robinson died hungry."

I have never understood young reporters who considered covering the cops the least desirable beat. The police beat is all about people, what makes them tick, what makes them become heroes or homicidal maniacs. It has it all: greed, sex, violence, comedy and tragedy.

Edna Buchanan, former police reporter, *The Miami Herald*

"In truth, Edna Buchanan doesn't write about cops. She writes about people," *Herald* editors wrote in the Pulitzer entry. Buchanan is the first to admit that: "You learn more about people on the police beat than any other beat," she said in a speech at a convention of investigative reporters.

She said she has reported more than 5,000 violent deaths. How does she keep from getting upset by them and burned out on the job? "The thing that keeps you going is that you realize you can make things better. You may be affected like everyone else by a terrible tragedy, but you're in a position to do something about it. That's the real joy of this job. We can be catalysts for change. We can bring about justice. Sometimes we are all the victim has got. Police stories do make a difference.

"You've got to be accurate and fair and very, very careful, particularly in crime reporting. A news story mentioning somebody's name can ruin their lives or come back to haunt them 25 years later. It is there in black and white on file. It's like a police record; you never outlive it. You can do terrible damage. So you knock on one more door, ask one more question, make one last phone call. It could be the one that counts."

As noted in Chapter 8, when Buchanan made those phone calls and someone hung up on her, she just redialed the number and said, "We were cut off." The second time, she might have gotten a relative or someone else who was willing to talk, or the first person might have changed his or her mind. But she didn't try a third time; that would be harassment, she said.

Crime Stories

Buchanan gathered her information from interviews and records. And then she wove them into stories with leads that hooked the reader. She said that crime reporters need to talk to witnesses and get color, background, ages and details—what people were wearing, doing and saying when they became crime victims or suspects. In other words, crime reporters need access.

Access

If you have the police beat, you should check the daily police log, also called the "blotter," to see the listing of all crimes recorded by police for that day. The log will list the names of the victims and suspects and the nature of the crimes. This is public record and should be available to the press and anyone else. However, the supporting documents—the actual reports filed by the officer at the scene—may not be available. Laws limiting access to these reports vary from state to state. Restrictions apply especially to records for cases under investigation, but if you develop good sources in the police department, you may gain access.

The arrest record, usually filed under the suspect's name, should contain the suspect's name and address, date and place of birth, sex, race, occupation, place of arrest, type of crime, a brief description of the incident, and names of witnesses. Of special importance to a reporter, the name of the arresting officer will be at the bottom of the report. For a major crime story, you will want to talk to the officer who was at the scene. However, police can withhold information about crimes that are under investigation.

To previous criminal records   If you are a good reporter, you will want to find out if a suspect has a previous criminal record for related charges. If you are lucky, you will be able to do that. But not necessarily from the police. Again, many states restrict access to previous criminal records.

However, if someone has been convicted of a crime, that court record is usually public and should be available to you in the court jurisdiction where he or she was convicted—unless the record is sealed by order of a judge. If the person was charged with a crime and found not guilty or charges were dropped, that record also is public. You need to look up the court file (and get the case file number) under that person's name.

Depending on how the records are filed in your city, you probably will need the year of the court case, too. Filing systems vary in every municipality, so ask the court clerk for help. The court file should contain all pertinent information, including names of the lawyers involved, description of the crime and all motions filed in the case. Most important, it will tell what happened—the disposition of the case—including specific terms of the sentence or probation or dismissal.

In some cases, a person convicted of a minor crime can have his or her record erased—"expunged"—after a number of years with permission of the court. In other cases, a judge may permit certain records to be sealed, meaning that they will be withheld from the public and only available to law enforcement officers.

To university records   Many universities withhold names on crime records because of a federal law. The Buckley Amendment to the Family Educational Rights and Privacy Act prohibits government agencies from releasing any personal data about students and employees in institutions that receive federal funding. Universities have claimed that if they release such crime records, they could lose federal funding.

In 1991, a federal judge in Missouri ruled that Southwest Missouri State University must release names and records of crimes at that school after Traci Bauer, editor of the campus newspaper, sued for access. That ruling did not apply to all universities. But in 1992, a new federal law exempted campus records from the restrictions of the Buckley Amendment. Although the new law makes access to police records easier at many universities, it doesn't guarantee access. Universities are still not compelled to release information on crime records, but they will no longer risk losing federal funds if they do release the names.

To records of juvenile offenders   All states have laws restricting the release of records that identify juvenile offenders, people under age 18. The names are withheld by all branches of the juvenile justice system, including the social services system, but a judge can authorize their release. If a juvenile is being tried as an adult—a decision that is made by a judge—or if the juvenile's name is mentioned in open court, the name can be used. This sometimes happens when the crime is particularly heinous or the juvenile has an extensive criminal record.

Most newspapers and broadcast stations have policies to withhold the names of juveniles, but that is more of an ethical decision than a legal one. The media may use the name if they receive it by legitimate means.

To the crime scene   Police have the right to protect the crime scene and limit access to the press. If it is public property, reporters and photographers can get as close as police will allow. If the crime scene is on private property, access is at the discretion of the police or the owners of the property. Generally, police will allow some access as long as the media do not interfere with the investigation of evidence at the crime scene.

Use of Names

Many newspapers withhold the names of suspects in crime stories until they have been charged formally with the crime. Being arrested means only that someone has been stopped for questioning in a crime. The person becomes an official suspect after charges are filed in a court, usually at a hearing called an "arraignment." (The process will be explained in the section about courts.)

Some newspapers also withhold the names of crime victims to protect their privacy. A growing controversy at newspapers and television stations is whether to withhold the names of complainants in rape cases. Again, the policy varies, but most of the media do not publish the names.

When names are used in crime stories, always get the full name, including the middle initial, and double-check the spelling. Do not rely on police reports; many names on reports are spelled incorrectly. Check the names in telephone directories whenever possible. If a discrepancy occurs between the name in the phone book and the one the officer gave you, call the officer again or go with the information from police.

Using full names with initials helps reduce confusion and inaccuracies; there could be a dozen John Smiths in the community. John T. Smith is more specific, especially when followed by age and address.

Wording of Accusations

Remember that all people are innocent until they are proved guilty in court or until they plead guilty. When a suspect is arrested, the person is not officially charged with anything. A person can be arrested after an officer gets a warrant or on suspicion of a crime. But the police cannot charge anyone with a crime; a member of the district attorney's office must file the charge officially with the court. (More about that later.) As a result, you must be careful with wording so you don't convict a person erroneously. Most media wait until the person has been charged with the crime, except in sensational cases when the arrest is important news.

If you are writing about an arrest before the official charge, do not say, "Sallie R. Smith was arrested for robbing the bank" (that implies guilt). Do say, "Sallie R. Smith was arrested in connection with the bank robbery." If you are writing about the suspect after charges have been filed, say, "Sallie R. Smith was charged with bank robbery" or "Sallie R. Smith was arrested on a charge of bank robbery."

Also be careful before you call anyone a crime victim. If a person was killed or visibly injured during a crime, it is probably clear that the person is a crime victim. In other cases, the suspect has to be proved guilty before you can say the other person is a victim. You can say "the *alleged* victim" or, if applicable, you can call the other person the accuser—for example, "The accuser in the rape trial was . . ."

Use the official charges when possible. If they are very awkward, and they often are, don't use them in the lead. Put them in the backup to the story. For example, one man who was accused of robbing a jewelry store was also accused of carrying a gun. But police didn't charge him with possession of a gun. They charged him with possession of an instrument of crime. And there are varying degrees in the charges, such as first-degree murder, which should be cited. But don't cite the other qualifications, such as Class E felony (a category for the crime), unless you are going to explain what they mean and why the reader must know. If categories are used at all, it is for explanation of the penalties, such as "The crime is a Class E felony, which carries a penalty of . . ." It is still preferable to explain the penalty without the category, which is meaningless to readers.

The word *alleged* is dangerous, so avoid it whenever possible. It means to declare or assert without proof. If you allege carelessly, you can be sued. Do not say, "Smith allegedly robbed the bank." You, the writer, are then the source of the allegation—and a good candidate for a libel suit. You can say, however, "Police accused Sallie R. Smith of robbing the bank" or "Police said Smith robbed the bank." If you must use *alleged,* say, "Police alleged that Smith robbed the bank." "Police accused Smith of allegedly robbing the bank" is redundant and awkward. Besides, police rarely allege; they accuse. An accusation is OK if it comes from police (and they are citing charges on record), not if it comes from you. Other permissible uses include "The bank was allegedly robbed" or "the alleged robbery," although such uses are not preferable.

Here's an example of the proper use of *alleged:* When William Kennedy Smith, the nephew of Sen. Edward Kennedy, was accused of rape at the Kennedy mansion in Palm Beach in 1991, newspapers properly wrote "The alleged rape at the Kennedy compound." Unless and until a court rules that the suspect is guilty, there is no proof that a rape actually occurred. So in this type of case, "alleged rape" is accurate. You also could use "the reported rape at the Kennedy compound." A jury later found Smith not guilty. The statement "the rape at the Kennedy compound" would have been inaccurate as well as libelous.

Also be careful when using the word *accused.* Follow the *Associated Press Stylebook* guidelines: A person is accused *of,* not *with,* a crime. In addition, you should not say, "accused bank robber Sallie R. Smith" (this convicts her). Instead, say, "Sallie R. Smith, accused of the bank robbery."

Attribution

Follow the guidelines for attribution explained in Chapter 3. In crime stories, make sure you attribute all accusatory information and much of the information you received secondhand (not by direct observation). Factual information does not need attribution. The location of a crime, for example, usually is factual. If someone has been charged with a crime, you can state that as a fact.

To reduce the use of attribution after every sentence, you can use an overview attribution for part of your story, especially when you are recounting what happened: "Police described the incident this way."

Newspaper Clips

The first thing you should do before you write your story is check newspaper clips in your library. They may make a big difference in your story.

In one case at *The Hartford* (Conn.) *Courant,* a man was arrested on a charge of rape. Small story for a big paper. But the reporter checked clips and discovered that the man had been arrested previously on rape charges and was free on bail when he was charged with this other rape— a much bigger story. Three months later, a different reporter was making police checks. A man had been accused of rape. The reporter checked the clips. It was the same man charged with a third rape, which occurred when he was free on bail still awaiting trial in the first rape case—a very big story. And this story led to a major front-page follow-up story on the system in Connecticut that allows rape suspects to be released on bail, no matter how many times they have been arrested and charged with that type of crime. (Bail is the amount of money, set by a judge, that the suspect has to deposit with the court to be released from jail pending a hearing or trial. If the suspect flees, the bail money goes to the court.)

One caution: Clips on file in your newspaper library or computer data base may not be up to date. They may contain stories of someone's arrest but not the disposition of the case. Always check to see if charges were dropped or if the person is still waiting trial or was convicted.

Guidelines for Reporting Crime Stories

In any story you will seek good quotes and answers to the five W's. Here are the basic questions to ask and the basic information to include in crime stories:

Victims: Get full names, ages, addresses and occupations, if available (use if relevant).

Suspects: Get full names, ages and addresses, if available; if not, get a description. Guidelines about whether to include race or ethnic background are changing. Check your newspaper's style. A general rule is to avoid mentioning race or ethnicity unless it is crucial to the story or to a description of a suspect.

Cause of fatalities or injuries: Also describe the injuries, where injured people have been taken and their current condition (check with hospitals). In stories involving property, specify the causes and extent of damage.

Location of incident: Don't forget to gather specific information for a graphic.

Time of incident: Be as specific as possible.

What happened: Make sure you understand the sequence of events; always ask about any unusual circumstances.

Arrests and charges filed: If people have been arrested, find out where they are being held, when they will be arraigned (a hearing for formal charges) or when the next court procedure will be. If they have already been arraigned, find out the amount of bail.

Eyewitness accounts: Comments from neighbors may also be relevant. Be careful about using accusations against named individuals. When in doubt, leave them out.

In addition to gathering the basic information, you may want to try some of these other reporting techniques:

Role-play: Imagine that it is your car in the accident, your home that was burglarized or burned in a fire, your friend or relative injured in a crime. What information would you want to know if you were personally affected by the story?

Play detective: What information would you want to gather to solve the crime?

Gather graphics: What information would you need to diagram the car accident, draw the crime scene or a locator map, write a highlights box or a chronology of events, or design a chart or graphic depicting how and where the crime occurred? Ask questions to gain the information you will have to convey to the artist who will draw the graphics for your story.

Use the telephone: Often you will gather information for crime stories over the telephone. Usually you will get the information from a dispatcher or public information officer who was not at the scene and is just reading a report to you. Make sure you ask police officials to repeat any information you did not hear clearly. Also ask the police officer releasing the information to give you her or his full name and rank. Police often identify themselves only by title and last name, such as Sgt. Jones. Ask the officer to spell the names of all people involved; you can spell them back to double-check the accuracy.

Stories About Specific Types of Crimes

For the first day of a major crime story, the preferred approach is a hard-news one. For follow-up stories and sidebars, consider some of the storytelling techniques.

Motor vehicle accidents   Vehicle accident stories usually are hard-news stories, unless there is an unusual angle. In addition to following the basic guidelines, make sure you have this information:

• Speed, destination, and directions of vehicles and exact locations at time of accident

• Cause of accident, arrests, citations and damages

• Victims' use of required equipment, such as seat belts and bicycle or motorcycle helmets

• Weather-related information, if relevant

• Rescue attempts or acts of heroism

It is customary to lead the story with fatalities and injuries. This example is very basic, structured in inverted pyramid form:

Summary lead: delayed identification, fatality and cause	A Santa Ana boy was killed when a van rear-ended the car he was riding in while it was stopped at a turn signal, police said. The van's driver was booked for vehicular manslaughter.
Identification	Robert Taylor, 10, died at UCI Medical Center in Orange.
When, where, other injured people	The 3:17 p.m. accident at First and Bristol streets in Santa Ana also critically injured the boy's mother, Griselda Taylor, 29, and his sister, Lynelle, 8. An 8-year-old boy in the car sustained minor injuries, police said. His name and relation to the Taylors were not released.
What happened	Taylor was waiting on the eastbound side of First, in the left-turn

lane, at a red light when a van driven by Don Currie Edwards, 49, struck the back of her car, police said. The impact pushed her car into the intersection, and it was then struck by a westbound car driven by Phillipe Hernandez, 18.

Who was involved

Taylor sustained a broken neck. She was in guarded condition at Western Medical Center in Santa Ana, hospital officials said. Lynelle sustained critical head injuries, police said.

Edwards was treated for minor injuries and arrested, police said. Hernandez was not injured.

Condition of injured people; hospital sources

The Orange County (Calif.) *Register*

Burglaries and robberies   A burglary involves entry of a building with intent to commit any type of crime; robbery involves stealing with violence or a threat against people. If you are away and a person enters your home and steals your compact disc player, that's a burglary. If you are asleep upstairs and the person is downstairs stealing the player, that's still a burglary. But if the person threatens you with force, that's a robbery. A burglary always involves a place and *can* involve violence against a person; a robbery *must* involve violence or threats against a person.

For both burglaries and robberies, ask the basics: who, what, when, where, why and how. Then add:

- What was taken and the value of the goods
- Types of weapons used (in robberies)
- How entry was made
- Similar circumstances (frequency of crime or any odd conditions)

In burglary and robbery stories, mention in the lead any injuries or deaths. Keep the tone serious when the story involves death or serious injuries. In other cases, use your judgment and lead with any unusual angles. If there are none, stress what was taken or how the burglars entered the building, if that is the most interesting factor.

Whether you write a hard or soft lead depends on how serious the crime was, if it is the first story on the crime and whether you have enough interesting information to warrant a soft approach.

Here's a hard-news version of a burglary story:

COUNCIL BLUFFS, Ia. (AP)—A first issue of "Iron Man" was among 44 rare comic books stolen from a Council Bluffs store.

The books, some valued at $200 to $225 each, dated back to the 1950s and '60s.

Other books stolen from Kanesville Kollectibles included a 1964 first issue of "Daredevil," 17 issues of "Spider Man," four issues of "The Incredible Hulk," "Mystery in Space," "Tales of Suspense," "Captain Marvel" and "Thor."

Police reports said rare comic books valued at $2,950, about 300 used rock 'n' roll compact discs valued at $2,200 and $50 in cash were taken from the business.

The Associated Press

In this burglary story, the tone is lighter and a soft lead is used, because of the subject matter:

Someone took Burger King's "Have It Your Way" slogan too literally this week and stole a three-foot-wide Whopper hamburger display costume from a van parked in northeast Salem.

Shannon Sappingfield, a marketing representative for local Burger Kings, said the missing burger was made of sponge.

The Whopper was in a van parked at Boss Enterprise, 408-A Lancaster Drive NE. The company owns nine local Burger Kings.

When Sappingfield came to work about 6 a.m. Tuesday, she saw that the van's window had been broken.

The cardboard box containing the Whopper costume was missing; two other boxes containing a milk shake costume and a french fry costume were untouched.

"I'm not convinced they realized what they had until they were away from the site and opened the box," she said.

She estimated that the costume was worth about $500.'But to get another one, the company would also have to buy another milk shake and french fry costume, which cost $500 each.

(Salem, Ore.) *Statesman-Journal*

This is a basic hard-news robbery story with a description of the suspects:

Two armed, masked men robbed a Huntington Beach restaurant late Tuesday, escaping with $2,000 in cash.

Police Lt. John Foster said the holdup occurred shortly before 11 p.m. at Jeremiah's, 8901 Warner Ave.

He said two men armed with shotguns and wearing stockings over their heads entered through the kitchen door, forced cooks into the main area of the restaurant, then made employees and patrons lie on the floor.

The robbers took the cash from a floor safe and fled, Foster said.

The men were described as Caucasian, wearing dark clothing. One was 6-foot-1 to 6-foot-3 with a thin build and dark, curly hair. The second was 5-foot-8, about 170 pounds with a medium to stocky build.

Detectives believe the same shotgun-wielding men robbed a Pizza Hut at 17342 Beach Blvd. about 9:40 p.m. Monday. The bandits took an undisclosed amount of cash and sped away in a small blue car, possibly a Toyota or Nissan.

The Orange County Register

In this robbery story, note the focus on the unusual angle:

A robbery was committed Tuesday with a can of deodorant spray, Des Moines police said.

James Vogel was at his insurance office at 3432 Forest Ave. when a masked man entered and displayed the deodorant spray. Police said the intruder attempted to spray Vogel and a struggle followed.

Vogel's glasses were broken, cutting his face, and the bandit grabbed Vogel's wallet, which contained about $20 cash and other items, and fled.

The Des Moines (Iowa) *Register*

This robbery story lends itself to a storytelling approach because no one was injured and the circumstances were unusual. The writer used a build-on-quote lead. Note that because the suspects are juveniles, their names are not used.

DES MOINES, Wash.—Police are calling it the "Two Stooges Robbery."

After robbing a Seafirst Bank branch in this Seattle suburb, police say, two teen-agers found that their beat-up getaway car had a dead battery.

When they got out to check under the hood, they locked their keys and the loot in the car.

Fleeing on foot, they ran straight to the car driven by a police detective dispatched to the crime scene.

"This was a bungled job from start to finish," Des Moines police Sgt. Mitch Barker said. "All we needed was Curly. We had Larry and Moe."

The 17-year-olds, one from Seattle and the other from Sumner, southeast of Tacoma, were in custody Friday at a juvenile detention center.

When the boys entered the bank, they handed a note to a teller that read, "Fast cash or die," court documents say.

Then, as the teen-agers turned to leave, the teller called them back and handed them additional money—including marked bills—which they took, according to court documents.

The Associated Press

Here is how the hourglass form can be used to eliminate some of the attribution in a crime story. The story on the left does not use the hourglass structure, but the one on the right does. Attributions are highlighted with underlining (note the overview attribution in the right-hand story).

Without hourglass structure

A robber took money from a clerk at Tom's Amoco, 3827 Topeka Blvd., early Sunday but had a change of heart, returned most of the cash and apologized before fleeing, police said.

The man showed no weapon but held what appeared to be a handgun beneath his sweater, said Detective Sgt. Greg Halford.

Halford said a 19-year-old male clerk was counting money inside the business about 4 a.m. when he saw the robber walk across Topeka Boulevard toward the service station.

The clerk told police he tried to get the money out of sight before the man came into the service station, but was unable.

The robber gave the clerk five nickels and asked for a quarter, Halford said, then announced the robbery as the clerk was getting the quarter.

The clerk asked the man if he was sure he wanted to go through with the robbery. The clerk then told him that three security guards from a nearby motel often come into the service station, Halford said.

At that point, the nervous-looking robber went behind the counter and grabbed the money out of the clerk's hands, the detective said. Some of the money dropped onto the floor, so the robber picked it up, Halford said.

The robber started to leave, Halford said, then came back, apologized, returned almost all of the money, said he needed only a small amount of cash and left with a small amount.

Topeka (Kan.) *Capital-Journal*

With hourglass structure

A robber took money from a clerk at Tom's Amoco, 3827 Topeka Blvd., early Sunday but had a change of heart, returned most of the cash and apologized before fleeing, police said.

The man showed no weapon but held what appeared to be a handgun beneath his sweater, said Detective Sgt. Greg Halford.

Halford described the incident as follows:

A 19-year-old male clerk was counting money inside the business about 4 a.m. when he saw the robber walk across Topeka Boulevard toward the service station.

The clerk tried to get the money out of sight before the man came into the service station, but was unable.

The robber gave the clerk five nickels and asked for a quarter, then announced the robbery as the clerk was getting the quarter.

The clerk asked the man if he was sure he wanted to go through with the robbery. The clerk then told him that three security guards from a nearby motel often come into the service station.

At that point, the nervous-looking robber went behind the counter and grabbed the money out of the clerk's hands. Some of the money dropped onto the floor, so the robber picked it up.

The robber started to leave, then came back, apologized, returned almost all of the money, said he needed only a small amount of cash and left with a small amount.

Homicides *Homicide* is the legal term for killing. *Murder* is the term for premeditated homicide. *Manslaughter* is homicide without premeditation. A person can be arrested on charges of murder, but he or she is not a murderer until convicted of the crime. Do not call someone a murderer until then. Also, don't say someone was murdered unless authorities have established that the victim was murdered—in a premeditated act of killing—or until a court determines that. Say the person was slain or killed. Some additional information to gather:

• Weapon (specific description, such as .38-caliber revolver)

• Clues and motives (from police)

• Specific wounds

• Official cause of death (from coroner or police)

• Circumstances of suspect's arrest (result of tip or investigation, perhaps at the scene)

• Lots of details, from relatives, neighbors, friends, officials, eyewitnesses and your own observations at the crime scene

For many first-day stories about death, you may choose to use a hard-news approach. You should get the news about the death in the lead. But if there is a more compelling angle, you could put it in the second or third paragraph. Again, you must use judgment in deciding whether the story lends itself to a hard-news or a storytelling approach.

This is a hard-news approach to a homicide story:

A 32-year-old man was charged Tuesday with killing his former girlfriend when she wouldn't leave the back porch of his home.

Lester Paul Stephens of 3357 N. 2nd St. was charged with first-degree intentional homicide while armed in connection with the death of Ruby L. Hardison, 42. Hardison was shot in the head Saturday.

According to the criminal complaint, Stephens told police that he and Hardison recently had ended their relationship. But Hardison came to Stephens' home Saturday and began knocking and banging on the door and front window.

Stephens told police he got upset about the noise, and went to the back door to tell her to leave him alone. Then he went back inside and got a .32-caliber semiautomatic pistol and walked back to the porch, the complaint says.

Stephens told Hardison to get off the porch and go home, then fired one shot in the air to scare her away.

The complaint says that he then put the pistol to the right side of her head, and after they continued to argue, the gun discharged.

Stephens, who faces life plus five years in prison if convicted, was being held on $50,000 cash bail. A preliminary hearing was scheduled for April 30.

The Milwaukee Journal

Here is an excerpt from a homicide story written in a storytelling style. This story includes reporting done according to most of the guidelines: interviews with neighbors, description based on observation, information from the police report and from officials. Remember that if you can't get to the scene, you can use your cross-directory to find neighbors to contact by telephone.

Soft lead

MELBOURNE, Fla.—June Anne Sharabati had planned every aspect of her children's lives, from their tasteful clothes to their exposure to classical music.

She missed only one detail: She forgot to plan a bullet for herself.

Backup for previous statement

The woman charged in the slaying of her two children Thursday night told deputies she would have committed suicide but she ran out of ammunition.

Basic news (five W's)

When deputies were called to her home at 2410 Washington Ave., they found Stephen Faulker, 14, dead on the floor of his bedroom. The Central Junior High School student had been shot in his stomach and head with a .38-caliber revolver.

Type of weapon

Two-year-old Aisha Sharabati was in her mother's bedroom dying from similar wounds.

Possible motive (note attribution)

Sharabati, who divorced Aisha's father in 1989, told deputies that Stephen had been a discipline problem, but she gave no explanation for her daughter's death, said Brevard County sheriff's spokeswoman Joan Heller.

Stephen's father died about nine years ago. Sharabati's former husband, Mohamad, lives in Canada and is en route to Melbourne, deputies said.

The first sign of the shootings came to light shortly before midnight Thursday with Sharabati's frantic calls to police and neighbors.

Narrative based on interview with neighbor

John Marrell said he was sleeping when the phone rang.

The call was from Sharabati, his 32-year-old neighbor. He had known her for 11 years and had helped her from time to time.

"She said, 'Didn't you hear the shots?' and I asked, 'What shots?'" Marrell said.

Dialogue

"And then she said, 'You need to get over here and get these kids. They've suffered enough.'"

Marrell said he grabbed a gun and a flashlight, thinking maybe a prowler was threatening the single parent and her children.

Instead, Sharabati met him at her screen door and told him she had "killed the kids."

Marrell said he ran home and called police, not knowing they had already been called.

When deputies arrived at the house, Sharabati met them unarmed on the doorstep and said, "Kill me. Kill me," Heller said. Sharabati was taken into custody, and deputies went in to find the bodies.

Information from officials

In the investigation report, Deputy Scott Nyquist said the suspect shot her son "in a fit of rage."

Police report

On Friday, many neighbors in the middle class neighborhood were struggling to understand how a seemingly "ideal mother" could have committed the slayings.

Reaction from neighbors

"She was the kind of mother who would attend parent-teacher conferences," said Frances Edwards, a retired high school guidance counselor who lives across the street from Sharabati. "She often said her children were her life. I sure didn't see this coming."

Occupation of neighbor (relevant to statement)

Sharabati's light blue, one-story home—like most in the wooded,

Observations

spacious subdivision—was well maintained. In the back yard, three lawn chairs were lined up alongside Aisha's child-sized chair.

Edwards said Sharabati wanted only the best for her children.

Backup for lead

"She bought them Mozart records to listen to and dressed them beautifully," she said. . . .

Reaction from relatives

"We are in deep shock—very, very deep shock," said Helen Faulker, Sharabati's mother.

Sharabati is being held in the Brevard County jail, where she is scheduled to make her first court appearance at 9 a.m. today.

Where suspect is, next step in court process

Laurin Sellers and Lynne Bumpus-Hooper, *The Orlando* (Fla.) *Sentinel*

Fires Although fire stories may not be crime stories, unless arson or other criminal behavior was involved, police reporters often are responsible for fire stories. These are the important elements:

• Time fire started, time fire companies responded, time fire was brought under control

• Number of fire companies responding, number of trucks at scene

• Evacuations, if any, and where people were taken

• Injuries and fatalities (make sure you ask if any fire officials were injured)

• Cause (ask if arson is suspected—intentional setting of fire), how and where fire started

• Who discovered the fire, extent of damage, insurance coverage

• Description of building

• Presence and condition of smoke detectors or sprinkler system (especially in a public building or apartment building, if city requires them)

• Fire inspection record, fire code violations (usually for a follow-up story, especially in public buildings)

When fatalities or injuries occur in a fire, they should be mentioned in your lead, preferably a hard-news lead. If no one is injured or if heroic rescue attempts are involved, a soft lead may be appropriate. Follow-up stories and sidebars provide many opportunities for storytelling techniques.

This example follows all the guidelines for reporting fires—including questions about smoke detectors:

Two young brothers were killed in a South Side fire early Friday, despite the efforts of neighbors who broke through the windows to try to reach the victims.

Corey and Keither Schaeffer, 10 and 11 years old, were killed in a blaze in the three-story building at 551 E. 38th Place. Four children were in critical condition.

Fire Department spokesman David McKoy said there were no smoke detectors in the home, which is part of the Chicago Housing Authority's Ida B. Wells complex.

Detective Charles Gardner of the Police Department's bomb and arson unit said the fire was ignited by the "careless use of smoking materials." He said it started in an overstuffed chair on the building's second floor and swept upstairs.

"I heard the little girl screaming and looked out the back door and saw smoke," said Tamra Jackson, 24, who lives next door. "The neighborhood got together and got the kids out, but we couldn't get two of them. There were a lot of people and they got bats and stuff, breaking the windows, trying to get the babies."

Some of the neighbors who helped rescue the children were treated for minor smoke inhalation, said McKoy.

The mother of the boys, Debra Schaeffer, and her boyfriend, Bobbie Stewart, were injured when they jumped from the burning building. They were treated and released from Michael Reese Hospital, a spokesman said.

Two more of Schaeffer's children—Wilbur, 6, and Wanake, 14—were listed in critical condition late Friday at Cook County Hospital, suffering from burns and smoke inhalation.

Two other children burned in the fire also were in critical condition Friday. Lisa Dotson, 2, was at Cook County Hospital, and Calvin Dotson, 3, was at Loyola University Medical Center.

Linnet Myers, *Chicago Tribune*

Court Stories

Writing about a crime is only the first step. The next step takes place in court. To cover courts, you need a basic understanding of the process and the terminology that is used. Court procedures vary from state to state and even in counties within states. You need to find out how the system works in the area where you are working.

A complete understanding of the courts would require a three-year course called law school. But you can learn most of what you need to know as you do your reporting. Whenever you hear a term you don't understand, seek a definition. And don't use legal terms in your stories unless you explain them. In fact, avoid them as much as possible. Go by this guideline: If you don't understand something, chances are the reader won't either. It's up to you to make the story clear.

Court cases are full of drama. They are the stuff of television series and movies. Yet many times newspaper stories about them are dull. Even if you use a hard-news approach to report a conviction or testimony, you can still use storytelling techniques of dialogue, description and narrative writing for portions of the story so the reader can experience the human drama that filled the courtroom.

Some basic guidelines for writing court stories:

• Get reactions, facial expressions, and gestures of the defendant and the accusers, attorneys, relatives and other people affected by the case, especially in trial stories and verdict stories.

• Use descriptive detail and color—lively quotes, dramatic testimony and dialogue.

• Translate all jargon, and avoid legal terminology.

• State exact charges in the story.

• Give the background of the crime, no matter how many stories have been published about this case.

• Include the name of the court where the trial or hearing is being held.

• Get comments from defendants, prosecutors, defense attorneys, relatives and plaintiffs (the people who brought suit or filed charges) and jurors in all verdict stories.

• In verdict stories, include how long the jury deliberated. Also include how many jurors were on the case; not all cases have 12-member juries, the most common number. In some cases, the amount of time the jury deliberated may be a major factor—as you will see in the following section, which is about the O.J. Simpson case. In all cases, however, the length of deliberations is part of the story.

• Write the next step—the next court appearance or, in verdict stories, plans for an appeal if the defendant is found guilty.

The O.J. Simpson Trial

The trial of former football player O.J. Simpson captured so much of the nation's attention for nine months that it was often referred to as "the trial of the century." But the jury deliberated less than four hours before reaching a verdict. That time element was the lead on Associated Press stories released shortly after the verdict. Later versions stressed the next step: how Simpson would resume his life as a free man. Although court stories often cite the makeup of the jury by sex, in this case the race of the jury was also included, because race was a factor in the defense. Simpson's lawyers claimed he had been framed because a detective on the case was biased against African Americans.

The following story shows how to apply the guidelines for writing court stories:

LOS ANGELES (AP)—O.J. Simpson was acquitted Tuesday of murdering his ex-wife and her friend, a suspense-filled climax to the courtroom saga that obsessed the nation. With two words, "not guilty," the jury freed the fallen sports legend to try to rebuild a life thrown into disgrace.

Simpson looked toward the jury and mouthed, "Thank you," after the panel was dismissed. He turned to his family and punched a fist into the air. He then hugged his lead defense attorney, Johnnie Cochran Jr., and his friend and attorney Robert Kardashian.

"He's going to start his life all over again," Cochran told reporters later.

"It's over from our viewpoint," District Attorney Gil Garcetti said.

After hearing nine months of testimony, the majority-black jury of 10 women and two men took less than four hours Monday to clear Simpson of the June 12, 1994, murders of Nicole Brown Simpson and her friend Ronald Goldman. The verdict was unsealed and read Tuesday.

The case seemed to come full circle after Simpson's release. Simpson was driven home in a white van along Southern California freeways, with news helicopters following and people waving, scenes eerily reminiscent of the slow-speed chase in a white Bronco just before he surrendered at his house on June 17, 1994. When he got home Tuesday, he embraced the driver of the Bronco, his friend A.C. Cowlings.

As the verdicts were read in court, Goldman's sister Kim broke into sobs. Her father sat back in his seat in disbelief, then embraced his daughter. Prosecutors Marcia Clark and Christopher Darden sat stone-faced.

Simpson's relatives smiled and wiped away tears. His son Jason sat in his seat, his face in his hands, shaking and sobbing. "Oh my God!" cried his grown daughter, Arnelle.

Later, Simpson's lawyers and relatives addressed reporters in the courtroom. "I was always in prayer," his frail mother, Eunice, said. "I knew my son was innocent." Jason Simpson read a statement from his father:

"I'm relieved that this incredible part of this nightmare of June 12, 1994, is over. My first obligation is to my young children, who will be raised the way Nicole and I had always planned.

"When things have settled a bit, I will pursue as my primary goal in life the killer or killers that have slaughtered Nicole and Mr. Goldman. They are out there somewhere."

At an emotional news conference, prosecutors shared their deep disappointment. Clark called the prosecution team members, "wonderful," and told them, "Please don't let this make you lose faith in our system."

"That is the verdict, that is the jury's position, and I accept that verdict," Darden said. "I'm not bitter and I'm not angry. I'm honored to have . . . ," he said, unable to complete his statement. He bowed his head, and, overcome by emotion, was surrounded by colleagues before he slowly walked away.

Goldman's father, Fred, fought back tears, saying, "Last June 13, '94, was the worst nightmare of my life. This is the second.

"This prosecution team did not lose today," he said. "I deeply believe that this country lost today. Justice was not served. I and my family will do everything in our power to bring about the kind of change that won't allow what happened today to ever happen to another family again."

Police Chief Willie Williams said he had no plans to reopen the murder investigation. "It doesn't mean there's another murderer," Williams said.

The jury of nine blacks, two whites and a Hispanic cleared Simpson of the murders of his 35-year-old ex-wife and her 25-year-old friend. Had he been convicted, Simpson would have faced life in prison without parole.

Instead, Judge Lance Ito ordered him taken to the sheriff's department and released "forthwith."

Outside the courthouse, a throng of 1,000 spectators erupted in cheers. The curious and an army of media began arriving at court early Tuesday, while police went on tactical alert to brace for possible trouble in the streets.

News helicopters roared outside. Barricades blocked the street. In the lobby, hundreds of people vied for the few precious seats in the courtroom. As their lottery numbers were pulled, the lucky few cheered.

The Associated Press

Criminal and Civil Cases

Court procedures fall into two categories: criminal and civil cases. Criminal cases are violations of any laws regulating crime. If you are arrested on suspicion of drunken driving, you could be charged in a criminal case.

Civil cases involve lawsuits between two parties. If your landlord says you have not paid the rent or you have damaged your apartment, he or she can bring a civil lawsuit against you. Divorces, malpractice, libel, contract disputes and other actions not involving criminal law are civil cases.

Federal Courts and State Courts

The court system functions on two levels: a federal level and a state level. Federal courts have jurisdiction over cases involving matters related to the U.S. Constitution (such as civil rights), federal tax and antitrust matters, and any other federal laws. Federal courts also hear cases between people from different states. The federal court system:

U.S. District Court: This is the lowest level of the federal judicial system, where most cases involving federal issues are first heard.

U.S. Court of Appeals: There are 12 of these courts for geographical areas, plus the U.S. Court of Appeals for the D.C. (District of Columbia) Circuit. It is the intermediary court, where cases from the federal district courts are appealed.

U.S. Supreme Court: This is the highest court in the nation. Cases may be appealed to this court, but the justices do not have to rule on all the cases.

Most states also have three levels of courts: a trial court, an appeals court and a state supreme court for appeals of the last resort on the state level. Cases from the state's highest court may be appealed to the U.S. Supreme Court if there is a federal angle, such as a constitutional matter—a First Amendment issue, for example—or a civil rights violation.

The names of the state courts can be confusing. In one state a superior court may be a trial-level court, whereas in others it may be an appellate court.

There also are municipal courts, where violations of local laws, such as traffic laws, or city ordinances may be heard.

In addition, within the state system there are juvenile courts (for cases involving people under age 18) and probate courts, where disputes involving wills and estates are heard.

When you write your court story, find out the proper name of the court—whether it is called a district court, a circuit court or a common pleas court—and write that in the story.

Criminal Court Process

Crimes are classified as misdemeanors or felonies. *Misdemeanors* are considered minor offenses that carry a potential penalty of up to a year in jail and/or a fine. *Felonies* are more serious crimes punishable by more than a year in jail. Criminal procedures differ from state to state, but there are some general processes in the court system that you should understand. Exhibit 23-1 outlines court procedures for both criminal and civil cases.

Arrest   The person is stopped by police for suspicion of having committed a crime and is taken to the police station for questioning or further action. Police are required to read a person his or her rights—to remain silent (if the person does not want to discuss the issue before a court procedure) and to retain an attorney. These are called the Miranda warnings, based on a court case by that name.

Exhibit 23-1

Process of criminal and civil cases

Courtesy of Bill Skeet

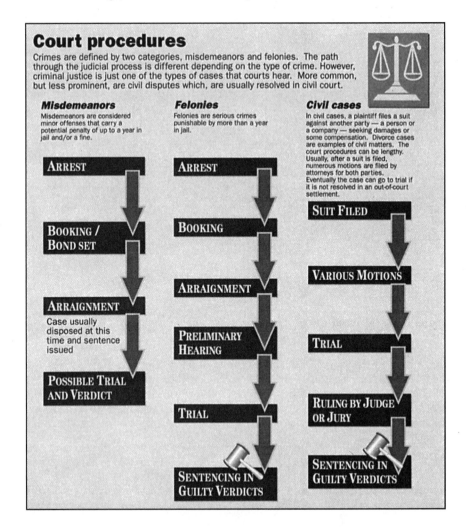

Court procedures

Crimes are defined by two categories, misdemeanors and felonies. The path through the judicial process is different depending on the type of crime. However, criminal justice is just one of the types of cases that courts hear. More common, but less prominent, are civil disputes which, are usually resolved in civil court.

Misdemeanors
Misdemeanors are considered minor offenses that carry a potential penalty of up to a year in jail and/or a fine.

ARREST

BOOKING / BOND SET

ARRAIGNMENT
Case usually disposed at this time and sentence issued

POSSIBLE TRIAL AND VERDICT

Felonies
Felonies are serious crimes punishable by more than a year in jail.

ARREST

BOOKING

ARRAIGNMENT

PRELIMINARY HEARING

TRIAL

SENTENCING IN GUILTY VERDICTS

Civil cases
In civil cases, a plaintiff files a suit against another party — a person or a company — seeking damages or some compensation. Divorce cases are examples of civil matters. The court procedures can be lengthy. Usually, after a suit is filed, numerous motions are filed by attorneys for both parties. Eventually the case can go to trial if it is not resolved in an out-of-court settlement.

SUIT FILED

VARIOUS MOTIONS

TRIAL

RULING BY JUDGE OR JURY

SENTENCING IN GUILTY VERDICTS

A person also can be arrested if someone has filed a complaint with police and the police find enough probable cause to believe the complaint is true. At this point the police can notify the person of the charge that will be filed—basically, why he or she is being arrested—but the charge is not official yet.

If someone is wanted for a crime, police also can seek a warrant for someone's arrest, a legal document provided by a judge that gives police the right to arrest a suspect.

Booking   The suspect is taken to a booking desk in the police station, where he or she is fingerprinted and photographed. Information about the person—age, address, physical description and so on—is then recorded in a police book, the log. At this point the person may be held in jail or released until formal charges are issued.

Charges   The arresting police officer confers with a member of the district attorney's office, who decides if a charge against the suspect should be filed with the court. It is important for the reporter to find out if the person has been charged officially with the crime, because many newspapers don't publish news of an arrest until charges have been filed.

Many states have standard bail fees for common or misdemeanor crimes, and the person may be able to post a bail bond at this time and be released without a hearing.

Arraignment   Usually within 24 to 48 hours, a suspect will have a first hearing. At this point the charges against him or her are read in court. In some places, at this time the suspect can enter a plea of guilty, not guilty or no contest—not admitting guilt but not contesting the charge either. In some jurisdictions, the arraignment may be held just to formally read the charges; the plea comes at a later hearing.

If the suspect pleads guilty, the sentence can be issued at this point, and the matter can be settled—or the judge may delay sentencing for another hearing. Misdemeanor cases often are settled at this level.

If the person pleads not guilty, he or she has the right to a trial, and the judge can set bail at this time.

At the hearing, the judge will determine bail. If the person fails to show up for the next court appearance, the total amount of bail is forfeited to the court. When the person has no previous record, the judge may release the suspect on his own recognizance (recognition) without any bail.

Preliminary hearing   In felony cases only, a judge weighs the facts presented by a prosecutor from the district attorney's office and by the defense attorney at a special hearing. Then the judge decides whether there is enough evidence (probable cause) to hold the person for trial. If not, the person is released, and charges are dropped.

Grand jury   In certain cases, particularly those involving political crimes or major drug cases and those in federal courts, a grand jury will be convened to investigate the circumstances of the case and determine if there is enough evidence—enough probable cause—that the crime has been committed.

Like a trial jury, the grand jury is a group of citizens, from 12 to 33 members, chosen to serve on the case. They listen to testimony from prosecutors and witnesses. Unlike the trial jury, however, the grand jury does not rule on guilt or innocence. It only recommends to a judge whether there is enough evidence to take the case to a trial.

If there is, the grand jury hands up (because the judge sits on a higher bench than the jury) an indictment, also called a "true bill." The defendant then enters a plea at another hearing. If the case goes to trial, another jury will be impaneled to serve at the trial.

Grand jury proceedings are secret; the jurors are sworn not to reveal deliberations to the media or anyone else (in most states). However, many reporters with good sources can find out the essence of what happened. After deliberations, if and when the grand jury issues a report, that is usually public record.

Pretrial hearings and motions   Before the trial, attorneys usually file a number of motions (formal requests to the court) seeking to have the case dropped, to have the trial moved to another location (called a change of venue) or to have evidence suppressed. The judge has to rule on each motion.

Trial   If the case goes to trial, a jury is selected and the case is heard. In some cases, particularly civil cases, a judge may decide the case without a jury.

For a not-guilty verdict, the *Associated Press Stylebook* says use the word *innocent* in the story. That rule is a holdover from the days of lead type to guard against the word *not* inadvertently being dropped. Many newspapers no longer adhere to this style rule.

Unanimous verdicts are required in criminal trials in most states. If the jury can't agree on a guilty or not-guilty verdict, it is called a "hung jury," and a mistrial is declared. The defendant is then technically not guilty.

If the defendant is judged guilty, you may then call him or her a murderer, rapist, or whatever accusatory term fits the crime involved. But do not use accusatory terms in stories before a guilty verdict.

Sentencing   After the trial, if the person is found guilty, there will be another hearing. The judge will then decide on a sentence. Sometimes the judge issues the sentence immediately after the verdict.

At any time during the criminal court process, the suspect may change his or her not-guilty plea to a guilty one and eliminate the need for a trial. To avoid a trial, lawyers often will engage in a process called plea bargaining. The defense lawyer and prosecutor will agree on a lesser charge in exchange for a guilty or no-contest plea. The defendant then forgoes a trial and gets sentenced to a lesser penalty.

Appeal A person convicted of a crime can appeal the decision to a higher court. It is logical to ask in all court trials with convictions whether an appeal is planned. The information should be included in the story.

Civil Court Process

A civil case starts with a suit filed by a person or a company. Anyone can file a lawsuit for a fee. After filing, the lawyers for both sides file various motions with the court. If the case is not settled between the two parties at a pretrial hearing, a court hearing date is set. Civil cases may be argued in front of a judge or before a jury if one is requested. Civil suits can drag through the courts for many years. If the case goes to trial, the process is the same as for criminal trials.

Most civil cases never even get to the trial stage. At any point after motions have been filed, the judge may dismiss the case or may grant a request for a summary judgment, a ruling on the case when both parties agree to forgo a trial.

Terms Used in Court Reporting

You should become familiar with these terms so you can better understand and explain court proceedings:

Acquittal: Finding by a court or jury that a person accused of a crime is not guilty.

Adjudicate: To make a final determination or judgment by the court.

Affidavit: Sworn statement of facts.

Appeal: Plea to ask a higher court to review a judgment, verdict or order of a lower court.

Appellant: Person who files an appeal.

Arraignment: Court hearing in which a defendant in a criminal case is formally charged with the crime and given a chance to enter a plea of guilty, not guilty or no contest (nolo contendere). At this time bail usually is set.

Bail: Amount of money set by the court that the defendant must guarantee to pay if he or she does not show up for a court trial. If the defendant can't raise the money through a bail bondsman or personal sources, he or she stays in jail.

Bond: Written promise to pay bail money on the conditions stated. The bond for bail is usually 10 percent of the total amount of bail set. The term is often used interchangeably with *bail.* Very often a person will borrow money from a bondsman. Then if the person flees, the bondsman loses the money.

Brief: Legal document filed with the court by a lawyer, stating the facts of the case and arguments citing how laws apply to this case.

Change of venue: Procedure to seek a change of location of the trial, usually when defense attorneys contend the defendant can't get a fair trial in the current location because of too much pretrial publicity.

Charge: Official allegation of criminal wrongdoing.

Civil suit: Lawsuit to determine rights, duties, claims for damages, ownership or other settlements in non-criminal matters.

Complaint: Formal affidavit in which one person accuses another of violating the law.

Condemnation: Civil action to acquire ownership of property for public use. When a municipality wants to build a road or sidewalk, the government will condemn the property to gain right of way.

Contempt: Action that disregards the order or authority of the court. A lawyer who screams obscenities at the judge probably will be found in contempt of court.

Defendant: In a civil case, the person being sued. In a criminal case, the person charged with breaking the law.

Deposition: Written statement of testimony from a witness under oath.

Discovery: Pretrial examination of a person (including depositions), documents or other items to find evidence that may be used in the trial.

Dismissal: Order to drop the case.

Docket: List of cases pending before the court. A trial docket is a list of cases pending trial.

Extradition: Procedure to move a person accused of a crime from the state where he or she is residing to the state where the crime occurred and where the trial will be conducted.

Felony: Major crime punishable by a sentence of a year or more. Crimes such as robbery, homicide and kidnapping are felonies; lesser crimes such as shoplifting are misdemeanors. Legally, a felony is defined as a crime punishable by death or imprisonment in a state prison.

Grand jury: Group of citizens selected by the court to investigate whether there is enough evidence or probable cause that a crime occurred and that the person should be charged, or indicted.

Hung jury: Jury that cannot reach a unanimous verdict, a requirement in most criminal trials.

Indictment: Recommendation by the grand jury that there is enough probable cause to charge a person or group of people with the crime under investigation. The grand jury hands up an indictment to the judge (because the judge sits on a platform higher than the jury); the judge hands down rulings. It's preferable to use the word *issued.*

Injunction: Order by the court instructing a person, group or company to stop the action that was occurring, such as picketing. For example, an injunction can order a group to stop marching outside an abortion clinic.

Innocent: Term used for a not-guilty verdict, according to Associated Press style. It is used as a safeguard so the word *not* will not be dropped accidentally from a story. But this usage is old-fashioned. *Not guilty* is the preferable wording.

Misdemeanor: Crime less serious than a felony; crime punishable by less than one year in jail and/or fines.

Mistrial: Trial that is set aside or declared invalid because of some mistake in proceedings or, in a criminal trial, because the jury cannot reach a unanimous verdict.

Motion: Request for the court to make a ruling or finding.

Nolo contendere: Latin for "I will not contest it" (no contest). This plea has the same effect as a guilty plea, but it is not an admission of guilt. It means the person will not fight the charge. If you agree to pay a fine for a traffic ticket but do not agree that you were speeding, you are pleading no contest. This type of plea is used as a form of bargaining to get the defendant a reduced charge in exchange for his or her agreement not to protest and to eliminate the need for a trial. Use the English *no contest* in a story, and explain briefly that it is not an admission of guilt.

Plaintiff: Person who sues in a civil case. The defendant is the one being sued.

Plea: Defendant's response to a charge, stating that he or she is guilty, not guilty or not willing to contest the charge.

Plea bargain: Agreement between the prosecutor and the defendant (or defense attorney) to accept a lesser charge and a lesser sentence in return for a guilty or no-contest plea. Plea bargaining is used extensively as a way to eliminate court trials. Once the defendant pleads guilty or no contest, there is no need for a trial. However, a plea bargain must be approved by the court.

Probable cause: Determination that there is enough evidence to prosecute a criminal case. Police officials also need probable cause—enough reason to believe a crime is being committed—when they seek a search warrant or any other warrant for a person's arrest.

Probation: Condition in which the person is released from serving a jail sentence if he or she meets certain terms, such as serving in the community, entering drug treatment or accepting whatever restrictions the judge decides.

Recognizance: Literally, "recognition." A person may be released from jail based on his or her own recognizance—meaning the recognition of a previously good reputation. This ruling is essentially the judge's way of saying that, because of the person's reputation, he or she is not considered a high risk for skipping the next court hearing or trial.

Subpoena: Court order commanding a person to appear in court or to release documents to the court.

Summary judgment: Procedure in a civil suit asking the court to give final judgment on the grounds that there are no further questions and no need for a trial.

Summons: Document notifying a defendant that a lawsuit or complaint has been filed against him or her.

Suspended sentence: Court order stating that the punishment of the defendant will be suspended if certain conditions are met. A person who receives probation gets a suspended sentence.

Temporary injunction: Court order to stop an action, such as a protest, for a specific amount of time until a court hearing and ruling whether the action should be enjoined, or stopped permanently.

Tort: Civil case involving damages, pain, suffering or other allegations of wrongdoing.

True bill: Indictment issued by a grand jury.

Verdict: Decision by a jury about guilt or innocence.

Warrant: Court order directing law enforcement officials to arrest a person. A search warrant gives officials authority to search a premise.

Court Story Examples

A court case is a continuing saga. From the time a person is arrested until the case is resolved, whether in a trial or a settlement, you will write many stories about it. But never assume the reader is familiar with the case, no matter how sensational it may be. Always include the background.

Whether you take a soft or hard approach, make sure your nut graph explains who is being accused of what, and place it high in the story.

If information is part of a court record, you may use it as fact—but it still may not be true. It's up to a judge or jury to decide whether the claims in court documents and trials are true. So you need to attribute your information, although not necessarily in the lead.

Unlike other stories, many court stories do not appear balanced. On any given day, one side in the case may present its arguments, so you won't always have a story that seems fair to both parties. The testimony will be biased; you should not be.

Some reminders:

- Explain charges and background.
- Describe defendants and witnesses.
- Specify the court where the proceeding takes place.
- Tell a good story.

When the verdict is issued in a major trial that has garnered interest locally or nationally, a hard-news story is appropriate. A soft lead also may work, but make sure you put the verdict very high in the story. The following story is an example of a basic hard-news approach. In this case, the judge sentenced the defendant immediately instead of at a separate hearing.

Summary lead: verdict, delayed identification	EXETER, N.H.—A high school instructor was convicted yesterday and sentenced to life in prison without parole after a sensational trial on charges that she manipulated her student-lover into murdering her husband.	hostage of the judicial system.

Summary lead: verdict, delayed identification

EXETER, N.H.—A high school instructor was convicted yesterday and sentenced to life in prison without parole after a sensational trial on charges that she manipulated her student-lover into murdering her husband.

Defendant's reaction, charges, name of court

Pamela Smart, 23, stood motionless as the Superior Court jury foreman pronounced her guilty of murder-conspiracy and being an accomplice to murder.

Relative's reactions

The victim's mother, Judith Smart, cried out as each verdict was read, and said afterward, "She got what she deserved."

Judith and William Smart then left the court for the cemetery where their son is buried.

"We're going to tell Gregg," William Smart said. "We're going to tell him that, by God, she did it."

Brief background

Gregg Smart, a 24-year-old insurance agent, was murdered May 1 last year, six days before his first wedding anniversary.

More reactions

Pamela Smart's parents, John and Linda Wojas, were stone-faced as they left the courthouse.

Descriptive detail

"You know how I feel about that," Linda Wojas said when asked if she thought her daughter had gotten a fair trial. Wojas wore a yellow ribbon every day, symbolizing her belief that her daughter was a

hostage of the judicial system.

"I feel terribly bad for the Wojas family," Judith Smart said. "I can imagine how I would feel and I feel very, very bad for them."

Reaction quotes

The jury, which heard three weeks of testimony, deliberated 12 hours over three days before returning its verdict. Smart also was convicted of witness-tampering for encouraging her student-intern to lie to police.

Jury information: time deliberated and length of trial

Other charges

Rockingham County Superior Court Judge Douglas Gray immediately announced the mandatory life sentence for the accomplice-to-murder charge. An appeal is expected.

Identification of court and judge, sentencing, expected appeal

Smart was the school district media coordinator when she met William Flynn, now 17, as one of his instructors in a self-awareness program at Winnacunnet High School in Hampton.

Background and highlights of trial

Prosecutors said the former high school cheerleader and college honor student tantalized and seduced Flynn, then 15 and a virgin, and then threatened to end their affair unless he murdered her husband. Smart testified that she broke off the affair just before the murder.

Prosecutors said Smart feared losing everything in a divorce, including her dog and furniture.

The defense called Flynn and

Fate of others involved (note plea bargain)

two confessed accomplices "thrill-killers" who shot Smart on their own, then framed his widow to avoid life prison terms. In plea bargains, they face minimum sentences ranging from 18 to 28 years.

Color details

The Boston Herald, which dubbed Smart the "Ice Princess," invited readers to call in their verdicts on a 900 number. They voted guilty, 543 to 101.

More highlights of trial

The most damaging evidence against Smart was four secretly recorded conversations she had with Cecelia Pierce, 16, her student-intern and confidante. The profanity-laden tapes, made after the murder, show that Smart urged Pierce to lie to police, that she feared being jailed herself, and that she had known her husband would be murdered.

Flynn, sobbing as he testified on March 12, admitted pulling the trigger on a .38-cal. pistol he held to Gregg Smart's head.

He and Patrick Randall, 17, testified that they entered the Smarts' condominium through a basement door that Pamela Smart had left unlocked for them and waited for Smart to arrive home. They also said they forced him to his knees as he begged for mercy.

Shortly before the verdict, John Wojas said people were misjudging his daughter.

"She's not a cold little woman like they're trying to describe her," he said. "She doesn't show a lot of outright emotion. She never has."

The Associated Press

Key testimony

Reaction quote kicker

Here is an excerpt from a story about testimony in a continuing trial. The writer weaves feature techniques of dialogue with a hard-news approach to convey the drama of this trial. Note that she includes descriptions of the courtroom and the defendant.

NEW LONDON, Conn.—Richard Crafts took the witness stand Thursday in the most dramatic moment of his 12-week murder trial, and calmly denied killing his wife and using a chain saw and wood chipper to dispose of her body.

"And do you know whether Helle Crafts is alive or not?" defense attorney J. Daniel Sagarin asked his client.

"I certainly hope she is," Richard Crafts replied. "I believe she is."

Crafts testified in a courtroom so crowded with more than 65 spectators and reporters that a sheriff stood at the door turning away latecomers. Despite the crowd, the courtroom was silent except for the exchanges between Sagarin and Crafts.

The 50-year-old airline pilot—who prosecutors say killed his wife by unknown means, cut up her body with a chain saw, and disposed of it with a wood chipper—testified with a voice and manner that was so calm it bordered at times on nonchalance. . . .

Helle Crafts was last seen Nov. 18, 1986. Richard Crafts testified she left their Newtown home in the early morning of Nov. 19, 1986, and her last words were, "I'm leaving now."

"She was all right the last time I saw her, the morning of Nov. 19, 1986," Crafts testified.

Lynne Tuohy, *The Hartford* (Conn.) *Courant*

Stories about upcoming court trials lend themselves to storytelling techniques. If the story is important enough to "advance" the trial, it probably has a good story behind it. A narrative writing technique was used to advance this trial in a story that uses almost no direct attribution, except for quotes. The story is based on court records and previous admissions by the defendant. If the defendant had not admitted the crime, this story would be too accusatory.

MIAMI—He was a distraught man that day, a man who sang lullabies and wept. With one hand, he held a gun. With the other, he stroked the smooth face of his daughter, a 3-year-old existing in limbo between life and death.

An hour before, he had given her what he thought was a fatal dose of Valium. But here she was still breathing, her tiny chest rising and falling rhythmically, if ever so slightly.

She was in a crib at Miami Children's Hospital, lying on her back. She had been there for eight months, since the day she nearly suffocated. He leaned over the crib railing and looked at her eyes. They were open. They stared ahead, mirrored no emotions, saw nothing. It was the same for her other senses. The damage to her brain was total and irreversible, and because of it, she couldn't hear his weeping, and she couldn't feel his last touch goodbye before he aimed the gun at her heart.

He shot her twice. He dropped the gun. He prayed that her suffering was over. He fell into a nurse's arms, cried and said he wanted to die. He said, "Maybe I should get the electric chair to make things even. I killed my daughter. I shot her twice. But I'm glad she's gone to heaven."

On Tuesday morning in a Miami courtroom, almost five months after the death of his daughter, Joy, Charles Griffith is scheduled to go on trial for murder. The defense, says Griffith's attorney, Mark Krasnow, will be mercy. "It was an act of love," Krasnow says, "not an act of malice."

David Finkel, *St. Petersburg (Fla.) Times*

The next example is a story about a lawsuit in a civil case that has not yet come to trial. When you cover a story about a suit that has been filed, always try to contact the people involved or at least their lawyers, whose names are listed in the suit. If you wade through all the legal writing, lawsuits can be very entertaining.

What has no arms or legs and wiggles in the night?

According to Gladys Diehl and her husband, John Brehm, it's their Sealy Posturpedic mattress.

In a lawsuit filed yesterday in Bucks County Court, Diehl and Brehm contend that they endured many nights of fitful slumber because an uninvited guest shared their bed—a 26-inch snake living inside the mattress.

"There was a lot of wiggling going on," said Stephen A. Shelly, the attorney representing the Quakertown couple.

Diehl and Brehm are seeking more than $20,000 from Sealy Mattress Co., the manufacturer, and Hess's department store, which sold the mattress. They say the incident traumatized them and caused sleep disorders.

According to the suit, the couple bought a mattress on May 13, 1988, from Hess's in Richland Township, Bucks County. Soon after, they began to notice an unfamiliar movement in their bed, which they "suspected could be a living creature."

In July, they exchanged the mattress at Hess's for another Sealy, hoping for a better night's sleep. They didn't get one. The replacement mattress also slithered and shimmied, according to the couple.

After four months of suspicious bumps in the night, Diehl and Brehm took the second mattress to Laboratory Testing Inc. in Dublin for examination. Inside, workers found a dead 26-inch ribbon snake. The species is not poisonous.

The suit contends that both the manufacturer and the department store breached their warranties. . . . No date has been set for a hearing on the case.

John P. Martin, *The Philadelphia Inquirer*

Most court stories are serious, but some have a humorous angle. Here is a light-hearted story in a conversational style that tries to involve the reader. It is an example of how a plea bargain works—or in this case, how it didn't work out very well. This story is written in pyramid form with the clincher at the end; unfortunately, the headline gives the twist away.

Man gambles on plea, loses

He admits guilt, then is acquitted

You're the defendant. You make the call:

You're Marvin E. Johnson, 40, convicted three times of drug possession. You're facing a minimum 15 years in prison without parole if convicted of being a felon in possession of a handgun.

On Wednesday, the jury at your federal trial in Kansas City deliberates three hours without reaching a verdict. On Thursday, the jury deliberates three more hours and announces it is hopelessly deadlocked. A hung jury and a new trial loom on the horizon.

The prosecutor, Assistant U.S. Attorney Rob Larsen, offers a deal. If you plead guilty, he'll reduce the government's sentencing request to a range of 15 to 22 months.

While you ponder that deal, the jury buzzes. It has a verdict.

Do you:

A) Sign the plea agreement and serve at least 15 months in prison? Or

B) Roll the dice with the jury's verdict? If it's guilty, you get at least 15 years; if it's not guilty, you walk away.

On Thursday afternoon, Marvin E. Johnson signed the plea agreement.

Five minutes later, the jury found him not guilty.

"I'm sure glad I struck that plea agreement," Larsen said.

"I can't win for losing," said Johnson's defense lawyer, John P. O'Connor.

Tom Jackman, *The Kansas City* (Mo.) *Star*

Exercises

1   Crime story: Although the police report in Exhibit 23-2 is labeled "Standard Offense Report," it is not. Each state has its own form; however, this one is similar to many. Most of the report is self-explanatory, with some exceptions. For instance, most information is in codes so the state bureau of investigation may insert the information into a computer data base. *ORI* stands for the organization where the report originated, followed by the number for that police department. The case number is important for reporters; if you want to follow the case through the court system, you need this number, which stays the same for all actions in the case. Time is computed as military time, from one to 24 hours. Where the stolen property is listed, codes are used to signify the type of property. A complete code sheet is usually on the back of the police report.

You acquired the police report earlier today, along with an attached narrative:

Exhibit 23-2

Police report

Standard Offense Report

Page 1

101. NAME OF AGENCY	102. ORI	103. CASE NO.
Ourtown, Allstate Police Dept.	0230100	92-123456

104. 1. DISPATCHED 2. CITIZEN 3. ON VIEW	105. DATE REPORTED 05-29-92	106. TIME REPORTED 22:56	107. TIME ARRIVED 23:01	108. TIME CLEARED 23:59	109. DATE OF OFFENSE 05-26-92/05-29-92	110. TIME OCCURRED 0:700/22:30

111. OFFENSE—LIST MOST SERIOUS FIRST

A. Burglary
B. Theft
C.

112. STATUTES

A. 21-3701
B. 21-3715
C.

113. LOCAL CODE

114. TYPE OF PREMISE:
1. STREET
2. SINGLE RESIDENCE
3. MULTIPLE RESIDENCE
4. COMMERCIAL
5. GAS STATION
6. CONVENIENCE STORE
7. PHARMACY/DOCTOR OFFICE
8. PUBLIC/COMMUNITY BLDG.
9. RESTAURANT
10. STORAGE/WAREHOUSE
11. TAVERN/BAR/LIQUOR
12. VEHICLE
13. BANK
14. OPEN AREA (PARK, FIELD, ETC.)
15. OTHER

115. LOCATION OF OFFENSE 2345 Felony Lane	116. REPORT AREA 124	TYPE (INSERT NUMBER): 2

CODES: V=VICTIM   B=BUSINESS   W=WITNESS   P=PARENT   DC=DISCOVERED CRIME   RP=REPORTING PARTY

117. NAME—LAST, FIRST, MIDDLE Doe, John	118. CODE DC/RP	119. RESIDENCE ADDRESS—PHONE 2337 Felony Lane, Ourtown, Allstate

120. RACE W	121. SEX M	122. AGE 25	123. DATE OF BIRTH 2/10/67	124. HT. 5 11	125. WT. 170	126. HAIR Bro	127. EYES Bro	128. OCCUPATION	129. BUSINESS ADDRESS—PHONE

130. NAME—LAST, FIRST, MIDDLE Smith, Jon J.	131. CODE V	132. RESIDENCE ADDRESS—PHONE 2345 Felony Lane, Ourtown, Allstate 555-4321

133. RACE W	134. SEX M	135. AGE 30	136. DATE OF BIRTH 3/10/62	137. HT. 6 00	138. WT. 195	139. HAIR Blo	140. EYES Blu	141. OCCUPATION	142. BUSINESS ADDRESS—PHONE

143. NAME—LAST, FIRST, MIDDLE	144. CODE	145. RESIDENCE ADDRESS—PHONE

146. RACE	147. SEX	148. AGE	149. DATE OF BIRTH	150. HT.	151. WT.	152. HAIR	153. EYES	154. OCCUPATION	155. BUSINESS ADDRESS—PHONE

156. DID VICTIM(S) RECEIVE MEDICAL ATTENTION? Vic. #1 _____ Vic. #2 n/a Vic. #3 _____	157. ADDITIONAL INFORMATION (LOCAL USE ONLY)

158. DESCRIBE BRIEFLY HOW OFFENSE WAS COMMITTED.

Person(s) unknown forced entry to the residence and removed items.

PROPERTY STATUS: S-STOLEN   RA-RECOVERED FOR YOUR AGENCY   RO-RECOVERED FOR OTHER AGENCY   F-FOUND

159. STATUS	160. QTY.	161. DESCRIPTION OF PROPERTY	162. CODE	163. MODEL-SERIAL-OWNER APPLIED NO.	164. VALUE	165. NCIC
S	1	Zenith VCR	0618	SNL-528VF3	400.00	
S	1	Smith & Wesson .38 cal. rev.	0702	E 92356	150.00	
S	1	Social Security check	0121	unk.	----	
S	1	Cockatoo (bird)	1002	N/A	1,500.00	

166. PROPERTY DAMAGE 100	167. TOTAL VALUE PROPERTY STOLEN 2050.00

168. REPORTING OFFICER Off. John Law	169. DATE 05-29-92	170. TYPED BY jl	171. DATE 05-29-92	172. REVIEWED BY	173. DATE	174. COPIES TO: __DET. __JUVENILE __KBI __OTHER __SO/PD __CO. ATTY. __KHP

1-'85   Page _____ of _____   KBI/IBR 1

At 22:56 the office was contacted by Mr. James Doe, next-door neighbor of the victim. He was watching Smith's house while Smith was away. Doe checked the door to Smith's residence at 07:00 before he went to work. When he returned home at 22:30, he again checked Smith's residence and noticed that someone had pried the deadbolt lock on the front door. I was dispatched to the residence. I searched premises but did not find any suspects. When Mr. Smith returned home, he advised that items missing were VCR, Smith-Wesson gun and cockatoo, who answers to the name of Homer. Owner described bird as white and 10 years old. He said the bird could say his name and had limited vocabulary of "damn," "rotten" and a few curse words.

You called the police to ask more about the theft of the bird, since that was unusual. The police told you that the bird was valuable and that was probably the reason it was stolen. They told you there is no rash of bird burglars, although there had been some thefts of birds several months ago. But this bird theft does not appear to be related to those, because other items were taken, the police said. The police are still investigating. Disregard the dates in this report; use yesterday as your time frame for date of offense and date reported.

Now write the story.

2   Fire story: You are making a routine call to the fire department to find out if any fires occurred overnight. Fire Battalion Chief Stephen McInerny gives you this information:

> A fire occurred in a ground-floor apartment in the 2700 block of Northeast 30th Place in your town at 1:12 a.m. today. Four fire engines and 16 firefighters responded at 1:15 a.m. Cause of fire: A stove was turned on and some cookbooks and towels on the stove ignited. When firefighters arrived, they found a 2½-year-old cocker spaniel at the front door. Estimated damage: $9,000 smoke damage to apartment. Other units not affected. Apartment is uninhabitable. Dog's name is Tito. McInerny said the dog apparently started the fire by jumping on the stove, using one of the knobs for foothold. The setting on the burner was on medium high. The dog apparently was looking for food. The dog crawled to the front door. "The dog was clinically dead; it had no pulse and no respiration." McInerney said firefighter Bill Mock took the dog outside and gave it cardiopulmonary resuscitation and oxygen, and the dog came back to life. The dog was taken to the animal hospital and treated for smoke inhalation. McInerney said it is not unusual for dogs to be caught in house fires, but it is unusual for them to be revived from the dead. "That's twice in a little more than a year we've revived dogs that have been clinically dead as a result of a fire. We're getting pretty good at it."

You interview Mark Alan Leszczynski, who rented the apartment and owns the dog. He said he and a house guest went to a bar before midnight and left the dog alone. "The dog is a little mischievous. I've caught him doing this before. He has a never-ending appetite. I had just reprimanded him for going into my house guest's suitcase and stealing some candy."

3   Court terms: You may use your imagination for this exercise. The point of it is to see if you can use court terminology in the proper context and spell the words correctly. Use the following terms: *change of venue, affidavit, felony, misdemeanor, subpoena, mistrial, bond, arraignment, suspended sentence, plea bargain.*

Use the terms to write a story about this situation: A college student, 19, named Gold E. Locks, has been charged with a felony: breaking and entering into the home of Pa Pa Bear and his wife, Ma Ma Bear, who lived at (you decide the address) with their child, Bay B. Bear.

4 Court hearing: If possible, go to your local courthouse and cover a hearing or a case in a municipal court. You might cover small-claims court, in which people represent themselves in civil cases where they are seeking damages. If you can attend an interesting trial, write a story based on that day's testimony.

5 Civil court case: Write a brief story about the following case, a petition for a name change, which was filed in the civil section of a county court (use your county court).

IN THE CIRCUIT COURT OF (YOUR COUNTY, YOUR STATE)

Joseph Weirdo, Petitioner   Case No. 97 C638

PETITION

Comes now the petitioner, Joseph Weirdo, and prays his cause of action and states as follows:

1. That he resides at 700 Louisiana St., Your City, Your State.

2. That the petitioner requests a change of name from Joseph Weirdo to Joseph Weir.

3. That the current name of the petitioner has caused him great embarrassment and suffering.

4. That petitioner is a citizen in good standing and the request for the name change is not to avoid any legal actions against said petitioner.

5. That petitioner is not seeking for redress as a means of avoiding any debts owed to any parties.

6. Wherefore, petitioner prays for favorable judgement from the court.

Joseph Weirdo

City, State, ZIP Code

On behalf of himself

You call Joseph Weirdo, and he tells you he was tired of being kidded about his name. "I didn't want to go through life being a Weirdo," he says.

You check with Circuit Court Judge Jack Musselman, who approved the petition. He says he signs hundreds of these, but most of them are name-change petitions from divorced women, foster children who want to take the name of the family they have stayed with or people with "an extremely ethnic name." "I can't recall anyone looking to play games. A lot of times people are trying to avoid creditors. There's no way of checking that out."

The court clerk tells you that more than 300 people filed to have their names changed this year. It costs $200 to file the papers.

COACHING

TIPS

Gather as much detail as possible for graphics and for your story.

Seek human interest stories and anecdotes.

Get information to reconstruct a chronology of events.

Use descriptive and narrative techniques for sidebars.

Double-check all information; initial reports and statistics will change quickly.

Use role-playing reporting techniques: If you were a relative of someone in a tragedy, what would you want and need to know?

Plan highlights boxes and empowerment boxes when you are reporting, so you get crucial information.

Disasters and Tragedy 24

J oy Mathis was sitting at her desk in *The Oklahoma Daily* newsroom when someone ran in and said there had been a bomb explosion in Oklahoma City. It was shortly after 9 a.m. As managing editor of this campus newspaper at the University of Oklahoma, Mathis wasn't too concerned. After all, it wasn't a university story. She watched the news on television for several minutes before she realized this was a major story. Then she sprang into action. She needed to send reporters to Oklahoma City, about 20 miles from the campus in Norman, Okla.

First she called the police reporter. He said he had classes in a few hours and said he couldn't go for more than an hour. She told him to go anyway. Then she tried other reporters and photographers. They all had classes or excuses.

"I got the same reaction," she says. "No one realized what a big deal it was."

Terrorists had bombed a nine-story federal building in Oklahoma City, and hundreds of people had been killed or wounded. The death toll was uncertain at this point. But as the students and the rest of the world would later realize, the bomb explosion on April 19, 1995, was the worst disaster of its kind in the United States. The fact that it happened in Oklahoma shattered the belief that the U.S. heartland was safe from terrorists. "Why Oklahoma?" would later be a headline on the campus newspaper. But for now, Mathis needed people to cover the event.

Within an hour, student reporters began to grasp the severity of the situation and started calling in, asking what they could do. Mathis didn't have a specific plan. "I was just screaming at people.

Death is always and under all circumstances a tragedy, for if it is not, then it means that life itself has become one.

Theodore Roosevelt

Omar Gallaga (left),
Joy Mathis (middle), and
Michelle Fielden working
on a story about the
Oklahoma City bombing
Photo by Anita Amarfio

I was saying, 'Get (University of Oklahoma) angles.' That's the kind of story I knew we could do better than anyone else."

By 1 p.m. she had at least 20 reporters and photographers gathering news on the scene in the city and around the campus. They kept calling in, asking her what she wanted, and she kept asking them what they had. The coverage wasn't organized at that point.

Then Mas'ood Cajee showed up. He wanted to put the newspaper on the Internet. Mathis didn't want to be bothered. The newspaper had no daily on-line version, and Mathis thought this was an inconvenient time to start one.

"We were frantically running around trying to do everything else, and he's trying to tell me what he wants to do with the (World Wide) Web version," Mathis says. "I was more annoyed than anything else. It was several hours before I realized the scope. He would set up something that would provide information. This was going to be huge."

The response was huge. In the next few days, more than 150,000 people from all over the world would access the University of Oklahoma on-line edition to read stories and view pictures the students had produced. But Mathis didn't foresee that response at the time.

Cajee wasn't deterred by Mathis' attitude. He was intent on doing something. He had to keep busy to divert his anxiety. He is a Muslim, and the initial reports linked the terrorism to Arabs. Within two days the FBI would arrest an American believed to have links to a U.S. paramilitary group. But on the day of the bombing, Muslims faced harassment and the wrath of the public because the first police reports described the suspects as Middle Eastern men. "I was in shock and disbelief," Cajee says. "I personally feared for my life."

At first Cajee planned to put on the Internet only reactions from local and Muslim groups. He had just stopped by the newsroom briefly after his 10:30 a.m. class to confirm the reports he heard about the explosion. As he walked to his apartment 10 minutes from the campus, he realized he wanted to do more. He was majoring in English and biochemistry, but he had close ties with the campus newspaper. He had written a column for two years and served on the editorial board. By publishing the campus newspaper on the World Wide Web, along with referrals to other Internet information, he thought he could provide a valuable service.

By afternoon he headed back to the newsroom and told Mathis, "You're going to need a big fly swatter because I'm going to pester you." Throughout the afternoon and evening, he went back and forth between the newsroom in the journalism school and the physics computer lab, where he and his friends developed an on-line newspaper. They used stories and photographs by the newspaper staff and added references to all sorts of Web sites where people could access information about the bombing.

By 7 p.m., most of the reporters and photographers had returned. Mathis and Tiffany Pape, editor of the newspaper, began organizing the stories and planning the pages.

"I was feeling a little panicky because we were just getting organized, and the reporters were freaking because they didn't have much time to write," Mathis says. "But by 8 p.m. we had every editor reading stories."

Their 16-page newspaper included six pages of explosion news and photographs, graphics, and information boxes about where to donate blood or get more information.

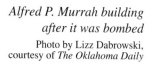

Alfred P. Murrah building
after it was bombed
Photo by Lizz Dabrowski,
courtesy of *The Oklahoma Daily*

Front page of
The Oklahoma Daily

THE OKLAHOMA DAILY

Thursday, April 20, 1995
The University of Oklahoma Norman, Okla. — Vol. 79, No.150

"Why Oklahoma City?"
Dr. Richard Havel, Goddard Health Center director

Bomb cripples OKC

DISASTER AREA — Police survey the rubble left of the Alfred Murrah Federal Building early Wednesday afternoon. Efforts continued through the night to remove victims.

WAITING FOR A SIGN — Brenda Jones, Carla Siplin and Michelle Marlowe watch as police push the public away from the bomb scene.

NOWHERE TO GO — These victims, who were inside the building at the time of the explosion, were bandaged quickly. However, it took two and a half hours before officials found them and told them to walk to a hospital.

EXPLOSION **COVERAGE**

- ❑ On the scene **2**
- ❑ Theories on bombers' motivation **2**
- ❑ OU campus reactions **2**
- ❑ Explosion quick facts **2**
- ❑ Real-life accounts **3**
- ❑ Clinton talks tough about attack **5**
- ❑ Pentagon orders relief **5**
- ❑ Muslims react to bombing **5**
- ❑ OKC citizens help blood drives **6**
- ❑ Bomb spurs Norman blood drives **6**
- ❑ Where to donate blood, supplies **6**
- ❑ Goddard, Norman help injured **6**
- ❑ HSC students help victims **7**
- ❑ HSC officials get bomb threats **7**

Explosion leaves at least 31 dead, 300 missing

Disaster — At least 200 people were injured.

By Rudolf Isaza
The Oklahoma Daily

At least 31 people died and 300 were still missing Wednesday after a car bomb gouged a nine-story hole in a federal office building.

A 9:04 a.m. explosion ravaged the north side of the Alfred Murrah Federal Building at 200 NW Fifth St. in downtown Oklahoma City. Most of the more than 500 employees were in their offices.

As of midnight Wednesday, the confirmed death toll was 31 people, 12 of those children. About 300

said Fire Chief Gary Marrs. More were feared trapped in the rubble.

"Firefighters are having to crawl over corpses in areas to get to people that are still alive," said Jon Hansen, assistant fire chief.

Gov. Frank Keating has called a state of emergency. Bomb experts from federal agencies have been called in to decipher the cause of the bombing and the Oklahoma National Guard has been called in.

Keating said he was told by the FBI that authorities were initially looking for three people in a brown pickup truck.

The Oklahoma Highway Patrol put out an all-points bulletin for three individuals, described as being Middle Eastern. One was

have been between 35 and 38.

Bob Ricks, head of the Oklahoma City FBI office, said the blast left a crater 20 feet long and eight feet deep directly outside the building, meaning the source of the explosion was probably outside.

An architect said the building was stable and was not in immediate danger of falling over.

Ricks said the shock was felt 50 miles away. Glass was reported shattered in businesses and homes within a 30-mile radius.

The search for people trapped in the rubble started as soon as the blast occurred, starting from the top floors down. People frantically looked for loved ones, including parents whose children were in the

"Firefighters are having to crawl over corpses in areas to get to people that are still alive."

Jon Hansen
Assistant fire chief

search because the elevator shaft was destroyed in the blast.

"The only way up the building is one staircase," Marrs said.

assumptions at this point," he said. "We've had hundreds, if not thousands, of leads." By midday, the government had received calls from six people saying they were from Muslim sects and claiming responsibility for the bombing.

A police source, who requested anonymity, said FBI agents were trying to piece together a van or truck that was believed to have carried the explosives. An aide of the vehicle was found about two blocks from the scene, the source said.

General concern was that this was a direct attack on the FBI. Ricks said although the FBI did not have an office in the building, 13 brother agencies did, including the Secret Service and the Bureau of

floor on the northwest side, was America's Kids, a day-care center for federal and county employees.

Seventeen children had been treated as of 10 p.m. Three were treated and released, and 20 were still unaccounted for.

Oklahoma City Chief of Police Sam Gonzalez said the Oklahoma City Police Department was in charge of perimeter control and monitoring streets, and had roped off four blocks in each direction.

Oklahoma City Mayor Ron Norick requested that all people who were in the building at the time of the explosion call 297-2424 or 397-2345 to establish an accurate count of people who were inside the building.

Of the 15 explosion-related stories, Mathis says she was most proud of the page filled with brief, emotional accounts of people on the scene. Like Michelle Fielden's story about survivor Rita Crews, who was on the ninth floor of the federal building when the bomb exploded:

"We slid over the door and down the stairwell," she said. "It was absolute, total fear. I just kept thinking, 'This has got to be a dream.' . . . Why did they pick us?" she kept asking. "Why did they pick us?"

Michelle Fielden, *The Oklahoma Daily*

Tiffany Pape began editing those stories while Mathis and other editors began editing the other stories: the main story, campus reaction, Muslims' reactions, bomb threats received at the University of Oklahoma Health Sciences Center, and several color stories with vivid scenes at hospitals and at the explosion site.

Deadline was 10 p.m. for the inside pages and midnight for the first three pages. Time was running out.

Pape knew they were going to put out a good paper. She didn't know why she was so confident. This wasn't the type of news that campus reporters usually covered. In fact, the biggest news in the paper recently had been about a power failure on campus. Nothing of this magnitude had ever happened.

"It all seemed surreal," Pape says. "Usually I'm overly emotional. I barely cried. Everyone was going about it like it's business."

Omar L. Gallaga had kept his emotions in check most of the day. Now he was tired. He had gotten up early that morning to cover a Board of Regents meeting for his campus administration beat. The meeting was boring, and he was glad to leave when he heard about the explosion. He returned to the newsroom and then headed for Norman Regional Hospital and the Norman Red Cross. But coverage wouldn't be easy.

"At the hospital a doctor said they had their first explosion victim," Gallaga says. "The man had been walking into an elevator when the building exploded. This was exactly what I'd been waiting and hoping for. Just when I felt it was time to approach the slightly wounded man, the (public relations) woman came in. She forbade me to speak to any patients." Everyone else was too busy to speak to him.

He headed for the Red Cross. He had better luck there. People were lined up for about two hours to give blood. He went to the waiting room. "In that waiting room I saw a poster whose content would become the lead for one of my bombing stories. It read ominously, 'A disaster can happen in any place, at any time!' WOW. I scribbled it down. I talked to some students who were getting ready to donate and left the scene. I returned to the newsroom where I would spend the rest of the day and night."

In addition to reporting, writing and editing, Gallaga became the newsroom liaison for the on-line newspaper pages. He began writing his stories about the Red Cross. "I was panicking because it was getting late and there were still details I needed. To add insult to devastating injury, I had to write a story about the regents in spite of what was going on. Those were about the toughest 10 inches I've ever had to compose."

He was emotionally composed until he read Rudolf Isaza's story about a grandmother who was awaiting news about her two grand-children, ages 5 and 3, who had been in the federal building's day care center. The woman had told Isaza about the youngest one:

> "He liked to draw," she said. "Just the other day he showed me a drawing of a tall and short man. I asked him who it was. He said it was Shaquille O'Neal and me."
>
> Seconds later, she was rushed into the hospital with the hope that there was some news of her grandchildren. After looking through pages of hospital fatalities and treated people, there came a tragic cry.

Rudolf Isaza, *The Oklahoma Daily*

"I began to cry when I read that," Gallaga says. "As the night wore on, we all pitched in to edit stories, and the stress was starting to wear us down."

It was close to deadline. Midnight came and went. By 12:30, only a half hour after deadline, the paper was ready for the printer.

It was time to relax. About 12 of the students headed for The Mont, a local bar. In an hour the newspaper's adviser, Jack Willis, arrived with the newspapers.

"It looked good," Gallaga says gleefully. "We had fantastic stories, first-rate photos and innovative layout. I was so proud."

Managing editor Mathis wasn't about to just sit around and gloat. As she sipped a rum and Coke, she took out a notebook. Time to plan tomorrow's paper. "I knew where I needed people," she says. "The next day was going to be fantastically organized."

It was 2 a.m. Time to go home and grab a few hours of sleep until tomorrow, when they would do it all again.

You may never have to cover a disaster of this magnitude, but all disasters require similar reporting and writing skills. If the story is about a major disaster, chances are you will be part of a team reporting and writing several stories. They include the hard-news accounts of what happened as well as many human interest sidebars about the effects on people in the area. Other sidebars could focus on history—other disasters of the same type or in the same area.

The techniques of reporting and writing these stories are the same as for any other story. But there are some differences in how you gather the information.

Reporting Techniques

Before you venture out of the newsroom, you should find out a few facts and take emergency precautions and supplies. Many major metropolitan newspapers have plans for covering disasters. In Fort Lauderdale, Fla., for example, the *Sun-Sentinel* has a detailed plan for coverage of disasters, particularly hurricanes. The plan spells out the responsibilities of each editor; assignments for reporters (hospitals, areas of the city, agencies); and telephone numbers of police, fire and rescue agencies, hospitals, utilities, and other places crucial to disaster coverage.

Cities also have major disaster plans, and police and fire departments frequently conduct drills to test them. If you have a municipal beat, find out if the government has such a plan and get a copy of it. If a disaster occurs, a good follow-up story is to check whether the plan was effective.

In the event of a disaster, you should follow these basic procedures before leaving your office or home:

• Check a map to see what routes lead to the scene. Are there alternative routes in case major arteries are blocked?

• Find out if temporary headquarters have been established for officials and media.

• Take plenty of change to make telephone calls to the newsroom to keep editors informed. If you have electronic equipment—a notebook computer or cellular telephone—make sure you have the right e-mail addresses and phone numbers. Take extra batteries as well. If you are calling in your story on deadline, remember that information changes frequently, and you will need to keep updating your editors.

• Take proper clothing, if necessary: boots, rain gear, a change of clothes (in cases of flood coverage) and emergency rations—food and beverage if you think you'll be stuck somewhere for an extended period, flashlight, and so on. You could be reporting for a long time in an area without utilities. It's a good idea to have this emergency kit of supplies in your car at all times.

• Make sure you have a full tank of gas for your vehicle.

• Take plenty of notebooks and pens. Don't rely on tape recorders or notebook computers at the scene of a disaster.

When you are covering the breaking news of a plane crash or earthquake or you are in the middle of a major storm, the sources of information are disorganized and unreliable. The news changes momentarily. The death toll often changes radically within the first few hours. Chaos reigns. You get the best information you can from eyewitnesses and officials at the scene. And then you check back repeatedly.

How do you know what to ask? You always need to ask the basics: who, what, when, where, why and how. But another way of thinking about questions is role playing, the "what if" technique of reporting. What if I were in this person's place? What if I were waiting to find out about a relative? What would I want to know?

For example: What if it were spring or winter break and you were expecting friends or relatives to visit you? Suddenly you hear over the radio that a plane has crashed at the international airport closest to you. What do you want to know? Make a list. Chances are that the information you want to know is the kind of information any reader would want to know. What airline, what plane, how many people died, who died, who survived, what caused the crash, how did it happen, where did it crash? Those questions will produce information for your lead and the top of your story. Then you gather details.

Think statistics. You need specifics: numbers of people killed and injured or evacuated.

Think human interest. How did people cope? How did they survive? What are their losses? What are their tragedies? Three hundred people could die in a plane crash, but the human interest stories of a few people make that crash vivid and poignant for the reader.

Think about narrative storytelling techniques for sidebars. How would you reconstruct the incident—what was the chronology? Try to gather information about the sequence of events if the story involves such disasters as explosions, plane crashes and other events that are not acts of nature. However, even with tornadoes, earthquakes, floods and hurricanes, it helps to get the sequence of events—specific times that events occurred, the minutes involved in destruction.

Think about helpful information for boxes. Where can people get more information, donate blood, volunteer their services and so on?

Graphics

Almost all disaster stories are accompanied by graphics—maps, illustrations, charts—to help the reader visualize where, when and how (see Exhibit 24-1). But only a few newspapers have graphics reporters. The job of supplying information to the graphic designer or artist falls to the news reporter.

You need to gather details. Get information about exact locations: streets, and measurements in yards or feet of where the accident, explosion or plane crash occurred. Try to get a map from a local gas station or convenience store. Consider whether the incident lends itself to a graphic using the time of the accident. Get a chronology in minutes or hours.

In the process of gathering all the information you need to describe the scene to a person who will draw it, you will be gathering some details you can use in your story. And, of course, the observation skills you

Exhibit 24-1

*Graphic accompanying a
story about a plane crash*

Courtesy of Jeff Dionise and
Jeff Goertzen, *The Detroit News*

Scene of fatal crash

According to reports, here's what
happened to Northwest Airlines
Flight 255 shortly after takeoff at 8:46
last night from Detroit Metropolitan
Airport.

**DC-9
MD-80**

Avis building

Wick Rd.

**Flight 255:
Destination:
Phoenix
Passengers: 144
Crew: 6
Off duty crew: 3**

Goddard Rd.
extension

Middle Belt

Wayne Co.   Detroit

Detroit Metropolitan
Airport

Detroit Metropolitan
Airport

Left side
of jet dips

Path of jet

Hits side of Avis
building with left
wing

Wick Rd.

Railroad

Debris hits truck
on I-94

Hits vecicle on
Middle Belt

I-94 Eastbound

I-94 Westbound

Portion of
cockpit
wreckage lands
here

Middle Belt Rd.

N

JEFF DIONISE AND JEFF GOERTZEN/The Detroit News

develop will help with all the descriptive writing you do to make the
reader see and care.

On-line Information

The Oklahoma City tragedy was not the first disaster in which people
turned to the Internet for information, but it was a turning point for on-
line communication because the Internet was used so extensively. As a
result of the intense interest in on-line information about this bombing,
the Internet Disaster Information Network (http://www.disaster.org), a
special network for disaster information, was created. The creators of
this service pledge to continue it as a central source of on-line information about any disaster in the future.

Although the Internet wasn't faster than television in reporting news, it offered access and information that other media could not offer as well or as completely because of space limitations. Thousands of people from all over the world were able to share information quickly in conversations in news groups. By clicking on a word or phrase, on-line readers could access scores of sites with information related to the disaster. For example, they could get reports from the Oklahoma governor's office, get media updates from newspapers and wire services, find out about paramilitary groups, connect to the on-line Voice of America, and even get advice on dealing with grief by connecting to a network called Griefnet.

Disaster information on the Internet is not limited to explosions. Special network sites exist to provide information about hurricanes, earthquakes, floods, nuclear disasters, avalanches and emergency public information for individual states.

The use of on-line information will continue to grow. You should consider gathering and printing information about where people can access on-line sites related to your stories. In addition to printing addresses and telephone numbers where people can get help, you should make Internet addresses part of the information. (Some of these sources are listed in the appendix.)

Disaster Basics

Whether you are a covering a natural disaster, such as an earthquake, or another kind, such as a plane crash or explosion, you need to gather some basic facts. With the exception of the five W's, which come first, the rest of the items are not listed in order of importance.

Who: How many people died or were injured and how many survived. These numbers will change constantly, but "who" should be one of your first questions. In a plane crash, get the name of the airline, the flight number and type of aircraft, takeoff and destination sites, and the number of passengers and crew members on board.

What and why: In many disasters, particularly airplane crashes, the cause is not immediately known. However, you should always ask and keep asking for follow-up stories. In natural disasters, get statistics about the height of rivers in floods, the intensity of earthquakes, the velocity of winds in hurricanes and similar information.

When and where: Find out exactly what time the disaster occurred and the location. Consider graphics and a reconstruction of the event.

Weather: For a weather-related disaster, get the specifics. If it is a plane crash, always find out about the weather, which could have been a factor.

Where people go: In case of evacuation—as in floods, hurricanes and earthquakes—find out where people are finding shelter.

Hospitals: Whenever people are injured, check hospitals.

Disaster scene: Gather every detail of sight, sound, emotion and other sensory feelings. You will need them for description in your stories.

Estimated cost of damages and property loss: Initially these accounts—from insurance agents, fire departments, police officials or state offices—are often inaccurate, but they add an essential element to the story.

Eyewitness accounts: Get accounts from eyewitnesses and survivors. People make the story real and emotional. You need them for quotes in the main story and for sidebars. Ask people to reconstruct where they were and what they were doing at the time of the disaster.

Government agencies involved: In plane crashes, the Federal Aviation Administration and National Transportation Safety Board always get involved in investigations. In major disasters, find out whether the National Guard is helping and which federal, state and local agencies will provide relief.

Consumer information: Find out where to go to give blood, to get help with insurance or rebuilding, to get further information. Consumer information may be included in your story or in separate boxes.

Red Cross and shelters: Always check with the Red Cross and other relief agencies for their role and their needs.

Safety precautions: Check with police and fire departments and with electric, gas and water utility companies to find out about the precautions people should take. You could refer to dangerous conditions in the main story or in a separate story.

Roads: Check highway departments to find out which roads are closed or dangerous and what alternate routes people can take.

Survivors: List those who are known to be alive.

Victims: The names of people who were killed often are not released for days, but try to obtain them from officials.

Crime: Check with police to find out about looting or other post-disaster crimes or arrests in cases of human-created disasters.

Perspective: Was this the worst, second-worst or ninth-worst disaster of its kind in a certain period of time? Check clips or an almanac to find out how this disaster ranks against previous disasters of its kind. If it is the worst of its type, that information should appear high in the story.

Background: Check the background of the airline involved in a plane crash or a business involved in a disaster. Readers will be interested in any history that may apply to this disaster.

Medical examiner: Check for information about progress in the identification of victims.

Here is how many of those basic elements worked in *The Oklahoma Daily*'s first-day story by Rudolf Isaza about the bombing in Oklahoma City. Many descriptive human interest stories were in sidebars or some of the 14 other stories.

Bomb cripples Oklahoma City

Explosion leaves 31 dead, 300 missing

At least 31 people died and 300 were still missing Wednesday after a car bomb gouged a nine-story hole in a federal office building.

A 9:04 a.m. explosion ravaged the north side of the Alfred Murrah Federal Building at 200 NW Fifth St. in downtown Oklahoma City. Most of the more than 500 employees were in their offices.

As of midnight Wednesday, the confirmed death toll was 31 people, 12 of those children. About 300 people were missing. At least 200 people were injured, 58 critically, said Fire Chief Gary Marrs. Many more were feared trapped in the rubble.

"Firefighters are having to crawl over corpses in areas to get to people that are still alive," said Jon Hansen, assistant fire chief.

Gov. Frank Keating has called a state of emergency. Nationwide bomb experts from federal agencies have been called in to decipher the cause of the bombing. The Oklahoma National Guard was called in.

Keating said he was told by the FBI that authorities were initially looking for three people in a brown pickup truck. The Oklahoma Highway Patrol put out an all-points bulletin for three individuals, de-

scribed as of Middle Eastern descent. One was described as being between the ages of 25 and 30. Another may have been between 35 and 38.

Bob Ricks, head of the Oklahoma City FBI office, said the blast left a crater 20 feet long and eight feet deep directly outside the building, meaning the source of the explosion was probably outside.

An architect said the building was stable and was not in immediate danger of falling over. Ricks said the shock was felt 50 miles away. Glass was reported shattered in businesses and homes within a 30-mile radius.

The search for people trapped in the rubble started as soon as the blast occurred, starting from the top floors down. People frantically looked for loved ones, including parents whose children were in the building's day-care center. Rescuers had problems initiating the search because the elevator shaft was destroyed in the blast.

"The only way up the building is one staircase," Marrs said.

Ricks would not speculate on any suspects. "We are making no assumptions at this point," he said. "We've had hundreds, if not thousands, of leads." By midday, the government had received calls from six people saying they were from Muslim sects and asserting they were responsible for the bombing.

A police source, who requested anonymity, said FBI agents were

trying to piece together a van or truck that was believed to have carried the explosives. An axle of the vehicle was found about two blocks from the scene, the source said.

General concern was that this was a direct attack on the FBI. Ricks said although the FBI did not have an office in the building, 13 brother agencies did, including the Secret Service and the Bureau of Alcohol, Tobacco and Firearms.

Also destroyed, on the second floor on the northwest side, was America's Kids, a day-care center for federal and county employees. Seventeen children had been treated as of 10 p.m. Three were treated and released, and 20 were still unaccounted for.

Oklahoma City Chief of Police Sam Gonzalez said the Oklahoma City Police Department was in charge of perimeter control and monitoring streets, and has roped off four blocks in each direction.

The explosion was similar to the terrorist car bombing that killed six people and injured 1,000 at New York's World Trade Center in 1993.

Oklahoma City Mayor Ron Norick requested that all people who were in the building at the time of the explosion call 297-2424 or 397-2345 to get an accurate number of people inside the building.

Rudolf Isaza, *The Oklahoma Daily*

Death Tolls   The day after the Oklahoma City bombing, the death toll had risen to 57. Each day thereafter, the number of dead and injured increased. The final toll was 168 people, including 19 children. In disasters, dealing with numbers of victims is difficult, because they change constantly. The first day you can report the facts as Isaza did, saying "At least . . . ," or use the words "an estimated" with the specific number. The following day your lead can state that the death toll has increased or you can just write the new death toll. You don't need to correct previous information. Readers know you haven't made an error; you are just giving the facts as they become available.

Here is how information about the death toll changed over a few hours when *The Detroit News* printed in several editions a story about a major plane crash. Note in the first story that no death toll was available and the number of passengers was incorrect.

First edition	**Fourth edition, about four hours later**
A Northwest Airlines passenger jet with 146 aboard crashed at about 8:45 p.m. Sunday shortly after takeoff en route to Phoenix from Detroit Metropolitan Airport.	A Northwest Airlines jet with 153 people aboard crashed just after takeoff Sunday night at Detroit Metropolitan Airport, killing at least 152 aboard and two people on the ground.

Interviews With Grief-stricken People   You have a list of people who died. Your editor wants you to call the families of victims to get biographical data and reactions. What do you do? Quit your job? Cry? Get sick? Many reporters feel like doing all three. But there are sensitive ways to cover grief. And it's difficult, if not impossible, to avoid dealing with such situations if you are going to be a newspaper or magazine reporter. So here are some suggestions about how you can cover such stories.

Jacqui Banaszynski, a former reporter for the *St. Paul* (Minn.) *Pioneer Press,* has covered numerous stories involving grief, so many that she claims she has the grief beat. She won the Pulitzer Prize in 1988 for her coverage of the story of a man who was dying of AIDS (discussed in Chapter 19). When she is reporting about tragedy, she often tells the people she interviews that if at the end of the interview they don't like the way she has conducted herself, she will offer them her notebook and won't write anything. So far, no one has ever taken her up on her offer.

How can you ask questions about grief? Try this classroom exercise: In groups of three or four, list all the fears and anxieties you have about interviewing people who are grieving. Then discuss some reporting techniques you can use to deal with each of these concerns. After compiling your concerns and solutions, discuss them with the class as a whole.

Here are some concerns students usually express during this activity:

What if the person hangs up on me? You could try the Edna Buchanan technique of calling back and suggesting you were disconnected. Or you could just forget that interview and try calling someone else. Another suggestion is to call a neighbor and ask if he or she knows someone in the house who might talk to you. Or call the house and ask if anyone could talk to you about the situation. You don't have to ask for the person who is in the greatest pain. If you are on the scene and the person does not want to talk to you, you might give him or her your card (or a note with your name and phone number) and ask if you could talk at another time.

What questions do I ask? Don't ask, "How do you feel about your son's death?" Obviously, the person feels terrible. You might instead ask specific questions about what the person was like, biographical questions. What was the person planning, or where was he or she going when the accident happened? Then you could ask for memories about the person.

What is the first thing I should say? Introduce yourself and state your purpose. You might also express your condolences.

What if I start to cry? You can be empathetic and even a little teary. Try not to weep. But be sincere. Do not fake your emotions.

What if the person I'm interviewing starts to cry? Stop interviewing and ask if you can get the person a glass of water or a tissue, or just be quiet for a while. You might also ask if the person would prefer you to come back another time, depending on the severity of the situation.

What if I say something insensitive without knowing it? Apologize.

Why do I have to interview people in times of grief? Because these types of stories make a news event more significant and real to readers. Because people relate to other people, not to vague generalities. And remember, for some people, talking about their pain is a form of catharsis. For others, grief is a very private matter. So some people will talk to you and others won't. Respect their needs. You won't get every story, especially if reporters from other newspapers and television stations already have talked to them. But the ones you do talk to can be wonderful.

Sidebars

Sidebars are not synonymous with soft news. Many sidebars are human interest stories, but they also can be hard-news stories or informational self-help stories. A sidebar is basically a story that gives the reader some new information or more information than the mainbar can provide. The mainbar in a disaster story is comprehensive; each sidebar should be very narrowly focused on one topic. The mainbar can allude to information that is in the sidebar, such as a quote from an eyewitness, but the sidebar should not be repetitious. A mainbar without emotional quotes from people would be boring. However, an entire sidebar about the people who have been quoted extensively in the mainbar is too repetitious.

Here are some ideas for sidebars and questions you can ask to determine whether you need them:

Helpfulness: If I were the reader, what information would I find helpful? For example, if a disaster affects utilities, as in a flood, should you have a sidebar on how to cope without electricity or fresh water? Or if it affects roads, consider a story about alternate routes. Or a story about how to get government aid.

Human interest: Is there a human interest story that the reader might find compelling? Does someone have a story that is unusual?

Perspective: Would the reader find it interesting to know the history of other disasters of this type?

The location: Is there a color piece that is compelling about the scene or a location affected by the disaster, such as a story about the hospital scene or the shelters where evacuated people were taken?

Other angles: Is there enough information worth telling about a specific angle of the story, such as the rescue efforts, the efforts of investigators or previous problems with that type of aircraft?

Analysis: If your community has been working on a disaster plan, is there a need for an analysis piece about how rescue or government workers coordinated the disaster operations?

In most cases, especially in human interest sidebars, you can use all the feature techniques of descriptive and narrative writing that you have studied. You should try to make the story vivid and compelling.

A sidebar still stands alone as a story, so you need to insert a reference to the main news—a brief line about the disaster or crash—especially if you have only one sidebar. If you have a huge package of several sidebars, you don't need to rehash the news statement in each one. You need to coordinate with the editor just how much of the main news needs to be in your story.

Here is an excerpt from one of the sidebars about grieving relatives in the Detroit plane crash. Notice from the quotes that the reporters did not ask "How do you feel?" The quotes and backup information contain specific memories and details about the people who died.

Grief cuts wide swath

Relatives draw close
as horror sinks in

By Jon Pepper
and Rachel Reynolds

The names of the dead trickled out slowly.

Among them was a professional basketball player. A weight lifter. A high school cheerleader and a successful businessman. A nursery school teacher from St. Clair Shores.

There were boyfriends and girl-friends, granddaughters and grand-sons, husbands and wives.

None of the dead were positively identified by this morning. The few names that trickled out came from friends and relatives.

Kurt Dobronski, 28, vice-president of a Scottsdale, Ariz., construction firm and a former star football player at Dearborn Edsel Ford High and Central Michigan University, had come home to Dearborn for the wedding of a friend and found his 10-day visit "the best vacation he ever had," said brother Karl Dobronski.

"Things were going great for him," Karl Dobronski said. "This is a shock."

Things were also going well for Nick Vanos, a 7-foot-2 center for the Phoenix Suns basketball team. After playing only sparingly in his first two years in the National Basketball Association, Vanos was expected to start for the Suns this fall. He had come to Detroit to visit a girlfriend and boarded Flight 255 for his return to Arizona, team officials said.

"Nick Vanos was a young man who was just beginning to come into his own as a professional athlete and was about to take a giant step," said Suns general manager Jerry Coangelo. "It was very sad because he gave everything he had with his abilities. . . ."

Bill Horton of Phoenix lost his wife, Cindy, 37, who had been visiting her parents in Wisconsin. She had flown to Detroit to catch a flight to Phoenix. At midnight Sunday, he tried to calm his two stepchildren, aged 11 and 7. "They're hysterical," Horton said, sobbing. "How do you explain something like this to them?"

The Detroit News

Follow-up Stories

All major disasters require follow-up stories for many days. The second-day story should attempt to explain the cause, if that was not clear the first day. If the cause still isn't clear, you can lead with what officials are investigating. If there isn't any new information, you can describe cleanup attempts at the scene. The death toll should remain in the lead, especially if it has changed from earlier reports, or should be in the first few paragraphs. Other follow-up stories may focus on rescue efforts, human interest elements, costs of rebuilding or any other related news.

In follow-up stories, you still need to mention what happened—when and where the plane crashed, when the earthquake occurred, and so on. In successive stories, that information can go a little bit lower. But it should still be high in the story on the second day.

Here is the second-day lead on the mainbar about the plane crash in Detroit:

Loose and broken parts caused the breakdown since mid-1985 of four jet engines like those on Northwest Flight 255, which crashed Sunday at Detroit Metropolitan Airport.

At least 154 people were killed after witnesses saw an explosion in or near the aircraft's left engine. However, the head of a National Transportation Safety Board team investigating the crash said other witnesses saw no such fire and "very preliminary" findings are that there was no failure or fire in the left engine.

Documents describing the engine failures, known to the Federal Aviation Administration (FAA) and the National Transportation Safety Board (NTSB) since April, were obtained in Washington Monday.

A U.S. Department of Transportation source claimed Monday that a serious fuel leak problem with the jet was reported by crew members less than two weeks ago. FAA officials refused to confirm such a report.

In Romulus, workers began the soul-bruising task of collecting human remains from the crash site for identification by pathologists, friends and relatives.

Ric Bohy, Fred Girard, Mike Martindale and Joel Smith, *The Detroit News*

Airplane Crashes

You may never have to cover a major airplane crash, but small plane crashes occur in almost every community. The principles for writing and reporting the news are the same, regardless of the size of the crash.

Almost all disaster-related information listed earlier also applies to an airplane crash. One of your first concerns should be the number of dead or injured people. Initially you will get only estimates, and most likely they will be wrong. But some accounting of the death and injury toll should be in the lead.

Although an actual cause may not be known for months, ask anyway, because you need some idea.

You should also seek the names, ages and home towns of victims and survivors. In major plane crashes, the list of passengers and their status usually is not released for a day or more, until the relatives have been notified. The names and status of the pilots and crew members may be available sooner.

In addition to getting accounts from eyewitnesses, reactions from relatives or people at the airport, and other human interest stories, make sure you get the following specifics: name of the airline and flight number of the plane; the type of plane and number of engines, especially for small planes; the origination and final destination sites.

Check for comments from the air controllers. The pilot's last words usually are not available until investigators get the plane's "black box" recording, but keep it in mind for follow-up stories.

Don't forget the perspective: how many plane crashes of this type have occurred in recent years or how this crash ranks in severity.

Here is an example of a plane crash story that follows most of the guidelines for disaster coverage:

20 die in La Guardia crash

The Associated Press

Lead: airline, number of people aboard, where crashed, when, death toll, destination, flight number

NEW YORK—A USAir jet carrying 51 people crashed in a snowstorm Sunday while trying to take off from La Guardia Airport and skidded part way into the frigid waters of Flushing Bay. Authorities said at least 20 people were killed.

Witnesses said USAir Flight 405, bound for Cleveland, left the ground, then fell back and exploded before sliding into the water.

Eyewitness account, color quote

"It looked like the sun coming up," witness Manny Dias told WNBC-TV. "The sky lit up. It was just about to take off. It just exploded."

Backup for lead: death toll, survivors, missing

Sgt. John Murphy of the Port Authority said 20 people were dead, 27 were known to have survived and four others were still missing.

Elaboration

Divers said they found passengers, and the plane's pilot, strapped upside down in their seats in the submerged part of the wreckage.

Status of airport, diversion of flights

The airport was closed after the accident, which occurred about 9:30 p.m. Incoming flights were diverted to nearby John F. Kennedy International Airport.

Elaboration

Twenty-one people climbed out of the plane in the water and to the Delta shuttle terminal, Port Authority police said.

Neither the airline nor the Federal Aviation Administration had any immediate explanation for what caused the plane to crash during takeoff or whether the bad weather was a factor. The National Transportation Safety Board sent investigators to the scene.

Suspected cause

Port Authority police said the plane veered left at the end of the runway and hit a snow-covered barricade just before the water.

Detail

The nose, wing and engine snapped off while the rest of the plane was in the water with its top sheared off.

At Cleveland's Hopkins International Airport, friends and relatives of passengers aboard the plane were in seclusion.

Relatives, friends: secluded (no reaction possible yet)

USAir spokeswoman Lynn McCloud in Arlington, Va., said 51 people were on the jet, including 47 passengers, two pilots and two flight attendants. The airline said the flight originated in Jacksonville, Fla., and five passengers were booked all the way through to Cleveland.

Airline official's comments substantiating earlier facts

Origination point

McCloud, the USAir spokesman, said the temperature was 31 degrees, wind about 15 mph, and the runway was wet with patches of snow. She said visibility was three-quarters of a mile.

Weather

The aircraft was a 6-year-old Fokker-28 4000 commuter jet, McCloud said.

FAA spokesman Fred Farrar described the plane as a "relatively small two-engine jet with both engines on the rear of the fuselage."

Detail about plane

It was the second time in three years a plane has skidded off a runway at La Guardia. Both were USAir flights.

Perspective: other crashes

Natural Disasters

All disaster stories should include the same basic information: death toll, survivors, eyewitness accounts, human interest quotes from survivors, and details of the scene and of recovery efforts. For natural disasters, add information about the natural forces at work, such as weather conditions. Any time you are writing about a weather-related disaster, be sure to include a weather forecast. If you are covering floods, find out how high the river crested—if that was a factor—or the height of water in feet. If winds were a cause of the destruction, get the specific miles per hour of the wind velocity. In the case of an earthquake, find out the magnitude and the location of the epicenter. Explain in simple terms how the natural phenomenon occurred. A graphic may be better than words (see Exhibit 24-2).

Tornadoes, earthquakes, hurricanes and floods all cause extensive damage and leave people homeless. Find out where people are finding shelter and what is being done to help them. Insurance is also a big factor in natural disasters. Include consumer information, such as areas readers should avoid and the names of impassable streets, or how people can cope. Utilities are often affected, so make sure you check about the safety of drinking water, food supplies and electricity.

Many of these consumer elements may be in sidebars. But when you write the first-day story, the format is similar to that of a plane crash or any other disaster. Give the basic facts and a death or injury toll in the lead.

FERNDALE, Calif.—A powerful earthquake rocked California's remote North Coast on Saturday, knocking brick facades off buildings, sparking fires that destroyed several businesses and two post offices, and sending at least 35 people to hospitals with cuts, broken bones and chest pains.

Los Angeles Times

Exhibit 24-2

*Graphic explaining
a natural disaster*
Courtesy of Paul Horn and
Dave Hardman, *Reno* (Nev.)
Gazette-Journal

A water spout is born

A water spout is similar to a tornado only created over water.

How they start

Fast winds

In and near a thunderstorm, higher winds move faster than winds along the ground due to friction with the Earth's surface. The air in between begins slowly rotating.

Slower winds

Rotating winds

A thunderstorm updraft — rising warm air — lifts the rotating air. If the rotation's diameter shrinks after being lifted, it speeds up and may become a spout.

Rotating winds

Updraft

Upward winds

Winds twist upward as air rushes into the bottom of the vortex. They usually rotate counterclockwise, but 1% of them spin clockwise.

Water spout sighting

Lake Tahoe

28

Zephyr Cove

Homewood

207

N

50

89

South Lake Tahoe

5 miles

50

Source: GNS research

Paul Horn and **Dave Hardman**/Gazette-Journal

Floods are the most prevalent natural disasters. Almost every part of the country has experienced disastrous flooding. Even in desert communities like Tucson, Ariz., heavy rains often cause flooding and fatalities. This flood story contains most of the crucial elements, including a weather forecast, specifics about flood levels and utility problems, and human interest:

Napa, Sonoma hit by floods—again

By Frank Sweeney, Janet Rae-Dupree and Michael Dorgan
Mercury News Staff Writers

Basic news lead

For the second time this winter, rain-swollen rivers flooded Napa and Sonoma county towns and vineyards Thursday, creating a colossal mess where weary residents were just getting their lives in order after fierce January storms.

Weather specifics

Howling out of the central Pacific, the storm slammed into the state late Wednesday with steady, torrential rain and winds blasting to 60 mph. And weather forecasters expect more of the same today.

But for a few brief respites, the relentless battering continued all day Thursday.

Torrential rains overpowered small streams and larger rivers throughout the region, triggering floods and mudslides. High winds

Power problems

snapped electrical power to 540,000 customers from Big Sur to Eureka, closed highways and shut down shipping in San Francisco Bay. New snow blanketed the Sierra Nevada.

Numerous rivers and streams were at or near flood stage throughout Northern California. Among communities threatened by the rising water were Susanville, Tehama and Hamilton City along the Sacramento River, Madison and Yolo near the city of Davis, and Lakeport on the western edge of Clear Lake.

Forecast

The National Weather Service warned residents to brace for another wave of rain spinning in from a strong low-pressure system in the northeastern Pacific before dawn today.

Forecaster Brandt Maxwell at the National Weather Service's Monterey office said some areas could get as much as two inches of rain today. "Of course, any amount is going to aggravate flooding."

The rain is forecast to taper off this afternoon, with showers tonight and Saturday.

A winter storm warning was issued for the Sierra Nevada with snow levels forecast to range from 5,000 to 6,000 feet today. As much as three feet of snow could fall above the 7,000-foot elevation, according to the National Weather Service.

History

It's starting to look like January, when a disastrous series of storms caused widespread flooding and $300 million in damage, killed 11 people and displaced thousands throughout California.

For residents of Napa and Sonoma counties, still recovering from the floods of January, it was an all-too-familiar story.

Evacuations

In St. Helena, a small town in the Napa Valley wine country, the Napa River flooded vineyards, homes, apartments and a mobile home park. Firefighters evacuated more than 1,000 people as the river rose to 19 feet—six feet above flood stage.

Several hundred others were rescued from the Vineyard Valley Mobile Home Park, which survived the January floods. On Thursday, two-thirds of the 300 mobile homes were under water.

Emergency workers in small boats evacuated people through waist-deep water that blocked access to apartment complexes. But even the rescuers had troubles. One rowboat, caught in the swift current, floated down the Napa River for five miles before another boat came to its rescue.

Human interest

Malia Barron Hendricks, about to give birth to her second child, and her husband, Charles, found the road to the hospital blocked by floodwaters. So they drove to a fire station where firefighters helped deliver a healthy baby girl. The woman and her newborn, Hope Bridget Hendricks, eventually were taken to St. Helena Hospital by an ambulance that had to negotiate flooded streets.

Shortly after the birth, the firefighters shared a bottle of expensive Napa Valley sparkling wine with the new mother and father.

By late afternoon, a sheet of water four feet deep covered much of the eastern Napa Valley, isolating flooded farmhouses in inundated vineyards.

Farther south in Napa, the river was expected to rise four feet above flood level, flooding Soscol Avenue, a main business artery. Helpless onlookers watched water creep into the street, growing deeper by the minute.

"We're waiting for the fire marshal to come tell us whether to shut down," said Carl Kada, 22, assistant manager of a movie complex near Soscol Avenue. "I already know the answer. We need to be out of here."

Mark Townsend, 41, owner of Soscol Antiques, hurriedly tried to waterproof his store, sealing the doors with tape and sandbags, putting his wares as high on shelves as he could, and hauling away the most valuable items in pickup trucks. He lost $10,000 worth of antiques in the flood two months ago.

"It's a little hard, but you have to remember we are going home tonight, and home will have booze and an espresso machine," Townsend said, "and there are a lot of people who don't get to go home tonight."

To the west in Sonoma County, the Russian River flooded low-lying parts of Guerneville, the waterside community submerged by floods only two months ago.

The water rose two feet an hour after eight inches of rain fell in 15 hours, officials said, although the rise slowed in late afternoon. At 5 p.m., the Russian River was $4\frac{1}{2}$ feet above flood level, and expected to crest at 43 feet late Thursday night—11 feet above flood stage. That would be $4\frac{1}{2}$ feet below the January flood line and would leave the main business area and most town residents dry, according to Sheriff's Capt. Bob Jarvis.

Sheriff's deputies in inflatable rubber boats rescued people stranded by rising water. The flood threat caused widespread alarm, particularly among those who have just completed cleanup and repairs from the last flood.

Landscaper Steve Chadwell, who lives in a low-lying section of town with his wife, Kathryn, and two young children, frantically loaded new furniture onto a flatbed truck Thursday afternoon. Already the homes of some of his neighbors were in several feet of water.

Chadwell bought an apartment-full of new furniture just a week ago to replace that ruined when the January flood put three feet of water in his second-story apartment.

"We weren't taking any chances," he said as his wife hoisted a big box of toys and other household items onto the truck. But the Chadwells have no plans to abandon the town where they have lived for four years.

"This is one of the most beautiful places in California," he said.

Flood levels

Personal Tragedy

In the beginning, hordes of reporters descended on the tiny town of Buckner, Mo., to cover the tragedy of three brothers who died in an icy pond. It was a personal tragedy of national magnitude.

Tad Bartimus, an award-winning writer for The Associated Press, was not among the initial reporters. Bartimus called the family several weeks later and said she wanted to do a story because she didn't think the real story about the boys had ever been told. To her surprise, the family consented. But Bartimus said it was a very painful story to write.

She said her reporting style for tragedy is to treat the family as though it were her own. "I can get anyone to tell me anything. And I can empathize with people. Those are my top two strengths."

But why do the media love to do stories about personal tragedies? The media are often criticized for their coverage of grieving families. A grief counselor in Bartimus' story expresses the reason well: "The human spirit is resilient beyond belief, and that is the hope here," said Ms. Howard. "At a time like this you can get swamped by the grinding pain of it. But out of that pain comes some of the most substantial character and human elegance to be found on Earth. You learn how people can rise up and care for one another."

And that is a theme of this story. Readers want to read about how people cope with tragedy.

Bartimus didn't ask the parents insensitive questions about how they felt. When parents lose their three children, the answer is obvious. Instead she focused on how the community reacted and the parents' memories of their children.

As a reporter, you undoubtedly will have to cover a personal tragedy at some point—probably many times—in your career. Many of those stories will focus on the community and how people cope with a tragedy that happens to their neighbors or members of their immediate family. Bartimus' story can serve as a model for questions to ask and approaches to take. It is similar to the personal tragedy story written by David Silverman (in Chapter 13) about the parents whose child was killed when a woman went on a shooting rampage in an elementary school in suburban Chicago. His approach focused more on the parents, three months after the tragedy.

As you read Bartimus' story, note the sources she used and the way she structured the story. Like Silverman, she also used a circular ending that returned to the beginning of the story for concept but focused on the future.

Band of brothers

Tad Bartimus
Associated Press

*"We few, we happy few,
we band of brothers . . ."*
William Shakespeare, *Henry V*

BUCKNER, Mo.—There is so little left.

A red cardboard valentine with torn paper lace, which proclaims, "I love you Mom." A carefully penned Thanksgiving essay in which the writer says he's grateful for his family "to have someone to love me." A child's "Life Story" book with extra pages left blank for future adventures.

Chad Eugene Gragg, 12, Aaron Wayne Gragg, 11, and Stephen Douglas Gragg, 8, died together at dusk on the cold afternoon of Feb. 4.

It was Aaron's 11th birthday. Despite admonishments from a teacher and a chum who rode home with him on the bus, he chose to celebrate it by sliding on the frozen surface of a farmer's pond.

The ice broke. Aaron fell into the frigid water. His big brother Chad, doing what his parents had always taught him to do, attempted to save him. He, too, fell in. Stevie, strong for his age, also tried to be his brothers' keeper. His body plunged through the thin crust.

A horrified neighbor boy ran for help. Frantic firemen pulled the brothers from the pond within 30 minutes. They weren't breathing and had no pulse. Two helicopters and an ambulance rushed them to three separate hospitals.

Thus began the agonizing pilgrimage of Charles and Mary Gragg, two ordinary people who now stagger in the footsteps of Job.

Meanwhile, word of the tragedy spread like woodsmoke over this western Missouri town of 2,800. The event would change forever Buckner's image of itself.

As doctors at St. Mary's Hospital in nearby Blue Springs told the parents their son Chad was dead, teachers and friends arrived to surround the stunned couple in a protective cocoon.

Hoping against hope, the Graggs next went to St. Luke's Hospital in Kansas City, only to be told Aaron, too, was gone.

By the time they reached Children's Mercy Hospital the Graggs were at the heart of a caravan of grief. They found Stephen on a life support system. At 10 p.m., he passed away.

In the space and time it took for the sun to set and the moon to rise, three healthy, happy, handsome little boys vanished from the lives of all who knew them.

They left behind bits of homework and smiling celluloid images, a puppy named Scooter who looks for them everywhere, empty school desks, classmates who struggle to remember their last words, teachers who wish they'd known them better.

They left behind the townspeople of Buckner, who were galvanized by the loss to dig deep within their hearts and pockets to bury the children with dignity, and continue to mourn them with honest tears.

They left behind their mother and their father, but Mary and Charles Gragg, both 41, are no longer parents. The sounds of laughter, of life, are gone from their empty house. The only noise comes from the television set. The door to the boys' bedroom is closed.

The unbearable must now be borne.

"In our age, children aren't eligible to die because our expectations have been set up that children can survive anything," said Kathryn Howard, a grief counselor with Comprehensive Mental Health Services in nearby Independence, Mo.

"All the time we read about children who fall into freezing water and survive. Why not Aaron, or Chad, or at least Stevie? They couldn't be saved because the water wasn't deep enough or cold enough. But because of modern medical miracles, we are conditioned to believe it is outrageous that they died."

Ms. Howard, whose nonprofit agency has contracts with both the local school district and fire department, had headed grief and death counseling in Buckner since the drownings. She also helped the Graggs plan their children's funeral.

"The human spirit is resilient beyond belief, and that is the hope here," said Ms. Howard. "At a time like this you can get swamped by the grinding pain of it. But out of that pain comes some of the most substantial character and human elegance to be found on Earth. You learn how people can rise up and care for one another.

"This is now a community that speaks with one voice. That phenomena is rare—too often we are too big and fragmented a society for this to happen. But if you listen to Buckner today, what you hear is, 'We care. This matters to us. They were our children, too.'"

The Graggs had no close relatives living nearby. Acting out of instinct and compassion, Buckner Elementary School Principal

Richard Thompson stepped into the abyss.

"The school in a sense became their family," said Thompson. "Working with me, Kathryn Howard, and Jerry Brown, the funeral director, Charlie and Mary decided to have the funeral in the junior high gymnasium. The parents wanted the teachers to speak, and to be pallbearers.

"This became a chance for the community to fulfill what a community is all about. Before the accident happened you could have counted on one hand the number of people who knew Charlie and Mary Gragg. Now everyone knows them and wants to help them."

The Parent-Teacher Association mobilized to take food to the Gragg home for the next two weeks. Secretly thanking God it wasn't their own kids, mothers reached into closets and brought forth suits and ties for the boys to wear to their graves.

Funds were established to accept donations to offset medical and funeral expenses. The local bank, the savings and loan and a florist donated flower sprays for the coffins.

"It is so hard to take it in," said James B. Jones, president of the First State Bank of Missouri, where nearly $20,000 was sent in the first two weeks after the accident.

Pondering the event's anguishing mathematics, Jones wondered, "If people had only one child and lost it, isn't that just as terrible as having three and losing them all? I don't know, I simply don't know, it's just so hard to make yourself think about it."

Mortician Brown tried not to think about his own boys, aged 7 and 8, as he plotted the funeral like a general planning a battle.

"We went into this with no idea there'd be any money to pay for it. I was estimating a minimum of $2,500 each. I went to my vault manufacturer and coffin supplier and explained the situation. They were willing to share the burden, no matter what happened," said Brown, whose family has served as Buckner's only morticians for three generations.

Brown decided on three identical coffins, three identical hearses. He reserved three side-by-side plots on a gently sloping hillside in the town cemetery.

From the graves you can look out over the walnut and oak trees, past the dormant farm pastures, and down toward the creek where an angry crawdad once bit Aaron's big toe, where Chad caught a two-pound lunker of a catfish, where Stevie loved to hunt for frogs.

Those are the same hills and hollows Brown scampered over as a child. He, too, remembers sliding across frozen ponds with his buddies.

Brown steeled himself not to think about any of those memories, or the event that brought him into the Graggs' circle, "because it is so overwhelming, so awesome, that it stops you in your tracks." He'd think later. First, he had a big job to do.

When he'd finished embalming and dressing the dead children in their new clothes, he tucked each boy's favorite toy into the silk-lined caskets.

As Brown ministered to the dead, Thompson and Ms. Howard, along with every clergyman in town, local teachers and reinforcements from other schools, consoled the living.

"The day after it happened we conducted emotional triage in the halls, the library, the cafeteria, and the classrooms," said Ms. Howard. "We had kids crying with counselors in corners everywhere you looked. Part of being young is learning how to deal with your pain. The kids were shown they could support one another and that they wouldn't be alone."

Teachers read "The Taste of Blackberries" to all fourth and fifth graders. The book relates the tale of a boy who loses his best friend. Younger children heard "The 10th Good Thing About Barney," a story of a little boy whose cat dies.

Thompson sent letters home with every student, detailing the day's upheaval and warning parents their children "might have tears or depression but that is expected and is normal in the grief process. . . ." Attached were four pages of guidelines for dealing with the situation.

"That day we just put a Band-Aid on it; we flew by the seat of our pants," recalled Thompson. "We decided to leave the Gragg boys' desks empty to stress the finality of death, to show some physical remains. We talked about the details. We tried to cope with the onslaught of the media but refused to let reporters talk to teachers or students. And we braced for the funeral."

Thompson is described by faculty, city fathers, and the Graggs as the glue that held everything together through that long weekend.

Besides organizing the school's response to the tragedy, Thompson set up the junior high gymnasium for the funeral, helped teachers prepare their farewell remarks, acceded to any family wishes, and comforted students who attended the open coffin visitation and closed casket funeral.

"It was tough trying to make an appropriate setting for a funeral out of a basketball court, but we did it," said Thompson.

He had a carpenter build a wooden schoolhouse which was then covered with flowers and presented by the students of Buckner. Thompson also gave the parents a brass school bell engraved with the boys' names. The gift usually is reserved for retiring teachers.

"We consider that your boys have retired to a heavenly school," Thompson told the Graggs.

More than 600 mourners heard fourth-grade teacher Jeanne Young describe the Gragg children as "three adventuresome, energetic little boys . . . each of us has a special place in our heart, locked and guarded—it's the place just for Chad and Stephen and Aaron."

Symbols of each boy's interests rested atop the blue-gray caskets: art materials for Aaron, a soccer ball for Stephen, a basketball for Chad.

Finally, the three brothers were laid to rest in the winter's hard ground.

Mortician Brown left town for a convention in Florida, allowing himself to cry most of the way.

Mental health counselor Kathryn Howard began planning a series of forums on death and dying for the Buckner community.

Principal Thompson fielded calls from People magazine and tried to get his school back to some semblance of normalcy.

"The tragedy will long be remembered in this community," said Thompson, pausing to wipe tears from his eyes and catch his breath over the big lump in his throat. "They were rambunctious country boys who were one for all and all for one.

"Two of the boys willingly gave up their lives for the other. That is the only thing that makes it comprehensible."

Mary and Charlie Gragg's relatives have gone home and neighbors visit less now. Gragg has resumed the commute to his metal treating company in Kansas City. His wife has returned to shift work for a janitorial contractor at the nearby Lake City Army Ammunition Plant.

The Graggs believe they'll stay in the neighborhood where dogs run free and kids' boundaries are defined by a stop sign on a country road.

They speak of their sons in the present tense.

Looking at a small pile of photographs, Mary Gragg remembers each of her sons as a sturdy blue-eyed, blond-haired baby.

"They were so good. They slept through the night every night.

"Aaron is my artist, my loner, he loves his dinosaurs. Chad is his daddy made over, my helper, everybody's helper, such a good student. He loves school, he never misses, and he loves riding his bicycle. Stevie's a little slow, a shy kid. Stevie loves Alf . . ."

Charlie Gragg takes up the sentence.

"You'll never see kids that alike, that close. If one goes out the front door the other two are right behind. . . . I wasn't surprised they all died trying to pull each other out of that pond.

"I always told them, 'No matter what happens, you help your brothers.' I told them that more than once. I told Chad he was responsible. He was in charge. He went to help Aaron, and Stevie followed."

Is there anything anyone can do for the Graggs? They say there is nothing. They are baffled that there might be an answer to such a question.

Soon it will be spring, time to go fishin' again, and frog huntin', and crawdad catchin'. That's when the children of Buckner Elementary School will plant three new trees in the memory of Aaron, Chad, and Stevie.

By then, the ice will be gone from the ponds.

Exercises

1 Disaster coverage: Brainstorm a package of stories about a disaster in your community. If you live in an area prone to weather disasters, such as earthquakes, tornadoes or floods, plan that type of coverage. Or you can brainstorm how you would cover a plane crash or an explosion in your community. List the stories you would do and places you should go for reporting on the type of disaster you have identified.

2 Internet exercise: Imagine that you are covering an earthquake. Find all the resources you can on the Internet related to disasters and earthquakes.

3   Deadline disaster writing: This exercise will test your ability to write on deadline and update your information repeatedly, just as the wire services do. Some of the initial information reporters get is inaccurate, but they must use what they get. In each succeeding part of this exercise, you will get additional information, some of which will differ from earlier information.

Write a lead for the first exercise, and then write a new lead and more information in each succeeding part of the exercise. Your original lead may hold for several editions; you have to decide when to change it. It doesn't help to look ahead, because you must act as a wire service reporter and write your story based on whatever you have at the time. Try to write each part in less than five minutes. When you get to part f, you may have more time; your instructor can set your deadlines. As the story builds, you may need to change only your lead and the first few paragraphs. Use today (name the day of the week) as your time frame.

The following information is based on the initial Associated Press wire coverage of the Oklahoma City bombing. Within 25 minutes of the explosion, which occurred at 9:04 a.m., the AP began sending dispatches. Then every few minutes throughout the day, AP updated its dispatches.

a   9:29 a.m.: There was an explosion in Oklahoma City today. It was at a federal building, the A.P. Murray building, downtown. A portion of the front of the building was blown away. Numerous injuries were reported. The building, which houses Social Security offices on the ground floor, has at least six stories. (The building name is wrong; fix it in "**c**" below.)

b   9:42 a.m.: Glass bricks and other debris were scattered over a wide area. Crews set up an emergency center near the building to treat people who were injured. Black smoke streamed across the skyline. The explosion could be felt as far away as 30 miles. The building houses the Social Security offices, Veterans Administration offices, a federal employee credit union and a day care center.

c   10:05 a.m.: Crews set up an emergency center near the building. Some injured people sat on the sidewalks with blood on their heads and arms. FBI spokesman Dan Vogel said he felt the blast as he was driving over a bridge. He called it "a tremendous explosion." He said FBI agents, including a bomb technician, were dispatched to the scene because federal property was involved. The A.P. Murrah building, which is at least six stories tall, is located at 200 N.W. Fifth St.

d   10:20 a.m.: The explosion at the tan, nine-story building occurred shortly after 9 a.m. It occurred on the second anniversary of the fire that destroyed the Branch Davidian compound at Waco, Texas. Dan Vogel, FBI spokesman in Oklahoma, wouldn't speculate if there was any connection. A man who was in the Journal Record Building about two blocks away said the force of the explosion blew people out of their chairs.

e   11:02 a.m.: Federal agents now say they think the building was bombed. An unexploded device was found in the building.

f   11:12 a.m.: From top to bottom, floors caved in. The north side of the nine-story building was obliterated. Burning debris and burning cars lined the streets. Dozens of people were injured, but there was no official word of deaths. Speculation about a second bomb sent emergency workers scurrying from the building and others running from the area. People including parents whose children were in a day care center in the building, were searching for loved ones. St. Anthony's Hospital downtown sent out an emergency call for blood and for all off-duty employees to report. Carol Lawton, 62, was sitting at her desk on the seventh floor when the explosion hit. "I was sitting there and all of a sudden the windows blew in. It got real dark and the ceiling just started coming down." She works for the Department of Housing and Urban Development in the building. She said she heard "the roar of the whole building crumbling." The floor around her fell onto the floor below, forcing her to crawl through a window into a hall and down some stairways. She was not injured. Jack Killorin, a spokesman for the Bureau of Alcohol, Tobacco and Firearms in Washington, said, "We believe this was a bombing and we are responding as if it was, but we do not have any forensic evidence to confirm that. The damage, however, appears consistent with a bombing." Oklahoma Gov. Frank Keating said, "The facts are not in but what we do know is that a terrible tragedy has occurred here in Oklahoma City." (Change your lead now if you have not already done so.)

g   3:36 p.m.: A car bomb caused the explosion, said Oklahoma City Mayor Ron Norick. He said it left a crater 8 feet deep. Mike Osburn, deputy chief of staff for Gov. Frank Keating, confirmed that at least eight people were dead, including six children, and at least 200 other people were injured. Other victims were trapped in the wreckage. The bomb was perhaps 1,000 to 1,200 pounds, said John Magaw, director of the Bureau of Alcohol, Tobacco and Firearms. Assistant Fire Chief John Hansen said, "We have to crawl on our stomachs and feel our way and we're talking to victims who are in there and reassuring them that we're doing everything within the good Lord's power to reach them and get to them. It's going to be a very slow process." More than 500 federal employees were assigned to the building, said Anne Marshall, a spokeswoman for the federal General Services Administration. From top to bottom floors caved in. The north side of the building was gone. Gov. Frank Keating said, "Obviously no amateur did this. Whoever did this was an animal." (Now that the information is more complete, you should rewrite your story.)

4   First-day airplane crash story: This is an exercise designed to help you learn how to organize massive amounts of information into one coherent story. Since it is not possible to simulate this reporting experience, you'll have to do some brainstorming. List the sources you would contact. List the information you think would be crucial to get for a main story. List the sidebars you would need for a large package.

For this assignment, you may consider yourself an Associated Press reporter if you want to write the story as the information is presented. If you want to make it more local—and more of a reporting lesson—substitute local sources, your nearest metropolitan airport and local hospitals for those named in the story.

Much of the information for this story is based on the actual crash of Delta Flight 191 at Dallas International Airport on Aug. 2, 1985. Some of the information is based on reports from the former *Dallas Times Herald* and *Sunshine* magazine of the *Sun-Sentinel* newspaper in Fort Lauderdale, Fla. Other parts are fictional.

You should check the chart at the end of the notes to include any perspective you think is necessary. Also, you may find conflicting information, as you would at the scene of any major disaster. You will have to decide how to handle it.

Before you begin reading this assignment and writing it, consider the writing process. In a story of this nature, you should use the FORK technique:

Focus: You have your focus—the news about the plane crash—for the mainbar.

Order: After you read all the information, you should jot down an order before you begin writing.

Repetition of key words: Consider key words as a tool to get you from one thought to another.

Kiss off: The kiss-off technique is most useful here. You will have many sources, far too many for the reader to remember. So use each one and then kiss her or him off. If you need to use a source again, re-introduce the person.

This is a deadline writing assignment. Limit yourself to about one hour writing time if possible—no more than 90 minutes.

Now, imagine that you are a reporter for the morning paper. It is 3 p.m. You hear on the police radio that ambulances are racing to the Kansas City (Mo.) International Airport and that the Kansas City fire department is also responding to a call for help. A plane has crashed. You call the city police department and find out that a major commercial airliner has crashed, but you can't get anything more at this time.

You call the airport public information department and learn that the plane was a Delta Airlines jetliner from Dallas–Fort Worth International Airport that was due to land in Missouri at 2:30 p.m. The spokeswoman, P.R. Informer, tells you the plane crashed at 2:55 p.m. and is in flames, but she can tell you nothing more at this time.

Your city editor sends you to the airport to get the main story and another reporter to get quotes from people at the terminal for a color sidebar. A third reporter is on standby in the city room waiting to hear from you to determine the extent of the crash and to make phone calls to get additional information for your story. This reporter will get background from clips and call hospitals. Your deadline for the first edition is 9 p.m. You will have to update for later editions until midnight.

It is raining hard. Lightning slices through the sky frequently as you drive to the airport. You arrive at the airport and head for the Delta Airlines terminal in the C concourse. You race to the runway where the plane has crashed and see the charred pieces of metal strewn over the edge of the runway. The tail section is intact; it has broken away from the rest of the plane and is resting on a stretch of grass, about 150 feet from the edge of the runway. The area is already cordoned off. The scene is chaotic. Scores of airport fire trucks and fire apparatus from all fire companies in the city and county, as well as ambulances, are at the scene. Firefighters are still spraying foam on the smoldering wreckage. The entire area is a sea of foam, as though the runway had been blanketed by a heavy snowstorm. Rescue workers are carrying bodies on stretchers. People are screaming.

It appears as though the nose of the plane exploded on contact with the ground, just at the edge of the runway. Wreckage is strewn over about 500 feet. Body parts, suitcases, pieces of clothing and mangled shreds of metal litter the ground.

You get to a roped-off area and talk to a man who seems to be in charge. He is the airport fire marshal, John L. Smoke. He has no specific figures, but he says it appears that more than 100 people are dead. The plane exploded as it hit the edge of the runway on its approach for a landing, he says. He says it seems that about 25 people who were in the rear of the plane survived, but he has no official count. Smoke says the airport authorities are taking care of the survivors who were not injured, but he is not specific about where they were taken. As he talks to you, injured passengers on stretchers moan and wail as they are loaded into ambulances. You are not allowed to get near them. Bodies draped in yellow plastic are still at the site. You count at least 20, but there is so much confusion you can't get an accurate count or even a good estimate.

You have been on the scene about 30 minutes, and by now the flames are out, helped by pouring rain.

The tail section is so covered with foam that you cannot make out any details. A dozen fire engines surround the plane.

You head back to the terminal to talk to airport authorities. On your way back, you corner an ambulance driver, Samuel L. Savior. He tells you this is the worst experience he has ever had. "It isn't the injuries that strike me," he says. "I have never seen so much terror in people's eyes. It's horrifying."

In the airport, you get to P.R. Informer, information director for the airport. She is conducting a news conference in a few minutes. At the news conference, she says it was a Delta Airlines L-1011, Flight 313 from Dallas International Airport. The plane was made by Lockheed Aircraft. She says many of the passengers originated at Kennedy International Airport in New York and changed planes in Dallas for the final destination to Kansas City. She says the three-engine plane was carrying 275 passengers and a crew of six flight attendants (plus the pilot and two co-pilots).

At this point it appears that at least 200 people are dead, including the pilot and two co-pilots. She says there are 25 survivors and she does not know the fate of others who are not accounted for yet. She says a passenger list will not be released to the press until all the families of the passengers have been contacted—which could take at least a full day and perhaps longer. Airport and Delta Airlines personnel will work around the clock, she says.

In answer to your questions, Informer says the dead are being held in an airport hangar until they can be identified. The injured are being taken to area hospitals. Most of them are being taken to the University of Kansas Medical Center, St. Luke's Hospital and Liberty Hospital.

"This is a terrible tragedy," Informer says. "We are doing everything we can to notify relatives as quickly as we can. This is the worst thing that has ever happened in this state. It was a freak accident. We flew 2 million passengers in and out of this airport last year and our safety record was perfect. The only thing we can ascertain at this time is that the weather may have been a factor."

"If the weather was so bad, why wasn't the airport closed?" you ask.

"We safely land and depart planes all the time in thunderstorms, and this one did not seem prohibitive to air traffic," Informer says. "We have just completed a $65 million airport expansion project, and our airport is one of the safest in the country."

She tells you the airport is closed to all traffic at this time and will remain closed until all rescue operations are completed. You check later and find out that the airport reopened five hours later but the northeast concourse will remain closed indefinitely. It will be at least three days and maybe a week before officials from the Federal Aviation Administration and the National Transportation Safety Board have investigated and the wreckage is removed.

About 50 firefighters and eight units responded.

A Delta Airlines spokesman, I.M. Devastated, says the plane had six flight attendants and three crew members. He says the pilot was Captain Ted Connors, the co-pilot was Rudy Price, and Nick Nassick was the flight engineer. All three crew members are confirmed dead. He says Connors was from Fort Worth and was 57. He had been with the airline for 30 years and was one of its most experienced pilots. He was due to retire in three years. Price was 42 and had been with the airline for 14 years. He was from Lithonia, Ga. Nassick was 43. He was from Atlanta. He had been with the airline for nine years. Devastated says it appears that the only survivors were in the rear of the plane. He says he does not know the fate of the flight attendants. He is not releasing their names until he is sure their relatives have been notified. "The airline is doing everything possible," he says.

Devastated says Delta Airlines has 35 L-1011s. He says this was a 125-ton jumbo jet with a capacity of 300 passengers and 11 crew members. "This is a terrible tragedy, and our company will do everything we can to give support to the loved ones of those who perished and those who were injured," he says.

Investigators from the National Transportation Safety Board arrive on the scene shortly before 6 p.m. They say they are looking for the black box that records the pilot's communications. Retired Coast Guard Adm. Patrick Bursely, a member of the NTSB team, says he has no official cause of the crash, but weather factors such as wind shears are suspected because of the violent thunderstorms that struck Kansas City shortly before the plane crashed.

Wind shears, which are sudden and violent changes in wind direction, were responsible for several other plane crashes, including the crash of a Pan American World Airways 727 jetliner that crashed after takeoff from Kenner, La., in 1982, killing 153 people.

You head for the Delta Airlines counter. Hundreds of people are jamming the area. Many are canceling flights. Others are waiting gloomily until the airport re-opens. Some are sitting on their luggage; others are lounging on the carpet. Others are in the airport bar. You see no sign of survivors or relatives. Airport personnel have taken them into a private room and will not allow the press to talk to them. At this point you meet up with Sarah Sidekick, the reporter who was assigned to get color. She says she was able to get some quotes from survivors and relatives before airline personnel got to them.

It is now 6:30 p.m. You call the city desk, and the editor tells you to come back and start writing. You are the main writer on the story. (In reality, someone inside the newsroom probably would be assigned to be the main writer, and you would stay at the scene.) You will take some of the color quotes from Sarah Sidekick and notes from other reporters who have done hospital checks, background and telephone interviews with officials.

Sidekick is writing a color sidebar with more reactions, but you need some quotes from her for your story.

Here is the information gathered by the other reporters:

Weather report: Severe thunderstorms started in the Kansas City area about 2 p.m. Winds in some parts of the city were as high as 65 mph. Trees were knocked down, and severe flooding occurred in some areas. The storm lasted for about two hours and then blew toward the west.

From survivor Milton I. Goldberg, 65, of New York: He was on his way to visit his daughter, Millie Muffin, 35, of 3600 Westbrooke, Lawrence (a city 30 miles west of Kansas City). "It was terrifying. Everyone was scream-ing and shouting. They were diving out of their seats and pushing. Some were getting trampled on. One of the flight attendants grabbed me and threw me out the emergency door. I'm lucky to be alive. I heard this earsplit-ting crackle. I think it was lightning. I was sitting in the back of the plane. I looked out the window and saw the wing crack. The next thing I heard was a deafening explosion. From that point on, all I heard was screaming. The cabin began to fill with smoke. There was mass panic." He began to sob and couldn't continue.

From Martha Mayhem, 59, of 2300 Harvard Road, Lawrence: She was waiting at the Delta Airlines gate where the passengers were supposed to come in when she heard the news of the crash. "I was waiting for my fiance. He was my childhood sweetheart. I waited for him all these years. I never married, but he did. Then we met in New York a year ago. He was widowed. We fell in love all over again. We were planning to get married this week. I can't believe that he isn't walking through that door. He told me he would take the first seat on the plane so he could get off fastest and never keep me waiting again. I don't think anyone in front of the plane survived. I feel like my life is over, too." Her fiancé's name was Joseph Heartfelt.

From Joseph I. Frightened, 35, of Kansas City, Mo.: He was at the Delta Airlines ticket counter canceling his travel plans to fly to San Francisco. "Too many plane crashes. I just don't feel safe on a plane anymore."

From Enid R. Intrepid, 25, a University of Kansas graduate student in journalism: She was waiting for a flight to Seattle to visit her parents. "It was a terrible tragedy, but the law of averages is on the side of safety. I'm going ahead with my plans. Hundreds of people die in traffic accidents, but you still get in a car. You can't let these things frighten you. This was a freak accident. The storm is over and the sun is shining. I just know I'll be safe when I fly."

From Sam Adams, 23, a computer technician from Kansas City, Mo.: He was driving past the airport on his way home. "I saw this big orange flash in the sky. I wondered if that was the sun coming out after the storm. It was so bright. Then I saw the horrible flames and smoke and heard what happened on the radio."

From a spokesperson at St. Luke's Hospital: "We've been told to expect 30 victims. We can't handle any more. All personnel have been called in, and our emergency room is full. We can't release any names at this time."

From a spokesperson at the Kansas University Medical Center: "We have five of the survivors in our intensive-care burn unit. Fortunately we have the best facility in the state, and we're doing all we can. We are expecting more injured people momentarily."

From Mayor Emanuel Cleaver of Kansas City: "Our hearts go out to the loved ones of those who died and were injured. It's a miracle that anyone survived. The state will lend all resources possible to investigators in this terrible tragedy. This is the worst tragedy imaginable. The city will provide hotel facilities for all the relatives, and we will do everything possible to assist in funeral arrangements for the victims. It appears as though our emergency disaster plan has been effective, but the city will do a thorough evaluation when the appropriate time comes. Right now every available rescue operator is working, and we are doing everything possible to cope with this disaster."

Your newspaper will run a separate chart on previous airplane crashes. For perspective, you can use the following information about previous U.S. air disasters. Check an almanac for further information on crashes during the past 10 years.

Sept. 8, 1994: USAir Boeing 737 crashed on approach to Pittsburgh International Airport; all 132 aboard killed.

July 2, 1994: USAir jetliner crashed near North Carolina's Charlotte-Douglas International Airport in a thunderstorm; 57 on board, 37 killed.

March 22, 1992: USAir Fokker F-28 crashed at La Guardia Airport during snowstorm; 51 aboard, 20 killed.

July 19, 1989: United Airlines DC-10 crashed in Sioux City, Iowa, while landing with a disabled hydraulic system; 111 killed.

Aug. 1, 1988: Delta Airlines Boeing 727 crashed and burned on takeoff at Dallas–Fort Worth International Airport; 104 on board, 13 killed.

Nov. 15, 1987: Continental Airlines DC-9 crashed on takeoff at Denver; 28 killed.

Aug. 16, 1987: Northwest Airlines MD 80 crashed on takeoff at Detroit; 156 killed.

Aug. 31, 1986: Aeromexico DC-9 hit small plane over Los Angeles suburb; 82 killed.

June 18, 1986: De Havilland Twin Otter plane and Bell 206 helicopter collided over Grand Canyon; 25 killed.

Sept. 6, 1985: Midwest Express Airlines DC-9 crashed after takeoff at Milwaukee; 31 killed.

Aug. 2, 1985: Delta Air Lines Lockheed L-1011 crashed at Dallas–Fort Worth; 133 killed.

Jan. 21, 1985: Chartered Galaxy prop-jet crashed after takeoff at Reno, Nev.; 68 killed.

July 9, 1982: Pan Am Boeing 727 crashed after takeoff at Kenner, La.; 153 killed.

Jan. 13, 1982: Air Florida Boeing 737 crashed after takeoff at Washington, D.C.; 78 killed.

COACHING

Observe descriptive details about the person and show the source in action.

Do background research to find unusual questions the subject will enjoy discussing.

Find a unifying theme that you can weave through your story.

Write an order for your story; think about organizing it by topics or time frames (present, past, back to present and future).

Use the GOAL method to frame your questions.

Profiles

Alan Richman walked into Bo Jackson's hotel room and got lucky. Bo Jackson was watching the soap opera "All My Children" on television. "I had a friend who wrote that episode of the soap opera, so I said, 'You want to know what's going to happen tomorrow on this show, I can tell you.' I called my friend and asked her what was going to happen. Bo loved this," Richman says. "Right away he thinks, 'This guy is not going to be as boring as the next guy.'"

Bo knows journalists. They always ask the same questions. The celebrated athlete, who for a time played both football and baseball, is reluctant to answer them.

Alan Richman knows athletes and celebrities. He interviews them all the time for profiles in *GQ (Gentlemen's Quarterly)*. He always asks something they haven't been asked before. It's a key to a successful celebrity profile.

With Boris Becker, that unique question came from a newspaper clipping about plans to list Becker in an encyclopedia. Richman handed him the clip and asked, "Why should you be in the 1991 World Book?" Becker was intrigued. He came back to the question six times during the interview. He speculated: Was it because he had done so much so young, that he was so well known, that he had won his first Wimbledon title at age 17?

"You've got to nail them with a question they like," Richman says. "They are so bored. I always ask myself, 'What question can I ask this guy that he'll enjoy answering.' It takes thinking."

That's good advice for any profile interview, whether for a magazine, a newspaper or a broadcast. Do your homework. Read

There's always something interesting about everybody. Nobody has lived a totally uneventful life.

Alan Richman, writer, *GQ*

(Gentlemen's Quarterly)

Alan Richman,
magazine writer
Courtesy of Alan Richman

clips about the person, and ask the subject's friends for anecdotes so you get ideas for interesting questions. But most important, whether it is a profile of a celebrity or just a person in your community, find a focus for the story. Decide why the person is newsworthy—the "so what" factor. What makes the person special enough to read about?

If you can master the skills of interviewing famous people, the less renowned people are easy. The basic techniques are similar.

"Everybody's got one good story to tell," Richman says. "If you talk to them long enough, you'll find it. Nobody has lived a totally uneventful life."

To find that story, Richman uses what he calls the "Columbo school of interviewing": "I sort of hang around looking harmless. I try to be as unthreatening as possible. Then I use a weave-and-jab style of questioning. You can't be afraid to be a little bit rude," he says. "If the point of the interview is that they were a bigamist, I'll say: 'We all want to have two wives; tell me how you got away with it.' If it's a profile of a man growing award-winning roses, I'll say: 'I can't believe someone would spend 15 years to grow a decent rose.'"

Writing Profiles

Richman has been writing about famous people for more than 20 years, first as a sportswriter for the defunct *Philadelphia Bulletin,* later as a sports columnist for *The Montreal Star,* which also folded. He also was a columnist and writing coach for *The Boston Globe* and a metropolitan reporter for *The New York Times.* Prior to his current job at *GQ,* he wrote profiles for *People* magazine.

"*People* was the hardest place to write for," Richman says. "They demand an incredible amount of information in a short amount of space. They want ages, parents and an extensive family history in every story."

Sometimes those background questions can be boring. So Richman just puts his subjects on notice. He tells them: "'It's that time now; I've got to ask these questions.' Basically they think I have some secret, that I'm going to ask them, 'Tell me about when you were 11 years old and you slept with a goat.' Then I tell them, 'I've got to go over your life.' They're relieved. I don't mess around and pretend it's going to be fun. It's more like, do me a favor. I don't trust press releases or clips. I always ask the background stuff. You never know what you are going to get."

Like these comments from Bo Jackson:

"I used to steal pocket change from my mother," he says. "I learned about sex from peeping in windows. I stole bicycles. I'd take them home, strip everything off the frame, throw the frame in the fire to burn the paint off, spray-paint the bike and ride it down the street. I was best known in the community for throwing rocks. I hit somebody every day with a rock. I was bad, the bully of the neighborhood. I beat up kids. I beat up girls. I beat the hell out of girls. I didn't care. I thought girls were just one of the guys."

He grew up in Bessemer, Alabama, just south of Birmingham, the son of Florence Bond and A.D. Adams, who never married. (His mother's maiden name was Jackson, her first husband was named Jackson, her second Bond.) The eighth of ten children, Bo was named Vincent after Vince Edwards, the actor then appearing in the popular television series "Ben Casey." As a child, says Bo, "I had tons of nicknames—my mother always called me 'sweetie'; sometimes 'knucklehead.'" The one that stuck came because he was such an ornery kid that friends compared him to a boar, or bo, hog.

That's a natural transition to Bo's mother (in Alabama) and her background, the *People* magazine technique Richman still uses in his current job:

Florence Bond sits in a small living room overstuffed with trophies, smiles fondly and talks about the child she "had to whip more than any of the others," the one she tried to educate with this basic message: "If you don't change your ways, you're going to be in jail or hell, sure as I'm sitting here."

Today, from her living room, she looks out onto Bo Jackson Avenue, shakes her head and wonders how that child of hers who liked stealing as much as he liked his stuffed animals could have turned out so well. The city fathers were not overly altruistic when they offered this narrow, soft-shouldered country lane in tribute to her son. At the speed Bo travels, approximately 100 yards every 9.5 seconds, he could traverse the length of it, dead end to dead end, in less than half a minute. The neighborhood is of mixed affluence, the houses ranging from practically middle-class to practically condemned. There are a few too many abandoned cars to classify it as suburbia. Bo wants his mother to move to a better place. She tells him, "I'm going to stay on this corner until God moves me."

Bo and his mother battled every day of his childhood. They're still at it today. He wants her to stop working at the motel where she cleans rooms. She tells him, "Look, honey, my working brought you up to where you are now. I'm proud of my job. All I've done is work."

Sometimes it seems Bo loves his mother more than anybody, even his wife.

"He better love his wife more," Florence warns.

His wife, who has a master's degree in counseling psychology from Auburn, says he couldn't possibly have been as bad a kid as he says he was or he wouldn't have grown into such a responsible man.

Alan Richman, *GQ*

Transitions   Richman's stories are virtually seamless. He weaves in background where it fits naturally. And he doesn't always put it in one block. It goes where it flows. One thought leads to another. Richman hates artificial transitions. The repetition-of-keyword technique is used all the time in *Sports Illustrated* and other magazines and newspapers—and it works, Richman admits. But he doesn't like it. "I want the story to conversationally slip from one paragraph to another. It should have a natural storytelling rhythm."

In a long profile—Richman's average is 6,000 words—that's not always possible. No problem. When it doesn't flow, he just puts in a break. "Eventually a train of thought has to drop," he says. "Someone once said, 'Nobody ever wrote a concert in one movement.' A break is good for the reader."

Theme

All Richman's profiles have a theme that binds the story. The nut graph is the "so what" reason you are doing the profile, but the theme is a unifying angle that weaves through the story, such as a recurrent image or concept, and ties the story together.

"I think the nut graph is even more important to the writer than the reader. You need to know what you are writing about," he says.

In the Bo Jackson profile, the theme is what makes this highly publicized but little-known athlete tick. The nut graph focuses on the fact that he was one of the few athletes to excel in both professional football and baseball, the "so what" factor. That's the reason for the story printed in 1990, before Jackson was injured and gave up football. Here is the lead; notice that the soap opera also made it into the lead:

> Bo is in bed this weekday afternoon, the blankets pulled so high over his head only two wary eyes peep out. Outside his Oakland-airport hotel room, frenzied kids roam the hallways keening for autographs, quote-starved writers probe for the secret of his two-sports life, a telethon bank of ladies in the lobby phone for a few minutes alone with the best body ever to play any game. When you're Bo Jackson, the inhuman highlight machine—star of Nike ads, baseball's All-Star Game and Sunday-afternoon NFL scoring clips—pulling the covers over your head seems a sensible way to hide.
>
> The eyes would be closed except the soaps are on, a lineup of people lying and stealing and screwing around, which is the stuff of nostalgia for Bo, inasmuch as he gave all that up years ago when he decided to make something of himself. "Nothing else to do until the game starts but sit in the hotel watching soaps," he says.
>
> Alan Richman, *GQ*

"I always go in with a preconceived idea for a theme," Richman says. "I hope something better will click for a theme during the interview."

The theme doesn't always work that well. "I go into all interviews with a notion of what I could write if all else fails." Everything did when he met Robert De Niro, another celebrity who, like Bo Jackson, hates to be interviewed. Richman was going to meet De Niro at a bar to see if the star would agree to an interview. He hadn't planned to do the interview at that time. He never got a second chance. This scenario from the *GQ* story—an exchange between De Niro and Richman—should convince you to be prepared from the minute you talk to a source:

He startles me by asking what my first five questions would be if we did an interview.

Does he mean any five, fire away? To ask anything at all of De Niro is surely a hyperventilating moment in celebrity journalism. My breath shortens. The genie has popped from the bottle and granted me five wishes. No, you fool, he doesn't mean that. This is a test. I have to come up with five questions he'll like. I'm not prepared. . . .

"A-hummina, hummina, hummina," I say.

He interrupts. He says two questions will be enough.

I haven't said a coherent word yet and I've blown 60 percent of this interview. Later, I'm told that I should have asked him about Brando. He loved Brando in "The Freshman," wants to do character roles like that, ones in which he doesn't have to carry the film.

I don't think of that. I choke and ask the obvious. I ask him why he's agreed to consider an interview if he hates them so much.

Alan Richman, *GQ*

De Niro gives a strained response. Richman is ready for question No. 2. He never gets to ask it. De Niro says he has to leave. He does. And Richman is stuck without a story.

So he calls De Niro's friends and associates. "After the interview failed, I went back and called all those people to figure how to make the story work," Richman says. "I asked them, what question can you ask that he (De Niro) would answer. Everybody told me something about De Niro you couldn't ask." Those comments about De Niro were probably more insightful than the actor would have been about himself.

And that was the theme of the profile: how to interview a celebrity who doesn't like to be interviewed.

The Writing Process

Richman returns from an interview and types all his notes into the computer; he doesn't use a tape recorder. "Then I immediately start writing. I try to write a first draft as fast as I can. It's fun because I know it won't make sense. By the time I finish, if the theme hasn't already emerged, I know it should. Then I write many drafts. I revise and revise and revise. Usually the second draft is the hardest for me, because that's the one that has to make sense.

"I'm not an outliner. I always know where I am going to end before I start. If I know that, I can get there. If I have a lead, a nut graph and an ending, I can write a 100,000-word story, and I know it's going to be OK."

In the revision process, Richman works on word choice. "If your language is not bright and interesting, people will get bored," Richman says.

His suggestion: "Tell a good story and look for something to make the reader smile"—perhaps an ending like this one from the Bo Jackson profile:

I ask him how he would have treated me if, as kids, I had wandered into his neighborhood. He looks me up and down, dismissing the thought of resistance.

"I'd probably have walked up to you and asked you for your money," Bo says.

If I didn't have any?

"I'd beat you up."

Okay, so maybe I did have some.

"If you had any, I'd take it, then beat you up so you wouldn't tell your mother."

Me, run crying to my mother? I guess it's true what they say in those Nike ads.

Bo knows.

Alan Richman, *GQ*

So does Alan Richman.

Basic Elements of Profiles

Celebrities are considered worthy of profiles because they have accomplished something more special than the average citizen has. But many profiles, especially in newspapers, focus on people in the community who have done something noteworthy but do not have celebrity status.

Regardless of the subject, all profiles need at least two elements:

Newsworthy angle: Why are you writing about this person now?

Focus: What is the main idea of the profile?

Say that someone has won an award. That's a reason for the story, but it won't carry a whole story. The focus could be developed around either of these questions: Why did the person win? What motivated that person to achieve? Or your story might have a coping focus: How did the person cope with success, failure or serious problems?

Coping is the subject of this campus-newspaper profile of a University of Florida nursing student who had been stabbed a year earlier, which was the newsworthy angle:

When Stacy LaRocca looks at a calendar today, she won't see that it's just Tuesday, April 10, 1990. Instead, her mind will flash back to Monday, April 10, 1989—the day 13-year-old David Rowe plunged a pocketknife with a three-inch blade into her body 17 times and almost killed her.

Much has changed since that day, both for Rowe and LaRocca. Rowe, now 14, has been convicted as an adult by a jury for attempted first-degree murder, and he awaits sentencing.

For LaRocca, a 21-year-old UF nursing student from Miami, much more has changed since the attack—physically and emotionally.

After undergoing five major operations the day of the attack to save her life, having other people feed and bathe her the following summer because she was too weak to do it herself, and testifying on the stand at Rowe's trial, LaRocca said she now has a different perspective on life.

"I think it's made me a lot stronger," she said in a recent interview. "I'm not afraid to stand up and speak out about something I feel needs to be said. It's certainly given me a different perspective on life. There are a lot of things I just don't take for granted anymore."

Duane P. Marsteller, *Florida Alligator*

Once you have determined why you are writing about the person, determine the scope. Will you write a whole-life profile, revealing the person's background from childhood to the present, or a partial-life profile, focusing only on the person's life as it relates to a current problem or news issue? If you are writing about people who are representative of a problem or issue, you will probably choose the partial-life profile. The previous example was a partial-life profile about the student's life as it related to the stabbing. If you are writing about a person who has received an award, you may opt for either type of profile.

Slice-of-life Profiles

Not everyone has a dramatic story, but everyone has some special talent or tale. Suppose you are interviewing a firefighter, a baker or even a candlemaker in your community for a slice-of-life profile, a story that simply shows people behind the scenes at work. How do you make the story compelling? Use the show-in-action technique. Spend a day or several hours watching your subject at work. That's what these writers did for these portraits of ordinary people at work in the community.

Baker

It's midnight and Mike Tennyson's day is about to begin.

He measures 80 pounds of flour, sugar, baking powder and yeast on a measuring scale the size of a home computer. Then he places the eggs and the rest of the ingredients into a 4-foot-tall mixer.

In the next five hours, Tennyson will bake more than 800 doughnuts, pastries and cinnamon rolls.

Tennyson owns and works as baker at Munchers Baker in the Hillcrest Shopping Center.

Charla Eisele, *Lawrence* (Kan.) *Journal-World*

The story continues by explaining how Tennyson became a baker, explaining what he likes and dislikes about his job, and showing him in action as he does it.

Candlemaker

Small candles blanket the table with a sea of color. On a table to the left, vanilla candles wait to be pulled from their metal molds.

The wax is warming, and Bob Werts adds vanilla fragrance to get it ready for pouring into empty molds. A metal mixing bucket hanging from the ceiling on a chain holds up to 60 pounds of wax.

Werts fills a pitcher with hot wax and walks over to the molds to begin pouring.

After 24 years as the owner of Waxman Candles, Bob Werts still participates in the daily process of making candles.

Valerie Crow, *Lawrence Journal-World*

The story continues about how and why Werts became a candlemaker.

When Zamora Jenkins interviewed a building inspector, she struggled to find a lead. What she saw in following him as he inspected buildings wasn't very exciting. "What struck you as interesting?" the editor said. Jenkins laughed as she recalled the fish tank in his office—not just an ordinary fish tank, but a tank for a piranha. It became a theme for the story about how he does his job and handles complaints.

> A three-foot clear water fish tank sits next to Lloyd Hoobler's desk in the Building Inspection Department of Lawrence City Hall. The tank is home to a six-inch piranha. Hoobler calls it his complaint department.
>
> Hoobler has been a structural engineer for the city since 1974. He is one of four building inspectors.

Zamora Jenkins, *Lawrence Journal-World*

The GOAL Method

Profiles should reveal not only what the person does but also what makes the person succeed or struggle in a job or in life. The GOAL Method (goals, obstacles, achievements, logistics), which was discussed in Chapter 8, can also work for you in profiles. To help find your focus or theme, consider the obstacles the person faced. These are often more interesting than the achievements. The achievements could be your nut graph—why you are writing the story—but the obstacles could be your theme—how you are presenting the story.

The GOAL method also works in the interviewing process. Some questions: What were the person's goals? What are the next goals? (These can work for an ending or even a lead and focus.) What obstacles did the person face in the past, and what new ones loom? What pleasure or pain have the achievements brought? What logistics—the background—led to the current condition? Don't stick to any particular order when asking these questions. Use a conversational interviewing approach.

Walter Dawson, managing editor of *The Herald* in Monterey, Calif., says that regardless of the profile subject, "the heart and soul of a profile is making sure the reader understands the twists and turns and intricacies of human life." Dawson directs his staff to consider the following universal elements:

Patterns: Some lives build to a climax, as for a law school student who becomes a judge.

Decisive moments or turning points: Patterns are important, but most lives take turns along the way. Take the law school student; maybe she wanted to be a great defense lawyer but became a prosecutor instead.

Or maybe your subject was an accountant who became head of a river-rafting company.

Future: Every profile subject has a future, and you need to explore the question. Ask your subject what could lie ahead, and let the person speculate, particularly about career goals. Ask the impertinent question: If this career doesn't work out, what could you do?

Some other basic elements to include in profiles:

Age and physical description: Use these facts only when they are relevant to the topic you are discussing. Make the details work for you. In this example from a profile of Willie Darden, a convicted killer who spent 11 years on Death Row in a Florida prison, the writer weaves in the age and physical description by relating them to the pressures of waiting for death:

Darden maintains a normalcy, a serenity, that is surreal. His forehead is not cleaved by worry lines. His hair has not gone gray. He lifts his shackled hands and displays unbitten fingernails. "Calmness is a nice thing to have in times of stress," he says.

He gives his age as 62, but prison records say he is 52. He looks 42. It's as if the man has not only cheated the executioner, but time itself.

Or maybe time just stops when there is no future.

"Prison does tend to sustain one's youth," Darden says with an ironic grin. "You're not doing anything that you would normally do on the outside—such as working hard every day. You've got no family problems. The wear and tear, so to speak, is on the inside."

Richard Leiby, *Sunshine* (Sunday magazine, *Sun-Sentinel*, Fort Lauderdale, Fla.)

Background: Describe the family, education and key experiences that led to the person's current success or failure. Before the interview, check clips and obtain a resume if one is available so you can check the background. When you write the story, insert the background where it fits naturally. In many profiles, the background is just plopped high in the story, as if to tell the reader, OK, now we launch into the past. When you plan your order, decide where the background is most relevant.

Other points of view: Seek comments from friends, family, colleagues and other people affected by the person at work, such as students for a profile about a professor or employees for a profile about a manager.

Graphics

Use graphics as a way to visualize your story in both the planning and writing stages. Outlining your profile by planning a facts (highlights) box can help you determine what topics to include in your story.

If the background is boring, break it out of your story. You can put key dates and such information as birthplace, education, career moves or similar items in a box. But if that information is an interesting and crucial part of your story, leave it in the body of the profile. You also can use a box to add information that doesn't fit well into your story but might be of interest, such as hobbies, favorite books, favorite saying, major goal. The major goal should also be mentioned in your story, but it works well in a facts box.

Several newspapers and magazines use graphic devices to substitute for written profiles; others use highlights boxes to enhance profiles. For example, *The Kansas City* (Mo.) *Star* Sunday magazine profiles celebrities with blurbs following these headings:

- Vital statistics (occupation, birthday, birthplace, current home, marital status and so on)
- My fantasy is . . .
- If I could change one thing about myself, it would be . . .
- The best times of my life . . .
- Behind my back my friends say . . .
- These words best describe me . . .

If you mention topics in a graphic, you don't have to repeat them in the story. And even if you don't present your profile in graphic form, you can use this concept to help organize the major topics.

Finding Profile Sources

When Mary Bishop wrote a profile of Billy Graham, she knew more about the evangelist's life than he did. She discovered that his mother walked a quarter-mile to pick beans the day before he was born, a fact he didn't know. For an in-depth profile, start in the cradle, if not in the womb, says Bishop, a reporter for the *Roanoke* (Va.) *Times & World-News.*

She uses records and human sources for her profiles. And she recommends that you think of yourself as an "amateur shrink." Put yourself in the subject's shoes. Check family photos, family background, classmates and teachers from the subject's school days—elementary school through college—old yearbooks, friends, relatives, neighbors and acquaintances.

In this profile about serial killer Jeffrey Dahmer (who was later convicted of killing 15 men and then was killed in prison), a picture in a high school yearbook provided the theme: his conflicting personality traits to seek attention and to hide his abnormal behavior.

On page 98 of Jeffrey L. Dahmer's Ohio high-school yearbook is a photograph of 45 honor society students lined up shoulder to shoulder; their hair well combed, their smiles confident.

One senior three rows from the top has no smile, no eyes, no face at all: his image was blacked out with a marking pen, reduced to a silhouette by an annoyed student editor before the yearbook went to the printer.

That silhouette was Mr. Dahmer in the spring of 1978, a couple of months before he says he killed his first person, with a barbell, 13 years before he confessed to one of the most horrific strings of slayings in modern times.

With grades that ranged from A's to D's, Mr. Dahmer fell far short of honor society standards, but he sneaked into the photo session as if he belonged. No one said a word until long after the flashbulb had popped and the shutter had clicked.

In all the years he cried out for attention, it was one of the few times he got caught. By then he had taught himself to live behind a mask of normalcy that hid his confused, often contradictory emotions. It was a mask no one pulled down until one night last month, when a man in handcuffs dashed out of Mr. Dahmer's bizarrely cluttered apartment in a tough Milwaukee neighborhood, called the police and stammered that Mr. Dahmer had been trying to kill him.

The authorities say that at least 17 other men did not get away: that Mr. Dahmer drugged their drinks, strangled them, cut up their bodies with an electric buzz saw; that he discarded bones he did not want in a 57-gallon drum he had bought for just that purpose; that he lined up three skulls on a shelf in his apartment, but only after spraying them with gray paint, to fool people into thinking that they were plastic models, the kind an aspiring artist or a medical intern might study. . . .

The facts—a home where parents went through a bitter divorce; a brother he long believed was the favorite in the family; a mother who he told police had had a nervous breakdown; his own lack of close friends—stop short of explaining why he did what he says he did. But the increasingly gruesome details that have emerged about Mr. Dahmer have all led back to one basic question: who is this man?

James Barron and Mary B.W. Tabor,
The New York Times

Most journalists interview the subject's friends, relatives and acquaintances before the scheduled interview. But Alan Richman, the writer for *GQ,* takes an unorthodox approach to other sources. He interviews them after he interviews the celebrity. "One of my rules is never call up friends or acquaintances of stars and ask what they think of the person, because they will always lie," Richman says. "If you were doing a profile of Hitler, most journalists would call up Goebbels and Himmler and they would say, 'What a guy!' Instead, ask them for facts or anecdotes."

Richman's point is well-taken. When you interview your sources, ask for specific details and anecdotes about your subject. General impressions yield only quotes with vague adjectives. On the other hand, anecdotes enliven the profile and help the reader understand the person's character.

To get anecdotes, however, don't ask people what was the most memorable moment or a similarly unfocused question. Give the person clues. Put the question in a time frame: When she was in college, what signs did you see that she would pursue this career?

When using description, try to elaborate with an anecdote, as in this example about the late publishing tycoon, Robert Maxwell:

In the 1950s, his reputation for tying up hotel switchboards and making unappeasable demands on the staff made him unwelcome in some of New York's best hotels. On one occasion, unable to reserve a room at the hotel of his choice, he ended up at the Winslow Hotel on Madison Avenue, which he promptly denounced as a "flea-pit." To make his point, he released 1,000 fleas in the hotel elevator shaft.

Alessandra Stanley, *The New York Times*

Organizing the Profile

There is no one way to organize a profile, other than having a lead, a body and an ending. Just make sure you have a focus.

Descriptive show-in-action leads, anecdotes, contrast leads and scene-setting leads work particularly well in profiles. As with any lead, those in profiles need good backup in the story.

The body of the story can be organized in many ways:

Supporting themes: Block each concept, use all relevant material, and go on to the next concept.

Time frames: Start with the present, go to the past, go back to the present, and end with the future.

Chronology: Look for a place in the story where chronological order might be useful, but don't write the entire profile in chronological order. A chronology might be most helpful for the background. It also might work if you are writing the profile in narrative style. In some cases, however, the story might lend itself to chronological order if a situation unfolds in that sequence. Just make sure your nut graph tells readers why you are writing about this person now.

Point/counterpoint: If the subject lends itself to pro-and-con treatment, you might consider this method. It can be helpful in profiles of politicians. You can include reaction quotes from other people after each controversial point is made. However, you still should use the kiss-off technique if you use this method.

Sections: Splitting the story into separate parts may work if the profile is very complex. For example, if you are doing an in-depth profile of a politician or crime victim or crime suspect, you might organize it in sections, either by time frames of the person's life, issues or different points of view.

Several types of endings work well with profiles. A quote kicker can be used to summarize a source's feelings about the subject or to summarize the subject's accomplishments. Or, with a circular ending, you can return to the lead for an idea and end on a similar note. An ending with a future theme tells what lies ahead for the person. Or try a simple factual sentence that conveys emotional impact.

Putting It All Together

The example in this section demonstrates a variety of techniques suggested in this chapter. It also has a clear focus, which is the one indispensable element of a compelling profile.

Notice that the three sections feature the present, past and future, although they are not so clearly delineated.

She is the finest of New Orleans' finest

*From a gritty past
to the city's best detective*

By Matthew Purdy
The Philadelphia Inquirer

Descriptive lead to create contrasts with past and present

NEW ORLEANS—The white frame house on Barrone Street is small and gated, just as it was when Jacklean Davis was a shy, serious-eyed little girl in a world of grownup horrors.

Here, 12 blocks from the muddy-brown Mississippi River, Davis was raised by a prostitute, raped by a sailor, sexually molested by an uncle and pregnant at age 16.

By then, folks in the neighborhood were whispering that Davis was headed for the same hard life as the aunt who had reared her: selling herself to strangers. In a sense they were right—but in an entirely different way.

Nut graph

Now 34, Jackie Davis cruises the city in a police car—not just any cop but the most successful detective in New Orleans, this humid capital of good times and jazz that also happens to be one of the deadliest cities in the South, with 346 murders last year.

Backup for nut graph (comment from colleague)

"She was the best I ever saw at solving a murder case," said David Morales, her boss during her five-year stint in the homicide unit. "There was nobody close to her in the history of the homicide division."

More backup for nut graph

Davis solved 88 of her 90 murder cases—a record better than any other detective and all the more impressive for the first black woman to join an elite corps of mostly white men who prodded her to fail.

Specifics: anecdotes

They destroyed her case reports, told tipsters she didn't work there, placed feces in her desk drawer, posted her mistakes on the bulletin board, and decorated her mailbox with a cartoon of a mop and bucket titled "black power."

Davis reacted by putting in longer hours. In solitary moments, exhausted, she would bow her head and sob.

"Every case that I got, I was looked at under a microscope: 'Well, what is she going to do now?'" Davis recalls matter-of-factly. "My biggest accomplishment, I consider, is not cracking under the pressure."

*More backup
for the "so
what" factor*

At a time when politicians have taken to bashing the poor for dragging on society, Davis stands out as a stunning example of someone who has succeeded precisely because of her harsh past. She is now the city's most celebrated officer— and the subject of a screenplay that has caught the eye of Whoopi Goldberg. . . .

In a life full of ironies and incongruities, Davis posed as a hooker, arresting so many men in the raucous French Quarter that 20 backup officers were assigned to her and her partner. But Davis' arrest rate so riled those in the tourist trade that her superiors had her wired to prove she wasn't entrapping men. Even so, business interest prevailed, and Davis was yanked off the street.

But not before she had nailed 300 johns.

"Having lived with a prostitute all my life, there are certain things you do, certain things you say," says Davis, chuckling over her record.

■

*New section:
arranged
topically to
reveal personal
side of source*

Christina Davis, 17, is a prep school senior with a B average who hopes to study engineering next year at Xavier University. It's Wednesday night in the blond-brick ranch home where she and her mother live with Gigi and Snoopy, their two dogs. Christina Davis is alone.

Her mother, like most officers in New Orleans, earns such a modest wage—$225 a week in take-home pay—that she has to work late-night security details for extra cash, stretching her workweek to 60 hours or more.

"I'm proud of her, but she had to sacrifice time with me and a lot of things we could have done together," Christina Davis says wistfully.

Losing days—and really, years— with her daughter is Jacklean Davis' greatest regret, she says one eve-

ning as she steers her unmarked Chevy through the bombed-out Desire housing project.

Her career started here 11 years ago, when she was the only woman street cop in the rough-and-ready urban squad, which worked the projects. . . .

A short woman with a stocky look about her, crimped hair combed into a tight ponytail, Davis always made it a point to later return to murder scenes in street clothes. It helped, she says, that she doesn't look like a cop: being a woman, looking young, using slang.

As she rolls through the broken streets, Davis says she worries about the good people in the projects who get ground down by the force of crime and neglect.

She could have been one of them.

Davis lost her father in a car accident when she was 3. Her bereaved mother squandered the insurance and had to give her children to an aunt.

As it turned out, Davis' grandaunt was a prostitute who bedded down with sailors. But she was a protective, strong-willed woman with a heart of gold, Davis said.

Davis' aunt was married to a merchant marine. When he was home, little Jacklean lived in stifled terror. He was sexually molesting her. Her aunt didn't know until Jacklean was 14 and her uncle was dying of cancer.

Trauma set in again when Davis was raped at 12 by a sailor who visited her aunt. By 16, she was pregnant and people in her working-class black neighborhood were whispering that she had picked up her aunt's habits.

Davis' aunt died when she was 17, about the time she was about to give birth to Christina. But she still managed to graduate from high

*Transition from
show-in-action
present to
past, including
background*

*Physical
description
made relevant
to job*

Turning point

school, faltering when it came to college. A better life seemed always out of reach, she thought as she worked clearing tables at ritzy restaurants and driving a bus.

It all hit bottom one winter when Davis found herself homeless for a two-week stretch, huddled in her parked car with Christina, danger lurking all around.

Quote kicker to section

"I knew this was it," she says. "There was no one else. I was on my own."

■

More background to bring reader back to present and on to future

The idea to become a cop came to Jacklean Davis when she dated a rookie in the department. Problem was, when she took the exam, she flunked it—again and again and again.

It took Davis five tries to pass the test—and two to overcome her fear of guns and make it through the police academy. It was 1981 before she got her first job at the urban squad. . . .

Comment from colleague

"She puts her heart into everything," said Wayne Farve, an old partner. "I've seen her at shootings where she'll kneel down in the blood right next to them and ask them who did it and where she can get more information."

Anecdote

Back in the old neighborhood, Davis got out of her car one night, in front of her home, eight blocks from where she grew up.

"Sssssss," a man hissed, pointing a gun.

Davis froze. Here she was, holding two bags of groceries, her own gun in her handbag, in the car. She screamed, slowly stepping away, as he closed in.

Unable to reach her gun, Davis screamed louder—and the man fled.

Davis dumped her groceries, grabbed her gun and opened fire as she chased him. Then suddenly, he turned and fired back, hitting her in the leg.

As she recovered in a hospital, she took heart. No longer a frightened child, Jacklean Davis had fought back this time and won. A few months later, police caught the man. He had raped 14 women. Davis testified against him, helping to lock him away in Louisiana's dreaded Angola prison.

Return to present

All told, it may be the stuff of movies, Davis concedes. An agent is negotiating for her, and the latest news is that Goldberg is reading the screenplay of her life.

Quote kicker on future note

"I don't even like to think about it," she says, admitting superstition. "I don't want to put a mojo on me."

Writing Snapshot Profiles

Julie Sullivan doesn't waste words. She writes snapshot profiles that let the reader see, hear and care about the character—quickly. Her skill earned her the Best Newspaper Writing Award from the American Society of Newspaper Editors for short news writing. The award was based on profiles she wrote for *The* (Spokane, Wash.) *Spokesman-Review*. They average 8 inches, less than 400 words. But she reveals a lifetime in her profiles.

Julie Sullivan, reporter
Courtesy of *The* (Spokane,
Wash.) *Spokesman-Review*

Her method: short sentences, few adjectives, few quotes, many details.

She began writing at a weekly newspaper in Alaska after she graduated from the University of Montana in 1985. "I started out leaning toward brevity," she said. "My first editor in Alaska would always tell me, every time you finish a story, go back over it. Figure out what words are extraneous. What can you leave out?"

She takes voluminous notes but discards about half of them. "I write everything down. I don't trust my memory," she says. That includes her observations. A cracked cement step. An automobile battery under the sink. Cockroaches scurrying across the kitchen table. A toothless smile.

How does she know which details to include in her stories? "I write what I remember without looking at my notes. What details stand out. Like Joe Peak's teeth were so significant and personal. The contrast struck me. His place was so neat that I couldn't figure out how somebody who paid so much attention to his surroundings wouldn't take the same care personally. Then I found out how he lost his teeth."

She is equally selective about the limited quotes she includes. "I really think readers glaze over quotes," she says. "I do few quotes because I think most people are pretty plain-spoken and simple. You don't need to use it just because it's in quotes."

Her tips for writing briefly: "Trust your instincts about what is important, what struck you during the interview. The rest is chaff. I generally bounce my lead and the most important details off my co-workers, and I can gauge from their reactions if I'm on the right track." That's the basic tell-it-to-a-friend technique.

She also stresses observation. "Pay attention to details, from the right spelling of names to finding out the date of people's birthdays."

On leads and kickers: "I tend to think readers read the beginning and the end. Never discount the lead you were throwing out. It could be a great kicker."

On structure: "You try to make a point with every paragraph."

On brevity: "Short has its place, but it won't replace more in-depth pieces; that's what a newspaper does best. I hope to continue to do both."

The two profiles that follow were part of a series about the problems of low-income residents in a deteriorating Spokane apartment building, the Merlin.

The second example, about Orval Aldrich, contains a racist term. "I thought about it and then realized it was too rich a detail to delete," Sullivan said. "The racism made me uncomfortable. How sad for someone to carry that around, especially since the only person who cared about him was a black woman. But in profiles, it's real easy to make people two-dimensional—the good guys and the bad guys. I tried not to succumb to that. I went in without a lot of preconceived ideas about the people in this series. They emerged as humans."

See if you agree. Notice the details—not just a watch, but a Seiko; not just a car but a 1977 Ford. And notice the strong factual kickers. As you read these profiles, consider what information came from observations and what came from questions. And then decide how you could say it all in as few words.

It took twice as many words to describe Sullivan's style as she used in these stories.

Donald 'Joe' Peak

Joe Peak's smile has no teeth.

His dentures were stolen at the Norman Hotel, the last place he lived in downtown Spokane before moving to the Merlin two years ago.

Gumming food and fighting diabetes have shrunk the 54-year-old man's frame by 80 pounds. He is thin and weak and his mouth is sore.

But that doesn't stop him from frying hamburgers and onions for a friend at midnight or keeping an extra bed made up permanently in his two-room place.

"I try to make a little nest here for myself," he says.

Chock-full of furniture and cups from the 32-ounce Cokes he relishes for 53 cents apiece, Peaks' second floor apartment is almost cozy.

A good rug covers holes in the kitchen floor, clean-looking blankets cover a clean-looking bed. Dishes are stacked neatly in the kitchen sink.

But cockroaches still scurry across his kitchen table.

"I live with them," he says with a shrug. "I can't afford the insecticides, pesticides, germicides. I don't have the money."

With a $500 per month welfare check and a $175 rent payment, Peak follows a proper diet when he can afford it. He shops at nearby convenience stores where he knows prices are higher but the distance is right. He has adapted to the noisy nightlife in the hallways and sleeps when he is too exhausted to hear it.

Part Seminole Indian, Chinese and black, the Florida native moved to Spokane 20 years ago to be near relatives in Olympia. He

quit school at 13 to help earn the family income and worked a string of blue-collar jobs. Along the way, someone started calling him Joe.

His voice is lyrical, his vocabulary huge, but Peak's experience with whites is long and bitter.

When conditions at the Merlin began worsening three months ago, junkies and gray mice the size of baby rats moved in next door. He hated to see it, but he isn't worried about being homeless.

He's worried about his diabetes. He's frightened by blood in his stool and sores on his gums. He wonders whether the white-staffed hospitals on the hill above him will treat a poor black man with no teeth.

Julie Sullivan, *The Spokesman-Review*

Orval Aldrich

They call him the Jockey.

At 82, he is bent from too many spills from a saddle and too many ex-wives to name. But it's the stress of his home that is breaking Orval Aldrich.

He moved into the Merlin 12 years ago to be close to his friends, who shared a passion for

horse racing, cards and "chewing the bull."

There was ample parking for his 1977 Ford. A dozen residents shared meals and long summer evenings together in the place they knew was rundown, but still livable.

"We had a pretty good bunch in here," he says.

Now Aldrich's friends have

moved to quieter, safer apartment buildings. The friendly faces have been replaced by ones he doesn't recognize or trust.

And the Ford's battery is under the sink in his room so thieves won't steal it.

Born in Liverpool, England, Aldrich worked as a jockey and construction boilermaker in jobs that took him from the Space

Needle in Seattle to refineries in eastern Montana.

He'll tell you he had six wives and show you pictures of two children, six grandkids and one great-grandchild, a pale blond beauty whose photo hangs in Room 8.

His gray room also has a stained sink on one wall and a gas stove on another surrounded by wisps of ash. Roach bombs must be set off every week.

The electricity is sometimes shut off for hours, and there are interruptions in water service.

Rent has risen from $50 to $100 since 1985.

The black residents bother him. He is afraid of them and calls them "niggers," though the woman who reminds him to take his medicine and calms him is black.

Lately, Aldrich's eyesight has begun failing. It takes two trembling hands to bring a small glass of beer to his lips. His family in Montana would like him to move, but he makes his own decisions, thank you.

The day the drug addict stole his watch and stuck a needle in her arm at his kitchen table, Aldrich sat stiffly on the crusty blankets of his bed.

"I'll get it back, you watch and see," he fumed later.

He did. The $50 Seiko was returned without explanation Thursday morning.

That night, they stole his food stamps.

Julie Sullivan, The Spokesman-Review

Here are some examples of vignettes written by journalism students who were following Julie Sullivan's style. The assignment was to find people behind the scenes on the campus of the University of Kansas. Students were instructed to write profiles filled with revealing details in fewer than 500 words—about one to one and a half double-spaced typewritten pages. They were also told to stress show-in-action techniques. The frame was the university at work.

Journalism school librarian

Yvonne Martinez has carefully picked out her wardrobe.

Dressed in a navy blue skirt patterned with white boxes and a white blouse with the same pattern in blue, she had come prepared for another day of work at the School of Journalism library.

However, her outfit would not be complete without her size 6 1/2 sneakers.

The 4-foot-11 librarian does not wear them simply because they help maintain a quiet atmosphere. That is just one of the added benefits.

She wears them because she is constantly on the move.

Whether it's searching for a student's request for the last two years' worth of *Folio* magazine or sorting through the seemingly endless stack of newspapers the library receives daily, she rarely has time to sit down.

Recent cuts in the library's budget and staff have increased Martinez's work load. The sneakers are crucial.

"I'd rather be comfortable than in pain," she said.

Her duties have grown during the two years she has been working behind the counter. But now her duties include repairing the copy machine.

It is the only copy machine the library can afford on its budget, Martinez said. Overuse causes it to break down at least once a day.

As she returns to the counter, she immediately is greeted by a professor who says the machine is out of ink. She reaches under the counter and pulls out a bottle of black ink.

As she pours, the bottle slips and ink covers her hands. More students who need to be helped arrive at the counter.

Martinez stands by the machine staring at her hands as if she were auditioning for the part of Lady Macbeth. She sighs and runs off to the restroom. She quickly returns to the counter and apologizes to the students.

After all, she is the only librarian on duty.

Ranjit Arab, The University Daily Kansan

Bus driver

The sounds of a screaming Mick Jagger shake the windows of the bus.

A basket of Jolly Rancher's candies sits on the dashboard. And the driver in the blue and white Rolling Stones baseball cap is smiling.

This is Hank's bus—slap him a high five on the way off, please.

Hank Jones, who is in the middle of his fifth year as a (University of Kansas) bus driver, likes doing something extra for his passengers.

"Why shouldn't I," he says. "A little extra effort can go a long way."

One passenger remembers Hank stopping his bus on Jayhawk Boulevard last Valentine's Day just to give her a candy heart. She's been a regular ever since.

Hank began driving those green and white buses when he needed some extra money and he enjoyed it so much, he stayed with it.

The students are the best part of the job, but Hank is not without his complaints.

"They're not too quick sometimes," he says. "But they're good kids, most of them."

He tries to keep it interesting—he never plays the same tape twice in one day on his portable Sony stereo.

"I'm always partial to the Stones," he says, cracking open his pack of Marlboro cigarettes. "But I'll play requests, too."

Hank plans to keep driving for KU as long as he still enjoys it—or until he finds a wife. At 34, he hasn't found the right woman yet.

But he's in no hurry.

"Who knows?" he says. "Maybe someone will get on my bus."

Kathy Hill

Flag raiser

Virginia Boyd is afraid of heights.

However, she does part of her job on top of Fraser Hall, one of the highest points on campus at the University of Kansas.

Boyd, an employee of the University's housekeeping staff, raises the flags on Fraser Hall each morning at 7 o'clock, where they fly nine stories above the ground.

After taking the elevator to the seventh floor, she climbs two flights of stairs before ascending two more 16-stair spiral staircases where the flag turrets are located. Climbing to the roof of the building is no easy task for her 51-year-old legs, she says.

"Kinda spooky, isn't it?" she says, wrinkling her freckled nose and gripping rickety wooden staircase railings covered with bird droppings.

She peers through the gratings over the vents in Fraser's turret and points to a trap door in the roof of the building.

"I used to peek out of there, just to see what it was like," she says.

Wind swirls around the tiny turret and Boyd looks up at the flagpole that sticks through the opening at the top.

"If the cord is whipping against that pole, it's too windy to put the flags up," she says.

She gently fingers the limp American flag attached to the cord at the bottom of the pole.

"As soon as it goes through that hole, it just gets sucked up," she says.

Boyd has only been on flag duty in Fraser Hall for about three weeks; she previously worked in the Art and Design building for two years.

She's thankful that she's only had to put the flags up three or four times since she has been working in Fraser.

"My knees just can't take this," she says, "so one of those young guys is going to take over."

Michelle Betts

Exercises   **1**   Write a profile about a newsworthy person on your campus or in your community.

2   Write a short profile about someone on your campus, using Julie Sullivan's style. Plan it as a vignette, considering it part of a package or a larger subject so it has a frame of reference.

3   Plan a celebrity profile of someone you would like to interview. If you enjoy sports, plan a profile of an athlete on your campus. Use Alan Richman's tips, and plan an interesting question you would use to begin the interview, as well as a preliminary theme you might pursue.

4   Coach a classmate on writing a profile. Ask your classmate some of the basic coaching questions: What's it about? What is the focus? Do you have a theme? Were there any patterns, any turning points? What anecdotes do you remember as most interesting? What is the point—why should the reader care? What order are you considering? As the writer discusses the profile, you as the coach can ask questions that occur to you.

5   **Slice-of-life snapshots:** Using the theme of "A Day in the Life" of your campus or your community, write vignettes about people and places. Each person in the class can take a different part of the campus or community.

Alice Klement, a writing coach and professor, used time frames to plan "A Day in the Life of Florida City" with her University of Miami journalism students. Each person captured a scene or vignette of someone at a different time of the day, from midnight one day to midnight the next. It started at midnight at the Circle K, a convenience store. Other students went to a police station, a truck stop, a bus station and so on through the night. During the day, students went to various places, including a school and a park. During the evening, they went to a bingo parlor, a restaurant and a bar. If you use this approach, you need to plan it as a class project so that each person has a different time period and place to cover.

As an alternative, you could do a late-night version of the slice-of-life vignettes by focusing on various places on campus or in the community that would attract people all night. Another alternative is to do slice-of-life portraits of people who work the night shift or work in unusual occupations. Brainstorm your own approach.

COACHING

TIPS

Keep a record of steps you take when you begin exploring the Internet.

Keep a file of electronic mail addresses for friends and sources.

Be patient when you explore on-line resources. You will learn more every time you navigate through the Internet, even when you fail.

Start a file of your favorite places on the Internet.

Start with spreadsheets when you begin using numerical data bases. Make a list of the problems and solutions you encounter.

Computer-assisted Journalism

26

Imagine a place like a giant supermarket where almost everything is free. In one aisle you can find opportunities for jobs or internships. In another aisle you can get free software for your computer. In other aisles you can find sources and documents you can use to write stories or research papers. If you prefer to shop for pleasure, you can find games, videos, and people who share your interests in music, hobbies or any other pastimes.

This treasure trove is the Internet, a vast interconnection of computer networks that offers access to thousands of places, people and programs for the price of a local phone call. If you use a commercial Internet provider, your membership fee buys you access to this supermarket.

Suppose you want to contact a friend or source but don't want to spend money on a fax or a phone call or wait several days for a letter to arrive. You can communicate via electronic mail in minutes and pay only for a local phone call. Communicating by e-mail with a person in another country is especially efficient. E-mail is another feature of the Internet, perhaps the one being used the most by millions of people all over the world.

Chances are you will need to know how to use e-mail and the Internet when you enter the work force. Throughout the world, companies in all types of industries are conducting business on line, so-called because the computer connections are made through telecommunications lines.

In journalism, knowing how to use these on-line services has become an important reporting skill. But it is just one form of computer-assisted reporting. The other way computers are

In this job market, the resume with average skills will end up in the discard pile. . . . The candidates with computer-assisted reporting skills stay. The candidates with on-line searching experience stay. All those without that experience are eliminated.

Christopher J. Feola, editor of new media, *Waterbury* (Conn.) *Republican-American* assisting journalists in their jobs is through programs that analyze data bases. For example:

• Reporter Scott Thomsen wanted to know if the police respond to crime scenes faster in some parts of Reno, Nev., than in others. He compiled a data base from police records of all the calls dispatched to the city's 26 patrol beats. Then, using computer software, he analyzed the figures and wrote a story for the *Reno Gazette-Journal,* showing the differences in response times. His story also included a chart listing response times for each section of the city and each type of crime so readers could see how safe they were or weren't.

• *Kansas City* (Mo.) *Star* reporter Mike McGraw won a Pulitzer Prize for using a computer program to analyze thousands of government documents about the U.S. Department of Agriculture meat inspection program (see Chapter 6). A year later McGraw used the Internet to track down federal Food and Drug Administration employees who had ruled that toxic food, contaminated by smoke from a food warehouse fire, could be distributed to the public. In this case he used the federal government bulletin board called FedWorld.

• Reporters at *The News and Observer* in Raleigh, N.C., use computer-assisted journalism in all types of stories, from features about what kinds of cars get the most tickets to major projects, such as a housing series that used U.S. Census data and other data bases.

Computer analysis of data bases and use of sources on the Internet will not replace the human stories you can get from traditional reporting skills. However, computer-based tools are becoming more valuable to reporters each year as access to the Internet becomes easier.

Computer Skills

The best way to learn how to use these journalistic resources is to explore them, so this chapter will be interactive; do it as you read it. The chapter will explain how to use e-mail, how to find sources and documents on the Internet, and how to use computer data bases. The chapter is geared toward beginners. If you already know how to create your own pages on the World Wide Web, you can probably skip most of the explanations and just do the interactive tasks. Terms spawned by the computer age will be explained as they are used, but a glossary also follows at the end of the chapter.

Tools You Need

To perform the tasks described in this chapter, you need the following:

Account with an Internet provider: This chapter's instructions for using e-mail and the Internet are for connection services provided free or at minimal cost to academic accounts. If you use a commercial service, follow its instructions. When you get your account, you will be given a user name, the name you use to sign on to your account. It can be your name, your initials, a combination of numbers and letters, or a pseudonym. You will also receive a password that gives you access to the computer network. Do not reveal your password to anyone; it is the only way you can keep your accounts secure.

Modem: If you are working from your home computer or a computer not directly connected to your college or university computer system, you will need this device. It connects your computer to a telephone line. Follow your modem's instructions for setting up and connecting to your computer account.

SLIP or PPP connection: If you are using a modem, you will also need a special Internet connection program, called a SLIP (Serial Line Internet Protocol) or PPP (Point-to-Point) connection. In an academic setting, a SLIP or PPP program should be available without charge from your computer center. To configure such a program, you need to ask a computer center technician for the main computer's address numbers, called IP numbers. If you are using a commercial service, the network connection will be provided by the service. Although newer computers already have such software installed, in an academic setting you will still need to get the IP address.

Internet browser: You also need software that allows you to explore the Internet with ease. This chapter discusses many types of browsers that will work on old and new computers. However, the preferred browsers for the Internet feature called the World Wide Web are Netscape and Mosaic. They can probably be obtained without charge for academic use from your computer center, the company that developed them or the Internet. (See the appendix for Internet sites where you may obtain these programs; if you are using a commercial Internet connection, the company will provide its own browsers.) Make sure you get the right version, for Macintosh or Windows.

The Connection to the Host Computer

Before you can use the Internet or use e-mail on an academic account, you need to know how to connect (log on) to your college or university computer system, called the "host" computer. You should receive instructions when you open your computer account. These are general instructions for most academic accounts that use Telnet, an Internet program that allows computers to communicate with each other:

1 If you are working from a computer center or a school with a direct connection to the host computer, find the command for the Internet connection, which may say *Telnet,* and click on it. If you are working from a personal computer with a modem, follow your modem instructions and dial into your host computer connection. If you are using a SLIP or

PPP connection, it should be set up to automatically insert your user name, password and host computer name. If so, you can skip the next three steps.

2   After you connect, you will be asked to write your user name. Then you will be asked for your password, which will not show up on the screen when you type it. The computer will verify your account, and if it is OK, you will see a symbol called a prompt. It may be a dollar sign ($), a percent sign, (%) or some other sign (such as >), depending on the type of computer program you are using.

3   Type the name that your college or university uses to connect you to the Internet (probably *telnet*) and the name of the machine your e-mail account uses. You should have received that name when you opened your account; it is probably part of your e-mail address.

4   When you are again asked for your user name and password, retype them. Because some programs are case sensitive, make sure you type your name and password in lowercase or uppercase letters as required by your account. You should now be connected to your host computer.

Electronic Mail

Electronic mail, known as e-mail, is a way of sending messages to people via a computer network. E-mail won't totally replace the U.S. Postal Service, a method of sending letters called "snail mail" by e-mail users, but it is becoming the preferred communication choice for millions of people because it is fast, cheap and convenient.

Suppose you want to send a message to a friend in Europe or Asia. Instead of spending several dollars on a long-distance phone call or waiting days for your letter to arrive via postal service, you can send an e-mail message in minutes. You pay only for the local phone call that connects you to your host computer network or time charges on commercial services.

In addition, you can check your e-mail anytime. If you travel and have a portable computer with a modem, you can get your e-mail anywhere. You can also attach documents to your e-mail messages.

For journalistic purposes, you can sometimes contact sources better by e-mail than by phone. But before you use anything from an e-mail message for a news story, make sure you tell the source that you plan to use the information. Check any anonymously sent information for accuracy.

Although the positive factors of e-mail greatly outweigh the negative ones, there are a few disadvantages to e-mail. One is that there's no guarantee of privacy. Your message could be read by the person who operates your computer network. Also, the tone of e-mail messages can easily be misunderstood. Unlike face-to-face contact, in which you can see gestures, or telephone conversations, in which you can hear the inflections in a voice, e-mail relies only on text, just as letters do. Sending angry or sarcastic messages is called "flaming."

To offset misinterpretation, some people use symbols called emoticons to show if they are happy, sad or just kidding. The most common emoticon is the "smiley" :-). To view it, turn your head sideways. You make a smiley with a colon, small dash and closing parenthesis. It's supposed to show that you're happy or that you mean the message in a friendly tone. If you are just kidding, put in a wink by using a semicolon for the eyes ;-). If you are upset or sad, use the reverse (opening) parenthesis at the end :-(. Although many people don't like emoticons, these symbols can help to convey the right tone and prevent misunderstanding.

If you are using a commercial service or if your word-processing software contains an e-mail feature, follow the instructions for use. This chapter focuses on free Internet e-mail programs that are readily available to almost anyone attending a college or university.

E-mail Basics

To use e-mail, you need to know the e-mail address of the person you want to contact. The first part of an e-mail address is the person's computer name, called a user name, login (the name the person uses to log onto the program) or user ID (user identification). The person's user name may be part of his or her name or initials, a nickname, a false name or numbers. The name is followed by the @ symbol (for "at") and the domain name, the address of the main (host) computer. The dots between the words or letters are a crucial part of the address.

For example, crich@falcon.cc.ukans.edu stands for Carole Rich at falcon (the name of the computer account); *cc.ukans* stands for the computer center at the University of Kansas; *edu* indicates that it is an educational account.

The easiest way to find a person's e-mail address is to ask for it, just as you might ask for a street address. Directories of e-mail addresses at universities and commercial services also exist. You can access these directories through the Internet, but it is not a very efficient method. When a person sends you an e-mail message, his or her e-mail address will be attached. You should begin a computer file (or card file) to save those addresses, just as you would create any source file, so you may contact the person again if needed.

To receive e-mail, you need to log on to the e-mail program and click on an icon or type letters to get to the folder that stores your mail. Most programs indicate when you have new mail; some audibly announce that you have mail if you have a sound component on your computer.

When writing an e-mail message, keep it brief. Write in uppercase and lowercase letters, just as you would when writing a letter. Don't use all capital letters, because they are very hard to read and are interpreted as shouting. Sign your name. Many e-mail programs insert your signature automatically.

The e-mail program you are using should have codes to write or boxes to click when you are ready to send the message. E-mail programs are continually getting easier to use as technology improves.

Pine   Pine is a free Internet e-mail program developed by the University of Washington. It is not as good as some commercial programs or the free Eudora program (which is explained in the next section), but it is readily available at most universities. Here is how to use Pine to read your mail:

1   Log on to your computer account.

2   Type *Pine* after the prompt; the main menu will appear. It will tell you if you have mail.

3   Read mail by selecting the *I* for the Folder Index, also called the Inbox (see Exhibit 26-1), which says *View messages in current folder*. Hit return.

Exhibit 26-1

Main menu for Pine e-mail program

```
* * * * * * * * * * * * * * * * * * * * * * * * * * * * * * * * * * *
You have new mail.
falcon:/homeb/crich $ pine

  PINE 3.91    MAIN MENU                         Folder: INBOX   9 Messages

        ?       HELP              -  Get help using Pine

        C       COMPOSE MESSAGE   -  Compose and send a message

        I       FOLDER INDEX      -  View messages in current folder

        L       FOLDER LIST       -  Select a folder to view

        A       ADDRESS BOOK      -  Update address book

        S       SETUP             -  Configure or update Pine

        Q       QUIT              -  Exit the Pine program




     Copyright 1989-1994.  PINE is a trademark of the University of Washington.

  Help                        PrevCmd                    RelNotes
  OTHER CMDS   [ListFldrs]    NextCmd                    KBLock
```

4   Instructions for processing your mail are at the bottom of the screen. After you have read your mail, you may save it or delete it. Hit *D* for delete. If you want to save your mail, just leave it there and it will automatically be retained. But don't let too much mail accumulate.

5   If you want to reply to the message, just hit *R*. Pine will automatically address your new message to the person who wrote to you. It will also ask if you want to include that person's previous message. Type *y* for yes or *n* for no.

6   To compose a new message, go to main menu (type *M*) and select *C* for *Compose message.* Fill out the e-mail address of the person you are writing to, as shown in Exhibit 26-2. You should write one or two words in the space for a subject; other items in the header are optional. Write your message using uppercase and lowercase letters, not all capitals. Sign your name. Hit *control-X* to send your message.

7   Quit the program by typing *q*. Type *y* for yes when the program asks if you want to quit. A system prompt will appear. Type *exit*. If you are dialing in from a modem connection, find the command for *Hang up* and click on it. It should be under *Phone* or another item on your menu at the top of the screen.

Exhibit 26-2

Pine message screen

```
 PINE 3.91   COMPOSE MESSAGE                      Folder: INBOX   1 Message

To      : Crich@falcon.cc.ukans.edu
Cc      :
Attchmnt:
Subject : how to send a message
----- Message Text -----

        Fill out the address under To.  CC is for carbon copy if you want
to send the message to other people.  Write the message and hit control X
for send.  If you change your mind, hit Control C. The computer will ask
you if you want to send your message.  Hit y and send it.  This is a
signature that is automatically inserted in  my messages.  The next steps
will show you how to make your own signature.

        ************************************************************
        *               Carole Rich                    *
        *   School of Journalism, University of Kansas  *
        *         Lawrence, Kansas 66045-2350           *
        *            (913) 864-7629 (o)                 *
        *         crich@falcon.cc.ukans.edu             *
```

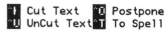

```
  Get Help     Send      R Read File  Prev Pg    Cut Text    Postpone
  Cancel       Justify     Alt Edit   Next Pg    UnCut Text  To Spell
```

Here's how to make a special signature in Pine that you can automatically insert at the end of any message:

1   When you get a system prompt (*$* or *%*), type *pico(space).signature* and hit Return (or Enter). Other computer programs may ask you to type *pico(space)pine.signature.*

2   After *Pico* comes up, start designing your signature. Include your name and e-mail address and any other information you wish, such as street address and telephone numbers or a brief quotation. Try to limit the signature to five lines. When you finish, hit *control-X* to save the file.

3   You will be asked if you want to save your signature to a buffer. Select *yes.*

4   You will be asked for a file name. You must write *.signature,* not your name. The period before the word is crucial. Write it as follows: *pico(space).signature.* If the dot signature appears automatically, just press Return and your signature will be saved.

5   You should now be back at the system prompt. Type *pine.*

6   Once in Pine, select *C* for Compose. Your signature letterhead will automatically be dropped into the text portion of your message. If you don't want to use it for any reason, just use *control-K* to wipe it out line by line.

7   If you want to permanently change the design or content of your signature, repeat the first five steps.

Eudora   Eudora is an excellent e-mail program, made by QUALCOMM, that is available free on the Internet. Eudora Pro is for commercial use; the free versions are called Eudora LightÅ for Macintosh platforms and Eudora Light for Windows platforms. Eudora is easier to use than Pine, but you need a SLIP or PPP connection if you are using a modem to access your host computer. A major advantage to this program is that it allows you to retrieve your mail messages and then read them off line at your leisure instead of tying up your phone line.

Eudora software is available on the Internet (at least for now) by using a file transfer protocol (ftp.qualcomm.com) or by downloading the program from the Qualcomm World Wide Web page (http://www.qualcomm.com). Information about searching and receiving programs from the Internet follows later in the chapter.

Once you have installed Eudora on your computer, it is very simple to use. The program allows you to create special folders and do many other things, and you can discover these capabilities through instructions that come with the program. Here are the most basic instructions:

1   Dial your host computer using your SLIP or PPP connection.

2   Call up Eudora by clicking on the appropriate icon. The top of your screen should look like Exhibit 26-3.

Exhibit 26-3

Main menu for Eudora e-mail program

File   Mailbox Message   Special Window

3 Pull down *File* and click on *Check mail.* The program will automatically retrieve your messages and store them in a folder on your computer. It will say that it is looking for the POP (Post Office Protocol) server. Create folders as you wish under *Mailbox.*

4 Reply or write a new message by clicking on the appropriate item under *message.*

5 To delete a message, hit *command-d,* or go to *Transfer* and pull down *Trash.* Then pull down *Special* and click on *Empty trash.*

6 To quit, pull down *File* or hit *command-q.* Close your computer connection by clicking *Disconnect* on your SLIP or PPP program.

Bulletin Board Discussion Groups

If you want to get a catalog from a mail-order store, you get on a mailing list. If you want to get information about a subject in which you share an interest with other people, you can get on an electronic mailing list called a bulletin board, forum or discussion group. Messages from that list will be sent directly to your e-mail address. Messages you send, or "post," to the list will be read by all its subscribers, which could be thousands of people. Some groups are managed by a person called a list operator or manager; other groups are known as "listserv" discussion groups because the discussion list is served to your e-mail address automatically via a computer program called Listserv. Most bulletin boards are free, but some—especially those that offer access to data bases—may charge subscription fees.

Suppose you are interested in learning more about on-line journalism. You could subscribe to a discussion group for on-line journalism. You and other people who want to discuss problems, concerns and news related to on-line journalism send messages to the list, and the person who manages the list sends the daily postings directly to your e-mail account. One note of caution: These discussion groups can generate hundreds of messages daily, so your e-mail account could be flooded with messages.

You don't have to actively participate in the discussion by sending messages. If you just want to read other people's messages to the list, you would be considered a "lurker."

To subscribe, you must address your request to get on the list to the person who manages the list; do not send your request to the name of the list itself. After you subscribe, you will receive a message confirming your request. Be sure to save the initial instructions you receive from the list manager for sending messages and for getting off the list if you decide you don't like it or can't handle the load of messages.

For example, to subscribe to the on-line journalism discussion group, address your e-mail message to majordomo@marketplace.com and write *Subscribe online-news,* followed by your e-mail address. Your request would be forwarded to the list manager (called the majordomo in this case), who would approve your subscription and send you a message confirming that you have been added to the list.

If you want to learn more about computer-assisted reporting, you could subscribe to the list called CARR-L by addressing your request to *listserv@ulkyvm.louisville.edu* (no period at the end). Your message should say *Subscribe CARR-L* and be followed by your e-mail address. This is one of the most popular lists for journalists, with more than 2,000 subscribers all over the world.

Another very useful bulletin board for journalists is FedWorld, operated by the federal government's National Technical Information Service to provide the public with on-line access to government information and documents. FedWorld offers information from scores of government agencies, such as the Department of Agriculture and the Centers for Disease Control. You may subscribe to this list by dialing with your modem into FedWorld at (703) 321-8020. An alternative is to use an Internet command. Type *telnet fedworld.gov* after the prompt when you have logged on to your host computer. You can also access FedWorld through the World Wide Web by using a browser, a technique described later in the chapter. (See the appendix for other resources for journalists.)

Newsgroups

Newsgroups are another form of discussion list, but they are not sent directly to your e-mail account. Instead, the messages are sent to your host computer, where you may read them when you call up the newsgroup you want. These newsgroups are part of an international network known as Usenet, which is a computer conference system on the Internet. There are thousands of newsgroups on subjects ranging from recreational topics to scientific ones. Because anyone may post messages to these newsgroups, you should not assume that information you read is accurate, and you should check everything before you use it in a news story.

There are many ways of accessing Usenet groups. When you get an academic computer account, you should receive instructions on accessing these groups from the type of terminal you are using. In general, however, first you have to log on to your computer account. Then you need to type the letters for a newsreader that will allow you to read the newsgroups. Some host computer systems ask you to type *news* after the prompt. Others require that you type *rn* for *Read news* or *nn* for *Network news.* Other access codes include *unews, usenet, trn* and *tin.*

Newsgroups are arranged by subject, indicated by prefaces such as *comp* for computers, *sci* for science issues, *rec* for recreation subjects, *misc* for miscellaneous topics and *alt* for alternative subjects, meaning any topics that don't fit into the other structured groups. Alt.journalism isn't alternative journalism but simply a discussion group on journalism, labeled *alt* because it is not grouped into science or recreation or the other Usenet topics.

The first time you use your newsreader, a list of all the newsgroups in your host computer system will appear. You will be asked if you want to register with a particular group. You don't have to subscribe. But if you do, the next time you access the newsreader, the groups you have selected will automatically be called up for you. You can also call up a newsgroup by the number, or you can scroll through the list of newsgroups and hit Return when you want to read the messages.

The newsreader may list the number of messages in the newsgroup. Use your cursor to scroll to the item you want to read, and hit Return if you want to see the message. You can use your cursor to go back to the previous message or list of newsgroups.

Some newsgroups relating to journalism are alt.journalism.freelance, alt.journalism.gay-press, alt.journalism.gonzo, alt.journalism.newspapers, alt.journalism.photo, alt.journalism.print, and alt.journalism.students.

The Internet

The Internet is a world-wide connection of networks that provides a mind-boggling array of information. It started in 1969 as a project of the U.S. Department of Defense to link military research contractors and universities doing military-funded research. Then the National Science Foundation got involved and set up regional networks, which grew primarily among academic institutions. Now it is available worldwide to commercial and academic organizations. As technology improves, navigating the Internet becomes easier.

The largest network on the Internet is called the World Wide Web, which is only one of many networks. It contains information ranging from government publications, such as U.S. census data, to videos of popular musicians. The World Wide Web is very easy to use because it relies on hypertext. Certain words and phrases are highlighted, and when you select them and click or hit Return, you are automatically linked to further details.

With good software programs called *browsers,* you can get sound and graphic images as well as text on the Internet. Most commercial services provide their own browsers to access information from the Internet; some of these services charge you for the time you are connected, and others charge a flat fee. You can access the Internet without time charges through most academic accounts. If you have a computer that cannot run graphical browsers because it lacks enough power or memory, you can still explore the Internet with a text-only browser, but the information is not as pleasant to read on your screen. However, some people prefer text-only browsers because text alone comes up faster than text with graphics. If you are working from a home computer, you don't need any special connections other than the basic software that comes with your modem.

The graphical/text browsers described in this chapter are Mosaic and Netscape, both available in free versions to academic users. If you are working through a modem instead of a direct connection to your host computer, you need a SLIP or PPP connection to use these browsers. You may be able to obtain Mosaic and Netscape on floppy disk from your computer center. Or you can access them on the Internet and transfer them to your home computer using a file transfer program (FTP), which should be available with your modem software. The appendix lists sites where you may get these browsers.

If you are using another browser, just follow its instructions for accessing the sites discussed in this chapter. Once you learn the main concepts of navigating the Internet, you can adjust to any differences in software.

URLs: Internet Addresses

Just as with e-mail, the Internet works on the concept of addresses. If you want to visit a person or place in any city, state or country, you need an address called a URL, or uniform resource locator. Many URL addresses are very long. Most of them on the World Wide Web start with *http://* (for hypertext transport protocol, followed by a colon and two slashes).

However, with the sophisticated technology of browsers, you don't even need to know a specific address to find the information you want on the Internet. You can use search engines, which are tools in a browser. You simply type the name of the subject you want, and these searchers then find Internet sites related to that subject. When you click on the name of a site, the browser takes you there. You can also just browse through topics linked with hypertext until you find a specific site you are seeking, but that method takes much longer.

The World Wide Web

The following are interactive exercises for exploring the World Wide Web. You can search for them using any browser. However, this section supplies detailed instructions for finding these sites using some specific tools.

• Find some sources or organizations on the Internet with information for a story about unidentified flying objects. (See Telnet Line-Mode Browser for complete instructions.)

• Find the site for U.S. federal government agencies and check what is available. Then find U.S. Government Information Sources and the Centers for Disease Control, and explore what CDC offers on the Internet. (See Lynx Line-Mode Browser for complete instructions.)

• Find your state on the list of World Wide Web servers, and then check whether your college or university has a site on the Web. (See World Wide Web Servers for more details.)

• Find Web sites for media organizations related to your major: public relations, broadcasting, newspapers and magazines, advertising, or photojournalism. (See Search Engines for more details.)

• Find your tarot reading (under Fortune Telling in the World Wide Web subject site) using a graphical browser. (See Mosaic for more details.)

• Find a list of journalism resources using a search engine in a graphical browser. (See Netscape for more details.)

Telnet line-mode browser   Let's begin by exploring the World Wide Web in the most primitive way, with a text-only, line-mode browser, which is accessible to almost anyone with an academic Internet account. If you have better tools, such as Mosaic, Netscape or other browsers, you can use them to locate the same information (and to complete the tasks listed for the other browsers).

Interactive task 1:   Find the site for UFOs using this line-mode browser, which requires you to scroll line by line and type numbers to get to the next link.

1   Log on to your computer account. At the first prompt, type *telnet(space) nxoc01.cern.ch* to connect to the World Wide Web at its headquarters at CERN, a research laboratory in Geneva, Switzerland. Here is the message you should see when the connection is made:

Welcome to the World-Wide Web

THE WORLD-WIDE WEB

This is just one of the many access points to the web, the universe of information available over networks. To follow references, just type the number then hit the return (enter) key.

The features you have by connecting to this telnet server are very primitive compared to the features you have when you run a W3 "client" program on your own computer. If you possibly can, please pick up a client for your platform to reduce the load on this service and experience the web in its full splendor. For more information, select by number:

A list of available W3 client programs[1]

Everything about the W3 project[2]

Places to start exploring[3]

Have fun!

1–3, Up, <RETURN> for more, Quit, or Help:

2 Type *3* for *Places to start exploring.* Press Return. You will see this message:

GENERAL OVERVIEW OF THE WEB

There is no "top" to the World-Wide Web. You can look at it from many points of view. Here are some places to start.

Virtual Library by Subject [2]

The Virtual Library organizes information by subject matter.

List of servers [3]   All registered HTTP servers by country

by Service Type [4] The web includes data accessible by many other protocols. The lists by access protocol may help if you know what kind of service you are looking for.

If you find a useful starting point for you personally, you can configure your WWW browser to start there by default.

1–5, Back, Up, <Return> for more, Quit or Help:

3 Type *2* for *Virtual Library by Subject.* This is a good way to see what subject matter is available. You can scroll (use your down arrow) to see all the subjects, which are listed in alphabetical order. If you want to see more specifics under any particular category, type *1.* Keep hitting Return to get to the entries that start with *U,* where the listing for unidentified flying objects is located. If you pass that entry, type *U* for *Up a page.*

4 When you find the entry for UFOs, type the number following it. The directory on UFOs should appear. Scroll through all the information so you have an idea what is available. For the purposes of this exercise and your hypothetical news story, find the organizations you might call to locate sources. Type the number after *Organizations;* you should get addresses for The Mutual UFO Network (MUFON), Operation Right to Know, The Center for UFO Studies, and Jeremy D. Zawodny, Bowling Green State University, who compiled the information for this Web site. The names of sources and sites may change, but if you have connected this far, you should have a good idea of how to access information the most difficult way.

5 To save a document you have found and wish to keep, follow the instructions for your modem software. You may have to save it in a file on your computer. Type *quit* when you are finished.

Lynx line-mode browser   Here's a way to navigate the Web with a free browser that requires no special software. It is the Lynx browser, which you can obtain from the University of Kansas, where it was developed. Lynx is easier and faster to use than Telnet. Instead of typing numbers, you use your cursor. With this activity, you will discover how vast the information is on the Web.

Interactive task 2: Find the site for U.S. federal government agencies. Then find U.S. Government Information Sources, and under that category find the Centers for Disease Control.

1 Log on to your computer account. When you see the prompt, type *telnet (space)lynx.cc.ukans.edu* (no period at the end). You will be asked to log in as lynxon*WWW*. You will get a message telling you that you can access KUFacts through the URL http://www.ukans.edu/, which you can do if you have other browsers like Mosaic or Netscape. To use Lynx, you can also type *telnet ukanaix.cc.ukans.edu* and log in as *KUFacts*.

2 The host computer will ask you to enter a terminal type, or it may say *Terminal type unknown*. Because the host operates on a VT 100 computer, type those letters or just hit Return.

3 Scroll to *Resources,* and hit Return when you get to the part that says *World Wide Web.* If you happen to log in and get *KUFacts,* you can connect by scrolling until you find *Reference Shelf* and, from there, *Internet Resources.* You can connect to *WWW Information by Subject* or *WWW Information by Type.*

4 Choose *WWW Information by Subject.* Once you connect to the Web, operate your cursors as indicated in the instructions at the bottom of each screen, which should look like this:

— press space for next page —

Arrow keys: Up and Down to move. Right to follow a link; Left to go back.

O)ther cmds H)elp K)eymap G)oto P)rint M)ain screen o)ptions Q)uit

5 Go to *Category Subtree,* hit Return to get to the World-Wide Web Virtual Library, and hit your space bar until you get to *U.S. Government Information Sources,* and hit Return. Then, using your space bar, find *Department of Health and Human Services* and scroll to *Public Health Service* to *Centers for Disease Control.* If you connected by KUFacts, go to *WWW Resources.* Then scroll to the National Center for Supercomputing Applications (NCSA) *meta-index* of Web resources. Scroll to the *WWW Virtual Library.* Then follow these links: *Category Subtree, U.S. Government Information Sources, Department of Health and Human Services, Public Health Service, Centers for Disease Control.*

6 Now explore *U.S. Government Agencies* by hitting your left arrow key to go back. Hit *b* to go back or *u* to go up to the previous page. Hit your space bar to discover all the departments and types of information available to you.

Using Lynx, you may also find the site for unidentified flying objects, as detailed in the Telnet exercise. See if you think the Lynx mode is faster.

World Wide Web servers   Servers are the people or organizations that put their information on the Internet. This exercise explores servers on the Web.

Interactive task 3:   Find your state on the list of World Wide Web servers, and then check whether your college or university has a site on the Web. Explore other sites your state has on the Internet.

1   Using Lynx, go back (keep hitting your left cursor) until you get to the part that asks if you want to connect to the Web by subject or by type.

2   Click on *WWW Information by Type* and hit Return. This site lists the Internet servers all over the world. When World-Wide Web servers is highlighted, hit Return, and using your down cursor, scroll to your country. If you start scrolling, you can explore any country you wish. To speed up the scrolling, you can hit your spacebar fast or hold it down. But be careful, because the program is very sensitive, and the list may scroll too fast.

3   To find your state and university in the United States, scroll down to *North America* and to your state. Then hit Return and find your state. Keep following the links until you find what your college or university or other sites in your state offer on the Internet.

Search engines   Suppose you know the topic you want to research and you don't feel like scrolling through lists from all over the world. No problem. You can find what you want by typing the words describing your topic into a program called a search engine or searcher. A list of Internet sources with information about that subject will appear on your screen. Your software program may have its own search engine, but this task uses the one on Lynx, which is available to everyone with a Telnet university account.

Interactive task 4:   Use a search engine to find a media organization related to your major: public relations, broadcasting, news (including newspapers and magazines), advertising or photojournalism.

1   If you are logged onto Lynx, get the menu and scroll to the World Wide Web, as in Interactive Task 2. But this time, move your cursor to *Inter-Links—Internet access made easy*.

2   Go to *Search the Net*. Hit Return.

3   Scroll to *Search the World-Wide Web*. Hit Return.

4   Choose one of the search engines, preferably ElNet Web Search or Webcrawler. Then type in your request—for example, *Journalism*. You should get a list of several sources, including electronic publications. If you are interested in other topics, just type those. One site has links to many others. You could also try Yahoo, which offers many sites and good links to journalism sources on the Web. If you are using some other browser, you can use the search engines it provides. Once you find the name of an organization related to your field, explore the links it offers.

Here are some search tips for specific majors:

Public relations: Look for the International Association of Business Communicators and the Public Relations Society of America. You could also try just searching *Public relations.*

Broadcasting: Search for RTNDA, the Radio-Television News Directors Association.

Newspapers and magazines: Search for the Society of Professional Journalists for starters. There are dozens of regional societies, too.

Photojournalism: Search for the National Press Photographers Association.

Advertising: Search for the American Association of Advertising Agencies.

Mosaic Mosaic is a graphical browser, which is much easier and more fun to use than the text-only browsers like Telnet and Lynx. It operates by clicking once on a link (clicking twice messes up the system). You must have a SLIP or PPP connection if you are dialing in to your host computer without a direct connection. Although retrieving information in graphic and text form may take longer, it is worth the wait because the information is so much easier to read and more exciting to view.

When using Mosaic, wait for the icon at the left side of the page to stop twirling before you click on anything. The top of the page should say Data Transfer Complete.

Interactive task 5: Using a search engine, find your tarot reading.

1 Dial into your host computer using your SLIP or PPP connection. Call up the NSCA Mosaic icon, so named because it was developed at the National Center for Supercomputing Applications at the University of Illinois, Urbana-Champaign. The top of the "home page" of Mosaic should appear like Exhibit 26-4 in the Mac OS or similar in Windows but without the apple on the left.

Exhibit 26-4

Mosaic home page

2 If you know the URL (the address) of a specific Web site, you may type it in the URL box, located under the Mosaic icon. Or you can pull down *File,* click on *Open URL* and type the address.

3 If you want to return to a previous page, use your left arrow. To get to the home page, click on the icon that looks like a house. Most often, however, you may navigate by clicking on highlighted links.

4 Hotlists: Once you find a site you like and plan to visit often, you can add its address to your hotlist so you don't have to type a URL or search for it again. Go to the top of your screen and pull down *Navigate.* Then click on *Hotlist,* and add the address to the list (hit *Save*). To call up an item already on your hotlist, go to *Navigate* and click on your *Hotlist.* A box like the one in Exhibit 26-5 will appear. Click on the item in your hotlist that you want and then click on *Load URL.* The site you want will appear.

5 To explore the World Wide Web, go to the Mosaic home page. Click on *Suggested Starting Points for the Internet.* You can explore at will or do

Exhibit 26-5

Hotlist in Mosaic

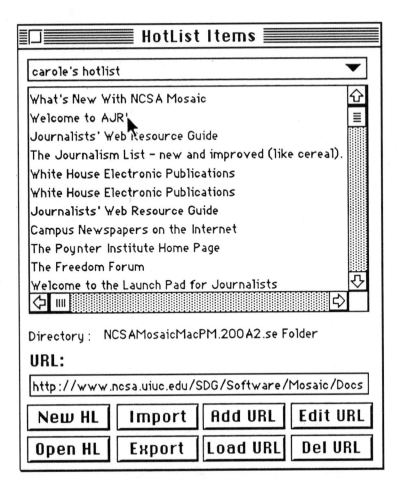

some of the previously suggested interactive tasks. Or you can get your fortune told. Call up *Web by Subject,* click on *Fortune telling,* and follow the instructions to get your own tarot reading. Be a bit patient; it may take some time for your tarot cards to transfer to your computer. But the wait is worthwhile, especially if you have a color terminal.

6   Search engines: Mosaic is developing new search engines so you can type your requests. You can use the Docfinder searcher by calling up http://docfinder.ncsa.uiuc.edu or use Yahoo by scrolling through Web servers or using this URL: http://www.yahoo.com.

7   To save any document, just go to *File,* pull down *Save* or *Save as,* and hit Return.

Now see if you can complete some of the other exercises, especially Interactive Task 6.

Netscape   This is a very popular browser because it is so easy to use. It is also a graphical browser that operates by hypertext links. By clicking on *Net Search,* you can access the InfoSeek search engine and type your request, which will generate many site names. You can also use other search engines.

After you click on a link, wait for movement to stop in the large *N* icon at the top right-hand side of your screen, which means the text has been loaded, before you try to click on another link. The bottom of your screen will also tell you what percentage of the document has been loaded and when the document is "done." If the site is too busy, meaning that it cannot accept any more viewers at this time, you will get the message *Connection refused by host.*

When you find a site you like and want to return to often, you can add it under *Bookmarks.*

Interactive task 6:   Using the Netscape search engine, InfoSeek, or any other search engine, find *Journalism* and explore the resources.

1   Log on to your computer using a SLIP or PPP connection if you don't have a direct connection to the host computer.

2   Click on the Netscape icon, and wait for the home page to load. The top of your screen should look something like Exhibit 26-6 (without the apple if you are operating in Windows).

3   Click on *Net Directory* if you wish to go directly to the Internet. The Yahoo search engine will be listed, along with World Wide Web servers.

4   To go back to the home page, click on the Home icon. To go back to the previous site you visited, click on *Back* or *Forward.* Use *Open* if you want to type in a URL address. Use *Find* to locate words within a document.

5   With Netscape, you can interrupt your search for a site by clicking on *Stop* if you change your mind while Netscape is in the process of loading it.

Exhibit 26-6

Netscape home page

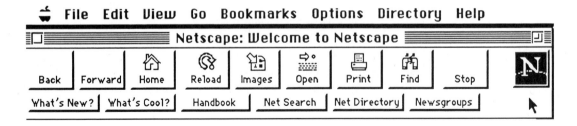

6 Searchers: Click on *Net search* to use InfoSeek, the Netscape browser that allows you to type in words to locate your topic, or other search engines, such as Webcrawler and Lycos. In addition, you can also click on *W3 Search Engines* or *CUSI* to access a large selection of searchers. Now type in *journalism resources*. You should get a list of sites, including John Makulowich's Awesome List and the Journalist's Toolbox or his list called The World Wide Web Virtual Library: Journalism. Check out related lists, such as Newslink. All these lists are worth exploring. While you are in any of these lists, you might want to explore on-line student newspapers.

7 To type the URL for a specific site, go to *File* and click on *Location*.

8 To save any document you want, just go to *File* and click on *Save*.

Gopher

Gopher is an Internet search system devised by the University of Minnesota and named after the school's mascot. In a computer context, a gopher is a scurrying animal that fetches documents for you by tunneling through the Internet. Gopher is arranged in menu form, listing Gopher servers, or sites that provide links to documents on many other networks that are part of the Internet but not part of the World Wide Web. If you have been exploring the Internet in the previous interactive tasks, you may already have noticed some links from the World Wide Web to documents in Gopher menus.

If you have a browser like Netscape or Mosaic, you don't need any other tools to run Gopher. You can also access Gopher menus by using the Lynx browser.

When you connect with a Gopher server, it will give you a menu that has "subject trees," or subheadings. You can scroll through them by topics. You can also explore the vast Gopher resources by clicking or scrolling on the menu item *All the Gopher servers in the world*.

The following exercises will familiarize you with Gopher:

• Find the Gopher site where you can get free software for your computer.

• Find out what is available through the Online Career Center and whether the service is used on your campus.

Accessing Gopher servers

If you know the name of a Gopher server whose information you want to explore, you can type that name as the address in your searcher or browser. A good place to start is with the University of Minnesota Gopher. Other good tools to use are Turbo-Gopher for Macintosh users and PCGopher for IBM, but you need a SLIP or PPP connection to use them from your modem.

Interactive task 7: Find the Gopher site where you can get free software for your computer. Check out *All the Gopher servers in the world.*

1 Using Netscape, Mosaic or any other browser that allows you to type a URL address, type *gopher://gopher2.tc.umn.edu/1* to get the University of Minnesota Gopher. Check under *Information about Gopher* and then under *Gopher software distribution.* Scroll until you find the software for your computer. Or you can go directly to this site by typing *gopher://boombox. micro.umn.edu:70/11/gopher* (unless that site address changes). This site provides only Gopher software. For all kinds of software from the University of Minnesota Gopher, follow this path: *Computer information* to *Type of computer* or *Internet file server (FTP) sites* to *Popular FTP sites via Gopher* to your computer type.

2 If you don't have a good browser, use the Lynx system described earlier in the chapter. Access Lynx by typing *telnet:ukanaix.cc.ukans.edu* and logging in as *KUFacts.* When you get the KUFacts directory, scroll to *Reference shelf* to *Internet resources* to *Gopher resources* and to *All Gopher resources.* Or go directly to the University of Minnesota Gopher. Then follow links from *Information about Gopher* to *Gopher software distribution.*

3 If you want to explore, check out *Gopher jewels* on the *Gopher resources* menu.

When you are getting free software from the Internet, be aware that there are two types: freeware and shareware. Freeware is just that, totally free with no restrictions. Shareware is software available for purchase at a nominal fee after a brief free trial period. Some shareware may have an expiration date, limiting the time it is functional. Other shareware has no limitations; you are on your honor to register and pay for it. In return, you will usually receive free updates. The software discussed here should be freeware.

Using Gopher search tools

If you know the subject you want to research and you don't feel like scrolling or clicking through links to many documents, you can take several shortcuts by using a Gopher address or by using a search engine that works with Gopher servers, such as Veronica, Jughead or WAIS. These tools work like other search engines, so if you have a good search engine in your browser, you can use that instead. However, if you are already linked to a Gopher site and want to find another site quickly, use the Veronica search engines, which also can retrieve documents from the World Wide Web and other resources.

Interactive task 8: Find out about available jobs and internships through the Online Career Center, and check whether this online job service is available on your campus. If you want information about other job opportunities, check under the listings for the professional organizations you discovered in Interactive Task 4.

1 Veronica: Veronica must be accessed through a Gopher site. When you call up the basic Gopher menu for the University of Minnesota or another site, choose *Other Gopher and information servers.* It should offer an option called *Search titles in gopherspace using Veronica.*

2 When you get the Veronica search tool, type the words for the topic you want. In this case, type *Online Career Center.* A menu of many choices should appear. Look for the Gopher site Online Career Center on Campus, and check if your campus is connected. The direct Gopher address is gopher://iq-occ.iquest.net:70/1/occ/campus (no period).

3 If you have Netscape or Mosaic, you can use a shortcut. Get to the Online Career Center through the World Wide Web or by using a search engine. Then follow the Gopher links. You can also access this site via a URL on the Web: http://www.occ.com/occ/TextHomePage.html.

4 WAIS: WAIS, for Wide Area Information Server, is another search tool for gopherspace. Unlike Veronica, which finds documents with titles that match the topic you requested, WAIS searches through the content of documents to find those that offer the specific information you request. You need a server that offers WAIS, such as Lynx or the University of Minnesota Gopher, and then you can type the words for the information you want.

File Transfers and FTP

Many directories on the Internet list information available via FTP, which means file transfer protocol. You may get these files from the directory (the FTP site) and transfer them to your own computer. Many files in FTP are offered via anonymous FTP. That means when you call up the directory and log in, you don't give your real name. You write the word *anonymous* and, when the program asks for your password, give your e-mail address. Do not use your real password. Sometimes the system will ask you to sign in as *Guest* instead. Just follow directions.

Transferring files via Telnet can be complicated, but you can get directions under *FTP* in the Lynx menu. If you are using a commercial browser or graphical browsers such as Netscape and Mosaic, you simply have to click on *Save* or *Download* when you find a document you want, and it will be saved on your own computer. These browsers are very easy tools for using FTP. If you don't have one of these browsers, you can get free software through the Internet (see Interactive Task 7) that makes file transfers easier than using Telnet.

Archie and Anarchie: Archie (for IBM users) and Anarchie (for Macintosh users) are search engines that help you find FTP files. If you have Archie or Anarchie software, you write the words of the topic you want to find, and the tool searches through thousands of documents to retrieve those relevant to your topic. Then you choose *FTP* from your menu and retrieve the files you want. If you don't have or can't get the Archie or Anarchie software, you can still use the search mechanism. To access an Archie server, a site that offers the Archie search program, without your own software, call up one of these servers: archie.ans.net, archie.rutgers.edu, archie.sura.net, or archie.unl.edu in the United States and archie.mcgill.ca in Canada. At the log-in prompt, type *archie*. Use the *help* command to get further instructions.

Kermit: This file transfer program was developed at Columbia University in New York and is available for all types of machines. It is accessible at http://www/columbia.edu. Once you have found the FTP files you want, click on *Kermit* and the program will retrieve them to your computer.

Although many Internet sites offer these programs without charge, the easiest way to find and download them is to use one of the search engines, such as Webcrawler, Yahoo, or InfoSeek. When you find a site that offers them, you can usually get them from the "public" directory. Many academic computer centers also offer these programs to students and faculty free of charge if you bring your own computer disk.

For further information about using FTP programs on the Internet, access one of the how-to guides available at almost every site or accessible under the Lynx program menu.

Data Bases

A data base is any collection of information. But in the context of journalism, it is considered a collection of facts, usually names and numbers, that can be logically grouped. A telephone book, for example, is a data base—whether it is in print or computer form.

Data bases can serve as an accuracy check. Suppose, for example, that you call the state fire marshal and ask which buildings on your campus are the most dangerous. He or she could give you an opinion based on inspections. But if you look at the records yourself, you might find that the problem is worse than the official says. You can get this information by checking paper records, but a computer data base allows you to calculate information much faster and easier. This capacity has encouraged journalists to use data bases to generate stories, not just to check them.

Some journalists still envision spending months or even years analyzing millions of numbers for major projects. And with good reason.

Many years ago, when reporters first began using computers to analyze data bases, they were usually working on investigative projects that took months or years to complete. Some projects still take a long time if they involve large data bases and difficult investigations. But at many newspapers, computer-assisted reporting is used on a daily basis for all kinds of stories.

Story Ideas from Data Bases

Here are some story ideas that can be researched quickly using data bases:

• Why don't people get married on the 13th day of the month? Reporters from the *News & Observer* in Raleigh, N.C., got the county's marriage data base. They analyzed which dates were the most popular wedding days and followed up with personal interviews. They found that people didn't choose the 13th of any month because they didn't want their anniversary to fall on any Friday the 13th.

• When do people die the most? During holidays, according to a *News & Observer* analysis of North Carolina's data base of deaths.

• Which public community college or university has the most fire code violations in your state? Reporters from the *Sun-Sentinel* in Fort Lauderdale, Fla., wrote this story by checking state fire inspection records.

• Where are the best places to meet eligible singles? Jennifer LeFleur, research analyst for the *San Jose* (Calif.) *Mercury News,* decided to find out. You could do the same story in your area by checking the U.S. census data base, particularly for cities with colleges and universities.

• What are the 10 most expensive homes in your area, and who owns them? A check of your county's property assessment data base can generate this information quickly.

• What types of dogs are the most popular, and what are the favorite names for these pets? If your county requires dog licenses, this is another quick and easy story.

• What type of vehicles are most likely to be ticketed for speeding? For example, do owners of red cars really get the most speeding tickets? And how do white cars compare? If your county keeps a data base of traffic tickets, this is another relatively easy story to compile.

• Who are the worst parking offenders on your campus? Is there one officer who writes the most parking tickets? All this information should be on a data base.

Although all these stories have a statistical foundation, reporters used the data bases to get names and then conduct interviews with the people behind the statistics. The numbers may be included in only one paragraph in the story, plus in a chart. Remember that you are still writing stories, not statistical reports. You still need the human element that comes from interviewing people. When you do use statistics, make sure you tell your readers what they mean, why they are significant and why readers should care.

Access to Data Bases

You can get data from the U.S. Census Bureau through your own computer if you tap the Internet. But getting local government data may be much harder, even if you are asking for public records. Universities also are often reluctant to release information. Officials frequently cite the Buckley Amendment, which protects the privacy of students and public employees by prohibiting the release of certain information, such as grades and personnel files. Local governments, especially those in small college towns, may not even have the information on a computer data base. And worst of all, you may be charged for the information. For example, even though vehicle licenses are public records, in Kansas and some other states the Department of Motor Vehicle Registration charges $3 for each license you wish to check. Public agencies may also charge you for downloading the information to a floppy disk, just as they might charge copying fees for paper records.

So the first thing you need to do is find out if the data base you want is available and if any fees apply. Then check whether you can get the information on a computer disk and whether the information will be compatible with your computer software.

Even if you get the data, you may not be able to use it without careful checking. When it converts to your computer software, it could be "dirty data," meaning many numbers could be out of line or contain typos and faulty codes that you must clean up. As a beginner in this type of computer-assisted reporting, you may be better served by starting with a relatively small data base that you compile yourself.

Spreadsheets and Relational Data Base Managers

The two types of computer software programs used most often to analyze data are flat-file and relational data base managers. Spreadsheets are considered flat-file data bases because all the data are entered into a sheet that contains only one type of table. Relational data bases allow you to make correlations among several types of tables. For example, in a spreadsheet listing contributions to politicians in your community, you could find out which politician received the most money by totaling the figures in each column. A relational data base manager might list the politicians and the amount of contributions in one table and the contributors to politicians in another. You could correlate which contributor gave the most money to which politician by asking the data base questions in a format called structured query language.

Spreadsheets are preferable when you have hundreds, instead of thousands, of numbers and when you want basic calculations, such as addition and percentages. These programs also allow you to make charts and graphs from your numbers. Relational data base managers, such as FoxPro and Paradox, are preferable when you use thousands or millions of numbers and you need to analyze a lot of links among data.

Rich Gordon, an expert in computer-assisted reporting at *The Miami Herald,* says if you want to build a solid foundation in this type of journalism, start with spreadsheets. That's good advice for basic reporting classes, so this chapter deals only with spreadsheets. The directions are for Microsoft Excel 5.0, a widely used program that is similar for both Macintosh and Windows platforms. The directions are similar to those in Lotus 1-2-3, another popular program. If you have another software program, follow those instructions. The instructions here cover just a few of the most basic skills.

Here are some basic terms you need to know before you start using spreadsheets:

Worksheet: Excel and some other software programs call the spreadsheet a worksheet.

Column: The columns are the vertical grids labeled alphabetically across the top of the document (see Exhibit 26-7). Use your right and left arrow keys to move the cursor from column to column.

Row: Rows are the horizontal grids labeled numerically on the left side—from 1 to 16,384 in Excel. Hit Return to move the cursor to the next row down or use your down arrow to move the cursor.

Microsoft Excel

Excel icon

Exhibit 26-7

Excel spreadsheet

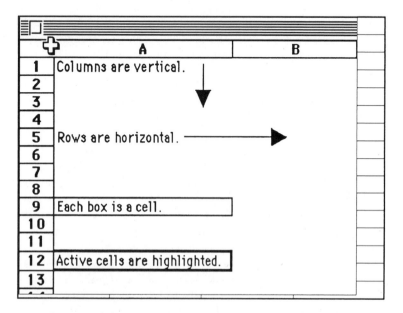

Cell: A cell is an individual box within the grid. To enter data, you must use the active cell, which has a highlighted box around it. Data entry is also indicated in the top line under the tool box. When you move your cursor to the right, the cell in the next column is highlighted. When you hit Return, the cursor moves down to the next cell in the column.

Interactive task 9:   Analyze which two sporting activities 18-to-25-year-olds participate in the most. This task uses the sorting function.

1   Open the Excel program by clicking on the Excel icon.

2   Insert the data in Exhibit 26-8 in your worksheet. You may enter data column by column—typing the names of each sport and hitting Return (or Enter)

Exhibit 26-8

Data on sports activity participation

Data from *The Statistical Abstract of the United States* (1992), based on a survey of 10,000 households by the National Sporting Goods Association

Activity	18-25 yrs.				
Aerobics	5771				
Backpacking	1547				
Baseball	1921				
Basketball	4896				
Bike riding	5547				
Bowling	7024				
Calisthenics	1583				
Camping	5297				
Equipment workout	6913				
Exercise walking	6310				
Fishing	4282				
Football	2762				
Golf	3048				
Hiking	2644				
Hunting	2614				
Racquetball	1980				
Running/jogging	4490				
Skiing - cross ctry	327				
Skiing - downhill	2601				
Soccer	1296				
Softball	2906				
Swimming	7690				
Tennis	3933				
Volleyball	5111				

after each word and then moving to the next cell in column A. Or you can enter data row by row (which is a little slower)—typing the name of the sport and the figure next to it in column B. For this method you use your right arrow to move the cursor to the next column; then hit Return and use your left arrow to get back to column A.

3 In the first row, write the headings *Activity* (in column A) and *18–25 Years* (in column B).

4 Save your worksheet under the title *Sports Activity Participation*. Hit *command-S* for save, and type a title for your worksheet. Do this before you begin entering data. Save (hit *command-S*) repeatedly as you enter data. Do not wait until you have finished typing all your numbers! If you make a mistake and lose your worksheet without saving the data, you will have to retype everything.

5 To widen column A so the complete names of the sports activities can be seen, place your arrow on the line between columns A and B and drag it to the right. If you make a mistake, put your cursor in the bad cell, and then hit Delete or click on the *X* in the top bar under the buttons (see Exhibit 26-9).

6 The next step is to sort by columns, ranking the sports from those with the highest participation to the lowest. Put your cursor at the top of column B (where the letter *B* appears), and drag your mouse to the left until both columns are highlighted. (You could also drag your mouse from the top of column B down the column and over to column A.) If you don't highlight both column B and column A, the sorted list of activities will not match the list of numbers. If you wanted to sort the activities in alphabetical order, as the chart in Exhibit 26-8 now appears, you would highlight column A first and then drag your mouse to highlight column B. Newer programs don't require highlighting the columns.

7 Go to *Data* in the menu bar and pull down *Sort*. You will see a box that looks like Exhibit 26-10. Click on the arrow next to *Activity* and move it to 18-25 years. Click on *Descending*. Click on *OK*, and the data should sort. For a shortcut, you can use the Sort buttons at the top of the screen (see Exhibit 26-11). The button with the *A* on top sorts data in ascending order (from lowest to highest), and the one with the *Z* on top sorts data in descending order. Are you surprised that the two most popular participatory sports are swimming and bowling?

Exhibit 26-9

Shortcut for deleting a cell in Excel

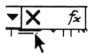

Exhibit 26-10

Excel sorting options

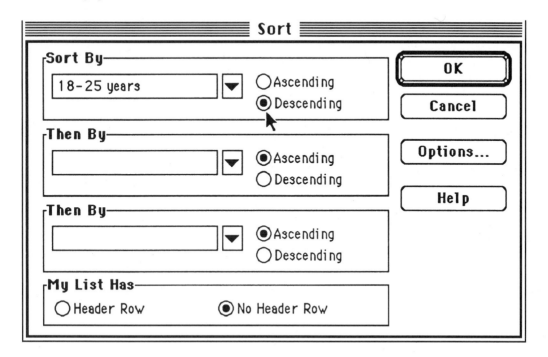

Exhibit 26-11

Shortcut for sorting data in Excel

Exhibit 26-12

Icon for selecting chart types in Excel

Now you can use your sorted figures to make a chart.

Charts   In Excel, you can make charts from your data in seconds with the click of a button, with the Chart Wizard feature. If you want to display the toolbar that tells you what types of charts you can make, click on *View* at the top of your screen and pull down *Toolbars*. Then click on *Chart* and *Showtools*. If you click on the arrow, you can see the types of charts you can create (see Exhibit 26-12). There are several ways to make charts, but here are some simple instructions.

Exhibit 26-13

*Horizontal bar chart
created with Excel*

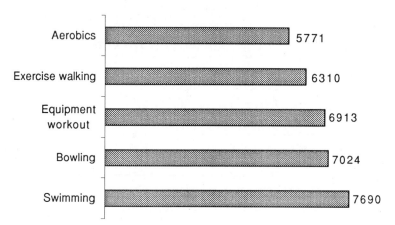

Sports Participation Chart

Aerobics	5771
Exercise walking	6310
Equipment workout	6913
Bowling	7024
Swimming	7690

Interactive task 10: Create a chart with the top five figures from your sorted results.

1 Using your mouse, highlight the top five categories in your table.

2 Go to *Insert* and click on *Chart.* In this case, let's add the chart to the spreadsheet, although you may create a separate chart if you prefer.

3 Click on *Chart Wizard,* and then click on *Next* in the dialogue box that appears. You should see a variety of sample charts. Click on the type of chart you wish to create. Click on *Finish.* You should see a chart. If you want to change the type of chart, go to the Chart Type button and select another chart or pull down Chart Type under Format at the top of your screen.

4 **Labels and legends:** If you click twice on the body of your chart, you can edit it. The Insert heading offers a variety of options, such as titles, data labels and a legend. The Format heading adds color or patterns to your bars or pie shapes. Simply click on the name of the element you want to change.

5 Try creating a variety of charts with the figures in your table. Exhibit 26-13 is an example of what you can do.

Calculations   Spreadsheet software and relational data base managers can be used to calculate new numbers from the data you provide. Here's an example.

Interactive task 11: Calculate college costs from data in *The Statistical Abstract of the United States* (in print or on the Internet).

1 Create a new spreadsheet. Go to *File* and click on *New.*

2 Widen the first row. Using your mouse, direct your pointer to the line at the top of the spreadsheet that separates the headings for columns A and B.

Exhibit 26-14

Data on college costs

Data from *The Statistical Abstract of the United States* (1992, 1993), based on an annual survey of colleges by The College Board on the costs for in-state undergraduate students

	A	B	C	D	E
					College Costs
1	Type of College and Item	1992-93	1992-93	1993-94	1993-94
2		Public colleges	Private colleges	Public colleges	Private colleges
3	Tuition and fees	$ 2,315	$ 10,498	$ 2,527	$ 11,025
4	Books and supplies	$ 528	$ 531	$ 552	$ 556
5	Room and board	$ 3,526	$ 4,575	$ 3,680	$ 4,793
6	Transportation	$ 497	$ 487	$ 557	$ 498
7	Other	$ 1,205	$ 936	$ 1,246	$ 974
8	Total	=SUM(B3:B7)			
9					

Exhibit 26-15

Autosum icon in Excel

The pointer should change from a thick cross to a thin cross. Using the thin cross, drag the line to the right to widen column A.

3   Type the information given in the chart in Exhibit 26-14. You might want to check the Internet for more current figures. Remember to save often as you type; don't wait until the end. The Total row will be blank until you do the addition.

4   **Addition:** Add the numbers in each column to get the total costs. Use the mouse to move your pointer to cell B8; outlining will indicate that it is the active cell. Then click on the autosum icon (see Exhibit 26-15) on the top row of your screen, and it will automatically insert in the active cell a code for the calculations (refer back to Exhibit 26-14). Hit Return and you will have your sum. Do the same for cells C8, D8, and E8. Instead of using autosum, you could manually write the calculation in the active cell by typing =*SUM(B3:B7).* The formula for addition is an equal sign, followed by the word *Sum* and, in parentheses, the numbers of the cells you want to add with a colon between the numbers. Some software uses the plus sign or "at" sign (@) instead of an equal sign. If your version of Excel or spreadsheet program differs, follow those instructions.

Other mathematical formulas All the mathematical formulas in Excel begin with an equal sign; other spreadsheet programs may use a slash (/). Here are the basic commands, called operators, for the most common mathematical functions:

+ (plus sign) for addition

- (hyphen for a minus sign) for subtraction

* (asterisk) for multiplication

/ (slash) for division

To insert a formula in the top formula row or the active cell, you would type the equal sign, then write the number of the cell you want in the formula or just click on it. Then you would write the operator—a plus, minus, asterisk or slash—and the number of the other cell in the formula. If you have many cells, you would use an operator between each.

Interactive task 12: Calculate how much more private colleges cost than public colleges in 1993–94, using the spreadsheet in Exhibit 26-14.

1 Move your cursor to cell F8. Then type the formula =E8-D8 (equal sign, cell E8, minus, cell D8) to subtract the total cost of public school ($8,562) from the total cost of private school ($17,846). You are clicking on or typing cell numbers instead of writing out all those figures.

2 Hit Return or Enter or click on the check. You should get the answer: 9,284. Remember that if you make a mistake or want to delete a cell, you may hit the Delete key or click on the *X*.

3 To add a dollar sign or percent sign, use the appropriate buttons (see Exhibit 26-16) before you write the formula.

Shortcut for deleting a cell in Excel

Exhibit 26-16

Dollar and percent buttons in Excel

Percentages If you plan a career in corporate public relations or news, chances are you will be dealing with budgets. You'll need to know how to figure percentage increases and decreases. A spreadsheet can help you calculate these figures easily.

Exhibit 26-17

Spreadsheet calculation of the percentage increase in a budget

	A	B	C
1	This year	$ 34,366,890	
2	Last year	$ 31,478,139	
3	Difference	$2,888,751	
4			
5	Percentage change	9%	
6			
7			

Interactive task 13:   Figure the percentage increase in a budget (see Exhibit 26-17).

1   Subtract the previous year's figure from the current figure. Outline cell B3. Type the formula, =B1-B2. Hit Return.

2   Divide the difference by the previous year's figure with the formula =B3/B2. Hit Return or Enter and you should get 0.09177007. Hit the percent sign to get the answer.

Glossary

Anonymous FTP: File transfer protocol that allows you to transfer documents by logging in with the user name *Anonymous* or *Guest*.

Bandwidth: Size or transmission capability of a channel carrying telecommunications. The bandwidth of an optical fiber cable the size of a human hair is about 1,000 times the bandwidth of radio frequencies, meaning that it can carry about 1,000 times as much information.

Baud rate: Measurement for the transfer speed of information (one signal per second) through modems. Preferred baud rates are 14.4 (14,400) or higher.

Bit: Binary digit; unit of data represented as a zero or one in computers.

Browser: Program that allows you to search through a network like the World Wide Web. Popular browsers are Netscape and Mosaic.

Bulletin board: Computer group discussion. See also *forum, newsgroup.*

Cyberspace: Computer-generated landscape. The term was created by William Gibson, author of a 1984 science fiction book, *Neuromancer.* Now the term is more commonly used to describe the world of networks that computer users navigate.

Digital Age: Term commonly used to describe the age of computers. Digits are the units of measurement, represented by zeroes and ones, that a computer reads.

Discussion group: Computer forum on a topic people wish to discuss.

Domain: Name given to the main or host computer on your network; the part of an Internet address that identifies the main computer network.

Download: To retrieve a file to your computer from another machine.

E-mail: Electronic mail transmitted through computer networks.

Emoticon: Symbol that reflects the tone of an e-mail message. Common emoticons are called "smileys" because they are happy faces when viewed sideways.

Eudora: Popular e-mail program.

FAQ: Frequently asked question, with the answer. Many computer programs on the Internet offer information in this form.

File transfer protocol: Method of transferring files from one computer to another.

Flaming: Transmitting an angry response to a computer message.

Forum: Computer discussion group or bulletin board.

Freeware: Software distributed free of charge.

Gopher: Information retrieval system, developed by the University of Minnesota, that provides menus for navigating through networks on the Internet.

Graphical browser: Program that allows you to search on the Internet for files containing both graphics and text.

Hardware: Machinery of your computer.

Host computer: Main computer that is directly connected to the Internet. The computer system at your college or university or a commercial system is the host computer.

HTTP: Hypertext Transfer Protocol; addressing system used by the World Wide Web. Most addresses on the Web start with *http* followed by a colon and two slashes.

Hypertext: Text that is highlighted and linked to other related topics.

Internet: Global network of thousands of smaller computer networks. The largest and most well-known network is the World Wide Web.

IP address: Numerical Internet address for a computer system. The IP number identifies a machine on the Internet.

LAN: Local area network; two or more computers connected via cables.

Line-mode browser: Tool for browsing the Internet that scrolls items line by line.

Listserv: Program that manages mailing lists by automatically sending messages to the e-mail addresses of people who subscribe to an interest group.

Log in: Name you use to gain access to your computer system.

Log on: Steps you take to gain access to your computer system.

Log out: Process of signing off or disconnecting from a computer network; also called log off.

Lurker: Person who reads messages but does not actively participate in a newsgroup or bulletin board discussion.

Lynx: Computer program used to read line by line on the Internet.

Majordomo: Name often used for the person who operates a bulletin board or discussion group.

Modem: Device that converts signals from your computer for transmission through a phone line.

Mosaic: Popular Internet browser that provides text and graphics.

Netscape: Popular Internet browser that provides text and graphics.

Newsgroup: Computer discussion group.

Newsreader: Computer program that allows you to read newsgroups.

On line: Overall term for connecting to computer networks through cable lines. The Associated Press style for the adjective form is *on-line,* but the one-word *online* is also commonly used.

Password: Secret name you use to gain access to a computer network.

Pine: E-mail program.

PPP: Point-to-Point Protocol; Program that allows you to directly connect to a computer network by dialing into the main computer through your telephone line.

Prompt: Symbol the computer system uses to indicate that it is ready to accept the directions you type.

Protocol: Set of rules used by computer systems to communicate with each other.

Search engine: Tool that allows you to find files on the Internet; also called *searcher.*

Shareware: Computer software that is provided without charge, to "share," for a limited period. The person who developed the software requests that you pay a fee to continue using the program.

SLIP: Serial Line Internet Protocol; like PPP, another program that allows you to dial in and directly connect to a main computer through your telephone line.

Smiley: Symbol (emoticon) that indicates the tone of your e-mail message.

Software: Computer program.

Surfing: Cruising or exploring the Internet.

Sysop: Computer system operator.

TCP: Transmission Control Protocol; language computers speak to transfer data. TCP/IP is a combination of Transmission Control Protocol and Internet Protocol, which is technical terminology for the rules computers use to communicate with each other.

Telnet: Internet program that allows you to access information on a remote computer.

Unix: Internet operating system in wide use among academic institutions.

URL: Uniform (or universal) resource locator; address of a site on the Internet.

Usenet: Worldwide network of discussion groups, also called newsgroups, on various subjects.

User name: Name you use to log on to your computer system; also called *user ID.*

Veronica: Software program whose name means "The Very Easy Rodent-Oriented Net-Wide Index to Computerized Archives." It is used to navigate through files connected through Gopher menus.

WAIS: Wide area information server; system that can search data bases on the Internet.

Web cruiser: Browser; way of searching files on the Internet.

World Wide Web: Interconnected group of computer networks throughout the world.

Exercises

1 Make a list of your favorite sites on the Internet.

2 Send an e-mail message to a student in your class. Add an emoticon at the end of your message. If you are using the Pine program, design your signature.

3 Find the alt.journalism.students newsgroup and other newsgroups related to journalism.

4 Find the Library of Congress Gopher menu, and explore information listed from your state. Here's how to access the Library of Congress Gopher:

- If you are using Netscape or Mosaic or some other good browser, write *gopher://marvel.loc.gov* for the URL. Then follow the hypertext links to *Government Information* until you get to your state.

- If you don't have a good browser like those, use Lynx by typing *telnet lynx.cc.ukans.edu,* as described in this chapter. Log into the KUFacts directory, and scroll to *Internet Resources.* Go to *Reference Shelf,* to *Internet Resources,* to *Gopher Resources,* to *All Gopher Resources.* Either scroll or search by typing in *Library of Congress.* You could also access the University of Minnesota Gopher and scroll from there. Then check under *Government Information* until you get to your state.

5 Search the Internet for the most recent press releases from the White House. (You can also access the White House through Gopher. Try *gopher://info.tamu.edu.)*

6 **Data base and the Internet exercise:** Use the Internet to find useful demographic information.

 a Check the U.S. Census site on the World Wide Web (http://www. census.gov). Assume you are writing a story about population growth in your state. Find state population projections. Check the statistics for your state for the 1990s, the year 2000 and the year 2020. Using Excel or another data base program, calculate the percent of change from most recent year to the years 2000 and 2020. Create a pie chart or bar chart showing the population estimates.

 b For comparative purposes, expand your data base by using the statistics for your neighboring states or for all 50 states. Which states have the highest projected growth rates?

 c Go to the table that shows the population growth rate for people over age 65 for the state you live in. Which state will have the highest growth rate of people over age 65? Make a chart of the states with the highest percentage rate of growth among people over 65.

 d Scroll through the tables in the U.S. Census data base, and add to the information in your own data base for a more complete story on population growth in your state. Use statistics for race, immigration, age and other information that you think is interesting and important.

 e Check the Social and Demographic Characteristics data base for statistics on computer use and ownership. Calculate the percentage of change in computer use over the past 10 years.

7 **Data base class project:** Compile a list of agencies on your campus or in your community (or both) that have data bases available to the media. Each student may be responsible for a few agencies. Then compile the information in a booklet, which you could file in your campus library for the benefit of other students. Include some of the following information: name of agency, type of data base available, form available (floppy disks, nine-track tape), costs, information not available on data base, chief source to contact.

COACHING

TIPS

Call the employer and find out the person to whom you should send your application. Make sure you have the correct name, title and sex of the person. Ask how to spell the person's first and last name.

Limit your cover letter to one page.

Proofread your application carefully to eliminate spelling and typographical errors.

Make a follow-up telephone call a few weeks after you send your application.

Media Jobs and Internships

27

Michael Strong wasn't a traditional journalism school graduate. He was 42 when he earned his degree at the University of Kansas, and he had a varied background prior to entering journalism school. But when he applied for a newspaper job, his original cover letter gave no clue that he was any different from the thousands of other journalism school graduates. It began: "I am graduating in May . . ."

He got few responses from editors. So he rewrote his cover letter, and this time it revealed a little more about him: "How many reporters do you know who have experience meeting people when they are nude? That isn't exactly traditional training for a reporter, but I'm not a traditional candidate for a reporting job."

Strong had been a massage therapist for a Kansas City athletic club, as well as a photographer, computer operator and astronomic surveyor for the U.S. Air Force. Every editor who received the revised cover letter responded; several called him for an interview and subsequently offered him a job.

Many employers prefer a simple, straightforward lead that clearly states why you are applying for the job. Use your judgment to determine whether a cover letter with a creative approach or one with a direct approach is appropriate for the job or internship you are seeking. In either case, your cover letter should reveal something special about you. It's the first impression editors get of you. You may be a straight-A student with a fabulous personality and wonderful reporting skills, but if you can't sell yourself, you are just another applicant from a journalism school.

I can't stress enough how important it is for the applicant to write a cover letter that is both clear and interesting. . . . If they're just saying they want a job, that doesn't excite me. I want that letter to entice me into their clips and resume.

Paul Salsini, former staff development director for *The Milwaukee Journal Sentinel*

Whether you are applying for a job in print or broadcast journalism or in public relations, most of the advice that follows applies.

Job Application Skills

For many years Paul Salsini reviewed cover letters and resumes from job applicants to *The Milwaukee Journal Sentinel,* where he was the staff development director and writing coach. He was appalled by the mistakes in these job applications. One applicant misspelled *Milwaukee* throughout her application. Another said, "I've always wanted to work at the *Minneapolis Star.*"

"Good for her," Salsini says. "Why should I care?"

One of the worst mistakes applicants make is that they fail to change the text in their word processors when they are sending out multiple applications, Salsini says.

"I can't stress enough how important it is for the applicant to write a cover letter that is both clear and interesting and tells me this person is a good reporter and writer," he says. "If they're just saying they want a job, that doesn't excite me. I want that letter to entice me into their clips and resume. The cover letter is the only original thing they send."

Salsini prefers cover letters with catchy leads that reveal something special about the applicant. Here's one he liked: "When I was 10 years old, I wanted to be a detective. When I was 12, I wanted to be a child psychologist, and when I was 13, I wanted to be a news reporter. That was the career choice that stuck. Ten years later I'm still basically a nosy kid who enjoys the challenge of storytelling." Some editors prefer a hard-news lead on a cover letter. Salsini says that whether it's a straight lead or feature, it should be a good lead to a personal account of the applicant.

Salsini also stresses that applicants should attach some explanation to their clips about how they wrote the story. "If they would just write a couple of sentences to explain whether this was their story idea and why the story was important, it would help to put the clip in context. It helps an editor understand the story. That doesn't take a lot of work and it is so important. I rarely get that in an application, but when I do, it's what I read first."

Internships and experience on campus newspapers are important. Editors want evidence of how you report and write or what you can do as a copy editor. They want clips of stories you have written or edited. However, clips are edited, so they aren't always indicative of the person's writing, Salsini says.

If you have skills in computer-assisted reporting or on-line journalism technology, it's important to stress those skills in your cover letter as well as in your resume. Many newspapers and magazines are going on line, and often the staffers already on board have little or no knowledge of the new media technology. As a result, editors want to hire people who have some training in these areas or who are receptive to learning.

But the majority of editors still mainly want evidence that you write and think clearly. You can demonstrate that you do in your cover letter.

Where to Apply

Here are some tips about where to look for a media job or internship.

Online Career Center If you want to use the Internet for your job search, you have a perfect way of reaching hundreds of companies and other potential employers: the Internet's Online Career Center. This World Wide Web site offers ways to put your resume on line, access to hundreds of job opportunities—not limited to journalism—and much other useful information. The site also includes college recruiting resources.

You can contact the Online Career Center at http://www.occ/img/occHome Page. The college center is at http://www.occ.com/occ/Universities.html.

The Internet also has sites where you can find an on-line resume form. You just have to type your information in the blanks provided in the form. A resume form is available at this Internet address: http://www.resumix.com/resume/resume-form.html.

Printed directories Check a directory of publications or broadcast stations in your field of interest for ideas about where to apply. These publications list the organization, telephone number, circulation, address and chief officers. But never rely on the publication for the names of editors or other people in charge. Journalists frequently change positions, and the directories cannot keep up with the changes. Always call and find out whom you should contact.

Here are some major directories:

For newspapers: Editor & Publisher Yearbook

For newspapers and magazines: Gale's Directory of Publications

For broadcast media: Broadcasting Yearbook, Television/Cable Factbook

For magazines and public relations (in-house) publications: Gebbie House Magazine Directory, Bowkers (publications of trade organizations)

Advertising: Standard Directory of Advertising Agencies

Whom to Contact

At most newspapers, you should apply to the managing editor, not the editor or publisher, unless the paper is very small and the editor or

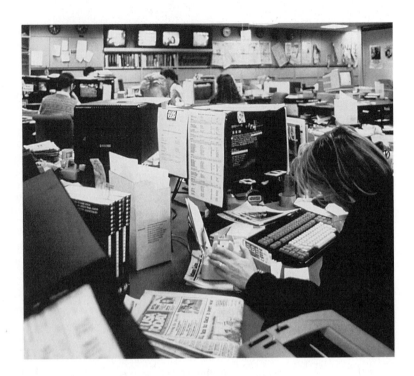

Newspaper newsroom
Courtesy of *The Gannetteer,*
Gannett Co., Inc.

publisher is the only person in charge. For other types of organizations, check to find out who reviews the applications.

Make sure you get the correct spelling of the person's name, the title and the gender. Some female editors and personnel directors have male-sounding names; some men's names are ambiguous, too. Remember, don't rely on directories for names of people whom you should contact; call the organization to find out. Your first step as a reporter or copy editor is to check the facts. Accuracy counts. Inaccuracy in addressing your application usually means you will not be considered.

How to Apply

Here are the basic steps to take when applying for most media jobs.

Cover letter   Try to limit the cover letter to one page. Always address it to a specific person, never *Dear Sir* or *Dear Madam*.

Write a good lead that tells something about you, but don't make it too flowery. Follow with a nut graph—your reason for writing. If you prefer a direct approach, lead with your reason for the letter. Write a few more paragraphs briefly explaining your experience, if any, and your major assets—why anyone should want to hire you—and why you want to work for this company. Then wrap it up with a brief paragraph thanking the editor for his or her attention.

Your cover letter is the employer's first impression of you. Make it clear, interesting and simple.

Resume   Make sure your resume is free of typos and spelling errors.

Give two or three references, and include phone numbers where they can be reached. Do not say "References available on request." Do everything you can to help the employer. By withholding references, you force the employer to spend more time checking on you.

You may have your resume printed on heavyweight paper and designed in an attractive way. But for most print and broadcast journalism employers, a printed resume is not essential. A neatly typed, simple resume will suffice. Something fancier may be more advantageous for public relations positions, because that is a promotional field. Your resume may reflect your ability to package promotional material. However, most employers really just want the facts in an easy-to-read form.

Clips or videotape   Include five or six clips (or videotape for broadcast journalists, although clips help in this area as well). Choose clips with good leads. Editors rarely read past a bad lead. Try to include a variety: features and hard news, short and long. Short is better, unless you have a major project. If you have some good enterprise stories, those you developed through your own ideas, include them. The significance of the news event is not important to editors; they want to see how you wrote more than what you wrote.

As Salsini suggests, attach a paragraph explaining how you got the story, why it was important or how much difficulty you might have had in getting interviews. Say something about each clip to explain why you think it is representative of your work or why you enjoyed doing it.

Follow-up phone call   A week or two after you have sent your letter, call the organization to ask if your resume was received and if you could come for an interview. Find out when the editor you are calling is on deadline or in meetings, and try to avoid these times.

Research for the interview   If you are granted an interview, make sure you get a few copies of the publication in advance and read them thoroughly. Check the library. Or call the circulation department of the newspaper or magazine and get them to send you a few copies. For a public relations job, try to get a media kit about the company. A little money and time invested before your interview may pay off in a paycheck.

Also do some research about the community. Find out if it has large ethnic groups. If you have special language skills that would be useful in this community, you can stress them in your letter and interview.

Follow-up phone call and thank-you note   After you have had an interview, wait a few weeks and then call to let the editor know you are aggressive and interested in the job. But don't be a pest.

Even if you are not interested in the job, send a note thanking the editor for the interview. That's just basic courtesy. And if you are interested in the job, the thank-you note lets the editor know something else about you: You're thoughtful.

Cover Letters

Make your first impression on the editor a good one. Use proper business letter form, and keep it brief—no more than one page. Editors and other employers are busy people. Double-check and triple-check your spelling. Make sure all the names and titles are correct. A misspelled name, typo or other mechanical error can disqualify you for consideration.

Be straightforward; not cute, not boring. Avoid starting with "I am graduating in May." So are thousands of other journalism majors. Instead, start with why you are applying to this organization or something about yourself that makes you worth noticing. But get to the point quickly, why you are applying. Specify whether you are seeking an internship or full-time job.

Explain why you are eager to work for this particular organization in the middle of your letter. Even though you are including a resume, mention its high points. Make special note of any unusual skills you may have, such as fluency in a second language or any relevant experience. If someone at the organization has encouraged you to apply, mention this person's name. The adage "It's not what you know but who you know" has some validity.

Here is some additional advice from editors, excerpted from an article that Judith Clabes, editor of *The Kentucky Post* in Covington, wrote for *Quill:*

> I'm editor of a medium-sized daily, and being deluged with letters to the editor comes with the territory.
>
> Believe me, by the time I've shuffled through the "Dear Stupid" letters to the editor, the "Dear Employee" memos from corporate, and the really important "Dear Resident" mail that somehow pours into the office, I'm in no frame of mind for a job-seeker's "Dear Mr. Clabes" letter.
>
> "Dear Mr. Judith Clabes" really ticks me off.
>
> Now, this may seem quirky, but we editors are entitled to an eccentricity or two.
>
> Idiosyncrasies aside, we editors do seem to agree on the issue of introductory letters from job-seekers. We prefer:

- Straightforward, one-page letters
- Simple resumes and
- Well-selected clips (yes, college newspaper clips are fine)

In the end, the clips speak loudest. But the introductory letter may determine whether a busy editor will even bother to listen.

"It's more important that the letter is not a turn-off than it's a turn-on," says Mike Phillips, editor of *The Sun-Tattler* in Hollywood, Florida. The following will automatically turn off an editor:

- Grammatical errors
- Typographical errors
- Misspelling the name of the newspaper
- Misspelling the name of the editor
- Form letters
- Incorrect titles, including courtesy titles
- Cutesy letters
- Bad writing, including poor sentence structure
- Phony sales pitches
- Lengthy, self-centered letters

"I'm impressed by the letter coming from someone who's got him or herself figured out, who knows personal strengths and weaknesses and has a flair for writing," says Phillips.

Typos are killers. "I can't remember bothering to interview an applicant whose letter contained typos or grammatical errors," says editor Dee W. Bryant of *The Leaf-Chronicle* in Clarksville, Tennessee. "If a person is that careless with letters, it raises the question about carelessness as a staffer."

Bryant's pet peeve, however, is the automatic—and mindless— "Mr." greeting. "If an applicant is seriously interested, he or she should have taken the time to find out. It irritates me that people make the invalid assumption that editors are men."

Bob Stiff, editor of *The Democrat* in Tallahassee, wants some evidence that the writer is familiar with the paper and the area. He prefers a follow-up phone call from the applicant, requesting a short interview.

Though we editors have our own pet peeves as well as hiring strategies, we shudder over the cute stuff, the gimmicks, the overzealous attempts at creativity.

Angus McEachran, editor of *The Pittsburgh Press* [before it folded], has compiled more than his share of to-the-editor eccentricities. . . . His attention was momentarily captured when he opened a letter and a stick fell out. The letter said:

"Dear Sir:

"Inside the envelope along with this letter I have sent you just what you don't need in filling editor slots at *The Pittsburgh Press*—

dead wood. Tired of dead wood? Give me a call. My phone number is . . ."

That letter writer's phone did not ring with McEachran's call.

What will work is a simple, professional approach. Throw away fuchsia paper and the gimmicks. Invest time in investigating the newspaper. Write a simple, well-crafted (and proofread) one-page letter that demonstrates your interest in journalism generally and in that particular newspaper specifically. Include a brief resume and five or six well-selected clips.

Before you write your cover letter and resume, do some research about the organization to which you applying. If you are seeking a job at a newspaper or magazine, read the publication. You can check on-line data bases, such as Lexis/Nexis, or get copies of the publication. If you are applying to a corporation for a public relations or advertising position, check data bases, such as Standard and Poor's Register of Corporations, and business publications to learn something about the organization. Don't just cite facts about the company; weave the information into the paragraph in your cover letter that explains why you want to work for the organization.

There is no single way to write an effective cover letter. The letter in Exhibit 27-1 has a storytelling lead. The nut graph, why this student is writing, is a little low in this letter, but because the letter is so brief, this placement is acceptable. Try to get your nut graph fairly high in the letter. Single-space your letter, with an extra line between paragraphs. Leave four spaces between "Sincerely yours" and the typed name so you can put your signature in the space.

The letter in Exhibit 27-2 has a more direct approach, but it is still somewhat creative to distinguish it from the hundreds of cover letters that employers receive. This letter effectively presents information about the company and about the student's abilities.

Student's home address
City, State, ZIP code
Date

Name of managing editor and title
Name of newspaper
Address

Dear ———:

When I was in first grade, my teacher asked me to write what I wanted to be when I grew up. I wrote down "Arthur." In confusion, my teacher called me up to her desk.

"Angelina, you want to be Arthur?"

"Yeah, Arthur, you know, like one of those people who write books."

She laughed and explained that the word was "author." She wrote it out in big, black printing. I practiced spelling it again and again: AUTHOR.

I still want to be an author, but now I want to write newspaper articles instead of books. Please consider me for a reporting internship this summer. I am a junior at the University of ———, where I am majoring in journalism.

From Day One I have known that I love to write and that I have a natural ability for it. I started a school newspaper in seventh grade, and I wrote for my school paper throughout high school. In the past year I wrote stories for my university paper. Now I want experience in the real newspaper world. I am eager to work for [name of newspaper] because it is a small newspaper, which will give me a chance to write a variety of news and feature stories. I know I can learn a great deal from the reporters and editors at your newspaper.

My experience is limited, but my ambition is endless. I hope you will grant me an interview so I can realize my childhood dream and become an author at your newspaper.

Sincerely yours,

[Signature]

Angelina Lopez

Exhibit 27-1

Cover letter with a storytelling lead

Student's home address
City, state, ZIP code
Date

Maureen Murray, Recruiter for Account Executives
Leo Burnett Company Inc.
35 W. Wacker Drive
Chicago, IL 60601

Dear Ms. Murray:

The basket of apples in your company logo indirectly led me to seek a career in advertising and to write this letter seeking a job in your agency. When I was growing up in Chicago, my grandparents told me a story about how your company used to hand out apples to people on the streets during the Depression as a good public relations gesture. I was impressed. I thought that your company would be the kind of place where I would like to work some day. Every time I see your logo, I remember that story.

Now, as a journalism student at the University of Kansas, I am even more impressed with the Leo Burnett Company, which is ranked the No. 1 advertising agency in the Midwest. Please consider me for a position as an assistant account executive in your client services division. I will graduate in December with a bachelor's degree in journalism. I have taken several advertising, public relations and news-writing courses. I would be eager to work on any of your accounts, such as Nintendo, Reebok, Hallmark Cards or Pillsbury. Any opportunity in your agency would be challenging, but a chance to assist on the Walt Disney account is my idea of the perfect job.

Although I have gained many skills from my academic training, I believe that my internships have offered me the best education. Currently I am a public relations intern for the Nelson-Atkins Museum of Art in Kansas City. I recently promoted and publicized the autobiographical exhibit of artist Andrew Wyeth. I also gained valuable experience last winter as an advertising intern for The Pioneer Press, a suburban Chicago newspaper chain. In that position, I created target account booklets, wrote reports and assisted sales representatives. When I worked in the advertising department of my college newspaper, *The University Daily Kansan,* I won an award as the best account executive.

I work well with people, and I am a good problem solver. In addition to my sales and advertising skills, I have written news stories for the university newspaper. I understand that you are seeking applicants with a broad educational background, and I believe that the variety of media experiences I have had make me a good candidate for your firm. Although I have much to learn, I offer boundless enthusiasm and a positive work ethic.

I will call you within the next two weeks to see if you will grant me an interview. I can be reached at (913) 000-0000. I am enclosing a resume and some examples of my work. Thank you for your consideration.

Sincerely yours,

[Signature]

Shelly Falevits

Exhibit 27-2

Cover letter that takes a direct approach

Resumes

The cover letter should be accompanied by a resume, preferably limited to one page. The resume should list your education, work experience and references (see Exhibit 27-3). Before you list anyone as a reference, make sure you ask the person for her or his permission. Also list any special skills and awards you have acquired and activities and organizations in which you have participated. You don't have to add the decorative lines shown in Exhibit 27-3, but if you know how to design your resume, it will be more attractive to potential employers.

Your Name

Permanent Address	Present Address
(if home address differs from address during the semester)	
Street	Street
city, state, ZIP code	city, state, ZIP code
Phone number with area code	Phone number with area code
	e-mail: name@_____

Position desired:	Reporting or copyediting internship for summer of . . .
Available:	May 19XX
Education:	University of ———— [Give dates, such as 1994 to present.]
	Degree expected: B.S. in journalism, 19XX
	Major: Journalism with emphasis in magazine
	Other colleges attended [if any]
	High school attended [optional]
Experience:	[List any full-time or part-time jobs, particularly any related to your field, in order starting from the most recent. Give the dates. You may add a line or two explaining your job duties.]
January–May 19XX	Reporter, *The Daily Campus* newspaper; covered university administration
July–August 19XX	Reporting internship with *City Newspaper;* covered general news for city desk and features
May–August 19XX	Waiter, Starving Students, City, State
Special skills and awards:	[Omit this category if you have no special skills.]
	Skilled in graphics programs and computer-assisted reporting
	Fluent in Spanish
	Scripps Howard Scholarship for College Journalism
Activities:	[List only important activities and memberships, especially those that show leadership or skills related to the job you are seeking. This category may be omitted.]
References:	[List only two or three people who have given you permission to list them. References may be listed on a separate page if you run out of room. List people's titles, addresses and phone numbers. Do not write "Available on request."]

Exhibit 27-3

Resume

Interviews

The interview is your chance to explain how much you want to work for the employer and why you would be a good choice. It is also your chance to find out more about the employer and to assess whether you would really like to work there.

Here are some tips:

Dress conservatively: Women should wear a suit or dress, stockings, and dress shoes (nice flats or heels). Men should wear a suit or sport jacket and tie. No jeans and no sneakers!

Be prompt: Be on time for your interview. You may arrive 15 minutes early, but don't get there too early. Never be late. That's equivalent to missing a deadline. And that's equivalent to saying you are not fit for the job.

Be prepared: Be informed about the publication, organization or station. Read copies of the publication, particularly the most recently published ones. Public relations applicants should try to gather research about the company and the types of promotions the firm does. Memorize the names of key editors in advance.

Understand the costs: Some organizations will pay for your transportation and hotel. If not, be prepared to pay for them yourself. Small newspapers and other organizations may not have the budget for your travel costs. You have to decide if the cost is worthwhile to you. If the organization is out of state, it's fair to ask if your transportation and lodging costs will be reimbursed.

Concentrate: When you are introduced to people, try to remember their names, especially those of key editors—such as the city editor or, if you are applying for a sports job, the sports editor. Homework helps.

Be enthusiastic: Your enthusiasm is your best asset, especially if you don't have experience. Show that you're interested in the job. Smile and enjoy the interview just as if you were doing an interview for a story. If you don't really want to work for the firm, don't waste everyone's time.

Be polite: Thank the editor or key person for granting you an interview, and thank the person at the end of it as well.

Be pleasant: Even if you are frightened, smile and be responsive.

Be yourself: Do not try so hard to make a good impression that you are insincere. Be honest about what you can and cannot do and what you want to learn. Never try to give a false impression of yourself.

Ask questions: The questions you ask are as important as the ones you answer. They show your curiosity and your concern about the job—qualities of a good reporter, editor or publicist.

Editors have their favorite questions, so it is hard to prepare for the interview. However, almost all of them will ask why you want to work for their organization and why you want to be a journalist. Try to be creative but sincere. "I've always wanted to write" is such a boring answer. Here are some other questions that are popular with newspaper editors (similar questions are often asked in other fields):

Why do you want to work for this organization? The answers are up to you: because you grew up in the area, want to remain in the area, are familiar with the community and so on. It's best to specify something you like about the paper if you are familiar with it. Or you could say you are seeking a variety of experiences, particularly if it's a small newspaper or television station, where reporters tend to do all types of stories. If it's a large organization, you could say you're attracted by the prestige of the paper or the chance to learn from very experienced journalists. If you are so eager that you will work anywhere, it's OK to say so. Just be honest.

Why did you want to become a journalist? Because it's more interesting than selling used cars, because you seek adventure, because you love the language, whatever. Here is your chance to give your real reason. It could be that someone influenced you or that you just like the type of work.

What are your goals as a journalist? You could say, "To get your job some day" or "To work here until *The New York Times* begs me to come there." If your goal is to be a foreign correspondent, at this point you might consider joining the Navy. Small papers don't have much use for foreign bureaus. Again, be sincere.

What books, magazines and newspapers do you read? Editors love this question. It tells them something about you.

What other interests do you have? This is another favorite question.

What can you do for this newspaper (organization), or why should I hire you? Don't say you can turn the paper around or make it wonderful. But do say something about the types of stories you would like to do, or say that you would be willing to do all types of stories. Don't be arrogant.

What do you think of this newspaper? Be cautious with this one. Don't say it's terrible and you can save it. Point out something good first. Then you might point out some weakness or area that you think could be improved. Perhaps you think it could use more human approaches to stories or more hard news. If you've read it, you have a right to your opinion. Just be diplomatic.

What was your favorite story that you wrote, and why did you like it? This is another question that gives insight into you—as well as your professional interests.

How would you cover this issue? The editor might give you an example of a topic that is of concern in that community. You'll have to think and do the best you can to come up with some interesting approaches.

What questions do you have? This question is very important. Here's where you get your chance to ask about the company, the workload, perhaps what the editors want or expect from reporters and copy editors. You could ask about a probationary period. You could also ask about salary, benefits and other compensation; generally, however, that shouldn't be your first question.

At the end of the interview, don't forget to thank the interviewer for his or her time and interest.

Exercises

1 Depending on your field of interest, interview three newspaper editors, television news directors, magazine editors or public relations employers about the qualities they seek in job candidates and the kinds of applications they want.

2 Write a few descriptive paragraphs about yourself in the third person (*she* or *he*). This exercise will give you a clue to what makes you special, and it may help you find a lead for your cover letter.

3 Write a cover letter and a resume for a job or internship you would be interested in getting.

On-line Sources for Journalists

Many of the address (URLs, or uniform resource locators) for the following Internet sites may have changed. If that is the case, use a search engine to find the new address. These are just some of the sites that may be useful to journalists. New sites are added to the Internet daily, so explore and add your own favorites to this list.

Follow the links in these sites to connect with others that are helpful. Many of the sites listed here duplicate the links to other sites in journalism and government.

You must type these URLs carefully. If you misplace a dot or a slash, you will not be able to connect to the site you want.

Disaster Sites

American Red Cross: http://www.crossnet.org

Federal Emergency Management Agency: http://www.fema.gov

ICES Disaster Resources: http://www.ag.uiuc.edu/~disaster/disaster.html (site with many links, operated by University of Illinois Cooperative Extension Service)

Internet Disaster Network: http://www.disaster.org

National Hurricane Center: http://www.nhc.noaa.gov

National Severe Storms Laboratory: http://www.nssl.uoknor.edu

Government-related Sites

Bureau of Labor Statistics: http://stats.bls.gov

Centers for Disease Control: http://www.cdc.gov

CIA World Factbook: http://www.odci.gov

Cop Net: http://police.sas.ab.ca/ (index to law enforcement sites on the Web, sponsored by the University of Wyoming, with links to campus, county, state and federal law enforcement agencies)

Environmental Protection Agency: http://www.epa.gov/gumpo/emap-dat.html

Federal agency servers: http://badger.state.wi.us:70/1/fed-info (Library of Congress, U.S. Federal Register, government gopher sites)

Federal Information Center: http://www.gsa.gov/et/fic-firs/fichome.htm (phone numbers of federal government agencies and personnel)

Federal legislation, including full text of U.S. Constitution: http://thomas.loc.gov

FedWorld: http://www.fedworld.gov, or telnet fedworld.gov, or by phone at 703-321-8020 (access to more than 120 government agencies)

FinanceNet: http://www.financenet.gov/whatis.htm (list of government assets sales and decisions of the controller of the General Accounting Office, plus other financial links)

General Services Administration: http://www.gsa.gov (policies on federal procurement)

Journalist's Toolbox of Government Information: http://www.jou.ufl.edu/commres/tbgovt.htm (excellent site for access to federal government agencies; includes FedWorld.)

Library of Congress: http://lcweb.loc.gov./homepage.online.html, or http://lcweb.loc.gov, or gopher.//marvel.loc.gov (for MARVEL, Machine Assisted Realization of the Virtual Electronic Library, offering links to hundreds of government resources via gopher)

Occupational Safety and Health Administration (OSHA): http://www.osha-slc.gov

U.S. Census: http://www.census.gov/

U.S. Department of Justice: http://www.usdoj. gov

U.S. House of Representatives: http://www.house.gov

White House: http://www.whitehouse.gov

Yahoo: http://www.yahoo.com/government/ (government agencies)

The Internet: Basic Resources

InterNIC InfoGuide: http://www.internic.net (World Wide Web server for finding general Internet-related information, operated by AT&T)

Lynx: telnet lynx.cc.ukans.edu, or http://www.ukans.edu, or telnet ukanaix.cc.ukans.edu (line-mode browser that provides text-only access to the Internet)

Mother of All Bulletin Boards: http://www.cs.colorado.edu/home/mcbryan/bb/summary.html

Telnet: telnet nxoc01.cern.ch (World Wide Web connection)

World Wide Web: http://www.w3.org

Job-related Sites

Editor and Publisher Interactive http://www.mediainfo.com/edpub/ep/jobs.htm

Journalism organizations and associations: Check sites below for media-related jobs

Online Career Center: gopher://iq-occ.iquest.net:70/11/occ/assist, or http://www.occ.com/occ/

Journalism-related Sites

American Association of Advertising Agencies: http://www.commercepark.com/AAAA/AAAA.html

American Journalism Review: http://www.inform.umd.edu:8080/News/AJR/ajr.html

Awards, grants and scholarships: http://www.inform.umd.edu:8080/News/AJR/awards.html

Campus Newspapers on the Internet: http://beacon-www.asa.utk.edu/resources/papers.html, or gopher://blick.journ.latech.edu

Clearinghouse for Subject-Oriented Resource Guides Related to Journalism: http://www.cais.com/makulow/vlj.html (massive list of media-related sites compiled by on-line expert John Makulowich

College and university home pages: http://www.mit.edu:8001/people/cdemello/univ.html

College News Publications: http://www.spub.ksu.edu/other/journ.html, or gopher://blick.journ.latech.edu

Communication and journalism academic sites: http://www.jou.ufl.edu/commres/jouwww.htm

CRAYON: http://www.eg.bucknell.edu/~boulter/crayon/how.html (site at Bucknell University to help you create your own cyberspace newspaper)

Ecola's 24-Hour Newstand: http://www.ecola.com/news/press/ (newspapers, magazines, computer publications and technical books; compiled by Bob Poulson of Ecola Design in Beaverton, Ore.)

Electronic Newstand: http://www.enews.com (selection of articles from magazines, newspapers, newsletters and catalogs)

Freedom Forum: http://www.freedomforum.org

International Association of Business Communicators: http://www.hooked.net/iabc.com/aboutiab.html

Investigative Journalism on the Internet: http://www.vir.com/~sher/julian.htm

Journalists' Web Resource Guide: http://www.inform.umd.edu/News/AJR/web.html (journalism resources listed by American Journalism Review)

MediaNet: By phone, 717-243-4285, or by e-mail 71344.2761@compuserve.com (journalist-owned and -operated free research service that helps journalists find sources)

National Press Photographers Association: http://sunsite.unc.edu/nppa/

National Scholastic Press Association: http://studentpress.journ.umn.edu

Newslink: http://www.newslink.org (hundreds of links to newspapers, broadcast organizations, magazines and other communication sites; compiled by Eric K. Meyer, a consultant and teacher at Marquette University)

Newspaper Association of America: http://www.infi.net/naa

Online Newspaper Services Resource Directory: http://www.mediainfo.com/edpub/e-papers.outing.html (comprehensive list compiled by Steve Outing)

Profnet: http://www.dgsys.com/~editors/profnet.html, or by e-mail, profnet@sunysb.edu, or by phone, 800-PROF-NET (network of schools that put the media in touch with professors who are experts on a variety of topics; responds only to journalists working on articles for publication, not students or professors doing work for classes)

Poynter Institute for Media Studies: http://www.nando.net/prof/poynter/home.html

Public Relations Society of America: http://www.prsa.org

Public Relations Web (PR Web): http://www.sme.com:80/prweb/default.htm

Society of Environmental Journalists: http://www.tribnet.com/environ/env_home.htm

Society of Professional Journalists: http://town.hall.org/places/spj

Yahoo Journalism List: http://www.yahoo.com/News/Journalism/

Broadcast Journalism Sites

Infosearch Broadcasting Links: http://www.xmission.com/~insearch/links.html

MU School of Journalism Broadcast News Department: http://www.missouri.edu/~jourmlm/bcstdept.html (from the University of Missouri)

National Association of Broadcasters: http://www.nab.org

National Association of College Broadcasters Gopher Service: gopher://rodent.cis.umn.edu:11152

Radio Stations on the Internet: http://wmbr.mit.edu/stations/list.html/wmbr/otherstations.html

Radio-Television News Directors Association: http://www.rtnda.org/rtnda

TV Net: http://TVnet.com/TVnet.html (comprehensive list of TV resources)

Journalism Bulletin Boards (Listservs)

Unless otherwise noted, you can subscribe to these bulletin boards via e-mail by writing the word *subscribe* and your name.

Center for Investigative Reporting: cir@igc.apc.org

Computer Assisted Reporting and Research: carr-l@ulkyvm.louisville.edu (to subscribe, write *listserv@ulkyvm.bitnet*)

Investigative Reporters and Editors: listserv@missou.1.missouri.edu (to subscribe, write *subscribe ire-L* and your name)

National Institute for Computer-Assisted Reporting: listserv@missou.1.missouri.edu (to subscribe, write *subscribe nicar-1* and your name)

Online News: Majordomo@marketplace.com (to subscribe, write *subscribe Online News* and your name)

Journalism Usenet Newsgroups

alt. journalism

alt. journalism.criticism

alt. journalism.freelance

alt. journalism.gay-press

alt. journalism.gonzo

alt. journalism.newspapers

alt. journalism.photo

alt. journalism.print

alt. journalism.students

alt. news-media

alt. politics.media

Legal Resources

American Bar Association: http://www.abanet.org

Freedom of Information Act or kits:
http://www.lib.umich.edu/chdocs/rights/foia.html

Legal and Ethical Internet Resources: http//www.nau.edu/legal.html

Legal Information Institute: http://www.law.cornell.edu (maintained by Cornell University law school)

Software

Eudora: http://www.qualcomm.com

Fetch: http://www.dartmouth.edu/pages/softdev/fetch.html

Gopher: gopher//boombox.micro.umn.edu   or
http://www.earn.net/gnrt/append-a.html

Kermit: http://www.columbia.edu/kermit

Mosiac: http://www.ncsa.uiuc.edu/SDG/software/Mosaic/NCSAMosaicHome.html

Netscape: http://home.mcom.com/index.html

Oak Software Repository: http://www.acs.oakland.edu/oak.html (at Oakland University)

Use of Lexis-Nexis

Lexis-Nexis is a data base that contains more than 60 million articles from a variety of publications. Lexis is the legal data base (court transcripts, law digests and so on). Nexis is the data base for newspapers, magazines, broadcast news transcripts, and business and trade publications. If this data base is not available in your college or university main library, it is usually available in a law school library. Use is limited because the service is expensive.

The following instructions use the Nexis portion of this data base, although the service comes as a package. Here is an abbreviated guide:

1   Log on: Your library probably lists this data base with others in a directory, so you simply have to scroll to Lexis-Nexis, select it, and hit Enter or Return. If this is not the case, follow the instructions provided by your library. When you log on, Lexis-Nexis may ask if you want to continue a previous search. Type *N* for no or hit the Enter or Return key.

2   Select News Library: Lexis-Nexis is arranged by libraries and by files. Libraries are broad topical categories—for example, real estate library, legal news library, news library. Select the news library by typing the number that appears next to it, or type the word *News*. If you have selected the wrong library or want to change libraries, type *.cl* and hit Enter.

3   Select a file: Choose *Mags, News* or an individual newspaper by typing the appropriate abbreviation. Then hit Enter or Return.

4   Search for an article: Narrow the scope of your topic. If it is too broad, you will get thousands of articles. For example, if you type *college costs,* you will probably get this message: "Your search has been interrupted because it probably will retrieve more than 1,000 documents. You may continue your search as it exists or edit your search." Type *E* for edit or *M* for modify, and hit Enter. Then narrow your search by adding more descriptive words and connecting words. Use any of these connecting words to narrow your topic: *and, or, not, w/ and pre/.* For example, typing $>>>$*and future* will give you stories about college costs in the future. Here are some other ways of narrowing the search:

To search by words: Type $>>>$*college pre/2 costs w/12 future and grants.* This command retrieves records about college costs where the word *college* is within two word (*pre/2*) of *costs,* where *future* is within 12 words (*w/12*) of *costs* and where *grants* also appears in the article.

To search by headline: Type $>>>$*headline (college and costs) and grants.* This command retrieves stories with the words *college* and *costs* in the headline and the word *grants* somewhere in the article.

To search by date: Dates may use just numerals (4/4/95) or numerals and words (April 4, 1995). Type $>>>$*college pre/2 costs and date aft april 4, 1995.* This command retrieves stories that use the word *college* within two words of *costs* and that were published after April 4, 1995. *Bef* indicates that you want stories published before the date you type.

5   Choose the display: After Nexis gets your list of stories, it will ask you to decide if you want a full record (type *.fu*), the list of citations (type *.ci*) or the sections of the articles where your key words appear (type *.kw*). You may also sort your documents by date, length or some other features before displaying them (type *s*).

6   View the document: Once you get your story, you can view it by typing the letters following the commands on your screen: *.np* for Next page; *.pp* for Previous page; *.fp* for First page; *.nd* for Next document; *.pd* for Previous document; *.ns* for Begin a new search; *.cf* for Change files. Type *h* for Help.

7   Print: You can generally print one screen at a time, depending on whether your library has connected this data base to a printer. You also may download the document to a floppy disk. Ask your librarian for help.

8   End the session: type *.so* for Sign off. Type *N* to indicate you do not want to have your search saved.

Lexis-Nexis provides another search method, called the "easy search." This search method is slightly easier because it provides a menu of choices for you to select when you look for documents. To use this alternative search method, after you log on to Lexis-Nexis, type the word *easy.* Then choose either *legal* or *news* for the library you want to enter.

The service will then ask you to click on a number or enter an equal sign followed by the number for the following topics:

$<<=1>>$ Major stories

$<<=2>>$ Every mention of a topic, person or place

$<<=3>>$ Specific story or author

$<<=4>>$ Companies and industries

<<=5>>   Entertainment and media

<<=6>>   Politics and government

<<=7>>   Quotations

<<=8>>   Experts

<<=9>>   Transcripts

<<=10>> Science and medicine

<<=11>> Hot topics

Be sure to type the equal sign before a number when you make your selection.

The menu will then offer you more choices, such as whether you want information about a topic, a person, or a city, state or country. Continue to select items from the menu by typing the equal sign and a number until you are asked to write the topic. After you select your topic, you will again choose menu items by equal sign and number until you have answered enough questions so the service can search for articles that match your requests.

To view the articles, use the commands that appear on the bottom of your screen. The commands for the original version and the easy version of Lexis-Nexis are the same.

Credits

Introduction

Eugene Roberts anecdote, *Washington Journalism Review* (now called *American Journalism Review*), February 1985, pp. 11–12. Reprinted with permission.

"Desperate days at the Merlin," *The Spokesman-Review,* Feb. 25, 1990. Reprinted with permission.

Edna Buchanan excerpts from *The Corpse Had a Familiar Face,* Random House, New York, 1987, p. 265.

Part One

Opening photo: Bill Snead/*The Washington Post*

Chapter 1

Chapter quote: *Coaching Writers: Editors and Reporters Working Together,* St. Martin's Press, New York, 1992, p. 173.

"Watkins detects fevers via the ear," *The University Daily Kansan,* Sept. 27, 1991. Reprinted with permission.

"Papers a lesson in criminology," *St. Petersburg* (Fla.) *Times,* Oct. 26, 1991. Reprinted with permission.

"Nevada regents OK raises," *Reno* (Nev.) *Gazette-Journal,* Oct. 4, 1991. Reprinted with permission.

Empowerment box: "Nursing home complaints surge," *Reno Gazette-Journal,* Oct. 24, 1991. Reprinted with permission.

Pull quote about Earvin "Magic" Johnson: *The Washington Post,* Nov. 8, 1991. ©1991 *The Washington Post.* Reprinted with permission.

Exhibit 1–1: "Students default on Uncle Sam," June 3–5, 1992. Copyright 1992, *USA Today.* Reprinted with permission.

Exercise based on "Lefties live shorter lives, new study says," *The* (San Bernardino, Calif.) *Sun,* April 4, 1991. Used with permission.

Chapter 2

Chapter quote: Burl Osborne, *The Next Newspapers,* American Society of Newspaper Editors, April 1988, p. 6.

"People demand politicians hear them," *The Charlotte* (N.C.) *Observer,* Jan. 19, 1992.

Exhibit 2–1: News 2000 pyramid and photo of Stockton Record; *The Gannetteer,* Gannett Co., Inc. Reprinted with permission.

Comments from Geneva Overholser, ombuds-

man of *The Washington Post:* "Newspapers as Wimps," *Editor & Publisher,* Feb. 1, 1992. Reprinted with permission.

"Damage catches residents by surprise," *Topeka Capital-Journal,* March 2, 1991. Reprinted with permission.

"Shawnee Heights ducks as funnels twist through," *Topeka Capital-Journal,* March 2, 1991. Reprinted with permission.

"26 hurt as school bus crashes head-on," *The* (Louisville) *Courier-Journal,* March 19, 1992. Reprinted with permission.

"71-year-old gets 8 years in drug case," *The Oregonian,* Dec. 4, 1990. Reprinted with permission.

"Man ticketed for walking his lizard," *St. Petersburg Times,* Feb. 6, 1991. Reprinted with permission.

"Michael Jackson sorry," *The Orange County Register,* Nov. 16, 1991. Reprinted with permission.

"Couple spends $6,000 looking for lost cat . . . ," *Rocky Mountain News,* Feb. 21, 1992. Reprinted with permission.

"Protesters gather to save schools," *Chicago Tribune,* May 22, 1991. Reprinted with permission.

"Speaking up about sexual harassment," The Associated Press, Oct. 10, 1991. Reprinted with permission.

"The proof is in the medical studies," Knight Ridder/Tribune News Service, Feb. 12, 1995.

"80-year-old gets draft notice," The Associated Press, March 7, 1995. Reprinted with permission.

"Injured violinist plans her return to concert halls," *Chicago Tribune,* March 22, 1995. Reprinted with permission.

"From sorrow comes art, 'Womanews,'" *Chicago Tribune,* Oct. 30, 1994. Reprinted with permission.

"Minority teens, police goals collide," *St. Cloud* (Minn.) *Times,* Jan. 30, 1995. Reprinted with permission.

"Today's libraries have more to check out than books," *The Milwaukee Journal-Sentinel,* Oct. 6, 1994.

Eyes on the News, by Pegie Stark and Mario Garcia, Poynter Institute for Media Studies, 1990.

"Water Shock," and Exhibit 2–2, "Water Cost Increase," *Reno Gazette-Journal,* Aug. 17, 1991. Reprinted with permission.

Chapter 3

"Basic costs at Stanford hit $21,262," *San Francisco Chronicle,* Feb. 14, 1991.

"Family sues in corpse mix-up," *St. Petersburg Times,* Jan. 10, 1991. Reprinted with permission.

"Salmon spawn a new crisis," *Los Angeles Times,* Nov. 15, 1990. Reprinted with permission.

"Amnesia victim recalls abduction," The Associated Press, Dec. 21, 1990. Reprinted with permission.

"Drunken driver, after six attempts to serve his 30 days, sues sheriff," Knight Ridder/Tribune News, Dec. 14, 1990. Reprinted with permission.

"11-year-old begins grad school," The Associated Press, March 19, 1995. Reprinted with permission.

"New seat-belt law simple to enforce," *The Oregonian,* Dec. 2, 1990. Reprinted with permission.

"Bush plans college grants to middle class," Feb. 5, 1991. Copyright 1991, *USA Today.* Reprinted with permission.

"Teen stabbed in school fight," *St. Petersburg Times,* Dec. 21, 1990. Reprinted with permission.

"Student's concern for society rises," Jan. 28, 1991. Copyright 1991, *USA Today.* Reprinted with permission.

"Man prowls dorms," *Iowa City Press-Citizen,* Sept. 22, 1990. Reprinted with permission.

"Thousands gather on Capitol steps for animal rights," The Associated Press, June 11, 1990. Reprinted with permission.

"Throw the book at them," The Associated Press, Sept. 4, 1990. Reprinted with permission.

"It's the water," Knight Ridder/Tribune News, Jan 3, 1991. Reprinted with permission.

"Police hear of campus cults," The Associated Press, July 23, 1991. Reprinted with permission.

Quote from sunbathing story, *St. Petersburg Times,* Jan. 11, 1991. Reprinted with permission.

"In Spitak, survivors comb ruins of devastated town," *The Washington Post,* Dec. 15, 1988. © 1988 *The Washington Post.* Reprinted with permission.

"A mom's anguish for wounded son . . . ,"

Chapter 11

Chapter 12

"A life in shambles ends a life full of promise," *The Hartford Courant,* April 25, 1993. Reprinted with permission.

Inverted pyramid exercise based on a story from The Associated Press, Oct. 17, 1991. Used with permission.

Wall Street Journal formula exercise based on: "Answer to idealism or joblessness," *Los Angeles Times,* March 27, 1992. Reprinted with permission.

Hourglass exercise based on "Couriers help foil robbery," *St. Louis Post-Dispatch,* Oct. 9, 1991. Reprinted with permission.

List exercise based on story from United Press International, March 14, 1991. Reprinted with permission.

Pyramid exercise based on story from McClatchy News Service, Oct. 1, 1991. Used with permission.

Chapter 13

Chapter quote: Bill Blundell, *The Art and Craft of Feature Writing,* New American Library. Copyright 1986, Dow Jones & Company, p. x.

"A cry in the night," *St. Petersburg Times,* June 12, 1988. Reprinted with permission.

"Adventures in babysitting," *St. Petersburg Times,* Oct. 2, 1988.

Christopher Scanlan anecdote from "Storytelling on deadline," *Best Newspaper Writing,* St. Petersburg, Poynter Institute for Media Studies, pp. 355–56.

"In an icy river, a heroic rescue," *The Hartford Courant,* March 2, 1991. Reprinted with permission.

"Now's the time for State Fair," *The Des Moines Register,* Aug. 15, 1990. Reprinted with permission.

William Ruehlmann quote, *Stalking the Feature Story,* Random House, N.Y., copyright by William Ruehlmann, 1977, p. 7.

Comments by Bruce DeSilva, *Coaches' Corner,* June 1990. Reprinted with permission.

"'Fat Albert' carves out an 891-pound niche," *St. Petersburg Times,* Nov. 10, 1985. Reprinted with permission.

"Smith found not guilty in less than 90 minutes," *Los Angeles Times,* Dec. 12, 1991. Reprinted with permission.

"Penn Relays: A carnival of sociability," *The Philadelphia Inquirer,* April 21, 1992. Reprinted with permission.

"George Burns: From has-been to superstar," *Chicago Tribune,* Feb. 2, 1986. Reprinted with permission.

Quotes from Jack Hart about verbs: "Second Takes," *The Oregonian* newsletter, April 1990. Reprinted with permission.

"Fielder puts final touch on season of triumph," *Detroit Free Press,* Oct. 4, 1990. Reprinted with permission.

"New life begins with help of coyotes," *Daily Forty Niner,* California State University, Long Beach, 1991. Reprinted with permission.

"Read-in attracts 400 to KC library," *Kansas City Star,* Feb. 3, 1992. Reprinted with permission.

"It couldn't happen to me: One woman's story," *The Des Moines Register,* Feb. 25, 1990. Reprinted with permission.

"Ghosts don't spook Down East couple," *Bangor* (Me.) *Daily News,* Aug. 6–7, 1983. Reprinted with permission.

"Clive woman's spell of success," *The Des Moines Register,* March 13, 1991. Reprinted with permission.

"Nov. 22, 1963: A day when time stopped," The Associated Press. Reprinted with permission.

Jon Franklin quote, *Writing for Story,* Mentor, N.Y., 1986, p. 78.

William Blundell organization tips, *The Art and Craft of Feature Writing,* New American Library, New York, copyright 1988 by William Blundell, pp. 98, 99.

"Nicky's story," *Chicago Tribune,* July 17, 1988. Reprinted with permission.

"A soldier's story," *Iowa City Press-Citizen,* Jan. 12, 1989. Reprinted with permission.

Narrative exercise based on "Memorial relives time of woman who aided Jews," *Chicago Tribune,* Dec. 6, 1987. Used with permission.

Chapter 14

"Paper Waste 'Irresponsible'" press release, InterCommunicationsInc., 1991. Reprinted with permission.

"Crayola Introduces Crayons That Are Literally 'Off The Wall,'" press release, Feb. 4, 1992, Binney & Smith Inc. Reprinted with permission.

"Crayola cleans up kids' act," Feb. 3, 1992. Copyright 1992, *USA Today.* Reprinted with permission.

"Crayola introduces a washable product," *The Wichita Eagle,* Feb. 13, 1992. Reprinted with permission.

"JC Penney to Study Site for Distribution Center," press release, June 22, 1989, J.C. Penney Inc. Reprinted with permission.

Chapter 15

Expocentre script excerpts, KSNT-TV, Topeka. Reprinted with permission.

Abortion ruling script excerpts, KSNT-TV, Topeka. Reprinted with permission.

Abortion ruling story, The Associated Press, June 30, 1992. Reprinted with permission.

"New Kansas law expected to stand," *Topeka Capital-Journal,* June 30, 1992. Reprinted with permission.

Exxon kidnapping story, The Associated Press broadcast wire, June 30, 1992. Reprinted with permission.

Nude camp excerpt, June 23, 1992, NBC News Channel wire. Reprinted with permission.

Korean merchants protest excerpt, June 23, 1992, NBC News Channel wire. Reprinted with permission.

Animal rights protest excerpt, The Associated Press broadcast wire, June 30, 1992. Reprinted with permission.

Toxic chemical spill excerpt, The Associated Press broadcast wire, June 30, 1992. Reprinted with permission.

Baldwin City water problems, September 1992, KSNT-TV, Topeka. Reprinted with permission.

Crime fighting teaser, June 30, 1992, KSNT-TV, Topeka. Reprinted with permission.

Exercise excerpt, June 23, 1992, NBC News Channel wire. Reprinted with permission.

Dentist's death teaser, June 23, 1992, NBC News Channel wire. Reprinted with permission.

Person of the Week script, July 13, 1992, KUSA-TV, Denver. Reprinted with permission.

"16-year-old boy with no license takes police on Highlands chase," *The* (Louisville) *Courier-Journal,* Feb. 23, 1992. Reprinted with permission.

Part Four

Opening photo: Bill Snead/*The Washington Post.*

Chapter 16

"The case of the dying child," *IRE Journal,* Fall 1986. Reprinted with permission.

"So what's wrong with pre-publication review?" *Quill,* May 1990. Reprinted with permission of the Society of Professional Journalists.

Comments by Bill Marimow made at convention of Investigative Reporters and Editors, Minneapolis, 1988.

Libel definition from *Mass Communications Law: Cases and Comment,* by Donald Gillmor, Jerome A. Barron, Todd F. Simon and Herbert A. Terry; West Publishing Co., St. Paul, 1990, p. 172.

Chapter 17

Survey by Ralph Izard for the Society of Professional Journalists, 1984–85 Ethics Report. Reprinted with permission.

Helen Benedict, *Virgin or Vamp: How the Press Covers Sex Crimes,* New York: Oxford University Press, 1992, p. 18.

"A Model of Respect: Beyond Political Correctness in the Campus Newsroom," *Journal of Mass Media Ethics,* Vol. 9, No. 1, pp. 43–45.

Arthur Sulzberger and Donald Graham comments about the "Unabomber manifesto," *The New York Times,* Sept. 19, 1995.

Code of ethics, Society of Professional Journalists. Reprinted with permission.

Code of ethics, Public Relations Society of America. Reprinted with permission.

Chapter 18

Exhibit 18–1, "Minorities at newspapers," April 8, 1992, Copyright 1992, *USA Today.* Reprinted with permission.

"A look at Asians as portrayed in the news," *Editor & Publisher,* April 30, 1994, pp. 46 and 56.

"It's official: They're American Indian, so they can get married," *The Philadephia Inquirer,* March 23, 1991. Reprinted with permission.

"Slipping from the scene," Women, Men and Media Project, Columbia University, 1995.

Exhibit 18–2, "Equal writes," April 25, 1992. Copyright 1992, *USA Today.* Reprinted with permission.

Jack Kammer, "She said. She said." *Editor & Publisher,* May 4, 1991, p. 120.

"Dress-up Dolly," *The Philadelphia Inquirer,* April 5, 1992. Reprinted with permission.

"Dolly bio scales career peaks," The Associated Press, Oct. 10, 1994. Reprinted with permission

"How to avoid sexism, stereotypes in writing," *The Gannetteer,* Gannett Co., Inc., June 1989. Reprinted with permission.

William Hilliard's comments from "Newsroom Diversity," *The Bulletin,* publication of the American Society of Newspaper Editors, May/June 1992. Reprinted with permission from William Hilliard.

Excerpts from "AIDS in the Heartland," *St. Paul Pioneer Press,* June 21, 1987, and July 12, 1987. Reprinted with permission.

Part Five

Opening photo: Lizz Dabrowski/*The Oklahoma Daily*

Chapter 19

"Youths wearing their hearts on their sleeves to honor dead friends," *The* (Louisville, Ky.) *Courier-Journal,* Nov. 7, 1994. Reprinted with permission.

"More girls turn to violent crime," *Reno Gazette-Journal,* May 21, 1995. Reprinted with permission.

"School officials trumpet QPA results, but debate over program remains," *Lawrence Journal-World,* May 27, 1995. Reprinted with permission.

"It fluttered and became Bruce Murray's heart," *The* (Syracuse, N.Y.) *Post-Standard,* May 12, 1984. Reprinted with permission.

"Curricula of color," *The Wall Street Journal,* July 1, 1991. Reprinted by permission of *The Wall Street Journal,* Dow Jones & Company, Inc. All rights reserved worldwide.

Jonathan Bor's guidelines, *Coaches' Corner,* September 1989. Reprinted with permission.

Karen F. Brown sportswriting tips, *Best Newspaper Writing 1991,* Poynter Institute for Media Studies, St. Petersburg, Fla., 1991, pp. 253–57. Reprinted with permission.

"Nova loses big to Boston College," *The Philadelphia Inquirer,* Feb. 16, 1992. Reprinted with permission.

"Mavericks bugged by loss to Nets," *Dallas Morning News,* Nov. 30, 1991. Reprinted with permission.

Chapter 20

Obituary of Lawrence Pompie "Mr. Buddy" Ellis, *Philadelphia Daily News,* Dec. 18, 1986. Reprinted with permission.

Obituary of Ella Hurst, *Philadelphia Daily News,* July 22, 1988. Reprinted with permission.

Apology for obituary of Dr. Rogers Fair, *Detroit Free Press.* Reprinted with permission.

Obituary of Lucy Davis Burnett, *The Dallas Morning News,* Nov. 24, 1991. Reprinted with permission.

Obituary of Hulda Kettler Stoner, *Los Angeles Times,* Feb. 1, 1991. Reprinted with permission.

Obituary of William Frank Peterson, *The Oregonian,* March 20, 1992. Reprinted with permission.

Obituary of Edward E. "Ace" Clark, *Philadelphia Daily News,* March 19, 1986. Reprinted with permission.

Obituary of Theodor "Dr. Seuss" Seuss Geisel, *The Philadelphia Inquirer,* Sept. 26, 1991. Reprinted with permission.

Obituary of Theodor "Dr. Seuss" Seuss Geisel, *The Orange County Register,* Sept. 26, 1991. Reprinted with permission.

Exercise based on obituary of Jim Henson, excerpts from *The New York Times,* Dec. 23, 1990. Copyright © 1990 by The New York Times Company. Reprinted with permission.

Chapter 21

"Commission votes down expansion," *Lawrence Journal-World,* April 19, 1995. Reprinted with permission.

"5 arrested during Dannemeyer speech," *The Orange County Register,* March 10, 1991. Reprinted with permission.

"Professor brings USF a provocative message on race," *St. Petersburg Times,* Feb. 26, 1992. Reprinted with permission.

"Official again scores alcohol use by young," The Associated Press, April 14, 1992. Reprinted with permission.

"Alcohol use tied to other teen problems," *USA Today,* April 14, 1992. Copyright 1992, *USA Today.* Reprinted with permission.

"Graffiti vandals may be 'tagged' by 1,000 hours of cleanup," *Chicago Tribune,* June 12, 1991. Reprinted with permission.

"Temple idea: All to take race class," *The Philadelphia Inquirer,* May 12, 1991. Reprinted with permission.

"City sets timetable for Simply Equal," *Lawrence Journal-World,* April 12, 1995. Reprinted with permission.

"Meeting addresses solutions to environmental problems," *The University Daily Kansan,* Feb. 7, 1991. Reprinted with permission.

"Water heater sculpture approved," *The Orange County Register,* March 20, 1991. Reprinted with permission.

Danville Public Safety Committee story, Danville, Ill. *Commercial-News.* Reprinted with permission.

Speech by Burl Osborne to American Society of Newspaper Editors. Reprinted with permission.

Earvin "Magic" Johnson highlights box, Nov. 8, 1991, *The Orange County Register.* Reprinted with permission.

Earvin "Magic" Johnson highlights box, Nov. 8, 1991, *Reno Gazette-Journal.* Reprinted with permission.

Earvin "Magic" Johnson press conference, The Associated Press, Nov. 8, 1991. Reprinted with permission.

Chapter 22

Chapter quote by Jim Steele, *Quill,* May 1993, p. 25.

"In Capitol, a bulb change carries a high price indeed," *The Philadelphia Inquirer,* June 8, 1990. Reprinted with permission.

"20 years' service, nine children and no job," *The Philadelphia Inquirer,* Feb. 22, 1991. Reprinted with permission.

"It may cost more to have fun in Pa.," *The Philadelphia Inquirer,* Feb. 8, 1991. Reprinted with permission.

Empowerment box from "Parking violators pay up," *Reno Gazette-Journal,* Nov. 2, 1991. Reprinted with permission.

"New York Air-Traffic Control: Pressures and Gains," Feb. 4, 1990, *The New York Times.* Copyright © 1990 by The New York Times Company. Reprinted with permission.

"Fontana landowners fear new general plan will trim values," *The* (San Bernardino) *Sun,* April 5, 1989. Reprinted with permission.

Rockford sales tax story, *Rockford Register-Star.*

"City officials get guidelines on handling controversies," Minneapolis *Star Tribune,* Feb. 21, 1991. Reprinted with permission.

"Alabama's Rivers: Endangered Resource," December 1990. *The Alabama Journal.*

"What the tax plan means in dollars," *The Philadelphia Inquirer,* March 28, 1991. Reprinted with permission.

"More drinking by lawyers found," The Associated Press, Dec. 7, 1990. Reprinted with permission.

"Universities' gender makeup changing," *Lawrence Journal-World,* Feb. 23, 1994. Reprinted with permission.

"Reported sexual assaults on slight rise in Portland," *The Oregonian,* Feb. 18, 1991. Reprinted with permission.

"Rainfall total is inching to record," *San Jose Mercury News,* May 2, 1995. Reprinted with permission.

"Storm brews over reappraisal," *Atlanta Constitution,* March 19, 1991. Reprinted with permission.

"Homeowners getting 1st break in 20 years," *The* (Hackensack) *Record,* May 15, 1991.

Philadelphia city budget, *The Philadelphia Inquirer.* Reprinted with permission.

"CSU board raises fees 20 percent," and Exhibit 22–1, *The Orange County Register,* March 14, 1991. Reprinted with permission.

Chapter 23

Edna Buchanan comments and quotes, from speech at conference of Investigative Reporters and Editors, Minneapolis, 1988.

"Boy dies in car crash," *The Orange County Register,* Feb. 21, 1991. Reprinted with permission.

"Rare comic books stolen from Council Bluffs store," The Associated Press, April 5, 1991. Reprinted with permission.

"Burger burglar makes off with a Whopper of a haul," *The* (Salem, Ore.) *Statesman Journal,* April 4, 1991. Reprinted with permission.

"Robbers sought," *The Orange County Register,* March 14, 1991. Reprinted with permission.

Deodorant spray robbery, *The Des Moines Register.* Reprinted with permission.

"Curly would join Stooges but he couldn't find bank," The Associated Press. Reprinted with permission.

"Robber does flip-flop," *Topeka Capital-Journal.* Reprinted with permission.

"Man charged in woman's death," *The Milwaukee Journal,* April 22, 1992. Reprinted with permission.

"Shattered dreams: 'Perfect' kids shot, mom jailed," *The Orlando Sentinel,* March 30, 1991. Reprinted with permission.

"Fire routs rescuers, 2 boys die," *Chicago Tribune,* June 15, 1991. Reprinted with permission.

"Simpson acquitted of murders," The Associated Press, Oct. 3, 1995. Reprinted with permission.

"N.H. Prosecutors get Smart," The Associated Press, March 23, 1991. Reprinted with permission.

"Crafts denies he killed wife," *The Hartford Courant,* June 17, 1988. Reprinted with permission.

"Joy Griffiths' killing: Act of love or murder?" *St. Petersburg Times,* Nov. 17, 1985. Reprinted with permission.

"A snake in a mattress twists its way into court," *The Philadelphia Inquirer,* April 4, 1991. Reprinted with permission.

"Man gambles on plea, loses," *The Kansas City Star.* Reprinted with permission.

Exercise 2 based on "Hungry pet starts kitchen fire," Fort Lauderdale, Fla., *Sun-Sentinel.* Used with permission.

Exercise 5 based on "Hundreds pay to get new name," Fort Lauderdale, Fla., *Sun-Sentinel,* Nov. 16, 1992. Used with permission.

Chapter 24

Excerpts from stories in *The Oklahoma Daily,* April 20, 1995, plus photographs and excerpts from the diaries of Omar Gallaga. Reprinted with permission.

Excerpts from "The crash of flight 255" and Exhibit 24–1, *The Detroit News,* special report, Aug. 17–23, 1987. Reprinted with permission.

"Bomb cripples Oklahoma City," *The Okla-homa Daily,* April 20, 1995. Reprinted with permission.

"Grief cuts wide swath," *The Detroit News,* special report, Aug. 17–23, 1987. Reprinted with permission.

"20 die in La Guardia crash," The Associated Press, March 23, 1992. Reprinted with permission.

Exhibit 24–2, water spout, Aug. 16, 1991, *Reno Gazette-Journal.* Reprinted with permission.

"6.9 quake rocks N. California coast," *Los Angeles Times,* April 26, 1992. Reprinted with permission.

"Napa, Sonoma hit by floods again," *San Jose Mercury News,* March 10, 1995. Reprinted with permission.

"Band of brothers," The Associated Press, February 1988. Reprinted with permission.

Deadline disaster exercise based on dispatches from The Associated Press, April 19, 1995. Used with permission.

Plane crash exercise based in part on material from the Fort Lauderdale *Sun-Sentinel.* Used with permission.

Chapter 25

"Only Bo knows Bo," *GQ,* March 1990. Courtesy GQ. Copyright 1990, 1992 by The Conde Nast Publications Inc. Reprinted with permission.

"You talkin' to Me?" *GQ,* January 1991. Courtesy GQ. Copyright 1990, 1992 by The Conde Nast Publications Inc. Reprinted with permission.

"Reflections: A year after her stabbing, Stacy LaRocca's painful memories remain," *Florida Alligator,* February 1991. Reprinted with permission.

"Night shift allows baker to concoct sweet surprises," *Lawrence Journal-World,* April 8, 1994. Reprinted with permission.

"Candle maker waxes eloquent about life as an entrepreneur," *Lawrence Journal-World,* April 8, 1994. Reprinted with permission.

"Inspector puts his stamp on construction," *Lawrence Journal-World,* April 8, 1994. Reprinted with permission.

"A time to die," *Sunshine* magazine, Fort Lauderdale *Sun-Sentinel,* July 28, 1985. Reprinted with permission.

"Clues in the life of an accused mass killer," *The New York Times,* Aug. 4, 1991. Copyright © 1991 by The New York Times Company. Reprinted with permission.

Robert Maxwell anecdote, *The New York Times,* March 17, 1991. Copyright © 1991 by The New York Times Company. Reprinted with permission.

"She is the finest of New Orleans' finest," *The Philadelphia Inquirer,* Feb. 3, 1992. Reprinted with permission.

Vignette profiles from "Desperate days at the Merlin," *The Spokesman-Review,* Feb. 25, 1990. Reprinted with permission.

Journalism school librarian vignette, *The University Daily Kansan,* Nov. 19, 1991. Reprinted with permission.

Vignette of bus driver, unpublished. Used with permission of Kathy Hill.

Vignette of flag raiser, unpublished. Used with permission of Michelle Betts.

Chapter 26

Quote from Christopher Feola, *Quill,* March 1994, p. 24.

Chapter 27

"Cutesy cover letters are like bricks," *Quill,* October 1988. Reprinted with permission of Judith Clabes.

Cover letter by Angelina Lopez. Reprinted with permission.

Cover letter by Shelly Falevits. Reprinted with permission.

Newspaper newsroom photo, courtesy of *The Gannetteer,* Gannett Co., Inc.

Index

Index